Models, Strategies, and Tools for Competitive SMEs

Rafael Perez-Uribe
Universidad Santo Tomas, Colombia

David Ocampo-Guzman
Santo Tomas University, Colombia & EAN University, Colombia

Luz Janeth Lozano-Correa
Universidad Santo Tomas, Colombia

Published in the United States of America by
   IGI Global
   701 E. Chocolate Avenue
   Hershey PA, USA 17033
   Tel: 717-533-8845
   Fax: 717-533-8661
   E-mail: cust@igi-global.com
   Web site: https://www.igi-global.com

Library of Congress Cataloging-in-Publication Data

CIP PENDING

ISBN13: 9798369340462
EISBN13: 9798369340479

Vice President of Editorial: Melissa Wagner
Managing Editor of Acquisitions: Mikaela Felty
Managing Editor of Book Development: Jocelynn Hessler
Production Manager: Mike Brehm
Cover Design: Phillip Shickler

British Cataloguing in Publication Data
A Cataloguing in Publication record for this book is available from the British Library.

ll work contributed to this book is new, previously-unpublished material.
he views expressed in this book are those of the authors, but not necessarily of the publisher.

Table of Contents

Detailed Table of Contents

Chapter 1

Terry Lantai, Inland Norway University of Applied Sciences, Norway
Atle Hauge, Inland Norway University of Applied Sciences, Norway
Xiang Ying Mei, Inland Norway University of Applied Sciences, Norway

While studies on immigrant enterprises are increasing, the smaller size and scale of such enterprises consisting of Immigrant Micro Enterprises (IMEs) in labour-intensive industries are still under-researched. This review paper provides an overview of scientific research consisting of journal articles on IMEs to understand the characteristics that influence innovation and business growth in the relevant industries. Findings are presented in a conceptual framework to set the precedence for future studies. IMEs experience additional difficulties than their native counterparts and those of larger sizes, including resource scarcity, language issues, lack of network, funding, government support, and local market knowledge. However, innovation in such enterprises is driven by the entrepreneurs' traits and characteristics, motivation, risk perception, non-economic capital, experience, and education level, impacting their business strategies and tool adaption. IMEs significantly contribute to the new home country, particularly rural regions, the local economy, and cultural diversity.

Chapter 2

Eurico Colarinho Navaia, Zambeze University, Mozambique
António Carrizo Moreira, University of Aveiro, Portugal
Cláudia Pires Ribau, University of Aveiro, Portugal

Although the relationship between competitive strategy and export performance has been addressed previously in the literature, the moderating effect of the competitive intensity of this relationship is little explored, especially in emerging economies. This study aims to address the moderating effect of competitive intensity in the relationship between differentiation competitive strategy and the export performance of Mozambican small and medium-sized enterprises (SMEs). The study involves the analysis of 250 questionnaires directed to Managers of Mozambican SMEs, using structural equation modeling and Partial Least Squares (PLS/SEM) algorithm (SmartPLS 3.0). The findings show that differentiation strategy has a positive influence on export performance. However, competitive intensity has a negative moderating effect on the relationship between differentiation competitive strategy and export performance.

This chapter examines the relationship between Colombian state entities and the competitiveness of private companies, focusing on human talent development and the internal control systems implemented by the State. Through an analysis of the Political Constitution and relevant laws, it explores how the public sector strengthens the national productive sector, improving its competitiveness locally and globally. The chapter highlights the importance of aligning state-owned and private companies, emphasizing training's role in facilitating agile responses to market demands. It also proposes integrating private sector management tools into the public sector to enhance administrative efficiency and support national economic growth. The methodology includes a comprehensive review of the theoretical underpinnings of internal control systems and their practical application within state entities.

Chapter 4

This paper introduces cultural insights by analyzing the similarities and differences between Filipino and Canadian cultures. It highlights the importance of building sustainable relationships to do business. By leveraging attitudinal and behavioral facets, communication styles, leadership and decision-making techniques, employee motivations, and conflicts in the workplace, the study emphasizes building sustainable business relationships between Filipinos and Canadians. As the researchers examined literature from academic researchers and government websites, the researchers recommended using the Us Approach to deepen the culturally diverse and sustainable partnership between Canada and the Philippines. By doing so, understanding differences, building trust, and recognizing gaps are established. That way, necessary adjustments will be completed depending on the cultural dissimilarities and relationship gaps. While these were deduced, one should be cautious of generalizing said analysis as certain deviations within Canadian and Filipino cultures exist.

The chapter explores how small and medium-sized enterprises (SMEs) can enhance competitiveness and innovation in a constantly evolving business environment. SMEs face significant challenges to remain relevant amid rapid technological evolution, shifts in consumer preferences, and increasing global competition To adapt, innovate, and thrive, SMEs must develop dynamic capabilities, comprising a set of skills, processes, and knowledge that enable them to integrate, build, and reconfigure their internal resources in response to environmental changes. To improve competitiveness and innovation, SMEs should foster a culture of innovation that values experimentation and creative thinking, promote collaboration through strategic alliances and agile methodologies, and manage organizational well-being by addressing mental health and stress management. These strategies collectively enhance resilience and adaptability, essential for navigating BANI environments

This research mainly aims to identify the financial behaviors and money beliefs in a business and military context. These analyses may lead to a partial reduction in the stress experienced by these households, thereby facilitating their focus on military activities and preparing them as entrepreneurs in the civil context. A survey was conducted to gather data about students' preferences and beliefs about money, using Klontz Money Script Inventory. The main findings explained students' attitudes on money that help to accomplish the personal financial goals, that are important to the SME´s success.

Chapter 7

The chapter titled highlights key approaches to enhance the competitiveness of small and medium-sized enterprises (SMEs) in developing countries. SMEs are key economic actors contributing significantly to employment and GDP growth. However, they often need help with unique challenges, including limited access to resources, technology and markets, that can hinder their growth potential. The chapter explores innovative strategies tailored to these contexts and highlights the need for an adaptable framework that considers local conditions and global market trends. It highlights the role of technology, particularly the adoption of digital tools and platforms, in improving operational efficiency, market reach and competitiveness. We also discuss the importance of entrepreneurial ecosystems that foster SMEs' collaboration, knowledge sharing, and skills development. The chapter also covers policy interventions and support mechanisms essential for enabling environments.

The strategic business analysis is essential to formulate strategies and tactical plans that allow companies to grow in an environment that is getting more and more competitive. Thus, the strategic analysis focuses on internal aspects of the company and external factors that affect it. This research focuses on a tool of internal analysis that has been applied in consulting processes performed by professors and students of the Politecnico Grancolombiano since the second semester of 2022. The tool uses the Excel spreadsheet; it includes modules of Marketing, Production, Human Resources, Technology, Administration, and Social Responsibility. Besides, by means of the calculation of ponderations, it generates specific and general scores that allow to classify each functional area of the company as competitively strong or weak. Thus, the results provided by the tool become an essential input for other models of strategic analysis, such as the Strategic Analysis of Fred David, or the dynamic capabilities model.

Chapter 9

SMEs are recognized as engines of growth and economic development worldwide. Yet they seem to be not contributing to their full potential. Many of them do not even survive for longer time and even if they do, they are not as competitive as they could be with proper resources and strategies. Adopting a qualitative approach the aim of this chapter is to explore how knowledge management and innovation in SMEs can enhance their competitiveness and aid in optimization of their potential and contribution to economic and sustainable development.

Chapter 10

The tourism sector is currently undergoing a digital transformation, with emerging technologies playing a pivotal role in redefining marketing strategies and improving the performance of small and medium-sized enterprises (SMEs). This study aims to examine, through a comprehensive literature review, the marketing applications of emerging technologies and the impact of these technologies on the business performance of SMEs. A rigorous methodology based on the PRISMA protocol for reference collection and NVIVO software for textual and thematic analysis was employed in this research. The objective was to demystify the complex relationship between emerging technology marketing applications and the business performance of tourism SMEs. The results revealed a convergence that linked these technologies to key performance indicators.

The study delves into the realm of Promotion and Fostering of Entrepreneurship (PFE) research, a domain of scholarly interest due to its potential to shape a future where economic growth aligns with societal well-being. This article presents the first-ever bibliometric analysis of academic research dedicated to PFE, spanning from 1956 to 2021. Utilizing bibliometric techniques as performance analysis and graphical mapping, the research examines academic output using the Scopus database, categorizing articles, authors, and institutions. Noteworthy journals like Journal of Business Venturing feature prominently. Crucial articles by authors like Walter, Auer, and Ritter gain attention, while influential institutions like the University of Toronto are emphasized. Graphical mapping of Keywords highlights the growing importance of PFE research, with a notable surge in studies over the last decade. Entrepreneurship ecosystems and the integration of PFE with sustainability and social responsibility issues stand out as new and prominent perspectives.

Chapter 12

The chapter aims to substantiate the significance of cultivating media education and information literacy, which empower civil society sectors to confront the VUCA environment and cater to their interests and needs. As a result, they fuel the economy and enable the establishment of small and large businesses. With the recognition that populism has an impact on the bonds of trust within civil society that are needed for creating sustainable, supportive, and cooperative economies, as well as production levels that strive for equity and creativity, the prolongation of a scenario marked by volatility, uncertainty, complexity and ambiguity becomes possible.

María Teresa Ramírez Garzón, Universidad de La Salle, Colombia
Carlos Mario Muñoz-Maya, Universidad de La Salle, Colombia
Olga Lucia Diaz-Villamizar, Universidad Militar Nueva Granada, Colombia

The objective of this research is to identify whether there is an association between sustainability and organizational management strategies in uncertain environments in micro and small enterprises. For this purpose, a survey was applied to 377 directors of MSEs in Bogota. To carry out the correlation, two dependent variables were considered: 1) sustainability and 2) organizational strategic management. Uncertainty was considered as an independent variable. Each of these variables was compared to different components. Empirical evidence of the relationship between uncertainty and organizational management and sustainability is shown, no correlation is found between the uncertainty variable and the main strategy variable of the company or between the main strategy of the company and the main problem of the company. There is a slight negative correlation between the uncertainty variable and the main problem variable of the company. Finally, a moderate positive correlation is found between the uncertainty variable and the sustainability and organizational management variable.

Froilan Delute Mobo, Philippine Merchant Marine Academy, Philippines
Mohammad Shahparan, Silk Road International University of Tourism and Cultural
* Heritage, Uzbekistan*
Abigail Gomez, Cavite State University, Philippines
Michael Bongalonta, Sorsogon State University, Philippines

ABSTRACT The paper indicates to the study of supply chain sustainability strategies, when the risks faced by all business farm in supply chains are so complex, diverse and sudden that it becomes more difficult than ever to predict and determine the probability of their materialization. It substantiates the relevance of supply chain management (Supply Chain Management SCM). It has been determined that in order to competitive advantages in the market sector, business sector need to improve supply chain management properly, which will reduce the cost of production to delivery, optimize times, as well as customer satisfaction. It is proposed to consider the risk management mechanism in business sector as a set of mutually agreed methods, procedures, management tools, taking into account the role of each subject of the supply chain. It is concluded that the correct risk assessment mechanism in the supply chain for business sector should constitute an appropriate tool for assessing the effectiveness of risk management from the point of view of all business sector in the supply chain.

This study examines the influence of FinTech technologies like crowdfunding, blockchain, and mobile payments on the entrepreneurial intentions of young Indian entrepreneurs. A quantitative research design was used to collect data from 150 respondents using a structured questionnaire. The study used exploratory factor analysis (EFA) and reliability tests to validate the components and analyze the links between these technologies and entrepreneurial inclinations. The findings show that crowdfunding lowers financial obstacles and raises entrepreneurial confidence, blockchain improves transparency and operational efficiency, and mobile payments increase transaction convenience and consumer reach. These findings demonstrate FinTech's major role in promoting entrepreneurship among young Indians.

Imark group S.A.S is a micro-company dedicated for 13 years to advising multiple Colombian companies in advertising communication, organizational communication, as well as in providing digital and lithographic printing solutions and sale of promotional material. The company has also provided advice on research of markets and design of digital marketing campaigns.The objective of this work is to show how, from a consultancy to a Colombian microenterprise, a strategic direction is formulated and how to relate it to business results in terms of better competitiveness, in this case of the company IMARK SAS. This work was carried out with the support of the owner of the company, the participation of the General Management and the accounting and financial support staff.The activities that were carried out through the application of the corporate strategic management (CSM) model which allowed the companies to structure their medium-term strategic direction and short-term action plan.

Preface

In today's rapidly evolving global market, the competitiveness of nations and regions is no longer an abstract concept but a tangible driver of economic growth and development. As defined by the World Economic Forum, competitiveness is "the set of institutions, policies, and factors that determine the level of productivity of a country." Productivity, in turn, underpins the attraction of both financial investment and human capital—essential components of sustainable growth and prosperity.

The global landscape is increasingly shaped by a competition for resources, talent, and innovation. Countries, industries, and metropolitan areas are striving to elevate their productivity in order to remain viable in this contest. Higher productivity is crucial not only for economic expansion but also for improving living standards and fostering development. This competitive environment places particular pressure on emerging economies, where challenges such as weak institutional frameworks, inadequate infrastructure, and a lack of trust in legal systems must be addressed if these regions are to close the gap with developed economies.

In this context, small and medium-sized enterprises (SMEs) play a pivotal role. These businesses, often the backbone of local economies, are faced with the challenge of navigating both domestic and international competitive landscapes. Yet, despite the importance of SMEs in the global economy, there remains a significant lack of accessible, comprehensive resources that address the specific challenges and opportunities they face in the context of competitiveness.

This book, *Models, Strategies, and Tools for Competitive SMEs*, aims to fill that gap. It brings together essential knowledge, practical models, and proven strategies, along with real-world experiences from various countries, to offer valuable insights for academics, entrepreneurs, and policymakers alike. Through this collection of work, we hope to contribute to the ongoing dialogue about how SMEs in emerging economies can strengthen their competitiveness, improve their productivity, and, ultimately, play a more prominent role in driving economic development.

We invite you to explore the concepts, case studies, and strategies presented in this book, with the hope that they will serve as useful tools in fostering the competitive capacity of SMEs globally.

ORGANIZATION OF THE BOOK

Chapter 1: A Review of Immigrant Micro Enterprises (IMEs) in Labour-Intensive Industries: Characteristics, Innovation, and Contribution

This chapter delves into the often-overlooked area of Immigrant Micro Enterprises (IMEs) in labor-intensive sectors. It provides a comprehensive review of existing literature to examine the unique characteristics that drive innovation and growth within these small, immigrant-run businesses. Despite facing additional challenges such as limited resources, language barriers, and lack of local market knowledge,

IMEs exhibit innovative behaviors driven by the entrepreneurs' personal traits, education, and risk perception. The chapter highlights the substantial contributions these enterprises make to local economies and cultural diversity, particularly in rural regions.

Chapter 2: Beyond Differentiation: How Competitive Intensity Shapes Export Performance for Mozambican SMEs

This chapter explores the intersection of competitive strategy and export performance within Mozambican SMEs, specifically focusing on the moderating effect of competitive intensity. Through a robust empirical study involving 250 SMEs, the findings reveal that while differentiation strategies positively influence export performance, intense competition can dampen this relationship. The study uses advanced statistical techniques, including structural equation modeling, to offer insights into how competitive environments shape business outcomes in emerging economies.

Chapter 3: Business Competitiveness Depends on Training and Control

Focusing on Colombia, this chapter examines the relationship between state entities and the competitiveness of private businesses. It underscores the role of human talent development and internal control systems in enhancing corporate competitiveness. By analyzing state policies and private sector practices, the chapter argues for closer alignment between public and private enterprises to improve market responsiveness and foster national economic growth. The integration of management tools from the private sector into state-run institutions is proposed as a method to boost administrative efficiency.

Chapter 4: Comparing Canadian and Filipino Culture for Sustainable Business Relationships

This chapter compares the business cultures of Canada and the Philippines, emphasizing the importance of understanding cultural differences to foster sustainable business relationships. By analyzing communication styles, leadership approaches, and workplace behaviors, the chapter offers recommendations for building trust and collaboration between Filipino and Canadian business partners. The chapter stresses that while cultural differences exist, they can be managed effectively to create long-lasting partnerships.

Chapter 5: Dynamic Capabilities to Drive Innovation and Competitiveness in a Changing Business World

In an era of rapid technological change and global competition, this chapter emphasizes the need for SMEs to develop dynamic capabilities to remain competitive. It offers practical strategies for fostering innovation, enhancing collaboration, and promoting organizational well-being. The chapter discusses how a culture of experimentation and strategic alliances can help SMEs adapt to volatile, uncertain, complex, and ambiguous (BANI) business environments, improving both innovation and resilience.

Chapter 6: Financial Behaviors and Money Beliefs in the Educational Sector: Case in the Business and Military Academic Context

This chapter explores the financial behaviors and money beliefs of students in business and military academic environments, utilizing data from a survey conducted with students. The findings highlight how students' financial attitudes influence their personal financial goals, which are critical to the success of SMEs. The chapter provides insights into how financial literacy in educational settings can prepare individuals for entrepreneurial ventures.

Chapter 7: Innovative Strategies for Enhancing SME Competitiveness in Emerging Economies

Focusing on developing economies, this chapter highlights innovative strategies that SMEs can adopt to enhance their competitiveness. It explores the role of technology, including digital platforms, in improving operational efficiency and market reach. The chapter emphasizes the importance of entrepreneurial ecosystems that foster collaboration, knowledge-sharing, and skills development, along with policy interventions that create enabling environments for SME growth.

Chapter 8: Internal Strategic Application Analysis Proposal

This chapter presents a practical tool for internal business analysis, designed by faculty and students of Politecnico Grancolombiano. The tool evaluates various business functions—marketing, production, human resources, and more—through weighted scores that identify strengths and weaknesses. The results of this analysis serve as critical inputs for other strategic models, helping companies align their internal operations with competitive business strategies.

Chapter 9: Knowledge Management and Innovation for Enhancing SMEs Competitiveness

This chapter examines how effective knowledge management and innovation practices can enhance the competitiveness of SMEs. Drawing on a qualitative research approach, it explores strategies that optimize the potential of SMEs to contribute to economic and sustainable development. The chapter provides practical insights into how SMEs can leverage knowledge management to improve business outcomes and sustain long-term growth.

Chapter 10: Marketing Applications of Emerging Technologies and Business Performance of Tourism SMEs: A Systematic Literature Review

This chapter explores the impact of emerging technologies on the marketing strategies and business performance of tourism SMEs. Through a systematic literature review, it examines how digital tools are reshaping the tourism sector and enhancing the competitiveness of SMEs. The chapter provides a detailed analysis of how technology adoption correlates with key performance indicators, offering insights into the digital transformation of the industry.

Chapter 11: Research on The Promotion and Fostering of Entrepreneurship in SMEs: A Bibliometric Study

This chapter presents a bibliometric study of research on the Promotion and Fostering of Entrepreneurship (PFE), spanning from 1956 to 2021. By analyzing academic output from influential journals and institutions, it provides a comprehensive overview of the evolution of PFE research. The study highlights emerging trends, including the integration of sustainability and social responsibility into entrepreneurship ecosystems.

Chapter 12: SMEs in VUCA and Populist Environments: The Imperative Need for Media Education and Information Literacy

This chapter emphasizes the importance of media education and information literacy in enabling SMEs to navigate volatile, uncertain, complex, and ambiguous (VUCA) environments, particularly in the face of populism. It explores how media literacy can strengthen civil society and foster sustainable business practices, ultimately contributing to the creation of equitable and creative economies.

Chapter 13: Sustainability and Strategic Organizational Management of MSEs in Bogotá in Uncertain Environments

This chapter investigates the relationship between sustainability and organizational management strategies in Bogotá's micro and small enterprises (MSEs) operating in uncertain environments. Through a survey of MSE directors, the chapter explores how uncertainty affects business strategies and sustainability efforts, revealing insights into how these businesses adapt to external pressures.

Chapter 14: Supply Chain Risk Management in Business Sector: From Modern Time Perspective

This chapter explores supply chain risk management strategies in the business sector, highlighting the complexities and uncertainties that modern supply chains face. It proposes a comprehensive risk management framework that considers the roles of all supply chain stakeholders. The chapter emphasizes the importance of effective risk assessment in maintaining competitive advantages and optimizing business operations.

Chapter 15: The Impact of FinTech on Entrepreneurial Intentions among Young Indian Entrepreneurs Using Crowdfunding, Blockchain, and Mobile Payments

This chapter examines how FinTech technologies, including crowdfunding, blockchain, and mobile payments, influence the entrepreneurial intentions of young Indian entrepreneurs. Through quantitative analysis, the chapter reveals how these technologies reduce financial barriers and enhance entrepreneurial confidence, operational efficiency, and market reach.

Chapter 16: Strategic Direction and Competitiveness: Case Imark Group S.A.S (IGS)

This final chapter offers a case study of Imark Group S.A.S, a Colombian microenterprise, to illustrate how strategic direction can improve competitiveness. Through a consultancy process, the chapter details how the Corporate Strategic Management (CSM) model helped the company develop a medium-term strategic direction and short-term action plan, resulting in enhanced business performance and competitiveness.

IN CONCLUSION

As editors of *Models, Strategies, and Tools for Competitive SMEs*, we are proud to present this comprehensive examination of the factors that shape the competitiveness of small and medium-sized enterprises (SMEs) in a rapidly evolving global market. The diverse perspectives offered across the chapters of this book highlight the complexity of challenges that SMEs face in both emerging and developed economies. These businesses, often seen as the backbone of local economies, are critical players in the pursuit of national and regional economic growth.

Through the collective insights of the contributing authors, it becomes evident that competitiveness is not a one-size-fits-all concept. It is shaped by a myriad of factors, including innovation, strategic management, financial behavior, technological adoption, and cultural understanding. From the entrepreneurial resilience of immigrant micro-enterprises in labor-intensive sectors to the strategic response of SMEs in volatile and uncertain environments, this book underscores the dynamic capabilities required to succeed in the modern business world.

What stands out across the chapters is the imperative for SMEs to adopt innovative strategies, build robust knowledge management systems, and leverage technology to enhance their operational efficiency and market presence. Moreover, the importance of fostering entrepreneurship, developing talent, and ensuring adaptability in the face of global challenges cannot be overstated. These elements, along with effective policy support and institutional frameworks, are crucial for unlocking the full potential of SMEs and enabling them to drive sustainable economic development.

We hope that the insights, models, and strategies presented in this book will serve as valuable resources for academics, policymakers, and practitioners alike. By addressing the critical elements of SME competitiveness, we believe that this collection contributes meaningfully to the broader discourse on economic productivity, resilience, and innovation.

In closing, we encourage readers to reflect on the lessons shared within these pages and apply them to their own endeavors, whether in research, business, or policymaking. As SMEs continue to navigate the complexities of the global market, we are confident that the knowledge contained in this book will provide essential tools for fostering growth and long-term success.

Rafael Pérez-Uribe
Universidad de la Salle, Colombia

David Ocampo Guzmán
Universidad EAN, Colombia

Janeth Lozano Correa
Universidad Santo Tomás, Colombia

Chapter 1
A Review of Immigrant Micro Enterprises (IMEs) in Labour–Intensive Industries:
Characteristics, Innovation, and Contribution

Terry Lantai
https://orcid.org/0000-0001-7354-8104
Inland Norway University of Applied Sciences, Norway

Atle Hauge
Inland Norway University of Applied Sciences, Norway

Xiang Ying Mei
https://orcid.org/0000-0002-9691-1540
Inland Norway University of Applied Sciences, Norway

ABSTRACT

While studies on immigrant enterprises are increasing, the smaller size and scale of such enterprises consisting of Immigrant Micro Enterprises (IMEs) in labour-intensive industries are still under-researched. This review paper provides an overview of scientific research consisting of journal articles on IMEs to understand the characteristics that influence innovation and business growth in the relevant industries. Findings are presented in a conceptual framework to set the precedence for future studies. IMEs experience additional difficulties than their native counterparts and those of larger sizes, including resource scarcity, language issues, lack of network, funding, government support, and local market knowledge. However, innovation in such enterprises is driven by the entrepreneurs' traits and characteristics, motivation, risk perception, non-economic capital, experience, and education level, impacting their business strategies and tool adaption. IMEs significantly contribute to the new home country, particularly rural regions, the local economy, and cultural diversity.

DOI: 10.4018/979-8-3693-4046-2.ch001

INTRODUCTION

Immigrants and immigrant-owned businesses have led to profound changes in many rural regions by being critical to broader socio-political and economic societal transformations (Mendoza et al., 2020). Studies on immigrants, in general, are increasing, including Dabić et al. (2020), Duan and Sandhu (2022), Malerba and Ferreira (2021) and Murnieks et al. (2020). However, limited studies have focused on such enterprises of smaller sizes, thereby Micro Enterprises (MEs), which are even smaller than Small and Medium-sized Enterprises (SMEs). While there are some discrepancies in the definition of MEs depending on the context, as it ranges from a maximum of five while others use fewer than ten employees (European Commission, 2021; Norwegian Government Security and Service Organisation, 2002), they are usually no more than ten employees in total. Many immigrant businesses are categorised as MEs, and although the number of such businesses together contributes significantly to the local economy and cultural diversity, there is a clear and urgent need for more attention to be given to Immigrant Micro Enterprises (IMEs) both academically and at the policy level. This is highlighted by the work of Arslan et al. (2022); Haq et al. (2021); Jones et al. (2019); and Malerba and Ferreira (2021).

Immigrant entrepreneurship is defined as business activities that immigrants carry out, such as business ventures, which create value (Mosquera & Jardim da Palma, 2020). Immigrant enterprises must deal with additional challenges than their native counterpart due to a lack of knowledge of the local market, language issues and discrimination (Mendoza et al., 2020). Furthermore, immigrant entrepreneurs are overrepresented in labour-intensive industries due to their relative ease of entry, low initial investments, and lack of requirement of specific skills, as tertiary education is not necessary (Mueller, 2014; United Nations, 2022). These include businesses such as eateries and restaurants, barbers and hairdressers, trade, retail, building and construction, and personal services. The relatively high risk, low profit margins, and often high efforts from long hours indicate that growth and survival in such industries are difficult.

The current research gaps call for more extensive research on IMEs in such industries (Liu & Cheng, 2018; Pikkemaat et al., 2019; Yachin, 2019), to review their unique characteristics and business constraints. Such factors arguably influence business practices, innovation strategies and tools that they may adopt, leading to long-term survival and contribution to their new home country despite the many challenges such businesses face compared with their native and large counterparts (Arslan et al., 2022; Haq et al., 2021; Jones et al., 2019; Malerba & Ferreira, 2021).

This conceptual paper aims to provide a systematic literature review (SLR) of existing literature consisting of a bibliographic search involving research topics that cover IMEs and business innovation. As IMEs in labour-intensive industries are still under-researched, this review considers the type of size, skills, business, industry, and regional location within the new home country they venture into, which have not been paid attention to in existing SLR papers (Duan & Sandhu, 2022). Based on the above discussion, three specific research objectives (RO) are developed for the paper.

- RO1: Gaining an overview of scientific research consisting of journal articles on IMEs.
- RO2: Reviewing the current research to understand the characteristics of IMEs and the strategies and tools they may adopt that influence innovation and growth.
- RO3: Developing a conceptual framework of IMEs' characteristics, business constraints, and contribution to the new home country.

The aim of the present paper is not merely to provide a systematic overview of existing literature, a criticism that systematics reviews have received (Xiao & Watson, 2019). It also seeks to discuss and understand the strategies and tools that IMEs may adopt and integrate into their business practices. These practices arguably differ from their native and larger counterparts in other industries due to the unique challenges experienced by IMEs in labour-intensive sectors. Further, the chapter also develops a conceptual framework to suggest a future research agenda on immigrant enterprises in this and similar categories.

BACKGROUND

The significant contributions made by IMEs to regional economies require more robust academic exploration. In numerous regional contexts, many immigrant-owned businesses are smaller in size and fall within labour-intensive sectors. However, there is a notable lack of specific focus on this segment within existing literature. Much of the research tends to group all immigrant-owned businesses into a single category, overlooking the unique characteristics and challenges faced by MEs. Furthermore, the broad category of Small and Medium Enterprises (SMEs) often used in research is insufficient to understand the intricacies and dynamics of IMEs. The realities and operational dynamics of a business with a maximum of ten employees vastly differ from those with a hundred employees. Grouping these diverse entities under the same category can lead to oversimplification, potentially obscuring essential insights.

In light of these gaps in the current body of research, a systematic review of literature specifically targeting IMEs can contribute significantly to the field of entrepreneurship and immigrant entrepreneurship studies. This under-researched area holds immense potential for new insights and understanding, particularly regarding the behavioural patterns of the owners of such businesses. This chapter sets the groundwork for future research topics by providing an overview of existing studies and identifying key themes. It aims to develop a conceptual framework to guide future investigations based on patterns and topics revealed in the relevant literature. By focusing on this particular segment, the chapter will shed light on these businesses' unique challenges, strategies, and strengths, thereby enriching the understanding of the broader landscape of immigrant entrepreneurship.

MAIN FOCUS OF THE CHAPTER

Research Methodology

Research Approach

This study completes an SLR to gather the necessary data to understand, investigate and analyse relevant studies on IMEs. SLR is chosen as the methodological approach to provide a thorough overview of the existing body of literature (Grant & Booth, 2009; Xiao & Watson, 2019). While SLRs have been criticised for their inability to develop new theories, they are typically not designed to do so (Xiao & Watson, 2019). Instead, the primary purpose is to systematically categorise the literature and synthesise and analyse existing research to comprehensively assess the evidence required to answer the defined research questions or objectives (Davies, 2019). Therefore, a sound SLR needs to define straightforward research objectives that can be used as a guideline for the process. By aggregating, interpreting, identifying, and integrating existing research, the SLR provides an account of the state of the literature when the review is conducted (Rousseau et al., 2008; Xiao & Watson, 2019). Such an approach has been used in several studies on immigrant entrepreneurship. Aliaga-Isla and Rialp (2013), Dabić et al. (2020), Duan and Sandhu (2022), Malerba and Ferreira (2021) and Murnieks et al. (2020). These studies prove that SLR is suitable for reviewing the current topic. While enterprise sizes are not specified in existing studies applying SLR, recognising that there are limited studies specifically on IMEs, existing systematic reviews are also included in the discussion in developing a conceptual framework. Some existing studies may be replicated as relevant data published in these two reviews are integrated into the current paper.

Data Collection Process and Analysis

There are many ways to carry out a systematic review. PRISMA is chosen as the appropriate approach in the present paper as such a method guides authors to report systematic reviews transparently, ultimately, and accurately, facilitating evidence-based decision-making (Page et al., 2021). Subsequently, it helps researchers to plan and conduct systematic reviews by ensuring that all relevant information is captured and also assists readers in assessing the appropriateness of the methods, the trustworthiness of the findings, and the applicability of the results to their setting (Page et al., 2021). Drawing on the process provided by Khan et al. (2003) and Moher et al. (2009), this review follows a five-step process of PRISMA consisting of (1) developing the research aim and relevant research objectives along with selection criteria, (2) systematically identifying relevant literature using the database and keyword searches set in step one (3) assessing and screen the relevant studies by excluding duplicates and unrelated work (4) summarising, categorising and organising the findings and finally, (5) interpret, present and discuss the findings. Setting specific criteria to locate and include the necessary and relevant literature is crucial. Studies in management, business, entrepreneurship, service, and hospitality were included. In addition, only literature in English was included.

Compared to the general literature on immigrant enterprises and innovation, limited studies exist on IMEs (Arslan et al., 2022; Haq et al., 2021). Recognising that not all literature uses the term 'micro' in describing IMEs as MEs are also a part of SMEs, both search words 'small' and 'SMEs' were also used. For the context of this paper, an ME is defined as fewer than five employees, small enterprises as between 6 to 20 and medium enterprises as 21 to 100 (NHO, 2022). Nevertheless, various publications may use different sets of criteria considered in the analysis. In addition, the search words 'immigr*', migra*, and 'ethnic' were applied to capture immigrant entrepreneurs. The search word 'foreign' was also used. However, none of the results were considered relevant and thus excluded altogether. Moreover, 'small businesses' as a search word resulted in many publications. Hence, this was further broken down by including the word 'innovation' to determine their relevance. Web of Science and EBSCO databases were used to source relevant literature. They are some of the most frequently used databases by researchers across disciplines to source relevant literature. (Duan & Sandhu, 2022; Xiao & Watson, 2019). Searches were conducted on the Web of Science first, and duplicates found in EBSCOhost were filtered out and not included in the 'Relevant' category. The timeframe was limited to 2000 to 2022, as two decades were evaluated to be suitable to capture the essence of the current topic of innovation and business growth.

To ensure that the publications located were relevant to the topics to be reviewed, researchers read each publication's title, abstract, and keywords to evaluate their relevancy. Discrepancies were discussed among the researchers to ensure consensus. Realising that there are limited articles on IMEs and immigrant SMEs and that some articles may not specify the size of the immigrant enterprises, the drawback is that relevant articles may not be found through database searches. Hence, drawing insights from Duan and Sandhu (2022), the reference lists of sourced articles were scanned to find additional relevant papers to include. This method is also called snowballing (Sedziniauskiene et al., 2019). Snowball sampling can be applied to document selection for research by identifying an initial set of relevant documents and then using references or citations within these documents to find other relevant sources. Despite its potential benefits, this method also presents some challenges. Snowball sampling can lead to discovering important sources that might not be found through traditional search methods. As one source leads to another, researchers may uncover valuable documents that were not initially apparent (Green et al., 2006). The snowball sampling process can provide a better understanding of the context of the research topic. By examining the references or citations in a document, researchers can gain insights into the broader intellectual landscape of the topic (Bailey, 2014). Since snowballing leverages existing references or citations, it can be a time and cost-effective way of sourcing relevant documents, mainly when the volume of potentially relevant literature is large (Green et al., 2006). Some drawbacks may exist when the selection of documents is not random but is based on connections to the initial documents. This may lead to overrepresenting certain perspectives and underrepresenting others (Bailey, 2014). Moreover, the scope of the document search may be limited by the initial set of documents. If these documents do not reference or cite important sources, these sources may be overlooked (Green et al., 2006). However, snowball sampling was deemed an effective method of document selection in the present research due to the large volumes of literature, such as SLR, and when the search words to locate relevant documents are unclear by covering a range of topics. This process led to an additional six publications. Table 1 details the search words and results.

Table 1. Search terms used and results

	Web of Science		EBSCOhost		
Search words	**Total**	**Relevant**	**Total**	**Relevant**	
Immigr* OR Migra* and SME	10	**2**	5	**1**	
Immigr* OR Migra* business and micro	76	**6**	4	**0**	
Immigr* OR Migra* and small business	337 ↓		225 ↓		
Immigr* OR Migra* and small business AND innovation	35	**7**	22	**5**	
Ethnic and microbusinesses	2	**1**	65	**6**	
Ethnic and small business	327 ↓		245 ↓		
Ethnic and small business and innovation	48	**5**	16	**7**	
		21		**19**	
Additional articles					6
Total					46

Source. Authors

Furthermore, while most systematic literature views limit their searches to include high-impact factors and most cited articles, this paper does not attempt to do so. This is due to the limited articles available on IMEs in general and the need to gain a complete overview of the extent of existing research on this topic to date. Nevertheless, only scientific peer-reviewed journal articles listed in selected databases, as indicated above, are included to ensure the quality of the articles to a certain extent. As the focal point was

IMEs in labour-intensive industries, the analysis also recorded whether publications focused on labour-intensive industries or other businesses of more high-wage and technology-intensive in nature, including accounting, management consultancy, technical engineering, R&D activities, design, services related to computer and information technology, and financial services (Baláž, 2004), or unknown/unspecified and both/mixed. In total, 46 publications are included in the review. A thematic analysis was applied to identify, organise, and understand patterns of themes across reviewed articles (Duan & Sandhu, 2022). Table 2 lists the journals in which the sourced articles are published.

Table 2. List of journals

Journals	IMEs	Immigrant SMEs	Mixed sizes
Entrepreneurship and Sustainability Issues	1		
Societies		1	
European Sociological Review	1		
Journal of Business Research	1		
Pacific Business Review International	1		
International Journal of Entrepreneurial Behaviour & Research	2		
Baltic Journal of Management		1	
Journal of Developmental Entrepreneurship		2	
African Journal of Business Management* not available full text			1
Sustainability	1		
Entrepreneurship and Regional Development		1	3
Journal of Entrepreneurship Management and Innovation			1
Economic Anthropology			1
Work, Employment and Society	1		
Journal of Small Business Management	1		
Small Business Economics		2	

continued on following page

Table 2. Continued

Journals	IMEs	Immigrant SMEs	Mixed sizes
European Management Journal			2
Journal of Enterprising Communities-People and Places in the Global Economy	1		
Small Business Economies		3	
Millennial Asia		1	
Competition Forum		1	
Scandinavian Journal of Hospitality and Tourism	1		
Research policy	1		
Journal of Small Business and Enterprise Development			1
Norwegian Journal of Geography			1
Geography Compass			1
Work, employment, and society			1
Kyklos			1
International Journal of Gender and Entrepreneurship	1		
Journal of Developmental Entrepreneurship		1	
Urban Studies			3
Local Economy	1		
Small Enterprise Research		1	
Journal of Economic Geography.		2	
Total			46

Source. Authors

Results and Findings

Overview of Current Research Production

While the studies are based on various countries and economies, innovation seems to be the overarching theme for all the articles. However, the search word 'innovation' was only used in conjunction with 'small business' and not with other terms referring to MEs, as illustrated in Table 1. Due to Schumpeter's earlier work, as well as other relevant publications in recent years, entrepreneurship and innovation have been strongly linked (Autio et al., 2014; Malerba & Ferreira, 2021; Schumpeter, 1934; Servantie & Rispal, 2020). Thus, the sourced articles on IMEs and immigrant SMEs focus naturally on innovation and business growth, as successful entrepreneurship entails innovation in any enterprise. Another commonality of the studies is that immigrant SMEs and IMEs are argued to be essential contributors to the economies of new home countries while acknowledging that such enterprises experience more constraints than their larger counterparts. For instance, four articles focused not on innovation or business growth but on the critical role of IMEs and immigrant SMEs in developing the local economy.

Undoubtedly, IMEs and small immigrant enterprises share some common traits and face similar challenges. However, it is important to acknowledge that there is a substantial difference between a MEs at the lower end of the scale, with perhaps only one employee, and one at the upper end, with up to ten employees. The drivers, barriers, and resource constraints can vary greatly depending on the size of the enterprise. The issue is compounded by the varying definitions of what constitutes a ME in terms of employee numbers. This lack of standardisation can lead to inconsistencies in research findings and make it difficult to draw comparisons across studies. Moreover, there is a prevalent trend in academic literature to group IMEs together with immigrant Small and Medium Enterprises (SMEs). While this approach may be convenient for broad-brush analyses, it fails to account for the unique characteristics and challenges of IMEs. The heterogeneity within the immigrant enterprise landscape is substantial, and lumping IMEs and SMEs together can mask important insights. For instance, IMEs, being smaller, may face more acute resource constraints and have fewer buffers against market fluctuations compared to their larger counterparts. On the other hand, their smaller size could also make them more resilient and able to adapt to changing market conditions more swiftly (Arslan et al., 2022; Fairlie & Lofstrom, 2015; Rath & Swagerman, 2016).

Therefore, there is a pressing need for more studies that exclusively focus on IMEs. By doing so, researchers can uncover nuances and patterns that are specific to these enterprises, thereby providing more accurate and relevant insights for policymaking and support initiatives. This focused research approach can contribute to a more nuanced and in-depth understanding of the unique characteristics, challenges, and potentials of IMEs.

The detailed key themes identified in existing literature include personal traits, characteristics, and innovation (n = 7), business constraints (n = 17), non-economic capital including human, social and cultural capital (n = 16), family dynamics (n = 10), education level (n = 6), contribution to new home country's economy and social development (n = 8). In addition, a majority of the paper examines IMEs and immigrant SMEs in the context of developed economies including Canada (n = 5), the United States (n = 6), Sweden (n = 4), Italy (n = 2), Germany (n = 1), the United Kingdom (n = 7), Finland (n = 2), Norway (n = 2), the Netherlands (n = 3), Spain (n = 3), Australia (n = 4), Taiwan (n = 1), New Zealand (n = 2), and mixed (n = 4). Others consider developing economies such as Malaysia (n = 4), South Africa (n = 5), the Kingdom of Saudi Arabia (n = 1) and Turkey (n = 1). The native ethnic profile/nationality of the immigrants consists of mixed (n = 17), Polish (n = 5), Italian (n = 4), Caribbean nations (n = 2), South Asian (n = 7), Pakistani (n = 6), Vietnamese (n = 2), Chinese (n = 7). In terms of industry, there is a mix of industries (n = 12) and labour-intensive industries (n = 14), as well as papers where the industry is unknown/unspecified (n = 20). Some publications focus exclusively on immigrant women entrepreneurs (n = 7). When it comes to methodology, there are quantitative methods (n = 15), followed by qualitative approaches (n = 12), a minor number mix methodology (n = 6), secondary data/existing databases (n = 6) and conceptual papers (n = 7).

Personal Traits, Characteristics, and Innovation

The business owner's immigrant status and the reasons for entering entrepreneurship affect innovation and business decisions (Martin-Montaner et al., 2018; Ostrovsky & Picot, 2021; Storti, 2014). For instance, maintaining, developing, growing, competing, surviving, and thriving would require specific innovative abilities (Addo, 2017; Chikwendu & Mutambara, 2020; Haq et al., 2021; Ostrovsky & Picot, 2021; Ruan et al., 2022; Zastempowski, 2022). Thus, the driver to innovation may lie in the personal characteristics of immigrant entrepreneurs, including qualifications and skills, relevant prior experiences, years of residence in the new home country, age and marital status (Martin-Montaner et al., 2018). Their initial motivation to venture into businesses may be out of necessity due to the lack of jobs available. However, IME owners also venture into entrepreneurship as a form of self-expression and identity-making and would be more proactive in their business decisions (Martin-Montaner et al., 2018; Storti, 2014). Ostrovsky and Picot (2021) explain that personal traits such as networking and social skills, perseverance, and language skills also impact innovation abilities. This is similar to the study of Ruan et al. (2022), arguing that personal traits impact business innovation, creativity and risk-taking. Although both studies emphasise immigrant SMEs and not IMEs, similar personal traits may also exist among ME owners. Risk-taking as an individual trait influencing innovation lies in the discussion rooted in immigrants' willingness to take risks, as migrating to a foreign country involves significant risks and uncertainties (Constant & Zimmermann, 2006; Neville et al., 2014; Vandor, 2021). Nevertheless, some discrepancies and inconclusive findings (Bonin et al., 2009; Kushnirovich et al., 2018; Naudé et al., 2017). Kushnirovich et al. (2018) explain that, on the contrary, since immigrants have already taken significant migration risks, further risk-taking would be limited. Subsequently, risk cannot be considered the sole factor to explain immigrants' approach to innovation and business growth. Arslan et al. (2022) further discovered that IME owners have great adaptability through quick adjustments in working conditions, innovative customer service, and supply chain adjustments. This leads to greater resilience during crises such as COVID-19 due to a low level of bureaucracy.

Business Constraints

Language barriers emerged as one of the critical constraints for immigrant entrepreneurs (Chikwendu & Mutambara, 2020; Hack-Polay et al., 2020; Jones et al., 2019; Ruan et al., 2022). Language skills, lack of government support programs, and lack of social networking are particularly relevant for immigrant SMEs compared with native SMEs (Ruan et al., 2022). Moreover, the ability of immigrant entrepreneurs to innovate may be impeded by insufficient proficiency in official languages or inadequate knowledge of markets in the new home country (Ostrovsky & Picot, 2021; Yeasmin & Koivurova, 2019). Unsurprisingly, a lack of language skills as a constraint is more prevalent in non-English-speaking new home countries such as Sweden and Italy and among non-native English speakers in English-speaking countries such as Canada and the US among Chinese and Polish immigrants, for instance (Addo, 2017; Aldén & Hammarstedt, 2016; Ostrovsky & Picot, 2021; Ruan et al., 2022; Van Hulten & Ahmed, 2013). Nevertheless, language may not be considered the most significant constraint if they have sound English language skills (Yeasmin & Koivurova, 2019).

Another critical business constraint is the lack of opportunities to access formal external funding (Abada et al., 2014; Abbasian & Yazdanfar, 2013; Aldén & Hammarstedt, 2016; Arslan et al., 2022; Bagwell, 2018; Jones et al., 2019; Tileva, 2022; Van Hulten & Ahmed, 2013; Yazdanfar et al., 2015; Yeasmin & Koivurova, 2019). Not seeking formal funding agencies may also be related to language barriers and difficulties in writing a comprehensive business plan (Tileva, 2022). In addition, they may also face discrimination based on their ethnic backgrounds, especially when it comes to funding from formal financial institutions and more prevalent among non-European immigrants than European counterparts, for instance (Aldén & Hammarstedt, 2016; Hack-Polay et al., 2020; Malki et al., 2022; Van Hulten & Ahmed, 2013). This leads to reliance on co-ethnic ties instead (Abada et al., 2014; Kloosterman, 2003; Szkudlarek & Wu, 2018).

Family Dynamics

Compared to their larger and native counterparts, IMEs and immigrant SMEs are much more reliant on family ties and assistance (Jones et al., 2019; Kerr & Kerr, 2020; Quigley & Rustagi, 2018; Yazdanfar et al., 2015). In labour-intensive industries, immigrants who venture into entrepreneurship have done so to build work opportunities for their families and communities (Kerr & Kerr, 2020). Thus, they rely more on finances and financial capital from family members than formal institutions such as government loans, banks, and other financial institutions (Abada et al., 2014; Arslan et al., 2022; Quigley & Rustagi, 2018; Ruan et al., 2022; Tileva, 2022; Yazdanfar et al., 2015). Moreover, the term family capital, a form of social capital obtained from family members (Abada et al., 2014; Tata & Prasad, 2015), is particularly relevant for IMEs. Nevertheless, family dynamics can both be a driver and barrier to the success of entrepreneurship owned by immigrant women specifically, which are generally classified as IMEs (Addo, 2017; De Vita et al., 2014; Wang, 2012). It depends on whether family members and spouses are available and supportive and whether they want to pursue business growth if the choice hinders their existing family and social relationships (De Vita et al., 2014; Munkejord, 2017).

Human, Social, and Cultural Capital

In addition to family ties, business development, growth, and success in IMEs depend on non-economy and financial capital, such as human capital and sociological factors (Addo, 2017; Chikwendu & Mutambara, 2020). This is similar to social and networking skills (Arslan et al., 2022; Martin-Montaner et al., 2018; Ruan et al., 2022; Yazdanfar et al., 2015). Such skills seem essential regardless of the economic context (developing and developed) but are primarily applicable to IMEs and immigrant SMEs than their native counterparts. Due to business constraints such as language barriers, as discussed, IMEs tend to rely on familiar networks and supplies such as fellow countrymen (Arslan et al., 2022). Thus, while lacking in financial and even human/cultural capital, such networks allow access to social capital (Bagwell, 2018; Wu, 2022).

Socio-cultural embeddedness, especially in rural areas, is how immigrant entrepreneurs embed themselves by building relationships with stakeholders in a new home environment, and it also determines their entrepreneurial success (Falavigna et al., 2019; Hack-Polay et al., 2020; Kloosterman, 2003; Storti, 2014; Szkudlarek & Wu, 2018). Haq et al. (2021) bring another perspective on social capital and discuss its significance in developing sound customer service and loyal customers. The close bond or relationship between the customers and the entrepreneur leads to innovation and improvement in business operations, as the entrepreneur is in close contact with customers and understands their needs and wants rather than using rigorous and formal customer feedback and survey processes to gain such knowledge. Such a strategy involves the willingness to make changes to adapt to such needs and wants quickly.

Education Level

It has been assumed that immigrant enterprises founded in labour-intensive and low-wage industries are generally from low-education immigrant groups (Duranton & Puga, 2004; Kerr & Kerr, 2020). Nevertheless, Addo (2017) investigated eateries and food businesses and found that all entrepreneurs possess higher education certifications from their native home countries. While Addo (2017) classified IMEs as fewer than six employees rather than five, the minimal discrepancy suggests that the findings apply primarily to IMEs and the definition used by this paper. Further, formal education helps them to achieve entrepreneurial goals such as business growth and establishing and sustaining business networks (Addo, 2017; Tata & Prasad, 2015). Formal education and prior experiences help IMEs in their business operations despite their lack of specific entrepreneurial education (Yeasmin & Koivurova, 2019). Nonetheless, once businesses are established, further education and training are not prioritised due to the costs, the lack of relevance, and the inability to be away from their businesses (Collins, 2003).

Contributions to New Home Country

Lundmark et al. (2014) especially emphasise rural regions and how immigrant businesses contribute to rural transformation and restructuring. The authors did not specify the size of immigrant enterprises in their study. However, since the focal point is self-employment in the tourism and hospitality sectors, it is assumed that most businesses in these sectors are MEs and SMEs (Camilleri & Valeri, 2021). In addition to economic contributions, IMEs offer immigrants the opportunity to pull themselves out of unemployment and social exclusion (Kloosterman, 2003). Social mobility is also created when IMEs employ other immigrants who experience difficulties in finding employment (Kloosterman, 2003; Wu, 2022). This, in turn, leads to further job creation and contribution to the new home country's economy (Yazdanfar et al., 2015). Moreover, Wu (2022) discovers that entrepreneurship in terms of self-employment among immigrant women in Taiwan outweighs native-born women, thus reassuring their economic contribution. Therefore, the contribution of IMEs to the new home country and its local economy is remarkable (Jones et al., 2019). Furthermore, immigrant SMEs, including IMEs, enrich the local culture, leading to cultural diversity in their regions (Collins, 2003; Jones et al., 2019; Lee, 2015).

Discussion of Findings

Business Strategies and Tools Unique for IMEs

Through their entrepreneurial endeavours, immigrants contribute significantly to the global economy. Despite facing challenges such as language barriers and cultural differences, as revealed in the findings, many have established businesses and made significant advances. Generally, incorporating strategic planning, adopting various tools at hand, and tapping into the resources offered by local communities and governmental entities can facilitate the growth and success of immigrant small businesses (Fairlie & Lofstrom, 2015). Strategic planning forms the foundation of any successful business. It involves setting both short-term and long-term goals, identifying potential challenges, and creating strategies to overcome them. Research has shown that strategic planning significantly improves business performance and growth (Brinckmann et al., 2010). For immigrant businesses in general, strategic planning also includes understanding the host country's business environment, which can be quite different from their home country. The role of strategic planning in business success cannot be overstated, as it provides a roadmap for growth and helps businesses navigate challenges. While strategic planning is not less important, for IMEs in the labour-intensive sectors, such a process may not be as formal, structured and meticulous as their larger counterparts. Firstly, in the labour-intensive sectors, the barriers to entry are arguably relatively low, which opens up opportunities for those lacking formal skills, as formal education may not be as needed as much. Hence, the entrepreneurs of IMEs may not follow the formal strategic planning processes as, in many instances, the 'gut feeling', learning by doing and learning from failing from previous experiences are more prevalent. Secondly, immigrants are also considered more hardworking than their native counterparts and more likely to venture into entrepreneurship as their businesses are their livelihood due to problems in finding suitable jobs (Faherty & Stephens, 2016; Fairlie & Fossen, 2020; Friberg & Midtbøen, 2018). Growing and succeeding are imperative as they believe they have no other choices. Thus, they also become more creative and adaptable by quickly changing their strategies and directions and being resilient to adverse situations (Arslan et al., 2022; Fairlie & Lofstrom, 2015; Rath & Swagerman, 2016).

Another finding is their reliance on community resources and support, including family members and people with similar backgrounds as themselves, either from the same home country or with similar immigrant status. Such resources would play pivotal roles in the success of IMEs in labour-intensive industries. As discovered, many immigrant businesses would employ other immigrants and even family members (Kerr & Kerr, 2020). In addition to the low number of employees in IMEs, this phenomenon evidently impacts the dynamic of the work environment, business operations, and decision-making compared with other smaller enterprises. Therefore, the significance of employees in IMEs should not be undervalued. This is particularly applicable to enterprises with a workforce of less than five individuals, where the creativity of each member can significantly influence the innovation capabilities. This includes formulating business strategies and being open to incorporating new tools and technologies into their business operations. In addition to providing financial assistance, as revealed in the findings, family and community members can provide extended networks and mentorship opportunities. Despite lacking formal funding support (Rath & Swagerman, 2016), government entities, community groups, and other non-profit organisations offer resources that immigrant entrepreneurs can leverage. Usage and access to such resources may impact their business strategy by gaining knowledge of various aids and tools that they can use to facilitate business operations and decisions. These resources include business training programs, networking events, and access to funding opportunities. Governmental support has been found to significantly impact the success of immigrant businesses (Newland & Tanaka, 2010). However, the extent to which such resources are actually utilised by IMEs in labour-intensive industries as part of their business strategies and the effect of such services need to be further explored.

The study results suggest that IMEs' strategies and tools in the relevant industries rely heavily on low-threshold solutions. The business strategies, strategic planning, and the selection of appropriate tools in labour-intensive industries do not stem from rigorous Research and Development (R&D) or any other formalised, structured processes. Instead, these strategies appear more spontaneous and rely on the wisdom, drive, and experience of the businesses' individuals. This includes the entrepreneurs and, in some other IMEs, extends to family members and community networks associated with the enterprise. Their collective knowledge and experiences can significantly influence the strategic direction of the IMEs. These findings underscore the importance of the human element as well as the critical role of human and social capital in shaping the strategic and operational decisions within these enterprises (Haq et al., 2021; Jones et al., 2014).

Furthermore, the absence of formalised processes and structures can be both a strength and a weakness for these enterprises. On one hand, it allows for a degree of flexibility and adaptability that may not be possible in larger, more structured organisations. On the other hand, it could lead to inconsistencies and inefficiencies in their operational processes, which could, over time, impact these enterprises' overall productivity and profitability (Almeida, 2024). Hence, while low-threshold solutions provide an accessible entry point and flexibility for IMEs, it is essential to recognise that the absence of structured processes and a reliance on individual knowledge and experiences may also present specific challenges. These challenges could include inconsistencies in operational processes, potential inefficiencies, and a heavy reliance on the knowledge and experiences of a limited number of individuals (Almeida, 2024; Istipliler et al., 2023). Overall, the findings highlight the unique strategic and operational dynamics within IMEs, which are heavily influenced by low-threshold solutions, individual knowledge and experience, and family and community networks. This underlines the importance of recognising these dynamics when developing support interventions and policies to promote these enterprises' growth and sustainability.

Proposed Conceptual Framework

As discussed, much of the findings can be applied to understand the innovation ability of immigrants venturing into micro-sized businesses in labour-intensive industries. IMEs share many of the challenges of being immigrant entrepreneurs in general. However, the review of existing studies confirms that they experience additional difficulties than their native counterparts and other immigrant entrepreneurs in larger enterprise sizes and industries (Addo, 2017; Ruan et al., 2022). Specific drivers and barriers exist that either promote or hinder innovation among such businesses stem from their personal traits and characteristics. While motivation was not a prominent theme that emerged from sourced articles, motivation can be considered a part of one's personal trait that impacts behaviour and decisions (Wasserman & Wasserman, 2020). The importance and influence of motivation were also revealed in the systematic review by Duan and Sandhu (2022). However, the size of immigrant enterprises is either not specified or unclear as various enterprises are grouped. The same issue is found in the systematic review by Malerba and Ferreira (2021) regarding business strategies and growth among immigrant enterprises. Although personal traits and characteristics can drive innovation and business growth, they can also hinder such processes regarding the willingness to take risks. Risk-taking is a contributing factor in business decisions. However, it cannot be considered the sole factor in explaining immigrants' approach to innovation and business growth due to discrepancies in existing studies (Barsky et al., 1997; Bonin et al., 2009; Kushnirovich et al., 2018; Naudé et al., 2017). Despite the various constraints, the number of IMEs that have experienced success in new home countries, especially in rural areas, contributes to the local economy and social and cultural development. ure 1 proposes a conceptual framework based on the analysis and findings of the present paper.

Figure 1. Proposed conceptual framework

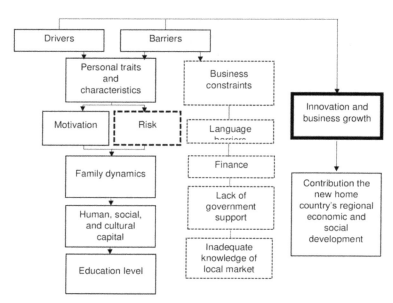

Source: Authors' own work

SOLUTIONS AND RECOMMENDATIONS

While IMEs naturally share some of the same characteristics as immigrant businesses in general, SMEs and MEs in general, and immigrant-owned SMEs, they also have unique traits. Hence, they should be treated as their own segment. Furthermore, studies should highlight the particular industry in which such enterprises are placed as entrepreneurial behaviour, and innovation would be vastly different in labour-intensive industries compared to other businesses of more high-wage and technology-intensive nature.

Essentially, IMEs should be better categorised and defined in studies as they are not homogenous with the general 'immigrant' businesses. Also, where they establish their business, whether in a regional or urban setting, would evidently impact their business practices and actions. The following section proposes some specific research directions.

FUTURE RESEARCH DIRECTIONS

This chapter provides some key topics based on a conceptual ground through a systematic literature review. The highlighted topics need further examination in empirical studies to explore their relevance and application in various contexts. These may include the motivations and characteristics of the owners of IMEs, who play a significant role in such enterprises in contrast to larger enterprises. In many cases, the owner may be the only person running the entire business, taking many and even all the roles necessary to keep the business afloat. Due to this, such enterprises may also be more vulnerable to crises and other major unexpected events. However, despite experiencing many business constraints, numerous IMEs survive and thrive, indicating that their entrepreneurial resilience and innovation behaviour are worth exploring.

Moreover, resources such as business training programs, networking events, and funding opportunities can have a substantial influence on IME's business strategy by acquiring knowledge of different aids and tools that can simplify business operations and strategic business planning and decision-making. Many of these resources are a part of governmental support and aid in contributing to the success of immigrant businesses. However, further exploration is required to understand the degree to which these resources are actually sought by IMEs in labour-intensive industries as integral components of their business strategies and the impact these services have.

Finally, many IMEs are also established in rural and regional areas; their socio-cultural contribution, in addition to their economic contribution, should not be underestimated. This is particularly prevalent in areas and regions that experience challenges associated with depopulation. How IMEs contribute to regional development and sustainability as a whole should be further investigated.

CONCLUSION

This chapter presents a comprehensive overview of the scientific research conducted so far, focusing on industry-specific, micro-sized immigrant businesses. The review of journal articles reveals the under-researched nature of IMEs. It underscores their unique traits, characteristics, and innovation potentials that contribute significantly to their new home countries' economic and socio-cultural development. IME owners often face many challenges and business constraints, from financial to cultural and language barriers. Nevertheless, despite these obstacles, many IMEs continue to succeed and thrive. This resilience under adversity is a testament to their determination and entrepreneurial spirit and indicates that their efforts should neither be ignored nor underestimated.

In recognition of IMEs' critical role in local economic landscapes, there are various governmental programs to support these businesses. These often include local government assistance schemes that offer financial aid and other forms of support. However, these initiatives must truly benefit IMEs and be accessible at a low threshold, acknowledging these enterprises' unique characteristics. Moreover, the extent to which such resources are actually known and utilised by the relevant immigrant entrepreneurs needs to be further explored, as well as the usefulness and effectiveness of such resources in aiding the strategic planning of such enterprises.

While this review has endeavoured to cover the breadth of literature on IMEs, it is essential to note that certain limitations exist in the current body of work. The classification and categorisation of micro-enterprises vary across studies, leading to potential discrepancies. Some research papers may conflate different sizes of immigrant enterprises, treating them as a homogeneous group. This may result in omitting relevant publications that classify these enterprises under different categories, such as self-employment, home-based, or family businesses. To advance the understanding of IMEs, this paper proposes a conceptual framework highlighting critical areas for future empirical studies. Another avenue deserving further investigation is family dynamics' role in innovation behaviour within IMEs. The concept of socio-emotional wealth (Berrone et al., 2012; Pikkemaat et al., 2019), considering emotional and non-financial aspects of family businesses, may provide valuable insights, given that many IMEs are owned and operated by family members. It is crucial, however, to recognise that although many IMEs are family businesses, not all family businesses are IMEs, and not all IMEs are family-owned. Furthermore, the role of employees in IMEs should not be overlooked. This is especially true for businesses with fewer than five employees, where individual creativity can significantly impact innovation capabilities, including business strategies and the willingness to adapt new tools and technologies as part of business operations. Also, the relationships and dynamics between IME owners and their employees are often distinct from those in other types of businesses and require further investigation.

As a concluding note, while the existing body of research on IMEs provides valuable insights, there is ample room for further examination. By understanding IMEs in labour-intensive industries and their unique challenges, characteristics, and potentials, policymakers, researchers, and practitioners can better support these critical contributors to the places, regions, and economies where such businesses have established their foothold.

REFERENCES

Abada, T., Hou, F., & Lu, Y. (2014). Choice or necessity: Do immigrants and their children choose self-employment for the same reasons? *Work, Employment and Society*, 28(1), 78–94. DOI: 10.1177/0950017013511870

Abbasian, S., & Yazdanfar, D. (2013). Exploring the financing gap between native born women- and immigrant women-owned firms at the start-up stage. *International Journal of Gender and Entrepreneurship*, 5(2), 157–173. DOI: 10.1108/17566261311328837

Addo, P. A. (2017). "Is It Entrepreneurship, or Is It Survival?': Gender, Community, and Innovation in Boston's Black Immigrant Micro-Enterprise Spaces [Article]. *Societies, 7*(3), 19, Article 20. https://doi .org/DOI: 10.3390/soc7030020

Aldén, L., & Hammarstedt, M. (2016). Discrimination in the Credit Market? Access to Financial Capital among Self-employed Immigrants. *Kyklos*, 69(1), 3–31. https://doi.org/https://doi.org/10.1111/kykl .12101. DOI: 10.1111/kykl.12101

Aliaga-Isla, R., & Rialp, A. (2013). Systematic review of immigrant entrepreneurship literature: Previous findings and ways forward. *Entrepreneurship and Regional Development*, 25(9-10), 819–844. DOI: 10.1080/08985626.2013.845694

Almeida, F. (2024). Causes of Failure of Open Innovation Practices in Small- and Medium-Sized Enterprises. *Administrative Sciences*, 14(3), 50. https://www.mdpi.com/2076-3387/14/3/50. DOI: 10.3390/ admsci14030050

Arslan, A., Kamara, S., Zahoor, N., Rani, P., & Khan, Z. (2022). Survival strategies adopted by microbusinesses during COVID-19: an exploration of ethnic minority restaurants in northern Finland. *International Journal of Entrepreneurial Behavior & Research*. https://doi.org/https://doi-org.ezproxy .inn.no/10.1108/IJEBR-05-2021-0396

Autio, E., Kenney, M., Mustar, P., Siegel, D., & Wright, M. (2014). Entrepreneurial innovation: The importance of context. *Research Policy*, 43(7), 1097–1108. https://doi.org/https://doi.org/10.1016/j.respol .2014.01.015. DOI: 10.1016/j.respol.2014.01.015

Bagwell, S. (2018). From mixed embeddedness to transnational mixed embeddedness. *International Journal of Entrepreneurial Behaviour & Research*, 24(1), 104–120. DOI: 10.1108/IJEBR-01-2017-0035

Bailey, S. (2014). *Academic writing: A handbook for international students*. Routledge. DOI: 10.4324/9781315768960

Baláž, V. (2004). Knowledge-intensive business services in transition economies. *Service Industries Journal*, 24(4), 83–100. DOI: 10.1080/0264206042000275208

Barsky, R. B., Juster, F. T., Kimball, M. S., & Shapiro, M. D. (1997). Preference Parameters and Behavioral Heterogeneity: An Experimental Approach in the Health and Retirement Study*. *The Quarterly Journal of Economics*, 112(2), 537–579. DOI: 10.1162/003355397555280

Berrone, P., Cruz, C., & Gomez-Mejia, L. R. (2012). Socioemotional Wealth in Family Firms: Theoretical Dimensions, Assessment Approaches, and Agenda for Future Research. *Family Business Review*, 25(3), 258–279. DOI: 10.1177/0894486511435355

Bonin, H., Constant, A., Tatsiramos, K., & Zimmermann, K. F. (2009). Native-migrant differences in risk attitudes. *Applied Economics Letters*, 16(15), 1581–1586. DOI: 10.1080/13504850701578926

Brinckmann, J., Grichnik, D., & Kapsa, D. (2010). Should entrepreneurs plan or just storm the castle? A meta-analysis on contextual factors impacting the business planning–performance relationship in small firms. *Journal of Business Venturing*, 25(1), 24–40. https://doi.org/https://doi.org/10.1016/j.jbusvent .2008.10.007. DOI: 10.1016/j.jbusvent.2008.10.007

Camilleri, M. A., & Valeri, M. (2021). Thriving family businesses in tourism and hospitality: A systematic review and a synthesis of the relevant literature. *Journal of Family Business Management, ahead-of-print*(ahead-of-print). https://doi.org/DOI: 10.1108/JFBM-10-2021-0133

Chikwendu, J. E., & Mutambara, E. (2020). Sociological factors influencing the success of African immigrant-owned micro businesses in South Africa. *Entrepreneurship and Sustainability Issues, 8*(1), 972-982. https://doi.org/https://doi.org/10.9770/jesi.2020.8.1(65)

Collins, J. (2003). Cultural diversity and entrepreneurship: Policy responses to immigrant entrepreneurs in Australia. *Entrepreneurship and Regional Development*, 15(2), 137–149. DOI: 10.1080/0898562032000075168

Constant, A., & Zimmermann, K. F. (2006). The Making of Entrepreneurs in Germany: Are Native Men and Immigrants Alike? *Small Business Economics*, 26(3), 279–300. DOI: 10.1007/s11187-005-3004-6

Dabić, M., Vlačić, B., Paul, J., Dana, L.-P., Sahasranamam, S., & Glinka, B. (2020). Immigrant entrepreneurship: A review and research agenda. *Journal of Business Research*, 113, 25–38. https://doi.org/ https://doi.org/10.1016/j.jbusres.2020.03.013. DOI: 10.1016/j.jbusres.2020.03.013

Davies, A. (2019). Carrying out systematic literature reviews: An introduction. *British Journal of Nursing (Mark Allen Publishing)*, 28(15), 1008–1014. DOI: 10.12968/bjon.2019.28.15.1008 PMID: 31393770

De Vita, L., Mari, M., & Poggesi, S. (2014). Women entrepreneurs in and from developing countries: Evidences from the literature. *European Management Journal*, 32(3), 451–460. DOI: 10.1016/j. emj.2013.07.009

Duan, C., & Sandhu, K. (2022). Immigrant entrepreneurship motivation – scientific production, field development, thematic antecedents, measurement elements and research agenda. *Journal of Enterprising Communities: People and Places in the Global Economy*, 16(5), 722–755. DOI: 10.1108/JEC-11-2020-0191

Duranton, G., & Puga, D. (2004). Micro-Foundations of Urban Agglomeration Economies. In Henderson, J. V., & Thisse, J.-F. (Eds.), *Handbook of Regional and Urban Economics* (Vol. 4, pp. 2063–2117). Elsevier., https://doi.org/https://doi.org/10.1016/S1574-0080(04)80005-1

European Commission. (2021). *Annual Report on European SMEs*

Faherty, U., & Stephens, S. (2016). Innovation in micro enterprises: Reality or fiction? *Journal of Small Business and Enterprise Development*, 23(2), 349–362. DOI: 10.1108/JSBED-11-2013-0176

Fairlie, R. W., & Fossen, F. M. (2020). Defining Opportunity versus Necessity Entrepreneurship: Two Components of Business Creation. In Polachek, S. W., & Tatsiramos, K. (Eds.), *Change at Home, in the Labor Market, and On the Job* (Vol. 48, pp. 253–289). Emerald Publishing Limited., DOI: 10.1108/S0147-912120200000048008

Fairlie, R. W., & Lofstrom, M. (2015). Immigration and entrepreneurship. In *Handbook of the economics of international migration* (Vol. 1, pp. 877–911). Elsevier.

Falavigna, G., Ippoliti, R., & Manello, A. (2019). Judicial Efficiency and Immigrant Entrepreneurs. *Journal of Small Business Management*, 57(2), 421–449. DOI: 10.1111/jsbm.12376

Friberg, J. H., & Midtbøen, A. H. (2018). Ethnicity as skill: Immigrant employment hierarchies in Norwegian low-wage labour markets. *Journal of Ethnic and Migration Studies*, 44(9), 1463–1478. DOI: 10.1080/1369183X.2017.1388160

Grant, M. J., & Booth, A. (2009). A typology of reviews: An analysis of 14 review types and associated methodologies. *Health Information and Libraries Journal*, 26(2), 91–108. DOI: 10.1111/j.1471-1842.2009.00848.x PMID: 19490148

Green, B. N., Johnson, C. D., & Adams, A. (2006). Writing narrative literature reviews for peer-reviewed journals: Secrets of the trade. *Journal of Chiropractic Medicine*, 5(3), 101–117. https://doi.org/doi. DOI: 10.1016/S0899-3467(07)60142-6 PMID: 19674681

Hack-Polay, D., Tenna Ogbaburu, J., Rahman, M., & Mahmoud, A. B. (2020). Immigrant entrepreneurs in rural England – An examination of the socio- cultural barriers facing migrant small businesses in Lincolnshire [Article]. *Local Economy*, 35(7), 676–694. DOI: 10.1177/0269094220988852

Haq, M., Johanson, M., Davies, J., Dana, L.-P., & Budhathoki, T. (2021). Compassionate customer service in ethnic minority microbusinesses. *Journal of Business Research*, 126, 279–290. https://doi.org/https://doi.org/10.1016/j.jbusres.2020.12.054. DOI: 10.1016/j.jbusres.2020.12.054

Istipliler, B., Bort, S., & Woywode, M. (2023). Flowers of adversity: Institutional constraints and innovative SMEs in transition economies. *Journal of Business Research*, 154, 113306. https://doi.org/https://doi.org/10.1016/j.jbusres.2022.113306. DOI: 10.1016/j.jbusres.2022.113306

Jones, T., Ram, M., Edwards, P., Kiselinchev, A., & Muchenje, L. (2014). Mixed embeddedness and new migrant enterprise in the UK. *Entrepreneurship and Regional Development*, 26(5-6), 500–520. DOI: 10.1080/08985626.2014.950697

Jones, T., Ram, M., & Villares-Varela, M. (2019). Diversity, economic development and new migrant entrepreneurs. *Urban Studies (Edinburgh, Scotland)*, 56(5), 960–976. DOI: 10.1177/0042098018765382

Kerr, S. K., & Kerr, W. (2020). Immigrant entrepreneurship in America: Evidence from the survey of business owners 2007 & 2012. *Research Policy*, 49(3), 103918. https://doi.org/https://doi.org/10.1016/j.respol.2019.103918. DOI: 10.1016/j.respol.2019.103918

Khan, K. S., Kunz, R., Kleijnen, J., & Antes, G. (2003). Five steps to conducting a systematic review. *Journal of the Royal Society of Medicine*, 96(3), 118–121. DOI: 10.1177/014107680309600304 PMID: 12612111

Kloosterman, R. C. (2003). Creating opportunities. Policies aimed at increasing openings for immigrant entrepreneurs in the Netherlands. *Entrepreneurship and Regional Development*, 15(2), 167–181. DOI: 10.1080/0898562032000075159

Kushnirovich, N., Heilbrunn, S., & Davidovich, L. (2018). Diversity of Entrepreneurial Perceptions: Immigrants vs. Native Population. *European Management Review*, 15(3), 341–355. https://doi.org/https://doi.org/10.1111/emre.12105. DOI: 10.1111/emre.12105

Lee, N. (2015). Migrant and ethnic diversity, cities and innovation: Firm effects or city effects? [Article]. *Journal of Economic Geography*, 15(4), 769–796. DOI: 10.1093/jeg/lbu032

Liu, C.-W., & Cheng, J.-S. (2018). Exploring Driving Forces of Innovation in the MSEs: The Case of the Sustainable B&B Tourism Industry. *Sustainability (Basel)*, 10(11), 3983. https://www.mdpi.com/2071-1050/10/11/3983. DOI: 10.3390/su10113983

Lundmark, L., Ednarsson, M., & Karlsson, S. (2014). International Migration, Self-employment and Restructuring through Tourism in Sparsely Populated Areas. *Scandinavian Journal of Hospitality and Tourism*, 14(4), 422–440. DOI: 10.1080/15022250.2014.967995

Malerba, R. C., & Ferreira, J. J. (2021). Immigrant entrepreneurship and strategy: A systematic literature review. *Journal of Small Business and Entrepreneurship*, 33(2), 183–217. DOI: 10.1080/08276331.2020.1804714

Malki, B., Uman, T., & Pittino, D. (2022). The entrepreneurial financing of the immigrant entrepreneurs: A literature review. *Small Business Economics*, 58(3), 1337–1365. DOI: 10.1007/s11187-020-00444-7

Martin-Montaner, J., Serrano-Domingo, G., & Requena-Silvente, F. (2018). Networks and self-employed migrants. *Small Business Economics*, 51(3), 735–755. DOI: 10.1007/s11187-017-9962-7

Mendoza, C., Morén-Alegret, R., & McAreavey, R. (2020). (Lifestyle) immigrant entrepreneurs in Spanish small villages: Rethinking international immigration in rural Alt Empordà, Catalonia. *Belgeo. Revue belge de géographie*(1). https://doi.org/https://doi.org/10.4000/belgeo.44107

Moher, D., Liberati, A., Tetzlaff, J., & Altman, D. G. (2009). Preferred reporting items for systematic reviews and meta-analyses: The PRISMA statement. *PLoS Medicine*, 6(7), e1000097. DOI: 10.1371/journal.pmed.1000097 PMID: 19621072

Mosquera, S., & Jardim da Palma, P. (Eds.). (2020). *Multidisciplinary Approach to Entrepreneurship Education for Migrants*. IGI Global. DOI: 10.4018/978-1-7998-2925-6

Mueller, E. (2014). Entrepreneurs from low-skilled immigrant groups in knowledge-intensive industries: Company characteristics, survival and innovative performance. *Small Business Economics*, 42(4), 871–889. DOI: 10.1007/s11187-013-9498-4

Munkejord, M. C. (2017). His or her work–life balance? Experiences of self-employed immigrant parents. *Work, Employment and Society*, 31(4), 624–639. DOI: 10.1177/0950017016667041

Murnieks, C. Y., Klotz, A. C., & Shepherd, D. A. (2020). Entrepreneurial motivation: A review of the literature and an agenda for future research. *Journal of Organizational Behavior*, 41(2), 115–143. https://doi.org/https://doi.org/10.1002/job.2374. DOI: 10.1002/job.2374

Naudé, W., Siegel, M., & Marchand, K. (2017). Migration, entrepreneurship and development: Critical questions. *IZA Journal of Migration*, 6(1), 5. DOI: 10.1186/s40176-016-0077-8

Neville, F., Orser, B., Riding, A., & Jung, O. (2014). Do young firms owned by recent immigrants outperform other young firms? *Journal of Business Venturing*, 29(1), 55–71. https://doi.org/https://doi.org/10.1016/j.jbusvent.2012.10.005. DOI: 10.1016/j.jbusvent.2012.10.005

Newland, K., & Tanaka, H. (2010). *Mobilizing diaspora entrepreneurship for development*. Migration Policy Institute Washington.

NHO. (2022). *Fakta om små og mellomstore bedrifter (SMB) [Facts about small and medium sized enterprises]* Norwegian Confederation of Businss. Retrieved 12 December from https://www.nho.no/tema/sma-og-mellomstore-bedrifter/artikler/sma-og-mellomstore-bedrifter-smb/

Norwegian Government Security and Service Organisation. (2002). *Prosjekt – DIFFERENSIERT regelverk for mikrobedrifter og nyetablert [Project - DIFFERENTIATED regulations for micro-enterprises and newly established]*.

Ostrovsky, Y., & Picot, G. (2021). Innovation in immigrant-owned firms [Article]. *Small Business Economics*, 57(4), 1857–1874. DOI: 10.1007/s11187-020-00376-2

Page, M. J., McKenzie, J. E., Bossuyt, P. M., Boutron, I., Hoffmann, T. C., Mulrow, C. D., Shamseer, L., Tetzlaff, J. M., Akl, E. A., Brennan, S. E., Chou, R., Glanville, J., Grimshaw, J. M., Hróbjartsson, A., Lalu, M. M., Li, T., Loder, E. W., Mayo-Wilson, E., McDonald, S., & Moher, D. (2021). The PRISMA 2020 statement: An updated guideline for reporting systematic reviews. *BMJ (Clinical Research Ed.)*, 372(71), n71. Advance online publication. DOI: 10.1136/bmj.n71 PMID: 33782057

Pikkemaat, B., Peters, M., & Bichler, B. F. (2019). Innovation research in tourism: Research streams and actions for the future. *Journal of Hospitality and Tourism Management*, 41, 184–196. https://doi.org/https://doi.org/10.1016/j.jhtm.2019.10.007. DOI: 10.1016/j.jhtm.2019.10.007

Quigley, B. Z., & Rustagi, N. K. (2018). Level of Education and Family Dynamics among Immigrant and Nonimmigrant Business Owners in the Case of Arlington County, VA. *Competition Forum, 16*(2), 90-95. https://login.ezproxy.inn.no/login?url=https://search.ebscohost.com/login.aspx?direct=true&db=s3h&AN=132606003&site=ehost-live&scope=site

Rath, J., & Swagerman, A. (2016). Promoting Ethnic Entrepreneurship in European Cities: Sometimes Ambitious, Mostly Absent, Rarely Addressing Structural Features. *International Migration (Geneva, Switzerland)*, 54(1), 152–166. https://doi.org/https://doi.org/10.1111/imig.12215. DOI: 10.1111/imig.12215

Rousseau, D. M., Manning, J., & Denyer, D. (2008). 11 Evidence in management and organizational science: Assembling the field's full weight of scientific knowledge through syntheses. *The Academy of Management Annals*, 2(1), 475–515. DOI: 10.5465/19416520802211651

Ruan, M. D., Baskaran, A., & Zhou, S. S. (2022). Mainland Chinese Immigrant-owned SMEs in Malaysia: Case Studies [Article]. *Millennial Asia, 13*(1), 5-34. *Article*, 0976399620977026. Advance online publication. DOI: 10.1177/0976399620977026

Schumpeter, J. A. (1934). *The theory of economic development: An inquiry into profits, capital, credit, interest, and the business cycle*. Harvard University Press.

Sedziniauskiene, R., Sekliuckiene, J., & Zucchella, A. (2019). Networks' Impact on the Entrepreneurial Internationalization: A Literature Review and Research Agenda. *MIR. Management International Review*, 59(5), 779–823. DOI: 10.1007/s11575-019-00395-6

Servantie, V., & Rispal, M. H. (2020). Bricolage, effectuation, and causation shifts over time in the context of social entrepreneurship. In *Social Entrepreneurship and Bricolage* (pp. 49–74). Routledge. DOI: 10.4324/9780429263767-3

Storti, L. (2014). Being an entrepreneur: Emergence and structuring of two immigrant entrepreneur groups. *Entrepreneurship and Regional Development*, 26(7-8), 521–545. DOI: 10.1080/08985626.2014.959067

Szkudlarek, B., & Wu, S. X. (2018). The culturally contingent meaning of entrepreneurship: Mixed embeddedness and co-ethnic ties. *Entrepreneurship and Regional Development*, 30(5-6), 585–611. DOI: 10.1080/08985626.2018.1432701

Tata, J., & Prasad, S. (2015). Immigrant family businesses: Social capital, network benefits and business performance [Article]. *International Journal of Entrepreneurial Behaviour & Research*, 21(6), 842–866. DOI: 10.1108/IJEBR-06-2014-0111

Tileva, A. (2022). Anything but micro-no small change: Informality practices at a nonprofit microlender in Washington, DC. *Economic Anthropology*, 9(1), 72–83. DOI: 10.1002/sea2.12193

United Nations. (2022). *Severe downturns in labour-intensive sectors spell trouble for global inequality*. United Nations. Retrieved January 15 from https://www.un.org/tr/desa/severe-downturns-labour-intensive -sectors-spell-trouble-global-inequality

Van Hulten, A., & Ahmed, A. D. (2013). Migrant entrepreneurs' access to business finance in Australia. *Journal of Developmental Entrepreneurship*, 18(01), 1350003. DOI: 10.1142/S1084946713500039

Vandor, P. (2021). Are voluntary international migrants self-selected for entrepreneurship? An analysis of entrepreneurial personality traits. *Journal of World Business*, 56(2), 101142. https://doi.org/https:// doi.org/10.1016/j.jwb.2020.101142. DOI: 10.1016/j.jwb.2020.101142

Wang, Q. (2012). Ethnic Entrepreneurship Studies in Geography: A Review1. *Geography Compass*, 6(4), 227–240. https://doi.org/https://doi.org/10.1111/j.1749-8198.2012.00482.x. DOI: 10.1111/j.1749-8198.2012.00482.x

Wasserman, T., & Wasserman, L. (2020). Motivation: State, Trait, or Both. In Wasserman, T., & Wasserman, L. (Eds.), *Motivation, Effort, and the Neural Network Model* (pp. 93–101). Springer International Publishing., DOI: 10.1007/978-3-030-58724-6_8

Wu, Y.-L. (2022). Entrepreneurship Experiences among Vietnamese Marriage Immigrant Women in Taiwan. *Sustainability (Basel)*, 14(3), 1489. https://www.mdpi.com/2071-1050/14/3/1489. DOI: 10.3390/ su14031489

Xiao, Y., & Watson, M. (2019). Guidance on Conducting a Systematic Literature Review. *Journal of Planning Education and Research*, 39(1), 93–112. DOI: 10.1177/0739456X17723971

Yachin, J. M. (2019). The entrepreneur–opportunity nexus: Discovering the forces that promote product innovations in rural micro-tourism firms. *Scandinavian Journal of Hospitality and Tourism*, 19(1), 47–65. DOI: 10.1080/15022250.2017.1383936

Yazdanfar, D., Abbasian, S., & Brouder, P. (2015). Business advice strategies of immigrant entrepreneurs in Sweden. *Baltic Journal of Management*, 10(1), 98–118. DOI: 10.1108/BJM-01-2014-0018

Yeasmin, N., & Koivurova, T. (2019). A factual analysis of sustainable opportunity recognition of immigrant entrepreneurship in Finnish Lapland: Theories and practice. *Journal of Entrepreneurship, Management and Innovation, 15*(2), 57-84. https://doi.org/https://doi.org/10.7341/20191523

Zastempowski, M. (2022). What Shapes Innovation Capability in Micro-Enterprises? New-to-the-Market Product and Process Perspective. *Journal of Open Innovation*, 8(1), 59. https://doi.org/https://doi.org/10.3390/joitmc8010059. DOI: 10.3390/joitmc8010059

ADDITIONAL READING

Chung, H. F. L., Yen, D. A., & Wang, C. L. (2020). The contingent effect of social networking ties on Asian immigrant enterprises' innovation. *Industrial Marketing Management*, 88, 414–425. https://doi.org/https://doi.org/10.1016/j.indmarman.2019.04.011. DOI: 10.1016/j.indmarman.2019.04.011

Hinterhuber, A. (2013). Can competitive advantage be predicted? *Management Decision*, 51(4), 795–812. DOI: 10.1108/00251741311326572

Masurel, E., & Nijkamp, P. (2004). Differences between first-generation and second-generation ethnic start-ups: Implications for a new support policy [Article]. *Environment and Planning. C, Government & Policy*, 22(5), 721–737. DOI: 10.1068/c0356

Munkejord, M. C. (2017). Becoming Spatially Embedded: Findings from a Study on Rural Immigrant Entrepreneurship in Norway. *Entrepreneurial Business and Economics Review*, 5(1), 111–130. DOI: 10.15678/EBER.2017.050107

Nunes, A. K. S., Morioka, S. N., & Bolis, I. (2022). Challenges of business models for sustainability in startups. *RAUSP Management Journal*, 57(4), 382–400. DOI: 10.1108/RAUSP-10-2021-0216

Tingvold, L., & Fagertun, A. (2020). Between Privileged and Oppressed? Immigrant Labor Trajectories in Norwegian Long-Term Care. *Sustainability (Basel)*, 12(11), 4777. https://www.mdpi.com/2071-1050/12/11/4777. DOI: 10.3390/su12114777

Wang, Y., & Warn, J. (2018). Chinese immigrant entrepreneurship: Embeddedness and the interaction of resources with the wider social and economic context. *International Small Business Journal*, 36(2), 131–148. DOI: 10.1177/0266242617726364

Williams, C. C. (2008). Beyond Necessity-Driven Versus Opportunity-Driven Entrepreneurship: A Study of Informal Entrepreneurs in England, Russia and Ukraine. *International Journal of Entrepreneurship and Innovation*, 9(3), 157–165. DOI: 10.5367/000000008785096647

Zettel, L., & Garrett, R. (2021). Building Entrepreneurial Resilience Through Adversity. *Proceedings - Academy of Management*, 2021(1), 10164. DOI: 10.5465/AMBPP.2021.10164abstract

KEY TERMS AND DEFINITIONS

Immigrants: Immigrants are individuals who move from their native country to another country with the intention of settling there permanently. They may make this move for various reasons such as seeking better economic opportunities, pursuing education, escaping conflict or natural disasters, or joining family members who have already immigrated.

Immigrant Micro Enterprises (IMEs): IMEs are referred to as small-scale businesses owned and operated by immigrants. These businesses typically have a small number of employees, which can vary from one to five or one to ten, and a low level of capital investment.

Labour-intensive Industries: These industries require a more significant proportion of workers or high human labour to produce goods or services. They are often characterised by a high ratio of labour costs to capital investment, and the focus is heavily on human skills, effort, and time. Examples including the tourism and hospitality industries, retail industries, cleaning services, beauty services, hairdressers and barbers.

Business Innovation: The term refers to how an enterprise introduces new processes, ideas, services, or products. It is a way for businesses to adapt to changes in the market, such as customer demands and competitive pressures, and improve their offerings, efficiency, and profitability.

Business Constraints: Business constraints refer to the limitations or obstacles that impede an enterprise's progress and successful operations. They may include financial constraints, language constraints (for immigrants), geographical and market constraints or the lack of knowledge of these. Moreover, this can include resource constraints, particularly for smaller enterprises.

Socio-cultural Embeddedness: The term refers to how individuals and entities are integrated within a social and cultural context through societal norms, values, traditions, and interpersonal relationships. It indicates that behaviour, actions, thoughts, and identities are shaped and constrained by the social and cultural environments in which individuals and entities are embedded.

Rural Region: A rural region is an area located outside towns and cities. It is typically characterised by low population density, small settlements, and vast amounts of open space. Common challenges faced by such regions are depopulation, a lack of core services, facilities and job opportunities, and low economic activities and business innovation.

Chapter 2
Beyond Differentiation:
How Competitive Intensity Shapes Export Performance for Mozambican SMEs

Eurico Colarinho Navaia
https://orcid.org/0000-0003-0216-4140
Zambeze University, Mozambique

António Carrizo Moreira
https://orcid.org/0000-0002-6613-8796
University of Aveiro, Portugal

Cláudia Pires Ribau
https://orcid.org/0000-0003-2796-0354
University of Aveiro, Portugal

ABSTRACT

Although the relationship between competitive strategy and export performance has been addressed previously in the literature, the moderating effect of the competitive intensity of this relationship is little explored, especially in emerging economies. This study aims to address the moderating effect of competitive intensity in the relationship between differentation competitive strategy and the export performance of Mozambican small and medium-sized enterprises (SMEs). The study involves the analysis of 250 questionnaires directed to Managers of Mozambican SMEs, using structural equation modeling and Partial Least Squares (PLS/SEM) algorithm (SmartPLS 3.0). The findings show that differentiation strategy has a positive influence on export performance. However, competitive intensity has a negative moderating effect on the relationship between differentiation competitive strategy and export performance.

INTRODUCTION

Michael Porter's (1980, 1985) seminal work on competitive advantage established the concept of differentiation and cost leadership strategies. This research received significant support in the literature and marked a turning point in the field of strategy. It integrated firm-specific factors into business performance models, previously dominated by the industrial organization perspective (Parnell, 2006).

DOI: 10.4018/979-8-3693-4046-2.ch002

Studies confirm that a firm's competitive strategy impacts its export performance. These strategies are influenced by the firm's intrinsic characteristics, particularly its resources and core competencies, as well as the industry it operates in (Aulakh et al., 2000; Morgan et al., 2004).

Exporting is a common initial step in the internationalization process, where firms gradually increase their global involvement (Johanson & Vahlne, 1977). Traditionally, internationalization research focused on multinational corporations (MNCs). More recently, there has been a growing interest in small and medium-sized enterprises (SMEs) (Mahamadou, 2021; Musso & Francioni, 2014; Ribau et al., 2015). While MNCs hold significant weight in the global economy, the perceived limitations of SMEs, particularly their resource constraints, are seen as a hurdle in international competition (Musso & Francioni, 2014). However, SMEs are key players in the development of African economies, which are largely reliant on them (Mahamadou, 2021). Current theories on the internationalization of African SMEs are often modeled after those developed in developed countries. It is crucial to consider the diverse economic environment in Africa, which varies in terms of political systems, resources, economic structures, and culture (Matenge, 2011). Internationalization discussions often focus on downstream activities, such as exporting products abroad. In this context, the applicability of these theories to African SMEs deserves further investigation, as emerging economies, particularly those in Africa, often have different ownership structures compared to developed countries (Amal et al., 2013; Maqsoom et al., 2021; Moreira et al., 2024).

Exporting firms in emerging markets face dynamic environments shaped by factors like fluctuating customer demand, evolving market needs and intense international competition (Khan & Khan, 2021). Most SMEs operate in turbulent economic environments, pressured to survive global economic crises while increasing revenue and profits. An effective differentiation strategy can provide a competitive advantage by offering customers greater value through superior products and services. This strategy can justify higher profit margins compared to competitors (Dervitsiotis, 2010).

Competition is central to firms' success. Adapting a firm's activities to an international competitive landscape can significantly contribute to its performance (Fuchs & Kostner, 2016; Leonidou et al., 2015; Morgan et al., 2004; Navarro-García et al., 2016; Porter, 1985). Competitive intensity, a dimension of the internationalization process, reflects the growing number of firms seeking opportunities in international markets to achieve their goals, secure their positions and ensure survival (Rasheed & Ahmad, 2022; Young et al., 1989). Research suggests a positive correlation between competitive intensity and export performance (Fuchs & Kostner, 2016; Lengler et al., 2016; Leonidou et al., 2015; Morgan et al., 2004; Navarro-García et al., 2016). As competition intensifies, a firm's actions and outcomes become heavily influenced by the actions and responses of its competitors, leading to decreased predictability and certainty (Auh & Menguc, 2005; Reimann et al., 2022).

Several studies have explored competitive strategies as determinants of export performance. Morgan et al. (2004) posit that the interaction between a firm's export resources and skills, its chosen competitive strategy and the competitive intensity of the export market determines its positional advantages. Aulakh et al. (2000) examine the effectiveness of cost leadership and differentiation strategies across different foreign market types. Their findings indicate a positive impact of competitive strategies on export performance, with differentiation being particularly effective for firms in developing economies. Rua et al. (2018) analyze the strategic determinants influencing export performance, considering the mediating effect of competitive strategy.

Building on the existing literature, our research offers a novel contribution by examining the moderating effect of competitive intensity on the relationship between a competitive differentiation strategy and the export performance of firms in emerging economies. We focus on two key aspects. First, we investigate the specific effect of a product and service differentiation strategy on export performance. Second, we analyze how competitive intensity moderates the relationship between differentiation strategy and export performance. This focus is particularly relevant for firms in emerging economies, such as those of Mozambique that are normally under-researched. As Aulakh et al. (2000) point out, firms in these economies face diverse competitive environments with distinct customer profiles in both developed and developing markets. This necessitates adapting competitive strategies to cater to the specific needs of each market type.

Mozambique's small and medium-sized enterprises (SMEs) are the backbone of the economy, constituting a significant 97.1% of all registered businesses. The National Institute of Statistics (INE) data from 2017 confirms this dominance, with most companies falling under the "small" category (INE, 2017). Similar to other nations, Mozambique's SMEs play a crucial role in driving economic growth and alleviating poverty (Kaufmann, 2020). INE's 2017 report further highlights their contribution, revealing a 23.4% share of the country's GDP.

As Table 1 shows, Mozambique currently boasts an estimated 49,734 SMEs, employing a workforce of 270,402. This segment can be further categorized: 1,996 are medium-sized, 27,426 are small, and the remaining 20,312 are micro-enterprises. Regarding national distribution, micro enterprises account for 40%, followed by small businesses at 53%, and lastly, medium-sized enterprises at 4%.

The employment picture is also noteworthy. According to INE (2017), SMEs provide jobs for 270,402 individuals, translating to 46.4% of the total workforce. Interestingly, large companies employ the remaining 53.6%, representing 312,381 workers.

Table 1. Distribution of companies by Size

Company size	Total Units		Total Workers		Average number of Workers
	No.	%	No.	%	
Micro	20 312	40	43 819	7.5	2.16
Small	27 426	53	167 537	28.7	6.11
Media	1 996	4	59 046	10.1	29.58
Total of SMEs	**49 734**	**97.1**	**270 402**	**46.4**	**5.5**
Large firms	1 503	2.9	312 381	53.6	207.8
Total	51 237	100.0	582 783	100.0	11.37

Source: (INE, 2017)

According to Kaufmann (2020), several key constraints and challenges hinder SME growth: access to finance, taxation, business management difficulties, workforce qualifications, underdeveloped infrastructure, limited market access, and inadequate stakeholder coordination. Mozambique exhibits characteristics of an emerging African economy with a vibrant SME sector and promising natural resources. However, addressing challenges in financing, infrastructure, and workforce development will be crucial to ensure inclusive and sustainable economic growth, a common goal for many African nations on the rise.

The remainder of this chapter is structured as follows. Section 2 presents a comprehensive literature review that explores competitive differentiation strategies, export performance and competitive intensity. We then develop our research hypotheses based on this review. Section 3 details the research methodology employed in our study. Section 4 presents the results of our analysis and discusses their implications. Finally, Section 5 concludes the chapter by summarizing the key findings, acknowledging any limitations of the study, and suggesting avenues for future research.

THEORETICAL BACKGROUND

Differentiation Strategy

Competitive strategy refers to the pursuit of a favorable position within an industry to achieve a sustainable and profitable advantage over competitors (Porter, 1980, 1985). It seeks to create a preferential competitive situation by differentiating the firm from its rivals. This differentiation allows the firm to establish a strong position in the face of competitive forces within the industry (Herzallah et al., 2014).

A differentiation strategy involves offering unique value to customers through various dimensions. Firms can differentiate themselves based on product attributes, delivery systems, marketing approaches, or a combination of factors (Porter, 1980, 1985). The goal is to provide superior products or services that better satisfy customer needs (et al., 2014). This often requires continuous product improvement and technological innovation, achieved through substantial investments in research and development (R&D) activities (Wang et al., 2024). Firms employing a differentiation strategy carefully select the attributes they will leverage to stand out, aiming for a unique position that commands a premium price (Porter, 1985). This premium price can be a key driver of firm performance (Acquaah, 2011; Carlson, 2023; Eulerich et al., 2023; Islami & Topuzovska Latkovikj, 2022; Lechner & Gudmundsson, 2014).

However, differentiation strategies are not without risks. The first risk concerns sustainability – competitors can imitate the differentiating factors, causing them to lose their significance to buyers. The second risk arises when costs become similar across offerings, negating the value proposition of differentiation. Finally, an overly focused differentiation strategy targeting a very specific niche market can limit overall sales potential (Porter, 1985).

Firms that implement a differentiation strategy hope to build a strong bond of loyalty with their target audience. Strategies based on differentiation and high-quality products are significant competitive weapons, especially in dynamic environmental, such as export markets (Leitner & Guldenberg, 2010). However, this strategy can present some risks when: 1) the differentiation strategy is unsustainable (competitors are able to imitate and the basis of differentiation becomes less important to buyers); 2) when there is similarity of costs between the different offers; and 3) when differentiation is very high, focusing on very specific market niches (Porter, 1985).

Export Performance

The globalization of markets and intensified global competition have prompted firms to increasingly seek opportunities in foreign markets to ensure long-term survival. In this context, exporting is the most common initial mode of international expansion, particularly for small and medium-sized enterprises (SMEs) (Lengler et al., 2014; Ribau et al., 2017, 2018). Exporting is also an important driver of economic development for nations. Understanding and mastering the factors that positively impact export performance is therefore crucial for academics, managers, and public institutions (Lengler et al., 2014).

Export performance reflects a firm's relative effectiveness in utilizing resources and translating them into strategies that maximize opportunities while minimizing threats and challenges in foreign markets (Ibeh & Wheeler, 2005). It also reflects the firm's specific approach to leveraging its resources and skills and is considered a key indicator of success in international operations (Beleska-Spasova et al., 2012; Pett & Wolff, 2017).

The literature offers various measurement approaches for export performance (Aulakh et al., 2000; Bonaccorsi, 1992; Cavusgil & Zou, 1994; Gemünden, 1991; Guan & Ma, 2003; Jantunen et al., 2005; Ribau et al., 2017; Sousa, 2004; Sousa et al., 2008; Yi et al., 2013; Zou & Stan, 1998), as shown in Table 2. For instance, Aulakh et al. (2000) developed a model examining the export strategies of firms in emerging economies and their performance in foreign markets. They used both financial variables (export sales and profits) and non-financial variables (export targets, satisfaction, and perceived success). Their findings suggest that differentiation strategies positively impact export performance in developing countries.

Guan and Ma (2003) considered several indicators to measure export performance, categorized as: structural factors (firm size, age, management systems, technology, and R&D); firm management factors (export expectations, profitability, risk, costs, and experience); and incentives and obstacles encountered during internationalization. Their research focused on the impact of innovation capabilities on the export performance of Chinese manufacturing firms. The results indicated that, apart from manufacturing innovation capability, all other factors (learning innovation capability, R&D, resource exploitation, marketing, strategic and organizational capabilities) had a direct positive relationship with export performance.

Table 2. Export performance measurement indicators

Indicators	Author
Financial – export sales and profits; Non-financial – firms' export objectives, satisfaction and perception of success.	(Aulakh et al., 2000; Jantunen, Puumalainen, Saarenketo, & Kylaheiko, 2005; Kuivalainen, Sundqvist, & Servais, 2007; Zou & Stan, 1998),
Export sales over total sales	(Yi et al., 2013)
Structural factors (size, age, management systems, technology and R&D); Management factors of the firm (export expectation, profitability, risk, costs and experience); and Incentives and obstacles in the internationalization process.	(Guan & Ma, 2003)
Intensity of exports; Growth in export sales; Profitability of exports; Export market share and overall satisfaction; Export performance; and Export Success.	(Sousa, 2004)
Economic (such as increased profits and sales); and Strategic (such as diversifying markets, gaining market share and increasing brand reputation).	(Cavusgil & Zou, 1994)
Size of the firm; and international experience.	(Sousa et al., 2008)

Source: Owner Elaboration

Ribau et al. (2017) applied various objective and subjective measures to assess export performance. Objective measures included financial ratios, economic measures, and non-economic measures. Subjective measures included items related to management decisions, export expansion strategies, target achievement, customer satisfaction and general subjective perceptions. These indicators helped them analyze factors influencing the export performance of SMEs and integrate the theories of international entrepreneurship and international strategies. Based on an extensive literature review, their model incorporates the key aspects of SME internationalization processes that influence export performance. The model by Ribau et al. (2017) highlights three important factors affecting a firm's entrepreneurial orientation: the industry sector, the environment, and the firm itself.

By studying the relationship between export performance and firm- and site-specific institutional idiosyncrasies, Yi et al. (2013) use export market sales over total sales as a measure of export performance. The results show that investment abroad, affiliation to the business group and the degree of commercialization of the region where the firm operates positively moderate the effects of innovative skills on export performance. Relations with the Government have a stronger positive moderating effect on the innovation-export relationship only in regions with a high level of commodification.

Competitive Differentiation Strategy and Export Performance

The literature suggests a positive relationship between competitive differentiation strategies and export performance (Aulakh et al., 2000; Boehe & Cruz, 2010; Falahat & Migin, 2017; Keskin et al., 2021; Leonidou et al., 2015; McGuinness & Little, 1981; Morgan et al., 2004; Peres et al., 2023). However, the nature of this relationship is explored from various perspectives. Morgan et al. (2004) propose that a firm's resources and competencies influence its choice of competitive strategies and the resulting positional advantages achieved in the export market, which ultimately affect export performance. Aulakh et al. (2000) go beyond examining differentiation and cost leadership strategies in isolation. They integrate marketing standardization and export diversification into their model.

Keskin et al. (2021) analyze 281 Turkish exporting manufacturing firms across various industrial sectors. They conclude that informational, relational, and marketing skills strengthen competitive advantages and influence both differentiation and cost leadership strategies. These skills enable firms to achieve superior performance in foreign markets.

Leonidou et al. (2015) investigate the internal and external determinants of environmentally friendly export business strategies and their effects on export competitive advantage and performance among Greek manufacturing firms. Their findings reveal that this business strategy was more prominent among larger firms with extensive export experience, firms producing high-tech industrial goods and those exporting to developed countries. Additionally, the study indicates a positive effect on the firms' export product differentiation advantage. This advantage, in turn, is positively associated with export market performance and the financial performance of exports.

Boehe and Cruz (2010) examine the contribution of corporate social responsibility (CSR) to product differentiation, quality, and innovation in the context of export performance within an emerging economy (Brazil). Their results support the positive effect of product differentiation on export performance. Similarly, Falahat and Migin (2017) test a theoretical framework that explores the relationships between international market orientation, business strategies and export performance among international new ventures in the emerging market of Malaysia. Their findings indicate that differentiation strategies positively impact export performance. They emphasize the importance of consistent monitoring and evaluation of business strategies to enable firms to add value for customers and consequently improve export performance.

However, some studies present contrasting evidence. Chung and Ho (2021) examine the effects of international competitive strategies (cost leadership and differentiation) on export performance (measured by market share and strategy) in New Zealand. Their research explores further into the roles of exploitative and exploratory organizational learning in the relationships between international competitive strategies and export performance. Their results suggest that the differentiation strategy does not have a positive influence on export performance. Halikias and Salavou (2014) explore the relationship between competitive strategies and export performance in an export context, drawing on Porter's (1985) framework. Their findings reveal that export performance is not contingent on all generic strategies employed by firms in the international arena. Notably, their results suggest that firms adopting a differentiation strategy tend to have lower export performance in terms of export sales intensity. They argue that while a differentiation strategy can enable firms with unique products or services to achieve higher domestic sales through premium pricing, this may not necessarily translate to export markets.

Competitive Intensity and Export Performance

Competitive intensity refers to the degree of competition within an industry (Boso et al., 2013). As the number of competitors in a market increases, the level of competition intensifies. This leads to a more dynamic environment characterized by frequent changes in pricing, marketing strategies and product offerings (Auh & Menguc, 2005). The outcome of a firm's actions becomes heavily influenced by the responses and countermoves of its rivals, leading to decreased predictability and certainty (Auh & Menguc, 2005). Highly competitive environments pressure firms to adapt and engage in proactive, and sometimes risky, activities. This may involve bold initiatives such as price wars, aggressive marketing campaigns, or rapid product innovation (Auh & Menguc, 2005; Ribau et al., 2017). Research suggests that the impact of competition varies. Weaker competitors have a less significant influence on stronger rivals, while strong competitors can significantly limit the opportunities of their weaker counterparts (Barnett, 1997).

Firm size can also play a role in competitive dynamics. Large firms may lose some competitive edge compared to smaller, more flexible rivals with less cumbersome structures (Barnett, 1997; Fuchs & Kostner, 2016). However, larger firms may be able to leverage institutional support mechanisms to mitigate challenges faced by weaker subsidiaries and improve their overall viability (Barnett, 1997). In such cases, smaller businesses may find themselves facing a more competitive landscape with strengthened larger rivals.

The relationship between competitive intensity and export performance is complex and has been explored in various studies (Arun & Yildirim Ozmutlu, 2024; Fuchs & Kostner, 2016; Lengler et al., 2016; Leonidou et al., 2015; Morgan et al., 2004; Navarro-García et al., 2016). Fuchs and Kostner (2016) investigated the relationships between organizational factors, the external environment (including competitive intensity), international marketing strategies and export success of Australian exporting SMEs. Their findings indicate that firms in more competitive environments increase their efforts to adapt and achieve higher export performance.

Lengler et al. (2016) examined the determinants of customer orientation and its quadratic effects on the export performance of Brazilian SMEs. Their results suggest that both technological and competitive intensity are key factors influencing export success. However, they also found a negative effect of competitive intensity, indicating that extremely high levels of competition can have a detrimental impact on export performance. Lengler et al. (2016) argue that firms in emerging markets entering developed economies face a need for continuous monitoring of competitors and frequent product/service adjustments. This is because the greater competitive intensity in developed markets demand more resource allocation towards enhancing offerings and meeting customer needs.

Navarro-García et al. (2016) explored the interrelationships between human resources, competitive intensity, export commitment, strategic behavior, and export performance (both strategic and operational) of Spanish SMEs. Their findings indicate that competitive intensity positively affects export performance. They attribute this effect to the dynamism of the international environment, which forces firms to be vigilant and react promptly to changes in foreign markets. Rapid response is crucial to avoid falling behind competitors.

The Moderating Effect of Competitive Intensity

The literature presents varied perspectives on the moderating effect of competitive intensity on export performance (e.g., Keskin et al., 2021; Khan & Khan, 2021; Lengler et al., 2014; Morgan et al., 2004). However, few studies examine competitive intensity as a moderator in the relationship between competitive strategy and export performance.

Drawing on the resource-based view (RBV) and the structure-conduct-performance (SCP) paradigm, Keskin et al. (2021) investigate the simultaneous effects of competitive strategies and firm competencies on achieving competitive advantages and export performance under varying levels of competitive intensity. Their findings reveal that competitive intensity negatively moderates the relationship between service advantages and export performance. Conversely, it does not moderate the relationships between cost advantages, product advantages and export performance. The authors explain this by suggesting that firms may not prioritize developing service competencies when competitive intensity is low. As a result, the marginal contribution of these competencies becomes more important for export performance when competition intensifies.

Similarly, Morgan et al. (2004) propose a conceptual model integrating the RBV and SCP perspectives to understand the dynamic performance process of exporting firms. They examine how a firm's available resources and skills, including competitive strategy and the competitive intensity of the export market, interact to determine positional advantage and export performance. Their results indicate that competitive intensity has a less significant direct effect on export performance. However, it does moderate the relationship between a firm's competitive strategies and its positional advantages.

Lengler et al. (2014) explore the moderating effect of competitive intensity on the relationship between the dimensions of market orientation and the export performance of Brazilian exporting firms. They find that the moderating effect of competitive intensity on competitor orientation and export performance is negative. This implies that as competition intensifies, competitor orientation has a diminishing marginal impact on export performance. In contrast, the interaction effect of customer orientation and competitive intensity positively influences export performance. Interestingly, their findings suggest that customer orientation alone does not directly impact export performance. However, when the moderating effect of competitive intensity is introduced, the interaction term has a positive effect on export success. This suggests that customer orientation becomes more valuable in highly competitive environments.

Khan and Khan (2021) draw on the RBV and dynamic capabilities approach to examine the role of marketing competencies (specifically, market responsiveness) in improving marketing performance for exporting firms in an emerging market (Pakistan) under conditions of highly competitive intensity. They find a moderately positive relationship, indicating that marketing performance improves with higher levels of competitive intensity. In this case, a highly competitive environment seems to play a positive role, allowing marketing competencies, through market responsiveness, to have a more positive influence on performance.

MAIN FOCUS OF THE CHAPTER

Hypotheses Development

Competitive differentiation strategies have a positive effect on export performance (McGuinness & Little, 1981; Aulakh et al., 2000; Morgan et al., 2004; Boehe & Cruz, 2010; Leonidou et al., 2015; Falahat & Migin, 2017; Keskin et al., 2021; Arun & Yildirim Ozmutlu, 2024). The literature suggests that export performance is strongly influenced by competitive strategic choices, with their competitive or positional advantages in the market and with the availability of key resources and skills (Morgan et al., 2004). Therefore, we raise the following hypothesis:

Hypothesis $_1$: Competitive differentiation strategies have a positive effect on the export performance of Mozambican SMEs.

Competitive intensity has a direct and positive impact on export performance, as exporting firms are those that have competitive advantages that allow them to compete in wider international markets (Fuchs & Kostner, 2016; Leonidou et al., 2015; Morgan et al., 2004; Navarro-García et al., 2016). On the other hand, the competitive intensity positively moderates the export performance (Khan & Khan, 2021; Lengler et al., 2014; Morgan et al., 2004). In this chapter, we will analyze the moderating effect of competitive intensity on the relationship between competitive strategy and export performance, so we propose the following hypotheses:

Hypothesis $_{2a}$: Competitive intensity positively influences the export performance of Mozambican SMEs.

Hypothesis $_{2b}$: The competitive intensity positively moderates the relationship between the competitive differentiation strategy and the export performance of Mozambican SMEs.

The conceptual model proposed is presented in Figure 1. This model suggests that competitive strategy is a determinant of export performance. Competitive intensity has a direct positive relationship with export performance, i.e., firms that adopt competitive strategies to differentiate their products or services survive in the intense competitive market have a high export performance. On the other hand, the competitive intensity of the market positively moderates the relationship between competitive differentiation strategies and export performance, which means that when competitive intensity increases, export performance also increases.

Figure 1. Proposal of the conceptual model

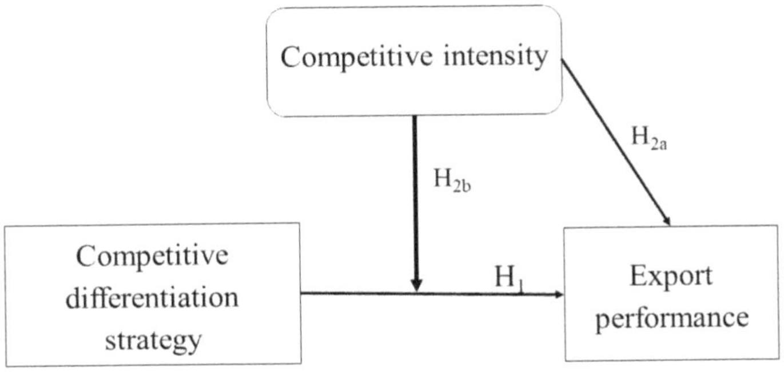

Source: Own elaboration

Method

Questionnaire Development and Measurement Scales

This study employed multidimensional scales adapted from previous research to measure the three key constructs: competitive differentiation strategy (Aulakh et al., 2000; Morgan et al., 2004), export performance (Aulakh et al., 2000; Jantunen et al., 2005; Kuivalainen et al., 2007; Zou & Stan, 1998) and competitive intensity (Jaworski & Kohli, 1993; Morgan et al., 2004).

Data collection involved a self-administered questionnaire distributed online through Google Drive LimeSurvey. The questionnaire was available in both English and Portuguese to cater to the target population. A seven-point Likert scale (1 = Strongly disagree, 7 = Strongly agree) was used to measure all constructs.

To ensure clarity and reduce respondent burden, the questionnaire underwent a pre-test with a convenience sample of eight individuals (university professors and managers). This pre-test helped refine the wording, organization, and formatting of the questionnaire, while assessing comprehension and completion time. Based on the feedback, terminology was simplified and the number of items per variable was minimized to maintain a reasonable questionnaire length. While telephone and in-person approaches were used to encourage participation, all responses were ultimately recorded online.

Sampling and Data Collection

A sample of 400 exporting SMEs from Mozambique was extracted from the Agency for the Promotion of Investment and Export (APIEX) database. From an initial pool of 305 completed responses to the survey sent out, 250 completed responses were obtained, representing a response rate of 62.5%. The sample included firms from various sectors: Agro-industry (19.2%), Wood Processing (35.6%), Fishery Products (26.8%) and Agricultural Products (18.4%). Most of these SMEs were small to medium-sized, with 67.2% employing 5-49 workers and 32.8% employing 50-100 workers. Notably, 84% of the surveyed SMEs exported to 1-3 countries.

Prior to analysis, the psychometric properties of the scales used (unidimensionality, reliability and validity) were assessed using established statistical tests (Hair et al., 2014). Internal consistency was confirmed through Cronbach's alpha coefficients.

Partial least squares structural equation modeling (PLS-SEM) with SmartPLS 3.0 software was employed for the main statistical analysis. This method is well-suited for this study due to its robustness with potentially non-normal data (Henseler & Chin, 2010) and its effectiveness with moderate sample sizes (Hair et al., 2011), although our sample size exceeded the minimum of 200 responses.

The measurement model was evaluated for reliability, convergent validity, and discriminant validity. Importantly, PLS-SEM utilizes bootstrapping to assess the statistical significance of relationships, making it appropriate even for non-normal variables that can arise when multiplying normally distributed variables (Bollen & Stine, 2014; Efron, 1988).

Measurement of Variables

Table 3 presents the analysis of the internal consistency of the scales of the three constructs, based on Cronbach's alpha and rho_A. The reliability coefficients all have values above the recommended value of 0.70 (Hair et al., 2011).

Table 3. Analysis of internal consistency

Variables	Cronbach's alpha	rho_A
Competitive differentiation strategy	0.924	0.925
Export performance	0.938	0.947
Competitive intensity	0.906	0.958

Source: Own elaboration

Table 4 presents factor loadings of the items, which were obtained through *bootstrapping* with 5,000 interactions. Items EP3 and SD5 were removed because they presented factor loadings lower than the minimum *threshold* value required. All other items have factor loadings equal to or greater than the minimum recommended limit of 0.7 (Götz et al., 2010).

Table 4. Factor loadings

Construct	Variables/Items	Factor loadings
Export Performance	Adapted from Jantunen *et al.* (2005); Kuivalainen *et al.* (2007); Aulakh *et al.* (2000);Zou & Stan (1998) (EP1) Exporting has contributed to the sales growth of our firm (EP2) Exporting has improved our firm's market share (EP3) Our export activity has made our firm more competitive (EP4) Exporting has contributed to our Profitability (EP5) Exporting has contributed to enter in new markets (EP6) Exporting has contributed to improve our international image (EP7) Exporting has contributed to improve the development of our know-how	0.889 0.847 - 0.864 0.878 0.918 0.837
Competitive Strategy	Adapted from Morgan *et al.* (2004); and Aulakh *et al.* (2000) Marketing differentiation (MD1) Improving/maintaining advertising and promotion (MD2) Building brand identification in the export venture market (MD3) Adopting new/innovative marketing techniques and methods Product/service differentiation (SD1) Maintaining higher quality standards for our products (SD2) Maintaining unique image for our products (SD3) Differentiating products and services from competitors (SD4) Achieving/maintaining quick product delivery (SD5) Achieving/maintaining prompt response to customer orders (SD6) Offering extensive customer service	0.830 0.778 0.865 0.703 0.844 0.834 0.757 - 0.851
Competitive Intensity	Adapted from Morgan *et al.* (2004); Jaworski and Kohli (1993) (CI1) Competition in our export market is cut-throat (CI2) There are many promotion wars in our export market (CI3) Anything that one competitor can offer others can match easily (CI4) Price competition is a hallmark of our export market (CI5) One hears of a new competitive move almost everyday	0.699 0.871 0.904 0.858 0.904

Source: Own elaboration

Table 5 describes the Average Variance Extracted (AVE), Composite Reliability (CR) and the correlations of each latent variable used. CR values are higher than the recommended minimum of 0.6 (Götz et al., 2010), indicating that all constructs have adequate internal consistency. In addition, the AVE of each construct is higher than the minimum expected limit of 0.5 (Götz et al., 2010), which guarantees its convergent validity. Finally, discriminant validity was obtained for each construct, since the square root of AVE is greater than the absolute value of all correlations with the other constructs, as shown in Table 5.

Table 5. Discriminant validity

Variables	Correlations		
	1.	**2.**	**3.**
1. Competitive strategy of differentiation	**0.810**		
2. Export performance	0.605	**0.873**	
3. Competitive intensity	0.586	0.518	**0.851**
Composite Reliability (CR)	0.938	0.950	0.929
Average Variance Extracted (AVE)	0.655	0.761	0.724

Note: Diagonal elements (in bold) are the square root of the AVE. Outside of diagonal elements are simple bivariate correlations between constructs

Source: Own elaboration

Hypotheses Testing

Linear regression analysis was used to test hypothesis H_1 and hierarchical regression analysis to test hypotheses H_{2a} e H_{2b} (Aguinis & Gottfredson, 2010; Arnold, 1982; Sharma et al., 1981).

Table 6 presents the results: the variable competitive differentiation strategy was used as independent variable in model 1, the variable competitive intensity as independent in model 2. The effect of competitive intensity is examined in model 3 with the inclusion of the two relationships to be tested: competitive differentiation strategy and competitive intensity (figure 2).

Model 1 validated the direct effect of competitive differentiation strategy on export performance ($\beta = 0.604$, $p < 0.001$), supporting H_1 (positive effect). Similarly, Model 2 tested the direct effect of competitive intensity ($\beta = 0.25$, $p < 0.001$), supporting H_{2a} (positive effect). Model 3 incorporated both independent variables and their interaction term. The results revealed a negative interaction effect ($\beta = -0.126$, $p < 0.001$), indicating that competitive intensity negatively moderates the relationship between differentiation strategy and export performance. Therefore, H_{2b} is not supported.

Table 6. Summary of regression analysis

Variables	Model 1	Model 2	Model 3
Competitive strategy of differentiation	0.604*	0.459*	0.369*
Competitive intensity	-	0.249*	0.224*
Competitive strategy of differentiation x competitive intensity	-	-	-0.126*

continued on following page

Table 6. Continued

Variables	Model 1	Model 2	Model 3
R²	0.365	0.407	0.432
R² Adjusted	0.362	0.402	0.426

Note: n = 250; non-standardized regression coefficients are reported; *p < 0.001
Source: Own elaboration

Figure 2. Moderating Effect of Competitive Intensity

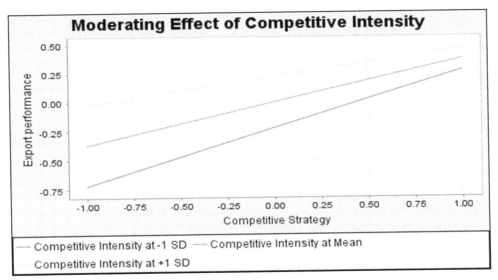

Source: Own elaboration

SOLUTIONS AND RECOMMENDATIONS

The results of model 1 confirm that competitive differentiation strategies have a direct positive influence on the export performance of Mozambican SMEs, which is in line with previous studies (Arun & Yildirim Ozmutlu, 2024; Aulakh et al., 2000; Boehe & Cruz, 2010; Falahat & Migin, 2017; Leonidou et al., 2015; Keskin et al., 2021; McGuinness & Little, 1981; Morgan et al., 2004). This result can be substantiated on the following factors: first, exporters from emerging economies can leverage positive consumer perceptions by differentiating their products based on the size of the country of origin and, over time, can build lasting brand reputations. In addition, the cost of implementing a differentiation strategy is lower in developing countries than in developed ones (Aulakh et al., 2000); second, firms in emerging economies concentrate on small groups of foreign markets and are therefore more successful in increasing their export performance by using a differentiation strategy rather than those that direct their exports to a large number of countries (Boehe & Cruz, 2010); and, third, differentiation strategies are leveraged on intangible resources and dynamic competencies that allow firms to overcome their limitations, which leads them to a superior export performance in international markets (Falahat & Migin, 2017). Thus, it is possible to validate Hypothesis 1.

The effect of competitive intensity increases the explanation power of the model, as presented in model 2. As Mozambican SMEs face international competition their performance improves, increasing the explanatory capacity of the model from 36.5% to 40.7%. Thus, as competition intensifies, Mozambican SMEs generally react positively to the stimulus of competitive intensity and stronger competitors, adjusting their competitive behavior to international markets (Auh & Menguc, 2005; Barnett, 1997; Westhead et al., 2004; Ribau et al., 2017). Thus, the H_{2a} can be validated.

The results presented by model 3 and Figure 2 reveal a negative interaction between the competitive differentiation strategy and the competitive intensity. This implies that the moderator effect tested is not validated, rejecting H_{2b}. From Figure 2 it is possible to conclude that the difference in export performance associated with an increased differentiation strategy is greater in firms facing lower competitive intensity compared to those facing higher competitive intensity. This indicates that Mozambican SMEs with a low level of competitive pressure may not need to invest heavily in developing significant differentiation advantages.

However, as the level of differentiation advantage increases, so does the export performance of Mozambican SMEs. As competition intensifies, so does the supply of differentiated products, as well as imitation, which results in two possible, although not exclusive, situations: greater difficulty in differentiation and a greater effort to adapt to the new competitive intensity, which implies that as competitive intensity increases, export performance is affected.

Thus, we can affirm that the increase in competitive intensity in international markets is a limiting factor in the development of Mozambican firms, hindering the increase in their performance (Auh & Menguc, 2005; Barnett, 1997; Ribau et al., 2017; Westhead et al., 2004). Furthermore, well-established firms with differentiation strategies, offering unique products or services at premium prices, may benefit from differentiation advantages and higher domestic sales volume. However, they may not achieve the same success in international markets due to increased competition and imitation in larger and more competitive markets (Halikias & Salavou, 2014).

This chapter presents two implications for theory development in the areas of business strategy and export performance. Firstly, it emphasizes the importance of competitive differentiation strategies for the export performance of SMEs from emerging economies, such as Mozambique. The second implication relates to the complex role of competitive intensity on export performance.

Insofar as competitive intensity, while providing a positive reaction for less established firms with differentiating advantages, leading to increased export performance, for highly differentiating firms, increasing competitive intensity does not necessarily translate to higher export performance, which may indicate the following:

- Mozambican SMEs have developed strategies that allow them to compete with some differentiation strategies in markets with low competitive intensity, however these skills are not enough to develop highly differentiated products and services in markets with highly competitive intensities, hence the difference in the increase in export performance between firms competing in environments with low and highly competitive intensity.
- There is a clear need for Mozambican SMEs to develop unique skills that will enable them to compete with products and services with higher marginal contribution to compete in markets with highly competitive intensity.

- There is a need for Mozambican SMEs to develop greater international experience, especially in competitive markets, in order to be able to develop products and services with high technological intensity, capable of facing international competitiveness, especially since differentiation strategies are positively associated with good performances in export markets.
- It is important to develop a public policy that allows for the further development of core and distinctive skills within Mozambican firms, to support their competitiveness in wider and more demanding markets, such as international markets.

As for the practical implications, the research reveals that exporting firms from emerging countries can take advantage of competitive differentiation strategies to increase their export performance. Moreover, when competitive intensity increases, more established firms in terms of differentiation advantages need to be more proactive, develop their internal competencies and international experience, as their export performance may decrease.

FUTURE RESEARCH DIRECTIONS

Future research could explore the combined effect of product or service differentiation strategies and export performance, while considering the mediating role of competitive or positional advantages held by exporting SMEs. This would allow for a more nuanced understanding of the relationship and facilitate comparisons across different contexts.

CONCLUSION

This research investigated the impact of competitive differentiation strategies on the export performance of firms and examines the moderating effect of competitive intensity on this relationship. The results reveal a direct positive effect of the differentiation strategy on export performance. By adopting a differentiation strategy for their products and services, Mozambican SMEs can potentially experience increased sales, improved market share, higher profit contributions, discovery of new markets and an enhanced image in international markets. However, competitive intensity has a negative moderating effect on the relationship between the competitive differentiation strategy and export performance. This means that as competitive intensity increases, the positive impact of differentiation on export performance diminishes as firms gain greater competitive advantages.

Limitations of this study include the use of one informant per firm and the cross-sectional nature of the research design. Longitudinal research, which captures changes over time, may need to be implemented to try to capture richer insights.

REFERENCES

Acquaah, M. (2011). Business strategy and competitive advantage in family businesses in Ghana: The role of social networking relationships. *Journal of Developmental Entrepreneurship*, 16(01), 103–126. DOI: 10.1142/S1084946711001744

Aguinis, H., & Gottfredson, R. K. (2010). Best-practice recommendations for estimating interaction effects using moderated multiple regression Estimating Interaction Effects Using Multiple Regression. *Journal of Organizational Behavior*, 31(6), 776–786. DOI: 10.1002/job.686

Amal, M., Awuah, G. B., Raboch, H., & Anderson, S. (2013). Differences and similarities of the internationalization processes of multinational companies from developed and emerging countries. *European Business Review*, 25(5), 411–428. DOI: 10.1108/EBR-08-2012-0048

Arnold, H. J. (1982). Moderator variables: A clarification of conceptual, analytic, and psychometric issues. *Organizational Behavior and Human Performance*, 29(2), 143–174. DOI: 10.1016/0030-5073(82)90254-9

Arun, K., & Yildirim Ozmutlu, S. (2024). The effect of environmental competitiveness, customer and competitor orientation on export performance. *Journal of Business and Industrial Marketing*, 39(2), 142–160. DOI: 10.1108/JBIM-01-2022-0019

Auh, S., & Menguc, B. (2005). Balancing exploration and exploitation: The moderating role of competitive intensity. *Journal of Business Research*, 58(12), 1652–1661. DOI: 10.1016/j.jbusres.2004.11.007

Aulakh, P. S., Kotabe, M., & Teegen, H. (2000). Export strategies and performance of firms from emerging economies: Evidence from Brazil, Chile, and Mexico. *Academy of Management Journal*, 43(3), 342–361. DOI: 10.2307/1556399

Barnett, W. P. (1997). The dynamics of competitive intensity. *Administrative Science Quarterly*, 42(1), 128–160. DOI: 10.2307/2393811

Beleska-Spasova, E., Glaister, K. W., & Stride, C. (2012). Resource determinants of strategy and performance: The case of British exporters. *Journal of World Business*, 47(4), 635–647. DOI: 10.1016/j.jwb.2011.09.001

Boehe, D. M., & Cruz, L. B. (2010). Corporate social responsibility, product differentiation strategy and export performance. *Journal of Business Ethics*, 91(2), 325–346. DOI: 10.1007/s10551-010-0613-z

Bollen, K. A., & Stine, R. (2014). Direct and indirect effetcs: Classical and bootstrap estimates of variability. *Sociological Methodology*, 20, 115–140. DOI: 10.2307/271084

Bonaccorsi, A. (1992). On the relationship between firm size and export intensity. *Journal of International Business Studies*, 23(3), 605–635. DOI: 10.1057/palgrave.jibs.8490280

Boso, N., Story, V. M., Cadogan, J. W., Micevski, M., Kadic-Maglajlic, S., & Kadić-Maglajlić, S. (2013). Firm innovativeness and export performance: Environmental, networking, and structural contingencies. *Journal of International Marketing*, 21(4), 62–87. DOI: 10.1509/jim.13.0052

Carlson, N. A. (2023). Differentiation in microenterprises. *Strategic Management Journal*, 44(5), 1141–1167. DOI: 10.1002/smj.3463

Cavusgil, S. T., & Zou, S. (1994). Marketing strategy-performance relationship: An investigation of the empirical link in export market ventures. *Journal of Marketing*, 58(1), 1–21. DOI: 10.1177/002224299405800101

Chung, H. F. L., & Ho, M. H.-W. (2021). International competitive strategies, organizational learning and export performance: A match and mis-match conceptualization strategies. *European Journal of Marketing*, 55(10), 2794–2822. DOI: 10.1108/EJM-04-2019-0309

Dervitsiotis, K. N. (2010). Developing full-spectrum innovation capability for survival and success in the global economy. *Total Quality Management & Business Excellence*, 21(2), 159–170. DOI: 10.1080/14783360903549865

Efron, B. (1988). Bootstrap Confidence Intervals: Good or bad? *Psychological Bulletin*, 104(2), 293–296. DOI: 10.1037/0033-2909.104.2.293

Eulerich, M., Eulerich, A., & Fligge, B. (2023). Analyzing the strategy–performance relationship in Germany – can we still use the common strategic frameworks? *Journal of Strategy and Management*, 16(3), 516–532. DOI: 10.1108/JSMA-09-2022-0157

Falahat, M., & Migin, M. W. (2017). Export performance of international new ventures in emerging market. *International Journal of Business and Globalisation*, 19(1), 111–125. DOI: 10.1504/IJBG.2017.085119

Fuchs, M., & Kostner, M. (2016). Antecedents and consequences of firm's export marketing strategy. An empirical study of Austrian SMEs (a contingency perspective). *Management Research Review*, 39(3), 329–355. DOI: 10.1108/MRR-07-2014-0158

Gemünden, H. G. (1991). Success factors of export marketing: A meta-analytic critique of the empirical studies. In Paliwoda, S. (Ed.), *Perspectives on International Marketing - Re-Issued* (pp. 222–246). Routeldge Library Edition International Business., DOI: 10.4324/9780203076613-8

Götz, O., Kerstin, L.-G., & Krafft, M. (2010). Evaluation of Structural Equation Models Using Partial Least Square (PLS) Approach. In Esposito Vinzi, V., Chin, W., Henseler, J., & Wang, H. (Eds.) *Handbook of Partial Least Squares*. Springer Handbooks of Computational Statistics (pp. 691–711). Springer, Berlin, Heidelberg. DOI: 10.1007/978-3-540-32827-8_30

Guan, J., & Ma, N. (2003). Innovative capability and export performance of Chinese firms. *Technovation*, 23(9), 737–747. DOI: 10.1016/S0166-4972(02)00013-5

Hair, J. F., Hult, G. T., Ringle, C. M., & Sarstedt, M. (2014). A Primer on Partial Least Squares Structural Equation Modeling (PLS-SEM). *Sage (Atlanta, Ga.)*.

Hair, J. F., Ringle, C. M., & Sarstedt, M. (2011). PLS-SEM: Indeed a silver bullet. *Journal of Marketing Theory and Practice*, 19(2), 139–152. DOI: 10.2753/MTP1069-6679190202

Halikias, J., & Salavou, H. E. (2014). Generic business strategies of Greek exporting firms. *European Journal of International Management*, 8(2), 127–140. DOI: 10.1504/EJIM.2014.059579

Henseler, J., & Chin, W. W. (2010). A comparison of approaches for the analysis of interaction effects between latent variables using partial least squares path modeling. *Structural Equation Modeling*, 17(1), 82–109. DOI: 10.1080/10705510903439003

Herzallah, A. M., Gutiérrez-gutiérrez, L., & Munoz, J. F. (2014). Total quality management & business excellence total quality management practices, competitive strategies and financial performance: The case of the Palestinian industrial SMEs. *Total Quality Management & Business Excellence*, 25(6), 635–649. DOI: 10.1080/14783363.2013.824714

Ibeh, K. I., & Wheeler, C. N. (2005). A resource-centred interpretation of export performance. *The International Entrepreneurship and Management Journal*, 1(4), 539–556. DOI: 10.1007/s11365-005-4777-4

INE. (2017). *Censo Geral da População de Moçambique*. Instituto Nacional de Estatística.

Islami, X., & Topuzovska Latkovikj, M. (2022). There is time to be integrated: The relationship between SCM practices and organizational performance - The moderated role of competitive strategy. *Cogent Business and Management*, 9(1), 1–26. DOI: 10.1080/23311975.2021.2010305

Jantunen, A., Puumalainen, K., Saarenketo, S., & Kylaheiko, K. (2005). Entrepreneurial orientation, dynamic capabilities and export performance. *Journal of International Entrepreneurship*, 3(3), 223–243. DOI: 10.1007/s10843-005-1133-2

Jaworski, B. J., & Kohli, A. K. (1993). Market orientation: Antrcendent and consequences. *Journal of Marketing*, 57(1), 53–70. DOI: 10.1177/002224299305700304

Johanson, J., & Vahlne, J. E. (1977). The internationalization process of a firm - A model of knowledge foreign and increasing market commitments. *Journal of International Business Studies*, 8, 23–32. DOI: 10.1057/palgrave.jibs.8490676

Kaufmann, F. (2020). *PME. Pequenas e Médias Empresas em Moçambique—Situação e Desafios*. ExperTS GIZ.

Keskin, H., Ayar Şentürk, H., Tatoglu, E., Gölgeci, I., Kalaycioglu, O., & Etlioglu, H. T. (2021). The simultaneous effect of firm capabilities and competitive strategies on export performance: The role of competitive advantages and competitive intensity. *International Marketing Review*, 38(6), 1242–1266. DOI: 10.1108/IMR-09-2019-0227

Khan, H., & Khan, Z. (2021). The efficacy of marketing skills and market responsiveness in marketing performance of emerging market exporting firms in advanced markets : The moderating role of competitive intensity. *International Business Review*, 30(6), 101860. DOI: 10.1016/j.ibusrev.2021.101860

Kuivalainen, O., Sundqvist, S., & Servais, P. (2007). Firms' degree of born-globalness, international entrepreneurial orientation and export performance. *Journal of World Business*, 42(3), 253–267. DOI: 10.1016/j.jwb.2007.04.010

Lechner, C., & Gudmundsson, S. V. (2014). Entrepreneurial orientation, firm strategy and small firm performance. *International Small Business Journal*, 32(1), 36–60. DOI: 10.1177/0266242612455034

Leitner, K., & Guldenberg, S. (2010). Generic strategies and firm performance in SMEs : A longitudinal study of Austrian SMEs. *Small Business Economics*, 35(2), 169–189. DOI: 10.1007/s11187-009-9239-x

Lengler, J. F., Sousa, C. M., & Marques, C. (2014). Examining the relationship between market orientation and export performance: The moderating role of competitive intensity. In *Advances in International Marketing* (Vol. 24, pp. 75–102). Emerald Group Publishing Limited., DOI: 10.1108/S1474-7979(2013)0000024008

Lengler, J. F., Sousa, C. M., Perin, M. G., Sampaio, C. H., & Martínez-López, F. J. (2016). The antecedents of export performance of Brazilian small and medium-sized enterprises (SMEs): The non-linear effects of customer orientation. *International Small Business Journal*, 34(5), 701–727. DOI: 10.1177/0266242615588837

Leonidou, L. C., Fotiadis, T. A., Christodoulides, P., Spyropoulou, S., & Katsikeas, C. S. (2015). Environmentally friendly export business strategy: Its determinants and effects on competitive advantage and performance. *International Business Review*, 24(5), 798–811. DOI: 10.1016/j.ibusrev.2015.02.001

Mahamadou, Z. (2021). Internationalization processes for sub-Saharan Africa' s small and medium-sized enterprises: The case of Ivory Coast. *Thunderbird International Business Review*, 63(4), 437–449. DOI: 10.1002/tie.22190

Maqsoom, A., Arif, I., Shafi, K., Umer, M., Nazir, T., & Nawab, S. (2021). Motives and competitive assets for internationalization: A comparison between emerging and developed economy international construction contracting firms. *Applied Economics*, 53(22), 2539–2553. DOI: 10.1080/00036846.2020.1863321

Matenge, T. (2011). Small firm internationalization – A developing country perspective. *International Journal of Business Administration*, 2(4), 103–111. DOI: 10.5430/ijba.v2n4p103

McGuinness, N. W., & Little, B. (1981). The influence of product characteristics on the export performance of new industrial products. *Journal of Marketing*, 45(2), 110–122. DOI: 10.1177/002224298104500211

Moreira, A. C., Ribau, C. P., & Borges, M. I. (2024). Internationalisation of SMEs: A comparative perspective between Africa and Latin America. *International Journal of Entrepreneurship and Small Business*, 51(4), 513–541. DOI: 10.1504/IJESB.2024.136944

Morgan, N. A., Kaleka, A., & Katsikeas, C. S. (2004). Antecedents of export venture performance: A theoretical model and empirical assessment. *Journal of Marketing*, 68(1), 90–108. DOI: 10.1509/jmkg.68.1.90.24028

Musso, F., & Francioni, B. (2014). International strategy for SMEs: Criteria for foreign markets and entry modes selection. *Journal of Small Business and Enterprise Development*, 21(2), 301–312. DOI: 10.1108/JSBED-10-2013-0149

Navarro-García, A., Arenas-Gaitán, J., Rondán-Cataluña, F. J., & Rey-Moreno, M. (2016). Global model of export performance: Moderator role of export department. *Journal of Business Research*, 69(5), 1880–1886. DOI: 10.1016/j.jbusres.2015.10.073

Parnell, J. A. (2006). Generic strategies after two decades: A reconceptualization of competitive strategy. *Management Decision*, 44(8), 1139–1154. DOI: 10.1108/00251740610690667

Peres, J. A. H., Geldes, C., Kunc, M. H., & Flores, A. (2023). The effect of local institutions on the competitive strategies of exporters. The case of emerging economies in Latin America. *Journal of Business Research*, 169, 114256. https://doi.org/https://doi.org/10.1016/j.jbusres.2023.114256. DOI: 10.1016/j.jbusres.2023.114256

Pett, T., & Wolff, J. (2017). Exploring competitive strategies: The role of managerial perceptions and motivations on internationalisation of SMEs. *International Journal of Entrepreneurial Venturing*, 9(2), 181–202. DOI: 10.1504/IJEV.2017.086484

Porter, M. E. (1980). *Competitive Advantage*. The Free Press.

Porter, M. E. (1985). *Competitive Advantage*. The Free Press.

Rasheed, B., & Ahmad, M. (2022). Competitive intensity: Bridging the gap between corporate social responsibility and competitive advantage. *Journal of Strategy and Management*, 15(4), 745–765. DOI: 10.1108/JSMA-08-2021-0177

Reimann, C. K., Carvalho, F. M., & Duarte, M. P. (2022). Adaptive marketing capabilities, market orientation, and international performance: The moderation effect of competitive intensity. *Journal of Business and Industrial Marketing*, 37(12), 2533–2543. DOI: 10.1108/JBIM-08-2021-0391

Ribau, C. P., Moreira, A. C., & Raposo, M. (2017). Export performance and the internationalisation of SMEs. *International Journal of Entrepreneurship and Small Business*, 30(2), 214–240. DOI: 10.1504/IJESB.2017.081438

Ribau, C. P., Moreira, A. C., & Raposo, M. (2018). SME internationalization research: Mapping the state of the art. *Canadian Journal of Administrative Sciences*, 35(2), 280–303. https://onlinelibrary.wiley.com/doi/pdf/10.1002/cjas.1419. DOI: 10.1002/cjas.1419

Rua, O., França, A., & Fernández Ortiz, R. (2018). Key drivers of SMEs export performance: The mediating effect of competitive advantage. *Journal of Knowledge Management*, 22(2), 257–279. DOI: 10.1108/JKM-07-2017-0267

Sharma, S., Durand, R. M., & Gur-arie, O. (1981). Identification and analysis of moderator variables. *JMR, Journal of Marketing Research*, 18(3), 291–300. DOI: 10.1177/002224378101800303

Sousa, C. M. P. (2004). Export performance measurement: An evaluation of the empirical research in the literature. *Academy of Marketing Science Review*, 9, 1–23.

Sousa, C. M. P., Martínez-López, F. J., & Coelho, F. (2008). The determinants of export performance: A review of the research in the literature between 1998 and 2005. *International Journal of Management Reviews*, 10(4), 343–374. DOI: 10.1111/j.1468-2370.2008.00232.x

Wang, X., Han, R., & Zheng, M. (2024). Competitive strategy and stock market liquidity: A natural language processing approach. *Information Technology and Management*, 25(1), 99–112. DOI: 10.1007/s10799-023-00401-2

Westhead, P., Ucbasaran, D., & Binks, M. (2004). Internationalization strategies selected by established rural and urban SMEs. *Journal of Small Business and Enterprise Development*, 11(1), 8–22. DOI: 10.1108/14626000410519065

Yi, J., Wang, C., & Kafouros, M. (2013). The effects of innovative capabilities on exporting: Do institutional forces matter? *International Business Review*, 22(2), 392–406. DOI: 10.1016/j.ibusrev.2012.05.006

Young, S., Hamill, J., Wheeler, C., & Davies, J. R. (1989). *International Market Entry and Development*. Harvester Wheatsheaf.

Zou, S., & Stan, S. (1998). The determinants of export performance: A review of the empirical literature between 1987 and 1997. *International Marketing Review*, 15(5), 333–356. DOI: 10.1108/02651339810236290

KEY TERMS AND DEFINITIONS

Competitive Advantage: A competitive advantage is an edge a company possesses that allows it to outcompete rivals. This edge can come from various factors like access to valuable resources, cutting-edge technology, or a highly skilled workforce. By offering greater value, higher quality, or a unique selling proposition to customers, a company can build this advantage, as it is possible to retain customers or foster brand loyalty.

Competitive Intensity: Competitive intensity captures the pressure companies face in crowded, competitive markets. When associated with international markets, it is normally associated with the way businesses aggressively fight for market share and growth. This intensity reflects the level of competition, with companies constantly reacting and adapting to each other's moves. Normally, the harsher the competition, the lower the business performance.

Differentiation Strategy: A differentiation strategy is a blueprint for a business to stand out from competitors. It involves offering (and providing) customers something unique, distinct from competitor products. The goal is to build a competitive advantage by understanding your strengths, customer needs, and the overall value you can deliver. There are two main approaches: broad differentiation, targeting a large audience with a general appeal, and focused differentiation, catering to a specific niche market with tailored features.

Export Performance: It is a specific type of performance that focuses on a company's success in selling goods or services in international markets. It essentially measures how effectively a company achieves its export goals. It is normally related with the way firms achieve growth in export sales volume and gain market share in foreign markets.

Moderation effects: They occur when the relationship between two variables (let's call them X and Y) is influenced by a third variable (M). This third variable is called the moderator and it changes the strength or direction of the effect X has on Y. In simpler terms, moderation helps us understand under what conditions a relationship between two variables holds true. The moderator variable acts like a dimmer switch, turning the effect of X on Y up or down depending on its level.

Performance: Generically, performance refers to the achievement of a goal or objective. It is a measure of how well something functions, operates, or produces the desired outcome. When linked to business performance, it is an indication of how well a business operates.

Chapter 3
Business Competitiveness Depends on Training and Control

German Fernando Medina
Universidad Nacional Abierta y a Distancia, Colombia

Pedro Rene Jimenez Hernandez
Worley-Jacobs, Colombia

Andrea del Pilar Barrera Ortegon
https://orcid.org/0000-0002-1286-2623
Universidad Nacional Abierta y a Distancia, Colombia

ABSTRACT

This chapter examines the relationship between Colombian state entities and the competitiveness of private companies, focusing on human talent development and the internal control systems implemented by the State. Through an analysis of the Political Constitution and relevant laws, it explores how the public sector strengthens the national productive sector, improving its competitiveness locally and globally. The chapter highlights the importance of aligning state-owned and private companies, emphasizing training's role in facilitating agile responses to market demands. It also proposes integrating private sector management tools into the public sector to enhance administrative efficiency and support national economic growth. The methodology includes a comprehensive review of the theoretical underpinnings of internal control systems and their practical application within state entities.

INTRODUCTION

In the contemporary business landscape, companies strive to enhance their competitiveness by fostering robust organizational cultures. Within this context, labor relations within companies tend to vary. One element that develops to a greater or lesser extent, depending on the organizational culture, is the

DOI: 10.4018/979-8-3693-4046-2.ch003

skill development of workers. This factor, closely tied to human capital, is directly associated with the competitiveness and productivity levels of companies.

Another critical aspect to consider in enhancing corporate competitiveness is the relationship between companies and the state, as the state functions as both a regulatory and controlling agent for the activities individuals carry out within a society. The more efficient the state becomes in facilitating procedures for both citizens and businesses, the more it acts as an economic agent that supports the competitiveness of organizations.

To achieve high levels of competitiveness in its management processes and in its interactions with companies, the state has developed a range of standards aimed at promoting self-regulation and ensuring a qualified workforce over time. These standards are grounded in regulations derived from the political constitution.

To maintain competitiveness in today's global economy, companies must prioritize the continuous training of human capital, ensuring that their workforce is prepared to meet current and future challenges.

Organizational Culture

In modern society, humans have made significant efforts to enhance productivity across various sectors, including the workplace. This necessity has led to the gradual development of different schools of thought, each with its own ideas and philosophies aimed at addressing this challenge. Ujar, A.C., Ramos, C.D., Hernández, H.E., and López, J. (2013) state, "The concept of organizational culture influences productivity, which is why it has gained great importance within organizations and has become a subject of study by various authors." This underscores the pivotal role of organizational culture in contemporary businesses, and recognizing its importance enables managers to direct their efforts toward improving organizational competitiveness.

A crucial yet often overlooked aspect of corporate training programs is the influence of cultural factors. Social norms, values, and beliefs held by employees can significantly affect their receptivity to new training practices. For instance, in some corporate cultures, resistance to change or hierarchical deference may limit the effectiveness of training initiatives, especially if cultural nuances are not considered in program design. Therefore, tailoring training programs to align with the organizational culture and the socio-cultural context of employees is essential to maximizing the effectiveness of training and ensuring that the knowledge acquired is translated into practice within the company.

Another scenario that must be considered is the diverse ways in which business leaders interact with the state: as private agents in various social, personal, and economic spheres, or, in some cases, as public servants or state contractors. Regardless of the role they play in maintaining societal cohesion, it is essential for them to understand, respect, and abide by the constitutional order established in their country of residence.

In Colombia, the current Political Constitution, promulgated in 1991, defines the rights and duties of citizens, as well as the structure of the Colombian State and the prevailing economic regime.

Workers function as productive agents, and their relevance in the productive sector is closely tied to their level of competence. When a company requires the development of new skills, it becomes necessary to organize training courses that promote the development of these competencies.

To establish the conditions necessary for companies to be competitive, both internally and externally, state entities also develop specific behaviors. A crucial aspect of their productivity is process optimization, which requires the continuous training of human capital. To achieve this objective, efforts must be aligned with regulations that facilitate these training processes, ensuring that the workforce is adequately trained to enhance its capabilities.

As Ujar et al. (2013) argue, "the relationships that organizational culture has with other constructs and variables can affect the behavior of the organization and the fulfillment of organizational objectives, such as continuous improvement, productivity, and competitiveness." Keeping these elements in mind allows for efficient management and fosters a clear and transparent relationship with state institutions, thus avoiding setbacks caused by non-compliance with state regulations, which could adversely affect the company's productivity.

Regardless of an employee's role within a company, ensuring a harmonious work environment requires adherence to company rules and respect for the organizational culture. To optimize resources, companies often implement technical training programs that can be swiftly integrated into the production process.

In many instances, employees' perceptions of the significance and relevance of training in their daily tasks can be ambiguous, as they may not fully grasp its importance. Organizational culture plays a pivotal role in the effectiveness of training initiatives. In organizations where continuous learning is a core value, employees are more likely to actively engage in training programs and apply their newly acquired skills in their daily responsibilities. In such cultures, leaders foster an environment where personal and professional development is seen as a long-term investment rather than a one-time event. A supportive organizational culture also provides a safe space for employees to make mistakes and learn from them, thereby promoting innovation and growth.

Business training

One of the most debated topics in the field of management is the pivotal role played by the workforce in enhancing the competitiveness of companies. These companies operate in highly competitive markets that demand continuous adaptation of their operational structures to meet evolving customer and market needs.

Technological advances, such as artificial intelligence (AI) and machine learning, are transforming the way companies train their employees, directly impacting their competitiveness. AI enables the customization of training programs, effectively tailoring content to the learning pace and specific needs of each employee. Moreover, these digital learning platforms can analyze large volumes of data to predict future skill requirements, allowing companies to stay ahead of trends and ensure that their talent is adequately prepared to address upcoming market challenges.

The use of automated learning platforms and learning management systems (LMS) has made training more accessible and efficient, reducing costs while improving learning outcomes by engaging employees in more interactive, user-centered learning experiences.

The effectiveness of any training initiative is intrinsically linked to the role of leadership within the organization. Leaders are not only responsible for providing the resources necessary for training, but they must also serve as role models by demonstrating a commitment to continuous learning. By exemplifying learning behaviors, leaders can inspire their teams to acquire new skills and knowledge with greater enthusiasm and openness.

As noted by Salas et al. (2012), the effectiveness of training programs depends not only on the content of the courses but also on how they are implemented and the organizational environment that supports them. Leaders play a critical role in fostering an environment that promotes continuous learning, which, in turn, significantly enhances employee performance.

Furthermore, leaders have the capacity to create an environment that encourages knowledge sharing and collaboration, both of which are essential for organizational learning. By ensuring that training is viewed not as an obligation but as an opportunity for personal and professional development, leaders can increase the effectiveness of training programs and ensure that learning leads to tangible improvements in organizational competitiveness.

While designing effective training programs is crucial, it is equally important to implement robust mechanisms to evaluate their effectiveness. Training evaluation allows companies to measure not only participants' satisfaction levels but also the actual impact the program has on their performance and overall organizational competitiveness. Common evaluation tools include satisfaction surveys, post-training performance observation, and key performance indicators (KPIs), which track improvements in productivity and other measurable outcomes. Additionally, feedback and adjustment processes should be tailored to adapt to changing market conditions, new technologies, and evolving employee needs.

Competitiveness

companies face a significant challenge, namely the scarcity of resources. As Salvatore D. (1996) defines, "the word scarce is closely linked to the concept of limited or economic, as opposed to unlimited or free. Scarcity is the fundamental problem of every society" (p. 2). It is due to this socioeconomic reason that companies must adopt a forward-looking vision with social responsibility, allowing them to optimize the use of available resources, including human resources, which can be strengthened through appropriate training techniques.

A relevant aspect in the market process, the satisfaction of needs and the consumption of scarce goods is what Polanyi, K. (2015) stated: "The general introduction of purchasing power as the means of acquisition turns the process of satisfaction of needs into an allocation of scarce resources with alternative uses (money). From this it follows that both the conditions of the choice and its consequences are quantifiable in the form of prices" This allows us to identify that a need such as business training is a good that organizations are free to acquire and choose in the market, according to their training needs, articulated with the levels of competitiveness that the company wants to have.

In the modern era, companies must meet the demands of their customers, which is the fundamental reason for their existence in the market. However, evaluating the quality of products in relation to customer needs can be an abstract concept. However, the International Standard ISO 9000:2015 has established a unifying quality standard.

The latest quality standard in Colombia is the Colombian Technical Standard NTC ISO 9001:2015, which corresponds to the Colombian version of the international standard ISO 9001:2015. This standard establishes the requirements for a quality management system that helps organizations demonstrate their ability to provide products and services that meet customer requirements and applicable regulations, and that aims to increase customer satisfaction through the effective application of the system, including processes for continuous improvement of the system and ensuring compliance with customer requirements and regulations.

In addition to the implementation of the Colombian Technical Standard NTC ISO 9001:2015, it is relevant to establish a comparison with the international standard ISO 9001:2015, which has been adopted by numerous countries as a reference standard for quality management. While both standards share a focus on ensuring that organizations can meet customer expectations through continuous improvement and process optimization, NTC ISO 9001:2015 is adapted to the particularities of the Colombian context, adjusting certain procedures and requirements to local regulations.

A comparative analysis highlights that, although the fundamental principles of quality are similar, key differences lie in the practical application of these standards within public and private organizations in Colombia, due to the specific regulations and institutional structure of the country. For example, the adoption of NTC is influenced by the regulatory and structural challenges specific to the Colombian public sector, while ISO 9001:2015 has greater flexibility when applied in a global context, where regulatory systems can vary significantly from one country to another.

This comparative analysis illustrates how the Colombian State, through the NTC, aligns its processes with international standards while addressing local needs for efficiency and competitiveness. Adapting regulations to national contexts facilitates more effective public and private management.

The quality of a product is ultimately determined by the customer, based on how well it meets their needs. To enhance product quality and market competitiveness, companies must implement quality management systems in line with ISO 9001 standards.

Kauffeld and Lehmann-Willenbrock (2019) found that companies investing in continuous employee training improve their competitiveness, as these investments allow them to adapt more rapidly to market changes and new technological demands.

When implementing a quality management system, companies must consider both internal and external factors that may impact its success. The organization's development plays a critical role in determining its competitive edge.

To effectively adjust processes, products, relationships, and structures, it is essential to train staff with the necessary skills to actively participate in the company's quality system. Given global trends, companies must prioritize training by defining its scope and frequency to ensure it positively impacts competitiveness.

Future challenges require organizations to adapt to shifting market dynamics. As producers and suppliers, companies rely on demand to remain competitive, and market volatility forces them to improve management practices, including training employees to respond to fast-changing markets and technological advancements.

In contemporary markets, competitiveness demands high productivity standards, where human talent plays a key role. In today's knowledge-driven world, employees' skills and expertise are critical for organizational success and a major factor in how the market values companies—something that draws the attention of entrepreneurs.

To achieve and maintain adequate levels of competitiveness, companies must pay special attention to human talent, as Giraldo (2006) comments: " It is now clear that one of the determining variables to achieve increased sustainable competitiveness of organizations and their sectors is the training of their human talent" which results in adequate training of workers helping companies maintain high levels of competitiveness in the markets.

Within the management of companies operating in local, regional, national or global markets, personnel play a crucial role. As companies increase their hiring of personnel, society has more resources available and, consequently, the demand for goods increases. This implies that the greater the number of companies, the greater the employment and, therefore, the relationship between supply and demand becomes more dynamic. The survival of companies, in turn, depends on their productivity.

Companies must strive to stay up to date to avoid falling behind in the market, adapting to its needs. This involves establishing training systems that align with their requirements and are organized effectively, as Ramírez and García (2006) point out, who comment:

"Training is often identified only with the modality used to transmit and share knowledge, that is, courses, diplomas, master's degrees, among others. However, the effectiveness of training rests largely on its approach as a process, the training process." (p.1)

In today's context, companies must invest not only in traditional training but also in advanced technologies to enhance program efficiency and accessibility. E-learning platforms offer unparalleled flexibility, delivering updated content swiftly and effectively. Additionally, virtual reality (VR) simulations provide experiential learning, enabling employees to navigate realistic scenarios in controlled environments. Combined with data analytics, these tools allow companies to create tailored training programs that meet individual employee needs, maximizing training impact and boosting competitiveness.

Alshammari (2020) found that in the banking sector in Saudi Arabia, well-structured training programs not only significantly improved employee performance but also contributed to enhancing organizational competitiveness. This study highlights the importance of investing in training programs that are tailored to market needs to maintain competitiveness.

In accordance with the above, it follows that companies must develop carefully designed training processes, considering both the formal and informal structure of the organization. This is done with the purpose of increasing productivity levels and competitiveness in the market.

Another concept that must be taken into account when studying the relationship between training and competitiveness is that proposed by Sutton (2001), who states:

Training is a fundamental tool for Human Resources Management, which offers the possibility of improving the efficiency of the company's work, allowing it to adapt to new circumstances that arise both inside and outside the organization. It provides employees with the opportunity to acquire greater skills, knowledge and abilities that increase their competencies, to perform successfully in their position. In this way, it also turns out to be an important motivational tool. (p.4)

When a company implements training processes, it aims to increase efficiency, a goal that requires staff collaboration. Identifying the necessary skills and topics for employee development is essential. Companies consistently seek to enhance competitiveness and productivity, achieving this through effective technological advancements and human talent development.

A crucial aspect is that training has a well-defined method to ensure that it fulfills its purpose effectively. According to Gore (1998) he comments:

Training is a systematic, planned and ongoing activity whose general purpose is to ensure that people do not make mistakes due to a lack of knowledge, skills and attitudes; preparing, developing and integrating human resources into the production process, through the delivery of knowledge, development of skills and attitudes necessary for the best performance of all workers in their current and future positions, contributing to adaptation to the changing demands of the context. (p.3)

Through training, employers aim to reduce errors in business management, avoiding reprocessing that may affect productivity and competitiveness. In addition, they seek to motivate workers by acquiring knowledge that they can develop and apply in future production processes.

Another sector that employs a large part of the workforce in the economy is public entities. These entities must be competitive and to achieve this it is essential to adequately train their staff. In the case of public service workers, training is regulated by article 4 of decree law 1567 of 1998, which establishes:

Training is understood as the set of organized processes related to both non-formal and informal education in accordance with the provisions of the general education law, aimed at prolonging and complementing initial education through the generation of knowledge, the development of skills and the change of attitudes, in order to increase individual and collective capacity to contribute to the fulfillment of the institutional mission, to the better provision of services to the community, to the effective performance of the position and to comprehensive personal development.

This definition encompasses training processes focused on fostering and strengthening public service ethics, grounded in the principles guiding administrative functions. Training is continuous and not limited to isolated courses; it must align with the competencies defined by the entity's manual, aiming to promote personal development within the work context.

In any company, training offers two main benefits: it stimulates workers to perform their tasks more effectively and facilitates the acquisition of knowledge applicable in the future. For the company, training directly reduces reprocessing and enhances both competitiveness and productivity.

Today, training programs must also integrate sustainability and ethical considerations, preparing employees to not only improve performance but also act responsibly. Companies that incorporate sustainability principles promote a corporate culture conscious of environmental and social impacts, such as minimizing the ecological footprint and adopting ethical policies that reinforce corporate social responsibility. By aligning with sustainability goals, companies enhance their public image and prepare their workforce for a future where ethical and sustainable practices are increasingly demanded.

It is essential for employers to understand the relationship between training and productivity. As Rico (2014) states, "The more trained an employee is, the better they will manage the resources at their disposal" (p. 2). Proper training optimizes resource use, contributing directly to business competitiveness.

To support the competitiveness of the real economy, the sector has adapted its processes to become more efficient, responding effectively to companies' needs for agility and ensuring efficient interactions between businesses and public entities, driving overall productivity

State competitiveness.

The competitiveness of state entities is closely linked to that of private sector companies. By examining this relationship, it becomes clear how the public sector can support the productive sector's development, thereby enhancing its competitiveness.

One key tool the State has implemented to modernize its operations is the management and internal control systems.

Citizens interact with the State in various ways: as private individuals in social, personal, and economic spheres, or as public servants and contractors. Regardless of their role, it is essential for citizens to understand and respect their country's constitutional framework to ensure societal harmony. In Colombia, the current Political Constitution, enacted in 1991, outlines citizens' rights and duties, as well as the structure of the State and the economic regime.

Endogenous development theories argue that regions possess the internal elements necessary for sustained economic growth. By implementing appropriate policies, favorable conditions for development can be created, ensuring citizen well-being and public trust in the State's management of public goods.

Modern companies maintain close ties with the State, complying with taxes, licenses, and permits. A harmonious relationship between businesses and the State depends on efficient administrative processes and the avoidance of errors that could affect service provision. For this, effective state control mechanisms are essential.

In today's business environment, the State remains a constant regulatory presence. While the extent of state intervention has grown significantly, its role as a regulatory and administrative body persists. This growth raises questions about the limits of state involvement and its impact on the private sector.

State-business relations vary, ranging from collaborative to confrontational, depending on the nature of the activity and the relationship between officials and business representatives. While collaboration offers potential benefits, it is not always feasible, highlighting the need for oversight and control of public entities.

The relationship between companies and the State is evident in regulations governing labor, patents, and other processes critical to production. Business owners must consider the constitutional framework when making decisions, ensuring compliance with regulations to avoid sanctions and take full advantage of opportunities provided by the State.

A thorough understanding of state processes allows entrepreneurs to participate successfully in government procurement, contributing to the State's constitutional functions. Thus, it is crucial that the State implements efficient processes that support private sector performance.

A significant aspect of Colombia's economy is its reliance on small and medium-sized enterprises (SMEs), which must remain competitive to survive. SMEs must understand their interactions with the State while maintaining a trained workforce suited to their business needs.

METHODOLOGY

In order to carry out research with high levels of scientific credibility, the triangulation procedure will be implemented in the process, mentioned by Briones G. (1981) where he comments "We refer to the principle of triangulation and convergence, which ultimately is the best known and most used technique in qualitative research" (p.38). What would allow to have adequate information and compare it with other sources, in this way an internal and external level of credibility of the research to be carried out will be achieved, since this method takes as a reference different sources, researchers and methods, which allows that it is not a single impression that gives validity to an event, but the combination of different methods allows to establish the reality of a fact and correct the possible biases that may arise in the statement of the problem.

In developing the principle of triangulation and convergence, the following aspects will be taken into account:

1. Methods and Techniques.
2. Data sources.
3. Researchers.

The triangulation procedure seeks to have a closer approach to the reality of the observed object, which is why information is collected in different places using various techniques, which will allow us to have the necessary elements to make judgments, as stated by Cerda (2002), "Information obtained through a document is confronted through an interview or observation" (p. 51). This facilitates the configuration of a reality by the researcher, which is built by consulting the different concepts and positions that are held in front of the object of observation, which allows to generate a broader knowledge by raising certain logical inferences in front of the analyzed phenomenon.

MAIN FOCUS OF THE CHAPTER

Globalization is widely recognized as an economic, technological, and cultural phenomenon with global impact, characterized by communication processes that create interdependence between countries in commercial matters. As Ramonet (2001) states, "Globalization does not aim to conquer countries, but markets." This phenomenon has significantly altered socioeconomic and political relations on a global scale.

Global dynamics shape the environment in which companies operate in global markets while maintaining a local perspective. To succeed, companies rely on state institutions that facilitate agile business operations, minimizing artificial barriers. The modern State plays a vital role as a regulator of national and international business activities.

In Colombia, commercial regulations are outlined in the Commercial Code, with oversight by both private and public bodies. Private entities, such as the Chamber of Commerce and Icontec, oversee company compliance, while public institutions—including municipal bodies like the Ministries of Finance, Health, and Environment—regulate aspects such as taxes and permits. National-level oversight is provided by entities like DIAN and various ministries of the national government.

For national companies to thrive, both locally and internationally, a robust and efficient State is essential. Effective organization of public-private sector relations is crucial to prevent unnecessary delays, which can increase operational costs for companies due to inefficiencies in public entities.

Since 1991, a critical aspect of state management in Colombia has been Internal Control, mandated by articles 109 and 269 of the National Political Constitution and further developed by Law 87 of 1993. This system aims to manage public affairs through self-regulation, ensuring efficient public administration. However, the current system lacks a technical tool for objective evaluation, making it difficult for final users of state services to provide accurate feedback on public entity performance.

The State

The State, like any organization, operates with limited resources, and the success of its management—encompassing planning, direction, execution, and control—is crucial for contributing to the social well-being of its communities. As an organizational entity, the State represents a society that determines how to structure its relationships to coexist within its territory. As Ignacio Molina (1998) notes, "The State is a central concept of Political Science that designates the quintessential form of legal-political organization. It arises alongside the idea of sovereignty and implies the static embodiment of this" (p. 18). Sovereignty allows the people to define their organizational structure and manage their resources.

A key concept for improving economic competitiveness in modern states is New Economic Geography (NEG), which emphasizes that regional growth follows a logic of "circular causation," where business networks lead to an accumulation of activities that self-reinforce over time (Moncayo, 2003, p. 38).

In light of NEG, the Colombian economy must have efficient and dynamic public organizations capable of responding to global challenges. These entities should facilitate free trade, promote the development of national companies, and leverage Colombia's geographic and natural advantages. This requires the State to implement policies and regulations that foster innovation and integration into global value chains.

Given resource scarcity, companies focus on maximizing efficiency through tools like strategic planning and the Balanced Scorecard. These tools provide critical support for decision-making, but their effectiveness relies on the quality and accuracy of data. Therefore, it is vital for companies to invest in data systems that ensure decisions are based on reliable, up-to-date information.

In corporate planning, managers must account for relationships with public entities. The technological and operational modernization of these entities is crucial for streamlining procedures and achieving business objectives. Companies should assess the efficiency and responsiveness of the public entities they interact with to ensure timely and effective support.

The current disparity between the control and evaluation processes of state entities and public perceptions of their effectiveness reveals a significant gap. This may stem from evaluation systems that are misaligned with societal needs or rely on inadequate performance indicators. To address this, it is essential to develop more robust evaluation models tailored to each state entity, aligning them with development plans and priority social needs. This would entail the following measures:

1. Review and Adjustment of Indicators: Evaluate and, if necessary, reformulate the indicators used to assess public management. This will ensure that they measure not only administrative efficiency but also the actual impact on societal well-being and needs.
2. Transparency and Accountability: Strengthen mechanisms for transparency and accountability to guarantee that public management information is accessible and comprehensible to the public.
3. Training and Modernization: Invest in staff training and modernizing internal management and control systems to enhance data collection quality and improve the accuracy of results evaluation.
4. Citizen Participation: Foster citizen participation in evaluation and control processes, enabling direct societal feedback on public management.

By implementing these measures, state entities could move toward more transparent and effective management, better suited to meeting the expectations and needs of Colombian society.

A state that strives for competitiveness

The Colombian State has undergone significant transformations in recent decades, driven by global phenomena such as globalization and interdependence between countries. These changes have redefined the roles and functions of the State, allowing it to adapt and modernize to face the challenges of the 21st century.

1. **Adaptation to Globalization:** Economic and cultural integration at a global level has forced the Colombian State to adjust its policies and administrative structures. This includes the need to facilitate international trade, promote foreign investment and actively participate in international agreements and treaties.

2. **Administrative Modernization:** In order to respond efficiently to the demands of an increasingly globalized society, the Colombian State has implemented administrative modernization processes. This involves the adoption of information technologies, improved efficiency of administrative procedures and strengthening of internal control systems.

3. **Transformation of Functions and Services:** There has been a redesign of the functions of the State to ensure that they are more effective and accountable. This includes the decentralization of certain responsibilities to local entities, the professionalization of public management and the improvement in the provision of basic services such as health, education and security.

4. **Incorporation of International Good Practices:** The Colombian State has adopted international good practices in governance, transparency and accountability. This seeks to strengthen citizen confidence and improve the efficiency of the state apparatus.

5. **Challenges and Opportunities:** Despite progress, the Colombian State faces persistent challenges such as corruption, social inequality and violence. However, continued modernization offers opportunities to strengthen public institutions, promote inclusive economic development and improve the quality of life of all Colombians.

In short, the modernization of the Colombian State is a dynamic and continuous process that responds to the demands of a globalized environment. This process not only seeks to improve administrative efficiency, but also to strengthen the State's capacity to promote sustainable development and guarantee the well-being of society as a whole.

The transition of the Colombian State from a benefactor role to a guarantor role, beginning in 1991, marked a significant change in its administrative structure and in the way public resources are managed. This change is aligned with concepts of "new public management" (NPM), an emerging global model since the 1980s that seeks to improve the efficiency and effectiveness of the public sector. Below are some key aspects of new public management and its impact on local governments and international relations:

1. **Focus on Efficiency and Effectiveness:** NGP promotes the adoption of results-oriented administrative practices, focusing on the efficient use of public resources and the effectiveness of the services provided. This implies a more professionalized management, based on performance metrics and continuous evaluation of public programs and policies.

2. **Decentralization and Local Autonomy:** As part of the NGP, administrative decentralization is encouraged, granting greater levels of autonomy to local governments. This allows for management that is closer to the specific needs of communities, improving the response to local problems and strengthening citizen participation in decision-making.

3. **Technological Modernization and Transparency:** The introduction of information and communication technologies (ICT) has been key in the modernization of public administration under NGP. These tools facilitate transparency in management, simplification of administrative procedures and improvement in the provision of public services.

4. **International Relations and Global Adaptation:** In the global context, NGP has encouraged local governments to adapt to international standards of good governance and public management. This includes active participation in international networks, the adoption of open government practices and the promotion of policies that facilitate economic and cultural integration at the international level.

5. **Challenges and Ongoing Adaptations:** Despite progress, NGP implementation faces challenges such as resistance to institutional change, the need for technical and leadership capabilities in the public sector, as well as ensuring equity and inclusion in the provision of public services.

In summary, the adoption of new public management in Colombia since 1991 has implied a profound transformation in the way the State manages its resources and provides services to citizens. This model seeks to promote a more efficient, transparent and results-oriented administration, adapting to global dynamics and strengthening the role of the State as guarantor of the well-being and development of society. In this model, national States have lost centrality and local government is strengthened, through a phenomenon called "new localism" (Brugué and Gomá, 1998).

In Latin America, Colombia has implemented various management instruments since 1991, with the aim of improving efficiency in State management. Some of these instruments include:

1. **Strategic Planning:** The adoption of strategic plans at national, regional and local levels has been fundamental to establish clear goals and align the government's efforts towards common economic, social and environmental development objectives.
2. **Performance-Based Budgeting:** This budgeting approach focuses on allocating public resources based on expected results and the evaluation of the performance achieved. It seeks to ensure that resources are used efficiently and effectively to achieve strategic objectives.
3. **Evaluation and Monitoring System:** Evaluation and monitoring systems have been established to measure the impact of public policies and social programs. This includes performance indicators that allow for assessing the achievement of goals and adjusting government actions as necessary.
4. **Administrative Modernization:** Administrative reforms have been implemented to improve efficiency in the provision of public services, reduce bureaucracy and strengthen transparency in public management. This includes the digitalization of procedures and the simplification of administrative processes.
5. **Open Government and Citizen Participation:** Open government is promoted as a way to strengthen transparency, accountability and citizen participation in decision-making. This is done through digital platforms, public consultations and mechanisms for access to information.
6. **Administrative Decentralization:** Progress has been made in administrative decentralization to empower local governments in resource management and service provision. This allows for a more agile and effective response to specific local needs.

These instruments have contributed significantly to the modernization of the Colombian State, strengthening its capacity to respond to socioeconomic challenges and improving the quality of life of citizens. However, they continue to face challenges such as consolidating technical capacities in the public sector and ensuring inclusive and equitable management throughout the country.

In the specific case of the Colombian state, management instruments such as the following have been implemented:

- Citizen participation, Art. 103 of the Political Constitution (CP)
- Administrative decentralization, Art.1 of the CP
- Political reforms of the parties, Art. 107 of the CP
- The concept of the administrative function, Art. 209 of the CP

- The adoption of internal control for public entities, Art. 269 of CP

The incorporation of aspects of New Public Management (NPM) into the Colombian Political Constitution has been a fundamental part of the State's modernization process. These changes have allowed state institutions to adapt and harmonize with new global and local needs, promoting efficiency in public management and facilitating both internal and external business processes.

These aspects have not only modernized state institutions but have also contributed to improving the environment for investment and economic development, facilitating business both within the country and internationally. However, it is important to continue advancing in the consolidation of these principles to guarantee an efficient State capable of responding to the challenges of the 21st century in an effective and equitable manner for all citizens.

New Public Management linked to competitiveness

New Public Management (NPM) is a model that seeks to modernize state entities by adopting efficient and effective practices that have proven useful in the private sector. Some of the key principles and tools promoted within NPM are: Specifically, NPM seeks to transfer successful practices from the private sector to the public sector to improve efficiency, quality of services and the State's ability to respond to the demands of society and the global economic environment.

NPM proposes a fundamental change in the way public entities operate and relate to citizens. NPM represents an innovative approach to modernize public administration, emphasizing efficiency, quality of service and orientation towards the real needs of citizens, with the goal of improving governance and strengthening the capacity of the State to fulfill its functions effectively in a dynamic and competitive environment.

In accordance with the contributions of Osborne and Gaebler (1992), the United States developed the concept of "reinventing government," whose main contribution is that a government can function as efficiently and productively as any private company. To achieve this goal, it is necessary to adapt its structure to meet the needs of the economy within the current legal framework.

It is correct to highlight that the restructuring of the public administration in Colombia has been driven by several laws and decrees that are based on the principles established in the 1991 Constitution. Here are some key points of the regulations you mentioned:

1. **Law 489 of 1998:** This law is fundamental to the administrative restructuring of the Colombian State. It establishes general principles for the organization and operation of the public administration, such as the elimination and simplification of procedures to improve efficiency and reduce bureaucracy.
2. **Law 790 of 2002:** This law provides for the merger of entities, national organizations and ministries with the purpose of optimizing resources, improving inter-institutional coordination and strengthening the State's capacity to respond to the demands of society.
3. **Law 962 of 2005:** This law focuses on the rationalization of administrative procedures and processes. Its objective is to simplify and streamline the processes that citizens and companies must comply with when interacting with the public administration, thus facilitating the relationship between citizens and the State.

These regulations are clear examples of how the Colombian State has sought to modernize its public administration, adopting New Public Management (NPM) practices to improve efficiency, transparency and the ability to respond to the needs of society.

The relationship between the 1991 Constitution, Law 27 of 1992 and Law 443 of 1998 is crucial to ensure that the Colombian State has a qualified and professional workforce to provide public service. Here I detail how each contributes to these objectives:

1. **Political Constitution of 1991:** Establishes the fundamental principles of the organization of the Colombian State, including provisions related to the administrative career. These principles include meritocracy, professionalization, and access to public service based on merit and ability.
2. **Law 27 of 1992:** This law regulates the administrative career in Colombia, establishing standards for the entry, promotion, transfer and retirement of public servants. It promotes job stability based on merit and performance, thus promoting a more efficient and professional public administration.
3. **Law 443 of 1998:** Modifies aspects of Law 27 of 1992 and reinforces the principles of meritocracy, promotion and stability in the administrative career. It introduces mechanisms to evaluate individual and organizational performance, rewarding the fulfillment of goals and objectives, and ensuring that public officials are evaluated and promoted based on their merits and capabilities.

These regulatory frameworks reflect principles of New Public Management (NPM), such as professionalization, performance evaluation and merit-based recruitment, which are essential for State entities to have competitive and trained personnel, capable of efficiently responding to the demands and challenges of the public and private sectors in the current globalized context.

Law 872 of 2003 and Decree 1145 of 2004 are fundamental instruments for the modernization and improvement of institutional performance in Colombian State entities. Here I briefly explain each one:

1. **Law 872 of 2003 - Quality Management System for State Entities:**
   o This law establishes the regulatory framework for the implementation of the Quality Management System in Colombian public entities.
   o Its main objective is to improve efficiency and quality in the provision of public services.
   o Provides guidelines for entities to develop and implement quality management systems that ensure user satisfaction and the optimization of public resources.
2. **Decree 1145 of 2004 - General Administrative Information System of the Public Sector (SUIP):**
   o This decree creates the General Administrative Information System of the Public Sector (SUIP), which is a platform for monitoring, evaluating and managing administrative information in state entities.
   o Facilitates the collection, processing and analysis of administrative data to improve decision-making and accountability.
   o Promotes transparency and efficiency in public management by establishing standards for the collection and exchange of information between public entities.

These instruments are part of the efforts to modernize administration and public management in Colombia, aimed at ensuring better service delivery, greater institutional efficiency and adequate accountability to citizens.

The implementation of processes for the modernization of public administration in Colombia can be identified with the incorporation of information technologies to modernize the administration of the online or electronic government in the entities of the national executive branch, which allows us to establish that the state is working to improve the competitiveness of its entities so that they adequately support the productive processes of the economy.

The importance of control to improve productivity

Control is crucial to the functioning of contemporary organizations. Ishikawa (1985, p. 71) emphasizes that control is not only about verifying compliance with standards and procedures, but also about ensuring that activities are carried out effectively and efficiently to achieve organizational objectives. This comprehensive approach to control involves monitoring performance, identifying deviations, and taking corrective action when necessary to ensure quality and efficiency at all levels of the organization.

Control also includes aspects such as continuous feedback, the use of key performance indicators and adaptation to changes in the organizational environment. It is essential to maintain alignment between strategic goals and daily activities, as well as to manage resources optimally and ensure customer and stakeholder satisfaction.

According to the above, control according to Ishikawa is not only a supervision process, but an integral tool to manage organizational performance and ensure competitiveness and sustainability in the current context of organizations.

For the correct functioning of contemporary organizations is control, Ishikawa (1985, p. 71) comments:

Dr. Taylor used to describe control with the words "plan, do, see." What does "see" mean? To Japanese high school students. It means simply looking at something. This does not convey the meaning that Taylor intended. So we prefer to say "plan, do, check, act." This is what we call the Circle of Control, and we need to get it moving in the right direction.

The idea presented by Dr. Ishikawa is a rather comprehensive control proposal, which is used today on an ongoing basis, especially in government entities, where it is applied in NTGP-1000-2009. The initial analysis resulted in a tool that, thanks to its broad approach, can be used in any type of organization, industry or process. The correct organization and execution of this control circle should foster a culture in all areas and people of the organization, promoting effective interaction and the development of critical judgments in an autonomous manner, without forgetting the importance of adequate supervision .

The concept of control in organizations has evolved significantly beyond the simple supervision of tasks. It has become a thorough and strategic process to ensure that the organization achieves its objectives effectively and efficiently. Control in modern organizations not only seeks to monitor the completion of tasks, but also plays a fundamental role in strategic planning, results analysis, decision making and risk management. It is an essential tool to maintain competitiveness and sustainability in a dynamic and changing business environment.

Control is a very important process within organizations, and it must be designed in organizations in a way that does not generate trauma to the processes and adds value to the production process, additionally according to Koontz (1998), "it is the process of verifying the performance of different areas or functions of an organization, usually involving a comparison between expected and observed performance, to verify whether objectives are being met" (p. 109). Therefore, control is an essential component of the administrative process, it performs multiple critical functions in any organization. Control is not only a fundamental administrative tool to measure the fulfillment of objectives and improve operational efficiency, but it also plays a crucial role in strategic planning, decision making, and the adaptability of organizations in the face of a dynamic and competitive environment.

In public institutions, those responsible for process management must understand that control is essential to verify execution in accordance with established policies and goals. Fred R. (2008) states that "control includes those activities undertaken to ensure that actual operations conform to those planned" (p. 135). When state-owned enterprises carry out adequate planning, they can perform control by comparing the results obtained with what was planned, which facilitates exhaustive analysis and evaluations. This allows critical areas to be identified and feedback to be applied in a timely and effective manner.

Control provides an ideal opportunity to conduct a thorough analysis of what has been established in planning. Fred R. (2008) comments that "control consists of fundamental steps: 1. Establish performance standards. 2. Measure individual and organizational performance. 3. Compare actual performance with established performance standards. 4. Take corrective action" (p. 156). Similarly, it is crucial to perform information measurements to examine situations where the results can be both positive and negative. This analysis facilitates decision-making in the face of unforeseen situations or the reactions of subordinate personnel. In these cases, the entity must provide prior training and orientation to personnel, preparing them to handle observations or necessary adjustments that improve procedures and results.

It should be noted that strategic planning is an important tool for modern companies, according to Palacios (2020) "The importance of adhering to new standards such as ISO is based on quality, allowing companies to commit to high levels of results, with acceleration and optimization in production processes." An aspect that has been taken into account by organizations, as long as they meet quality requirements, they will be more competitive in the market. To achieve this purpose, it is important to have adequately trained personnel.

Innovation in productivity with the internal control system

Since the 1991 Political Constitution, internal control has experienced a regulatory development that has facilitated its implementation and evolution in the Colombian context. For example, articles 209 and 269 of the Constitution establish the principles that regulate both the administrative function and internal control in the State. This makes internal control a significant advance that supports and facilitates the management of state entities, promoting self-control to guarantee the proper use of public resources.

Law 87 of 1993 regulates the Internal Control System (ICS), and Presidential Directive 002 of 1994 establishes the guidelines for the ICS. This allows for effective control that streamlines the management of public entities, strengthening their capacity to adequately support the management of the business sector.

Modern states need to have agile and adaptable administrative apparatuses that can respond effectively to the new demands of global markets. "The need to make the institutions of the [Colombian] State efficient and effective made public administration in general turn its attention to modern administrative theories… among them the controls that must be in place throughout the organization" (Charry, 1996, p. 17). This is essential to ensure that institutions can respond quickly and effectively to the needs of both society and companies.

The Political Constitution, in articles 209 and 269, establishes that public administration must be governed by the principles of equality, morality, efficiency, economy, speed, impartiality and publicity. Consequently, public entities must design and apply internal control methods and procedures appropriate to the nature of their functions, as well as implement management and results evaluation systems.

The Constitution, in its article 267, eliminated the prior control carried out by the comptroller's offices, considering it a process that slowed down the activities of public entities. Instead, it established a subsequent and selective control to supervise and evaluate the fiscal management of the State, as well as that of individuals or entities that manage funds or assets of the nation. In 1993, Laws 87 and 42 normatively developed these constitutional provisions. Law 42 of 1993 grants the comptroller's offices the function of supervising the State through financial controls, management legality, results and the evaluation of the internal control systems of each entity.

Aspects to consider in the modernization of companies

To modernize processes in companies, it is important to work on training the workforce and the management tools of the State and strive to align with globalization; it is important to adopt management instruments that have been developed in the private sector.

To consolidate highly efficient public companies that drive the improvement of their competitiveness and support the development of the private sector, it is crucial to implement tools such as:

- The systemic approach
- Technological surveillance
- Competitive intelligence
- Critical surveillance factors.

Systemic approach

In the document "Organizations and methods of understanding them", prepared by Alexandra Montoya Restrepo and Iván Alonso Montoya Restrepo (2003), a comparison is established between administration and other sciences. It is suggested that, by studying the similarity between organizations and living organisms, as biotics does, teaching and learning processes can be developed that allow understanding the evolution of organizations.

One of the main themes discussed is the variety of approaches to making comparisons. According to Stafford Beer, "there are several levels of comparison at which the scientist might try to work" (cited by Montoya, 2003, p. 2). This suggests that there are multiple levels of comparison available to any scientist interested in analyzing diverse objects, including the evolution and management of organizations.

Many public officials may have implicit knowledge about the control they exercise in their functions, although they are often not aware of it. This lack of awareness can lead them to rely on new internal control processes or external controls, resulting in unnecessary delays in meeting external client requirements. This situation affects the management of public servants and distorts the quality of services perceived by the citizens who use them.

Technological surveillance

A fundamental characteristic of the production of goods and services at a global level, whether by private, public or mixed companies, is that it is conditioned by the specific natural characteristics of each country. This leads to various economies, making use of their comparative advantages, specializing in the production of certain goods or services to maximize their productivity. Mankiw comments that "productivity is the quantity of goods and services produced in each hour of work performed" (1998, p. 51). According to what has been said, economic actors seek to maximize their productivity by making the most of the available natural conditions. In this sense, both public and private companies must use competitive intelligence to compete effectively in the markets and meet the needs of society.

Organizations in Colombia, both public and private, must prioritize improving their competitiveness to expand both in the local and international markets. This means taking advantage of the opportunities offered by unilateral and multilateral trade agreements signed between the country and other industrialized or emerging economies.

Technology management is defined as the business strategy that encompasses the identification, analysis, planning and implementation of technological developments and applications. Its objective is to significantly improve the performance of business processes, creating differentiation through competitive added value (Sánchez, 2002). This suggests that implementing an effective technology management process is essential for the development of competitive organizations.

Competitive intelligence

The administration of organizations requires high levels of professionalism. In this sense, the professionals in charge must adequately manage the company's resources, seeking to optimize their use to achieve business objectives.

One of the fundamental resources in organizations, whether public or private, is the efficient and timely management of available information. In this sense, it is crucial to analyze how to collect information and determine the most appropriate method for its storage and processing, with the objective of developing Competitive Intelligence (CI) in organizations. It is not enough to simply have computer equipment to process information; it is also necessary to select the appropriate equipment that meets the specific needs of the organization.

According to the above, efficient management of organizations must cultivate specific skills, such as the ability to identify the hardware and software required for their operations. It must also manage internal and external information in a way that improves productivity and allows for the efficient development of its processes. This is crucial to fulfill the institutional mission entrusted by the State in the exercise of the administrative function.

Critical Surveillance Factors (CSF)

Companies that adopt management models focused on competitive intelligence do so to have a tool that facilitates decision-making based on extensive information. Therefore, they seek to understand how their environment evolves, observing variables such as product development, competition, customers, marketing processes, among other aspects relevant to the organization, which can have significant impacts on its performance at any given time.

In order for state companies to be able to anticipate opportunities and threats in the environment, it is essential to adopt an efficient Strategic Technological Management (GET) model, based on technological surveillance and competitive intelligence. In this sense, Álvaro Pedroza (2001) proposes a five-stage GET model that integrates technological strategy with corporate strategy, enhancing key factors such as internal management efficiency, innovation capacity and strategic resource alignment. This approach is complemented by competitive intelligence and technological surveillance tools, providing a more robust framework for decision-making in competitive environments. Pedroza's model prioritizes the identification of market/product pairs, establishing a direct relationship with the ability of companies to quickly adapt to market changes, thus optimizing their competitiveness. This approach allows the development of capabilities to meet growing global demands.

The model proposed by Pedroza (2001) begins with the determination of the market/product pairs of interest, using matrix tools such as the information matrix of the product lines. This matrix details aspects such as product categories, market categories, year of introduction of the product, average sales in the last three years and percentage of the company's total sales. In addition, market-product analysis matrices are used that show the market segments served by the company's products, considering variables such as total sales, annual growth rate, contribution to profits and market share. These matrices prioritize cells based on factors such as the difficulty of competing, the growth of the customer market and strategic intuition.

In today's business environment, competition is fierce and companies must constantly adapt to stand out. It is not just about offering low prices or high-quality products, but innovation has become a key factor. Companies that manage to introduce new products or improve existing ones have a significant advantage. This not only helps them attract and retain customers, but also allows them to differentiate themselves in a market. Alzate (2012).

Technology surveillance is a key tool that can help companies avoid wasting time and resources on innovations that are already protected by patents. By conducting advance analysis, they can identify which ideas are already on the market and thus focus their efforts on areas where they can really contribute something new. This not only saves money, but also fosters a more efficient innovation environment.

FUTURE RESEARCH DIRECTIONS

The impact of emerging technologies on corporate training can be explored by examining how tools like artificial intelligence, machine learning, and augmented reality are transforming training programs and their link to organizational competitiveness. Additionally, it would be valuable to assess the integration of sustainable and socially responsible practices in training, their long-term impact on organizational performance, and the metrics for measuring effectiveness.

Another key area of interest is the relationship between organizational culture and technological adaptation, focusing on how internal culture influences a company's ability to navigate technological and market changes, and the strategies that facilitate this transition.

International comparative studies on ISO 9001 implementation could also investigate how local adaptations affect competitiveness and business outcomes in different contexts. Lastly, analyzing the effectiveness of internal control models in public management could help refine methods to better assess public entities' performance and their impact on private sector competitiveness.

CONCLUSIONS

In contemporary society, entrepreneurs must acknowledge the State's influence on daily activities and strategic planning for building competitive businesses. Although state intervention evolves, its presence has grown significantly in recent decades, raising questions about its limits.

To enhance competitiveness and maintain effective relations with the State, companies must efficiently manage interactions with both the private and public sectors. For exporters, proper management of procedures and taxes is essential to comply with current regulations. Efficient administrative processes are critical to avoid obstacles in service provision, and the State must implement effective control mechanisms that do not create unnecessary burdens for businesses.

While collaboration between the State and businesses is often promoted, it is not always feasible. This dynamic is common across many countries, highlighting the importance of oversight and control of public entities.

In the knowledge-driven era, human capital is a key strategic element for sustainable competitiveness. The development of human talent is crucial, as competitiveness relies on productivity, creativity, and innovation—factors influenced by human capabilities and decision-making processes.

REFERENCES

Alshammari, M. (2020). The impact of training on Employee performance: A study of the banking sector in Saudi Arabia. *International Journal of Business and Management*, 15(3), 1–12. DOI: 10.5539/ijbm. v15n3p1

Alzate, BA, Giraldo, LT, & Barbosa, AF (2012). *Technological surveillance: methodologies and applications* . Electronic Journal of People Management and Technology, 5(13).

Colombian Political Constitution. 1991, Congress of the Republic, Law 27 of 1992.

Congress of the Republic, Law 87 of 1993. file:///C:/Users/User/Downloads/Dialnet-FormacionDel-TalentoHumano-2934638.pdf file:///C:/Users/User/Downloads/KarlPolany_Economy-as-an-institutionalized-activity%20(1).pdf

Fred, R. (2008). *Strategic Management Concepts* (11th ed.). Pearson education.

Giraldo, A. M., Arango, M. J., & Castillo, M. B. (2006). *Training of human talent: a strategic factor for the development of sustainable productivity and competitiveness in organizations. Guillermo de Ockham: Scientific Journal, 4* (1), 43-81. https://www.redalyc.org/articulo.oa?id=477847114019 https://www .researchgate.net/profile/Marco-Vivarelli/publication/228001376_Impacto_social_de_la_globalizacion _en_los_paises_en_desarrollo/links/5a02fb77a6fdcc6b7c9a4f94/Impacto-social-de-la-globalizacion -en-los-paises-en-desarrollo.pdf https://www.scielo.sa.cr/scielo.php?script=sci_arttext&pid=S1659 -49322020000200006

Ishikawa, K. (1995). *The Essence of Quality Control.* Available in https://jrvargas.files.wordpress.com/ 2011/02/que_es_el_control_total_de_la_ calidad_-_ -kauro_ishikawa.pdf.

Kauffeld, S., & Lehmann- Willenbrock, N. (. (2019). The role of training in improving organizational competitiveness: A systematic review. *Journal of Business Research*, 101, 1–12. DOI: 10.1016/j.jbus-res.2019.01.011

Koontz, H. (1998). *Management: A Global Perspective.* McGraw- Hill.

Law 1499 of 2017.

Mankiw, N. G. (1998). *Principles of Macroeconomics.* Mc Graw-Hill.

Molina, I. (1998). *Fundamental Concepts of Political Science.* Alianza Editorial.

Moncayo, J, E. (2003). *New Theories and Approaches*

Palacios Rodríguez, M. Á. (2020). Strategic Planning, a functional instrument within organizations. *National Journal of Administration*, 11(2).

Polanyi, K. (2015). The economy as an institutionalized activity. Journal of critical economics, (20), 192-207.

Ramonet, I. (2001). *Impact of globalization on developing countries. Memoria magazine, 143* .

Restrepo Restrepo, A. M., & Montoya Restrepo Restrepo, I. A. (2003). Organizations and methods of understanding them. *Innovar (Universidad Nacional de Colombia)*, 13(22), 63–72.

Salas, E., Tannenbaum, S. I., Kraiger, K., & Smith-Jentsch, K. A. (2012). The science of training and development in organizations: What matters in practice. *Psychological Science in the Public Interest*, 13(2), 74–101. DOI: 10.1177/1529100612436661 PMID: 26173283

Salvatore Dominick. (1996) *Microeconomics*. Mc Graw Hill, Third Edition. Mexico.

Sanchez, P. A. (2002). Soil fertility and hunger in Africa. *Science*, 295(5562), 2019–2020. DOI: 10.1126/science.1065256 PMID: 11896257

Ujar, A. C., Ramos, C. D., Hernandez, H. E., & Lopez, J. (2013). *Organizational Culture: evolution in measurement. Management Studies. vol.29 no.128 Cali*. http://www.scielo.org.co/scielo.php?pid=S0123-59232013000300010&script=sci_arttext

Chapter 4
Comparing Canadian and Filipino Culture for Sustainable Business Relationships

Resti Tito Villarino
https://orcid.org/0000-0002-5752-1742
Cebu Technological University, Philippines

Maria Lavina M. Alonzo
https://orcid.org/0009-0004-3201-6207
Université du Québec à Montréal, Canada

Michel Plaisent
Université du Québec à Montréal, Canada

Prosper Bernard
Université du Québec à Montréal, Canada

ABSTRACT

This paper introduces cultural insights by analyzing the similarities and differences between Filipino and Canadian cultures. It highlights the importance of building sustainable relationships to do business. By leveraging attitudinal and behavioral facets, communication styles, leadership and decision-making techniques, employee motivations, and conflicts in the workplace, the study emphasizes building sustainable business relationships between Filipinos and Canadians. As the researchers examined literature from academic researchers and government websites, the researchers recommended using the Us Approach to deepen the culturally diverse and sustainable partnership between Canada and the Philippines. By doing so, understanding differences, building trust, and recognizing gaps are established. That way, necessary adjustments will be completed depending on the cultural dissimilarities and relationship gaps. While these were deduced, one should be cautious of generalizing said analysis as certain deviations within Canadian and Filipino cultures exist.

DOI: 10.4018/979-8-3693-4046-2.ch004

INTRODUCTION

Internationalization is crucial for developed and emerging economies in today's interconnected world. It has transformed from a one-sided resource extraction model to a mutually beneficial system. Previously, internationalization involved transferring resources from developing countries to developed ones, often at lower prices (Jones et al., 2023).

However, the end of the 20th century saw a shift. Outsourcing work to countries with lower labor costs, initially to China and then to surrounding Southeast Asian nations like the Philippines, fueled economic growth in these emerging economies (World Bank, 2022). This international exchange fosters the creation of new networks, which are particularly important for small and medium-sized enterprises (SMEs). Through internationalization, SMEs can build client bases and relationships that transcend geographical borders.

Countries like Canada and the USA have a long history of being built by immigration. Foreign workers bring expertise in specific fields and a willingness to take on challenging jobs, often at lower wages, which are more affordable for SMEs. The Philippines is globally recognized for its labor mobility, with Overseas Filipino Workers (OFWs) playing a significant role in economic growth (International Labour Organization, n.d.; OECD & Scalabrini Center, 2017). April to September 2020 saw 1.77 million OFWs working abroad, generating 134.77 billion pesos in remittances (Philippine Statistics Authority, 2022). Canada, a key destination, has a large Filipino community of 837,130, making it a top contributor to the country's immigrant population (Embassy of the Philippines in Ottawa, n.d.).

The increased contact between people from different countries has led to a new phenomenon: developing countries becoming popular tourist destinations. This, in turn, has driven the growth of the hospitality and tourism sectors (United Nations World Tourism Organization, 2023). Effective communication between locals and foreigners is essential for successful business ventures in this environment. This is where cultural understanding becomes paramount. Studying cultural norms is not just an academic exercise; it's a practical necessity for businesses to thrive internationally.

Leveraging tourism, the Philippines' National Tourism Development Plan for 2016-2022 maximizes employment generation and income distribution through socially responsible and sustainable tourism development (Department of Tourism, n.d.). The country aims to expand community participation in various tourist destinations and other development areas by focusing on national and local tourism targets. Using such marketing initiatives, more sustainable growth is to be achieved while considering the contribution of Filipino society, namely SMEs.

This chapter commemorates the longstanding diplomatic relationship between Canada and the Philippines, marking its 75th anniversary (Government of Canada, 2024). Building upon collaborative research and exchange programs, this chapter fosters knowledge-sharing networks, emphasizing the need to understand cultural similarities and distinctions between the two nations. This understanding is crucial for facilitating sustainable business partnerships, particularly for small and medium-sized enterprises (SMEs).

The Philippines and Canada established a Joint Economic Commission (JEC) to enhance economic cooperation (Global Affairs Canada, 2022). Both nations seek to diversify trading partnerships. Experts recommend a Canadian focus on security and cultural understanding to boost trade within ASEAN (Charbonneau, 2017). Research emphasizes the need for SMEs to adopt sustainable practices and enhance competitiveness to establish lasting international business relationships (Lopez-Torres, 2023; Mishra et al., 2023). Developing countries face various barriers, but this chapter aims to mitigate challenges arising from cultural differences (Moshtari & Safarpour, 2023). Canada's chairing of the Comprehensive and Progressive Agreement for Trans-Pacific Partnership in 2024 positions itself to expand policies on digital trade and foster relationships with underrepresented groups in trade, particularly SMEs (Government of Canada, 2024b).

The Canadian Minister of International Trade, Export Promotion, Small Business and Economic Development signed a memorandum of understanding establishing a Joint Economic Commission (JEC) with the Philippines' Department of Trade and Industry (Global Affairs Canada, 2022). Through this, the Government of Canada recognizes the Philippines as a vital trading partner and an economic player in the Indo-Pacific area. Furthermore, the Asia Pacific Foundation encourages Canada to focus on culture to bridge and boost trade with ASEAN (Charbonneau, 2017).

The Philippines holds a unique position within ASEAN. It is closer to Canada than other ASEAN countries, by sharing Christian values, language, and Latin roots. Its shared history with Spain, English fluency, and cultural links to the United States offer the potential for strengthened economic ties with Canada. It reflects Canada's commitment to the Indo-Pacific region, evidenced by the Strategic Operations Centre in Manila (Government of Canada, 2023) and significant trade growth with the Philippines, reaching $3.1 billion annually (Global Affairs Canada, 2022).

Given the illustrated ties between Canada and the Philippines, various studies call for the establishment of sustainable business relationships. A study conducted on small and medium enterprises (SMEs) emphasized the importance of building and enhancing sustainability practices by first acknowledging the complexities that come along with these while developing strategies that promote both sustainability and competitiveness (Lopez-Torres, 2023).

This chapter aims to cultivate a deeper cross-cultural understanding in support of successful economic partnerships, acknowledging the role of cultural nuances in business interactions. The chapter also examines cultural similarities and differences, providing actionable insights into communication, workplace dynamics, and business practices. It addresses preferred leadership styles, decision-making processes, workplace conflict resolution, and motivations, all critical for building robust, sustainable business relationships between Filipino and Canadian enterprises. Another objective of this research is to facilitate the elaboration of sustainable business relationships between Filipinos and Canadians.

BACKGROUND

Importance of Culture for Sustainable International Business Relationships

Research demonstrates the critical role of organizational culture in facilitating change, driving performance, and achieving operational goals (Sahoo, 2022). Culture is a complex set of attitudes, behaviors, beliefs, and values of a special group of people at a given time. It was reported to have a significant influence on the informal economy of SMEs (Tomos et al., 2020). Semrau et al (2016) surveyed 1248 SMEs from 7 different national contexts to discover that the relationship between Entrepreneur orientation and performance was moderated by culture.

The Ethnocentric Perspective is the predisposition that one's cultural values, norms, and beliefs are far superior to the rest (Mukhopadhyay, n.d.). Graham (2010) analyzes the cultural differences of Slovakia SMES and what they mean for developing effective management practices. One reason is that SME employees are often issued of the same culture and SMEs hire in the vicinity, based on a familiar common contact instead of an anonymous national job website. The owner plays also an important role in decision-making and is near his employees so the probability of homogeneity of culture is greater in SMEs than in big enterprises.

Organizations seeking to expand internationally must move beyond ethnocentric perspectives that can hinder cross-cultural collaboration (Mukhopadhyay, n.d.). Effective intercultural communication demands cultural awareness, adaptability, and a commitment to building trust-based relationships (Luu, 2023). While core human values often transcend cultural boundaries, their behavioral expression may vary significantly (Hanel et al., 2018). Successful cross-cultural interactions depend on understanding and respecting these contextual differences (Durant & Shepherd, 2009).

This perspective also entails the strong inclination to be in control of business procedures and stereotyping other countries while ignoring the people factor in other cultures by neglecting relationship building and solely focusing on work-driven goals. With that, it has been posed that opposition to ethnocentric perspective must include adjustments to the understanding of cultural-related ethical differences, modifications in one's attitudes toward both work and life and the strengthened importance of building professional and personal relationships. Studying how to improve the exportation capacities of Vietnamese SMEs Selvarajah & Sukunesan (2019) recall the importance of developing cultural competencies, not only foreign language to communicate effectively with foreigners and their environment, namely the variations arising from social institutions, history, religion, family, etc. These cultural competencies would contribute to the development of best practices for exportation among an experimental group of SMEs in Vietnam.

Swank presents the same ideology of building long-lasting relationships within an organization through the Young Entrepreneur Council (2019). The author highlighted that two levels of interaction are necessary to build and maintain a connection, namely personal where characteristics, feelings, emotions, and culture are considered, and business where skills and knowledge of products and services are considered. Furthermore, maintaining sustainable business relationships and establishing professional connections will only be possible when both parties feel mutually comfortable and friendly towards each other. A similar understanding was presented in the study of strategic entrepreneurship of SMEs where the role of organizational change forces such as leadership, engagement, adaptive culture, and environment were highlighted (Luu, 2023).

In a study on cross-cultural differences and similarities in human value instantiation, the researchers claim that people generally carry similar values across other countries and even instantiate them comparably to a certain extent (Hanel et al., 2018).

Despite that, the researchers also accentuated that people coming from different countries and backgrounds can exude disparity in the behaviors that are perceived as typical instantiations of values but still acknowledge similar ideas about their abstract meaning and importance. With that, it has been concluded that intercultural understanding and communication must be considered as cross-cultural differences were claimed to be linked to various contextual factors.

MAIN FOCUS OF THE CHAPTER

Hofstede's cultural framework offers a valuable lens for understanding dimensions such as power distance, uncertainty avoidance, individualism/collectivism, gender roles, long-term orientation, and indulgence (Hofstede, 2011). While the model has limitations, analyzing how countries rank on these dimensions can provide valuable insights for businesses navigating cultural complexities (Soloviov, 2022). While some researchers like Soloviov (2022) question Hofstede's cultural framework based on a lack of linkages with other variables such as innovation, Hofstede claims that by having these dimensions in considering organizational culture, an analysis of high and low scores of opposing cultures is possible in understanding the validation of country dimension index rankings even in the event of culture change. Understanding the limitations of any single model allows for a more subtle intercultural comparison.

Comparing Filipino and Canadian Culture

The reader is invited to examine how Canada and the Philippines compare on critical dimensions; the scores were obtained from The Culture Factor Club Country Comparison tool (Hofstede Insights, n.d.) and part of their description is reported below in a synthesis by the authors of their view in conjunction with literature.

The power distance index for most countries, presented in this section are freely available easily on websites like https://clearlycultural.com/geert-hofstede-cultural-dimensions/power-distance-index/ . It was designed by Hofstede from three questionnaires i) how often employees fear expressing a disagreement with their boss; ii) their perception of their boss' decision style (among authoritarian paternalist, egalitarianism, and transformational leadership); iii) their preference for their boss's decision style.

Power Distance

This dimension measures how society views power distribution. Canada's egalitarian values and focus on interdependence lead to relatively flat organizational structures where employees' expertise is valued by managers. In contrast, the Philippines has a hierarchical society where rigid structures are accepted, and employees expect clear direction from superiors (The Culture Factor club, n.d.).

This dimension emphasizes the unequal distribution of power and how society accepts and expects such inequalities in one's country (The Culture Factor club, n.d.). It is also illustrated as the measure in which the less powerful openly accept the unequal distribution of power in society this dimension studies the range that exists in an egalitarian-hierarchical perspective (Hofstede et al., 2009).

Having a score of 39, Canada values egalitarianism, where class distinctions are low while interdependence is high (The Culture Factor club, n.d.). Such Canadian culture is also reflected in Canadian organizations where hierarchy is only deemed for convenience. With that, managers seek assistance from their subordinates for their expertise as staff members could also openly rely on their supervisors.

Unlike Canada, the Philippines scored 94, proving the existence of a hierarchical society within the country (The Culture Factor Club, n.d.). This reflects how Filipino employees accept such a rigid structure where they are expected to be instructed on their tasks and responsibilities. This Filipino culture also transcends to accepting the reality of inequalities and hierarchical order within the entire system.

Uncertainty Avoidance

This dimension refers to a society's comfort level with ambiguity. Canada welcomes innovation and change with less emphasis on strict rules (The Culture Factor club, n.d.). The Philippines shares a similarly relaxed attitude toward change and punctuality (Hofstede Insights, n.d.).

The dimension focuses on the degree of comfort ability in unknown situations (The Culture Factor club, n.d.). Furthermore, it is the measurement of how a society manages said uncertainties through the creation of certain beliefs, norms, and institutions to control such ambiguity. Having a score of 48, Canadian culture is perceived as accepting of these situations. As a society that promotes freedom of expression, Canada also celebrates innovation whether it be in best business practices or technology. Canadian culture also includes welcoming new ideas instead of being rules oriented.

Counting closely with Canada is the Philippines with a score of 44 (Hofstede Insights, n.d..). This is interpreted as having a low preference for said dimension. In fact, it is claimed that the Philippines perceives innovation as not threatening and that rules should be changed if it is not working efficiently for the organization.

Individualism vs. Collectivism

This highlights the relative importance of individual goals versus group cohesion. Canada's highly individualistic culture prioritizes the self and immediate family, with promotions based on personal merit (The Culture Factor club, n.d.). The Philippines' collectivist culture emphasizes loyalty, group harmony, and building relationships. This is reflected in the 'bayanihan' (reciprocal labor) concept, where mutual support influences career advancement (Hays, 2015).

The dimension highlights independence and interdependence. As Canada scored 80, the country is taken as a highly individualist society. Like other individualist countries, Canada tends to look solely after themselves and their immediate family. Having such background, it could be deduced that Canadian culture in the business setting translates to prioritizing initiative and self-reliance as promotions are heavily based on merit.

Conversely, the Philippines is a collectivist society scoring 32 in this dimension (Hofstede Insights, n.d..). Unlike Canada, the Philippines relies heavily on loyalty and long-term commitment. As it values both immediate and extended families, the Philippine culture nurtures building strong linkages and relationships among themselves. In the workplace, a collectivist setting relies on the management of groups even during hiring and promotion. With that, shame and loss of face are considered in team decisions where everyone takes responsibility for the rest of the group.

Masculinity

This dimension examines a society's drive for success. Canada balances ambition with a strong focus on work-life balance (The Culture Factor club, n.d.). The Philippines exhibits a highly competitive culture with a strong emphasis on career advancement (Hofstede Insights, n.d..).

As a cultural dimension, masculinity refers to how society is driven by success and the achievement of goals. With a score of 52, Canadians are goal-oriented but still prioritize work-life balance at the end of the day. This moderately masculine culture stems from Canadians' appreciation of the quality of life, family gatherings, and leisure alongside work. On the contrary, the Philippines earned a score of 64

(The Culture Factor Club n.d.). Just like other highly masculine countries, the Philippines relies heavily on being the best and prioritizes the career ladder. It is also claimed that superiors in the Philippines are expected to assert competition and productivity within the workplace.

Long-Term Orientation

This refers to a society's focus on long-range planning vs. short-term results. Canada and the Philippines are "normative" societies, respecting traditions while emphasizing present outcomes over multi-year plans (Hofstede Insights, n.d.).

In relation to achieving success, long-term orientation is the dimension that highlights how society considers the past while also focusing on the present and future (Hofstede Insights, n.d.). With a score of 36, Canada is considered a normative society striving to highlight the truth. Even in the workplace, Canadian culture respects traditions and prefers attaining quick results.

Just like Canada, the Philippines is a normative society (Hofstede Insights, n.d.). The Philippines maintains and preserves traditions with a low score of 27 in this dimension. In addition, Philippine culture emphasizes normative thinking. Instead of heaving planning on the future, Philippine society works on the "now" and what could be achieved "today".

Indulgence

This dimension measures the degree to which a society enjoys leisure and gratification. Canada's indulgent culture prioritizes leisure and personal enjoyment (Hofstede Insights, n.d.). In contrast, the Philippines is more restrained, emphasizing societal norms and focusing less on leisure activities (Hofstede Insights, n.d.).

The last dimension of Hofstede, indulgence, focuses on the ability to control basic human desires and impulses (Hofstede Insights, n.d.). With a score of 68, Canada is claimed to be an indulgent society. Canadians are to enjoy life by giving in to their desires. In the workplace, they show a high inclination towards optimism and a predisposition to the importance of leisure.

On the other hand, the Philippines generally practices restraint as it scored a low mark of 42 (Hofstede Insights, n.d.). Instead of optimism and vulnerability, Filipinos are said to project tendencies of pessimism in the workplace. Filipinos tend to be restrained by societal norms while neglecting the importance of leisure and personal gratification.

Multiculturalism

A significant contrast exists between Canadian and Filipino approaches to multiculturalism. Canada actively promotes diversity and inclusion through robust governmental policies (Government of Canada, 2020a; Ertorer et al., 2020). This focus aims to increase cultural awareness and participation across all levels of society.

Founded on governmental policies focused on multiculturalism and interculturalism, Canada aims to assert respect for people, including their backgrounds, identities, traditions, and religions (Ertorer et al., 2020). The significance of multiculturalism in Canada transcends to building program-specific initiatives that support the community (Government of Canada, 2020a). Leveraging on said programs and initiatives, Canada aims to increase awareness of its cultural diversity and encourage participation at all societal levels. The Philippines, on the other hand, also acknowledges the diversity within the country through the various social organizations and cultural expressions among the Indigenous Peoples communities (Minority Rights Group International, n.d.).

Values and Personality

Canadians generally value politeness, kindness, and a commitment to democratic ideals, emphasizing equality, freedom, and the rule of law (Beattie, 2020; Government of Prince Edward Island, n.d.). In contrast, Filipinos prioritize family, hospitality, and the maintenance of social harmony. This emphasis manifests in key cultural concepts like 'kapwa' (shared identity), 'pakiramdam' (shared inner perception), and 'kagandahang loob' (shared humanity) (de Leon, n.d.; Hays, 2015).

Canadians, in general, are also perceived as polite (Beattie, 2020). In a study conducted by Beattie (2020), the participants of the research also viewed Canadians as smart and kind. Other attributes associated with Canadians are friendly, nice, and even accepting. As Canada highlights democracy, its values also revolve around it, namely equality, respect for cultural differences, freedom, peace, and law and order (Government of Prince Edward Island, n.d.).

Equality translates to having everyone voice their opinions, even if that entails receiving disagreement from the rest (Government of Prince Edward Island, n.d.). This value also equates to the government treating its citizens and their rights with utmost respect and dignity. Respect for cultural differences is when the cultural norms and traditions of those born in Canada and those naturalized citizens are understood and appreciated. This could also translate to respecting the cultural backgrounds of newly landed immigrants and their families. Freedom as a value, on the other hand, promotes and celebrates the basic freedoms of every Canadian including but not limited to freedoms of thought, speech, religion, and of peaceful assembly. In relation to freedom is peace, where Canada serves not only as peacekeepers within the country but internationally as well. The value also accentuates its zero tolerance for violence within the society. Lastly, the value of law and order emphasizes the importance of due process in the Canadian system. This transpires from respecting the rule of law, which promotes transparency and accountability, especially within the government.

On the other hand, Filipinos are perceived to be friendly, fun-loving, sensitive and hospitable (Hays, 2015). The spirit of camaraderie or pakikisama is also highlighted in the Filipino culture as it portrays working together for a common good even if that entails not obtaining monetary rewards. With that, Filipinos are known for their strong sense of family and community. In fact, they are recognized as a warm community that loves to hang out with family and friends. They enjoy making jokes and holding conversations where gossips or chismis spread easily. Filipinos are also accused of the attitude of caring only about the present and ignoring the future or bahala na. Despite that, the Filipino culture leverages protecting self-esteem to maintain harmony within the community.

Furthermore, Filipino core values consist of shared identity or kapwa, shared inner perception or pakiramdam, and shared humanity or kagandahang loob (de Leon, n.d.). The levels of Filipino social interaction are also classified into two by the author, namely among outsiders and among insiders. For outsiders, the dimensions outlined are courtesy or pakikitungo, mixing or pakikisalamuha, joining or pakikilahok, adapting or pakikibagay, and getting along with or pakikisama. As for Filipino social interaction among insiders, the highlighted levels are rapport or pakiki pagpalagayang loob, involvement or pakikisangkot, and oneness or pakikiisa. With that, the societal values highly associated with Filipinos that they prioritize most are freedom or kalayaan, justice or katarungan, and honor or karangalan.

Language and Conversations

Canada is officially bilingual, with English and French as its main languages (Government of Canada, 2017). Canadians generally communicate directly (Todaytranslation, n.d.), emphasizing active listening and clarity (Government of Canada, 2016a; The Culture Factor club, n.d.). Conversations typically focus on general topics like weather and sports rather than personal matters (Today Translations, n.d.). Titles and formal greetings are important (Santander Trade, 2022). Salutations are also heavily used in Canada (Santander Trade, 2022). Mr., Mrs., Monsieur, or Madame are also commonly used together with their titles such as Doctor, Attorney, Professor, etc.

On the other hand, the Philippines also has two official languages, Filipino and English (Embassy of the Philippines in Hague, n.d.). English is also acknowledged as a medium of instruction in various educational institutions in the country. Some languages with a variation of dialects also include Bicolano, Cebuano, Hiligaynon or Ilonggo, Ilocano, Pampango, Pangasinense, Tagalog, and Waray. Despite having regional languages as auxiliary languages across their areas, it has been accentuated that these do not fully replace Filipino and English (Catacataca, n.d).

Filipinos are also distinguished as respectful or "magalang" (Hays, 2015). This translates to the use of titles and honorifics including po/opo in everyday conversations and not just in business transactions. Unlike Canadians who practice humor with caution, Filipinos have a unique sense of humor in that they can laugh, make jokes easily, and tease each other comfortably.

Communication Styles

Canadians value strong eye contact and appropriate personal space during interactions (Today Translations, n.d.). Handshakes are standard in professional settings. Filipinos, conversely, are keenly attuned to non-verbal cues (`pakiramdam`) (Hays, 2015; de Leon, n.d.). The 'pagmamano' gesture signifies respect for elders.

Canadian business transactions rely heavily on body language, particularly strong eye contact (TodayTranslations, n.d). Without a good amount of eye contact, Canadians would generalize that the other end is insecure and all the more insincere. Maintaining distance is also notably considered as Canadians should keep a two-feet distance while French Canadians tend to maintain a slightly closer distance. Greetings in the form of handshakes tend to be the most appropriate in professional and business settings and meetings with Canadians.

Just like handshakes, Filipinos, too, are known for their own set of body language and gestures (Hays, 2015). Pagmamano or bless, a gesture relatively similar to hand-kissing, is a sign of respect to elders and people in authority. As Filipinos are identified as those with sharp intuitive senses and are tacit knowing or pakiramdam, they are also acknowledged as observant of non-verbal communication (de Leon, n.d.). In return, it has been claimed that business counterparts must be sensitive to a Filipino's non-verbal cues including facial expressions and body language to gauge what said Filipino is trying to convey.

Just like most Westerners, Canadians strictly adhere to time ethics (TodayTranslations, n.d). Canadians believe that punctuality and meeting deadlines should be prioritized especially in business meetings and other social events. With that, arriving up until 15 minutes late is acceptable, if an excuse is provided, but arriving later than 30 minutes is considered disrespectful as it is wasting other people's time. Meetings should also be expected to end in the aforementioned duration (Santander Trade, 2022). As for dress code, it is expected for managers and employees to be formal with the use of sober-colored suits and dresses while some industries encourage their staff to dress casually.

A Gender-based Analysis Plus was an advancement created by the government to critically analyze policies and programs that affect women and other diverse groups. Despite those initiatives, it has been claimed that a wide gap still exists as more women continue to be victims of sexual and domestic violence. According to Statistics Canada of 2017, Canadian women who work full-time only receive 87 cents to every dollar earned by Canadian men, while the Canadian Board Diversity Council 2017 Report Card claimed that a gap exists in women in executive positions as they only represent 23% of board positions in Canada's top 500 business. In addition, a wide gap also exists in the proportion of men to women elected to the national Parliament (Statistics Canada, 2021).

Unlike Canadian workplace time, Filipinos are mostly late for business meetings and other social gatherings (Hays, 2015). It has also been claimed that other people who are meeting up with Filipinos should not expect them to arrive exactly on time. Despite the lack of punctuality, Filipinos are still deemed to be hard workers. In addition, regardless of rank and position in the office, Filipinos perceive themselves as well-groomed as they associate such with social attractiveness (de Leon, n.d.). With that, a Filipino employee dresses cleanly and neatly to look and smell good (de Leon, F.M., n.d.; Hays, 2015).

Unlike Canadian women in the workforce, Filipinos experience a relatively smaller margin of gender pay gap on a per-hour basis (Investing in Women, 2017). Despite that claim, the call for female representation in Filipino businesses and government settings remains high. This is in relation to Filipino women's demand to be more involved in decision-making processes for policies that include family leaves, equitable recruitment, and just and fair promotion.

Workplace Environment

Punctuality is highly valued in Canadian business; meetings have a fixed duration (Santander Trade, 2022; Today Translations, n.d.). Professional dress is generally formal, though some industries are more casual. Despite government initiatives like Gender-based Analysis Plus, a gender gap remains in pay, board representation, and political leadership (Government of Canada, 2022b; Statistics Canada, 2021, 2017).

Business Relationships

Canadians prefer scheduling meetings in advance, with clear objectives. Small talk is common initially (Santander Trade, 2022). Presentations should be concise, and agreements documented. Business lunches are brief, and alcohol is uncommon (Today Translations, n.d.). Gift-giving is reserved for established partnerships. Filipinos, in contrast, are comfortable sharing personal details even in formal settings (de Leon, n.d.). They value ('pasalubong') gifts after trips (Hays, 2015). Regardless of status, respect (`galang`) is crucial in both cultures.

Ideally before getting to business, an appointment made by telephone or email for the first meeting must be set (Santander Trade, 2022). A thorough explanation of the objectives for the meeting request must also be established when dealing with Canadian meetings. During the initial meeting, the Canadians usually hand out business cards in English and French after the introductory handshake. Small talk as a form of breaking the ice is common before the formal meeting. During the meeting itself, presentations must be short and clear while agreements must be indicated in writing and supported by documentation.

Business lunches are also possible, but they must be kept short as alcohol is not usually included (TodayTranslations, n.d). It must also be remembered that Canadians value privacy, which is why professional life is separate from personal life, especially at the beginning of establishing a business partnership (Santander Trade, 2022). On the other hand, business gifts are mostly offered only after a partnership closes a deal.

Unlike Canadians, most Filipinos are comfortable in sharing personal aspects of their lives even during formal meetings (de Leon, n.d.). As for gifts, Filipinos are known for handing out pasalubong (Hays, 2015). These quasi-sacred ritual gifts are mostly from trips wherein some Filipinos are not shy to demand one after completing the journey (de Leon, F.M., n.d.; Hays, 2015). Despite the differences in establishing personal relationships with business partners, it should be noted that both Filipinos and Canadians place much importance on respect or galang regardless of rank and status (Hays, 2015; TodayTranslations, n.d.). Filipino workplaces can be less time-strict (Hays, 2015). Employees prioritize a well-groomed appearance (de Leon, n.d.). Additionally, Filipino women seek greater inclusion in business and political decision-making (Investing in Women, 2017).

Workplace Conflict

Canadians encourage respectful voicing of differences during meetings (Santander Trade, 2022). Employees are expected to manage minor disputes independently (Evason, 2016a). On the contrary, despite valuing social harmony (`hiya`), Filipinos tend to avoid direct confrontation (Hays, 2015). They may use intermediaries to address sensitive issues.

Canadian culture emphasizes how disagreements and differences of opinion are allowed and encouraged even in the middle of business meetings (Santander Trade, 2022). Such concerns may be directed as long as they come from a place of respect and diplomacy. According to Cultural Atlas, a discrete and non-confrontational way of settling disputes among employees should be openly performed before seeking assistance from the manager (Evason, 2016a). This is also concerning how managers expect their employees to deal with work and conflict with minimal supervision.

As the Philippines is identified as a highly masculine society, conflicts are said to be resolved by mostly fighting them out (Hofstede Insights, n.d.). Despite that notion, shame or hiya is also deeply rooted in Filipino culture and Filipinos stray away from confrontation (Hays, 2015). This is to ensure that the other person does not lose face and is not humiliated in front of a crowd. According to the Philippines Australia Business Council, situations that lead to hiya are oftentimes dealt with by a third-party intermediary. Indirect messaging of unpleasant information could be coursed through human resources and managers to avoid workplace conflict.

Motivation

Canadians are financially motivated but value workplace development opportunities (Evason, 2016a; Government of Canada, 2022a). Pension plans are essential for younger and older workers (HOOPP, 2022).

Filipinos are renowned for their work ethic (`bayanihan`), particularly OFWs who are driven by family (Darvin, 2016). Farmers, though facing challenges, demonstrate remarkable resilience (Shah et al., 2017). Praise is a powerful motivator for Filipinos, while public criticism can be demotivating (de Leon, n.d.).

Canadians, especially those in their early 20s to mid-40s, are highly motivated by money to a certain extent, but some are still driven by rewards and benefits for improvement in job productivity (Evason, 2016a). In fact, the Government of Canada (2022a) itself drafted a tool that would enforce job enhancement and essential skills in the workplace. This tool targets employers who aim to support their employees' skill sets by creating opportunities for growth and development. The survey conducted by the Healthcare of Ontario Pension Plan (HOOPP), on the other hand, revealed that 66% of Canadians would rather have a pension plan or a better plan despite having a lower salary than a higher salary but with no or worse pension plan (2022). The survey also revealed that not only the older Canadians are interested in prioritizing pension over salary but also the young workers, aged under 35 years old, would have come up with the same decision. This stems from the young workers' recognition of the societal value of pension which translates to their understanding of creating an effective way of saving up for retirement.

Just like Canadians, Filipinos are hardworking employees (Hays, 2015). In a study on migrant workers in Canada, the findings revealed that Filipinos are deemed hardworking migrants who are mostly in the health and manual labor industries (Darvin, 2016). Motivated by their will to bring their families abroad, OFWs risk-taking contracts that would require them to commit to uninterrupted service, causing them to be separated from their children for two years or more. Just like OFWs, farmers in the Philippines are notorious for being resilient as they endure financial loss, various ecological damages, and other water-related risks (Shah et al., 2017). Farmers are said to be optimistic and motivated in working the entire day as they hope for a brighter future for themselves and their families. Filipino workers are also motivated by praise done in public while demotivated if criticism is shared in front of a crowd (de Leon, n.d.). This stems from the Spanish concept of amor-propio or self-esteem, resulting in conflict if confrontation is risked.

Leadership Styles

Canadian leaders adhere to the Key Leadership Competency Profile (Government of Canada, 2016b). They should exemplify integrity, respect, and flexibility. Constructive feedback, innovation, collaboration, and a broad vision are valued. Filipinos admire leaders who are nurturing, morally upright, courageous, fair, and intelligent (`makatao`, `matapat`, etc.) (de Leon, n.d.). Arrogance is strongly disliked. Leaders must be role models, both firm and selfless.

In Canada, leaders and managers are bound by a Key Leadership Competency profile set by the government (Government of Canada, 2016b). This profile is updated to provide examples of effective and ineffective behaviors of leaders in public service. Canadian leaders are expected to uphold integrity and respect wherein they exude trust within the workplace. It is important for leaders to encourage collaboration through the sharing of opinions while demonstrating flexibility in understanding different perspectives. With that, constructive and respectful feedback is expected by employees from managers. Canadian leaders also promote innovation and intelligent risk-taking to achieve results. Canadians are drawn to leaders who can take on challenging decisions and see the bigger picture. As they positively motivate their employees, they collaborate and work closely with the organization's partners and stakeholders. At the end of the day, Canadians tend to appreciate leaders who are open to alternatives instead of those who are strictly authoritarian.

As for Filipinos, they are said to likely follow a leader who adheres to a specific set of characteristics, namely makatao, matapat, malakas ang loob, makatarungan and magaling (de Leon, n.d.). The first cluster, makatao, entails mapagkalinga and may magandang kalooban meaning a leader possessing nurturant qualities. The second cluster, matapat, follows matuwid, maka-Diyos and may moralidad meaning a leader who is upright, God-centered, and has moral judgment. Malakas ang loob, on the other hand, refers to leaders who are courageous and possess political will. Makatarungan is a leader who is demokratiko and pantay-pantay ang tingin sa lahat meaning someone who is always fair and just in any situation. Lastly, Filipinos tend to lean towards leaders who are magaling or marunong which means people who are intelligent, capable, and competent.

Following those leadership guidelines, Filipinos are also very particular about arrogance (de Leon, n.d.). Being a know-it-all who exudes arrogance contradicts the Filipino concept of shared identity or kapwa where no one, regardless of status, is more important than the rest. With that, humility must be present at all times. Filipinos also expect that their managers lead by example and that they are firm but selfless. With that, it is also claimed that successful leadership in the Philippines equates to being skilled in problem-solving and managing interpersonal relations.

Hierarchy and Decision-Making

Canada has a less rigid hierarchy than the Philippines. While experience is respected, younger employees can voice opinions readily (Evason, 2016a). Subordinates typically consult their immediate manager before escalating issues (Santander Trade, 2022). While final decisions lie with management, employee input may be considered. Despite progress, women remain underrepresented in Canadian decision-making structures (Canadian Women's Foundation and Platform, 2021).

The Philippines maintains a strong hierarchical model (Scroope, 2017a). While top-down decision-making prevails, achieving consensus is important (de Leon, n.d.). Decision processes can be slower as various perspectives are sought (Scroope, 2017a). Despite a matriarchal society, Filipino women have more access to leadership than in some countries (Investing in Women, 2017). However, traditional gender roles persist, with men seen as primary providers and women as caregivers (Pinzon, 2021).

In Canadian culture, a definitive hierarchy of age or gender does not exist (Evason, 2016a). Despite that, it is mostly claimed that managerial roles are usually given to more experienced ones. With that, younger employees are generally encouraged to share their opinions, especially in the avenues of innovation, while supervisors cultivate these ideas before they reach top management. Using that line of decision-making, subordinates are expected to refer to their immediate supervisor first before reporting to top management. At the end of the day, managers are to set the final decision but, in some cases, employees' opinions are taken into consideration as well (Santander Trade, 2022).

As a patriarchal society, women in decision-making remain underrepresented (Canadian Women's Foundation and Platform, 2021). This slow process is evident in Canada's rigid political landscape where women's decisions and voices are said to be missing from the discourse of societal issues. Moreover, it has been claimed that multiple systemic gaps and barriers to women's equitable participation in decision-making processes still exist in today's workplace.

On the other hand, the Philippine culture builds on a rigid hierarchical structure with a top-down approach (Scroope, 2017a). Unlike Canadian culture where the manager lays out final decisions, Filipinos put much value on achieving consensus (de Leon, n.d.). While employees tend to refer final decisions to top management, they also expect that everyone's opinions are considered and at least asked (Scroope, 2017a). By doing so, decision-making tends to be slower as the propositions are also considered.

As a matriarchal society, women in decision-making in the Philippines are accounted for as evident in the supervisory positions that they are likely to be claimed in service, sales, and other professional industries (Investing in Women, 2017). In politics, the country has also had two women Presidents and three Vice Presidents. While this is the case, men are still viewed as head of the family or haligi ng tahanan who is expected to provide for the family financially, and yet women are claimed as pillars of the home or ilaw ng tahanan who are solely in charge of caring for the children (Pinzon, 2021).

Religion and Social Celebrations

Canada embraces religious pluralism (Evason, 2016c). While Christianity is dominant, secularism and other faiths are respected. Canadians generally avoid overt religious discussion in the workplace. Public holidays include Christmas and New Year's Day, but many businesses remain open year-round (Evason, 2016b; Santander Trade, 2022).

The Philippines is deeply religious, with Catholicism heavily influencing societal norms (Hays, 2015; Scroope, 2017b). Religious holidays like Holy Week and Christmas are significant (Syrek et al., 2018). Religion can be more openly expressed in the Filipino workplace. Sundays are generally reserved for family and religious observance. (Hays, 2015).

Canadian culture upholds pluralism and freedom where everyone has the right to practice any religion of their comfort and preference (Evason, 2016c). A large portion of the population practices Christianity while secular alternatives and non-Christian faith also exist in Canada. Minority faiths have also been increasing in the past few years due to labor migration. While this is true, Canadians are perceived as not regularly attending religious services. They also do not openly discuss religion in public such as the workplace while preaching during conversations could lead to confrontations and negative implications. Some of the social celebrations that they put much importance on are Halloween, Christmas, Boxing Day, and New Year's Day but companies and businesses are still said to be open all year round (Evason, 2016b; Santander Trade, 2022).

The Philippines, on the other hand, is a deeply religious country, with a large majority of the population being Roman Catholic, several other Christian denominations especially among the Indigenous groups, a portion are Muslim, and some identifying with other religions and other non-religious group (Hays, 2015; Scroope, 2017b). While the Constitution mandates the separation of Church and State, it has been evident throughout the years that Catholicism has been integral in both political and societal affairs (Scroope, 2017b). Religion has a strong influence on Filipinos and it even serves as the foundation of some of the values and norms that they uphold (Hays, 2015). In fact, according to the Canadian Center for Intercultural Learning, social celebrations in the Philippines such as Holy Week, Easter and Christmas are closely related to the spiritual fervor that the country exhibits. It should also be taken into account how the Philippines celebrates the longest Christmas in the world (Syrek et al., 2018). Having said that, religion is practiced and exemplified by Filipinos in various aspects including in the workplace (Hays, 2015). The Canadian Center for Intercultural Learning also accentuates that Sunday is deemed a day of obligation for family and religion which is why working on Sundays is mostly avoided by Filipinos.

Sustainability and Environmentalism

Canada prioritizes responsible business practices, encouraging sustainability as an ethical and competitive imperative (Government of Canada, 2021c). The Responsible Business Conduct Strategy helps companies mitigate risks and contribute to global sustainability goals.

Filipinos' attitude towards sustainability stems from frequent exposure to natural disasters (Reyes, 2015). They may hold a somewhat pessimistic outlook, making efforts toward biodiversity conservation and environmental education crucial.

According to Honorable Mary Ng, P.C., M.P, Minister of International Trade, Export Promotion, Small Business, and Economic Development, the Canadian way of management equates to the commitment to implementing responsible strategies, promoting sustainable business growth, and building a better and safer future not just for the company but for everyone (Government of Canada, 2021c). The Government's Responsible Business Conduct Strategy serves as a tool in guiding companies in following responsible business protocols that will contribute to sustainable development. In addition, it accounts for a framework for recognizing the shifting global environment where one must calculate and mitigate sustainability risks to survive.

The attitude of Filipinos towards sustainability and environmentalism today stems from the country's long history of natural disasters (Reyes, 2015). Filipinos claim a pessimistic view of the environment given the problems they faced throughout the years. With that, biodiversity, conservation ecological facets, and environmental behavior must be considered, moving forward. In addition, environmental education is recommended to address sustainability and environmentalism concerns from the roots.

Inclination Towards Migration

Canada actively embraces immigration as a critical economic driver. Government policies promote diversity and inclusion, recognizing the benefits of immigration for strengthening the labor market, boosting innovation, and filling critical gaps (Ertorer et al., 2020; Government of Canada, 2021b). Immigration is also seen as essential to counterbalance Canada's aging population.

In contrast, the Philippines has historically been a labor-exporting nation, consistently ranking among the top sources of global migrants since 2000 (Kang & Latoja, 2022). Economic factors are a major driver; salary differences between the Philippines and receiving countries motivate OFWs to seek better opportunities abroad (Rivera & Tullao Jr, 2020). This applies to high-skilled professionals seeking career advancement and less-skilled workers escaping poverty. Remittances sent back by OFWs significantly contribute to the Philippine economy.

Canada is known as a country of immigration where collective respect for diverse customs, identities, languages, and religions is enforced (Ertorer et al., 2020). Business experts and economists acknowledge how immigration strengthens the labor market, reinforces innovation, and addresses labor gaps and shortages especially in the health sector (Government of Canada, 2021b). As Canada recognizes immigration as the driver of its economy, it also mitigates issues with the increasing aging population. With that, it continuously welcomes immigrants for the improvement of its labor force growth.

The Philippines has been known as a labor-sending country as it has been one of the top sources of global migrants since the year 2000 (Kang & Latoja, 2022). The overall average of Filipino migrants that have relocated in North America equates to a straight 50% of the said population. Due to salary differentials between their home country and the labor-receiving country, OFWs tend to maximize the country's exporting labor as a means of addressing unemployment. Despite the risks of underemployment, educated Filipino manpower lean towards seeking growth from the labor-receiving country while average and low-skilled Filipino workers pursue working abroad as a means of getting out of poverty in the Philippines. As a result, collective remittances from OFWs benefit the Philippine economy (Rivera & Tullao Jr, 2020).

SOLUTIONS AND RECOMMENDATIONS

This chapter elucidates the potential for a strengthened Canada-Philippines partnership, recognizing existing collaborations and the need to address cultural differences for sustained success. To maximize this potential, the following policy recommendations should be considered:

Strategic Labor Mobility

Both nations must prioritize streamlined, efficient labor mobility channels. Canada needs targeted programs to recruit skilled Filipino workers and address its SME labor shortages. The Philippines should, in turn, implement expedited visa and work permit processes for Canadians. A formal bilateral agreement is essential, outlining transparent terms, equitable wages, and protections against worker exploitation.

Reciprocal, Skills-Based Immigration

Canada can benefit from easing restrictions for Filipino workers seeking permanent residency, with a focus on in-demand skills. The Philippines should simultaneously create attractive pathways for Canadian entrepreneurs, investors, and specialized professionals. Such policies must prioritize fair market integration with clear qualifications and safeguards to prevent displacement within local labor markets.

Fostering Cultural Fluency

Beyond economic benefits, sustainable collaboration requires cultural understanding. Initiatives must transcend academic scholarships to actively support artist-in-residence programs, high-profile cultural exchanges, and diverse media representation. This combats stereotypes, fostering the subtle cultural awareness crucial for success in cross-cultural business environments.

FUTURE RESEARCH DIRECTIONS

This chapter highlights the need for a deeper examination of cultural similarities and differences between Canada and the Philippines, offering a foundation for future research. Here are crucial areas for further study:

Cross-Cultural Perception Survey

A comprehensive survey comparing how Canadians and Filipinos perceive each other can provide empirical data, validating the observations noted in this work. Such research could inform targeted training and awareness programs for businesses and policymakers.

Adaptation and Integration

Research examining the ease with which Filipinos adjust to Canadian culture (and vice versa) is vital. Identifying factors contributing to successful adaptation can help SMEs develop onboarding and support strategies, maximizing the benefits of a diverse workforce. This is particularly valuable given Filipino employees' positive impact on workplace culture, as noted.

Leveraging Differences

Beyond overcoming barriers, the research could focus on how cultural differences could be transformed into competitive advantages for businesses. For instance, understanding Filipino perspectives on innovation and problem-solving could help SMEs unlock new approaches and reach untapped markets.

CONCLUSION

This comparative analysis emphasizes the opportunities and potential complexities inherent in a strengthened Canada-Philippines partnership. Understanding vital cultural differences, as outlined through Hofstede's framework, is essential for successful business ventures:

Power Dynamics

Filipinos' acceptance of hierarchical structures contrasts Canada's egalitarian values. SMEs must be mindful of establishing leadership styles, decision-making processes, and communication channels.

Individualism vs. Collectivism

Canada's individualistic culture prioritizes personal goals, while Filipinos' collectivist approach emphasizes group harmony and loyalty. SMEs should tailor recruitment messaging and reward structures, fostering inclusive workplaces that harness both perspectives.

Work Ethic and Ambitions

The Filipino emphasis on career advancement contrasts with Canadians' focus on work-life balance. SMEs must demonstrate awareness of these priorities, offering growth opportunities for Filipino employees alongside flexible or family-friendly policies.

Critical Recommendations for Sustainable SME Engagement

Prioritize Targeted Training

Comprehensive cross-cultural training programs should go beyond awareness, equipping SME employees with practical communication, conflict resolution, and team-building skills. This is vital for maximizing a diverse workforce's potential.

Flexible Approaches

Successful SMEs will develop adaptable business models that draw on the strengths of both cultures. For instance, blending elements of hierarchical structures with Canadian-style consultative processes can prove effective.

Building Trust and Reciprocity

Cultural sensitivity is a foundation, but genuine trust is paramount. This requires demonstrating long-term commitment, understanding Filipino concepts like 'kapwa', and actively seeking mutually beneficial outcomes.

Embracing Diversity as Strength

When navigated thoughtfully, SMEs must recognize that cultural differences can be a source of innovation and resilience. Internal variations within each country must also be acknowledged for adaptive approaches.

REFERENCES

Beattie, M. (2020). 'Like an American but without a gun'?": Canadian national identity and the Kids in the Hall. *Participations*, 17(2). https://www.participations.org/Volume%2017/Issue%202/2.pdf

Blanchet, N. (2021). *Immigrant-led SME exporters in Canada.* /https://www.international.gc.ca/trade -commerce/assets/pdfs/inclusive_trade-commerce_inclusif/Immigrant-led-SME-Exporters-canada-en.pdf

ca/guides/spotlight-pleins_feux/intercultural-business-interculturelle-des-affaires.aspx?lang=eng

Canada.ca. (n.d). The Honourable Rechie Valdez. https://www.pm.gc.ca/en/cabinet/honourable-rechie -valdez

Canadian Women's Foundation and Platform. (2021). *Resetting normal: Gender, intersectionality and leadership.*https://fw3s926r0g42i6kes3bxg4i1-wpengine.netdna-ssl.com/wp-content/uploads/2021/04/ Resetting-Normal-Gender-Intersectionality-and-Leadership-Report-Final-EN.pdf

Catacataca, P. D. (n.d). *The use of Filipino in official transactions, communication, and correspondence.*https://ncca.gov.ph/about-ncca-3/subcommissions/subcommission-on-cultural-disseminationscd/ language-and-translation/the-use-of-filipino-in-official-transactions-communication-and-correspondence/

Charbonneau, J. (2017). *To win at trade with ASEAN, Canada must also focus on security and Culture.* https://www.asiapacific.ca/blog/win-trade-asean-canada-must-also-focus-security-and-culture

City of Toronto. (n.d.). *Strong economy.*https://www.toronto.ca/business-economy/invest-in-toronto/ strong-economy/

Darvin, R. (2016). Mediating identities: Language, media, and Filipinos in Canada. https://dx.doi.org/ DOI: 10.14288/1.0347617

de Leon, F. M., Jr. (n.d.). *Understanding the Filipino* [PowerPoint Slides]. SlidePlayer. https://slideplayer .com/slide/4211242/

Department of Foreign Affairs. (n.d.). *Mission, vision, and core values.*https://dfa.gov.ph/about/mission -vision-core-values

Department of Tourism. (n.d.). *National tourism development plan.*http://www.tourism.gov.ph/NTDP.aspx

Department of Trade and Industry. (n.d.). *ASEAN 50: 50th year of being one ASEAN.* Association of Southeast Asian Nations. https://www.dti.gov.ph/asean/

Durant, A., & Shepherd, I. (2009). 'Culture' and 'communication' in intercultural communication. *European journal of English studies*, 13(2), 147-162. Page 4

Embassy of the Philippines in Hague. (n.d.). *General information.* https://thehaguepe.dfa.gov.ph/79 -about-us/98-general-information#:~:text=Two%20official%20languages%20%E2%80%94%20Filipino %20and,of%20instruction%20in%20higher%20education

Embassy of the Philippines in Ottawa. (n.d.). *Filipinos in Canada: The Filipino diaspora in Canada.* https://ottawape.dfa.gov.ph/index.php/2016-04-12-08-34-55/filipino-diaspora

Ertorer, S. E., Long, J., Fellin, M., & Esses, V. M. (2020). Immigrant perceptions of integration in the Canadian workplace. *Equality, Diversity and Inclusion*, Vol. ahead-of-print No. ahead-of-print. https://doi.org/DOI: 10.1108/EDI-02-2019-0086

Evason, N. (2016a). *Canadian Culture: Business Culture.* https://culturalatlas.sbs.com.au/canadian-culture/canadian-culture-business-culture

Evason, N. (2016b). *Canadian Culture: Dates of Significance.* https://culturalatlas.sbs.com.au/canadian-culture/canadian-culture-dates-of-significance

Evason, N. (2016c). *Canadian Culture: Religion.* https://culturalatlas.sbs.com.au/canadian-culture/canadian-culture-religion

Gazette, O. (n.d.). *Philippine Government.* https://www.officialgazette.gov.ph/about/gov/

Gazette, O. (n.d.). *The Philippines.* https://www.officialgazette.gov.ph/about/philippines /

Global Affairs Canada. (2022). *Minister Ng establishes the Canada-Philippines joint economic commission.* https://www.canada.ca/en/global-affairs/news/2022/05/minister-ng-establishes-the-canada-philippines-joint-economic-commission.html

Gouvernement du Québec. (2022). *Importance of French in Quebec.* https://www.quebec.ca/en/immigration/french-in-quebec#:~:text=According%20to%20the%20Charter%20of,work

Government of Canada. (2012). *Discover Canada – Canada's economy.* https://www.canada.ca/en/immigration-refugees-citizenship/corporate/publications-manuals/discover-canada/read-online/canadas-economy.html

Government of Canada. (2016a). *Effective interactive communication.* https://www.canada.ca/en/revenue-agency/corporate/careers-cra/information-moved/cra-competencies-standardized-assessment-tools/canada-revenue-agency-competencies-april-2016/effective-interactive-communication.html

Government of Canada. (2016b). *Key leadership competency profile and examples of effective and ineffective behaviors.* https://www.canada.ca/en/treasury-board-secretariat/services/professional-development/key-leadership-competency-profile/examples-effective-ineffective-behaviours.html

Government of Canada. (2017). *About official languages and bilingualism.* https://www.canada.ca/en/canadian-heritage/services/official-languages-bilingualism/about.html

Government of Canada. (2018a). *About the Crown.* https://www.canada.ca/en/canadian-heritage/services/crown-canada/about.html

Government of Canada. (2018b). *Mandate - Immigration, Refugees, Citizenship Canada.* https://www.canada.ca/en/immigration-refugees-citizenship/corporate/mandate.html

Government of Canada. (2020a). *Community support, multiculturalism, and anti-racism initiatives program.* https://www.canada.ca/en/canadian-heritage/services/funding/community-multiculturalism-anti-racism.html

Government of Canada. (2020b). *The creation of Canada.* https://www.canada.ca/en/canadian-heritage/services/origin-name-canada.html

Government of Canada. (2021a). *Aging and chronic diseases: A profile of Canadian seniors.* https://www .canada.ca/en/public-health/services/publications/diseases-conditions/aging-chronic-diseases-profile -canadian-seniors-report.html

Government of Canada. (2021b). *Canada welcomes the most immigrants in a single year in its history.* https://www.canada.ca/en/immigration-refugees-citizenship/news/2021/12/canada-welcomes-the-most -immigrants-in-a-single-year-in-its-history.html

Government of Canada. (2021c). *Responsible business conduct abroad: Canada's strategy for the future.* https://www.international.gc.ca/trade-commerce/rbc-cre/strategy-2022-strategie.aspx?lang=eng

Government of Canada. (2021d). *The constitutional distribution of legislative powers.* https://www.canada .ca/en/intergovernmental-affairs/services/federation/distribution-legislative-powers.html

Government of Canada. (2021e). *Spotlight on intercultural business.* https://www.tradecommissioner.gc

Government of Canada. (2022a). *Job enhancement and essential skills.*

Government of Canada. (2022b). *What is gender-based analysis plus.* https://women-gender-equality .canada.ca/en/gender-based-analysis-plus/what-gender-based-analysis-plus.html

Government of Canada. (2023). *Canada opens operations centre in the Philippines to boost global immigration processing capacity.* https://www.canada.ca/en/immigration-refugees-citizenship/news/ 2023/03/canada-opens-operations-centre-in-the-philippines-to-boost-global-immigration-processing -capacity.html

Government of Canada. (2023). *Notice – Supplementary information for the 2024-2026 immigration level plans.* https://www.canada.ca/en/immigration-refugees-citizenship/news/notices/supplementary -immigration-levels-2024-2026.html

Government of Canada. (2024a). *Canada-Philippines relations.* https://www.international.gc.ca/country -pays/philippines/relations.aspx?lang=eng

Government of Canada. (2024b). *Canada's chairing of the CPTPP Commission in 2024.* https://www .international.gc.ca/trade-commerce/trade-agreements-accords-commerciaux/agr-acc/cptpp-ptpgp/ commission-2024.aspx?lang=eng

Government of Canada. (2024c). *State of trade 2023: Inclusive trade.* https://www.international.gc.ca/ transparency-transparence/state-trade-commerce-international/2023.aspx?lang=eng. ISSN 2562-8321

Government of Prince Edward Island. (n.d.). *Canadian citizenship.* http://www.gov.pe.ca/photos/original/ WI_KCanadianCit.pdf

Graham, J. (2010, April). The influence of national culture on SME management practices. In *Proceedings of the Management Challenges in the 21st Century Conference*, Bratislava, Slovakia (pp. 91-99).

Gupta, R. (2024). Exploring the impact of socio-cultural factors on entrepreneurship development in emerging markets. DOI: 10.21203/rs.3.rs-3938479/v1

Hanel, P. H. P., Maio, G. R., Soares, A. K. S., Vione, K. C., de Holanda Coelho, G. L., Gouveia, V. V., Patil, A. C., Kamble, S. V., & Manstead, A. S. R. (2018). Cross-cultural differences and similarities in human value instantiation. *Frontiers in Psychology*, 9(849), 849. Advance online publication. DOI: 10.3389/fpsyg.2018.00849 PMID: 29896151

Hays, J. (2015). *Filipino character and personality: Hiya, amor propio, emotions and the influences of Catholicism, Asia and Spain. Facts and Details.*https://factsanddetails.com/southeast-asia/Philippines/sub5_6c/entry-3867.html

Healthcare of Ontario Pension Plan. (2022). *2022 Canadian retirement survey.*

https://hoopp.com/docs/default-source/default-document-library/abacusresearch2022_execsummary.pdf

Hofstede, G. (2011). Dimensionalizing Cultures: The Hofstede Model in Context. *Online Readings in Psychology and Culture*, 2(1). Advance online publication. DOI: 10.9707/2307-0919.1014

Hofstede, G. J., Jonker, C. M., & Verwaart, T. (2009). Modeling power distance in trade. In David, N., & Sichman, J. S. (Eds.), Lecture Notes in Computer Science: Vol. 5269. *Multi-agent-based simulations IX. MABS 2008.* Springer., DOI: 10.1007/978-3-642-01991-3_1

International Labour Organization. (n.d.). *Labour migration in the Philippines.*https://www.ilo.org/manila/areasofwork/labour-migration/lang--en/index.htm

International Monetary Fund. (2022). *Philippines: Datasets.*https://www.imf.org/external/datamapper/profile/PHL

International Trade Centre. (2020). *Promoting SME competitiveness in the Philippines: Compete, connect, and change to build resilience to crises.* ITC.

Investing in Women. (2017). *Filipino women in leadership: Government and industry.*https://investinginwomen.asia/knowledge/filipino-women-leadership-government-industry/

Jones, K., Ksaifi, L., & Clark, C. (2023). 'The biggest problem we are facing is the running away problem': Recruitment and the paradox of facilitating the mobility of immobile workers. *Work, Employment and Society*, 37(4), 841–857. DOI: 10.1177/09500170221094764

Kang, J. W., & Latoja, M. C. (2022). COVID-19 and overseas Filipino workers: Return migration and reintegration into the home country – the Philippine case. *ADB Southeast Asia Working Paper Series*, 21. https://dx.doi.org/DOI: 10.22617/WPS220002-2

https://www.canada.ca/en/services/jobs/training/initiatives/skills-success/tools/job-enhancement.htm l

Lopez-Torres, G. C. (2023). The impact of smes' sustainability on competitiveness. *Measuring Business Excellence*, 27(1), 107–120. DOI: 10.1108/MBE-12-2021-0144

Luu, T. D. (2023). Fostering strategic entrepreneurship of smes: The role of organisational change forces. *Management Decision*, 61(3), 695–719. DOI: 10.1108/MD-08-2021-1024

Martinez, A. (2023). A paper about the influence of Philippines' unique social culture in business. *ASEAN Journal of CI-EL and Applied Philosophy*, 1(1). Advance online publication. DOI: 10.22146/arcelap.v1i1.9732

Minority Rights Group International. (n.d.). *Philippines: Indigenous peoples.*https://minorityrights.org/minorities/indigenous-peoples-6/#:~:text=The%20other%20concentration%20of%20indigenous,Talandig%2C%20and%20Tiruray%20or%20Teduray

Mishra, M., Chaubey, A., Khatwani, R., & Nair, K. (2023). Overcoming barriers in automotive smes to attain international competitiveness: An ism approach modelling. *Journal of Business and Industrial Marketing*, 38(12), 2713–2730. DOI: 10.1108/JBIM-12-2022-0546

Moshtari, M., & Safarpour, A. (2023). Challenges and strategies for the internationalization of higher education in low-income East African countries. *Higher Education*, ●●●, 1–21. PMID: 36713135

Mukhopadhyay, S. (n.d.). *International Projects* [PowerPoint Slides]. SlidePlayer., https://slideplayer.com/slide/13936018/

OECD, & Scalabrini Migration Center. (2017). *Interrelations between public policies, migration and development in the Philippines. OECD Development Pathways.*https://doi.org/DOI: 10.1787/9789264272286-en

OECD. (2017). SME and entrepreneurship policy in Canada. OECD Studies on SMEs and Entrepreneurship. *OECD Publishing, Paris.*https://doi-org.lib-ezproxy.concordia.ca/10.1787/9789264273467-en

Philippine Statistics Authority. (2022). *2020 overseas Filipino workers (final results).* https://psa.gov.ph/content/2020-overseas-filipino-workers-final-results

Pinzon, M. J. L. (2021). *Defamiliarized family: The "Anak ng OFWs" emergent narratives on mediated communication and parent-child relationships.* https://scholar.archive.org/work/fm6e4hv6nzgvtctoi vd3uujohu/access/wayback/http://www.plarideljournal.org/download/6098/

Reyes, J. A. L. (2015). Environmental attitudes and behaviors in the Philippines. *Journal of Educational and Social Research*, 4(6), 87–102. DOI: 10.5901/jesr.2014.v4n6p87

Rivera, J. P. R., & Tullao, T. S. Jr. (2020). Investigating the link between remittances and inflation: Evidence from the Philippines. *South East Asia Research*, 28(3), 301–326. DOI: 10.1080/0967828X.2020.1793685

Sahoo, S. (2022). Lean practices and operational performance: The role of organizational culture. *International Journal of Quality & Reliability Management*, 39(2), 428–467. DOI: 10.1108/IJQRM-03-2020-0067

Saskatchewan. (n.d.). *Key economic sectors.*https://www.saskatchewan.ca/business/investment-and-economic-development/key-economic-sectors

Scroope, C. (2017a). *Filipino culture: Business culture.*https://culturalatlas.sbs.com.au/filipino-culture/filipino-culture-business-culture

Scroope, C. (2017b). *Filipino culture: Religion.*https://culturalatlas.sbs.com.au/filipino-culture/filipino-culture-religion

Selvarajah, C., Le, T. D., & Sukunesan, S. (2019). The Vietnam project: Developing conceptual knowledge on cross-cultural skills for training in SME internationalization. *Asia Pacific Business Review*, 25(3), 338–366. DOI: 10.1080/13602381.2019.1598076

Semrau, T., Ambos, T., & Kraus, S. (2016). Entrepreneurial orientation and SME performance across societal cultures: An international study. *Journal of Business Research*, 69(5), 1928–1932. DOI: 10.1016/j.jbusres.2015.10.082

Shah, S. H., Angeles, L. C., & Harris, L. M. (2017). Worlding the intangibility of resilience: The case of rice farmers and water-related risk in the Philippines. *World Development*, 98, 400–412. DOI: 10.1016/j.worlddev.2017.05.004

Soloviov, V. (2022). Re-examining the links between cultural values and innovation. *Economics & Sociology (Ternopil)*, 15(2), 41–59. DOI: 10.14254/2071-789X.2022/15-2/3

Statistics Canada. (2021). *Table 10-10-0137-01 Representation of women and men elected to national Parliament and of ministers appointed to federal Cabinet.* https://doi.org/DOI: 10.25318/1010013701-eng

Swank, G. (2019). *The importance of building lasting relationships for your organization.* https://www.inc.com/young-entrepreneur-council/the-importance-of-building-lasting-relationships-for-your-organization.html

Syrek, C. J., Weigelt, O., Kühnel, J., & de Bloom, J. (2018). All I want for Christmas is recovery–changes in employee affective well-being before and after vacation. *Work and Stress*, 32(4), 313–333. DOI: 10.1080/02678373.2018.1427816

The Culture Factor club (n.d). *Country Comparison tool Hofstede Insigths.* https://www.hofstede-insights.com/country-comparison-tool?countries=canada https://www.hofstede-insights.com/country-comparison-tool?countries=philippinies

The Philippine Atmospheric Geophysical and Astronomical Services Administration. (2022). *Flood information.* https://www.pagasa.dost.gov.ph/flood#flood-information

The Philippine Atmospheric Geophysical and Astronomical Services Administration. (n.d.). *Climate of the Philippines.* https://www.pagasa.dost.gov.ph/information/climate-philippines#:~:text=Using%20temperature%20and%20rainfall%20as,season%2C%20from%20December%20to%20May

The World Bank. (2021). *GDP (current US$).* https://data.worldbank.org/indicator/NY.GDP.MKTP.CD

TodayTranslations. (n.d.). Doing business in Canada. https://www.todaytranslations.com/consultancy-services/business-culture-and-etiquette/doing-business-in-canada/

Tomos, F. A., Thurairaj, S., Balan, O., & Hy.ams-Ssekasi, D. (2020). Effects of Culture on Women Entrepreneurs' Success: A Cross-Country Study. *Gender Studies, Entrepreneurship and Human Capital.,* 269-295. .DOI: 10.1007/978-3-030-46874-3_15

Trade, S. (2022). *Canada: Business practices.* https://santandertrade.com/en/portal/establish-overseas/canada/business-practices

United Nations Office for Disaster Risk Reduction. (2019). *Disaster risk reduction in the Philippines: Status report 2019.* https://www.unisdr.org/files/68265_682308philippinesdrmstatusreport.pdf

Villarino, R. T. H., Villarino, M. L. F., Temblor, M. C. L., Bernard, P., & Plaisent, M. (2022). Developing a health and well-being program for college students: An online intervention. *World Journal on Educational Technology.*, 14(1), 65–78. DOI: 10.18844/wjet.v14i1.6638

KEY TERMS AND DEFINITIONS

Attitudinal Facets: Aspects related to the attitudes or predispositions of individuals or groups towards various subjects or situations.

Behavioral Facets: Elements that concern individuals' or groups' observable actions or reactions in different situations.

Cross-culture: a concept that refers to the differences observed among people from different nations' expression and behavior, namely their ethnicity, view of life, and relations. This also defines the connections and interactions sustained by and through the various layers of cultural diversity. Cross-cultural knowledge is essential in building and honing business relationships in the context of new markets.

Culture: from the Latin "cultura," nicknamed "the software of the mind," is a concept that refers to a set of values and beliefs, a way of thinking, expressing and reacting, behaving, formalized by social institutions, learned and shared in a community, often defined geographically, that guide and explain behavior and attitudes. It also refers to the deeply rooted customs, backgrounds, and traditions that shape one's identity and being, which are mostly highly influenced by a collective.

Cultural Insights: Understanding gained through examining a specific cultural group's characteristics, behaviors, and norms.

Hoftstede's Cultural Framework: an empirically deducted categorization into six characteristics of the main traits, explicative of differences observed among nations and countries, named power distance, uncertainty control or avoidance, individualism vs collectivism, masculinity (motivation towards achievement), long-term orientation, indulgence vs. restraint. This framework illustrates a structural tool for analyzing the complexities of cultural similarities and differences that shape organizational culture.

Organizational culture: a unique combination of values, beliefs, and attitudes specific to an enterprise and its DNA, guiding and explaining its practices, favoring the integration of newcomers but limiting the capacities of change. This also refers to the shared understanding that strengthens the organization's vision and goal.

Relationship Gaps: Lacks or deficiencies in the understanding, communication, or connection between parties, which can hinder the development of effective and sustainable relationships.

Sustainable Relationships: characteristics of a relation between partners based on a long-term strategy guaranteed by transparency to the other, sincere involvement, stability of the relation, and win-win conception of transactions. These relationships are founded on mutual respect, trust, and understanding from all parties involved.

Chapter 5
Dynamic Capabilities to Drive Innovation and Competitivenss in a Changing Business World

Andrea del Pilar Barrera
https://orcid.org/0000-0002-1286-2623
Universidad Nacional Abierta y a Distancia, Colombia

Pedro Rene Jimenez-Hernandez
Worley-Jacobs, Colombia

German Fernando Medina-Ricaurte
Universidad Nacional Abierta y a Distancia, Colombia

ABSTRACT

The chapter explores how small and medium-sized enterprises (SMEs) can enhance competitiveness and innovation in a constantly evolving business environment. SMEs face significant challenges to remain relevant amid rapid technological evolution, shifts in consumer preferences, and increasing global competition To adapt, innovate, and thrive, SMEs must develop dynamic capabilities, comprising a set of skills, processes, and knowledge that enable them to integrate, build, and reconfigure their internal resources in response to environmental changes. To improve competitiveness and innovation, SMEs should foster a culture of innovation that values experimentation and creative thinking, promote collaboration through strategic alliances and agile methodologies, and manage organizational well-being by addressing mental health and stress management. These strategies collectively enhance resilience and adaptability, essential for navigating BANI environments

INTRODUCTION

In today's business landscape, characterized by rapid technological evolution, shifting consumer preferences, and increasing global competition, small and medium-sized enterprises (SMEs) face significant challenges in remaining competitive in a business environment characterized by volatility, uncertainty,

DOI: 10.4018/979-8-3693-4046-2.ch005

complexity, and ambiguity. To survive and thrive in this context, it is essential for SMEs to develop capabilities that enable them to quickly adapt to changing market conditions.

In this context, businesses need to develop tools that allow them to adapt swiftly to changes and effectively manage uncertainty. This is where dynamic capabilities come into play, enabling organizations to identify opportunities and reconfigure their strategic resources in response to the changing demands of the BANI environment. The following section explores the key characteristics of dynamic capabilities and their relevance to SMEs

The rise of dynamic capabilities is closely linked to the profound transformations the business world has experienced since the 1990s, with the advent of the Internet and globalization. The digital era has marked a paradigm shift in how companies operate, interact with customers, and compete in the marketplace (Teece, 2018). This shift has generated a business environment characterized by uncertainty, volatility, and complexity, where organizations must be agile and adaptable to survive and succeed.

In response to these profound transformations, businesses have increasingly relied on dynamic capabilities to navigate this new landscape. Dynamic capabilities refer to the ability of organizations to integrate, build, and reconfigure internal and external resources in response to changes in their environment (Teece et al., 2016). These capabilities are critical for innovation, adaptation, and maintaining a competitive edge in a constantly evolving business landscape.

The development of dynamic capabilities is not just an abstract concept but can be translated into practical strategies that drive competitiveness and innovation, particularly for SMEs. These strategies enable SMEs to leverage their resources and adapt to shifting market demands. The following section outlines key strategies that support the development of dynamic capabilities and promote competitiveness in SMEs.

Dynamic capabilities foster innovation within organizations by enabling the identification and understanding of emerging market opportunities, including new customer needs, technological advances, and industry trends (Eisenhardt & Martin, 2000). This capacity energizes organizations, allowing them to rapidly adjust their internal resources, promote learning from past experiences, and pave the way for new ideas and solutions (Teece, 2018). Consequently, an organizational culture that is sensitive to environmental changes, continuous learning, and adaptation is promoted, encouraging experimentation, creative thinking, and risk-taking necessary for successful innovation (Eisenhardt & Martin, 2000).

In this regard, dynamic capabilities serve as a significant driver of innovation and competitiveness in a changing business environment. These elements must be developed to facilitate adaptation and organizational learning, thus forming a fundamental basis for sustained competitiveness.

BACKGROUND

Small and Medium-Sized Enterprises-SMEs

Small and medium-sized enterprises (SMEs) are a vital component of the global economy. Representing most businesses, they are crucial to driving economic growth, job creation, and innovation. SMEs constitute approximately 90% of businesses worldwide and employ more than 50% of the global workforce (World Bank, 2020). In developed economies, they account for 60-70% of total employment and contribute around 55% of GDP. The importance of this sector underscores the need for public policies that promote their growth and sustainability, including access to finance and digitalization (IFAC,

2020). Regardless of the size or the specific activity of an SME, they generally share three key characteristics: they exert significant influence over national economies, are major drivers of innovation, and are typically resource-constrained (Sanford & Moskowitz, 2015; OECD, 2021).

SMEs play an especially vital role in developing economies, where they represent a significant source of employment and economic growth. SMEs account for 90% of businesses and employ approximately 60-70% of the workforce in most OECD member countries. They are essential for fostering economic dynamism and reducing unemployment, with their contributions being particularly significant in developing economies (OECD, 2021). This importance is further highlighted by their role in job creation (Beck et al., 2005) and their substantial contribution to GDP and employment in emerging economies, which supports sustainable economic development (Ayyagari et al., 2021). Additionally, SMEs contribute to building social capital and social cohesion, strengthening local communities (Audretsch & Keilbach, 2004).

Given their smaller size, SMEs tend to be more agile and flexible compared to large corporations, allowing them to adapt more quickly to shifting market demands (Lee et al., 2020). This agility enables SMEs to respond rapidly to changes in their environments, making them key actors in innovation and market adaptation.

SMEs are recognized for their capacity to innovate and adapt swiftly to market changes. They actively engage in networks and collaborations, implementing strategies that significantly enhance their innovative performance (Albats et al., 2020). Participation in these networks fosters improved innovation outcomes and overall competitiveness (Vătămănescu et al., 2020)

Competitiveness

Competitiveness is a concept that emerged alongside the theoretical development of economics. Adam Smith, through his concept of absolute advantage, described it as the abundance of a nation's productive factors—capital, land, and labor—supported by the wealth of natural resources each nation possesses. This abundance differentiates nations and drives the development of productive capacity (Smith, 1776). In this sense, productivity can be viewed as the foundation of competitiveness, tied to the division and specialization of labor. Smith's approach was complemented by David Ricardo in 1817 with his theory of comparative advantage, which laid the groundwork for the concept of international trade. Ricardo posited that a country has a comparative advantage based on opportunity cost: the cost of producing good A relative to good B. The country with the lower opportunity cost will have the comparative advantage (Krugman & Obstfeld, 2000). Thus, competitiveness is based on cost differentials and the intensity of productive factors each country possesses (Bajo, 1991). Initially, comparative advantage generated differences between nations and fostered the development of competitive trade.

The concept of national competitiveness can be understood as the intrinsic ability of a country to produce goods and services that meet international market standards while maintaining the real income of its citizens (Scott & Lodge, 1985). From this perspective, national competitiveness is linked to a country's industrial capacity to improve, shaped by the conditions of its productive factors, the demand for its goods, related industries, and their structure, as well as the development of strategy and firm rivalry (Porter, 1991).

At this point, the development of comparative advantage can be seen as a pillar of competitiveness theory, emphasizing the creation of comparative advantages through strategies or policies that mitigate the scarcity of productive factors within a nation (Lombana & Rozas, 2009). Comparative advantage, then, is based on a country's provision of productive factors, where firms in the same industry do not inherently have advantages over one another but develop strategies that create competitive advantages (Mahmood & Ezeala-Harrison, 2000). This advantage stems from the differences in how firms transform inputs to maximize utility. According to Porter, a nation's prosperity is linked to competitiveness, which is primarily rooted in microeconomic development. For example, a company's strategies and operations contribute to revitalizing the industrial environment, thereby demonstrating that understanding the micro-level characteristics of an industry enhances the development and implementation of national economic policy (Porter, 1991). Porter's analysis of competitive advantage, particularly his "competitiveness diamond," illustrates how a nation's conditions influence business competitiveness. His model highlights the importance of factors such as natural resources, infrastructure, local demand for products and services, and the intensity of local competition.

Competitiveness must also account for the implications that globalization has introduced to the concept. Although initially centered on the development of foreign trade, the contemporary phenomenon of globalization—accelerating in the late 20th century and continuing throughout the 21st century—has broadened the meaning of competitiveness. Advances in technology have reshaped how the world is perceived.

Globalization can be defined not only as the extension of social relations on a global scale but as the intensification of those relations, connecting all regions of the planet in direct contact. Globalization is no longer simply about movements or connections "crossing borders," but about relationships characterized by immediacy, where local events are inherently tied to distant occurrences (Mateus & Brasset, 2002).

Competitiveness is intrinsically linked to economic, social, and political factors and can be analyzed at various levels: national, industrial, and firm (Gutiérrez et al., 1998). At the national level, macroeconomic aggregates provide insight into the conditions of the macroeconomic environment that support industrial sectors and, consequently, firms. Analysis at the industry level provides information on market dynamics and sector-specific conditions, which creates a mesoeconomic environment serving as a bridge between the macro and micro levels. Finally, at the firm level, analysis focuses on the internal and external factors that strengthen competitiveness in the microeconomic environment. The aggregate of these analyses provides a comprehensive view of national competitiveness (Malavé, 1996).

The vision of the international market, in which a specific region or country seeks to increase its global market share while maintaining the quality of life for its citizens, relies on the efficient production of goods and services and the ability to adapt to changing international market conditions (Fagerberg, 1996). In global terms, global competitiveness is shaped by institutions, policies, and factors that determine a country's productivity (Schwab, 2018).

Thus, competitiveness can be understood at three levels of analysis: 1) the firm, 2) the industry or sector, and 3) the macroeconomic environment of a nation. These levels are interdependent, revealing the importance of a favorable economic environment for the development of industries and firms. Consequently, efforts should be focused on improving endogenous factors to enhance competitiveness.

The conceptualization of competitiveness is complex and depends on the level at which it is analyzed. National competitiveness, for example, requires different variables than competitiveness at the industry or firm level (Nelson, 1992). For the purposes of this analysis, we will focus on firm-level competitiveness.

Business Competitiveness

Business competitiveness is supported by the possession and exploitation of valuable, rare, inimitable, and non-substitutable resources (VRIN). In this context, internal resources such as human capital, technology, and organizational capabilities become particularly relevant (Barney, 1991). Competitiveness, therefore, is linked to the resources and capabilities that a company possesses. A company is competitive when it has the capacity to design, produce, and sell better-quality products at a lower cost, which in turn results in greater profitability and improved market share (Buckley et al., 1991).

Understanding business competitiveness involves examining various levels, each relating to different variables that impact company performance (Montenegro-Velandia & Álvarez-Rodríguez, 2011). This relationship allows for a direct connection between the development of business management and competitiveness. Meeting certain characteristics contributes to business strengthening and sustained presence in the global market (Hill et al., 2004).

Survival in the global market requires not only market knowledge but also the development of models that enable companies to compete and sustain their business (Porter, 2000). Two types of models are commonly proposed: the cluster model, where companies in the same industry concentrate and engage in complementary activities to compete globally (Forcadell, 2004); and the resource-based model, which suggests actions to enhance organizational competitiveness, such as cost reduction, strategy development, value addition, human talent management, environmental monitoring, and fostering collaborative industry relations (Bonilla & Martinez, 2009). Thus, promoting strategies that enhance business competitiveness, particularly by fostering innovation and adopting new technologies, is essential (Kotler & Keller, 2012). In this way, strategic formulation offers opportunities to generate competitive advantages that drive business competitiveness.

The generation of competitive advantages and added value is fundamental to competitiveness, allowing companies to become central actors in strategy development and as key units of competitiveness. This also helps to bridge gaps in comparative advantage, enabling companies to produce competitively, contribute to performance indicators, and generate utility and expansive growth. Expansive growth involves managing and controlling a company's endogenous factors, which influence exogenous factors at the industry and national levels, thereby creating a competitiveness ecosystem.

The focus here is on identifying the factors critical to developing business competitiveness and gaining competitive advantage. By improving production methods and administrative processes—particularly those concerning product pricing and quality—key factors influencing market share can be impacted. Considering the aspects or variables involved in process development and administrative functions is directly related to management efforts and strategy formulation aimed at achieving company goals (Musik & Romo, 2005).

Focusing on strategy impacts both market positioning and market share expansion (Ferraz et al., 2004). This focus leads to strengthened competition, closely linked to the development of marketing strategies within organizations.

When seeking models to measure the factors influencing organizational competitiveness, Michael Porter's framework can be utilized. Porter's model includes 188 variables grouped into 12 factors:

Performance indicators: General characteristics of a country's performance.

Macro environment: The investment climate, political and social stability of the economy.

Technology and innovation: The country's technological standing relative to other nations.

ICT: Connectivity aspects and the use of mobile devices.

Infrastructure: Quality and quantity of infrastructure, along with transportation availability.

Public institutions: Credibility and performance of public institutions.

Public powers: Levels of corruption and embezzlement.

Domestic competencies: Legal frameworks, including legalization and dispute resolution.

Cluster development: Aspects of partnership, specialized services, and installed capacity.

Business operations and strategy: Management and administrative tasks across the organization.

Environment: Environmental management and regulations.

International institutions: The role played by international organizations.

This model addresses competitiveness at a general or macro level. Among the factors contributing to competitiveness, the model includes both operational and strategic aspects related to the competencies and skills necessary for effective business management. Furthermore, the development of competitive advantage serves as the cornerstone of competitive strategy, referring to the ability to execute an action, while competitiveness reflects the capacity to leverage that ability and sustain a presence in the market. Thus, business competitiveness functions as an indicator of a company's ability to compete and remain in the market (Porter, 1991). From this perspective, Porter's "competitiveness diamond" framework consolidates the proposal for analyzing competitiveness.

The competitiveness diamond includes six factors: a) supply factors, which comprise the resources companies use to produce goods and services that are competitive in the market; b) demand factors, related to the elements that enable companies to understand preferences, tastes, segmentation variables, consumption structures, and trends, along with identifying their competitors; c) integration factors with related companies, aimed at enabling the company to analyze its strengths and weaknesses and articulate itself with other firms; d) factors associated with market opportunities, referring to the company's ability to interpret the context and identify favorable conditions that may provide benefits; e) institutional support, which refers to conditions that influence the industry's performance; and f) business strategy factors, which consist of information and environmental elements useful for structural and strategic decision-making within the company (Porter, 1991).

The functional strategies and competitiveness model proposes the use of perceptual analysis variables from the manager's perspective. These include productivity strategies, research strategies, technological strategies, marketing strategies, human resources strategies, organizational strategies, and financial strategies. This perceptual analysis is combined with objective measurements of indicators within each strategy, providing clear quantitative results on performance (Sharma & Fisher, 1997).

The world-class firm model identifies three key variables that define the gap a company must close to achieve world-class status. These variables are: a) market impacts, which involve anticipating customer needs, offering added value, establishing clear supplier requirements, and exceeding customer expectations; b) light operation, which refers to the company's ability to produce without errors, in a flexible and integrated manner, while minimizing waste; and c) balanced culture, which encompasses shared beliefs, common goals, teamwork, a well-trained workforce aligned with company objectives, empowerment, leadership, and a unified organizational vision (Smith, 1995).

In reviewing various competitiveness models, Jiménez-Ramírez proposed an integrated business competitiveness model that presents six key factors to consider:

Commercial management: Actions related to market knowledge, marketing, market participation, pricing policy, advertising, and e-commerce.

Financial management: Involves profitability, equity value, liquidity, financing sources, financial statements, and debt management.

Production management: Addresses installed capacity, cost structures, raw material acquisition, and inventory systems.

Science and technology: Includes research and development, the application of technology within processes, and patent development.

Internationalization: Focuses on identifying potential markets.

Managerial management: Considers the managerial skills and competencies required for effective business management.

According to this model, general management, which oversees administrative functions, and commercial management, specifically focusing on marketing as an integrating element, are key factors in the development of business competitiveness

Innovation and its contribution to competitiveness.

Innovation is a key driver of economic growth, enhancing productivity and job creation (Fagerberg et al., 2013), as well as contributing to competitiveness and sustainable development. It involves the implementation of new ideas, products, services, processes, or methods that significantly improve an organization's ability to achieve its objectives.

Innovation can be viewed as the capacity to assimilate and apply knowledge that translates into the development of a competitive advantage (Cohen & Levinthal, 1990). This capacity allows companies to differentiate themselves by adapting to technological changes and responding to evolving consumer demands (Tidd & Bessant, 2018). The innovation process includes incremental innovation, which helps maintain competitiveness in the short term and improves operational efficiency (Henderson & Clark, 1990). Incremental innovation focuses on continuous, gradual improvements to existing products, services, or processes, refining what already exists (Dosi, 1982).

Incremental innovation is complemented by radical innovation, which addresses unmet demand and creates new markets, often driven by the development of technologies that more efficiently satisfy that demand (Christensen, 1997). This type of innovation introduces significant changes that can transform entire industries and create new business opportunities (Leifer et al., 2000). By identifying unmet needs in emerging markets, radical innovation generates products that reshape market structures and can even displace leading firms from dominant market positions (Christensen et al., 2015). Disruptive innovation becomes a key strategy for entering new markets and consolidating a foothold in them (Gans, 2016).

As markets become more sophisticated and demanding, it is crucial to maintain high levels of innovation through the development of products and processes that are not only profitable but also environmentally and socially responsible (Hall & Vredenburg, 2012). This vision of sustainable innovation promotes the creation of new paradigms to address environmental challenges such as climate change and resource scarcity (Bocken et al., 2014). Sustainable innovation balances the creation of economic, social, and environmental value (Boons & Lüdeke-Freund, 2013), enabling the development of business models that support sustainable development and corporate social responsibility (Geissdoerfer et al., 2017).

The development of open innovation broadens the horizon for companies by utilizing both internal and external ideas and pathways to create innovative products and services that enable market expansion (Chesbrough, 2003). This shift from the traditional closed innovation model, which is constrained by organizational boundaries, promotes collaboration between organizations in pursuit of common goals (West & Bogers, 2014). Open innovation enhances internal capabilities and contributes to success and competitiveness by providing access to new market opportunities.

One of the key elements of competitiveness is the recognition that organizations face limited resources. This challenge has led to the rise of frugal innovation, through which products and services are developed to provide efficient, affordable, and sustainable solutions using minimal resources. This approach creates greater economic and social value by utilizing fewer resources (Radjou et al., 2012). Frugal innovation emphasizes functionality, accessibility, and sustainability, eliminating superfluous features and unnecessary costs. From a business perspective, this type of innovation enhances cost efficiency, which improves the organization's competitive indicators (Zeschky et al., 2014). It can be seen as a response to the economic and sustainable needs of both emerging markets and established economies, creating significant value for a broad range of consumers and contributing to global economic and social development (Bhatti & Ventresca, 2013).

Dynamic capabilities

Rooted in the Resource-Based View (RBV), which emphasizes the importance of valuable, rare, inimitable, and non-substitutable (VRIN) resources, the development of dynamic capabilities emerges as a set of skills, processes, routines, patterns, and knowledge that organizations develop and leverage to create, expand, and modify their resources and capabilities. These capabilities enable organizations to adapt effectively to changes in the business environment (Teece et al., 2016). This concept elucidates how firms can continuously renew their competencies to sustain competitive advantages in dynamic markets (Sharma & Sharma, 2020).

The study of dynamic capabilities demonstrates their connection to a firm's ability to detect and exploit opportunities and threats, maintaining competitiveness through the enhancement and reconfiguration of assets. The significant increase in academic interest in this topic since 2012 underscores the relevance of these capabilities in contemporary strategic management (Yudistira et al., 2022).

Dynamic capabilities theory offers an analytical framework for understanding the conceptual interrelationship between business model innovation and dynamic capabilities. It positions innovation as a strategic process grounded in a firm's higher-order capabilities (Najmaei, 2011). Dynamic capabilities enable firms to integrate, build, and reconfigure their internal and external competencies to cope with rapidly changing environments, thereby maintaining a sustainable competitive advantage (Teece et al., 2016; Eisenhardt & Martin, 2000). Consequently, a firm's ability to continuously innovate and adjust its business model becomes essential for long-term survival and success (Najmaei, 2011).

The crucial role of business intelligence and data analytics (BIDA) in enhancing dynamic capabilities is also noteworthy. BIDA facilitates knowledge discovery, supports decision-making, and predicts changes and risks, allowing firms to not only adapt to change but also capitalize on it, thereby improving their competitiveness in turbulent environments (Dabab & Weber, 2018).

The development of innovation and business competitiveness fosters a company's ability to adapt to changes, promoting flexibility and agility in responding to new challenges and opportunities. In this context, continuous innovation focuses on the creation of new products and processes that meet emerging market needs, maintaining competitive advantages and enabling the constant renewal of resources and capabilities to ensure long-term survival.

The development of dynamic capabilities is characterized by three key elements (Burinskienė & Daškevič, 2023): identification, which allows firms to detect opportunities and threats in the environment, positioning them as pioneers in new markets or technologies; mobilization, which involves utilizing resources to capitalize on identified opportunities, resulting in greater operational efficiency and innovation capacity, supported by agile decision-making processes for reconfiguring and implementing new strategies (Augier & Teece, 2009); and transformation, which arises as a logical consequence of the previous processes, enabling firms to adapt to environmental changes and strengthen their competitive position (Helfat et al., 2007).

The development of dynamic capabilities permeates various dimensions of an organization (Ali & Anwar, 2021), from the creation of competitive strategies and innovation culture to the emphasis on management ethics and innovative ideas. These dimensions significantly impact the development of a company's competitive advantage.

Changing Business Environments

Business environments are continuously evolving, and understanding these dynamics is crucial for companies to adapt and thrive. Two conceptual frameworks that have gained prominence in recent decades to describe these changes are VUCA and BANI.

The term VUCA, coined by the U.S. military in the 1990s, refers to a world characterized by Volatility, Uncertainty, Complexity, and Ambiguity. This framework has been widely used to describe the global business environment and the strategies needed to navigate it. VUCA was adopted in the business field as a response to market changes driven by increasing globalization and technological advancements in the late 20th and early 21st centuries (Lawrence, 2013). VUCA represents a global reality defined by the following characteristics:

Volatility. Refers to the rapid and unexpected changes in an environment marked by instability and unpredictability, where events evolve quickly and often without warning (Billions, 2019).

Uncertainty, Denotes the lack of predictability regarding future events (Bader et al., 2019), making planning and decision-making more challenging (Lawrence, 2013).

Complexity, Involves the presence of multiple interconnected variables, procedures, and networks, not always easily identifiable, that affect decision-making (Bennett & Lemoine, 2014; Rodriguez & Rodriguez, 2015).

Ambiguity, Describes the lack of clarity in interpreting events and data, leading to confusion when trying to discern threats or opportunities (Kaivo-oja & Lauraeus, 2018). This ambiguity complicates understanding and responding to environmental shifts (Lawrence, 2013).

The accelerated occurrence of disruptive events, often difficult to comprehend in a globalized world, impacts the robustness of systems and exacerbates the complexity that hinders the understanding of causal relationships and their prediction. This environment fosters subjective emotional responses, intensified by a chaotic and incomprehensible setting, which heightens the emotional dimension when faced with large-scale challenges. This perspective offers a more nuanced understanding of contemporary realities. A new context is emerging, one characterized by chaos. Political, environmental, societal, and technological changes amplify stress, leading to a paradigm shift that includes instability, chaotic situations, and incomprehensibility. This shift has given rise to BANI environments (Cascio, 2020).

BANI environments describe a world that is not only volatile, uncertain, complex, and ambiguous, but also brittle, anxious, non-linear, and incomprehensible. Each of these elements provides deeper insights into the modern business landscape:

Brittle refers to systems and structures that may appear solid but can quickly collapse under pressure. For example, an over-reliance on global supply chains, which can easily be disrupted by events such as pandemics or natural disasters.

Anxious, Reflects the anxiety and stress experienced by individuals and organizations as they navigate constant uncertainty and pressure. Employees and leaders alike must continuously adapt to rapid technological and market changes, which heightens stress levels.

Non-linear, describes situations where the effects and causes are not always directly aligned or proportional. Small actions can lead to significant consequences, and vice versa. For instance, negative news can go viral on social media, causing severe reputational damage to a person or company.

Incomprehensible, Highlights the difficulty of understanding and predicting events due to the overwhelming complexity and volume of available information. For example, predicting financial market movements becomes nearly impossible due to the interaction of countless global variables.

MAIN FOCUS OF THE CHAPTER

Methodology

This research is based on a qualitative, descriptive approach, aiming to describe the constructs and compare them with reality to offer an interpretation of specific phenomena from our own perspectives. The study adopts a qualitative approach of a descriptive nature, with the primary objective of providing an in-depth understanding of the constructs under analysis. The focus is on describing the analyzed phenomena and comparing them with real-world scenarios to offer contextualized interpretations (Cazau, 2006).

To conduct this research, the content analysis technique is used as the principal tool. This technique was selected for its suitability in formulating reproducible and validated inferences from the data collected (Krippendorff, 1990). The methodological process adheres to rigorous scientific standards, utilizing the triangulation and convergence procedure proposed by Guillermo Briones (1981). This methodology is chosen with the aim of collecting diverse information from various sources, ensuring both the internal and external credibility of the study.

The selection of sources and authors follows an exhaustive criterion, considering diverse perspectives and approaches. The study is structured using the Pozas scheme, combined with the approaches of Rafael Popper (2008), which outline several steps for the research process: reviewing formal sources and bibliographic information, defining relevant characteristics, systematizing the information, and analyzing the results. The variety of sources consulted enriches and validates the analysis (Cerda, 2002).

The choice of this methodological approach is justified by its capacity to meet the specific objectives of the research, offering a detailed understanding of the addressed phenomena and allowing for contextualized and nuanced interpretations.

RESULTS

Strategies to Improve Competitiveness and Innovation in BANI Environments

Development of Dynamic Capabilities:

Dynamic capabilities are essential for small and medium-sized enterprises (SMEs) to adapt, innovate, and maintain their competitiveness in a constantly evolving business environment. The development of competitiveness in SMEs must be accompanied by well-formulated strategies. In this regard, the following strategies are proposed

Detection Strategies, involve the development of robust environmental monitoring and data analysis systems that capture early signals of change. In this context, it is crucial to implement data analysis and technological surveillance tools to build market intelligence, enabling SMEs to predict market shifts and adjust their strategies accordingly (Lee et al., 2020). Furthermore, the development of innovation and participation networks allows SMEs to stay updated on the latest trends and technologies, fostering their ability to remain competitive in a dynamic environment (Albats et al., 2020).

Utilization Strategies focus on enabling quick decision-making and the implementation of effective strategies to capitalize on new opportunities. To achieve this, the adoption of flexible organizational structures is recommended, alongside fostering a culture of continuous innovation. Such structures allow SMEs to adapt more easily to market changes, thereby improving operational efficiency (O'Reilly & Tushman, 2020). This culture of innovation must be supported by the training and development of employees to enhance their capabilities and improve the organization's overall adaptability (Kump et al., 2019).

Transformation strategies contribute to long-term sustainability by enabling companies to remain competitive through continuous adaptation. These strategies involve the implementation of advanced technologies to optimize business processes, enhancing the company's capacity to reconfigure its operations in response to market changes. This includes the adoption of automation tools and integrated management systems (Schilke, 2014). Additionally, restructuring teams and processes to better align with evolving market demands allows organizations to maintain a significant competitive advantage (Eisenhardt & Martin, 2000).

Fostering a Culture of Innovation

Promoting an environment that values experimentation, creative thinking, and calculated risk-taking is essential for fostering innovation. This can be achieved through the establishment of ongoing training programs for employees in innovation and change management methodologies.

Balancing incremental innovations with radical innovations, while integrating social responsibility and sustainability, can enhance operational efficiency and create new business opportunities (Henderson & Clark, 1990; Christensen, 1997). This approach not only fosters innovation but also improves competitiveness in increasingly demanding markets (Bocken et al., 2014).

Collaboration and External Networks

Collaboration and the exchange of ideas foster the development of new knowledge and resources, supporting open innovation (Chesbrough, 2003). Open innovation leverages external ideas and resources to provide efficient and sustainable solutions, aligning with the principles of frugal innovation, which focuses on using minimal resources to achieve maximum impact (Radjou et al., 2012). The adoption of agile methodologies to manage innovation projects further enhances competitive capacity by allowing for faster and more flexible responses to market changes (Pavlou & El Sawy, 2011).

In the realms of competitiveness and innovation, it is crucial to promote strategic alliances with other companies, academic institutions, and research centers to drive the development of new products and technologies.

Stress Management and Organizational Well-being

Resilience emerges from the development of dynamic capabilities, enabling organizations to more effectively navigate BANI environments, and improving their ability to respond to market disruptions and changes (Cascio, 2020). To achieve this, it is essential to implement organizational stress management and foster a culture of continuous innovation that helps overcome anxiety and uncertainty in BANI environments (Eggers, 2020).

This effect is facilitated through the implementation of well-being policies that address mental health and stress management, mitigating anxiety in BANI environments. These policies contribute to the development of a positive work environment that promotes resilience and adaptability among employees.

To enhance competitiveness and innovation in BANI environments, SMEs must focus on developing dynamic capabilities, fostering a culture of innovation, establishing strategic collaborations, and utilizing adaptive tools and methodologies

From theory to practice

To illustrate how dynamic capabilities and the associated strategies can be applied in practice, let us examine the case of a small Colombian business specializing in stuffed potatoes and empanadas. This SME successfully adapted to the challenges imposed by the COVID-19 pandemic, demonstrating how the rapid implementation of digitalization and innovative strategies enabled it to survive and thrive in a volatile environment

When examining how a company develops its dynamic capabilities, the case of a stuffed potatoes and empanadas SME in Colombia offers valuable insights. Before the pandemic, this SME operated under a traditional model, relying on physical stores to sell food. Their product offering consisted of stuffed potatoes and empanadas, accompanied by beverages such as soft drinks, juices, and coffee. The business was well-known among its local customers for the flavor of its products, and people enjoyed a dedicated physical space where they could savor the food.

With the onset of the pandemic, the SME faced a significant challenge as social distancing measures and the closure of commercial premises severely restricted face-to-face interaction with customers. The company faced a dilemma: how could it survive in an environment where physical customer interaction was not possible? This situation compelled the business to seek strategies that would enable it to adapt to the new reality.

One of the first steps was the adoption of digital technologies to maintain customer contact. The company implemented an ordering system via WhatsApp, a widely accessible and popular platform in Colombia. This allowed them to efficiently manage orders directly with consumers, enabling customers to order their products from home during a time when store access was limited. This action represented an accelerated digitalization strategy.

As a second measure, the company adapted its production capacity to accommodate the orders received through digital channels. They integrated digital payments and the use of virtual wallets, which allowed transactions to be securely processed from mobile devices, eliminating the need for handling cash. This move exemplified a resource configuration strategy.

The third measure focused on completing the customer service cycle. The company organized a delivery system with strict health protocols, ensuring that consumers felt confident their products were delivered safely. The home delivery system enabled the business to continue operating without the need for physical space, maintaining its sales volume. This step represented the establishment of a delivery strategy.

The rapid implementation of these strategies, leveraging the dynamic capabilities of the SME, allowed the business to maintain a steady income flow during the pandemic, even as many similar businesses were forced to close their doors.

Through digitalization and home delivery, the company not only survived but also expanded its reach by attracting new customers who appreciated the convenience of the service.

Now let's analyze how this SME developed its dynamic capabilities by applying the strategies described in the previous section.

Detection Strategies. in this case, the ability to detect opportunities allowed the SME to navigate the restrictions imposed by the pandemic. While they did not implement a high-tech monitoring system with advanced data analysis, the use of WhatsApp as a direct communication platform with customers was a practical and effective strategy for real-time demand monitoring. Although this system is basic, it provided a robust way to monitor their environment, allowing them to identify early signals of changes in consumer habits and preferences, and adjust their production accordingly.

Leverage Strategies. The SME demonstrated a strong ability to capitalize on opportunities, reflected in the rapid implementation of a digital ordering system and a delivery service. This quick decision-making enabled them to meet the needs of consumers who sought home-delivered food during the pandemic. This reflects the company's organizational flexibility and its adoption of virtual wallets and digital payments, showcasing an agile organizational structure and a culture of innovation. This aligns with the idea that companies with flexible structures are better able to adapt (O'Reilly & Tushman, 2020).

Transformation Strategies. The adoption of new technologies, such as WhatsApp for orders and digital payments, along with the reconfiguration of the business model to focus on home delivery, exemplifies the transformation strategy. The SME successfully restructured its operations and adapted to new market demands, ensuring quality and service. This transformation, though relatively simple, improved the SME's long-term competitiveness. By integrating these digital solutions, the company maintained its competitive advantage in a BANI environment (Schilke, 2014; Eisenhardt & Martin, 2000).

Fostering a Culture of Innovation While the SME may not have a formal innovation training program, it demonstrates a practical culture of innovation by experimenting with new operational methods, such as digital ordering and delivery. This ability to foster incremental innovation, combining digital solutions with traditional operations, improved their operational efficiency. The company effectively balanced maintaining its core operations while adopting radical innovations to reach and serve customers, enhancing its competitiveness by integrating both radical and incremental innovations (Henderson & Clark, 1990).

Collaboration and External Networks. The adoption of delivery protocols can be seen as a form of external collaboration, requiring cooperation with external entities to complete the customer service cycle. This use of external resources to achieve sustainable results with minimal internal resources aligns with the concept of open innovation (Chesbrough, 2003; Radjou et al., 2012).

Stress Management and Organizational Wellbeing. In response to the pandemic, the SME demonstrated strong organizational resilience by quickly adapting its business model, which helped mitigate the negative effects of change and maintain employee motivation. The internal reorganization reflects effective management of organizational stress in BANI environments (Cascio, 2020; Eggers, 2020).

This case illustrates how a small company can leverage dynamic capabilities to rapidly adapt to unforeseen and severe changes in its environment. The digitalization and reconfiguration of resources were key to its success. Today, the SME has not only overcome the challenges of the pandemic but has also adopted a more resilient business model, positioning itself to be more flexible in the face of future crises.

The case of the Colombian SME highlights how dynamic capabilities and well-executed strategies can allow small businesses to respond effectively to sudden disruptions. Drawing from this example, the following conclusions summarize the key takeaways regarding the role of dynamic capabilities in driving innovation and competitiveness in SMEs.

SOLUTIONS AND RECOMMENDATIONS

Challenges in the Implementation of Dynamic Capabilities in SMEs

The implementation of dynamic capabilities in small and medium-sized enterprises (SMEs) presents significant challenges due to the intrinsic characteristics of these organizations, such as limited resources, more rigid organizational structures, and the fast-paced, volatile markets in which they operate. Several critical factors hinder the adoption of dynamic capabilities, which are essential for competitiveness and innovation in business environments such as VUCA and BANI.

One major challenge is resistance to organizational change. In many SMEs, the organizational culture is deeply rooted in traditional processes, making it difficult to adopt more agile and flexible strategies. A more open and agile mindset is required to facilitate change (Pappas et al., 2021). This resistance is particularly pronounced in uncertain environments, where employees and leaders may be reluctant to abandon established methods that, while inefficient, are perceived as safe. The transformation towards dynamic capabilities requires a significant cultural shift, where innovation and continuous adaptation become central (Pavlou & El Sawy, 2011; Kump et al., 2019).

Lack of resources also limits SMEs' ability to implement rapid strategic changes, placing them at a competitive disadvantage compared to larger companies that have greater capacity to invest in innovation and adaptability (Vătămănescu et al., 2020). To address this, SMEs can leverage strategic alliances with other companies, fostering collaboration through networks to share resources and knowledge, facilitating the development of dynamic capabilities without incurring excessive costs (Dabić et al., 2020).

Another significant barrier is the lack of personnel with technological skills required to adopt and apply emerging technologies (Khin & Ho, 2019). There is a need for upskilling in fields such as big data analysis and artificial intelligence, which are essential for remaining competitive (Teece, 2019).

The complexity of decision-making is another challenge, especially when SMEs lack the necessary systems to interpret and utilize data in a timely manner (Eggers, 2020). This deficiency places actions related to detection and utilization at a disadvantage, thereby affecting effective decision-making, particularly in times of uncertainty (Pavlou & El Sawy, 2011).

The integration of emerging technologies also poses challenges for SMEs due to insufficient technological infrastructure, limiting their ability to adapt to an increasingly digitalized business environment (Khin & Ho, 2019). This shortfall affects the reconfiguration of processes and impairs long-term competitiveness (Radicic & Petković, 2023).

A key question that arises when defining strategies for enhancing competitiveness is how an SME can successfully develop each of these strategies. It is important to recognize that every organization is made up of people, and the development of dynamic capabilities in BANI environments is no exception. Therefore, a two-dimensional approach is necessary: viewing the SME as an independent entity, while also recognizing it as a convergence of individual talents contributed by its members. These individuals must develop essential skills to navigate BANI scenarios (Barrera-Ortegon et al., 2024), including competencies in digitalization and environmental risk management. SMEs must invest in market intelligence and technological surveillance to anticipate and adapt to emerging trends.

FUTURE RESEARCH DIRECTIONS

While the current analysis provides valuable insights into the importance of dynamic capabilities for SMEs, there remain several areas that warrant further exploration. The following lines of research are suggested to deepen our understanding of how SMEs can continue to evolve in BANI environments and capitalize on emerging technologies to enhance their adaptability and resilience

The development of dynamic capabilities to promote competitiveness requires balancing economic growth with environmental and social responsibility. Future research should explore business models that place integral sustainability at their core, ensuring that SMEs can achieve long-term success while addressing ecological and societal challenges.

Another promising research direction focuses on the impact of emerging technologies, such as artificial intelligence, the Internet of Things, and automation, in the development of dynamic capabilities. Investigating how the implementation of these technologies contributes to the operational and innovation efficiency of SMEs will provide valuable insights into their role in fostering competitiveness.

Additionally, further research is needed to develop efficient collaboration models for SMEs. Such models should identify key aspects and insights of strategic alliances, establishing the critical success factors necessary for their successful implementation.

Finally, the identification of theoretical frameworks, practices, and tools that enable SMEs to navigate BANI environments more effectively represents a critical area for future study. Understanding how SMEs can better cope with volatility, uncertainty, complexity, and ambiguity will provide essential strategies for maintaining competitiveness in increasingly dynamic markets.

CONCLUSION

The importance of dynamic capabilities for innovation and competitiveness in a BANI environment for SMEs is a crucial factor in enabling rapid adaptation to market changes. By fostering a culture of innovation and collaboration, SMEs can remain competitive and agile.

The evolving nature of environments such as BANI highlights the need to implement flexible and adaptive strategies that allow companies to not only survive but also thrive. This can be achieved through the development of proactive and resilient management practices.

Sustainable economic development must be regarded as a fundamental pillar for strengthening competitiveness. A model of collaboration and technological implementation that aligns with the complexities of a more dynamic world is essential.

The analysis of dynamic capabilities for innovation and competitiveness in SMEs shows a comprehensive alignment with the management components necessary to face the BANI scenario (Barrera-Ortegon et al., 2024). The proposed strategies, development of specific capabilities, promotion of a culture of innovation and resilience, and the implementation of flexible and efficient practices are key elements that enhance organizational adaptability, antifragility, and responsiveness to disruptive events in changing environments such as BANI.

The implementation of market intelligence and technological surveillance, combined with a culture of organizational well-being that emphasizes effective stress management, enables organizations to withstand disruptive impacts. This approach fosters continuous learning and proactive strategic planning, optimizing both operational efficiency and employee well-being. In this way, organizations are better equipped to anticipate and adapt to emerging trends, thereby consolidating their competitive position.

REFERENCES

Albats, E., et al. (2020). Networks for Innovation: Accelerating Innovation through Networked Relationships.

Ali, B. J., & Anwar, G. (2021). Business strategy: The influence of Strategic Competitiveness on competitive advantage. International Journal of Electrical. *Electronics and Computers*, 6(2), 1–9.

Audretsch, D. B., & Keilbach, M. (2004). Entrepreneurship and Regional Growth: An Evolutionary Interpretation. *Journal of Evolutionary Economics*, 14(5), 605–616. DOI: 10.1007/s00191-004-0228-6

Augier, M., & Teece, D. J. (2009). Dynamic capabilities and the role of managers in business strategy and economic performance. *Organization Science*, 20(2), 410–421. DOI: 10.1287/orsc.1090.0424

Ayyagari, M., Demirguc-Kunt, A., & Maksimovic, V. (2021). "Small vs. Young Firms across the World: Contribution to Employment, Job Creation, and Growth." Policy Research Working Paper, World Bank.

Bajo, O. (1991). *Theories of international trade*. Antoni Bosh.

Barney, J. (1991). Firm resources and sustained competitive advantage. *Journal of Management*, 17(1), 99–120. DOI: 10.1177/014920639101700108

Barrera-Ortegon, A., Medina-Ricaurte, G. F., & Jimenez-Hernandez, P. R. (2024). Organizational Elements to Confront Turbulent and Fragile VUCA to BANI Scenarios. In *Organizational Management Sustainability in VUCA Contexts* (pp. 20–43). IGI Global. DOI: 10.4018/979-8-3693-0720-5.ch002

Beck, T., Demirguc-Kunt, A., & Levine, R. (2005). SMEs, Growth, and Poverty: Cross-Country Evidence. *Journal of Economic Growth*, 10(3), 199–229. DOI: 10.1007/s10887-005-3533-5

Bhatti, Y., & Ventresca, M. (2013). How Can 'Frugal Innovation' Be Conceptualized? SSRN Electronic Journal.

Billiones, R. (2019). Thriving (and not just surviving) in a VUCA healthcare industry. *Medical Writing*, 28(1), 67–69.

Bocken, N. M. P., Short, S. W., Rana, P., & Evans, S. (2014). A literature and practice review to develop sustainable business model archetypes. *Journal of Cleaner Production*, 65, 42–56. DOI: 10.1016/j.jclepro.2013.11.039

Bonilla, M., & Martínez, M. (2009). *Analysis of the methodology for evaluating competitiveness: the case of the World Economic Forum and the Colombian business reality*. Bogotá, Colombia: Universidad del Rosario.

Boons, F., & Lüdeke-Freund, F. (2013). Business models for sustainable innovation: State-of-the-art and steps towards a research agenda. *Journal of Cleaner Production*, 45, 9–19. DOI: 10.1016/j.jclepro.2012.07.007

Briones, G. (1981). *Methods and Techniques of Research for the Social Sciences. The Formulation of Social Research Problems*. Uniandes.

Buckley, P. J., Pass, C. L., & Prescott, K. (1991). Measures of International Competitiveness: A Critical Survey. *Journal of Marketing Management*, 4(2), 175–200. DOI: 10.1080/0267257X.1988.9964068

Burinskienė, A., & Daškevič, D. (2023). CONTEMPORARY CONCEPT OF BUSINESS COMPETITIVENESS. *Management/Vadyba (16487974), 39* (1).

Cascio, 2020 Facing the Age of Chaos https://medium.com/@cascio/facing-the-age-of-chaos-b00687b1f51d

Cazau, P. (2006). Introducción a la investigación en ciencias sociales.

Cerda Hugo. (2002). The Elements of Research. Editorial el Buho Ltda. Bogotá. 3rd reprint.

Chesbrough, H. W. (2003). *Open Innovation: The new imperative for creating and profiting from technology.* Harvard Business School Press.

Christensen, C. M. (1997). *The Innovator's Dilemma: When New Technologies Cause Great Firms to Fail.* Harvard Business Review Press.

Christensen, C. M., Raynor, M. E., & McDonald, R. (2015). What is disruptive innovation? *Harvard Business Review*, 93(12), 44–53. PMID: 17183796

Cohen, W. M., & Levinthal, D. A. (1990). Absorptive capacity: A new perspective on learning and innovation. *Administrative Science Quarterly*, 35(1), 128–152. DOI: 10.2307/2393553

Dabab, M., & Weber, C. (2018). Business Intelligence and Data Analytics as a Driver of Dynamic Capability Strategic Approach. *Portland International Conference on Management of Engineering and Technology (PICMET)*, 1-9. DOI: 10.23919/PICMET.2018.8481750

Dabić, M., Maley, J., Dana, L. P., Novak, I., Pellegrini, M. M., & Caputo, A. (2020). Pathways of SME internationalization: A bibliometric and systematic review. *Small Business Economics*, 55(3), 705–725. DOI: 10.1007/s11187-019-00181-6

Dosi, G. (1982). Technological paradigms and technological trajectories: A suggested interpretation of the determinants and directions of technical change. *Research Policy*, 11(3), 147–162. DOI: 10.1016/0048-7333(82)90016-6

Eggers, F. (2020). Masters of Disasters? Challenges and Opportunities for SMEs in Times of Crisis. *Journal of Business Research*, 116, 199–208. DOI: 10.1016/j.jbusres.2020.05.025 PMID: 32501306

Eisenhardt, K. M., & Martin, J. A. (2000). Dynamic capabilities: What are they? *Strategic Management Journal*, 21(10-11), 1105–1121. DOI: 10.1002/1097-0266(200010/11)21:10/11<1105::AID-SMJ133>3.0.CO;2-E

Fagerberg, J. (1996). Technology and Competitiveness. *Oxford Review of Economic Policy*, 12(3), 39–51. DOI: 10.1093/oxrep/12.3.39

Fagerberg, J., Mowery, D. C., & Nelson, R. R. (2013). *The Oxford Handbook of Innovation.* Oxford University Press.

Ferraz, J. C., Kupfer, D., & Iootty, M. (2004). Industrial competitiveness in Brazil. 10 years after liberalization. *CEPAL Review*, 82(82), 91–119. DOI: 10.18356/a99f5747-en

Forcadell, F. (2004). *Business growth from a resource-based approach. Towards an integrative model.* Rey Juan Carlos University.

Gans, J. (2016). *The Disruption Dilemma.* MIT Press. DOI: 10.7551/mitpress/9780262034487.001.0001

Geissdoerfer, M., Savaget, P., & Evans, S. (2017). The Cambridge business model innovation process. *Journal of Cleaner Production*, 142, 1550–1567.

Gutiérrez, R., Martínez, C., Sfeir-Younis, A., Fairbanks, M., Lindsay, S., Holden, P., & Brugger, E. (1998). Challenges for the new millennium in Latin America. Sustainable development, competitiveness and second-generation reforms. Bogotá, Colombia.

Hall, J. K., & Vredenburg, H. (2012). The challenge of innovating for sustainable development. *MIT Sloan Management Review*, 45(1), 61–68.

Helfat, C. E., Finkelstein, S., Mitchell, W., Peteraf, M. A., Singh, H., Teece, D. J., & Winter, S. G. (2007). *Dynamic Capabilities: Understanding Strategic Change in Organizations.* Blackwell Publishing.

Henderson, R. M., & Clark, K. B. (1990). Architectural innovation: The reconfiguration of existing product technologies and the failure of established firms. *Administrative Science Quarterly*, 35(1), 9–30. DOI: 10.2307/2393549

Hill, M., Ireland, R., & Hoskisson, R. (2004). *Global Economy. Strategic Management, Competitiveness and Concepts of Globalization.* Thomson.

IFAC (2020). The Foundation for Economies Worldwide Is Small Business. IFAC Report.

Jimenez-Ramírez, M. H. (2006). Modelo de competitividad empresarial. *Umbral científico*, (9), 115-125.

Kaivo-oja, JRL and Lauraeus, IT (2018), " *The VUCA approach as a solution concept to corporate foresight challenges and global technological disruption* ", foresight, Vol. 20 No. 1, pp. 27 - 49 .

Khin, S., & Ho, T. C. (2019). Digital technology, digital capability and organizational performance: A mediating role of digital innovation. *International Journal of Innovation Science*, 11(2), 177–195. DOI: 10.1108/IJIS-08-2018-0083

Kotler, P., & Keller, K. (2012). *Marketing Management.* Addison-Wesley.

Krippendorff, K. (1990). *Content analysis methodology: theory and practice.* Editorial Paidos.

Krugman, P., & Obstfeld, M. (2000). *International Economics: Theory and Policy.* Addison-Wesley.

Kump, B., Engelmann, A., Kessler, A., & Schweiger, C. (2019). Toward a dynamic capabilities scale: Organizational measuring sensing, seizing, and transforming capacities. *Industrial and Corporate Change*, 28(5), 1149–1172.

Lawrence, K. (2013). *Developing leaders in a VUCA environment.* UNC Executive Development.

Lee, N., Sameen, H., & Cowling, M. (2020). Access to Finance for Innovative SMEs since the Financial Crisis. *Research Policy*, 49(2), 103900.

Leifer, R., McDermott, C. M., O'Connor, G. C., Peters, L. S., Rice, M., & Veryzer, R. W. (2000). *Radical Innovation: How Mature Companies Can Outsmart Upstarts*. Harvard Business Review Press.

Lombana, J., & Rozas Gutiérrez, S. (2009). *Analytical framework of competitiveness: Foundations for the study of regional competitiveness. Thought & management, (26), 1-38*. Porter.

Mahmood, A., & Ezeala-Harrison, F. (2000). *Comparative versus competitive advantage, and competitiveness in developing countries. Socioeconomic Development in the 21st Century*. International Institute for Development Studies.

Malavé, J. (1996). Competitiveness: Current state of the debate. *IBM Debates*, 3, 38.

Mateus and Brasset (2002). Globalization: its effects and benefits. *Economy and Development, 1* (1).

Montenegro-Velandia and Alvarez-Rodriguez. (2011). Approach to the concept of organizational competitiveness. *National Research Journal, 9* (16).

Musik and Romo. (2005). On the concept of competitiveness. *Foreign Trade, 55* (3).

Najmaei, A. (2011). Dynamic Business Model Innovation: An Analytical Archetype. *3rd International Conference on Information and Financial Engineering*, 12, 165-171. IACSIT Press, Singapore.

Nelson, R. (1992). Recent Writings on Competitiveness: Boxing the Compass. *California Management Review*, 34(2), 127–137. DOI: 10.2307/41166697

O'Reilly, C. A., & Tushman, M. L. (2020). *Lead and Disrupt: How to Solve the Innovator's Dilemma*. Stanford University Press.

OECD (2021). SME and Entrepreneurship Outlook 2021. OECD Report.

Pappas, N., Caputo, A., Pellegrini, M. M., Marzi, G., & Michopoulou, E. (2021). The complexity of decision-making processes and IoT adoption in accommodation SMEs. *Journal of Business Research*, 131, 573–583. DOI: 10.1016/j.jbusres.2021.01.010

Pavlou, P. A., & El Sawy, O. A. (2011). Understanding the Black Box of Dynamic Capabilities: A Dynamic Process Model of Sensing, Seizing, and Transforming. *Academy of Management Review*, 35(1), 60–79.

Popper, R. (2008). How are foresight methods selected? *foresight, 10*(6), 62-89.

Porter, M. (1991). *The competitive advantage of nations*. Ed. Vergara.

Porter, M. (2000). *Being competitive. New contributions and conclusions*. CECSA.

Radicic, D., & Petković, S. (2023). Impact of digitalization on technological innovations in small and medium-sized enterprises (SMEs). *Technological Forecasting and Social Change*, 191, 122474. DOI: 10.1016/j.techfore.2023.122474

Radjou, N., Prabhu, J., & Ahuja, S. (2012). *Jugaad Innovation: Think Frugal, Be Flexible, Generate Breakthrough Growth*. Jossey-Bass.

Ricardo, D., & Reeder, J. (1817). *Principles of Political Economy and Taxation*. Pyramid Editions.

Rodriguez, A. and Rodriguez, Y. (2015), " *Metaphors for today's leadership: VUCA world, millennial, and cloud leaders* ", Journal of Management Development, Vol. 34 No. 7, pp . 854 - 866.

Sanford, L. & Moskowitz. (2015). The Small and Medium-Sized Enterprise (SME). DOI: 10.1016/ B978-0-12-800353-4.00004-X

Schilke, O. (2014). On the contingent value of dynamic capabilities for competitive advantage: The non-linear moderating effect of environmental dynamism. *Strategic Management Journal*, 35(2), 179–203. DOI: 10.1002/smj.2099

Schwab, K. (2018). The Global Competitiveness Report 2018. World Economic Forum.

Scott, B. R., & Lodge, G. C. (1985). US Competitiveness in the World Economy. *Harvard Business Review*.

Sharma, B., & Fisher, T.Sharma and Fisher. (1997). Functional strategies and competitiveness: An empirical analysis using data from Australian manufacturing. *Benchmarking for Quality Management & Technology*, 4(4), 286–294. DOI: 10.1108/14635779710195122

Sharma, S., & Sharma, S. K. (2020). Probing the links between team resilience, competitive advantage, and organizational effectiveness: Evidence from information technology industry. *Business Perspectives and Research*, 8(2), 289–307. DOI: 10.1177/2278533719887458

Smith, A. (1776) . *The Wealth of Nations: Books I-II-III and selection of Books IV and V*. Alianza editorial.

Smith, S. (1995). Elaborate World Class Competitiveness. *Managing Service Quality*, 5(5), 36–42. DOI: 10.1108/09604529510100387

Teece, D., Peteraf, M., & Leih, S. (2016). Dynamic capabilities and organizational agility: Risk, uncertainty, and strategy in the innovation economy. *California Management Review*, 58(4), 13–35. DOI: 10.1525/cmr.2016.58.4.13

Teece, D. J. (2018). Business models and dynamic capabilities. *Long Range Planning*, 51(1), 40–49. DOI: 10.1016/j.lrp.2017.06.007

Teece, DJ (2019). A capability theory of the firm: an economics and (strategic)

Tidd, J., & Bessant, J. (2018). *Managing Innovation: Integrating Technological, Market and Organizational Change*. Wiley.

Vătămănescu, E. M., Cegarra-Navarro, J. G., Andrei, A. G., Dincă, V. M., & Alexandru, V. A. (2020). SMEs Strategic Networks and Innovative Performance: A Relational Design and Methodology for Knowledge Sharing. *Journal of Knowledge Management*, 24(6), 1291–1316. DOI: 10.1108/JKM-01-2020-0010

West, J., & Bogers, M. (2014). Leveraging external sources of innovation: A review of research on open innovation. *Journal of Product Innovation Management*, 31(4), 814–831. DOI: 10.1111/jpim.12125

World Bank (2020). Micro, Small and Medium Enterprises Economic Indicators. World Bank Report .

Yudistira, Y., Arkeman, Y., Andati, T., & Jahroh, S. (2022). A bibliometric review on dynamic capability. *Indonesian Journal of Business and Entrepreneurship*, 8(1), 158–167. DOI: 10.17358/ijbe.8.1.158

Zeschky, M., Widenmayer, B., & Gassmann, O. (2014). Frugal innovation in emerging markets. *Research Technology Management*, 57(4), 38–45. DOI: 10.5437/08956308X5404007

KEY TERMS AND DEFINITIONS

Organizational Adaptability: The ability of an organization to adjust its strategies, structures and processes in response to changes in the environment.

Strategic Alliances: Collaboration agreements between two or more organizations to achieve common objectives and share key resources and knowledge.

Industrial Clusters: Concentrations of interrelated companies, suppliers and other institutions that collaborate to increase competitiveness and innovation in a specific industry.

Competitiveness: A company's ability to offer products and services that surpass those of its competitors in terms of quality, price and added value.

Open Communication: Practice of encouraging the free and transparent exchange of information within an organization, promoting collaboration and trust.

Creativity: Ability to generate original and valuable ideas that can be transformed into practical and innovative solutions.

Knowledge Management: The process of effectively discovering, distributing, and using knowledge within an organization to improve decision making and innovation.

Frugal Innovation: Strategy to create efficient and sustainable solutions using minimal resources, for emerging needs.

Market Intelligence: Systematic collection and analysis of market information, including trends, competitors and consumer preferences, for decision making.

Technological Surveillance: Continuous monitoring of new technologies and developments in the scientific and technical field to identify opportunities and threats for the organization

Chapter 6
Financial Behaviors and Money Beliefs in Educational Sector:
Case in the Business and Military Academic Context

Albert Dario Arias Ardila
Escuela Militar de Cadetes José María Córdova, Colombia

Adolfo Hernando Hernandez Hernandez
https://orcid.org/0000-0002-1367-6021
Escuela Militar de Cadetes José María Córdova, Colombia

Irma Neli Gutierrez Almendarez
https://orcid.org/0009-0005-6605-2502
Universidad Abierta y a Distancia de México, Mexico

ABSTRACT

This research mainly aims to identify the financial behaviors and money beliefs in a business and military context. These analyses may lead to a partial reduction in the stress experienced by these households, thereby facilitating their focus on military activities and preparing them as entrepreneurs in the civil context. A survey was conducted to gather data about students' preferences and beliefs about money, using Klontz Money Script Inventory. The main findings explained students' attitudes on money that help to accomplish the personal financial goals, that are important to the SME´s success.

INTRODUCTION

According to authors such as Carlson et al. (2016) and Luther et al.(1998), there is a limited number of research studies associated with financial topics related to military and business households. These analyses may lead to a partial reduction in the stress experienced by these households, thereby facilitating their focus on military activities and prepare them as entrepreneurs in the civil context. According to Appiah & Agblewornu (2024), there is strong positive association between financial literacy and SMEs' financial performance showing that financial literacy is a crucial requirement for SMEs' success,

DOI: 10.4018/979-8-3693-4046-2.ch006

however when people have a wide or strong access to credit the association becames statistically weak. A situation that is very common among military personnel due to the stability provided by the origin of their monetary resources. Moreover, it can positively impact their well-being and management skills by enhancing financial knowledge. This process is intertwined with these individuals' perception of money management, and consequently, with factors associated with beliefs regarding money, which can be understood through studies aimed at comprehending beliefs about money (B. Klontz et al., 2011). The existence of financial education among university students has been positively associated with higher scores in each of the composite indices of short-term financial behaviors (Henager, 2017). In the case of business and military university students, it is gnoteworthy that they graduate with significant loan debts, often struggling to manage finances and comprehend the lifelong effects of student loan repayments (Loux, 2021) in other words the can be called financial homo ignorans because the individual avoid and dismissed information to maintain a favorable self-image and defend identity-based beliefs (Barrafrem et al., 2024).

At first glance, there is still a gap in field research on financial education and beliefs within the Colombian context, which could further develop and expand on crucial aspects compared to available literature on the subject. Similarly, there is a lack of research direction aimed at enhancing these skills to serve as a foundation for improving money management and financial commitments faced by recent graduates entering military service (Loux, 2021). It is important to clarify that financial behavior and management remain the primary challenge for Micro, Small, and Medium Enterprises (MSMEs), especially among their owners, indicating insufficient knowledge of financial management. Additionally, decisions are often made based on emotions (Agustina & Nurulistanti, 2022). Furthermore, based on other studies, three key aspects can be defined: financial knowledge (education, experience, perception, and opinion; knowledge of products and services; socialization agents), financial attitude (attitude towards money, expenditure, income level), and financial awareness (savings and investment, retirement planning), all crucial for assessing SME strategy to determine its sustainability (Damayanti et al., 2018). The study revealed that the majority of entrepreneurs lack adequate financial knowledge. It found that financial skills, financial knowledge, financial attitude, past experiences, support and guidance, and financial socialization directly influenced levels of financial literacy among entrepreneurs (Polisetty et al., 2021). The results indicated a positive relationship between financial self-efficacy, financial socialization agents, attitude toward money, mindfulness, and financial literacy (Riaz et al., 2022).

Higher levels of student knowledge correlate with improved financial behavior. They trust their ability to make sound financial investments, expecting these investments to generate significant income in the future, thereby shaping their financial behavior. Perceived financial confidence and attitude toward money influence financial behavior. The attitude toward money has successfully mediated the influence of financial education and perceived financial confidence on student financial behavior (Susilowati & Latifah, 2017). Three main types of money attitudes were identified: prestige and power, money management, and goal-oriented attitudes (Henchoz et al., 2019). Measures to foster general solidarity in society and expand financial education programs among entrepreneurs are expected to significantly improve the environment for law implementation (Tanyushcheva & Kunitsyna, 2021).

Financial knowledge and the presence of financial education among military officers have been positively associated with higher scores in each of the composite indices of short-term financial behaviors according to empirical studies conducted on military households (Henager, 2017). Previous studies on the development of applications or technological tools have found that such developments lead to intentions to save more, spend less, and earn more income, thereby significantly improving financial behavior and savings (Amagir et al., 2022). It is important to note that well-being in military organization contexts, where work is carried out according to permanent general operating procedures and routine orders, shows that interpersonal relationships are one of the most important components of workplace well-being and performance (Smaliukiene & Bekesiene, 2020). Thus, analyzing characteristics, perseverance, and financial behavior can promote practices in the future to improve well-being.

Well-being in the Colombian context is crucial for the development and improvement of services and quality of life. According to the CONPES document, the Colombian market presents an insufficient number of financial products and services, limited access to financing, high informality in credit, and a limited legal framework for alternative financial services, along with limited skills for efficient economic and financial decision-making (Departamento Nacional de Planeación [DNP], 2020).

Therefore, analyzing financial determination and education in the military field becomes crucial as military families experience "unique" difficulties, including low salaries for low-ranking members, increased deployment-related costs such as childcare and communication expenses, frequent relocations, easy access to quick loans, spouses who are often uninformed about financial matters, disruption of military spouses' employment due to military personnel deployments, and offers from low-reputation vendors near military bases (Varcoe et al., 2002).

BACKGROUND

Financial behaviors refer to the actions and decisions individuals make regarding the management of their money, including saving, investing, spending, and budgeting. These behaviors are often studied in the context of financial literacy, which encompasses the knowledge and skills needed to make informed and effective financial decisions (Lusardi & Mitchell, 2017). Money beliefs, on the other hand, are the underlying attitudes and perceptions individuals hold about money, which can significantly influence their financial behaviors. These beliefs are shaped by various factors, including cultural, social, psychological, and economic influences (Lim et al., 2014). The theoretical framework often employed in studying these concepts includes behavioral finance theories, which integrate psychological insights with traditional economic theories to explain deviations from rational financial behavior (Thaler, 2016).

Financial behaviors and money beliefs are integral components of personal finance management, influencing individuals' financial decisions, savings, spending habits, and overall financial well-being. Understanding these aspects is crucial for developing effective financial education programs and interventions aimed at promoting better financial practices among various demographics. This research background delves into the recent literature on financial behaviors and money beliefs, examining their definitions, influencing factors, and implications for financial literacy and well-being (Fernandes et al., 2014).

The study of financial behaviors and money beliefs has advanced significantly over the past decade, driven by interdisciplinary research and technological innovations. Psychological factors, cultural and social influences, technological advancements, and policy interventions all play crucial roles in shaping financial behaviors. The integration of behavioral economics insights has enriched our understanding of these behaviors, while fintech innovations have transformed personal financial management and promoted financial inclusion.

Psychological factors, such as self-control, risk tolerance, and financial anxiety, play a crucial role in shaping financial behaviors. Strömbäck, et al. (2017) found that individuals with higher levels of self-control tend to engage in more prudent financial behaviors, such as saving regularly and avoiding unnecessary debt. Similarly, financial anxiety can lead to both avoidance of financial issues and compulsive financial behaviors, highlighting the complex relationship between emotions and financial decision-making (Archuleta et al., 2013). Cultural and social contexts significantly influence money beliefs and financial behaviors. For instance, individualistic cultures, which emphasize personal achievement and independence, tend to encourage financial behaviors focused on personal savings and investment (Gutter et al., 2010). In contrast, collectivist cultures, which prioritize family and community well-being, may influence individuals to make financial decisions that support familial and communal financial health (Shim et al., 2010).

Economic factors, such as income level, employment status, and economic stability, also impact financial behaviors and money beliefs. Higher income levels are generally associated with better financial behaviors, such as increased savings and investment activities (Xiao et al,.2014). Conversely, economic instability and unemployment can lead to adverse financial behaviors, such as increased debt and reduced savings (Falahati & Paim, 2011). Financial education is a critical factor influencing financial behaviors and money beliefs. Lusardi and Mitchell (2017) emphasize the importance of financial literacy education in enhancing individuals' ability to make informed financial decisions. Educational programs that improve financial knowledge can lead to more positive financial behaviors, such as budgeting, saving, and investing (Fernandes et al., 2014).

The rise of financial technology (fintech) has transformed personal financial management. Mobile banking, budgeting apps, and robo-advisors provide tools that facilitate better financial decision-making. Gomber et al. (2017) discuss how fintech innovations offer real-time information and personalized financial advice, enhancing users' ability to manage their finances effectively. Fintech also plays a crucial role in promoting financial inclusion. Ozili (2018) highlights how digital financial services have expanded access to banking for underserved populations, reducing barriers to financial participation and fostering more inclusive economic growth. The accessibility of digital financial tools helps bridge gaps in financial literacy and inclusion.

Emerging trends, such as sustainable financial behaviors, gender differences and the impact of the COVID-19 pandemic continue to shape the landscape of financial behaviors and money beliefs. As research progresses, it is essential to develop and implement effective educational programs and policy measures that enhance financial literacy and well-being across diverse populations. By addressing the multifaceted nature of financial behaviors and money beliefs, we can foster a more financially resilient and inclusive society.

There is growing interest in sustainable financial behaviors, reflecting broader societal shifts towards sustainability. Research by Vermeir and Verbeke (2016) suggests that environmentally conscious consumers are increasingly considering sustainability in their financial decisions, such as investing in green funds and supporting ethical banking practices. This trend highlights the intersection of financial behaviors and broader ethical and environmental concerns. Gender differences in financial behaviors continue to be an important area of study. Falahati and Paim (2011) found that women often exhibit different financial behaviors and face unique financial challenges compared to men. Recent research aims to understand these differences better and develop targeted interventions to address gender-specific financial needs and barriers. The COVID-19 pandemic has had profound effects on financial behaviors and money beliefs. Clark, Lusardi, and Mitchell (2020) highlight how the economic uncertainty and financial strain caused by the pandemic have underscored the importance of financial resilience and emergency savings. Studies indicate that individuals with higher financial literacy were better equipped to navigate the financial challenges posed by the pandemic (Hasler, Lusardi, & Oggero, 2020).

MAIN FOCUS OF THE CHAPTER

Research Methodology

The type of research selected for this study is quantitative. Quantitative research focuses on the collection and analysis of numerical and statistical data to identify patterns and relationships between variables. This approach is appropriate to the nature of the structured survey, which allows obtaining objective and comparable data through standardized responses. The research approach adopted is descriptive and exploratory, descriptive because the study aims to describe the characteristics of a specific population or phenomenon. In this case, the aim is to describe and classify the individuals in the sample based on their responses to the survey. Exploratory because this approach is used when the objective is to explore an understudied problem. Although classifying individuals based on surveys is common practice, this study also aims to explore new forms of data segmentation and analysis that may not have been widely researched.

This research performs a survey between students in the seven and eight level of studies at Colombian Army Military Academy "General José María Córdova" that studied business and military career, that belong to the highest level of formation. According to the inventory of B. Klontz et al. (2011) the survey use a list of items related for the evaluation regarding to money beliefs and financial behaviors, the list of items about: 1. Money Worship (8 items), 2. anti-rich (6 items), 3. money is bad (5 items), 4. money mistrust/openness (12 items), 5. frugality/fiscal responsibility (11 items) 1,6. money anxiety (8 items), 7. money status/worth (18 items) and 8. money is unimportant (3 items). A sample of 50 students were invited to participate to the survey, 48 responds the questions, with the acceptance and help to the research and signed an agreement to participate to the study. The demographic profile of the students will be explained in the figures below:

Measures

We used a Likert scale applying the same measures of (B. Klontz et al., 2011) study that measure a six-point coded where 1= strongly disagree, 2=disagree, 3= disagree a little, 4=agree a little, 5=agree, and 6= strongly agree.

On the other hand, Gender was coded with 1=Male 2=Female, Age was coded with 1= (20-22 years old), 2 = (23-25 years old), Ethnicity 1= Hispanic-white 2 = Afrodescent, Education 1=Secondary, 2=Technical Professional, 3=Underdegree., Nationality 1=Colombia, 2=Panamá, 3=Paraguay; Socioeconomic Status 1, 2, 3, 4, 5, 6 level of socioeconomic conditions, Mother´s Educational Level 1=Primary School, 2=Secondary School, 3=Technical School, 4=Technological, 5= Underdegree, 6=Posgraduate, Father´s Educational Level 1=Primary School, 2=Secondary School, 3=Technical School, 4=Technological, 5= Underdegree, 6=Posgraduate. Monthly Family Income USD, 1= 0-250 USD 2=251-500 USD, 3=501-1.000 USD, 4-1.001-1.500 USD, 5-1.501-2.000 USD,6= 2.001-2.500 USD, 7-2.501-3.000 USD, 8= more than 3.000 USD, Family members) Number of members, Level of Education 1=VII

2=VIII, Net Worth 1=Unknown, 2=1-25.000 USD, 3=25.001 -62.500 USD, 4=62.501-125.000 USD, 5=125.001-150.000 USD, 6=> 150.000 USD.

Credit card 1 =Yes 2=Not, *Student Loan 1 =Yes 2=Not, how do you mainly finance your studies? 1= Own resources (Parents), 2= Family financial aid (Other than Parents), 3= Education Loans (Government) 4= Education Loans (From Banks). The home where you live is (family group). 1= Own without mortgage credit or housing leasing, 2= Own with mortgage credit or housing leasing, 3= Rent.

Results analysis

This part presents the descriptive analysis according to the adapted survey from the original inventory o B. Klontz et al. (2011):

Figure 1 shows that much of the group (63.8%) have an education level of VIII, while the remaining 36.2% have an education level of VII.

Figure 1. Level of Education of the Participants.

Frequencies of *Level of Education

*Level of Education	Counts	% of Total	Cumulative %
1=VII Level	17	36.2%	36.2%
2=VIII Level	30	63.8%	100.0%

Source: The authors

Figure 2 shows that most of the group (70.2%) have between 20 to 22 years old, and 29.8% have between 23 to 25 years old.

Figure 2. Age of the participants

Frequencies of *Age

*Age	Counts	% of Total	Cumulative %
20-22 y	33	70.2 %	70.2 %
23-25 y	14	29.8 %	100.0 %

Source: The authors

Figure 3 shows that most of the sample (93.6%) belongs to Hispanic- White ethnicity and only the (6.4%) percent belong to the Afro-descendant ethnic group.

Figure 3. Ethnicity of the participants

Frequencies of *Ethnicity

*Ethnicity	Counts	% of Total	Cumulative %
Hispanic-white	44	93.6%	93.6%
Afro-descent	3	6.4%	100.0%

Source: The authors

Figure 4 shows that most of the group (85.1%) are male, while a smaller percentage (14.9%) are female, the explanation of that is because female students are interested in military studies.

Figure 4. Gender of the participants

Frequencies of *Gender

*Gender	Counts	% of Total	Cumulative %
1=Male	40	85.1%	85.1%
2=Female	7	14.9%	100.0%

Source: The authors

The data in the Figure 5 shows that much of the group (93.6%) are from Colombia, with smaller percentages from Panamá (4.3%) and Paraguay (2.1%), the other nationalities that there are not Colombian were included because students from different Latin American countries participate in military and business studies for bilateral agreements between governments.

Figure 5. Nationality of the participants

Frequencies of *Nacionality

*Nacionality	Counts	% of Total	Cumulative %
1=Colombia	44	93.6%	93.6%
2=Panamá	2	4.3%	97.9%
3=Paraguay	1	2.1%	100.0%

Source: The authors

Figure 6 shows that most of the students (66%) come from the secondary school (8.5%), from technical studies that probability they did before coming the Military School and (25.5%), under degree that explain those students just finished the program where the survey was conducted.

Figure 6. Educational Level of the participants

Frequencies of *Education

*Education	Counts	% of Total	Cumulative %
Secondary	31	66.0%	66.0%
Technical Professional	4	8.5%	74.5%
Underdegree	12	25.5%	100.0%

Source: The authors

Figure 7 shows the socioeconomic stratification that is defined by the National Administrative Department of Statistics (DANE) and the municipal administrations, stratification in Colombia aims to assign subsidies and contributions for household public services (water, electricity, gas, etc.). Lower strata2 (1, 2, and 3) usually receive subsidies, while higher strata (5 and 6) contribute with surcharges. The data explained that 80.9% of the students belongs to 1, 2, 3 Lower Strata, and (17%) Medium and (2.1%) medium- high.

Figure 7. Socioeconomic status of the participants

Frequencies of *Socioeconomic Status

*Socioeconomic Status	Counts	% of Total	Cumulative %
1	4	8.5%	8.5%
2	17	36.2%	44.7%
3	17	36.2%	80.9%
4	8	17.0%	97.9%
5	1	2.1%	100.0%

Source: The authors

Figure 8 shows that the most common family size in the group is 4 members (40.4%), followed by families with 5 members (31.9%). Families with 2, 6, or 8 members are less common

Figure 8. Number of Family Members of the participants

Frequencies of *Family Members

*Family Members	Counts	% of Total	Cumulative %
2	1	2.1%	2.1%
3	8	17.0%	19.1%
4	19	40.4%	59.6%
5	15	31.9%	91.5%
6	3	6.4%	97.9%
8	1	2.1%	100.0%

Source: The authors

Figure 9 shows the Mother´s Educational Level as we see (29.8%) have Under degree, follows by (23.4%) Technical school and secondary school (21.3%), primary school (8.5%) and Postgraduate program (8.5%) are less common.

Figure 9. Participants Mother´s Educational Level

*Mother´s Educational Level	Counts	% of Total	Cumulative %
1= Primary School	4	8.5 %	8.5 %
2= Secondary School	10	21.3 %	29.8 %
3=Technical School	11	23.4 %	53.2 %
4=Technological	4	8.5 %	61.7 %
5= Underdegree	14	29.8 %	91.5 %
6= Posgraduate	4	8.5 %	100.0 %

Source: The authors

Figure 10 shows the father´s educational Level as we see (27.7%) Secondary studies, follows by (27.7%) Technical school and technological (14.9%), primary school (10.6%) and Postgraduates studies (10.6%) are less common.

Figure 10. Participants Father´s Educational Level

Frequencies of *Father´s Educational Level

*Father´s Educational Level	Counts	% of Total	Cumulative %
1=Primary School	5	10.6 %	10.6 %
2=Secondary School	13	27.7 %	38.3 %
3=Technical School	11	23.4 %	61.7 %
4=Technological	7	14.9 %	76.6 %
5= Underdegree	6	12.8 %	89.4 %
6= Posgraduate	5	10.6 %	100.0 %

Source: The authors

Figure 11 shows monthly family income in USD dollars, we assume the price of the dollar were 4.000 Colombian Pesos, the most common income range is 251-500 USD (27.7%), followed by 501-1,000 USD (23.4%) and 1,001-1,500 USD (19.1%).

Figure 11. Participants Monthly Family Income

Frequencies of *Monthly Family Income USD

*Monthly Family Income USD	Counts	% of Total	Cumulative %
1= 0-250 USD	2	4.3 %	4.3 %
2=251-500 USD	13	27.7 %	31.9 %
3=501-1.000 USD	11	23.4 %	55.3 %
4=1.001-1.500 USD	9	19.1 %	74.5 %
5=1.501-2.000 USD	6	12.8 %	87.2 %
6= 2.001-2.500 USD	4	8.5 %	95.7 %
7=2.501-3.000 USD	1	2.1 %	97.9 %
8= more than 3.000 USD	1	2.1 %	100.0 %

Source: The authors

Figure 12 shows Net Worth from family in USD dollars, we assume the price of the dollar were 4.000 Colombian Pesos, the most common net worth category is "Unknown" (46.8%) the most common is (46.8%), follows by that range is 62.501-125.000 USD (21.3%) and 25.001-62,500 USD (17%).

Figure 12. Participants Family Net worth

Frequencies of * Net Worth

* Net Worth	Counts	% of Total	Cumulative %
1=Unknown	22	46.8 %	46.8 %
2=1-25.000 USD	3	6.4 %	53.2 %
3=25.001 -62.500 USD	8	17.0 %	70.2 %
4=62.501-125.000 USD	10	21.3 %	91.5 %
5=125.001-250.000 USD	2	4.3 %	95.7 %
6=> 125.000 USD	2	4.3 %	100.0 %

Source: The authors

Figure 13 shows if the students have credit cards results are mixed 34% of them have credit cards and 66%, they have not.

Figure 13. Participants Credit Card Holding

Frequencies of *Credit cards

*Credit cards	Counts	% of Total	Cumulative %
1=Yes	16	34.0 %	34.0 %
2= Not	31	66.0 %	100.0 %

Source: The authors

Figure 14 shows if the students have student's loans, results are mixed 38,3% of them have student loan to financing their studies and 61,7%, they have not.

Figure 14. Participants Student loans

Frequencies of *Student Loan

*Student Loan	Counts	% of Total	Cumulative %
1=Yes	18	38.3 %	38.3 %
2= Not	29	61.7 %	100.0 %

Source: The authors

Figure 15 shows how students financing the most common are from their parents (Own resource: The authors) 57.4%, and Educational Loan-Government (34%), less likely to Family financial aid (4.3%) and Educational Loans from Banks (4.3%).

Figure 15. Participants Source: The sources of Funding

Frequencies of *How do you mainly finance your studies?

*How do you mainly finance your studies?	Counts	% of Total	Cumulative %
1= Own resources (Parents)	27	57.4 %	57.4 %
2= Family financial aid (Other than Parents)	2	4.3 %	61.7 %
3= Education Loans (Government	16	34.0 %	95.7 %
4= Education Loans (From Banks)	2	4.3 %	100.0 %

Source: The authors

Figure 16 shows that many families (85.1%) own their homes without mortgage credit or leasing arrangements, while a smaller percentage (4.3%) own their homes with mortgage credit or leasing. Additionally, 10.6% of families rent their homes.

Figure 16. Participants type of housing

Frequencies of *The home where you live is (family group)

*The home where you live is (family group)	Counts	% of Total	Cumulative %
1= Own without mortgage credit or housing leasing	40	85.1 %	85.1 %
2= Own with mortgage credit or housing leasing	2	4.3 %	89.4 %
3= Rent.	5	10.6 %	100.0 %

Source: The authors

We just applied Cronbach's alpha values that indicate the internal consistency or reliability of the scale measuring attitudes or beliefs about money that are represented in the following Figures that indicate the internal consistency of the entire set of statements regarding Klontz Money Script inventory related to Money worship, anti-*rich, Money is bad, Money mistrust /openness, frugality /fiscal Responsibility, money anxiety, Money Status /worth, Money is unimportant, all items such as suggesting a high degree of reliability in measuring the construct of "money script inventory".

On the other hand, we introduced fourth questions that are related to how father, mother, partner and I manage the money that indicate the internal consistency or reliability of the scale measured.

Figures 17 and 18 suggest that higher net worth and specific methods of financing studies are associated with higher levels of Money Worship, further analysis and interpretation may be needed to understand the practical significance of these findings.

Figure 17. Internal consistency of the survey per dimension (Dimensions 1 to 4)

Item Reliability Statistics	Cronbach's α
1.1 "Money would solve all my problems	0.743
1.2 " Things will get better once I have more money	0.747
1.3 " Money buys freedom	0.738
1.4 " It is hard to be poor and happy	0.736
1.5 " More money will make you happier	0.728
1.6 " Rich people have no reason to be unhappy	0.740
1.7 " Money is power	0.734
1.8 "Money is what gives life meaning.	0.733
"Money Worship	0.810

Item Reliability Statistics	Cronbach's α
2.1" People get rich by taking advantage of others.	0.722
2.2"Rich people are greedy.	0.713
2.3" The rich take their money for granted	0.730
2.4"It is hard to be rich and be a good person	0.761
2.5" The rich should give the most to charity	0.759
2.6" Most rich people do not deserve their money	0.757
Anti-rich	0.772

Item Reliability Statistics	Cronbach's α
3.1 " Money is the root of all evil.	0.766
3.2 " Money corrupts people	0.751
3.3 " Having a lot of money separates you from others	0.744
3.4 " Being wealthy means you cannot know whether someone loves you or your money	0.737
3.5 "Being rich means you no longer fit with old friends and family	0.737
"Money is Bad	0.753

Item Reliability Statistics	Cronbach's α
4.1"I work hard, so cheating the government is okay now and the	0.741
4.2" You cannot trust people around money	0.731
4.3" It is okay to keep secrets from your partner around money.	0.738
4.4"You cannot trust banks	0.736
4.5" If you have money, someone will try to take it away from you	0.733
4.6"You should not tell others how much money you have or make	0.733
4.7"It is wrong to ask others how much money they have or make	0.747
4.8" If you loan money to someone you should not expect to get it back.	0.743
4.9" If someone asked me how much I earned, I would probably tell them I earn more less I actually do	0.739
4.10" It is not polite to talk about money	0.744
4.11" If someone asked me how much I earned, I would probably tell them I earn more less I actually do	0.740
4.12" You cannot be rich and trust what people want from you	0.732
Money Mistrust/Openness	0.863

Source: The authors

Figures 17 and 18 suggest that higher net worth and specific methods of financing studies are associated with higher levels of Money Worship, further analysis and interpretation may be needed to understand the practical significance of these findings.

Figure 18. Internal consistency of the survey per dimension (Dimensions 5 to 9)

Item Reliability Statistics	Cronbach's α
5.1* It is important to save for a rainy day	0.722
5.2*Life is short. It is better to spend money while you have it.	0.724
5.3* If I had to borrow money to get what I want I would do it.	0.720
5.4* I deserve money.	0.719
5.5*If something is not considered the "best." It is not worth buying	0.725
5.6* I am entitled to money	0.717
5.7* If you cannot pay cash for something, you should not buy it.	0.735
5.8*You should always try to pay less than retail price for something	0.725
5.9 *You should always look for the best deal before buying something, even if it takes more time	0.719
5.10* There will always be someone I can turn to for money	0.718
5.11* I will not buy something unless it is new (e.g., car, house	0.731
Frugally /Fiscal Responsability	0.792

Item Reliability Statistics	Cronbach's α
6.1* There will never be enough money.	0.751
6.2* You can never have enough money	0.743
6.3* Investing money in the stock market is no way to secure your future	0.739
6.4* I will never be able to afford the things I really want in life	0.747
6.5* I have to work hard to be sure I have enough money	0.762
6.6*Taking risks with money is foolish	0.747
6.7* It takes money to make money.	0.750
6.8* I would be a nervous wreck if I did not have money saved f	0.742
Money Anxiety	0.853

Item Reliability Statistics	Cronbach's α
7.1*People are only as successful as the amount of money they earn	0.753
7.2*Your self-worth equals your net worth	0.749
7.3*Poor people are lazy.	0.748
7.4*If you are good, your financial needs will be taken care of	0.753
7.5* As long as you life a good life you will always have enough money	0.750
7.6* Most poor people do not deserve to have money.	0.748
7.7* Giving money to others is something people should do	0.756
7.8* People should work for their money and not be given financial handouts.	0.754
7.9* There is virtue in living with less money	0.753
7.10*I don't deserve money	0.746
7.11*Money I did not earn (e.g. inheritance, insurance settlement, etc.) is not really mine to spend.	0.749
7.12* It is extravagant to spend money on oneself.	0.753
7.13* It is hard to accept financial gifts from others.	0.748
7.14*There will always be enough money for the things I want	0.751
7.15* I do not deserve a lot of money when others have less than me	0.747
7.16* It is not okay to have more than you need	0.748
7.17* The poor have no money because they do not want to work.	0.749
7.18* I would be embarrassed to tell someone how much money I make.	0.748
Money Status / Worth	0.943

Item Reliability Statistics	Cronbach's α
8.1.* Money is not important	0.807
8.2.* The less money you have, the better life is.	0.792
8.3.*Good people should not care about money	0.807
Money us Unimportant	0.794

Item Reliability Statistic	Cronbach's α
9.1* I believe that my father handles money appropriately	0.826
9.2* I believe that my mother handles money appropriately	0.843
9.3* I consider that in general my partner handles money adequately	0.813
9.4* I think that in general I manage money properly.	0.891

Source: The authors

Figure 19 explains that factors such as education, mother's education, socioeconomic status, family size, and net worth can influence Anti-rich sentiment, were some categories showing stronger effects than others, although factors such as age, ethnicity, gender, nationality, monthly family income, level of education, credit cards, student loan, how do you mainly finance your studies and the home where you live, do not show statistically significant effects.

On the other hand, categories such as age, ethnicity, education, mother´s educational level, gender, nationality, socioeconomic status, monthly family income, family members, level of education, Net worth, credit cards, student loan, how do you mainly finance your studies and the home where you live, do not show statistically significant effects on "Money is bad" sentiment.

Figure 19. Predictors Analysis

Predictor				
Money Worship				
*Net Worth	Estimate	SE	t	p
2 – (1-25.000 USD)	-3.263	10.97	-0.2975	0.776085
3 – (25.001 -62.500 USD)	-1.465	6.04	-0.2425	0.816434
4 – (62.501-125.000 USD)	6.630	4.59	1.4449	0.198611
5 – (125.001-250.000 USD)	-0.804	19.31	-0.0416	0.968140
6 – (> 150.000 USD)	26.795	10.28	2.6074	0.040261
*How do you mainly finance your studies?:				
2 – Family financial aid (Other than Parents)	31.683	9.52	3.3274	0.015858
3 – Education Loans (Government)	37.480	14.26	2.6290	0.039114
4 – Education Loans (From Banks)	16.804	12.91	1.3018	0.240714

Source: The authors

Figure 19, explains that factors such as education, mother's education, socioeconomic status, family size, and net worth can influence Anti-rich sentiment, were some categories showing stronger effects than others, although factors such as age, ethnicity, gender, nationality, monthly family income, level of education, credit cards, student loan, how do you mainly finance your studies and the home where you live, do not show statistically significant effects.

On the other hand, categories such as age, ethnicity, education, mother´s educational level, gender, nationality, socioeconomic status, monthly family income, family members, level of education, Net worth, credit cards, student loan, how do you mainly finance your studies and the home where you live, do not show statistically significant effects on "Money is bad" sentiment.

Figure 20 Shows that results suggest that higher socioeconomic status and higher monthly family incomes are associated with increased Money Mistrust/Openness. Individuals with higher incomes and higher socioeconomic status may have different attitudes towards money and finance, possibly influenced by their financial stability or experiences.

Figure 20. Anti-Rich Predictors Analysis

Predictor				
Anti-rich	**Estimate**	**SE**	**t**	**p**
*Education:				
2 – Technical Professional	18.520	4.81	3.850	0.0084614
3 – Underdegree	-1.528	3.44	-0.444	0.6728494
*Mother´s Educational Level:				
2 – Secondary School	-13.622	5.25	-2.595	0.0409238
3 – Technical School	-9.557	4.52	-2.114	0.0789865
4 – Technological	-21.660	6.65	-3.257	0.0173148
5 – Underdegree	-14.167	4.63	-3.058	0.0222721
6 – Posgraduate	-21.659	4.25	-5.097	0.0022281
*Socioeconomic Status:				
2 – 1	5.032	4.21	1.196	0.2767290
3 – 1	4.419	4.06	1.089	0.3180923
4 – 1	13.454	4.77	2.818	0.0304410
5 – 1	-10.697	16.65	-0.642	0.5443170
*Familiy Members:				
3 – 2	-56.142	14.09	-3.985	0.0072458
4 – 2	-54.376	14.96	-3.635	0.0109044
5 – 2	-54.986	13.20	-4.165	0.0059112
6 – 2	-55.599	15.77	-3.526	0.0124282
8 – 2	-63.558	18.44	-3.447	0.0136770
* Net Worth:				
2 – 1	5.842	5.57	1.049	0.3344295
3 – 1	-0.332	3.07	-0.108	0.9172689
4 – 1	-1.316	2.33	-0.565	0.5925035
5 – 1	-27.305	9.80	-2.786	0.0317347
6 – 1	8.637	5.22	1.656	0.1488733

Source: The authors

Categories such as age, ethnicity, education, mother´s educational level, gender, nationality, socio-economic status, monthly family income, family members, level of education, Net worth, credit cards, student loan, how do you mainly finance your studies and the home where you live, do not show statistically significant effects on "frugality/fiscal responsibility" sentiment. (Figure 21).

Figure 21. Money Mistrust/ Openness Predictors Analysis

Money Mistrust/Openness

Predictor	Estimate	SE	t	p
*Socioeconomic Status:				
2 – 1	12.29	10.50	1.170	0.2861961
3 – 1	12.21	10.13	1.205	0.2734155
4 – 1	23.05	11.92	1.934	0.1012562
5 – 1	186.16	41.56	4.480	0.0041936
*Monthly Family Income USD:				
2 – 251-500 USD	117.80	28.33	4.158	0.0059609
3 – 501-1.000 USD	115.77	29.24	3.960	0.0074524
4 – 1.001-1.500 USD	110.19	27.18	4.055	0.0066917
5 – 1.501-2.000 USD	106.54	30.37	3.508	0.0127058
6 – 2.001-2.500 USD	112.84	27.47	4.107	0.0063057
7 – 2.501-3.000 USD	74.48	25.95	2.870	0.0284106

Source: The authors

Nationality, monthly family income, and possession of credit cards are associated with differences in Money Anxiety levels. Individuals from Panamá and Paraguay, lower- and middle-income brackets, and without credit cards tend to experience higher levels of Money Anxiety. Although factors such as age, ethnicity, gender, nationality, monthly family income, level of education, Mother´s and Father´s education, student loan, how do you mainly finance your studies and the home where you live do not show statistically significant effects on "Money Anxiety" (figure 22).

Figure 22. Money Anxiety

Money Anxiety

Predictor	Estimate	SE	t	p
*Nacionality:				
2 – Panamá	73.99	26.54	2.7878	0.031669
3 – Paraguay	92.15	33.70	2.7348	0.033971
*Monthly Family Income USD:				
2 – 251-500 USD	69.50	27.24	2.5517	0.043388
3 – 501-1.000 USD	65.11	28.10	2.3168	0.059713
4 – 1.001-1.500 USD	73.14	26.13	2.7996	0.031181
5 – 1.501-2.000 USD	78.35	29.20	2.6834	0.036371
6 – 2.001-2.500 USD	64.54	26.41	2.4439	0.050205
7 – 2.501-3.000 USD	62.13	24.94	2.4911	0.047095
*Credit cards:				
2 – Not	-19.60	7.32	-2.6778	0.036645

Source: The authors

Nationality and monthly family income are associated with differences in perceived Money Status/ Worth. Individuals from Panamá and higher income brackets tend to perceive themselves as having higher Money Status/Worth. These findings provide insights into how socio-economic factors influence individuals' perceptions of their financial status and worth. Although factors such as age, ethnicity, gender, nationality, monthly family income, level of education, Mother´s and Father Education, student loan, how do you mainly finance your studies and the home where you live do not show statistically significant effects on "Money Status /Worth" (figure 23).

Figure 23. Money Mistrust/ Openness Predictors Analysis

Money Status / Worth

Predictor	Estimate	SE	t	p
*Nacionality:				
2 – Panamá	132.794	50.6	2.6246	0.039342
3 – Paraguay	141.025	64.2	2.1954	0.070544
*Monthly Family Income USD:				
2 – 251-500 USD	121.225	51.9	2.3347	0.058265
3 – 501-1.000 USD	129.524	53.6	2.4175	0.052037
4 – 1.001-1.500 USD	127.557	49.8	2.5611	0.042845
5 – 1.501-2.000 USD	118.668	55.7	2.1320	0.076996
6 – 2.001-2.500 USD	132.599	50.3	2.6337	0.038869
7 – 2.501-3.000 USD	83.995	47.5	1.7665	0.127738

Source: The authors

In the regression model for "Money is Unimportant," several predictor variables have estimated co-efficients, but none of them are statistically significant at conventional levels ($p < 0.05$). Age, ethnicity, education, mother's educational level, gender, nationality, socioeconomic status, monthly family income USD, family members, level of education, net worth, credit cards, student loan, how do you mainly finance your studies; the home where you live is (family group), coefficients for different groups of variables are not statistically significant on the perception that "money is unimportant".

Figure 24 shows the correlations in between Klontz money Script inventory the scales explain issues about accumulation of money (worship), how people think about rich (anti-rich), how people think about money (money is bad, avoidance), money mistrust /openness, Frugal and fiscal responsibility, money anxiety money status /Worth, provide insights into how different attitudes towards money are interrelated. All questions are positive correlated, and we can find that a higher belief that "Money is bad" correlates with money mistrust and openness, and money status and anxiety about money. Similarly, a belief that "Money Is Bad" correlates moderately with anti-rich sentiments

Figure 24. Klontz Money Script Inventory Correlations Analysis

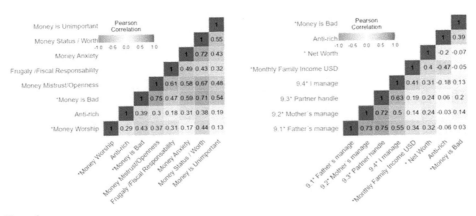

In Table 1 we can see the definitions of every aspect of the money inventory, that help professionals to help and change aspects of their life´s and help researchers to understand behaviours and help to introduce some aspects:

Table 1. Money Inventory definitions

Money worship	"Accumulate Money" It means that people understand that with more money things will be better.	At their core, money worshipers are convinced that the key to happiness and the solution to all of them are money. People with higher scores ignore financial situation, give money to others even without think if they can pay it and area depend from others. (B. T. Klontz & Britt, 2012).More likely to have lower income, lower net worth, and be trapped in a cycle of revolving credit card debt. Some of the problems associate includes overspending, workaholism hoarding.(B. Klontz & Klontz, 2009).
Money avoidance	It means that people feel that they try to avoid money matters.	People that perform with high scores money is seen as a source of fear, anxiety, or disgust, because they have a negative association with money, believe that people of wealth are greedy and corrupt, and believe there is virtue in living with less money. These people reject financial matters, and have excessive risk aversion and the spend less may sabotage their financial success. (B. Klontz & Klontz, 2009).
Money Status	Differentiate one´s self from other socio-economic classes	They think that is a positive and perfectly relationship between self-worth and net worth. Higher scores explain that money is status and related with socioeconomic classes.(B. Klontz et al., 2011) They have lower net worth, lower income, and tend to grow up in families with a lower socioeconomic status. People can be compulsive spenders and they can predict pathological gambling.(B. T. Klontz & Britt, 2012)
Money Vigilance.	Keep one´s money issues private.	Higher scores explain that this person could be alert, watchful, and concerned about their financial welfare. On the contrary they do not spend compulsively, enable others financially, and ignore their finances. They have higher income and higher net worth, they are anxious and secretive about their financial status, and they won't lie to partner about spending. (B. T. Klontz & Britt, 2012).

After obtaning the results scores less and equal than 2 suggest you do not shown the money script. Scores between 2 and 3 imply that may be more beliefs associated with the money script. Scores between 3 and 4 shown some characteristics of the money script. Scores higher than 4 suggest that person have some or many characteristics of the money script (CIMA, 2018).

Figure 25 reveals that 59.5% of respondents exhibit numerous characteristics indicative of a predisposition towards, or existing struggle with, money worship. These individuals are likely to believe that money is the solution to their problems or that it can buy happiness. In contrast, only 8.5% of respondents show no significant tendencies towards money worship.

Figure 25. "Money Worship" Frequencies

Frequencies of **Money Workship

**Money Workship	Counts	% of Total	Cumulative %
>4	9	19.1 %	19.1 %
3-4	19	40.4 %	59.6 %
2-3	15	31.9 %	91.5 %
<2	4	8.5 %	100.0 %

Source: The authors

The 63.8% of respondents exhibit characteristics indicative of a predisposition towards, or an existing struggle with, anti-rich sentiment. This sentiment is often associated with money avoiders who believe that wealthy individuals are inherently greedy. These respondents are likely to feel that they do not deserve money. In contrast, only 10.6% of respondents show no significant tendencies towards anti-rich sentiment (figure 26).

Figure 26. "Antirich" Frequencies

Frequencies of **Antirich

**Antirich	Counts	% of Total	Cumulative %
>4	8	17.0 %	17.0 %
3-4	22	46.8 %	63.8 %
2-3	12	25.5 %	89.4 %
<2	5	10.6 %	100.0 %

Source: The authors

The 61.8% of respondents exhibit characteristics indicative of a belief that money is inherently negative. This sentiment is often associated with money avoiders, who view money as harmful or morally questionable. These respondents are likely to be at a greater risk of holding money-avoidant beliefs. In contrast, only 8.5% of respondents show no significant tendencies towards the belief that money is bad (figure 27).

Figure 27. "Money is Bad" Frequencies

Frequencies of ***Money is bad

***Money is bad	Counts	% of Total	Cumulative %
>4	4	8.5 %	8.5 %
3-4	25	53.2 %	61.7 %
2-3	14	29.8 %	91.5 %
<2	4	8.5 %	100.0 %

Source: The authors

The 72.3% of respondents exhibit characteristics indicative of mistrust and a negative perception of openness towards financial matters. This sentiment is often associated with money avoiders who may avoid reviewing bank statements or engaging with financial institutions due to a lack of trust. These respondents are likely at a greater risk of developing beliefs that undermine trust and openness regarding financial management. In contrast, only 4.3% of respondents show no significant tendencies towards mistrust and a lack of openness in financial matters (figure 28).

Figure 28. "Money Mistrust /Openness" Frequencies

Frequencies of ***Money Mistrust/Openness

***Money Mistrust/Openness	Counts	% of Total	Cumulative %
>4	6	12.8 %	12.8 %
3-4	28	59.6 %	72.3 %
2-3	11	23.4 %	95.7 %
<2	2	4.3 %	100.0 %

Source: The authors

Figure 29 shows that 72.3% of respondents exhibit characteristics indicative of frugality and fiscal responsibility, coupled with a negative perception of money vigilance. These individuals prioritize saving, paying for everything in cash, and avoiding credit. This sentiment is often associated with money vigilants, who are highly concerned about their financial welfare. In contrast, only 2.13% of respondents show no significant tendencies towards frugality and fiscal responsibility. Consequently, money vigilants typically achieve higher net worth and income due to their prudent financial practices.

Figure 29. "Frugally/ Fiscal Responsibility" Frequencies

Frequencies of **Frugaly /Fiscal Responsability

**Frugaly /Fiscal Responsability	Counts	% of Total	Cumulative %
>4	19	40.4 %	40.4 %
3-4	27	57.4 %	97.9 %
2-3	1	2.1 %	100.0 %

Source: The authors

Figure 30 reveals that 78.7% of respondents exhibit characteristics indicative of money anxiety. These individuals perceive money as a source of fear, anxiety, or disgust, a sentiment typically associated with money avoiders. When analyzing this information alongside socioeconomic status, it is notable that 23.4% of respondents come from the 3-Strata and 19.1% from the 2-Strata. In contrast, only 6.4% of respondents show no significant tendencies towards money anxiety.

Figure 30. "Money Anxiety" Frequencies

Frequencies of **Money Anxiety

**Money Anxiety	Counts	% of Total	Cumulative %
>4	9	19.1 %	19.1 %
3-4	28	59.6 %	78.7 %
2-3	7	14.9 %	93.6 %
<2	3	6.4 %	100.0 %

Source: The authors

Figure 31 indicates that 57.4% of survey respondents are concerned with money status and worth, equating their net worth with their self-worth, as suggested by B. T. Klontz & Britt (2012). This mindset can lead individuals to engage in riskier financial behaviors, such as overspending and projecting an appearance of greater wealth than they possess. In contrast, only 10.6% of respondents show no significant tendencies toward concerns about status and worth.

Figure 31. "Money Status" Frequencies

Frequencies of **Money Status / Worth

**Money Status / Worth	Counts	% of Total	Cumulative %
>4	5	10.6 %	10.6 %
3-4	22	46.8 %	57.4 %
2-3	15	31.9 %	89.4 %
<2	5	10.6 %	100.0 %

Source: The authors

Figure 32 indicates that 57.4% of survey respondents are concerned with money is not important, people think with less money better is the life, and associated with the perception of good person do not care about money. In contrast, only 21.3% of respondents show no significant tendencies toward that money is unimportant.

Figure 32. "Money is Unimportant" Frequencies

Frequencies of **Money is Unimportant

**Money is Unimportant	Counts	% of Total	Cumulative %
>4	6	12.8 %	12.8 %
3-4	21	44.7 %	57.4 %
2-3	10	21.3 %	78.7 %
<2	10	21.3 %	100.0 %

Source: The authors

CONCLUSION

The main purpose of this research is to identify the financial Behaviors and Money Beliefs in Small and medium sizes enterprises in the educational sector to acomplish the objetive a small sample of a higher education in Colombia that have students from Panama and Paraguay, a survey were conducted using Klontz Money Script Inventory. As we see the survey found that most of the students from the Military School have some issues about the money attitutes scores bigger than 3 shown some characteristics of the money script. Money Workship 59.6%, sentiments against to rich people (anti-rich) 63.8%, Money is bad (61.7%), money trust and oppeness 72.3%, frugaly and fiscal responsabitility (97.9%), anxiety (78.7%), Money status /worth (57.4%) and money is not important (57.4%). These behaviors will concern that students should have better knowledge and awareness of money and financial literacy to performe in wellbeing concern by the finance matters as we showed anxiety and frugality and fiscal responsibility have the highest score so probably there is a high risk aversion and financial denial, that may be help in the future to self-sabotage abusing of credit cards (B. Klontz & Klontz, 2009) or they think a money as a secret (vigilance) so it would be consider that for example 46.8% of people that is okay to keep secrets from your partner around money.

If we see trust and openness 51.1% (ranked 1 or 2) expressed that they follow the rules so is not okay to cheating the government, in contrast this number should be bigger because military cadets would manage governments resources, 23.4% (ranked 1 or 2) they do not think that "money corrupts people" so we can explain that behavioral dimension of money ethic and financial behavior as positive relationship (Aydin & Akben Selcuk, 2019), in other words most of them think that money is bad.

On the other hand we just have a new sample in military school that check the reliability of the test and find aspects that are not considered, this survey was conducted in students that were finalizing their studies in the military field as well as a business studies, so 70.2% were from 20 to 22 years old, 59.6% with up to 4 familiy members, 74% earn less 1.500 USD a monthly familiy income, were their parents reached technical school (mother 53.2% and fathers 61.7%). So these aspects and portraits explains why money represent status to 57.4% of them (ranked 3 of more) and why may be younger individuals have potencial destructive beliefs about money from the prespective of financial professional such as: counselors, educators and therapist.(B. Klontz et al., 2011).

We presume for the monthly family income that students at ESMIC should have low monthly allowance, so the study of (Sari et al., 2020), it could be a huge advantage for military students that if we improve or have better understanding of financial literacy with low amount of allowance so they can manage finances well, compared with students who have high allowance and do not understand financial literacy.

Probably this study may be influenced how professionals can approach to students in the military field that is necessary to have the ability to fulfill and reaches financial goals in the middle and long term, in contrats cadets 63% belief that they can manage money properly, these factors they can be used in the adulthood that can improve support from their families and improve family communication about money that's plays a key role in developing certain sets of financial behaviors (Vijaykumar, 2022), and financial discussion with parents during childhood positively influences financial well-being of young adults (Pandey et al., 2020), that´s why 67.4% belief that their mother can manage money properly and 78.3% belief that their father can manage money properly.

Moreover, 76.1% belief that their partner can manage money properly so analyse factors such as a financial planning for marriage contributes to happier, more satisfying and longer-lasting unions (Koe & Yeoh, 2021) that usually happen after students finish their studies.

At the end, there are contradictive statements that should be explain with further studies related to money behaviors that should considered for the students to help to acomplish the personal financial goals, that are important to the SME´s success.

SOLUTIONS AND RECOMMENDATIONS

According to the analysis of the results obtained in the previous chapters and the main findings, some opportunities for improvement are evident in the development of this research, which allows us to propose some recommendations as shown below:

It is recommended to expand the sample size to include more academic institutions and extend the geographical scope to more countries, encompassing diverse contexts beyond that of military education. This will enable the application of the information collection instrument in a variety of settings, facilitating the analysis of a larger dataset and allowing for more conclusive results.

Additionally, it is suggested to promote the use of the tools employed in this chapter of the book by disseminating them across a greater number of institutions and various localities. This will broaden the research's reach, involving not only more current students but also alumni and professors from these institutions. This broader participation will provide a more comprehensive understanding of the impact of financial behaviors and beliefs about money, extending beyond the confines of academia.

It is crucial to adapt the information collection instrument to different higher education settings, considering diverse characteristics of the institutions, such as their legal nature (public or private), potential religious influences, and the size of the institution in terms of student enrollment, among other factors. This adaptation will allow for a more precise and relevant application of the instrument in various educational contexts.

FUTURE RESEARCH DIRECTIONS

This section highlights the need for comprehensive and targeted research to address multifaceted financial behaviors and challenges within the context of higher education. By delving deeper into these areas, future studies can significantly contribute to improving the financial well-being of students, alumni, faculty, and even the institutions, that help individuals to locus of control in financial knowledge, financial attitude and financial behaviour intention (Sam et al., 2022). While the previous chapters show the basics, several aspects may require further exploration to fully understand the financial dynamics of individuals in higher education institutions and SME´s that would contribute to the formalization from informal businesses to formal SME´s through to targeted policies and strategies (Mehjabeen & Khan, 2024). As a recommendation for future research, the development of longitudinal studies is proposed to understand how financial behaviors evolve over time among students. These studies could monitor the financial health of such students from joining the institution to graduation and beyond, examining the relationship between mental health and financial behavior in the context of higher education and exploring how financial stress affects academic performance and decision making in the student population. You can also evaluate the role of mental health support services in mitigating financial stress and understanding how students manage financial crises and develop financial resilience tools.

REFERENCES

Agustina, Y., & Nurulistanti, L. (2022). How money circulates in indonesian smes: An analysis of financial literacy, business performance, financial management behavior, and financial attitude. Educational Administration: *Theory and Practice, 28*(2), 122-132. *Scopus.* Advance online publication. DOI: 10.17762/kuey.v28i02.425

Amagir, A., van den Brink, H. M., Groot, W., & Wilschut, A. (2022). SaveWise: The impact of a real-life financial education program for ninth grade students in the Netherlands. *Journal of Behavioral and Experimental Finance, 33.Journal of Behavioral and Experimental Finance,* 33, 100605. Advance online publication. DOI: 10.1016/j.jbef.2021.100605

Antonak, R. F., & Livneh, H. (1988). *The measurement of attitudes toward people with disabilities: Methods, psychometrics and scales.* Charles C Thomas, Publisher.

Appiah, T., & Agblewornu, V. V. (2024). Financial Literacy, Financial Access, and Small Business Performance in Secondi-Takoradi Metropolis of Ghana: The Mediating Effect of Financial Capability. *African Journal of Business & Economic Research*, 19(2), 299–321. DOI: 10.31920/1750-4562/2024/v19n2a13

Archuleta, K. L., Dale, A., & Spann, S. M. (2013). College students and financial distress: Exploring debt, financial satisfaction, and financial anxiety. *Financial Counseling and Planning*, 24(2), 50–62.

Atkinson, A., & Messy, F. A. (2012). Measuring financial literacy: Results of the OECD/International Network on Financial Education (INFE) pilot study. OECD Working Papers on Finance, Insurance and Private Pensions, No. 15. *OECD Publishing.*

Aydin, A. E., & Akben Selcuk, E. (2019). An investigation of financial literacy, money ethics and time preferences among college students: A structural equation model. *International Journal of Bank Marketing, 37*(3), 880-900. *Scopus.* Advance online publication. DOI: 10.1108/IJBM-05-2018-0120

Barrafrem, K., Västfjäll, D., & Tinghög, G. (2024). Financial Homo Ignorans: Development and validation of a scale to measure individual differences in financial information ignorance. *Journal of Behavioral and Experimental Finance*, 42, 100936. DOI: 10.1016/j.jbef.2024.100936

Carlson, M. B., Nelson, J. S., & Skimmyhorn, W. L. (2016). Military personal finance research. *Handbook of consumer finance research*, 251-264.

CIMA, R. (2018). Identify and understand clients' money scripts: A framework for using the KMSI-R. *Journal of Financial Planning*, 31(3), 46–55.

Clark, R., Lusardi, A., & Mitchell, O. S. (2020). Financial fragility during the COVID-19 pandemic. *NBER Working Paper No. 28207.* National Bureau of Economic Research.

Damayanti, R., Al-Shami, S. S. A., Bin Rahim, A. B. R., & Marwati, F. S. (2018). Factors that influence financial literacy on small medium enterprises: A literature review. [Scopus.]. *Opción*, 34(86), 1540–1557.

Departamento Nacional de Planeación [DNP]. (2020). Política nacional de inclusión y educación económica y financiera. *Documento CONPES 4005, 1,* 94.

Falahati, L., & Paim, L. H. (2011). Gender differences in financial well-being among college students. *Australian Journal of Basic and Applied Sciences*, 5(9), 1765–1776.

Fernandes, D., Lynch, J. G.Jr, & Netemeyer, R. G. (2014). Financial Literacy, Financial Education, and Downstream Financial Behaviors. *Management Science*, 60(8), 1861–1883. https://www.jstor.org/stable/42919641. DOI: 10.1287/mnsc.2013.1849

Gomber, P., Koch, J.-A., & Siering, M. (2017). Digital Finance and FinTech: Current research and future research directions. *Journal of Business Economics*, 87(5), 537–580. DOI: 10.1007/s11573-017-0852-x

Gutter, M. S., Copur, Z., & Garrison, S. (2010). Which students are more likely to experience financial socialization opportunities? Exploring the relationship between financial behaviors and financial well-being of college students. *Journal of Family and Economic Issues*, 31(3), 387–397. PMID: 20835377

Hasler, A., Lusardi, A., & Oggero, N. (2020). Financial fragility in the US: Evidence and implications. *NBER Working Paper No. 26383*. National Bureau of Economic Research.

Henager, R. (2017). Financial Behaviors of Military Households: The Role of Financial Literacy and Financial Education. *Consumer Interests Annual, 63*.

Henchoz, C., Coste, T., & Wernli, B. (2019). Culture, money attitudes and economic outcomes. *Swiss Journal of Economics and Statistics, 155*(1). *Swiss Journal of Economics and Statistics*, 155(1), 2. Advance online publication. DOI: 10.1186/s41937-019-0028-4

Klontz, B., Britt, S. L., Mentzer, J., & Klontz, T. (2011). Money beliefs and financial behaviors: Development of the Klontz Money Script Inventory. *Journal of Financial Therapy*, 2(1), 1–22. DOI: 10.4148/jft.v2i1.451

Klontz, B., & Klontz, T. (2009). *Mind over money: Overcoming the money disorders that threaten our financial health*. Crown Currency.

Klontz, B. T., & Britt, S. L. (2012). How clients' money scripts predict their financial behaviors. *Journal of Financial Planning*, 25(11), 33–43.

Koe, J. H. N., & Yeoh, K. K. (2021). Factors influencing financial planning for marriage amongst young malaysian couples. *International Journal of Business and Society, 22*(1), 33-54. *Scopus*. Advance online publication. DOI: 10.33736/ijbs.3161.2021

Loux, M. D. (2021). *Strategies to Provide Financial Literacy to Military Students*. Colorado Technical University.

Lusardi, A., & Mitchell, O. S. (2017). How ordinary consumers make complex economic decisions: Financial literacy and retirement readiness. *The Quarterly Journal of Economics*, 122(1), 207–252.

Luther, R. K., Leech, I. E., & Garman, E. T. (1998). The employer's cost for the personal financial management difficulties of workers: Evidence from the US Navy. *Personal Finances and Worker Productivity, 2*(1).

Mehjabeen, M., & Khan, S. N. (2024). Motivating factors affecting formalization of small informal enterprises: Evidence from an emerging economy. *Business Strategy & Development*, 7(3), e426. DOI: 10.1002/bsd2.426

Ozili, P. K. (2018). Impact of digital finance on financial inclusion and stability. *Borsa Istanbul Review*, 18(4), 329–340. DOI: 10.1016/j.bir.2017.12.003

Pandey, A., Ashta, A., Spiegelman, E., & Sutan, A. (2020). Catch them young: Impact of financial socialization, financial literacy and attitude towards money on financial well-being of young adults. *International Journal of Consumer Studies, 44*(6), 531-541. *Scopus*. Advance online publication. DOI: 10.1111/ijcs.12583

Polisetty, A., Lalitha, N., & Singu, H. B. (2021). Factors affecting financial literacy among budding entrepreneurs. *Universal Journal of Accounting and Finance*, 9(5), 1085-1092. *Scopus*. Advance online publication. DOI: 10.13189/ujaf.2021.090518

Riaz, S., Khan, H. H., Sarwar, B., Ahmed, W., Muhammad, N., Reza, S., & Ul Haq, S. M. N. (2022). Influence of Financial Social Agents and Attitude Toward Money on Financial Literacy: The Mediating Role of Financial Self-Efficacy and Moderating Role of Mindfulness. *SAGE Open, 12*(3). *SAGE Open*, 12(3). Advance online publication. DOI: 10.1177/21582440221117140

Sam, P. A., Frimpong, S., & Kendie, S. (2022). Personal finance behaviour: A reasoned action approach. *International Journal of Social Economics*, 49(8), 1119–1131. DOI: 10.1108/IJSE-02-2021-0097

Sari, D. E., Narimo, S., & Saputra, R. C. (2020). The effect of financial literacy and pocket money on consumer behavior of universitas muhammadiyah surakarta (Ums) students. [Scopus.]. *International Journal of Scientific and Technology Research*, 9(2), 4235–4237.

Shim, S., Barber, B. L., Card, N. A., Xiao, J. J., & Serido, J. (2010). Financial socialization of first-year college students: The roles of parents, work, and education. *Journal of Youth and Adolescence*, 39(12), 1457–1470. DOI: 10.1007/s10964-009-9432-x PMID: 20938727

Smaliukiene, R., & Bekesiene, S. (2020). Towards sustainable human resources: How generational differences impact subjective wellbeing in the military? *Sustainability (Basel)*, 12(23), 10016. DOI: 10.3390/su122310016

Strömbäck, C., Lind, T., Skagerlund, K., Västfjäll, D., & Tinghög, G. (2017). Does self-control predict financial behavior and financial well-being? *Journal of Behavioral and Experimental Finance*, 14, 30–38. DOI: 10.1016/j.jbef.2017.04.002

Susilowati, N., & Latifah, L. (2017). College student financial behavior: An empirical study on the mediating effect of attitude toward money. *Advanced Science Letters*, 23(8), 7468-7472. *Scopus*. Advance online publication. DOI: 10.1166/asl.2017.9500

Tanyushcheva, N. Y., & Kunitsyna, N. N. (2021). Assessment of public opinion on compliance with anti-cleaning legislation. *Monitoring Obshchestvennogo Mneniya: Ekonomicheskie i Sotsial'nye Peremeny*, 2, 213-233. *Scopus*. Advance online publication. DOI: 10.14515/monitoring.2021.2.1730

Thaler, R. H. (2016). Behavioral economics: Past, present, and future. *The American Economic Review*, 106(7), 1577–1600. DOI: 10.1257/aer.106.7.1577

Thaler, R. H., & Sunstein, C. R. (2008). *Nudge: Improving decisions about health, wealth, and happiness*. Yale University Press.

Varcoe, K. P., Emper, N., & Lees, N. (2002). Working with military audiences to improve financial well-being. *Journal of Family and Consumer Sciences*, 94(1), 33.

Vermeir, I., & Verbeke, W. (2016). Sustainable food consumption among young adults in Belgium: Theory of planned behaviour and the role of confidence and values. *Ecological Economics*, 64(3), 542–553. DOI: 10.1016/j.ecolecon.2007.03.007

Vijaykumar, J. H. (2022). The Association of Financial Socialization with Financial Self-Efficacy and Autonomy: A Study of Young Students in India. *Journal of Family and Economic Issues, 43*(2), 397-414. *Scopus*. Advance online publication. DOI: 10.1007/s10834-021-09797-x

KEY TERMS AND DEFINITIONS

Belief: Condition where some attitudes are learned behavior manifestation, result of some interactions with others (Antonak & Livneh, 1988).

Financial behaviors: Decisions and actions taken by individuals regarding their finances, such as spending, saving, investing, financing and budgeting (Klontz et al., 2011).

Financial distress: Psychological discomfort caused by financial challenges, that already were taking and affect the actual a future condition of well-being, this unease occasionally came from high level of debt, insufficient savings, or financial insecurity (Klontz et al., 2011)

Financial Literacy: Process where individuals acquire a better understanding of basic financial concepts, that are needed to take financial decisions with awareness and these decisions should be informed in terms of risk that would improve their well-being OECD. (2005)

Financial well-being: The state of being financially "happy" with its own financial conditions that gives perception of stable, secure, and able to meet financial goals (Klontz et al., 2011).

Money avoidance: A money script characterized by fear or evading of face off financial issues (Klontz et al., 2011). For further information see table 1.

Money beliefs: Perceptions, attitudes and values that persons have about money and its role in their lives associated with a mindset related to family background and how individuals take decisions (Klontz et al., 2011).

Money scripts: List of inner beliefs and attitudes about money that influence decision-making. And financial behaviors (Klontz et al., 2011). For further information see table 1

Money status: A money script focused on the association of money with self-worth and social status (Klontz et al., 2011). For further information see table 1.

Money vigilance: A money script characterized by careful and aware behavior towards financial decisions and money management (Klontz et al., 2011). For further information see table 1.

Money worship: A money script characterized by the belief that money is the key to success and happiness (Klontz et al., 2011). For further information see table 1.

ENDNOTES

[1]   *1 item was not included in the items "money should be save not spent".

[2]   **Strata** refers to a socioeconomic classification system used in Colombia to categorize residential properties, each strata reflects different levels of income and living condition. The classification ranges from Stratum 1 to 6, with 6 being the highest, which represents a small percentage of the population with the highest income.

Chapter 7
Innovative Strategies for Enhancing SME Competitiveness in Emerging Economies

Muhammad Usman Tariq
https://orcid.org/0000-0002-7605-3040
Abu Dhabi University, UAE University College Cork, Ireland

ABSTRACT

The chapter titled highlights key approaches to enhance the competitiveness of small and medium-sized enterprises (SMEs) in developing countries. SMEs are key economic actors contributing significantly to employment and GDP growth. However, they often need help with unique challenges, including limited access to resources, technology and markets, that can hinder their growth potential. The chapter explores innovative strategies tailored to these contexts and highlights the need for an adaptable framework that considers local conditions and global market trends. It highlights the role of technology, particularly the adoption of digital tools and platforms, in improving operational efficiency, market reach and competitiveness. We also discuss the importance of entrepreneurial ecosystems that foster SMEs' collaboration, knowledge sharing, and skills development. The chapter also covers policy interventions and support mechanisms essential for enabling environments.

INTRODUCTION

Many economies rely heavily on Small and Medium Enterprises (SMEs) to propel growth, employment and innovation. However, SMEs frequently face major obstacles that can obstruct their growth and sustainability in a market that is becoming increasingly competitive and dynamic. Creative solutions are essential to overcome these obstacles. This introduction examines the different creative tactics that SMEs can use to boost growth, increase operational effectiveness, and become more competitive. We hope to shed light on how SMEs can use innovation to prosper in the current fast-paced business environment by looking at real-world examples and describing workable solutions. SME innovation primarily consists of using technology to improve productivity and optimise processes. The achievement of operational effi-

DOI: 10.4018/979-8-3693-4046-2.ch007

ciency depends heavily on digital transformation. For example, cloud computing frees SMEs from costly infrastructure investments required to access powerful computing resources (Manotas & Gonzalez, 2020).

One prominent example is the use of cloud-based accounting software such as Xero or QuickBooks which help small and medium-sized businesses (SMEs) automate repetitive tasks, work with remote teams and manage their finances in real time. In addition to lowering operating expenses, this study also uses data analytics to offer insightful information that helps companies make wise decisions. The use of agile approaches is another cutting-edge strategy for enhancing responsiveness and project management. Originally created for software development, agile practices have shown advantages in several sectors. To improve collaboration, expedite project delivery, and adjust to evolving client demands, small design firms and marketing agencies have effectively adopted agile frameworks such as scrum. SMEs can remain adaptable and responsive to market demands by segmenting their projects into manageable sprints and continuously iterating based on feedback. Ultimately, this results in better outcomes and higher client satisfaction. SMEs can profit from novel business models that challenge established norms and technological breakthroughs (Sarwar and Atif, 2023).

Subscription-based services are one such model that boosts customer loyalty and offers a consistent revenue stream. Businesses that provide customers with convenience and tailored experiences, such as Netflix and the Dollar Shave Club, have proven the viability of this business model. Subscription models are used by SMEs across a range of industries, including professional services and food delivery, to establish a steady clientele and steady income streams. This strategy helps SMEs retain customers, while facilitating more efficient operations. Another creative tactic that SMEs can use to spur growth is collaboration and partnership. SMEs can gain access to new market resources and technologies by forming strategic alliances with other companies' academic institutions and industry experts. For example, smaller tech startups frequently work with larger corporations to take advantage of their knowledge resources and funding sources. One effective example is the collaboration between pharmaceutical companies and small biotech businesses, where the latter benefits from novel discoveries and provides resources for research and development. Through these partnerships, SMEs can overcome their resource constraints and grow quickly. SMEs can also be used to improve customer experiences and set themselves apart from rivals (Manotas & Gonzalez, 2020).

In the current market, personalisation and customer-centric strategies are crucial. For instance, small retail companies utilise data-driven insights to better target their marketing campaigns, develop customised offers, and enhance client relationships. Brand loyalty and strong customer relationships have been fostered by companies such as Glossier which have successfully implemented direct-to-consumer models and made use of social media. SMEs can create a devoted clientele and differentiate themselves in a competitive market by concentrating on providing outstanding customer experiences. In summary, creativity is essential if SMEs successfully negotiate the intricacies of contemporary business settings. SMEs can stay ahead of competition, increasing operational efficiency and spur growth by embracing technology agile methodologies, disruptive business models, strategic partnerships, and customer-centric approaches. Adopting and iteratively improving these cutting-edge tactics will be essential to SMEs' long-term success and sustainability, as the business environment changes (Sarwar and Atif, 2023).

Small- and medium-sized enterprises (SMEs) are key drivers of economic growth and development in emerging markets, playing a key role in creating jobs and fostering innovation and entrepreneurship. This chapter provides an overview of the SME landscape in emerging markets, discusses their role in economic development, and examines the unique challenges and opportunities faced by these enterprises. SMEs represent the majority of enterprises in emerging markets and contribute significantly to the GDP and employment. For example, in countries such as India and Brazil, SMEs account for a large proportion of employment and play a central role in diversifying economic activity across various sectors such as manufacturing, services, agriculture, and technology (World Bank, 2023). These enterprises often form the backbone of local economies, especially in rural areas, where larger enterprises have a limited presence. The role of SMEs in economic development goes beyond simply contributing to GDP. These companies are flexible and innovative, and often introduce new products and services that meet local market needs. This dynamic not only increases economic resilience, but also contributes to technological advancement and industrial modernisation in emerging markets (IMF, 2022). In Vietnam, SMEs in the technology sector have contributed significantly to the country's digital transformation. Companies such as the FPT Corporation have not only expanded economic opportunities, but also increased Vietnam's global competitiveness in software development and IT services (Nguyen & Pham, 2021).

Despite their significant contributions, SMEs in emerging markets face several challenges that impede growth and competitiveness. These challenges include a lack of access to finance, regulatory complexity, infrastructure deficits, and skill shortages (OECD, 2021). Access to finance remains a significant barrier for SMEs in the emerging markets. A lack of collateral or credit history means that SMEs are often viewed as risky investments in traditional banking systems, resulting in limited access to affordable credit (Marovic and Islam, 2021).

In addition, informal sources of finance, when available, often have high interest rates and limited scalability. For example, despite efforts to improve financial inclusion In Nigeria, SMEs have struggled to access finance. The lack of collateral and high interest rates from informal lenders limits their ability to invest in technology and expand their businesses (Okafor & Eze, 2023). Regulatory frameworks in emerging markets are complex and inconsistent, posing significant challenges to SMEs. Compliance costs, bureaucratic delays, and political uncertainty inhibit entrepreneurial efforts and investments (UNDP, 2020). These regulatory hurdles disproportionately affect SMEs that lack the resources to effectively address legal complexities. In Brazil, SMEs in the manufacturing sector face regulatory challenges related to environmental compliance and taxation (Akomea and Osei, 2023).

Complex tax laws and frequent changes in regulations impose additional costs and administrative burdens on these businesses (Silva & Santos, 2022). The lack of infrastructure also affects the competitiveness of SMEs in emerging markets. Inadequate transport networks, unreliable electricity supplies, and limited access to technological infrastructure increase operational costs and reduce efficiency (Asian Development Bank, 2021). These challenges are particularly acute in rural areas, where infrastructure development lags that of urban centres. In Bangladesh, SMEs in the textile industry face logistical challenges owing to poor transport infrastructure, affecting their ability to meet export demand and become globally competitive (Ahmed et al., 2023). Despite these challenges, SMEs in emerging markets have unique opportunities to drive growth and sustainability. Rapid urbanisation, a growing middle-class consumer market, and increasing digital connectivity are creating new opportunities for market expansion and innovation (UNCTAD, 2021).

Technological advances such as digital platforms and e-commerce enable SMEs to reach a wider customer base and streamline their operations. The rise of e-commerce platforms in Southeast Asia has revolutionised market access for SMEs. Companies, such as Shopee and Lazada, have provided SMEs with digital storefronts that facilitate direct-to-consumer sales and improve market visibility (UNCTAD, 2022). Furthermore, to realise the full potential of SMEs in emerging markets, supportive policies to increase SME competitiveness, improve access to finance through innovative financing solutions, and invest in infrastructure development are essential (IFC, 2023). Governments and international organisations play a key role in creating an environment that supports SME growth and entrepreneurship. SMEs in emerging markets play a key role in economic development through job creation, innovation, and diversification. Although SMEs face significant challenges such as access to finance, regulatory hurdles, and infrastructure deficits, they also benefit from the unique opportunities presented by digital transformation and growing consumer markets. Addressing these challenges requires concerted efforts by policymakers, financial institutions, and the private sector to create an enabling environment for SMEs to thrive and contribute to sustainable economic growth (Akomea and Osei, 2023).

BACKGROUND

Organizations must perform the crucial task of talent acquisition to recruit and maintain talent. Artificial intelligence (AI) has become a potent ally in this area in recent years, providing several advantages that boost the effectiveness of hiring procedures and enhance the applicant's experience. AI also adds the capacity for data-driven decision making and can help advance diversity and inclusion in recruiting procedures. In this section, we explore the essential advantages of AI for hiring. Adopting new technologies and embracing digital transformation have become essential tactics to increase the competitiveness and sustainability of small and medium-sized enterprises (SMEs). Although digital tools and platforms play a significant role in improving the operational effectiveness market reach and overall competitiveness, it is unclear from the chapters discussion whether they concentrate on digital tools in particular or on more general strategies for SME competitiveness. With the goal of addressing these topics in-depth, this assessment demonstrates how digital innovations can help SMEs grow and gain strategic advantage. Owing to their substantial increase in operational efficiency, digital technologies are essential for helping SMEs become more competitive. SMEs can obtain computing power and storage capacity on demand owing to cloud computing which is a prime example. Large hardware investments and continuous IT maintenance expenses were eliminated using this on-demand approach. SMEs can scale their operations more effectively in response to seasonal variations and market demands by utilizing cloud services. To maximize resource allocation and operational agility, for example KPMG (2023) emphasizes how cloud computing gives SMEs the freedom to modify their infrastructure in response to their immediate needs.

By overcoming geographic barriers that previously prevented SMEs from accessing international markets, digital platforms and e-commerce solutions helped them reach a wider audience. By connecting SMEs with customers outside their local areas through online marketplaces, they can expand their clientele and reduce their dependency on conventional brick-and-mortar stores. For instance, local artisans and SMEs can reach a worldwide consumer base through the Indian e-commerce platform Craftsvilla. Artists can exhibit and market their handcrafted goods globally via the Craftsvilla digital marketplace, greatly increasing their market reach and revenue (Craftsvilla 2020).

These platforms serve as examples of how digital tools that increase market access can boost visibility and encourage company growth. Digital marketing strategies are essential for increasing SMEs competitiveness and broadening their market reach. SME brand awareness and customer acquisition are enhanced by strategies such as search engine optimization (SEO), social media marketing, and targeted online advertising. These tactics work especially well for targeting niche markets and fostering individualized interactions that increase brand loyalty. According to Chaffey and Ellis-Chadwick (2021), digital marketing tools afford SMEs an affordable means of engaging with their customers, enabling them to compete with larger companies.

Using social media and digital marketing to attract clients dissatisfied with traditional banking services, Nubank transformed the Brazilian financial industry. Owing to its easy-to-use app and customer-focused philosophy, Nubank has become the top digital bank in Brazil and has experienced rapid growth (Nubank 2023). Adopting new technologies is not enough for a digital transformation to be successful; a thorough redesign of business procedures and an innovative culture is also necessary. Several case studies have demonstrated how SMEs can use digital transformation to gain a competitive edge and sustain growth. For example, the provision of mobile financial services by Safaricoms M-Pesa revolutionized the financial landscape in Kenya. SMEs in rural areas have benefited most from this innovation which has facilitated transactions, decreased cash-handling costs, and improved financial inclusion (Safaricom 2021). Comparably customers can use SMS or mobile applications to confirm the legitimacy of medications with M-Pedigrees digital solution increasing consumer safety and faith in the medication supply chain (M-Pedigree 2022). These illustrations show how digital solutions can completely change SMEs and emphasize the importance of incorporating technology into corporate strategies. SME competitiveness is further increased by utilizing data-driven insights and cutting-edge technologies such as big data analytics, Internet of Things (IoT), and artificial intelligence (AI). These technological advancements offer SMEs an enhanced comprehension of consumer behavior, operational inadequacies, and market trends, empowering them to make well-informed decisions and consistently enhance their procedures (Accenture 2021).

Furthermore, digital transformation cultivates a culture of responsiveness and agility which is essential for adjusting to the rapidly shifting demands of customers and the dynamics of the market (Deloitte 2022). Finally, the chapter should clarify whether it concentrates on digital tools exclusively or on more comprehensive strategies, even though its goal is to investigate how digital tools and platforms can improve SME competitiveness. Adopting digital technologies is crucial for SMEs seeking to increase market reach, boost operational effectiveness, and achieve long-term growth. Examples of case studies that demonstrate the substantial influence of digital solutions on SMEs are M-Pesa M-Pedigree and CraftsVilla. Businesses can break through conventional barriers to gain new opportunities and prosper in the digital economy by making strategic investments in technology and digital tools (Marovic and Islam 2021).

MARKET EXPANSION STRATEGIES

Market expansion strategies are important for businesses seeking to grow and expand their reach, both domestically and internationally. This expansion often involves identifying new opportunities and implementing effective strategies for entering and competing in these markets. These strategies are particularly important for small and medium-sized enterprises (SMEs), which must overcome challenges such as limited resources, unknown regulatory frameworks, and intense competition. In this discussion, we examine different approaches to market expansion and provide examples and insights into how businesses can effectively enter new markets (Alkahtani and Khan, 2020). Identifying new market opportunities is the first step toward market expansion. This requires thorough market research and analysis to uncover potential gaps, unmet needs, or underserved segments (Tariq, 2024).

For example, a software development company specializing in educational tools expects a growing demand for digital learning platforms in emerging markets, where the traditional education infrastructure is limited (Akpan & Adebisi, 2022). When companies recognize these opportunities, they can tailor their products and services to meet their specific market needs. A Silicon Valley-based technology startup conducted extensive market research and identified Southeast Asia as an emerging market for fintech solutions. Given the increasing penetration of smartphones and acceptance of digital payments in the region, the company is developing a mobile payment app aligned with local preferences and regulatory requirements. This strategic move allows startups to benefit from the growing demand for convenient and secure digital payment solutions in the region (Akomea & Osei, 2023).

Entering foreign markets can be difficult for SMEs because of their limited resources and lower brand recognition compared to larger companies (Tariq, 2024). However, strategic approaches can help SMEs overcome these challenges and gain a foothold in international markets. These strategies often include market-entry modes, partnerships, product/service customization, and cultural localization. An Italian family-owned winery wants to expand its presence in the United States. (Akpan & Adebisi, 2022). Rather than entering the market directly on their own, which can be expensive and risky, wineries form sales partnerships with local importers specializing in fine European wines. The partnerships not only give Italian SMEs access to established distribution channels but also benefit from importers' knowledge of local market preferences and regulations. By adopting a marketing strategy that highlights wine's origin and quality, wineries can successfully appeal to American consumers seeking authentic European wine (Akpan & Adebisi, 2022). The implementation of market expansion strategies varies depending on factors, such as market characteristics, industry trends, and company resources. These strategies range from geographic expansion to diversifying product offerings to leveraging digital platforms for a global reach (Le and Ikram, 2022). A multinational consumer goods company has decided to expand its presence in Africa by targeting a growing middle-class population. Through a series of strategic acquisitions of local brands known for organic and natural products, the company has strengthened its portfolio to cater to evolving consumer preferences for sustainable and health-conscious products (Edeh and Ramos, 2020).

By combining global expertise in product development and sales with local market knowledge gained through acquired brands, the company has successfully expanded its market share in several African countries. Despite the potential benefits of market expansion, companies face a variety of challenges that must be carefully addressed. These challenges include cultural differences, regulatory complexities, competitive pressures, and operational logistics. A successful market expansion strategy requires thorough risk assessment, adaptation to local conditions, and the flexibility to respond to changing market conditions. A European fashion retailer plans to enter the Asian market starting with China (Manotas & Gonzalez, 2020).

The brand's European collections have been well received for their high fashion appeal, but retailers face the challenge of adapting size standards and design aesthetics to Asian consumers' preferences. By collaborating with local designers and influencers to create a unique collection tailored to Asian tastes, retailers can not only overcome cultural barriers but also increase the brand's resonance with its target group (Caballero, 2021). This strategic adjustment enables retailers to effectively compete with local and international fashion brands operating in the region. In summary, market expansion strategies are important for companies seeking growth opportunities, both at home and abroad. Identifying new market opportunities and implementing effective strategies can help companies leverage their strengths to overcome challenges and achieve sustainable growth. Strategic market entry, adaptation to local conditions, and leveraging partnerships are crucial for successful expansion into foreign markets, especially for small and medium-sized enterprises. As global markets continue to evolve, companies must maintain a flexible and innovative approach to capitalize on new opportunities and gain a competitive advantage (Edeh & Ramos, 2020).

Talent Management for Competitive Advantage

Talent management plays a key role in shaping the competitive advantage of companies, especially small- and medium-sized enterprises (SMEs), by focusing on attracting, retaining, and developing talented employees. This holistic approach not only improves productivity but also fosters innovation and agility, which are essential for sustainable growth in dynamic market environments.

Attracting talent

Attracting the best starts by creating a compelling employer brand that resonates with the potential employees. For SMEs, showcasing unique aspects such as entrepreneurial spirit, growth opportunities, and a collaborative work environment can attract candidates seeking career opportunities and meaningful work experience. Effective recruitment strategies often involve leveraging digital platforms, networking events, and employee referrals to create diverse candidate pools. Technology startups in competitive markets such as Silicon Valley focus on innovative culture and flexible work arrangements to attract software engineers and developers. By highlighting its commitment to cutting-edge technology and collaborative working environments, the startup appeals to tech-savvy professionals seeking opportunities to contribute to impactful projects and drive innovation in dynamic environments. This strategic positioning helps startups attract top talent and align themselves with their growth goals in the competitive technology industry (Manotas and Gonzalez, 2020).

Talent Retention

Talent retention is equally important for small and medium-sized businesses that want to maintain continuity and avoid the costs associated with high turnover. Effective retention strategies include competitive salaries and benefits, career development opportunities, mentoring programs, and a supportive work-life balance. Creating a positive work culture in which employees feel valued and recognized for their contributions can increase retention. A leading marketing agency invests in individual employee career development plans including training workshops and certifications for digital marketing trends. By providing opportunities for upskilling and professional growth, the agency retains talented marketing staff and strengthens its ability to deliver innovative marketing strategies to clients. The collaborative and inclusive culture cultivated within the agency fosters loyalty among employees who value continuous learning and career development (Caballero, 2021).

Talent Development

Talent development involves developing the skills and capabilities of employees to meet the current and future needs of the organization. Small businesses can implement development initiatives such as mentorship programs, cross-functional projects, and leadership training to prepare promising talent for leadership positions. By investing in talent development, companies can increase their employee engagement and build a pool of skilled professionals that can drive innovation and adaptability. An architectural firm specializing in sustainable design has integrated a mentorship program in which young architects work on eco-friendly projects with experienced partners (Naradda and Rajapakshe, 2020). Through hands-on experience and mentorship from experienced professionals, budding architects can gain valuable insights into sustainable design principles and project management skills. This structured development approach not only improves employees' technical expertise but also prepares them for leadership positions within the company, contributing to the firm's reputation as a leader in sustainable architecture (Caballero, 2021).

Company culture and innovation

Company culture plays a central role in driving innovation and agility in SMEs. A culture that encourages open communication, risk taking, and continuous improvement allows employees to try new ideas and approaches. Encouraging diversity in thinking and a growth mindset allows companies to create a dynamic work environment in which innovation can thrive. Fintech startups value transparency and collaboration, encouraging employees to participate in brainstorming sessions and cross-functional teams to develop innovative financial solutions. By fostering a culture of creativity and inclusivity, startups accelerate their product development cycles and attract talent who want to contribute to breakthrough innovations in financial technology. This collaborative culture makes the startup agile in responding to market trends and customer needs, positioning it as a disruptive force in a competitive fintech environment (Manotas and Gonzalez, 2020).

Agility and Adaptability

In today's rapidly changing business environment, agility and adaptability are key for SMEs to navigate uncertainties and capitalize on new opportunities. Talent management practices that emphasize flexibility, rapid decision-making, and cross-functional collaboration enable companies to respond quickly to market shifts and customer demands. By enabling employees to embrace change and learn from setbacks, SMEs can foster a resilient culture that delivers long-term competitive advantage. A logistics company faces challenges as global supply chains are disrupted by geopolitical events (Farida and Setiawan, 2022). The company has improved its operational resilience by implementing an agile workforce planning strategy and cross-functional training for logistics operations and customer service employees. This proactive approach mitigates the risks associated with supply chain disruptions and strengthens employee engagement by providing opportunities for diversification of skills and career growth. Thus, a company can continue to adapt to market fluctuations and maintain its competitive advantage in the logistics industry (Caballero, 2021). Effective talent management is essential for SMEs to gain competitive advantage by attracting, retaining, and developing qualified employees. By fostering a positive company culture that prioritizes innovation, agility, and talent development, SMEs can build a motivated workforce that drives sustainable growth and adaptation to dynamic market environments. By leveraging talent management best practices, companies can position themselves as employers of choice and strategic leaders in their respective industries, positioning them for long-term success and resilience in the face of evolving challenges (Safari and Balicevac, 2022).

Leveraging Strategic Partnerships and Alliances

Leveraging strategic partnerships and alliances is an important strategy for SMEs (small and medium-sized enterprises) that want to improve their market position, access resources, and achieve sustainable growth. These partnerships involve collaborations with other companies, academic institutions, or organizations that have complementary strengths and common goals. By pooling resources, expertise, and networks, SMEs can leverage strategic alliances to expand their market reach, innovate more effectively, and minimize the risks associated with limited scale and resources. Forming strategic partnerships to improve SMEs' market position and access to resources offers several benefits that can have a significant impact on their market position and operating capabilities. First, partnerships allow SMEs to access resources and skills that would otherwise be out of reach, owing to financial constraints or limited in-house expertise. This includes access to the technology, expertise, distribution channels, and financing options offered by larger companies and research institutes. A biotech startup specializing in personalized medicine enters a strategic partnership with a pharmaceutical company known for its extensive R&D capabilities (Caballero, 2021). This alliance provides start-up access to the pharmaceutical company's state-of-the-art laboratories, regulatory expertise, and distribution networks. This partnership accelerates the development and commercialization of new drug therapies and strengthens startups' credibility and market visibility in the healthcare industry. Strategic partnerships allow SMEs to combine complementary strengths and expand their competitive advantages. This could involve partnering with companies with expertise at different stages of the value chain, or with complementary technologies. By leveraging their strengths, SMBs can offer more comprehensive solutions to their customers and differentiate themselves from competitors. An IT service company specializing in cybersecurity has partnered with a cloud computing provider to offer an integrated cybersecurity solution for SMBs (Farida & Setiawan, 2022).

IT services companies focus on threat detection and incident response, whereas cloud providers offer secure hosting and data management services. Together, they build a robust cybersecurity platform that meets the evolving needs of SMBs who want to protect their digital assets from cyber threats. This strategic partnership not only expands service offerings but also improves competitiveness in the IT security field (Sarwar & Atif, 2023). Strategic partnerships facilitate market entry into new geographic regions and industries. For SMEs looking to expand internationally, working with local companies and traders familiar with the market and regulatory environment can accelerate market penetration and reduce market-entry risks. A European fashion boutique partner with a local Asian retailer enters the Asian market. The dealer has established relationships with retail chains and understands consumer preferences in the region (Manotas & Gonzalez, 2020). This partnership provides boutique access to a network of retailers and insights into the local market, allowing them to effectively introduce European fashion brands to Asian consumers. This collaborative approach not only minimizes logistical challenges, but also increases brand awareness and sales growth in new geographic markets. Additionally, forming strategic partnerships can help SMEs navigate industry disruptions and technological advances more effectively. Working with innovative start-ups and research institutes helps SMEs remain at the top of emerging trends and introduce new technologies that drive operational efficiency and product innovation. Renewable energy start-ups are partnering with research universities specializing in sustainable energy technologies to develop next-generation solar panels. The university provides research facilities, access to scientific expertise, and funding opportunities through government grants (Manotas and Gonzalez, 2020). Through this partnership, the start-up will accelerate the development of highly efficient solar modules and establish itself as a leading player in the renewable energy sector. The partnership not only strengthens the research capabilities of both companies, but also gives them a competitive advantage in a rapidly evolving market around clean energy solutions (Farida & Setiawan, 2022). In summary, forming strategic partnerships allows SMEs to access resources, improve their market position, and capitalize on growth opportunities that would be difficult to achieve alone. Working with partners with complementary strengths and strategic goals helps SMEs drive innovation, expand their market reach, and remain competitive in a dynamic business environment.

Successful collaboration between SMEs and large corporations or academic institutions: Successful collaboration between SMEs and large corporations or academic institutions demonstrates the transformative effect of strategic partnerships on business growth and innovation. These collaborations often leverage each partner's unique capabilities to achieve common goals and create value for customers and stakeholders (Anwar and Shah, 2021).

IBM and Box

IBM, a global technology leader, has partnered with Box, a cloud content management platform, to leverage IBM's AI and machine learning capabilities in Box's cloud storage and collaboration tools. The goal of this collaboration is to improve data security, optimize workflow automation, and increase productivity for enterprise customers. By combining IBM's cognitive computing expertise with Box's intuitive cloud platform, these two companies can now offer comprehensive solutions that meet the evolving needs of businesses in a digital-first environment (Alkahtani and Khan, 2020).

Google and Shopify

Google, known for its digital advertising and cloud computing services, has partnered with Shopify, a leading e-commerce platform for small and medium-sized businesses. This partnership brings together Google's advertising tools and Shopify's e-commerce capabilities, enabling small businesses to reach a wider audience and increase their online sales. The partnership seamlessly integrates Google marketing insights and analytics into Shopify's merchant solutions, helping small businesses optimize their online presence and efficiently scale their business (Storz & Zou, 2022).

Siemens and Local Motors

Global technology group Siemens collaborated with Local Motors, a pioneer in autonomous vehicle development and additive manufacturing. This partnership focused on advancing digital manufacturing technologies and accelerating the production of 3D printed electric vehicles. By leveraging Siemens' expertise in industrial automation and digitalization and Local Motors' innovative vehicle design capabilities, the partnership aimed to disrupt the automotive industry by introducing sustainable and adaptable mobility solutions to urban environments (Storz & Zou, 2022).

Johnson and Johnson Innovation and Biotech Startups

Johnson and Johnson Innovation, the venture capital arm of healthcare giant Johnson and Johnson, works with numerous biotech startups worldwide to innovate and accelerate drugs, medical devices, and consumer health products. Through strategic investments, partnerships, and mentorship programs, Johnson and Johnson's innovation supports early-stage biotech companies in advancing breakthrough therapies and technologies. These collaborations not only advance scientific discovery and clinical development but also expand Johnson & Johnson's portfolio of innovative healthcare solutions for global markets (Farida & Setiawan, 2022).

Toyota and Tesla

Toyota, a leading automaker, joined Tesla, a pioneer in electric mobility, to develop and manufacture electric vehicles and battery technology. The purpose of the partnership was to combine Toyota's manufacturing expertise and global sales network with Tesla's innovative electric drive technology. Although the alliance eventually dissolved, it laid the foundation for advances in electric vehicle technology and sustainability efforts in the automotive industry. These examples illustrate how strategic partnerships between small and medium-sized enterprises and large corporations, or academic institutions can create synergies, accelerate innovation, and drive market growth (Anwar and Shah, 2021). By leveraging each partner's strengths and resources, these collaborations create value propositions that meet market needs, increase competitiveness, and capture new opportunities in various industries. In summary, strategic partnerships and alliances are crucial to the growth and competitiveness of SMEs, enabling them to access resources, expand their market reach, and innovate effectively. Working with partners that share complementary strengths and strategic goals enables SMEs to overcome industry challenges, capitalize on growth opportunities, and provide sustainable competitive advantage in a dynamic business environment. These examples demonstrate the transformative impact of successful partnerships between SMEs and larger corporations and highlight the strategic benefits of joint initiatives in driving business innovation and market leadership (Alkahtani & Khan, 2020).

Access to Finance and Sustainable Funding Models

Small and Medium-sized Enterprises (SMEs) need access to financing to succeed and remain viable in emerging economies. These businesses frequently have difficulty obtaining the funding required for growth innovation and managing financial instability. Typical obstacles include insufficient collateral, elevated interest rates, restricted credit data, and inadequate financial infrastructure. The absence of the collateral required by traditional financial institutions is one of the biggest obstacles for SMEs. Many SMEs lack the property or fixed assets required to support their loan applications. This restriction makes it more difficult for them to obtain financing from traditional lenders such as banks. For instance, in Kenya, a small manufacturing company may have trouble obtaining bank loans because it does not have any property or equipment to pledge security. A major additional obstacle is high interest rates (Sarwar and Atif, 2023). The financial stability of SMEs can be significantly affected by these rates which are influenced by variables such as inflation and currency volatility. Owing to high inflation, for example, an SME in Argentina may have to pay exorbitant interest rates which would affect its profitability and ability to reinvest in growth. This makes it difficult for companies to obtain loans. An insufficient credit history is another significant problem. Financial institutions perceive SMEs as high-risk borrowers because they frequently lack complete credit history or sufficient documentation. This condition may make it difficult for SMEs to obtain credit on favorable terms. For example, due to insufficient documentation or a weak credit history, a Nigerian tech startup may refuse a loan or be given unfavorable terms (Edeh & Ramos, 2020).

These problems are exacerbated by weak financial institutions in the emerging markets. Limited financial products and services such as angel investor networks and venture capital restrict the amount of capital available for business development. An underdeveloped financial system in Vietnam, for example, might make it difficult for small agricultural businesses to find investors or financial products that meet their needs. However, a few creative financing options are starting to appear to assist SMEs in overcoming these obstacles. For example, peer-to-peer (P2P) lending platforms eliminate middlemen by directly linking individual investors with small and medium-sized enterprise (SME) borrowers. These platforms facilitate SMEs' access to affordable credit by evaluating their creditworthiness using alternative metrics. For instance, the Funding Circle has made it easier for small businesses across several nations to access capital that traditional banks may not be able to provide through peer-to-peer (P2P) financing. Providers of small loans and financial services to marginalized markets and microfinance institutions (MFIs) also have a significant impact. In contrast to traditional banks, MFIs employ flexible lending strategies such as group lending and nontraditional security types. For instance, Bangladeshi Grameen Bank has been successful in offering microloans to small enterprises, allowing many to flourish despite having little collateral. Impact investment funds present an additional beneficial option by lending money to small- and medium-sized enterprises (SMEs) that tackle environmental or social issues while yielding profits. Agribusiness and renewable energy are two common industries that focus on these funds (Sarwar and Atif, 2023).

To assist SMEs in emerging economies and advance both socially and economically, organizations such as Acumen concentrate on raising impact capital. Venture capital (VC) and private equity (PE) are significant sources of equity funding for high-growth SMEs. These financiers offer the company strategic support to enable them to grow and innovate, as well as substantial funding in return for equity stakes. Sequoia Capital, for instance, has backed several tech startups by giving them the money and know-how required for substantial expansion. SMEs can raise money from the public online through crowdfunding platforms. These platforms engage people who can contribute to, or invest in, business ventures through digital networks. For instance, crowdfunding platforms such as Kickstarter and Indiegogo have assisted numerous small and medium-sized enterprises globally to obtain capital for creative initiatives, thereby transforming members of the community into investors and stakeholders (Safari & Balicevac, 2022). Thus, a multimodal approach is necessary to address the financing challenges faced by SMEs in emerging economies. SME access to the capital required for expansion and growth can be facilitated by utilizing cutting-edge financing options such as impact investing in crowdfunding P2P lending microfinance and venture capital. Furthermore, SMEs can become more competitive and sustainable in the ever-changing emerging market environment by implementing strategies to strengthen their creditworthiness, financial management, and engagement with government programs. SMEs may more successfully navigate the economic realities of emerging economies and attain long-term success by utilizing these funding sources and financial tools (Safari and Balicevac, 2022).

Information and security systems that safeguard small data businesses usually depend on larger corporations for expansion. Data security is crucial in the modern digital world, but many small businesses lack the resources to implement strong security measures on their own. Small businesses can benefit from large companies' advanced information and security systems through partnerships, cloud services, or outsourced solutions. Small businesses can reduce the risk of cyberattacks by complying with legal requirements and protecting sensitive data using these systems (Edeh & Ramos, 2020). To avoid having to invest in their own data centres or security infrastructure, small businesses can take advantage of scalable and secure cloud solutions offered by providers, such as Microsoft Azure and Amazon Web Services (AWS). These services are essential for safeguarding information that is vital to the operation of the business and include threat detection data backups and encryption. These cutting-edge security features are available to small businesses for a fraction of the cost of building and maintaining an internal system. However, although these alliances and programs offer crucial assistance, they are not without difficulties. It can be challenging for entrepreneurs to obtain funding without giving up control over their companies. Giving up equity is necessary for many funding options, including venture capital and angel investments which can reduce the founder's ownership and influence decisions (Caballero, 2021).

Many small business owners are deeply concerned about the trade-off between capital and control because they want to preserve their independence while obtaining the resources they need to expand. Small businesses should consider a few suggestions to manage these difficulties. First, other financing options that do not involve giving up control, such as government grants or revenue-based financing, can supply the required funds while maintaining ownership. Second, forming strategic alliances or joint ventures with big businesses can provide access to cutting-edge resources and systems without requiring direct financial commitments (Caballero, 2021). To improve internal data protection procedures and lessen dependency on external systems, small businesses should also invest in cybersecurity awareness and training. However, these tactics do not remove all restrictions. Barriers, such as the high expense of sophisticated security systems or difficulties in overseeing outside services, can still affect small businesses. Furthermore, if big businesses experience disruptions or hacks, small businesses may be at risk of over-reliance on them for data security. Thus, to maintain control while achieving growth, small businesses must strike a balance between their reliance on external systems and efforts to fortify their internal security procedures and investigate a variety of funding options.

Policy Recommendations for Supporting SME Competitiveness

Promoting the competitiveness of SMEs by applying appropriate policies and measures can remain an important means of enhancing economic development, employment opportunities, and technological advancement in both developed and developing countries (Anwar and Shah, 2021). Every businessperson knows that SMEs make up a substantial percentage of companies around the world, provide employment opportunities, and boost GDP and the economy in general. However, they are subject to numerous constraints that limit their growth, such as finance, regulatory mechanisms, markets, and a shortage of skilled personnel. Thus, reform solutions targeting the creation of a favorable environment for the development of SMEs can meet the above-mentioned challenges and unlock the potential of SMEs for sustainable development (Edeh & Ramos, 2020).

Access to Finance

Thus, strengthening SMEs' access to financing is deemed the primary requirement. Some actions could and should be undertaken here, including forming specific institutions for financing SME's, extending guarantees for loans, venturing into capital, and Angel Investment networks. In addition, increasing the awareness of SMEs regarding financing and standardising loan application procedures can help develop better connections between small businesses and capital to expand, innovate, and reinvest in employees (Manotas & Gonzalez, 2020).

Reducing regulatory burden

Removing excessive legislation and optimizing administrative requirements are critical tasks for improving SMEs' positions. The government can revise certain policies by making it easier to register businesses, ensure consistent policies on licensure, and implement analyses that would determine the effectiveness of some regulations on small businesses. Moreover, depending on the sector, increasing the digital presence for compliance with regulations and offering rewards for compliance can improve operational performance and regulatory compliance (Alkahtani and Khan, 2020).

Facilitating Market Access

The intensification of market access for SME's entails the removal of trade barriers, encouragement of export initialization programmers, and creation of opportunities for integration into global value chains. Policymakers can offer trade preferences to partners, facilitate export credits and guarantees, and encourage export promotion practices, such as exporting SME's participation in fairs and exhibitions abroad. Furthermore, the creation of export promotion agencies and trade facilitation centers can help type-2 SMEs gather export-related information and coordinate to enter international markets (Anwar & Shah, 2021).

Technology Adoption

Promoting innovation and use of technology is essential for success to Small and Medium Enterprises in the current generation. For R&D, policymakers should offer grant funding and tax credits and promote collaborative project initiatives between SMEs, research facilities, and expansive organisations. Investing in the growth of infrastructure, especially digital ones, has the potential to encourage the development of skills training programs to support SMEs' integration into the digital economy, the development of appropriate clusters, and the support of incubators targeting technological startups (Manotas & Gonzalez, 2020).

Vocational Training Progammes

One of the significant focuses of SMEs is their skill gap and attempts to improve human capital. This makes it easier for policymakers to encourage and support vocational training programs, apprenticeships, and relationships with learning institutions to ensure that the workforce is adequately trained in the new market. Moreover, deploying lifelong learning, upskilling for Digital Literacy, and Entrepreneurship can enhance human capital through constant learning development for a skilled and appropriate talent pool to support SMEs in various sectors (Anand & Narula, 2021).

Entrepreneurship and SME Development

To cultivate an environment for SMEs and business development, steps must be taken starting from encouraging the spirit of entrepreneurship. Public policies can create physical space and funding opportunities to encourage post-startup support, mentorship, networking, and access to capital for new entrepreneurs. Awareness campaigns, annual SME awards, and recognition programs have been suggested to help foster entrepreneurial culture within organizations and thus promote fresh ideas for the growth of SMEs in Kenya (Manotas & Gonzalez, 2020).

Enhances Access to Finance

Regarding suggestions to enhance SME financing, the first is to encourage the formation of more targeted SME financing institutions for novel financial products. This comprises microfinance banks' non-bank institutions, venture capitalists' funds, and angel funding networks that support SMEs. Specific measures that can help increase the effectiveness of finance management and access to capital include the application of credit guarantee schemes and strengthening efforts to ensure proper financial literacy among SMEs (Anand and Narula, 2021).

Simplified regulatory frameworks

Easing the process of business registration and reducing bureaucracy in costs may help decrease the compliance expenses. The government should encourage the use of the Internet when submitting documents to legal bodies, harmonize the approach to issuing licenses across regions, and conduct periodic audits to remove barriers that hinder the functioning of organizations (Manotas & Gonzalez, 2020).

Promote exports and market access

To enhance SME access to a particular foreign market, policymakers need to formulate trade policies involving access to export markets, the introduction of trade credit facilities for export insurance services, and export development services. The expansion of trade promotion agencies and assistance to SMEs in the procurement of certifications and licenses in foreign markets makes them competitive at the international level (Edeh & Ramos, 2020).

Stimulates Innovation and Technology Adoption

Governments should encourage SMEs to increase their R&D intensity through grant, tax relief, and partner funding. Promoting technological innovation by supporting technology transfer and initiatives, collaborating between SMEs and research institutions, and developing digital infrastructure can drive the growth in competitiveness among SMEs in emerging industries.

Invest for skill development

Eliminating the gaps in matches between the demand and supply of skills and strengthening capabilities of workers in the labor market remain critical for policymakers, and thus need to strengthen vocational training, apprenticeship, and continuing education and training systems. Of particular interest is the conjoining of initiatives that engage educational institutions in the design of curricula tailored to the needs of modern industries and call for increasing the availability of digital skills training that would provide SME with a pool of a workforce capable of fostering innovation and growth (Anwar & Shah, 2021).

Support Entrepreneurship Ecosystems

Developing an environment for entrepreneurship requires fostering incubation centers, accelerators, and other types of hubs that will help start-ups obtain mentorship, networking, and funding solutions. The government should raise public awareness of the importance of entrepreneurship, encourage innovation through the identification of successful SMEs and entrepreneurs, and organize forums in which information and knowledge are freely shared among stakeholders (Anwar & Shah, 2021). Accordingly, the policy implications for improving the competitive environment and boosting SME development in emerging economies include improving SME financial access; reducing regulatory constraints; expediting access to markets; embracing innovation, technology, and skills development; and entrepreneurship infrastructure. Through these measures, there is no doubt that policymakers will be preparing the right environment for SMEs to unlock their growth potential and thereby foster economic development and more importantly unlocking the potential of small business as key drivers of innovation, employment and sustainable prosperity within these countries (Alkahtani & Khan, 2020).

Future Trends and Emerging Opportunities

The main reason SMEs need to look forward to and practice dynamic planning is to be ready for change and capture opportunities as they emerge. Many origins influence businesses, such as shifts in the global economy, technology, and sustainability concerns, which have created new opportunities for SMEs.

Digital Transformation

This shift towards digital transformation is strong and adds pressure to changing industries across the globe. Today, organizations that use modern technologies, such as artificial intelligence, machine learning, big data and data analytics, automation, and cognition, can have competitive advantages by optimising their business activities, managing client interactions, and implementing new strategies, methods, and models. Consider the opportunity to expand into foreign markets and effectively compete with large online stores. Simultaneously, consumers and businesses actively turn to digital solutions and services. SMEs need to become digital to respond to new market requirements and effectively use digital tools to develop and create a presence in foreign markets (Anand & Narula, 2021).

Shift Towards e-commerce and online platforms

The availability of e-shops and Internet platforms is also a huge opportunity for SMEs to expand to foreign locations and spread risks and revenue. Given the developments in the trend towards buying products and services through virtual stores and social networks, these organizations can have a wider market reach, fewer location constraints, and better management of their production and demand. Therefore, SMEs can leverage Internet comical sales and next-generation consumer routines by enhancing e-commerce functionalities, using digital media promotions, and developing customer experience strategies (Anwar & Shah, 2021).

Focus on sustainability and green technology

Lifestyle changes, specifically environmental consciousness and several regulatory authorities, have put high pressure on the use of recyclable products and services. In these industries, especially those that embrace sustainability in products and processes through the development of green technologies, renewable energy solutions, and sustainable manufacturing practices, the benefits of innovation include differentiation of industrial products and service portfolios, attracting environmentally conscious consumers, and compliance with emerging complex markets and regulatory standards. The implementation of sustainability in business not only positively impacts corporate image and its sustainable benefits but also provides an opportunity to improve the bottom line and sustainable business returns in the face of sustainable global change (Anand & Narula, 2021).

Global economic shift and market diversification

Market conditions, such as demographic structure alterations, political instability, and changes in trade policies, are potential risks to the same industrial efficiencies and opportunities to look for amines for the same markets. It is strategically important for SMEs to seek new export opportunities, enter into satisfactory partnerships, and respond to changing customer needs, as all these actions help the former diversify their customer base. Therefore, they can minimize their vulnerability to domestic economic fluctuations. Trade policies, agreements, and international affiliations are crucial for easing global market entry and expansion (Anwar and Shah, 2021).

FUTURE RESEARCH DIRECTIONS

Emphasis could be placed for new research on the application of the following concepts for micro, small and medium-sized enterprises:

AI, IoT, blockchain, and 5G connectivity are among today's worthy technological revolutions that threaten traditional industries and provide SMEs with a way to set up a niche in the market. If SMEs adopt emerging technologies, they can enhance the efficiency of the process or procedure that may take place and provide customized products according to customers' needs. Therefore, entering technology partnerships, adopting digital value chains, and enacting cybersecurity protocols can make SMEs relevant in the evolving digital age and in tune with changing trends to sustain a competitive edge in their respective industries (Anand & Narula, 2021).

Focusing on corporate social responsibility (CSR) and sustainable development goals (SDG) among the population means that SMEs can capture this spirit to drive their operations to associate with new ethical business standards, entice a growing number of consumers who are becoming aware of the effects they leave on society, and contribute positively to the well-being of society. When sustainability is viewed as part of SMEs' operations, they can develop new environmentally friendly products while also supporting the principles of efficient usage of resources and the supply of more sustainable credentials (Edeh & Ramos, 2020).

Activities, such as sustainability certification, green financing, and stakeholder associations, improve credibility and customer loyalty. SMEs can set standards apart from others, as corporations responsible for the environment and growth. To summarize, making predictions, looking for new opportunities, and forecasting future changes are critical. These are the fundamental strategic activities of SMEs that must provide competitive sustainability and growth in the contemporary environment (Farida and Setiawan, 2022).

When challenged by numerous obstacles, from the highly competitive markets to global changes in economic and technological dynamics, sustainability issues, and responsibility for digital transformation, e-commerce platforms, and so on – SMEs have all the chances to remain competitive, overcome problems, and build opportunities. Adopting innovation, agility, and a forward-looking approach will help SMEs uncork opportunity deficiency trends for sustainable success in today's complex global business environment.

CONCLUSION

In conclusion, fostering competitiveness for SMEs in emerging economies needs to be done holistically while seeking to mitigate current challenges and harness future opportunities through change drivers such as emerging global trends and technology adoption. The following treatment has been recognized during this narrative as a significant approach to SMEs' success in changed and complex economies. First, it underlines the strategy of increasing product accessibility through financial access. By creating specific organizations for SME funding; increasing knowledge about the financial market and proper financial management; and offering microfinance and venture capital, authorities can help SMEs invest in growth, development, innovation, and talent promotion. Reducing regulatory compliance costs and easing other bureaucratic procedures are critical for enhancing SME competitiveness (Anwar and Shah, 2021).

Second, there is significant emphasis on utilizing digital transformation capabilities. Companies that adopt digital technologies can improve their internal operational processes, extend their markets through online platforms for sales, and foster innovation in products and consumer relations. Therefore, SME growth can be pegged to investments in training and enhancing digital infrastructure, which makes companies work their way through the complexities of a digital economy to become competitive at both the national and international levels (Haddad & Dwyer, 2020).

However, creating a program culture that supports innovation, and sustainability can only be described as critical for sustaining future growth. As such, SMEs can distinguish themselves when they incorporate sustainability into business methods and implement green technologies as consumers become more sensitive and aware of ethical practices. Innovativeness that comes with R&D innovation, the development of integration between firms and universities, and organizations integrating themselves with other firms or industries assist SMEs to avert new changes in the market and bring new concepts in the business organization that challenge other established business models (Heenkenda, 2022).

Future strategies for SMEs in the global environment and in the ever-evolving new world order depend on adaptiveness and sound planning. This rise in innovation in the digital age shows that shifts in technology, such as artificial intelligence, blockchain, or IoT, will continue to reshape industries and open new opportunities for the growth and development of SMEs. Mitigating the risk factor is paramount to fueling market presence; a resilient supply chain, geopolitics of globalization, and other market opportunities are critical success factors in international trade (Haddad & Dwyer, 2020).

It can be stated that while SMEs in emerging economies operate in various restraining environments, they have several opportunities available only to them due to numerous worldwide tendencies and technological developments. Spiritual: It also triggers a strategic move towards finance, digital transformation, innovation, and sustainability goals, and is used by SME to boost competitiveness and economic growth, as well as to identify several opportunities within the evolving global environment. Embrace change is, therefore, a wise approach that can help SMEs plan and prepare for the challenges of an uncertain environment and build on areas of competitive advantage to create new solutions that fit the customer needs and demands of future markets (Heenkenda, 2022).

REFERENCES

Akomea, S. Y., Agyapong, A., Ampah, G., & Osei, H. V. (2023). Entrepreneurial orientation, sustainability practices and performance of small and medium enterprises: Evidence from an emerging economy. *International Journal of Productivity and Performance Management*, 72(9), 2629–2653. DOI: 10.1108/IJPPM-06-2021-0325

Akpan, I. J., Udoh, E. A. P., & Adebisi, B. (2022). Small business awareness and adoption of state-of-the-art technologies in emerging and developing markets, and lessons from the COVID-19 pandemic. *Journal of Small Business and Entrepreneurship*, 34(2), 123–140. DOI: 10.1080/08276331.2020.1820185

Alkahtani, A., Nordin, N., & Khan, R. U. (2020). Does government support enhance the relation between networking structure and sustainable competitive performance among SMEs? *Journal of Innovation and Entrepreneurship*, 9(1), 1–16. DOI: 10.1186/s13731-020-00127-3

Anand, J., McDermott, G., Mudambi, R., & Narula, R. (2021). Innovation in and from emerging economies: New insights and lessons for international business research. *Journal of International Business Studies*, 52(4), 545–559. DOI: 10.1057/s41267-021-00426-1

Anwar, M., & Shah, S. Z. (2021). Entrepreneurial orientation and generic competitive strategies for emerging SMEs: Financial and nonfinancial performance perspective. *Journal of Public Affairs*, 21(1), e2125. DOI: 10.1002/pa.2125

Caballero-Morales, S. O. (2021). Innovation as recovery strategy for SMEs in emerging economies during the COVID-19 pandemic. *Research in International Business and Finance*, 57, 101396. DOI: 10.1016/j.ribaf.2021.101396 PMID: 33558782

Edeh, J. N., Obodoechi, D. N., & Ramos-Hidalgo, E. (2020). Effects of innovation strategies on export performance: New empirical evidence from developing market firms. *Technological Forecasting and Social Change*, 158, 120167. DOI: 10.1016/j.techfore.2020.120167

Farida, I., & Setiawan, D. (2022). Business strategies and competitive advantage: The role of performance and innovation. *Journal of Open Innovation*, 8(3), 163. DOI: 10.3390/joitmc8030163

Haddad, M. I., Williams, I. A., Hammoud, M. S., & Dwyer, R. J. (2020). Strategies for implementing innovation in small and medium-sized enterprises. *World Journal of Entrepreneurship, Management and Sustainable Development*, 16(1), 12–29. DOI: 10.1108/WJEMSD-05-2019-0032

Heenkenda, H. M. J. C. B., Xu, F., Kulathunga, K. M. M. C. B., & Senevirathne, W. A. R. (2022). The role of innovation capability in enhancing sustainability in SMEs: An emerging economy perspective. *Sustainability (Basel)*, 14(17), 10832. DOI: 10.3390/su141710832

Le, T. T., & Ikram, M. (2022). Do sustainability innovation and firm competitiveness help improve firm performance? Evidence from the SME sector in Vietnam. *Sustainable Production and Consumption*, 29, 588–599. DOI: 10.1016/j.spc.2021.11.008

Le Thanh, T., Huan, N. Q., & Hong, T. T. T. (2021). Determinants for competitiveness in the context of international integration pressure: Case of small and medium enterprises in emerging economy–Vietnam. *Cogent Business & Management*, 8(1), 1893246. DOI: 10.1080/23311975.2021.1893246

Manotas, E. C., & Gonzalez-Perez, M. A. (2020). Internationalization and performance of small and medium-sized enterprises from emerging economies: Using hazards methodology for competitiveness study. *Competitiveness Review*, 30(5), 635–663. DOI: 10.1108/CR-03-2019-0028

Markovic, S., Koporcic, N., Arslanagic-Kalajdzic, M., Kadic-Maglajlic, S., Bagherzadeh, M., & Islam, N. (2021). Business-to-business open innovation: COVID-19 lessons for small and medium-sized enterprises from emerging markets. *Technological Forecasting and Social Change*, 170, 120883. DOI: 10.1016/j.techfore.2021.120883

Naradda Gamage, S. K., Ekanayake, E. M. S., Abeyrathne, G. A. K. N. J., Prasanna, R. P. I. R., Jayasundara, J. M. S. B., & Rajapakshe, P. S. K. (2020). A review of global challenges and survival strategies of small and medium enterprises (SMEs). *Economies*, 8(4), 79. DOI: 10.3390/economies8040079

Safari, A., Saleh, A. S., & Balicevac Al Ismail, V. (2022). Enhancing the export activities of small and medium-sized enterprises in emerging markets. *Journal of Business and Industrial Marketing*, 37(5), 1150–1166. DOI: 10.1108/JBIM-08-2020-0388

Sarwar, H., Aftab, J., Ishaq, M. I., & Atif, M. (2023). Achieving business competitiveness through corporate social responsibility and dynamic capabilities: An empirical evidence from emerging economy. *Journal of Cleaner Production*, 386, 135820. DOI: 10.1016/j.jclepro.2022.135820

Storz, C., Ten Brink, T., & Zou, N. (2022). Innovation in emerging economies: How do university-industry linkages and public procurement matter for small businesses? *Asia Pacific Journal of Management*, 39(4), 1439–1480. DOI: 10.1007/s10490-021-09763-z

Sulistyo, H., & Ayuni, S. (2020). Competitive advantages of SMEs: The roles of innovation capability, entrepreneurial orientation, and social capital. *Contaduría y Administración*, 65(1), 156. DOI: 10.22201/fca.24488410e.2020.1983

Surya, B., Menne, F., Sabhan, H., Suriani, S., Abubakar, H., & Idris, M. (2021). Economic growth, increasing productivity of SMEs, and open innovation. *Journal of Open Innovation*, 7(1), 20. DOI: 10.3390/joitmc7010020

Tariq, M. U. (2024). Emotional intelligence in understanding and influencing consumer behavior. In Musiolik, T., Rodriguez, R., & Kannan, H. (Eds.), *AI impacts in digital consumer behavior* (pp. 56–81). IGI Global., DOI: 10.4018/979-8-3693-1918-5.ch003

Tariq, M. U. (2024). Fintech startups and cryptocurrency in business: Revolutionizing entrepreneurship. In Kankaew, K., Nakpathom, P., Chnitphattana, A., Pitchayadejanant, K., & Kunnapapdeelert, S. (Eds.), *Applying business intelligence and innovation to entrepreneurship* (pp. 106–124). IGI Global., DOI: 10.4018/979-8-3693-1846-1.ch006

Tariq, M. U. (2024). Multidisciplinary service learning in higher education: Concepts, implementation, and impact. In S. Watson (Ed.), *Applications of service learning in higher education* (pp. 1-19). IGI Global. https://doi.org/DOI: 10.4018/979-8-3693-2133-1.ch001

Tariq, M. U. (2024). Enhancing cybersecurity protocols in modern healthcare systems: Strategies and best practices. In Garcia, M., & de Almeida, R. (Eds.), *Transformative approaches to patient literacy and healthcare innovation* (pp. 223–241). IGI Global., DOI: 10.4018/979-8-3693-3661-8.ch011

Tariq, M. U. (2024). Advanced wearable medical devices and their role in transformative remote health monitoring. In Garcia, M., & de Almeida, R. (Eds.), *Transformative approaches to patient literacy and healthcare innovation* (pp. 308–326). IGI Global., DOI: 10.4018/979-8-3693-3661-8.ch015

Tariq, M. U. (2024). Leveraging artificial intelligence for a sustainable and climate-neutral economy in Asia. In Ordóñez de Pablos, P., Almunawar, M., & Anshari, M. (Eds.), *Strengthening sustainable digitalization of Asian economy and society* (pp. 1–21). IGI Global., DOI: 10.4018/979-8-3693-1942-0.ch001

Tariq, M. U. (2024). Metaverse in business and commerce. In Kumar, J., Arora, M., & Erkol Bayram, G. (Eds.), *Exploring the use of metaverse in business and education* (pp. 47–72). IGI Global., DOI: 10.4018/979-8-3693-5868-9.ch004

KEY TERMS AND DEFINITIONS

Small and Medium-Sized Enterprises (SMEs): Businesses with a limited number of employees and revenue.

Emerging Economies: Nations with developing industrial bases and lower-to-middle income levels that are transitioning towards more advanced economies.

Digital Transformation: The integration of digital technology into all areas of a business, fundamentally changing how SMEs operate and deliver value to customers.

Market Expansion: Strategies used by SMEs to grow their customer base by entering new domestic or international markets.

Talent Management: A strategic approach to attracting, developing, and retaining skilled employees to gain a competitive edge.

Strategic Partnerships: Collaborations between SMEs and other businesses, institutions, or larger corporations to leverage shared resources.

Access to Finance: The ability of SMEs to obtain capital or funding from financial institutions or alternative sources.

Chapter 8
Internal Strategic Application Analysis Proposal

Ronald Mauricio Martinez-Contreras
Politecnico Grancolombiano, Colombia

Nydia C. Hernandez-Mora
https://orcid.org/0000-0003-3051-4734
Politecnico Grancolombiano, Colombia

Carlos Salcedo-Perez
https://orcid.org/0000-0002-4433-5537
Politecnico Grancolombiano, Colombia

ABSTRACT

The strategic business analysis is essential to formulate strategies and tactical plans that allow companies to grow in an environment that is getting more and more competitive. Thus, the strategic analysis focuses on internal aspects of the company and external factors that affect it. This research focuses on a tool of internal analysis that has been applied in consulting processes performed by professors and students of the Politecnico Grancolombiano since the second semester of 2022. The tool uses the Excel spreadsheet; it includes modules of Marketing, Production, Human Resources, Technology, Administration, and Social Responsibility. Besides, by means of the calculation of ponderations, it generates specific and general scores that allow to classify each functional area of the company as competitively strong or weak. Thus, the results provided by the tool become an essential input for other models of strategic analysis, such as the Strategic Analysis of Fred David, or the dynamic capabilities model.

INTRODUCTION

As the society, technology, and knowledge move forward, companies must make more efforts to keep being competitive in a dynamic market. To do so, it is necessary to have a strategic plan that sets the path for an organization, so it can develop or maintain a competitive advantage, providing tools to achieve the company´s vision. A clear assessment of the company, including strengths and weaknesses, is essential to design such strategic plan, to implement actions for improvement. There are methodolo-

DOI: 10.4018/979-8-3693-4046-2.ch008

gies for strategic analysis, such as the model of Fred David, the strategic prospective, and the model of dynamic capabilities.

An essential component of said methodologies is the analysis the company's internal factors, whether they are called strengths, weaknesses, resources, or capabilities. Therefore, an Excel software of internal strategic analysis was created; such software is used by students of the Business Administration Program of the Politecnico Grancolombiano, during the business consulting process that they develop during their last academic term.

This software includes several different questions that are applied in different areas of the company, automatically generating performance indicators. It uses a scale to determine the main strengths and weaknesses; besides, there is a weighing system to classify the company and each one of its internal dimensions, into different categories, being considered competitively strong If the score obtained is five or above, or competitively weak if the score is lower.

To validate the user's perception of the software, 171 surveys were answered by teams of students who performed consulting activities during the first semester of 2024. The survey included 16 questions that evaluated the components and differentiating factors of the software. This chapter presents the methodology used to evaluate companies based on this software, its usefulness for companies, and the results of the surveys that measured the satisfaction of users regarding the tool, to validate its pertinence.

LITERATURE REVIEW

Business Consulting

Consulting in business must be performed by highly qualified professionals that can provide advice to different organizations, thus helping companies to identify and solve management problems in an independent and objective manner (Kipping & Clark, 2012). According to Kubr (1997), business consulting can have two approaches: a service provided by a professional and a method to provide advice and help at practical level.

The development of a consulting process can be linked to two main trends. Psychologists, sociologists, and social scientists represent the neoclassical trends, while specialists in technical and technological fields represent the engineering trend, focusing on rational thinking. Thus, specialists in human and social sciences follow the humanistic approach, while the rational approach is followed by rational thinkers. Organizations try to identify and apply both approaches (Szeiner, Ladislav, Horbulak, & Póor, 2020).

From a strategic point of view, there is a trend to align strategic consulting and direction, based on cause-and-effect observations among different areas of the organization (Flores, Pincay, & Vargas, 2018). In a study conducted in Medellin (Columbia), aimed at identify characteristics of business consulting oriented to human resource management, researchers identifies key needs of companies, being the most solicited: quality assurance, evaluation or organizational climate, strategic planning, competency management, empowerment, etc. (Lopez, Sepulveda, & Arenas, 2010).

Evolution of Business Strategic Analysis

At strategic level, organizations' needs have evolved. The term strategy was initially used in war matters. Later, it became a matter of interest in business administration, and nowadays, it is used to project and execute the direction and as a methodology to plan organizational actions (Garrido, 2003).

According to Mintzberg (1993), strategy is presented as a plan to integrate policies and goals, with a logic sequence of actions to develop. To review internal deficiencies and the resources of an organization is necessary to foresee projects and prevent changes in the environment.

Strategic thought is part of the comprehensive process of the business context (Labarca N, 2008). Strategic thought has been researched during the last 40 years, through different schools and thoughts. Mintzberg (1993) divides nine schools of thoughts into two groups: prescriptive and descriptive thoughts.

Due to the complexity of the different types of organizational structures, managers retake the theoretical principles that can be applied to organizations in different environments, starting from the key successful factors. Some schools of thought that have created valid and still useful concepts can be studied as the base of strategic planning (Labarca N., 2007).

Figure 1. Evolution of the Concept of Strategy in the Prescriptive and Descriptive Schools

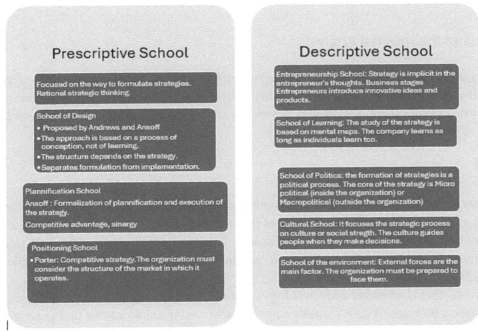

Source: The authors based on Mintzberg & Quinn (1993)

SWOT Analysis

The analysis of internal and external factors constitutes a basic element of planning. The SWOT Analysis originates from research developed by researchers of the Stanford Research Institute. This analysis identifies opportunities and threats related to economic, social, political, cultural, demographic, ecological, environmental, and competitive (David, 2003). It also includes internal factors from different organizational dimensions.

The SWOT Analysis is a tool that helps to identify the impact of the staff of the different areas of the organization, narrowly focusing on the areas of services and the culture of customers in the initial stages of the strategic plan, and how these people influence in the objectives and strategic actions (Belue, et al, 2024).

A study of the use of networks and advanced computing proposes, through a SWOT Analysis, to enhance the infrastructure of e-science in Colombia (Gonzales & M, 2017). In the same way, an analysis of the electrical industry identified the internal and external factors to define strategic indicators to diminish the losses due to users' unauthorized use. (Perez, Vasquez, Luna, & J, 2011).

There are studies about the systemized tools that allow businessmen to develop the SWOT Matrix, from the relation of opportunities and threats with the strengths and weaknesses. These tools allow to automate processes and design strategies from the analysis of the organization (Mariño, Cortez, & Luis, 2008).

Dimensions of the Internal Analysis

Strengths and weaknesses come from activities under the control of the organization; such activities come from the dimensions of management, marketing, finances, accounting, production, operations, R&D, systems, among others. Companies search for strategies that enhance strengths and eliminate weaknesses. (David, 2003).

Marketing

Digital marketing and brand promotion have increased the relevance of this dimension; buyers adopt specific characteristics generated from the use of new technologies (Pitre, Builes, & Hernández, 2021). Segments are defined from the research on customer behavior; for example, after the Covid-19 pandemics consumers, from different ages groups, buy and value purchases through electronic channels. (Chambi, 2023).

Content marketing accelerates sales; weblogs became a need in a digital communication specialized in different topics (Gomez, 2021). Customer loyalty, achieved through actions that generate customer satisfaction, is a key factor of analysis for the marketing department; it is possible to determine emotions and topics of interest of consumers by analyzing content (Atarama & Vega, 2020).

Human Resources

The HR department plays an important role in the workers' experience; a study on SME's shows that organizations want to have an impact on careers, professions and continuous feedback, however, learning and development of management based on competences is not widely used. (Solano, Chalco,

& Luis, 2023). Therefore, the development of human resources is directly related to quality and sales services (Hernandez, Chumaceiro, & Atencio, 2009).

It is important to evaluate and organize this department, since human talent recruitment requires solid processes. Small companies usually lack processes that help to reduce risk (Moncada, Zambrano, Falcones, & Angulo, 2022).

Production

The production process is related to the activities to transform input into final products. Functions related to capacities, processes, inventories, and quality are performed in this area (David, 2003). This process has an important impact on companies' profitability; they require to be more competitive and increase the quality of their products. Simulation of systems in critical stages of production increases efficiency and reduce production time (Paola A. Sánchez, 2015).

Technology

The main functions of this area are the management of infrastructure and of information, which helps in the process of decision-making, therefore, it is necessary to have information with data from different areas to improve such process and its outputs. (David, 2003).

Nowadays, the evaluation of security threats is considered essential for organizations. An analysis by the Universidad Distrital of Bogota, aimed at preventing cyber-attacks through implementation of infrastructure, allowed to efficiently find pit falls, by designing a system to register information related to the attacks, and to establish effective solutions (Leguizamon, 2020).

Administration

Ramirez and Ramirez (2016) provide a set of different definitions of administration from different authors such as George Terri, who defines it as a process of planning, organize, direct, execute and control of the work. This definition includes elements of the administrative process. A well-takeng administration process is essential for the good performance of the company.

Corporate Social Responsibility

Truong (2019) states that CSR is usually referred to as the philanthropic and community contributions made by the organization. Chumarina and Abulkhanova (2021) cite Simchenko and Piskun (2019) who state that CSR in business today can be divided into four broad categories: environmental measures (actions to reduce pollution), humanitarian actions (help charities and local programs), ethical treatment of the workforce (treat employees fairly), and voluntary contributions (attending volunteers' events).

Finance

Weston and Copeland (1992) mentioned that the basic financial functions are investment, financing, and decisions about dividends; they also stated that the goals of the financial administrator are to plan, obtain, and use the funds to maximize the value of the organization. To do so, some of the responsibilities include to obtain funds at the lowest possible cost and use it in an efficient way, and to make changes if the conditions of the environment and the competition makes it necessary to do so.

Models of Strategic Consulting

Strategic consulting models search to integrate internal strengths and weaknesses with external opportunities and threats to identify the current state of the company and an ideal scenario or goal that the company wishes to achieve. Drucker (1954) stated that the starting point for an organization to reach its vision or desired situation is to have an adequate analysis of its current situation.

The main elements of an internal analysis were previously covered in this document, so, at this point, it is important to cover some components of the external strategic analysis to comprehensively approach the models of strategic analysis used nowadays. Fahey and Narayanan (1986) designed a model of analysis of external factors that later they themselves complemented, called PESTEL, which includes political, economic, social, technological, environmental, and legal factors.

Porter (1980) stated that there are five forces that influence the competitive dynamics of an industry; these forces measure the relation of the company with its suppliers, customers and competitors.

There are different methodologies to perform such analyses. Three of the main models of strategic analysis and their characteristics are explained below.

Model of Fred David

This model developed by David (2003), takes internal and external factors that impact the company, to create, the EFI (Internal Factor Evaluation) Matrices and the EFE (External Factor Evaluation). The former evaluates the strengths and weaknesses of the company, weighing them relative to their importance, and thus classifying them using the following scale:

Major Strength (4 points)
Minor Strength (3 points)
Minor Weakness (2 points)
Major Weakness (1 point)

Then, results are added to obtain a final score. A company is considered to have a strong internal competitive position if it scores above 2.5, and a score below that number indicates a weak internal competitive position.

The EFE matrix is used to evaluate the capacity of the company to take advantage of the opportunities and to overcome the threats. It evaluates this in a similar way as with the EFI matrix.

The scale used for the EFE matrix is:

Superior Response (4 points)
Above the Average Response (3 points)
Average Response (2 points)
Poor Response (1 point)

Just as with the EFI matrix, results are added to obtain a final score. A company is in a competitive position to take advantage of the opportunities of the environment if it scores above 2.5. The company is in an unfavorable position to develop its strategic plan if the score obtained is lower than 2.5.

Then, the DOFA Matrix is used to determine strategies for each quadrant of such matrix. Such quadrants are Strength-Opportunity (SO), Strength-Threat (ST), Weakness-Opportunity (WO), and Weakness-Threat (WT). Such strategies are analyzed along with the SPACE Matrix (Rowe & Mason, 1982) to identify the strategic position of the company. The relation between both matrices is shown in Table 1.

Table 1. Correlation between SWOT and SPACE Quadrants

SWOT Quadrant	SPACE Quadrant
Strength – Opportunity	Aggressive
Strength – Threat	Competitive
Weakness – Opportunity	Conservative
Weakness – Threat	Defensive

Source: The authors based on the SWOT and SPACE Matrices

These are the characteristics of said quadrants:

Aggressive

It includes the strategies that use the strengths of the company to take advantage of the opportunities of the environment. For a company to take an aggressive approach it must have a clear competitive advantage and a strong financial capability.

Competitive

The company must use its strengths to face the threats of the environment. For a company to take a competitive approach it must have a strong financial position to implements its strategy, however, it must develop a competitive advantage to be able to successfully compete against its competitors.

Conservative

It includes the strategies to follow to take advantage of the external opportunities in order to diminish the company's weaknesses. If a company is in a competitive environment, it means that it has competitive advantages but its capacity to apply its strategy is limited due to its financial limitations.

Defensive

It is the most challenging situation for a company. Strategies of this quadrant focus on transform weaknesses into strengths to face external threats. The company is in a hostile environment, its financial position is evidently weak, it has few or no competitive advantages, and depending on the complexity of the situation, it is valid to consider selling the assets, or liquidate the company.

After identifying the strategic quadrant, the process ends with the application of the Quantitative Strategic Planning Matrix, which evaluates the attractiveness of the strategies proposed in the quadrant of the SPACE in which the company is located. This assessment is made by evaluating each strategy regarding the previously analyzed opportunities, threats, strengths, and weaknesses.

The evaluation scale ranges from 1 to 4 thus:

Very attractive (4 points)
Attractive (3 points)
Slightly attractive (2 points)
Not attractive at all (1 point)

Finally, the scores of each strategy are added. The company should implement the strategy that obtains the highest score.

Strategic Prospective Approach

This model proposes the creation of future scenarios to determine the organization's corporate strategy. Its origins date back to 1945, when the Department of Defense of the USA develops the Delphi Methos as one technique to analyze the future (Dalkey & Herlmer, 1962). However, it is in France, where the prospective analysis as we know it was formed; first, Bertrand de Jouvenel proposed the existence of multiple possible futures (Mojica, 2006), and later, Godet (2000) unified and developed a set of methodologies to apply prospective in business strategic analysis.

The final purpose of the prospective analysis is to identify, from a series of possible future scenarios, the scenario under whose conditions the company will work. Godet (2000) defines a series of steps to find such scenario. First, to identify and analyze those trends that will be relevant for the company in a specific future year (5, 10, or more years from the date of the analysis). Then, to develop the Cross-impact Matrix. This matrix permits to quantify each variable according to its level of dependence and influence regarding all the other variables. The dependence refers to how much the result of the analyzed variable depends on the results of each one of the other variables, while the influence refers to the degree of influence of the analyzed variable in the result of each of the other variables that affect the company. Both, the dependence and the influence are qualified using a scale ranging from 0 to 3, which measures the level of the impact.

The next step is to generate the MIC MAC chart, which results from locating, in a cartesian plane, the points corresponding to the sumatory of the values obtained with the Cross-impact Matrix. The cartesian plane is divided into four quadrants, each of them including a different group of variables:

Driving factors

Key trends that will support the organization's strategic plan, since these are variables that have a higher degree of influence on the results of other variables; the results of the variables of this quadrant barely depends on other variables.

Linkage factors

These are variables that influence others, but their outcome depends on variables outside the control of the company. The company may find that is complex to manage these variables.

Dependent factors

Variables that barely influence others, but whose results greatly depends on other variables.

Autonomous factors

Trends with little effect on the company´s future, since their degree of influence and dependence is low. This matrix allows to identify the most important trends for the organization, either because of their strategic value or their risk level.

The next step, based on the key trends identified previously, is to formulate hypotheses regarding the most probable results to obtain in the future year analyzed. Then, by combining all hypotheses, this results in obtaining all the possible scenarios that the company may face; from these scenarios, the most likely to occur are identifies, and finally, the final scenario is selected. Based on this final scenario, the company will sustain its vision, and structure its strategic plan.

Dynamic Capabilities

Edith Penrose is the forefather of this model; according to Kor, Mahoney, Siemens and Tan (2016) her main contributions were: the company is a set of productive resources and its services, making it possible to boost the company's singularities; managers play an important role to transform input into services; services are important since they shape the vision of the company; the managers' knowledge of the resources along with their business imagination shape the way in which the company perceives the demand and the opportunities it will take advantage of.

Wernerfelt (1984) proposed the Input-Product Matrix, that allows to identify the company's available resources to compete in the market, so, its best resources help to improve those factors in which the company is weaker. Barney (1991) proposed a relation between the strategic resources of the company and its capacity to generate a sustainable competitive advantage; such analysis is based on four empirical indicators: valuable, rare, imperfectly imitable, and imperfectly substitutable.

The concept of Dynamic capabilities developed by Teece, Pisano, and Shuen (1998), refers to contexts of rapid technological change, in which wealth creation depends on the improvement of technological, organizational, and managerial processes of the company. Lately, different classifications of Dynamic capabilities have been proposed; Cardazco, Zapata and Lombana (2021) state that capabilities to detect, change, and take advantage are the key capabilities that companies must rely on to make decisions to face a changing environment.

In all three methodologies, the internal factors of the company are essential to structure the strategic plan of the organization, but it is in the dynamic capabilities model in which they gain more relevance. Still, internal organizational factors, whether called strengths, weaknesses, resources, or capabilities, are essential for organizations to develop a sustainable competitive advantage.

Next, this chapter will include a detailed description of the characteristics of the Software of Internal Strategic Analysis developed and implemented in consulting processes performed by students and processors of the Business Administration Program of the Politecnico Grancolombiano.

METHODOLOGY

The software of Internal Strategic Analysis was applied by students of last semester of the online program of Business Administration of the Politecnico Grancolombiano during the first semester of 2024. A total of 1527 students participated, divided in groups of 5 students in average (305 teams). Each team that participated in the study had to use the software and apply it in a consulting process in a Colombian SME in order to evaluate internal factors. This becomes the basic input of the consulting process, which also includes external factors, the SWOT Analysis, the Space Matrix, the QSPM, and the development of the strategic proposal by using the Balance Score Card.

After the students finished their consulting processes, a survey was applied; it was answered by 190 teams (higher than the 171 surveys necessary to have a confidence level of 95% and an margin of error of 5%).

The population is composed by college student. Other data about the population that participated in the study is: women composed 67.63% of the population and men 32.37%; 48.92% have some type of marital union; 56.84% have at least one kid; 73.38% are employees, 10.79% are entrepreneurs, and 12.23% are unemployed.

The questionnaire included 16 questions, 5 of them to characterize the population, and the remaining 10 questions were questions to select a number in a numeric scale from 1-10. The last one was an open-ended question to get the perceptions of the participants regarding the use of the software. The objective was to evaluate the usefulness of each of the dimensions and the general perception of the usefulness of the software to fulfill its purpose.

Description of the Software

Its main purpose is to aid to perform an objective evaluation of strengths and weaknesses of the organization, to make a comprehensive assessment of its capabilities and opportunities for improvement. One characteristic that makes this software different it that it works under the use of a questionnaire, and, as questions are answered, the software automatically generates the results of performance indicators of the following six dimensions:

- Marketing
- Production
- Human Resources

- Technology
- Administration
- CSR

Then, the software generates a series of tools, so the analysis becomes easier for the consultant. This process can be divided into the following four sections:

- Basic information
- Internal dimensions
- Analysis of indicators
- Results

Basic Information

This section includes basic data of the company such as its industry, location, products, number of employees, sales, assets, and the last year for which information is available. This data provides an overview of the company; later, this data is used to calculate performance indicators based on formulas included in the software.

Figure 2. Basic Information Section (Spanish is the language in which the software is designed; the figures include the original images of the software in said language. The chapter explains the contents of the figures).

Importancia	Indicador	Dimensión	2022	2023	2024	Impacto
1	vinculación y desarrollo de carrera para madres	Responsabilidad_Social	0.0000	0.0000	3.0000	5
2	Índice de Creatividad	Talento_Humano	0.5556	0.4000	0.8182	5
3	Ventas de nuevos productos	Tecnología	0.3333	0.4211	0.5000	5
4	Concentración de Ingresos	Mercadeo	0.3333	0.2632	0.1300	5
5	Porcentaje de ingresos por exportación	Mercadeo	0.4444	0.4737	0.9000	5

Source: Taken from the Software of Internal Strategic Analysis created by professors of the Politecnico Grancolombiano

Internal Dimensions

This section includes the six internal dimensions (previously mentioned) analyzed in the software. Each section contains a questionnaire, indicators, and calculations. Figure 4 shows a small sample of how the questionnaire looks (as it is seen by the respondent), which includes two columns: one request information or data, and the other is for the respondent to fill the information requested.

Figure 3. Internal Dimensions

Figure 4. Example of the structure of the questionaire

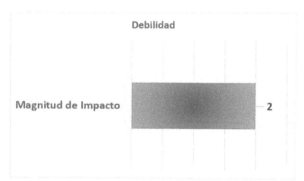

After collecting the information, the software automatically, based on formulas included, generates a series of predetermined indicators. This is one of the main added values of this software, since it automatically generates results, allowing its use by novel consultants (as it is the case used for this chapter). Figure 5 shows how an indicator looks to the consultant in the software.

Figure 5. Visual Sample of Indicators in the Software

Source: Taken from the Software of Internal Strategic Analysis created by professors of the Politecnico Grancolombiano

Finally, indicators are classified based on their impact. The software offers another added value that is the automatic categorization of the indicators based on the elements of the SWOT Analysis, specifically of the internal quadrants, this is, it classifies every indicator as strength or weakness depending on the numeric result. Such classification is suggested, meaning that the consultant may change it if he/she considers it so. Figure 6 shows a visual sample of how the classification appears on the software. The first column is the one the software suggests, and the column in the middle is the one in which the consultant can keep or change such suggestion.

Figure 6. Visual Sample of Classifications in the Software

Importancia	Dimensión	Puntaje
20%	Dimensión de Mercadeo	5.92
20%	Dimensión de Talento Humano	6.91
14%	Dimensión de Producción	4.60
14%	Dimensión Tecnológica	5.60
14%	Dimensión Administrativa	5.70
18%	Dimensión Responsabilidad Social	5.78
100%	TOTAL	5.83

Source: Taken from the Software of Internal Strategic Analysis created by professors of the Politecnico Grancolombiano

Finally, there is a column of magnitude of the impact, with a 0-5 scale with the following levels (Table 2):

Table 2. Scale of magnitude of the impact of strengths and weaknesses

Magnitude	Level
0	Nule
1	Low
2	Lower middle
3	Middle
4	High
5	Very high

Source: the authors based on the structure of the software of internal strategic analysis.

The purpose of this categorization is to identify the most important internal factor and to assign them a numeric weighing to each internal dimension analyzed, so the consultant finds it easier to perform the internal assessment of the company.

Analysis of Indicators

The menu of indicators that make this section up are shown in Figure 7.

Figure 7. Menu of Analysis of Indicators

Indicador	Dimensión	2022	2023	2024	2025
Tasa de renovación de maquinaria y equipo	Tecnologia	0.3393	0.8125	0.0345	5%
PLAN DE ACCIÓN PROPUESTO					

Source: Taken from the Software of Internal Strategic Analysis created by professors of the Politecnico Grancolombiano

The first item of this section is the summary. This section includes the consolidated of all performance indicators, separated by each of the internal dimensions analyzed. Besides the information of each of these dimensions, a weighing of factors is generated; the later will later allow to identify the internal strategic global position for each dimension. Figure 8 shows how this ponderation is visualized in the software (the weighing depends on the magnitude of the impact and its categorization in the SWOT Matrix either as strength or weakness).

Figure 8. Section of Factors' Weighing

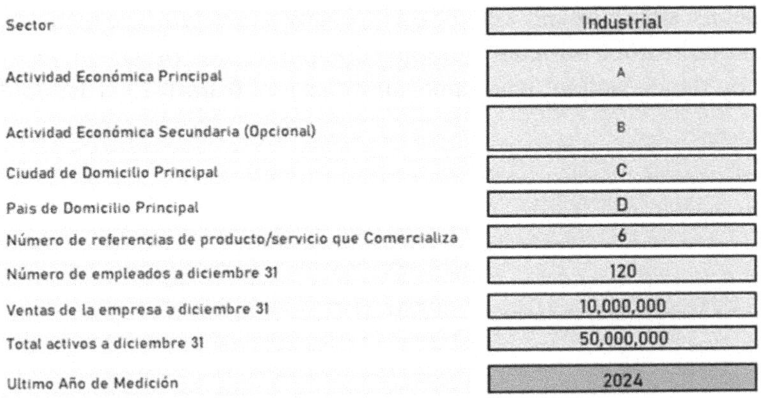

Sector	Industrial
Actividad Económica Principal	A
Actividad Económica Secundaria (Opcional)	B
Ciudad de Domicilio Principal	C
Pais de Domicilio Principal	D
Número de referencias de producto/servicio que Comercializa	6
Número de empleados a diciembre 31	120
Ventas de la empresa a diciembre 31	10,000,000
Total activos a diciembre 31	50,000,000
Ultimo Año de Medición	2024

Source: Taken from the Software of Internal Strategic Analysis created by professors of the Politecnico Grancolombiano

Strengths are weighed in a scale from 6-10 depending on the magnitude of the impact, as follows:

Table 3. Weighing of strenghts' impact

Magnitude	Weight
1	6
2	7
3	8
4	9
5	10

Source: the authors based on the structure of the software of internal strategic analysis.

As the previous table shows, the higher the magnitude the higher the score. Weaknesses are weighed as shown in Table 4.

Table 4. Weighing of weaknesses' impact

Magnitude	Weight
1	5
2	4
3	3
4	2
5	1

Source: the authors based on the software of internal strategic analysis

For weaknesses, the higher the impact the lower the score; this, so the more important strengths increase the global score of the company to a score close to 10, and the more important weaknesses decrease the score closer to 1. Thus, later, the inflection point of the weighing will be 5. A dimension with a score over 5 has a strong internal position, and a dimension with a score lower than 5 has a weak internal position.

In the next four menus, strengths and weaknesses are shown in detail. The menu of strengths included the 15 most important indicators, with an additional column called *"Importancia"* (Importance). Such column is filled out by the consultant who ranks all indicators from 1-15, 1 being the most important for the company.

Figure 9. Menu of Strengths

Source: Taken from the Software of Internal Strategic Analysis created by professors of the Politecnico Grancolombiano

After the performing the previous process, the menu of strengths is automatically placed in order (same for weaknesses). Figure 10 shows how it is visualized in the software.

Figure 10. Menu of Strengths (in order)

Cuestionario		Datos
Digite los ingreso totales de la industria en el periodo	2024	100.000.000
Digite los ingreso totales de la industria en el periodo	2023	90.000.000
Digite los ingreso totales de la industria en el periodo	2022	80.000.000

Source: Taken from the Software of Internal Strategic Analysis created by professors of the Politecnico Grancolombiano

Finally, this section includes the detailed menu by indicator, which shows a graph of the behavior of each of the indicators analyzed (ideal to present in the final consulting report). By using dropdown lists, it is possible to select the indicator to review. Figure 11 shows a sample of the graphical visualization of indicators.

Figure 11. Graphical of Visualization of Indicators

Indicador	Fórmula	Resultados Empresa		
		2022	2023	2024
Participacion en el mercado	PM=Ventas de la empresa/Ventas de la Industria	8.75%	10.56%	10.00%

Source: Taken from the Software of Internal Strategic Analysis created by professors of the Politecnico Grancolombiano

The first graph shows the historical behavior of the selected indicator, while the second shows if it is a strength or weakness and its magnitude in a scale from 1-5 included in the software.

Figure 12. Visualization of the Magnitude of the Impact

DOFA (Sugerido)	DOFA	Magnitud del Impacto
Fortaleza	Fortaleza	3

Source: Taken from the Software of Internal Strategic Analysis created by professors of the Politecnico Grancolombiano

Menu of Results

The main menu of the Results Section shows the scores of each dimension and the total score obtained by the company of its internal strategical situation.

Figure 13. Components of the Menu of Results

RESUMEN

FORTALEZAS

FORTALEZAS ORDENADAS

DEBILIDADES

DEBILIDADES ORDENADAS

DETALLE POR INDICADOR

Source: Taken from the Software of Internal Strategic Analysis created by professors of the Politecnico Grancolombiano

As mentioned above, a score above 5 indicates a strong internal position, and a score below 5 indicates a weak internal position

Figure 14: Menu of Results

DOFA	Magnitud d Impacto	Ponderación		
		Debilidades	Fortalezas	Global
Fortaleza	3	0.0	8.0	8.0
Debilidad	1	5.0	0.0	5.0

Source: Taken from the Software of Internal Strategic Analysis created by professors of the Politecnico Grancolombiano

To improve the relevance of the total score, the consultant may assign a level of importance to each dimension, in a way that, depending on the specific characteristics of the industry and the company, he/she can assign a higher percent weighing. As an example, in the case of the sample shown, the marketing (*mercadeo*) and human resources (*talento humano*) dimensions are assigned a 20%, so they have a higher importance when calculating the final score.

The menu Graph of Results shows a graph of the results obtained in the menu of results.

Finally, the Menu of Action Plans includes the five major weaknesses previously identified; such menu is aimed at generating a specific action plan for each of such weaknesses.

Figure 15. Menu of Action Plans

Indicador	Dimensión	2022	2023	2024	Impacto	Importancia
¿Cómo calificaría la efectividad del programa de vinculación y desarrollo de carrera para madres gestantes?(de 1 a 5)	Responsabilidad_Social	0.0000	0.0000	3.0000	5	1
Indice de Creatividad	Talento_Humano	0.5556	0.4000	0.8182	5	2
Ventas de nuevos productos	Tecnología	0.3333	0.4211	0.5000	5	3
Concentración de Ingresos	Mercadeo	0.3333	0.2632	0.1300	5	4
Porcentaje de ingresos por exportación	Mercadeo	0.4444	0.4737	0.9000	5	5
Efectividad en la Contratación	Talento_Humano	1.0000	0.8000	1.0000	5	6
Efectividad en la Contratación	Talento_Humano	1.0000	0.8000	1.0000	5	7

Source: Taken from the Software of Internal Strategic Analysis created by professors of the Politecnico Grancolombiano

This menu also determines the goal to reach for each indicator that needs to be addressed, so the proposed action plan must be aligned with such goal. At this point, the consulting process ends.

Such proposed action plans must be analyzed considering the financial situation of the company to determine the feasibility of their implementation. Then, the expected result is to achieve an improvement in the management of the company and the strengthening of its capabilities. On the other side, this process is an input for deeper models of strategic analysis such as the Strategic Prospective Model, the Model of Fred David, or the Model of Dynamic Capabilities.

Methodology

The software of Internal Strategic Analysis was applied by students of last semester of the online program of Business Administration of the Politecnico Grancolombiano during the first semester of 2024. A total of 1527 students participated, divided in groups of 5 students in average (305 teams). Each team that participated in the study had to use the software and apply it in a consulting process in a Colombian SME in order to evaluate internal factors. This becomes the basic input of the consulting process, which also includes external factors, the SWOT Analysis, the Space Matrix, the QSPM, and the development of the strategic proposal by using the Balance Score Card.

After the students finished their consulting processes, a survey was applied; it was answered by 190 teams (higher than the 171 surveys necessary to have a confidence level of 95% and an margin of error of 5%).

The population is composed by college student. Other data about the population that participated in the study is: women composed 67.63% of the population and men 32.37%; 48.92% have some type of marital union; 56.84% have at least one kid; 73.38% are employees, 10.79% are entrepreneurs, and 12.23% are unemployed.

The questionnaire included 16 questions, 5 of them to characterize the population, and the remaining 10 questions were questions to select a number in a numeric scale from 1-10. The last one was an open-ended question to get the perceptions of the participants regarding the use of the software. The objective was to evaluate the usefulness of each of the dimensions and the general perception of the usefulness of the software to fulfill its purpose.

Results

Regarding the questions related to the general perception of the quality of the software to assess strengths and weaknesses, the score obtained was 8.63/10, meaning that users overall have a positive perception of the software. The other questions of the survey focused on valuing the pertinence and effectiveness of the performance indicators used, whose results are shown in Table 5.

Table 5. Results of scores for each dimension

Dimension	Score
Marketing	8.60
Human Resources	8.75
Production	8.70
Technology	8.69
Administration	8.73
CSR	8.70

Source: Taken from results of the survey applied to students of last semester of Business Administration of the Politecnico Grancolombiano who performed consulting processed during the first semester of 2024.

The average score was 8.69/10, showing that users have a very good perception of the software. Overall, the scores obtained for all dimensions are similar. Human Resources and Administration obtained the highest scores. In contrast, Marketing obtained the lowest score (even though is a very good score); therefore, it is worth to analyze opportunities for improvement of such dimension.

Besides, the survey asked about differential aspects of the software. The first question was related to the automatic generation of results for performance indicators, which was evaluated positively by 84.17% of respondents. About the differential regarding the methodology of the software to identify the main strengths and weaknesses of the company, the score obtained was 8.83/10, with 67.62% of participants assigning grades or 9.0 or higher.

Regarding the results section, which is the most important section of the software, students were asked about its pertinence to determine the internal competitive position of the company. This section obtained the highest result, with a score of 8.90; this implies that users perceive the software as a tool that really allows them to perform a high-quality internal assessment of the company.

Finally, participants commented about their perception of the software, including ideas such as:

- It allows to look in more detail the internal processes of companies to identify strengths and weaknesses.
- Good tool since it includes formulas and links.
- It is an easy-to-use tool, with good tools to analyze results.
- Very complete, practical, and interactive.
- It is notorious the effort to create it and structure it, thinking about the comfort and easiness to fill out by the student, to find tools to get adequate results.

Such perceptions are valuable to keep using the software in business consulting process; they highlight its practicality, interactivity, and especially that it is a tool with which it is easy to get results that can be analyzed in future stages of the consulting process.

However, participants also mentioned opportunities for improvement such as:

- Review that macros can be edited correctly, aligning, and texts; this to have a better presentation
- Regarding the matrices, it is necessary provide more explanation about the functioning of Excel functions, to know what is being evaluated; in addition, to explain more about how this type of matrix id designed and how it works, since this will help as an experience to work with Excel.
- Small and medium companies do not have all the information required by the software. Leaving such data in blank worries students.
- About comments regarding opportunities for improvement, there were very few comments; the most relevant one was provided by one respondent who indicated that a few indicators do not apply for small and medium companies, which can make the consulting process difficult.
- Regarding the explanation of the internal structure of the software, it is worth to propose a workshop to explain suers the internal details of the programming and functioning of the software.
- Besides, because of comments regarding the presentation of the tables, the structure must be reviewed, to make the presentation of results easier and visually more attractive.
- Overall, results of the survey allow to infer that the software serves its purpose, and users are highly satisfied with it. Users highlight that results obtained are valuable for business consulting processes and to move forward towards other stages of the consulting process.

Outcomes

Between 2022 and 2024 the software has been applied to consulting processes in 1,032 Colombian companies from a variety of industries. Of such 1,032 companies, 45% belong to the service industry, 30% to trade activities, 22% are manufacturing companies, and 3% are companies that perform agricultural activities. By using this software, the School of Administration and Competitivieness of the Politecnico Grancolombiano has been able to consolidate industry indicators by grouping compiled data of the companies analyzed, therefore allowing the unit of industry studies, which is in charge of monitoring the behavior of indicators related to areas of human resources, markegint, CSR, and production, among others.

FUTURE RESEARCH

Based on the comments of previous users, the authors consider important to provide extra training to new users about the design of the software. The authors also may consider to include additional questions, and if necessary and always based on the current software, to create new software with information tailored to specific sectors of the economy. In the short term, the software will keep being used to perform consulting services in more Colombian companies. As there is more information available, the data obtained can be used to perform a precise characterization of Colombian companies, initially by industry and by geographic location.

CONCLUSION

The business strategic analysis is essential so organizations can identify and develop a sustainable competitive advantage to reach its vision. Diverse methodologies for that type of analysis such as the Model of Fred David, the Strategic Prospective Model and the Model of Dynamic Capabilities are available. These methodologies have one thing in common: the internal aspects of the organization are the core of the business assessment.

Therefore, this chapter presented a software of internal strategic analysis which is used as a tool for processes of business consulting by students of Business Administration of the Politecnico Grancolombiano. Besides, the perception of users regarding the characteristics of the software was evaluated. Results showed a high level of satisfaction by users, with an average general result of 8.63/10, a score of 8.83/10 regarding its easiness to use to analyze strengths and weaknesses, and a score of 8.90/10 regarding the methodology used to identify the internal strategic position of the company (the most important component of the software).

Some opportunities for improvement were identified: 1) the presentation and visualization of data; and 2) the difficulty of its implementation in small companies since some of them did not have all the data required by the software.

Overall, the software was well valued by users, and it is worth to keep using it in processes of business consulting, as well as to improve it so consultants and users from the company analyzed can have a better experience during the consulting process.

The application of this tool has allowed students to increase their competencies to conduct consulting processes later in their careers. Small Colombian companies in which students have performed the consulting processes have benefited greatly, since they can have access to a professional consulting process at no cost (the academic institution and the company sign a contract that specifies that the company will not have to reimburse any money for the process). The tool is applied by students under the guidance of a trained professor who advises students based on the results obtained to develop a strategic path for the company. Many small companies cannot afford hiring a professional consulting team, which may lead them to have no strategic orientation whatsoever. By using this software, students, academics and entrepreneurs can reduce time and synthetize information during the process, since the software also allows to prioritize actions, because it includes spaces to rank activities and factors (as mentioned earlier). The former helps to find out what are the main focuses for companies.

There is criticism related the lack of relation between the academic world and the private industry; the consulting processes performed, facilitated by the use of this software, fills such gap, since it links the academy (students and professors) with private companies, providing them with a real benefit that helps them to better understanding the environment and to lead them to create a strategic path that increases their competitiveness and the possibility of success in the market.

REFERENCES

Atarama, T., & Vega, D. (2020). *Comunicación corporativa y branded content en Facebook: un estudio de las cuentas oficiales de las universidades peruanas*. Revista de Comunicación.

Barney, J. (1991). Firm Resources and Sustained Competitive Advantage. *Journal of Management*, 17(1), 99–120. DOI: 10.1177/014920639101700108

Belue, R., Tayllor, K., Anakwe, A., Bradford, N., Coleman, A., & Ahmed, M., & D, A. (2024). Poner la Cultura en primer lugar en la planificación estratégica organizativa de la Comunidad. *Organization Development Journal*, ●●●, 80–90.

Cadrazco-Parra, W., Zapata-Domínguez, Á., & Lombana-Coy, J. (2021). Capacidades dinámicas: Aportes y tendencias. *Revista Lasallista de Investigacion*.

Chambi, P. (2023). *Segmentación de mercado: Machine Learning en marketing en contextos de covid-19*. Industrial Data.

Chumarina, G. & Abulkhanova, G. (2021). Corporate Social Responsibility Management. *International Journal of Financial Research*. Vol 12 No. 1.

Dalkey, N., & Helmer, O. (1962). An Experimental Application of the Dephi Metod to the Use of Experts. *Rand Co*, 27. https://www.rand.org/content/dam/rand/pubs/research_memoranda/2009/RM727.1.pdf

David, F. R. (2003). Conceptos de Administración Estratégica. Naucalpan de Juárez: Pearson Education.

Drucker, P. F. (1954). The Practice of Management: A Study of the Most Important Function in America Society. *Harper & Brothers*.

Fahey, L., & Narayanan, V. K. (1986). *Macroenviromental Analysis for Strategic Management*. West Publishing Company.

Flores, J., Pincay, D., & Vargas, P. (2018). Esquema de alineamiento estratégico: Una perspectiva teórica desde la consultoría empresarial y la gerencia aplicada. *CIENCIA UNEMI*, 41-56.

Garrido, S. (2003). *Direccion estrategica*. Mc Graw Hill.

Godet, M., Monti, R., Meunier, F., & Roubelat, F. (2000). *La caja de herramientas de la Prospectiva*. Librairie des Arts et Métiers.

Gómez, G. (2021). Los cibergéneros especializados: Análisis sobre la modalidad de gestión de contenidos en weblogs independientes de moda. *Cuadernos del Centro de Estudios en Diseño y Comunicación. Ensayos*.

Gonzales, L. (2017). Gestión estratégica de la Comunidad Colombiana de Cómputo Avanzado 3CoA® mediante análisis DOFA y cocreación. *Ingeniare. Revista Chilena de Ingeniería*, 25(3), 464–476. DOI: 10.4067/S0718-33052017000300464

Hernandez, J., Chumaceiro, C., & Atencio, E. (2009). Quality of Service and Human Resources: Case study of a department store. *Revista Venezolana de Gerencia*.

Kipping, M., & Clark, T. (2012). *The Oxford Handbook of Management Consulting*. Oxford University Press.

Kor, Y. Y., Mahoney, J. T., Siemsen, E., & Tan, D. (2016). Penrose's The Theory of the Growth of the Firm. *Production and Operations Management Society*, 1727-1744.

Kubr, M. (1997). La consultoría de empresas: Guía para la profesión. Geneva.

Labarca, N. (2007). *Consideraciones Teóricas de la Competitividad Empresarial*. Zulia: OMNIA 13.

Labarca, N. (2008). Evolución del pensamiento estratégico en la formación de la estrategia empresarial. *Publicaciones científicas Universidad de Zulia*.

Leguizamon, M. (2020). Análisis de ataques informáticos mediante Honeypots en la Universidad Distrital Francisco José de Caldas. *Ingeniería y competitividad*.

Lopez, E., Sepulveda, C., & Arenas, A. (2010). La consultoría de Gestión Humana en empresas medianas. *Estudios Gerenciales*, 146-168.

Mariño, A., Cortez, F., & Luis, G. (2008). Herramienta de software para la enseñanza y entrenamiento en la construcción de la matriz DOFA. *Ing. Investig*.

Mintzberg, H., & Quinn, B. (1993). *El proceso estratégico: Conceptos, Contextos y casos*. Prentice Hall.

Mojica, F. J. (2006). Concepto y aplicación de la prospectiva estratégica. *Revista Med Volumen 14.*, 122-131. https://www.redalyc.org/pdf/910/91014117.pdf

Moncada, L., Zambrano, L., Falcones, J., & Angulo, R. (2022). Company "Corp. Naula S.A.S" and the Importance of an Audit of the Human Talent Department. *Universidad y Sociedad*.

Paola, A., & Sánchez, F. C. (2015). *Análisis del Proceso Productivo de una Empresa de Confecciones: Modelación y Simulación*. Ciencia e Ingeniería Neogranadina.

Perez, L., Vasquez, C., & Luna, M., & J, P. (2011). Indicadores estratégicos para incrementar la efectividad de las inspecciones para las operadoras del servicio eléctrico Venezolano. *Universidad, Ciencia y Tecnología*.

Pitre, R., Builes, S., & Hernández, H. (2021). *Impacto del marketing digital a las empresas colombianas emergentes*. Revista Universidad y Empresa.

Porter, M. (1980). *Las 5 fuerzas de Porter*. Harvard Business School.

Ramirez, C., & Ramirez, M. (2016). *Fundamentos de Administración*. Ediciones ECOE.

Rowe, A., & Mason, K. D. (1982). *Strategic Management and Business Policy: A Methodological Approach*. Addison-Wesley.

Solano, V., Chalco, F., & Luis, N. (2023). Estrategias de gestión de talentos humanos en pequeñas y medianas empresas peruanas. *Revista Venezolana de Gerencia*.

Szeiner, Z., Ladislav, M., Horbulak, Z., & Póor, J. (2020). *Management Consulting Trends in Slovakia In the Light of Global and Regional tendencies*. IEECA. DOI: 10.15549/jeecar.v7i2.390

Teece, D. J., Pisano, G., & Shuen, A. (1998). Dynamic Capabilities and Strategic Management. *Strategic Management Journal*.

Truong, L. (2019). *Corporate Social Responsibility and Job Pursuit Intention: A Study of Moderating Role of Personal Values*. RCISS's Working Papers.

Wernerfelt, B. (1984). A Resource-Based View of the Firm. *Strategic Management Journal*, 5(2), 171–180. DOI: 10.1002/smj.4250050207

Weston, J., & Copeland, T. (1992). *Finanzas en administración* (9th ed., Vol. I). McGraw Hill.

ADDITIONAL READING

Goryachev, A., Kabakova, T., Krasnyuk, I., Kuvshinova, N., Lemeshchenko, E., Afanas'Ev, O., & Davidov, S. (2020). Analysis of Influence of External and Internal Environment Factors on Pharmacy Production of Infusion Medicinal Drugs. *Systematic Reviews in Pharmacy*, ●●●, 532–537.

Porter, M. (2008). *How Competitive Forces Shape Strategy*. Readings in Strategic Management.

Porter, M. E., & Kramer, M. R. (2011). Creating Shared Value. How to Reinvent Capitalism and Unleash a Wave of Innovation and Growth. *Harvard Business Review*, ●●●, 1–17. https://www.communitylivingbc.ca/wp-content/uploads/2018/05/Creating-Shared-Value.pdf

Sumba, R. C. (2020). La planeación estratégica: Importancia en las PYMES ecuatorianas. *FIPCAEC*, 114-136

KEY TERMS AND DEFINITIONS

Functional Areas.: They represent a way of administrative division of the company; the main are finances, marketing, production, and human resources. However, depending on the company's size, there may appear variations to the traditional administrative division.

Chain Value.: It is a graphic representation of the primary and secondary activities of the company. Primary activities are directly related to the productive and commercialization processes. Secondary are support activities required for the good functioning of primary activities.

Competitive Advantage.: A competitive advantage is composed by a set of attributes that allow the company to be able to make something differently, and better than its competitors. To be considered so, it must bs sustainable through time.

KPI.: They help the company to measure its performance; they are essential to measure the progress of its strategic plan.

SWOT Analysis.: A technique that allows companies to assess its strengths, weaknesses, opportunities and threats.

Chapter 9
Knowledge Management and Innovation for Enhancing SME Competitiveness

Neeta Baporikar
https://orcid.org/0000-0003-0676-9913
Namibia University of Science and Technology, Namibia & SP Pune University, India

ABSTRACT

SMEs are recognized as engines of growth and economic development worldwide. Yet they seem to be not contributing to their full potential. Many of them do not even survive for longer time and even if they do, they are not as competitive as they could be with proper resources and strategies. Adopting a qualitative approach the aim of this chapter is to explore how knowledge management and innovation in SMEs can enhance their competitiveness and aid in optimization of their potential and contribution to economic and sustainable development.

INTRODUCTION

Unlike most Knowledge Management (KM) studies, which focus on large enterprises, this study focuses on SMEs, which represent large percentage of the total business establishments, the largest percentage of establishments in any country. With the emergence of knowledge-based economy, knowledge is considered as the essential way to create wealth and prosperity and it is the important driving force for business success (Baporikar, 2018). Knowledge is a critical source of an organization's competitive advantage; hence organizations attempt to look for ways that strengthen the management of knowledge resources in order to cope with the company's challenges in competing environment for improved business performance (Baporikar, 2017a; 2017b). Knowledge management (KM) has increasingly become a topic of interest in all kinds of organizations due to the growing awareness of the importance of knowledge for the organization's prosperity and survival (Baporikar, 2016a). That is why KM should be included in the SMEs' daily activities so that they become more successful and stay longer (Baporikar, 2016b).

However, KM no longer stands out as a sufficient factor that can lead to improved business performance in today's highly competitive environment where pressures for businesses to meet multiple customers' demands are a challenging task. Other factors that are needed to achieve business performance and many

DOI: 10.4018/979-8-3693-4046-2.ch009

a times the poor performance and failure of SMEs mainly derived from the "me-too" syndrome that is, carrying out similar businesses and lacking innovation (Baporikar, 2015a) Innovation involves the transformation of an idea into a new product or service that meets and satisfies the needs and expectations of customers. Other studies also emphasize the vital role of innovation in business performance. Ordoñez de Pablos, (2014) supports the same view arguing that for a business to achieve better performance and remain competitive, knowledge needs to be managed not only effectively but also innovatively.

So far, there has been limited research on how innovation and knowledge management can enhance SMEs competitiveness that is the role of role of innovation in the relationship between KM and business performance (e.g. Alrubaiee, Alzubi, Hanandeh, & Ali, 2015). Most of existing literature investigates the mediating role of innovation in the relationship between business performance and other factors, such as organizational learning, manufacturing flexibility, retailers' strategic orientations, personal mastery. Therefore, the desire to understand the role of KM and innovation in the relationship of business performance of SMEs motivated this study with the aim of chapter being to examine how KM and innovation can enhance SMEs competitiveness that is the role of role of innovation in the relationship between KM and business performance of SMEs. In the context of this chapter, KM refers to knowledge acquisition, knowledge sharing and knowledge application, while innovation implies the processes of introducing new products and markets or improving the existing ones. As for business performance, it is viewed from the perspective of profits, sales growth and market share. This chapter argues that without effective KM, there may not be any innovation, and without innovation, SMEs may not perform well. Hence, effective KM along with innovation can better explain the variances in business performance of SMEs.

BACKGROUND

In today's modern, turbulent and uncertain marketplace, companies are faced with constant challenges, such as cost reduction, changing purchasing behaviors, increased customer service, mature markets and globalization. In reference to Drucker (2020), the most vital economic resource to achieving competitive advantage is knowledge. Such collective knowledge resides in the minds of its suppliers, employees, customers (Mahr, Lievens, & Blazevic, 2014), which happens to be the most important resource that guarantees a firm's stable growth, more important than the traditional factors of production (i.e. land, capital and labor). Knowledge management (KM), according to Baporikar (2018), includes identifying and analyzing the required and available knowledge, as well as planning and controlling actions to expand further knowledge assets to accomplish company objectives. Many researchers, past and present, have recognized and acknowledged the importance of efficient knowledge use as a primary source for developing core competencies, improving performance, creating value, and attaining competitive advantage, which ensures an organization's success. A firm's ability to innovative relies heavily on its intellectual assets and its ability to utilize knowledge, taking on the viewpoint that innovation process is the utmost knowledge-intensive business process (Baporikar, 2015a; 2015b). Further, knowledge spillovers positively affected its ability to innovate and collaborate among firms situated at the science and technology parks.

KM does not only promote high innovative performance, it also develops a firm's competitive advantage (CA). For a firm to be competitive, it depends on the firm's ability to expand consistently its capabilities in the products and services offered. It is insufficient to have assets and resources alone, as a firm needs to have strong KM competency to develop and support work practices and routines in order to remain competitive. This is particularly so for firms that are competing in the fast moving dynamic markets as being competent in KM enable firms to innovate and respond faster to the shifting market conditions, and attain sustainable competitive advantage (Baporikar, 2021). In line with this, Andreeva and Kianto (2012) also empirically confirmed that information communication technology (ICT) and human resource management (HRM) practices that are used to manage knowledge have been found to significantly affect both financial performance and firm competitiveness.

With the introduction of the knowledge economy era, it has proven that intangible assets have turn out to be a vital source of firm's competitive edge. Both knowledge and technology are considered an enterprise's strategic asset and a main source to create competitive advantage. With innovative technology comes the development of distinct products and service; and successful innovation relies heavily on the knowledge resources a firm possess. KM was found to improve the innovation, which affect the new product development performance in the machine tool industry.

While extensive literature can be found to promote the existence of KM, there is a worrying shortage of empirical evidence to demonstrate the actual linkage between the three concepts of KM, Innovation and CA. Furthermore, empirical evidence on whether KM practices, Innovation and CA are found to be insufficient. Additionally, there is a dearth of empirical research being conducted on the Small Medium Enterprises (SMEs), in particularly from the perspective of developing countries (Baporikar, 2020). KM, according to Baporikar (2019), was created and developed in large enterprises, which is to be applied later on in SMEs. In other words, most of the KM studies have been concentrated on the large enterprises, neglecting the SMEs due to issues of knowledge transfer (Baporikar, 2017b). SMEs have often been described as the backbone of a country's economy as they provide employment for 60–70 percent of its working population. SMEs play a fundamental role in the nation's economic development (OECD, 2018). In order to bridge this gap, this research purports to offer new insights on how SMEs nurture and cultivate their knowledge to achieve a higher level of Innovation to gain CA like no other. It is essential for the SMEs managers to comprehend the specific nature and a source of firm's innovation and CA due to the unique nature of the SMEs. They do not manage knowledge in a way that large firms do, and that they have a different organizational culture as well as a less complex organizational structure that is generally less bureaucratic in their decision-making.

LITERATURE REVIEW

Knowledge management evolves as a body of knowledge following the dawning of knowledge economy era (Baporikar, 2018). It is believed that the knowledge informs and transforms the business arena by means of continuous improvement, or radical innovation, both of which promote change for the better as a result of assimilating new and relevant knowledge inside an organization. Knowledge is one of the enterprise's most important assets that influence its competitiveness. One way to capture an enterprise's knowledge and make it available to all its members is through the use of knowledge management practices. Small and medium-sized enterprises (SMEs) are known for too much implicit knowledge, limited resources, insufficiently shared between managers and other employees. So, in the context of SMEs, KM can be used to capture knowledge and experience generated during their operations, activities, and processes.

The environment in which businesses operate today can be summarized in terms of five key trends: globalization and the increasing intensity of competition; changing organizational structures; new worker profiles, preferences and predispositions; advances in information and communication technology;

and the rise of knowledge management KM. The basic assumption of KM is that organizations that manage organizational and individual knowledge better will deal more successfully with the challenges of the new business environment. KM is seen as a key factor in realizing and sustaining organizational success for improved efficiency, innovation and competition. In SMEs (small and medium enterprises) individual competences usually represent the cornerstone of a firm's knowledge and a key determinant of organizational performance. The increasingly fierce competition deriving from globalization and ICT has challenged this approach calling for new ways to develop, diffuse and retain knowledge in SMEs. Starting from the assumption that SMEs' core capabilities and intellectual capital are deeply rooted in personal knowledge, this paper identifies a knowledge management model for managers working in SMEs in order to best utilize and harness the knowledge of their workers.

In the context of SMEs, KM can be used to capture the knowledge and experience generated during the operations and processes. Reusing knowledge can prevent the repetition of past failures and guide the solution of recurrent problems. Also, we must not forget that collaboration is one of the most important knowledge sources for SMEs. The current focus and study of knowledge management is not for the sake of academics only, but a realization that knowing about knowledge is critical to business growth and business survival. Knowledge, if properly utilized and leveraged, can drive organizations to become more competitive, innovative and sustainable, KM is an emerging discipline that promises to capitalize on enterprises' intellectual capital. The concept of knowledge is far from new and phrases containing the word knowledge, such as "knowledge bases" and "knowledge engineering", have been around for a while.

With reference to KM in SMEs, knowledge is a fluid mix of framed experience, values, contextual information, and expert insights and grounded intuitions that provides a framework for evaluating and incorporating new experiences and information. It originates and is applied in the minds of the knower. In SMEs, knowledge often becomes embedded not only in documents or repositories, but also in organizational routines, processes, practices, and norms (Baporikar, 2022). Knowledge is increasingly recognized as a key organizational asset and its creation, dissemination, and application as a critical source of competitive advantage. At the level of SMEs, investments on intangible resources and the creation of capabilities are quite problematic because of the necessity to increase the efficiency scale or size, in addition to the difficulties related to the internal and external growth through fusions or acquisitions. However, alliances and cooperation may allow SMEs to reach a sufficient dimension to obtain the advantages of being large and, at the same time, keep the advantages of SMEs in terms of specialization, reduction in costs, and flexibility. That is why we consider it interesting to look at whether, from the SMEs' perspective, it is possible to obtain competitive advantage by the promotion of intangible factors and capabilities as large firms do.

An increasing body of research maintains that, in the knowledge economy, knowledge, no other assets, represents the critical resource for both business and individuals. In SMEs, it is individual competencies, which represent the cornerstone of a firm's intellectual capital and a key competitive factor. The increasingly fierce competition deriving from globalization and ICT has challenged this approach, asking for new ways to develop, diffuse and retain knowledge in SMEs. Shortening time to market, reducing costs and increasing product quality and customer service, all drive innovation in SMEs and force these companies to update their competencies and skills. SMEs are heavily dependent on tacit knowledge, which is very mobile. If a person with critical knowledge about processes and practices suddenly leaves the organization, severe knowledge gaps are created (Baporikar, 2023). Therefore, it is more important for SMEs to exploit and manage their intangible assets in contrast to their physical assets (Prusak, 2019).

Knowledge management is now a well-established discipline in many organizations. However, what is its status and role in small and medium enterprises?

Most management studies agree on the importance of knowledge as a firm's strategic asset. Building on the concept of a firm as a bundle of routines, an increasing body of research focuses on how firms can capture value from knowledge and dynamic capabilities. Indeed, intellectual capital comprises two types of knowledge and knowing; the individual and the organizational. In SMEs, where organizational structures and management systems are usually informal, and where some key people, such as the owner/ entrepreneur, family members, managers and partners, play the most relevant roles, individuals represent the main and sometimes exclusive repository of organizational knowledge. Therefore, the personal, tacit knowledge and knowing tends to be the core component of a firm's intellectual capital. Nonaka and colleagues (Takeuchi & Nonaka, 2000), studied the individual knowing part of intellectual capital, how individual learning processes contribute to the organizational knowledge creation process. Less emphasis has been put on studying the individual component of intellectual capital related to personal knowledge, i.e. the endowment of competencies that is at the basis of a person's learning and actions, and, consequently, on the relation between individual competence and organizational capabilities.

In SMEs, one can identify two types of knowledge:

1. Knowledge embedded in the products (artifacts), since they are the result of highly intellectual creative activities.
2. Meta-knowledge, that is, knowledge about the products and processes.

Knowledge

There have been many definitions made on the topic of knowledge within organizations and as discussed earlier a variety of philosophical discussions on the true meaning of knowledge. Davenport and Prusak (1998; 2005) offer working definition of knowledge within organizations, as follows: 'Knowledge is a fluid mix of framed experience, values, contextual information, and expert insight that provides a framework for evaluating and incorporating new experiences and information. It originates and is applied in the minds of knower. In organizations, it is often becomes embedded not only in documents or repositories but also in organizational routines, processes, practices, and norms. Knowledge is increasingly claimed to be a key critical resource and source of competitive advantage in the modern global economy, it is also increasingly claimed that all organizations will have to excel at creating, exploiting, applying, and mobilizing knowledge. The resource-based view of the firm suggests that organizations will need to be able combine distinctive, sustainable, and superior assets, including sources of knowledge and information, with complementary competencies in leadership and human resource management and development to realize fully the value of their knowledge.

When examining one's own experience, knowledge is much more obscure than definitions allow. 'Knowing is a human act, whereas information is an object that can be filled, stored and moved around. Knowledge is a product of thinking, created in the present moment, whereas information is fully made and can sit in storage. To share knowledge, we need to think about the current situation, whereas we can simply move information from one mailbox to another. However, knowledge is more than you think. Knowledge settles into our body. It is a kind of "under the fingernails" wisdom, the background expertise from which we draw. Most of us find it hard or impossible to articulate what we know; whereas information can be written or built into machinery. We acquire knowledge by participating in a community using the tools, ideas, techniques, and unwritten artifacts of that community, whereas we acquire information by reading, observing, or otherwise absorbing it.

Organizations have a wealth of knowledge, which, is embedded in people's head, work practices, and systems. The challenge for organization is to be able to capture that knowledge and to leverage it throughout the organization. This challenge has driven organization to codify knowledge. Codification describes the process of converting knowledge into a form, which is accessible, easy to find, and portable. Knowledge within organization can be classified into two types, one which is structured explicit-formalized and expressed knowledge and the other tacit knowledge-complex, resides within the individual, difficult to articulate or communicate adequately, and is based on practical skills and actions. This dynamic process of converting tacit to explicit is the basis for knowledge creation within organization. The need to codify, transfer and leverage knowledge within organizations, is one of many tasks that organizations need to undertake. Four ambitions are prevalent when knowledge is put on the agenda. These are: 1) a strengthening of the competitiveness, 2) an increase in the benefit for the customers, 3) a stimulation of the innovative abilities and 4) an improvement of the work climate. This last point should be considered from the point of view that knowledge oriented enterprises should be driving forces in improving the standards for creation of attractive places to work. In this respect, it should also be mentioned that the key to development lies in the pocket of the knowledge worker. For that reason, it is clear that the question of management of people and processes has a high priority on the managerial agenda.

Knowledge Management

Knowledge management (KM) is the process of creating, capturing, and using knowledge to enhance organizational performance, such as documenting and codifying knowledge and disseminating it through databases and other communication channels. KM is often seen as involving the recognition, documentation, and distribution of both explicit and tacit knowledge residing in organizations' employees, customers, and other stakeholders. Drucker (2020) considers knowledge the main resource in a post-industrial society. It is the only unlimited resource, and business leaders or consultants the chief asset of organizations and the key to a sustainable competitive advantage (Davenport and Prusak 1998). Knowledge management is the corollary, actually, of decision-making and decisions support systems: since knowledge is raw material, work in process and the finished good of decision-making.

SMEs Considerations

There are an increasing number of studies focusing on the main competitive factors of SMEs. The literature on this field shows that intangible factors, such as structure and organizational change, human resource management, innovation, and technological resources, among others, are elements that clearly contribute to the SMEs' competitiveness and success. The internationalization of economy, the frequent and uncertain changes, and the greater competition among firms, the need for continuous innovations, and the growing use of information technologies force companies to face the challenge of improving their competitiveness. These difficulties are greater for small and medium enterprises (SMEs) because their economies of scale and their resources are less than those of large firms are. However, what compensates for these weaknesses is the fact that SMEs may enjoy greater flexibility because of the simplicity of their internal organization, being faster at adapting and responding to changes. This new situation reveals the need to suggest or find more efficient management processes so that SMEs can apply strategies that allow them to achieve a better performance.

The new knowledge-based economy is built on information technology and the sharing of knowledge and intellectual capital. In such a knowledge-based economy, competitive advantage will be with those enterprises that have the capacity to deliver fast and have innovative forms of processes that raise productivity (Baporikar, 2018). In such an environment, small and medium-sized enterprises (SMEs) have tremendous opportunities. Implicit promises include access to world markets, low-cost entry into new markets and the ability to gain efficiencies in business processes. However, these promises may be illusory for most SMEs. Technological, organizational and marketing hurdles are also making it more difficult for SMEs to succeed in knowledge-based economies. The European Commission introduced the European Union (EU) definition for small and medium size enterprises (SMEs) in 1996. SME is classified in three groups including medium, small and micro enterprises. Its definition is based on the number of paid employees, turnover, balance sheet total, and independence. Independence is the ultimate criterion to justify enterprises to be a SME. Independence means less than a quarter owned by one large company or several companies.

However, talking about SMEs there are other important considerations to take into account other than the legal or formal consideration. SME are quite different between themselves, they do not share a common vision and are usually not rich in resources. Usually, roles in these kinds of companies are poorly defined. It is common to find the same person sharing different roles. Finally, SME do not participate in the Stock Market, so all the market capitalization methods must be rejected. Competition requires small and medium-sized enterprises (SMEs) to seek both external and internal knowledge and to establish external and internal relationships with partners such as customers and suppliers.

Knowledge in SMEs

In today's economy, many of the high value-added SMEs are likely to be knowledge intensive; in the processes, they deploy or the products and services they produce and sell. The normal way that a body of knowledge evolves from tacit to explicit, provides commercialization opportunities at every stage. When individuals team up to solve a problem (or to develop a product), they form a community of practice. When individuals communicate and exchange information related to a common topic, but for solving different problems within or outside a company, they form communities of interest, such as groups of Java programmers. These communities heavily utilize web technology for knowledge sharing. KM is seen as a strategy that creates, acquires transfers, brings to the surface, consolidates, distills, promotes creation, sharing, and enhances the use of knowledge in order to: improve organizational performance; support organizational adaptation, survival and competence; gain competitive advantage and customer commitment; improve employees' comprehension; protect intellectual assets; enhance decisions, services, and products; and reflect new knowledge and insights.

Organizational Memory for SMEs

Learning from experience requires remembering history. Individual memory is, however, not sufficient and the entire organization needs a memory to explicitly record critical events. There are at least seven distinguishable forms of organizational memory (Takeuchi & Nonaka, 2000):

1. Memory consisting of regular work documents and other artifacts that were developed primarily to assist development of the product.
2. Memory consisting of entities that were developed specifically to support the organizational memory.
3. Technological memory refers to knowledge on products, techniques, services or production and manufacturing processes, project experiences, problem solving expertise, design rationale, composition of the project team.
4. Financial memory relates to knowledge on budget, cost of workforce, cost of on-the-shelf products, financial results.
5. Internal risk memory means knowledge on insurance, reserves, risk with new technologies, organizational risks, risks about sub-contractors.
6. Pricing memory deals with knowledge on clients, competitors, market, and marketing strategy.
7. External risk memory includes environmental risks, risk of money currency changes, risk of lessening company brand image.

KM and SMEs

Success in an increasingly competitive marketplace depends critically on the quality of the knowledge, which organizations apply to their business processes. The challenge of using knowledge to create competitive advantage becomes more crucial. Shorter time-to-market, better quality and better productivity present the increasing number of goals to be achieved. To meet these requirements, SMEs have tried to better use one of their most important resources: the organizational knowledge.

Historically, this knowledge has been stored on paper or in people's minds. When a problem arises, we look for experts across our work, relying on people we know, or we look for documents. Unfortunately, paper has limited accessibility and it is difficult to update. On the other hand, in a large organization, it can be difficult to locate who knows what, and knowledge in people's minds is lost when individuals leave the company. Important discussions are lost because they are not adequately recorded. Therefore, knowledge has to be systematically collected, stored in the corporate memory, and shared across the organization. In other words, knowledge management (KM) is vital. Creation of knowledge in any organization is inevitably incessant. Its appropriate use and handling are strategic to the competitiveness of the organization. In many small-and medium-sector enterprises (SMEs), while specific knowledge generation is a continuing activity, importance of its apt management could be crucial to its very existence. In order to compete effectively in global markets and achieve competitive advantage, enterprises need to use effective knowledge management practices.

In SMEs, the managers are in most cases the owners, which imply that decision-making is centralized, and fewer layers of management. This means that decision-making is shorter than in large organizations. The advantage for the owners in SMEs is that they become the key drivers for knowledge management implementations, assuming of course that they appreciate the importance of knowledge management. Another distinction to be made is that management of SMEs has to look after every aspect of the business, which gives them limited time to focus on the strategic issues relating to knowledge management. SMEs have an advantage over large enterprises in respect to their structure, in implementing knowledge management as they usually have a simple, flatter, less complex structure, which will facilitate a change initiative across the organization since functional integration both horizontally and vertically, is easier to achieve, and fewer complications will be encountered.

SMEs tend to have a more organic and fluid culture, than larger organizations. Smaller number of people is usually united under common beliefs and values, which implies that it easier for smaller organizations to change and implement knowledge management. It is easier to create a knowledge sharing culture in smaller organization than in larger ones. In smaller organizations, the owners can influence the cultural values and beliefs of the employees. This can be a problem if the owner does not trust his employees or does not encourage the culture of sharing and transferring knowledge. In this case, the owner can obstruct the development of knowledge rather than develop it.

SMEs have a problem in attracting high caliber, experienced employees. These experienced people, tend to go to larger organizations, where they will be paid higher salaries and bonuses. Furthermore it also a problem for SMEs to retain, specialized employees, because of limited opportunities for career progression, and the constant appeal of larger organizations, who can provide better prospects. SMEs are mostly seen by some employee as a stepping-stone to move to larger organization. The departure of highly knowledgeable employees is a major threat to SMEs, unless that knowledge is captured, codified, and transferred throughout the organization. In SMEs, there is a collective, complex, and creative effort. As such, the quality of a product/ service heavily depends on the people, organization, and procedures used to create and deliver it. In other words, there is a direct correlation between the quality of the processes and the quality of the product/ service developed.

For SMEs, the drivers for knowledge management are (Davenport and Prusak, 2005):

- Customer driven: the need for better customer knowledge to meet their needs
- Process improvement: the need to become more efficient is often a powerful motivator
- Product-related: knowledge of technologies and marketplace to help the development of new products
- Restructuring: as small businesses grow, they need to add new functions and restructure; this often creates the need to be more explicit with what was previously informal knowledge
- Joint ventures: knowledge to help the creation and effectiveness of a joint venture
- Succession planning: knowledge to fill the gap when the owner/manager retires or moves on (they often hold much knowledge of the business in his or her head)

SMEs not only require knowledge about its own domain, but also about the domain for which product/ service are being developed. Domain knowledge that no one in the organization possesses must be acquired either by training or by hiring knowledgeable employees. KM however, can, enable the acquisition of new knowledge and it can help identify expertise as well as capture, package and share knowledge that already exists in the organization.

Challenges and Opportunities for KM in SMEs

Implementing KM in any organization is a challenge because of the time and effort that is required before there is a return on the investment. SMEs seem to have even less time than others because of the fast pace of the business. The most problematic challenge to KM is that most of the knowledge in SMEs is tacit and will never become explicit. It will remain tacit because there is no time to make it explicit. A way to address this problem can be to develop a knowledge sharing culture, as well as technology support for KM, never forgetting that the main asset of the organization is its employees. It is clear that a KM system needs to be supported by appropriate IT infrastructure. While IT can be intimidating to many people, this is not the case for SMEs (Schneider, 2001).

IMPLEMENTATION OF KM

Implementing a KM system might, however, not be so simple, involving both challenges and obstacles. Examples include:

- Technology issues: KM involves software technology, but it is not always simple or even possible to integrate all the different subsystems and tools to achieve the level of sharing that was planned. While the idea behind KM is to share knowledge, it is important not to share knowledge assets with the wrong audience (e.g., competitors and former employees). This issue might limit the extent to which knowledge can be shared in the organization. Further, different parts of the organization might use terms and concepts in different ways. This lack of standards can inhibit sharing of knowledge between them.
- Organizational issues: It is a mistake to focus only on technology and not on methodology. It is easy to fall into the technology trap and devote all resources to technology development without planning for a KM implementation approach.
- Individual issues: Employees do not have time to input knowledge or do not want to give away their knowledge.

KNOWLEDGE MANAGEMENT AND BUSINESS PERFORMANCE

KM is considered the best strategy that businesses can use to improve their competition level since knowledge is a strategic resource that allows them to obtain a higher level of competitiveness and innovation. KBT advocates that competitive advantage of the firm come from intangible assets, such as firm-specific knowledge (explicit knowledge), the tacit knowledge of its people and the ability to apply knowledge resources. Besides, knowledge leads to performance improvement when it is well managed. KBT suggests that KM practices, such as knowledge acquisition, knowledge creation, knowledge sharing, and knowledge storage and knowledge implementation play a vital role in achieving superior performance. Thus, businesses that strive to remain competitive ought to put more effort on the management of their knowledge resources that are necessary to increase their profits, sales growth, and market share. Furthermore, scholars like Seba and Rowley (2010) reported that firms that use suitable KM practices enhance their capabilities, resulting in improved business performance.

INNOVATION

Innovation is the implementation of a new organizational method in business practices, workplace organization, or external relations. Innovation is the process of translating an idea or discovery into a good or service that makes value to meet and satisfy the needs and expectations of customers. Similarly, innovation is the creation, adaptation and utilization of a value added, novelty in business and manufacturing domains, renewal and expansion of a product, services and markets, making of new ways of product development and establishing new management system. However, organizational innovations are measured based on product, process and administrative innovations, while innovation can be measured using product, process and market innovations.

Innovation and business performance

Owing to the current levels of intense competition and turbulent business environment, SMEs need to monitor their competitive edges vis-à-vis their competitors through rapid innovations. This partly explains why innovations are more vital to business performance levels. Innovations have significant influence on organizations' performance, survival and competitiveness. Similarly, innovations provide firms with a strategic orientation to achieve sustainable competitive advantage. Previous researchers have tested the association between innovations and business performance and have found significant positive relationships. For instance, business performance depended on the number of innovations, the nature of those innovations and the firm resources invested in the innovations (Baporikar, 2015a; 2015b). While, product and process innovations led to superior performance, performance is measured by sales, market share and profitability. The positive and significant relationships between innovations and business performance were also found in SMEs industry within different business sectors. Other studies on the effect of innovation on business performance came up with similar or slightly different results. For instance, Rosli and Sidek's (2013) study revealed a positive impact of product and process innovations on firms' performance in manufacturing sector in Malaysia but no direct relationship between market innovations and firms' performance were established. Salim and Sulaiman (2011) focused on ICT companies in Malaysia and confirmed the same results. Yet, another study done in Kenya, Ndalira, Ngugi, and Chepkulei (2013) revealed that innovations influenced the growth of garment SMEs. It also showed that the tendency of owners to engage in new ideas and creative processes resulted in new products and processes, which had great influence on the performance of SMEs. Lastly, Ndesaulwa and Kikula, (2016) conducted a literature survey to investigate the relationships between innovation and business performance of SMEs.

Knowledge management and innovations

Zaied, Louati, and Affes, (2015) associated knowledge resources to innovation and argued that these resources determine the capacity of the firm to innovate. Similarly, innovation is the transformation of knowledge into new products, practices, and processes and services. Hence, the influence of KM through acquisition, sharing, and application of innovation is acknowledged in the cited literature. To be specific, knowledge acquisition is the process of obtaining available knowledge from somewhere and it refers to the use of existing knowledge or capturing new knowledge (Lin & Lee, 2005). Internally, the company can acquire knowledge using explicit knowledge from existing documents or the tacit knowledge of its people into its repositories. Externally, business can acquire knowledge by employing individuals with the required knowledge and by purchasing knowledge assets, such as patents and research documents. Besides, a close relationship with customers may allow business managers to have a direct and faster knowledge flow and this may help them to improve their ability to capture the customers' knowledge, competitors' actions and behavior, market trends, and other developments (Baporikar, 2018).

It is important to emphasize that when there is acquisition of new knowledge within the company, the capacity of the employees' increases and they become more able to transform the new knowledge and generate the new ideas. Consequently, the stocks of knowledge increase and the business takes advantage of new opportunities by applying and exploiting acquired knowledge to produce innovative results. Scholars confirm the relationship between knowledge acquisition and innovation. Moreover, information acquired from alliance partners affects knowledge creation of the organization, which in turn leads to innovations. There is also a positive and significant relationship between knowledge acquisition and technological innovation (process and product innovation).

It can be stated that knowledge sharing is the exchange of knowledge, experiences and skills across the whole organization and members of the organization share and exchange knowledge to prompt their level of participation to increase. This contributes to the development of innovative ideas (Chen & Huang, 2009). Thus, a positive association can be assumed between knowledge sharing and innovation. Lastly, knowledge application (responsiveness to knowledge) is very necessary. It is the utilization of acquired knowledge to make useful decisions regarding business. Therefore, knowledge application can stimulate innovative activities. Factual evidences adduced from several studies have found a positive and significant relationship between KM and innovation. Thus, the way knowledge is managed determines the success of innovations in businesses. Further, effective KM process through knowledge creation, storage, distribution and application contributes to innovation in the firm. However, there is a positive relationship between the effectiveness of acquisition, sharing and application of knowledge and product innovation.

KNOWLEDGE MANAGEMENT - INNOVATION AND BUSINESS PERFORMANCE

Some researchers have identified a gap in the innovation field, especially in the determination of the critical factors that have a direct effect on innovation to improve business performance (Camisón & Villar López, 2010). That is why managers with the desire to increase their business performance pursue innovations in order to remain competitive since they are operating in a changing environment (Baporikar, 2015a). In this regard, scholars confirmed that the achievement of superior business performance requires that effective KM lead to innovation. Hence, effective KM through knowledge acquisition, knowledge sharing and application is very important because it comes to support management decision-making to enhance business performance and increase the capacity for creativity and innovation. Leal Rodríguez, Leal Millán, Salgueiro, and Gutiérrez, (2013) stated that when knowledge is effectively managed in different levels of the organization, it leads to the capabilities that are unique which in turn contribute to better performance through innovation. KM practices (i.e. knowledge acquisition, knowledge dissemination and responsiveness to knowledge) contribute to increased sales through new product development, adaptations and improvements in innovation. Other scholars, such Schiuma (2012) demonstrated a significant indirect effect of KM, where KM supported by IT facilitates the generation of innovation which results in increased business performance of SMEs in the technology sector. Figure 1 gives how KM practices impact innovation performance leading to business performance through products and services, management practices and business models.

Figure 1. KM Practices Impact on Innovation Performance Leading to Business Performance

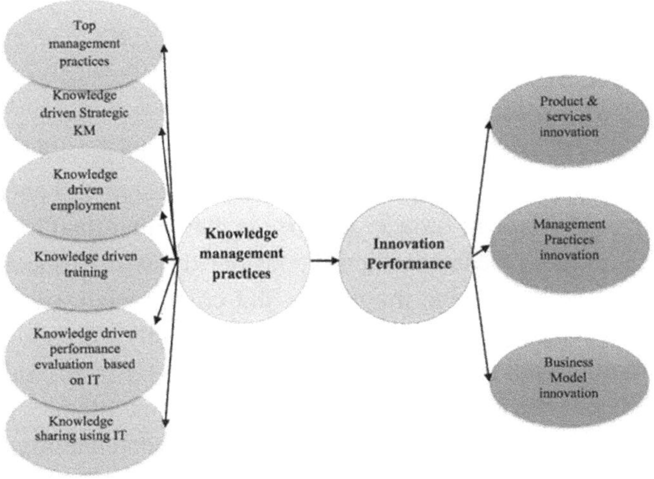

Source: Self Developed

SOLUTIONS AND RECOMMENDATIONS

SMEs can benefit from developments in KM. Knowledge is the most powerful and ubiquitous resource of any enterprise in general and SMEs in particular. Therefore, implementing KM in SMEs is useful and necessary. This study examined the KM and innovation in the relationship between KM and enhancing competitiveness and business performance. Innovation acts wholly as a conduit in the relationship between KM and business performance levels. The study has proven that KM, on itself, cannot influence business performance of SMEs, implying that knowledge resources that are acquired, shared and applied must be used to improve the quality of products, production processes and markets in order to achieve improved business performance.

KM remains a fundamental factor that promotes SMEs innovations. This is true because the generation of new ideas is through proper management of knowledge, which is a seed of innovations. Overall, KM does not have a direct effect on business performance except through innovation. This study emphasizes the power of innovation in the relationship between knowledge management as an antecedent to business performance.

The practical implications of this study are that owner-managers of manufacturing SMEs should pay keen interest in translating their available knowledge resources into the development of new products, processes, and markets to improve on their business performance levels. Utilizing well-qualified staff, motivating, and empowering employees through short courses and enabling them to attend seminars, conferences, and exhibitions to acquire new knowledge, can achieve this. Besides, knowledge-sharing culture within an enterprise should to be strengthened and the new knowledge should be utilized to enhance innovative activities for better business performance. In this connection, it would be prudent for policy-makers (ministries in charge of SMEs, government agencies, and stakeholders) to implement the findings of this study that should help them to formulate sound policies and support program which are necessary to boost the performance of SMEs.

FUTURE AREAS OF RESEARCH

Knowledge management in SMEs is still a relatively new topic, and research continues to understand its unique characteristics. Managers should encourage further research and encourage more initiatives that provide practical help to SMEs. Our broader premise is that rather than focus solely on knowledge management within SMEs, future researches should consider the wider aspect of "knowledge for the development of SMEs' e.g. the knowledge innovation and commercialization process. This study is based on literature review and exploratory in approach, so it is highly recommended that future studies on the subject employ a longitudinal method to compare any long-term variations in the results. Alternatively, qualitative studies could be conducted to supplement the quantitative findings because through methodological triangulation, it may be possible to gain a better understanding of the effect of KM and innovations on the relationship enhancing competitiveness leading to better business performance.

CONCLUSION

Knowledge management (KM) as a concept has become important because of the growing awareness of the importance of knowledge for the organization's prosperity and survival. As a result, knowledge has been identified with two fundamental characteristics, namely, tacit knowledge and explicit knowledge. According to Davenport and Prusak (2005), tacit knowledge involves the complex process of comprehension, which may not be easy to understand because it is hard to digest. It is assessed in the form of capabilities, skills, and ideas, which individuals may possess mentally. This type of knowledge can be transferred only by means of interactions with other people in the organization through experiences, practice, feelings, and attitudes among others. On the other hand, explicit knowledge means the information that can easily be articulated or codified, transferred, and shared to others in the form of manuals, fact sheets, pictures, charts, and diagrams. KM has been operationally defined differently because of its multi-dimensional nature. KM is the process of identifying and analyzing accessible knowledge that is needed to achieve organizational objectives. There is no generally agreeable definition of innovation. KM has also been examined as a process of acquiring, storing, understanding, sharing, implementing knowledge and all actions taken in the learning process in tandem with strategies of the organizations concerned. Further, KM is effort to explore the tacit and explicit knowledge of individuals, groups and organizations and to convert this treasure into organizational assets that are used by managers to make organizational decisions. Knowledge intensive enterprises have realized that a large number of problems are attributed to uncaptured and unshared product and process knowledge, as well as the need to know 'who knows what' in the enterprise, the need for remote collaboration, and the need to capture lessons learned and best practices. These realizations have led to a growing call for KM. Knowledge is a valuable resource of any enterprise. Any activity that does not leverage its power is clearly a sub-optimal utilization of the resources. In SMEs, a highly complex and intellectually intensive activity is not an exception. It involves intellectual effort by individuals in teams on projects with deadlines and deliverables that often change over the lifetime of the project leading to innovations that enhance the competitiveness.

REFERENCES

Alrubaiee, L., Alzubi, H. M., Hanandeh, R. E., & Al Ali, R. (2015). Investigating the relationship between knowledge management processes and organizational performance the mediating effect of organizational innovation. *International Review of Management and business research, 4*(4 Part 1), 989.

Andreeva, T., & Kianto, A. (2012). Does knowledge management really matter? Linking knowledge management practices, competitiveness and economic performance. *Journal of Knowledge Management,* 16(4), 617–636. DOI: 10.1108/13673271211246185

Baporikar, N. (2015a). *5. Innovation Knowledge Management Nexus. Innovation Management.* GRUYTER.

Baporikar, N. (2015b). Drivers of Innovation. In Ordoñez de Pablos, P., Turró, L., Tennyson, R., & Zhao, J. (Eds.), *Knowledge Management for Competitive Advantage During Economic Crisis* (pp. 250–270). Business Science Reference. DOI: 10.4018/978-1-4666-6457-9.ch014

Baporikar, N. (2016a). Organizational Barriers and Facilitators in Embedding Knowledge Strategy. In *Business Intelligence: Concepts, Methodologies, Tools, and Applications* (pp. 1585–1610). Business Science Reference. DOI: 10.4018/978-1-4666-9562-7.ch079

Baporikar, N. (2016b). Understanding Knowledge Management Spectrum for SMEs in Global Scenario. [IJSODIT]. *International Journal of Social and Organizational Dynamics in IT*, 5(1), 1–15. DOI: 10.4018/IJSODIT.2016010101

Baporikar, N. (2017a). Knowledge Management for Excellence in Indian Public Sector. [IJSESD]. *International Journal of Social Ecology and Sustainable Development*, 8(1), 49–65. DOI: 10.4018/IJSESD.2017010104

Baporikar, N. (2017b). Knowledge Transfer Issues in Teaching: Learning Management. In Baporikar, N. (Ed.), *Innovation and Shifting Perspectives in Management Education* (pp. 58–78). Business Science Reference. DOI: 10.4018/978-1-5225-1019-2.ch003

Baporikar, N. (2018). *Global Practices in Knowledge Management for Societal and Organizational Development.* IGI Global. DOI: 10.4018/978-1-5225-3009-1

Baporikar, N. (2019). Knowledge Management Dynamics and Public Sector Organization Development. In Albastaki, Y., Al-Alawi, A., & Abdulrahman Al-Bassam, S. (Eds.), *Handbook of Research on Implementing Knowledge Management Strategy in the Public Sector* (pp. 55–71). IGI Global. DOI: 10.4018/978-1-5225-9639-4.ch003

Baporikar, N. (2020). Role and Room for Knowledge Management in Small and Medium Enterprises. In Idemudia, E. (Ed.), *Handbook of Research on Social and Organizational Dynamics in the Digital Era* (pp. 115–134). IGI Global. DOI: 10.4018/978-1-5225-8933-4.ch006

Baporikar, N. (2021). Knowledge Management for Business Sustainability. In Geada, N., & Anunciação, P. (Eds.), *Reviving Businesses With New Organizational Change Management Strategies* (pp. 30–44). IGI Global. DOI: 10.4018/978-1-7998-7452-2.ch002

Baporikar, N. (2022). Strategies to Manage and Preserve Indigenous Knowledge. In Tshifhumulo, R., & Makhanikhe, T. (Eds.), *Handbook of Research on Protecting and Managing Global Indigenous Knowledge Systems* (pp. 207–222). IGI Global. DOI: 10.4018/978-1-7998-7492-8.ch012

Baporikar, N. (2023). Intergenerational Leadership for Improved Knowledge Transfer. In Polat, S., & Çelik, Ç. (Eds.), *Perspectives on Empowering Intergenerational Relations in Educational Organizations* (pp. 114–139). IGI Global. DOI: 10.4018/978-1-6684-8888-1.ch005

Camisón, C., & Villar-López, A. (2010). Effect of SMEs' international experience on foreign intensity and economic performance: The mediating role of internationally exploitable assets and competitive strategy. *Journal of Small Business Management*, 48(2), 116–151. DOI: 10.1111/j.1540-627X.2010.00289.x

Davenport, T. H., & Prusak, L. (1998). *Working knowledge: How organizations manage what they know.* Harvard Business Press.

Davenport, T. H., & Prusak, L. (2005). What do we talk about when we talk about knowledge? *I. NONAKA, Hg. Knowledge management. Critical perspectives on business and management. London: Routledge*, 301-321.

Drucker, P. F. (2020). *The essential drucker.* Routledge. DOI: 10.4324/9780429347979

Leal Rodríguez, A. L., Leal Millán, A., Roldán Salgueiro, J. L., & Ortega Gutiérrez, J. (2013). Knowledge management and the effectiveness of innovation outcomes: The role of cultural barriers. *Electronic Journal of Knowledge Management*, 11(1), 62–71.

Lin, H. F., & Lee, G. G. (2005). Impact of organizational learning and knowledge management factors on e-business adoption. *Management Decision*, 43(2), 171–188. DOI: 10.1108/00251740510581902

Mahr, D., Lievens, A., & Blazevic, V. (2014). The value of customer cocreated knowledge during the innovation process. *Journal of Product Innovation Management*, 31(3), 599–615. DOI: 10.1111/jpim.12116

Ndalira, D. W., Ngugi, J. K., & Chepkulei, B. (2013). Effect of the type of innovation on the growth of small and medium enterprises in Kenya: A case of garment enterprises in Jericho, Nairobi. *European Journal of Management Sciences and Economics*, 1(2).

Ndesaulwa, A. P., & Kikula, J. (2016). The impact of innovation on performance of small and medium enterprises (SMEs) in Tanzania: A review of empirical evidence. *Journal of Business and Management Sciences*, 4(1), 1–6.

OECD. K. (2018). *OECD science, technology and innovation outlook 2018.* Paris: OECD publishing.

Ordoñez de Pablos, P. (Ed.). (2014). *Knowledge management for competitive advantage during economic crisis.* IGI Global.

Prusak, R. (2019). Analysis of selected elements of knowledge management in the context of the size of the enterprise and the specifics of its activity. *Management*, 23(1), 90–104. DOI: 10.2478/manment-2019-0006

Rosli, M. M., & Sidek, S. (2013). The Impact of innovation on the performance of small and medium manufacturing enterprises: Evidence from Malaysia. *Journal of Innovation Management in Small & Medium Enterprises*, 2013, 1–16. DOI: 10.5171/2013.885666

Salim, I. M., & Sulaiman, M. (2011). Organizational learning, innovation and performance: A study of Malaysian small and medium sized enterprises. *International Journal of Business and Management*, 6(12), 118. DOI: 10.5539/ijbm.v6n12p118

Schiuma, G. (2012). Managing knowledge for business performance improvement. *Journal of Knowledge Management*, 16(4), 515–522. DOI: 10.1108/13673271211246103

Seba, I., & Rowley, J. (2010). Knowledge management in UK police forces. *Journal of Knowledge Management*, 14(4), 611–626. DOI: 10.1108/13673271011059554

Takeuchi, H., & Nonaka, I. (2000). Classic work: Theory of organizational knowledge creation.

Zaied, R. M. B., Louati, H., & Affes, H. (2015). The relationship between organizational innovations, internal sources of knowledge and organizational performance. *International Journal of Managing Value and Supply Chains*, 6(1), 53–67. DOI: 10.5121/ijmvsc.2015.6105

KEY TERMS AND DEFINITIONS

Approach: Method used in dealing with or accomplishing.

Barriers: Anything serving to obstruct, or preventing, access, or progress or something, which limits a quality or achievement or the act of limiting or the condition of being limited or cause delay. Barriers come in many forms and from many sources. They can be temporary or permanent. When evaluating a barrier, it is necessary that one looks at all the activities that precede the delay as well as the activities that follow the delay.

Challenges: Something that by its nature or character serves as a call to make special effort, a demand to explain, justify, or difficulty in a undertaking that is stimulating to one engaged in it.

Competitive Advantage: An advantage that firms has over its competitors, allowing it to generate greater sales or margins and/or retain more customers than its competition. There can be many types of competitive advantages including the knowledge, skills, structure, product offerings, distribution network and support.

Core competences: Knowledge based technical and human abilities and skills. Decision-Making: A rational and logical process of choosing the best alternative or course of action among the available options.

Innovation: Something new or different introduced, it is the act of innovating, which includes introduction of new things or methods. Innovation is also introduction of a new idea into the marketplace in the form of a new product or service, or an improvement in organization or process. The process of translating an idea or invention into a good or service that creates value or for which customers will pay.

Knowledge: The fact or condition of knowing something with familiarity gained through experience or association, acquaintance with or understanding of a science, art, or technique, the range of one's information or understanding, the circumstance or condition of apprehending truth or fact through reasoning or the fact or condition of having information or of being learned. Knowledge is acquaintance with facts, truths, or principles, as from study or investigation; general erudition, familiarity or conversance, as with a particular subject or branch of learning including acquaintance or familiarity gained by sight, experience, research or report.

Knowledge Management: The systematic process of finding, selecting, organizing, distilling and presenting information that improves the comprehension in a specific area of interest.

Organization: A group of persons organized for some end or work; an organized structure or whole for a business or administrative concern united and constructed for a particular end or a body of administrative officials, as of a political party, a government department, etc. It is act or process of organizing; a structure through which individuals cooperate systematically to conduct business and/or the administrative personnel of such a structure.

Small and Medium Enterprises (SMEs): is a term for segmenting businesses and other organizations that are somewhere between the "small office-home office" size and the larger enterprise. Country to country this term may vary, but it is usually based on the criteria of investment, number of employees and turnover, etc.

Tacit: Expressed or understood without being directly stated or put into words, to involve or indicate by inference, association, or necessary consequence, to contain potential sense.

Chapter 10
Marketing Applications of Emerging Technologies and Business Performance of Tourism SMEs:
A Systematic Literature Review

Mourad Aarabe
https://orcid.org/0009-0003-9772-6683
National School of Business and Management of Fez, Morocco

Nouhaila Ben Khizzou
National School of Business and Management of Fez, Morocco

Lhoussaine Alla
https://orcid.org/0000-0002-7238-1792
National School of Applied Sciences of Fez, Morocco

Ahmed Benjelloun
https://orcid.org/0009-0004-9673-2747
National School of Business and Management of Fez, Morocco

ABSTRACT

The tourism sector is currently undergoing a digital transformation, with emerging technologies playing a pivotal role in redefining marketing strategies and improving the performance of small and medium-sized enterprises (SMEs). This study aims to examine, through a comprehensive literature review, the marketing applications of emerging technologies and the impact of these technologies on the business performance of SMEs. A rigorous methodology based on the PRISMA protocol for reference collection and NVIVO software for textual and thematic analysis was employed in this research. The objective was to demystify the complex relationship between emerging technology marketing applications and the business performance of tourism SMEs. The results revealed a convergence that linked these technologies to key performance indicators.

DOI: 10.4018/979-8-3693-4046-2.ch010

INTRODUCTION

The prevailing trend is the restructuring of the global economic order, facilitated by the advent of new technologies. According to the United Nations Conference on Trade and Development (UNCTAD Technology and Innovation Report 2023), the volume of the technology market was estimated at 1.5 trillion dollars in 2018, with the potential to reach 9.5 trillion dollars by 2030. Small and medium-sized enterprises (SMEs) represent 95% of the economic fabric and contribute significantly to the creation of over 60% of jobs, according to OECD statistics. These figures illustrate the significant role that small and medium-sized enterprises (SMEs) can play in the global economy. The recent years have been marked by an unprecedented health and economic crisis, which has accelerated the digital transformation. This transformation is of paramount importance for the recovery and growth of the economy (UNCTAD Technology and Innovation Report 2021).

Several authors have demonstrated the complex and dynamic interplay between the commercial performance of small and medium-sized enterprises (SMEs) and the marketing application of technological advances. In recent years, there has been a notable increase in the utilization of technological advances, including Big Data (Bag et al., 2021), blockchain technology (Boukis, 2019; Ertemel, 2019; Stallone et al., 2021), artificial intelligence (Chintalapati & Pandey, 2022; Han et al., 2021; Verma et al., 2021) and the Internet of Things (Grewal et al., 2020). Kumar et al., (2021a) have identified the potential impact of new technologies on businesses and customers. In a similar vein, Deltour & Lethiais, (2014) have drawn attention to the positive impact of information and communication technology (ICT) on the performance of small and medium-sized enterprises (SMEs), particularly in conjunction with innovation. Nizeyimana et al., (2023) & Saoudi et al., (2023) contribute to this debate by emphasizing the potential of digital transformation to enhance the performance and success of SMEs.

The tourism sector has undergone significant transformations as a result of the emergence of new technologies, which have enabled the redefinition of marketing strategies and the development of the commercial performance of small and medium-sized enterprises (SMEs) (Lara et al., 2017). In order to survive, grow, and build a relationship of trust and co-creation of value with customers, SMEs in the tourism sector must differentiate themselves by rapidly and effectively integrating technological advances into their processes (Perera, 2021). This research examines the potential of emerging technologies to enhance the commercial performance of small and medium-sized enterprises (SMEs) in the tourism sector.

The objective of this study is to address the following central question: How does the marketing adoption of emerging technologies affect the commercial performance of tourism small and medium-sized enterprises (SMEs)? To provide answers to this crucial question, our work will first explore the various marketing applications of emerging technologies. This will be followed by an examination of the indicators of the company's commercial performance, with the aim of proposing a conceptual model explaining the relationship between the two concepts that can be transposed to the context of tourism SMEs. To this end, we endeavor to implement a meticulous literature review methodology, in accordance with the guidelines set forth by the PRISMA protocol and the utilization of NVIVO software for comprehensive textual and thematic analysis.

The present research is divided into four sections. The initial section will investigate the background of this research, with a particular emphasis on the theoretical and conceptual aspects of emerging technologies, their marketing applications, and the key performance indicators for small and medium-sized enterprises in the tourism sector. The second part will examine the chapter's main focus, emphasizing the current state of the art of the relationship between these two concepts, the research methodology, and the findings and discussions. The third and fourth parts present, respectively, the solutions and recommendations and the future research orientations. In conclusion, the research will be summarized, its limitations identified, and prospects for future research suggested.

BACKGROUND

Emerging technologies and SMTE marketing

A number of researchers have sought to conceptualize the notion of emerging technologies due to its inherent complexity and multidimensionality (Aarabe et al., 2024a). Godé, (2021) defines emerging technologies as "*all new innovations that are still in the early stages of development and are experiencing rapid growth.*" Bobillier Chaumon, (2021) supports this view, using Anastassova's (2006) four criteria to assert that new technologies represent breakthroughs in full development. These technologies possess distinctive characteristics, a limited range of applications, and the potential to significantly transform the social and economic landscape Bobillier Chaumon, (2021).

The features and applications of emerging technologies are continuously infiltrating business practices. Bobillier Chaumon, (2021) identifies collaborative robots, ambient technologies, artificial intelligence, big data, and immersive environments as innovative technological devices. (Agrawal et al., 2023) posit that organizations that leverage emerging technologies, including TD printing, the Internet of Things, artificial intelligence, nanotechnologies, social media, and databases, can provide a personalized and immediate customer experience while maintaining a competitive position in an uncertain and turbulent market.

Several authors have observed that emerging technologies have the potential to transcend the traditional boundaries of marketing, influencing the way companies interact with their customers and shape their brand image. Strategic and operational actions are now interconnected with artificial intelligence (Chintalapati & Pandey, 2022; Davenport et al., 2019, 2020; Haleem et al., 2022; Stone et al., 2020; Verma et al., 2021; Vlačić et al., 2021), blockchain technology (Boukis, 2019; Ertemel, 2019; Gleim & Stevens, 2021; Stallone et al., 2021), the Internet of Things (Grewal et al., 2020; Hoffman & Novak, 2018), and big data (Agrawal et al., 2023; Bag et al., 2021; Rosário & Dias, 2023) were identified as key areas of interest.

The diverse applications of emerging technologies have significantly transformed marketing practices. In accordance with the findings of Grewal et al.,(2020), these technologies facilitate the comprehension of shifts in consumer behavior and the sustenance of the dynamics of increasingly intricate markets. Kotler et al., (2021) distinguish the five components of Marketing 5.0, which are predicated on the integration of emerging technologies. These include Predictive Marketing, Data-Driven Marketing, Augmented Marketing, Agile Marketing and Contextual Marketing. Both authors concur on the pivotal role of new technologies in the advancement and optimization of the customer experience.

The tourism sector has not been exempt from the transformative impact of emerging technologies. Indeed, the adoption of artificial intelligence, big data, and other technologies has facilitated improvements in the commercial performance of small and medium-sized tourism enterprises (SMTEs) (Arce et al., 2024). These technologies afford businesses the capacity to customize customer preferences, which has a positive impact on customer satisfaction and sales (Ansari et al., 2022). Furthermore, they facilitate marketing automation and the personalization of advertising campaigns, thereby increasing efficiency and reducing costs (Arce et al., 2024). Consequently, the potential of virtual reality (VR) as a marketing technology for small and medium-sized enterprises (SMEs) in the tourism sector is underscored by its capacity to enhance customer engagement and offer immersive experiences (Lara et al., 2017). The adoption of blockchain technology facilitates the confidentiality and security of transactions (Lara et al., 2017). Coltey et al., (2022) propose an AI-driven market platform designed to assist small businesses in coping with market disruptions caused by events such as the COVID-19 pandemic. The study underscores the value of AI in automating market research and adapting to changing conditions, which is of paramount importance for tourism SMEs confronted with fluctuating demand patterns. In conclusion, the integration of advanced technologies can significantly enhance the competitiveness and resilience of SMEs in the tourism sector (Samara et al., 2020).

Business performance of tourism SMEs

Due to its complexity and polysemy, the concept of performance is inherently multidimensional, giving rise to a wealth of debate. The term "performance" is derived from the verb "to perform" which signifies the act of realizing and executing a given task. The English word "performance" is identical in form to the verb "to perform," which refers to the action of successfully achieving a goal. A number of authors have sought to conceptualize the concept of performance, linking it to three essential dimensions: action, result, and desired success (Bourguignon, 1995; Otley, 1999; Lebas and Euske, 2002). As defined by Nabaoui, (2023),performance is the evaluation of the degree to which an objective has been achieved in a specific temporal and spatial context. Deschamps and Nayak (1997) introduce a social dimension to this concept by associating performance with stakeholder satisfaction. This perspective broadens the scope of performance beyond tangible results to encompass social relations and effects (Nabaoui, 2023). A number of authors (Kalika 1988; Kaplan et Norton, 1992 & 1993; Morin et al., 1994 cited par Bentalha et al., 2020) have broadened the scope of the concept of performance to encompass elements such as the quality of goods and services, employee commitment, the workplace atmosphere, production, and customer satisfaction. Alazard (2007) and Marion et al. (2012) introduce an operational component to performance, taking into account factors such as effectiveness, efficiency, consistency, and relevance (Nabaoui, 2023). This operational combination constitutes a component of the management control optimization approach.

In the commercial context, Gafa, (2020) proposes a comprehensive approach to evaluating business performance. The author posits that business performance is not solely determined by quantitative indicators, such as sales, profits, and market share. Rather, it encompasses a broader range of qualitative indicators, including the capacity for innovation, customer satisfaction, perception of quality, and reputation. This combination of qualitative and quantitative criteria allows for a comprehensive evaluation of the company, considering financial, social, economic, perceptual, and organizational factors.

Table 1. Summary of the main mechanisms of the performance concept

Author	Mechanisms
Bourguignon (1995)	Action, result, success
Otley (1999)	Success, results
Bouquin (2009)	Meeting stakeholder expectations
Kalika, 1988 ; Kaplan et Norton, 1992, 1993 ; Morin et al., 1994	product and service quality, employee motivation, work climate, productivity, customer satisfaction
Marion et al. 2012	Effectiveness, Efficiency, Consistency, Relevance

Source: inspired from Bentalha et al., (2020)

Additionally, numerous scholars have put forth suggestions for quantifying the commercial success of tourism SMEs. These include financial indicators such as sales growth, market share, competitiveness, and profitability, as well as non-financial indicators such as customer satisfaction and loyalty, the number of complaints, the number of new businesses, repeat purchases, and employee skills and capabilities (Panno, 2020). Additionally, innovative practices and governance have been identified as playing a significant role in improving the business performance of SMEs in the tourism sector (Seow et al., 2021). Consequently, customer orientation, leadership skills, internal marketing, and reputation are the primary determinants of the performance of small tourism businesses (Komppula & Reijonen, 2006). Furthermore, the utilization of a dashboard facilitates the most effective control over the performance measurement process in tourism SMEs (Phillips & Louvieris, 2005).

The extant literature has identified a number of internal and external factors that influence the performance of small and medium-sized tourism businesses. The degree of integration of these technologies is of particular importance (Seow et al., 2021). Organizational capabilities linked to employee training and managerial change play a pivotal role in the effective implementation of these technologies (Ali Qalati et al., 2020). The competitiveness of the tourism sector, the structure of competition, and market dynamics exert a direct influence on the commercial performance of companies (Setiowati et al., 2015). Institutional and regulatory support facilitates the adoption of technology and the development of SMEs (Setiowati et al., 2015). Consumer behavior, influenced by socio-demographic and cultural factors, is a determining factor in the development of marketing strategies and sales performance (Seow et al., 2021).

The profile of investors in tourism SMEs is shaped by a number of performance-specific factors. These include an in-depth understanding of sector-specific performance levers, the necessary orientation of investment towards sustainable value creation, and heightened sensitivity to issues of social and environmental responsibility. Indeed, this type of business requires a more nuanced understanding of the key success factors (Aldebert & Gueguen, 2013), as well as a more sophisticated analysis of the potential risks and opportunities (Favre-Bonté & Tran, 2013). Secondly, the investor must possess a long-term strategic vision (Loufrani-Fedida & Aldebert, 2013) and demonstrate an active commitment to strategic support (MAKHLOUFI, 2021). Ultimately, the entrepreneur must integrate ESG criteria into their decision-making process (NIANG, 2024) and demonstrate a commitment to generating a positive impact on all stakeholders (Aziz & RAHOUA, 2020).

MAIN FOCUS OF THE CHAPTER

State of the art

A review of the literature reveals a general consensus regarding the impact of emerging technologies on the business performance of tourism companies. As posited by (Lara et al., 2017), the advent of new technologies has had a discernible impact on the structure of the tourism market and the manner in which small and medium-sized enterprises (SMEs) within the sector are managed. In order to remain competitive and survive in a tumultuous digital environment, it is imperative that businesses differentiate themselves. In contrast, (Ashari et al., 2014) emphasizes the growing potential of the strategic use of information and communication technologies to improve the internal processes and managerial innovations of tourism SMEs in order to develop their business performance. (Cuevas Vargas et al., 2021; Perera, 2021; Pothineni, 2023) have demonstrated that the commercial performance of SMEs can be enhanced through the adoption of digital transformation and the marketing of emerging technologies.

The advent of new technologies has revolutionized the tourism industry, offering innovative solutions to enhance the competitiveness of small and medium-sized enterprises (SMEs) and tourism destinations, and promote an inclusive and sustainable economy (O'Connor, 2023). These technologies have facilitated the emergence of e-tourism and smart tourism, which have improved the interaction between tourism businesses and destinations and the consumer. This has optimized their experience and increased their satisfaction during their stay or (Aarabe et al., 2024b; Buhalis, 2019).

Bag et al., (2021) have investigated the relationship between emerging technologies, such as artificial intelligence and big data, and the development of consumer and market knowledge, which in turn facilitates rational decision-making and improves overall company performance. Akpan et al., (2022) corroborate this study, emphasizing the significance of Big Data and the Internet of Things in enhancing operational efficacy and establishing a resilient competitive edge. Wamba-Taguimdje et al., (2020) present case studies demonstrating the significant impact of artificial intelligence on organizational and process performance levels through the mobilization of the theory of computational capabilities. The authors describe AI as a technological configuration that is characterized by complexity and diversity of applications in the business context. It is of paramount importance to reassess AI-based marketing as a pivotal strategic asset for enhancing the performance of small and medium-sized enterprises (SMEs) (Abrokwah-Larbi & Awuku-Larbi, 2023). In a related vein, Nuryyev et al., (2020) have demonstrated the beneficial impact of blockchain technology adoption on the business performance of SMEs in the tourism and hospitality sector.

Gafa, (2020) corroborates the significance of innovative capacity in the commercial performance of small businesses, adopting the market orientation approach of Kohli and Jaworski (1990) and Narver and Slater (1990). The author proposes a conceptual model adapted to small businesses, emphasizing the necessity of adopting more innovative approaches as an essential dimension of emerging technologies to ensure their business performance. In contrast, Mikalef & Gupta, (2021), demonstrate a correlation between advances in artificial intelligence capabilities and improvements in organizational creativity and business performance, using the RTB theory of resources.

Despite the benefits of adopting these technologies, challenges remain, such as the cost of adoption and employee training (Cuevas Vargas et al., 2021; Pothineni, 2023). This summary of the main empirical findings reveals a convergence of perspectives on the positive impact of the marketing application of emerging technologies, in particular big data and artificial intelligence, on the commercial performance of companies. The studies cited by Bag et al., (2021) and Wamba-Taguimdje et al., (2020) provide empirical evidence to support this assertion, with a particular focus on the impact on small businesses (Gafa, 2020).

Research Methodology

The systematic literature review employs a rigorous methodology to synthesize prior research on specific topics, such as technology adoption in small and medium-sized enterprises (SMEs) (Zamani, 2022). This process requires defining the research question, determining inclusion and exclusion criteria, and identifying appropriate databases (Shah et al., 2015; Zamani, 2022). SLRs are a widely utilized methodology for investigating a multitude of facets of SMEs, including the drivers and impediments to technology adoption in SMEs (Zamani, 2022), the impact of market orientations on performance (Shah et al., 2015), and the effectiveness of SME marketing (Bocconcelli et al., 2018). In the context of tourism, SLR has sought to examine the marketing implications of emerging technologies, including the metaverse (Sánchez-Amboage et al., 2024), digital marketing adoption (Sharma & Sharma, 2024), the challenges of implementing social networks (Al-Haidari et al., 2021) and numerous other perspectives that have either been previously discussed or identified as potential areas for future research.

In order to provide answers to our questions, we conducted a textual and literary analysis of 43 references selected according to the PRISMA protocol (Moher et al., 2009; PRISMA-P Group et al., 2015; Shamseer et al., 2015). This method is based on rigorous standards and guides to ensure the relevance of selected references (Mateo, 2020). The initial step was to identify over 3,687 references related to our queries (emerging technologies, Internet of Things, IoT, Virtual Reality, Augmented Reality, Artificial Intelligence, AI, marketing, marketing applications, business performance, performance indicators, tourism SMEs, tourism enterprises, tourism industries) in reputable databases such as PubMed, ScienceDirect, SCOPUS, and Springer. Subsequently, a series of filters were applied, including those based on research field, document type, and full-text availability. The 43 articles selected were included definitively after a thorough examination of their titles, abstracts, and keywords.

Figure 1. Flow chart – PRISMA

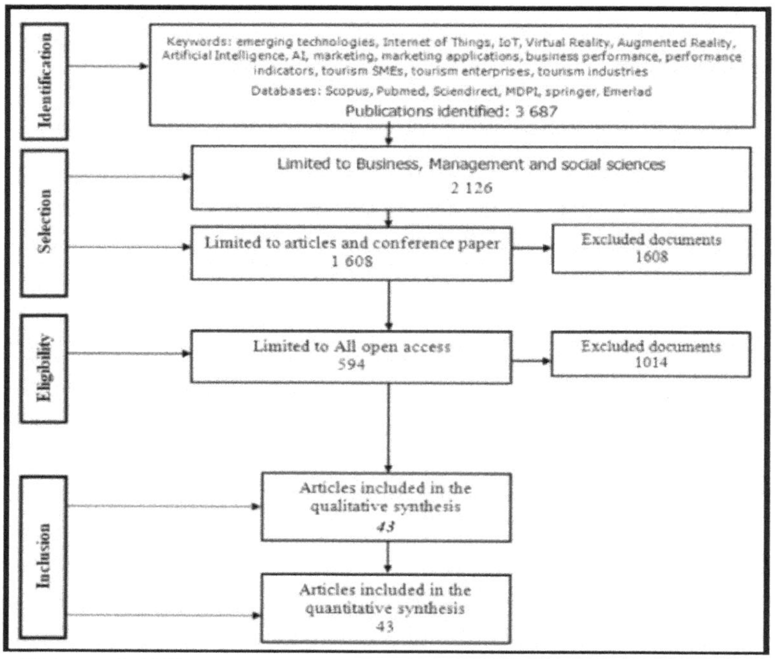

Source: Adapted from (Moher et al., 2009)

A descriptive and qualitative analysis was conducted using a corpus of 43 articles.

FINDINGS AND DISCUSSION

A textual analysis of the marketing applications of emerging technologies and the business performance of SMEs

A word cloud is a visual representation of the most significant features of a data set. The prevalence of English as the dominant language of scientific communication is also evident. Four clusters emerge from the word cloud. The main cluster relates to the field of research, i.e. SMEs in the tourism sector, with keywords such as "tourism; travel; hospitality; SME". There is also the management aspect with keywords such as "management; adoption; marketing; strategic; performance", the technological aspects "digital; technology", the business aspects "enterprise" and "management". This clustering shows the importance of the adoption of emerging technologies by SMEs in the tourism sector in order to improve their performance and competitiveness, thus demonstrating the relevance of the corpus studied. The word cloud below illustrates the main elements of the data set.

Figure 2. Word Cloud

The following table presents a breakdown of the articles by year. In recent years, there has been a growing interest in topics related to emerging technologies.

Table 2. References by Publication Year

Year	Number of corresponding sources	%
2024	4	9%
2023	6	14%
2022	7	16%
2021	5	12%
2020	4	9%
2019	2	5%
2018	2	5%
2017	1	2%
2016	1	2%
2015	1	2%
2014	3	7%
2007	1	2%
2006	1	2%
2005	2	5%
2000	1	2%

continued on following page

Table 2. Continued

Year	Number of corresponding sources	%
1998	1	2%
1997	1	2%
Total	43	100%

Source: Authors

The table below presents a comprehensive overview of the articles published in various academic journals. It demonstrates the diverse range of topics covered, from journals specializing in marketing to those focusing on management and technology. This reflects the interdisciplinary and multidimensional nature of research on our subject.

Table 3. Distribution of references by publication journal

Source	Number of corresponding sources
Sustainability	2
Tourism Review	2
Journal of Business Research	1
Systèmes d'information et management	1
RUFSO Journal of Social Science and Engineering	1
Revue internationale PME	1
Information & Management	1
International Journal of Information Management	1
Tourism Through Troubled Times: Challenges and Opportunities of the Tourism Industry in the 21st Century	1
Journal of Tourism Futures	1
European Scientific Journal, ESJ	1
International Journal of Academic Research in Accounting, Finance and Management Sciences	1
International Journal of Business Strategy and Automation (IJBSA)	1
JOURNAL OF SOCIAL SCIENCES DEVELOPMENT	1
International Journal of Economics, Business and Management Research	1
Tourism Recreation Research	1
Journal of Small Business & Entrepreneurship	1
Journal of Entrepreneurship in Emerging Economies	1
International Journal of Contemporary Hospitality Management	1
Measuring business excellence	1
Asian Journal of Technology Innovation	1
Journal of Travel Research	1
Journal of Small Business Management	1
Review of Integrative Business and Economics Research	1
International Journal of Business and management invention	1

continued on following page

Table 3. Continued

Source	Number of corresponding sources
Management decision	1
Migration Letters	1
Journal of Hospitality and Tourism Technology	1
International Journal of Tourism and Hospitality in Asia Pasific (IJTHAP)	1
Entrepreneurship, Innovation and Inequality	1
World Scientific News	1
Journal of Convergence for Information Technology	1
Journal of Business and Retail Management Research	1
ETRI Journal	1
Management Science	1
SN Computer Science	1
International journal of hospitality management	1
Smart Tourism	1
International Conference on Machine Learning, Big Data, Cloud and Parallel Computing (COM-IT-CON)	1
Strategic Direction	1
Journal of Competitiveness	1
Total	43

Source: Authors

A thematic analysis of the main marketing applications of emerging technologies.

The initial results on the areas of emerging technologies studied in the 43 articles were extracted using Zotero and NVIVO. The analysis of our corpus reveals that the following main emerging technologies are most prevalent: The following emerging technologies were identified: big data, blockchain technology, artificial intelligence, and the Internet of Things. Table 4 presents the principal authors who have addressed the four principal categories of emerging technologies in the corpus under study.

Table 4. Thematic analysis of the main areas of emerging technologies

Category	Definition	Authors
Big data	This is a substantial corpus of data, encompassing both structured and unstructured elements, derived from a multitude of points of contact between the customer and the brand. Such touchpoints may include social networks, online booking platforms, connected devices and appliances, and so forth.	(Akpan et al., 2022; Ali Qalati et al., 2020; Alla et al., 2022; Ansari et al., 2022; Camilleri, 2019; Kumar et al., 2021a; Mariani et al., 2018; Pothineni, 2023; Topsakal et al., 2022)
Blockchain	This technology is based on secure, decentralized data storage and transaction verification via interconnected computer nodes.	(Akpan et al., 2022; Ansari et al., 2022; Camilleri, 2019; Kumar et al., 2021b; Nuryyev et al., 2020; Perera, 2021; Pothineni, 2023; Saoudi et al., 2023; Topsakal et al., 2022)
Artificial Intelligence (AI)	This is a set of devices designed to emulate the cognitive processes of the human mind in order to perform tasks or solve problems based on data created by other technological advances.	(Akpan et al., 2022, 2022; Ansari et al., 2022; Mariani et al., 2018, 2018, 2018; Pothineni, 2023)
Internet of Things IoT	These are physical objects or devices that are interconnected and linked to communication technologies for the purpose of collecting important data. The data can be utilized to facilitate data-driven decision-making.	(Abrokwah-Larbi & Awuku-Larbi, 2023; Akpan et al., 2022; Ansari et al., 2022; Camilleri, 2019; Kumar et al., 2021b; Pothineni, 2023; Topsakal et al., 2022)

Source: Authors

An analysis of the four categories enables us to summarize the emerging technologies that are particularly relevant in the context of SME tourism marketing. These technological advances are essential for optimizing marketing practices. Table 5 provides a summary of the main marketing applications of emerging technologies.

Table 5. Main marketing applications for emerging technologies

Emerging technologies	Main applications	Dimensions of marketing practices
Big data	• Big data collection and storage • data analysis • Analysis of tourists' fingerprints • Using APIs to access social network data • Data cleansing and understanding methods for online review platforms	• Real-time analysis of tourist behavior • Customize offers according to customer preferences • Using social media to collect data and understand tourist behavior • Special offers and personalized experiences • Identifying critical business issues • Development of mobile customer relationship management applications for tourist destinations
Blockchain	• Data protection and transaction security • Creating a secure digital identity • Smart contracts • Product transparency and traceability	• Digital payments • Creation of new offers • Marketing automation • Programmatic marketing • Programmatic advertising campaigns • Reservations management • Authenticate user reviews
Artificial Intelligence (AI)	• Data processing and analysis • Deep learning • Digital twins • 3D visualization • VR/AR	• Personalized travel • Destination recommendations • Segmentation of customers into specific groups according to their preferences, behaviors and needs • Automate customer support with chatbots and virtual assistants • Optimizing advertising campaigns
Internet of Things IoT	• Real-time monitoring and management • Virtual and augmented reality • Collaborative networks and shared decision-making • Process automation	• Co-creating value with customers • Personalizing customer experiences • Innovation marketing • Interactivity and commitment • Marketing automation

Source: Authors

In the field of small and medium-sized enterprise (SME) marketing, the uzing of emerging technologies is becoming increasingly prevalent, due to their substantial impact on business performance. A number of authors have identified the significance of practices such as big data, blockchain, artificial intelligence (AI), and the Internet of Things (IoT) in the development of various key performance indicators.

In the context of big data, the authors have focused on the crucial role of these technologies in the collection, storage, and analysis of massive data (Mariani et al., 2018). The analysis of tourism data enables companies to gain insight into customer behavior and preferences in real time (Camilleri, 2019). This enables the creation of offers and experiences that are tailored to the specific needs of travelers. Consequently, tourism organizations are able to optimize their marketing campaigns and enhance customer engagement (Topsakal et al., 2022).

Blockchain technology offers valuable solutions in terms of security and transparency in the tourism industry (Kumar et al., 2021b; Nuryyev et al., 2020). The creation of authentic digital identities and the protection of data security are crucial factors in enhancing privacy and facilitating product traceability (Camilleri, 2019). Smart contracts facilitate the automation of processes such as reservations, advertising campaigns, and e-reputation management (Camilleri, 2019).

Artificial intelligence has transformed the tourism sector by streamlining data processing and analysis through machine learning and deep learning (Arce et al., 2024). Consequently, the creation of digital twins has enabled enhanced 3D visualization and immersive experiences (VR and AR) (Akpan et al., 2022; Topsakal et al., 2022). These capabilities facilitate travel personalization, destination recommendation, and customer segmentation. Chatbots and virtual assistants can be utilized to automate customer support, optimize advertising campaigns, and enhance the quality of company-customer interaction (Ansari et al., 2022).

The Internet of Things has transformed the tourism industry, facilitating real-time monitoring and management, as well as enhanced experiences in augmented and virtual reality (Kumar et al., 2021b). The co-creation of value with customers and the personalization of their experience are facilitated by these technological advances (Abrokwah-Larbi & Awuku-Larbi, 2023).

Each emerging technology category offers distinctive advantages to tourism small and medium-sized enterprises (SMEs), facilitating their capacity to innovate, adapt to changing consumer needs, and create personalized customer experiences while promoting efficiency and confidentiality.

Thematic analysis of improved key business performance indicators

The following table presents a summary of the key performance indicators for small and medium-sized tourism enterprises (SMEs) that are likely to be affected by the marketing adoption of emerging technologies.

Table 6. Main business KPIs improved by the use of emerging technologies

Emerging technologies	Business KPIs
Big data	• Innovative applications boost revenue • Customer satisfaction with services provided • Enhanced reputation for tourism businesses • Reduce operating costs while maintaining customer satisfaction • Better decision-making thanks to Big Data-powered business intelligence • Creating value for stakeholders and customers • Improving competitiveness through • Increasing tourist numbers through data-driven strategies
Blockchain	• Reduce costs, improve transaction security and transparency • Increase customer satisfaction and service levels • Improved customer loyalty and operational efficiency • Optimize marketing campaigns and boost ROI • Increased transparency and consumer confidence
Artificial Intelligence (AI)	• Conversion rates • Satisfaction • Commitment • Profit margin • Loyalty rate
Internet of Things IoT	• Customer satisfaction, Product quality • Customer loyalty, Increased sales • Purchase intention, Customer commitment • Efficient decision-making processes • Lower operating costs

Source: Authors

The findings of the literature review demonstrate how emerging technologies can enhance business performance for a variety of marketing purposes. The studies indicate that new technologies, such as artificial intelligence, big data, blockchain technology, and the Internet of Things, are crucial to improving the marketing effectiveness of small and medium-sized enterprises (SMEs).

Big data enables companies to collect, analyze, and make effective use of vast amounts of data, enabling them to significantly increase revenues, improve customer satisfaction, cut costs, and boost competitiveness. Blockchain technology, for instance, can help reduce costs, increase the security and transparency of transactions, boost satisfaction, optimize marketing campaigns and return on investment, and optimize the customer experience. Similarly, artificial intelligence can improve conversion rates, customer satisfaction, engagement and loyalty. Ultimately, the Internet of Things can enhance the customer experience and respond in real time to customer needs to increase sales and customer engagement by optimizing marketing decisions and product quality improvement processes.

The model examines the impact of new technologies applied to marketing on the performance and efficiency of small and medium-sized enterprises (SMEs) in the tourism sector. It assesses how these technologies affect customer engagement, trend forecasting, campaign management, segmentation, personalization, data analysis, customer experience, as well as product tracking. Marketing effectiveness is combined with a wide range of quantitative and qualitative measures of business performance. It is possible that other factors may serve to moderate this relationship, including the prevailing culture within the management structure, the specific characteristics of the sector in question, and considerations related to time and space. The model provides tourism SMEs with a comprehensive understanding of the strategic implications of these technologies.

Figure 3. Outline Analysis Model

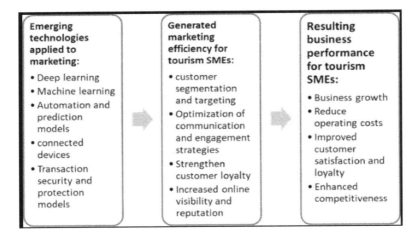

Source: Authors

Issues and Challenges

Indeed, the marketing adoption of emerging technologies by tourism small and medium-sized enterprises (SMEs) presents a multitude of opportunities for enhancing business performance. However, it also gives rise to significant challenges for management, ethics, and privacy. It is incumbent upon managers to address these issues with prudence in order to fully leverage the potential of these innovations while upholding ethical standards, respecting customer trust, and adhering to the relevant regulations.

Table 7. Issues and challenges in adopting emerging technologies

	Dimension	References
Operational barriers	The complexity and velocity of technological evolution	(Akpan et al., 2022; Kumar et al., 2021a)
	The costs associated with investment and maintenance	(Deltour & Lethiais, 2014; Mariani et al., 2018)
	The difficulty of integrating the technology into existing processes	(Perera, 2021; Topsakal et al., 2022)
	The complexities inherent in managing and analyzing massive data sets	(Mariani et al., 2018)
	The difficulties associated with personalization and customer experience	(Camilleri, 2019)
	The lack of requisite skills and knowledge	(Camilleri, 2019)
	Data protection, privacy and confidentiality	(Kumar et al., 2021b)
	The necessity of adapting to evolving consumer expectations	(Lara et al., 2017)
Safety and ethical	Personal data protection	(Abrokwah-Larbi & Awuku-Larbi, 2023; Camilleri, 2019)
	Transparency and consent	(Nuryyev et al., 2020)
	Data and transaction, privacy	(Camilleri, 2019; Kumar et al., 2021b)
	Algorithmic bias and discrimination	(Ansari et al., 2022)
	Technological dependency	(Abrokwah-Larbi & Awuku-Larbi, 2023; Arce et al., 2024)
	Digital divide	(Lythreatis et al., 2022; Nizeyimana et al., 2023)
	Environmental impact	(Pattinson, 2015)

Source: authors

It is evident that the adoption of emerging technologies presents a substantial opportunity for SMEs in the tourism sector. However, the implementation of such an approach necessitates a more creative and innovative approach on the part of managers (Mariani et al., 2018), as well as a combination of common sense, humility, and realism (Topsakal et al., 2022), pedagogy, and foresight (Akpan et al., 2022; Camilleri, 2019).

Similarly, the success of such a challenge depends on effective governance of the ecosystem as a whole (Nizeyimana et al., 2023; Perera, 2021), as well as support from supervisory bodies to facilitate the implementation of these significant organizational changes in a manner that is not constrained by the limitations of the present moment or the mere imitation of existing practices.

SOLUTIONS AND RECOMMENDATIONS

The advent of new technologies presents unparalleled prospects for small and medium-sized enterprises (SMEs) operating within the tourism sector. The implementation of augmented reality allows tourism SMEs to enhance the visitor experience and differentiate themselves from competitors (Cranmer et al., 2021). As the authors posit, SMEs can leverage these technologies to develop distinctive business models and offer valuable benefits to visitors and stakeholders alike, including enhanced accessibility and job security (Cranmer & Jung, 2017). To ensure the successful implementation of augmented reality, small and medium-sized enterprises (SMEs) must form partnerships with technology developers or academic and professional institutions. This will enable them to generate revenue, increase profits and reduce costs (Cranmer et al., 2018). Business models based on augmented reality (AR) provide a framework for small and medium-sized enterprises (SMEs) to effectively implement AR and capitalize on its potential benefits, including added value and economic sustainability and competitiveness (Cranmer et al., 2021). The adoption of new technologies by SMEs in the tourism sector is an effective means of improving performance and competitiveness (Ashari et al., 2014). These advances facilitate improvements in management innovation, the strengthening of marketing strategies, and the development of internal procedures (Ashari et al., 2014). Through the adoption of these technologies and strategies, tourism SMEs can enhance competitiveness and adapt to market demand (Ashari et al., 2014). The following table presents a summary of the principal solution and recommendations pertaining to the marketing adoption of emerging technologies by tourism small and medium-sized enterprises (SMEs).

Table 8. Key solutions and recommendations

Authors	Solutions and recommendations
(Ansari et al., 2022; Ashari et al., 2014; Cranmer et al., 2021; Lara et al., 2017; Shaikh, 2022)	• Leverage augmented reality (AR) to enhance the visitor experience and increase customer engagement. • Innovative Business Models to differentiate in the market and integrate the value proposition. • Flexibility and agility of SMEs in adopting new technologies • Collaboration with stakeholders • Staff training and awareness to overcome reluctance to adopt new technologies. • Assessing return on investment • Integration of marketing and management efforts through advanced technology platforms • Train and educate employees on the use of new technologies • Innovation and flexibility to technology and market changes • Differentiation and innovation in products/services and marketing • Customize customer experience • Unique value proposition • Integrate IoT technologies to meet specific and personalized customer needs • SMEs can adopt new IoT technologies with minimal cost and effort. • Adopt IoT to reinvent business models of tourism SMEs • Collect real-time data with IoT and AI technologies

Source: Authors

FUTURE RESEARCH DIRECTIONS

The marketing applications of emerging technologies, including artificial intelligence, the Internet of Things, and augmented reality, by small and medium-sized enterprises (SMEs) in the tourism sector present both significant opportunities and challenges. Future research should concentrate on investigating the ways in which artificial intelligence can be utilized in marketing to analyze customer-company interactions, including social media posts, with the objective of enhancing customer engagement (Abrokwah-Larbi & Awuku-Larbi, 2023). Furthermore, it would be beneficial to examine how tourism SMEs can leverage immersive technologies, such as augmented reality, to enhance their competitiveness and optimize the customer experience, while considering the flexibility of SMEs in navigating barriers to adopting such technologies (Cranmer et al., (2021). As well as Developing strategic approaches that take into account consumer preferences and staff needs for successful adoption of artificial intelligence and big data technologies (Ansari et al., 2022). The following table provides a comprehensive overview of the primary areas of focus within the field of futures research.

Table 9. Main directions of futures research

Auteurs	Directions of futures research
(Ashari et al., 2014; Cranmer et al., 2021; Lara et al., 2017)	• Exploration of sustainable and innovative tourism SME business models • Identifying specific barriers to the adoption of new technologies by SME • Cooperation between tourism SMEs and other sectors • Deepening research on the use of data and artificial intelligence for personalizing tourism experience • Investigate the utilization and effects of social media in the context of tourism marketing. • Digital marketing strategies specific to tourism SMEs • Investigate the impact of networking and collaboration between tourism SMEs and other industry players on innovation and competitiveness.

Source: Authors

CONCLUSION

In conclusion, this literature review aims to explore the ways in which the marketing applications of emerging technologies can enhance the performance of small and medium-sized enterprises, with a particular focus on the tourism sector. The findings demonstrate that the integration of diverse technologies can facilitate business efficiency in SMEs through strategic and operational decision-making. These decisions are predicated on the company's capacity to gather information and anticipate changes in the external environment. The study emphasizes the pivotal role of technology in enhancing the efficacy of marketing decisions, thereby optimizing sales efficiency. Consequently, the enhancement of the customer experience through the application of emerging technologies has the potential to influence the company's long-term performance.

However, it is important to note that all research is subject to limitations. The concepts defined are variable and evolving, which may require adaptation to possible changes in contexts. As a result, while the conceptual framework is general, there is a risk of neglecting geographical, dimensional, or even environmental specificities. Moreover, from a methodological standpoint, the dearth of data on SMEs in the tourism industry constrains the representativeness and applicability of the findings, potentially introducing a selection bias due to the irrelevance of the selected references.

The study provides valuable insights for future research. It highlights the need for further analysis, particularly in adapting the study to the marketing characteristics specific to small and medium-sized enterprises (SMEs). To enhance the recommendations for SME performance, it is essential to consider cross-cultural and managerial differences, as well as spatial and temporal disparities. Additionally, a deeper exploration of the conceptual frameworks is required to understand their evolving nature better and to tailor the study to the unique marketing needs of SMEs, emphasizing the importance of holistic theories. Methodologically, it is crucial to empirically test the proposed model to verify and refine its components and to delve deeper into the complex relationship between emerging technology marketing practices and company performance.

From an empirical standpoint, it would be beneficial to employ participant observations to monitor fluctuations in SME economic performance indicators. Segmenting SMEs by business sector, size, structure, and management style provides a comprehensive overview. The advancement of new technologies through policies and initiatives necessitates an integrated approach, international comparisons, and stakeholder involvement to formulate recommendations for professionals. This study constitutes a significant contribution to the marketing of small and medium-sized enterprises and establishes the foundation for future research and practical applications.

REFERENCES

Aarabe, M., Khizzou, N. B., Alla, L., & Benjelloun, A. (2024a). Marketing Applications of Emerging Technologies : A Systematic Literature Review. In *AI and Data Engineering Solutions for Effective Marketing* (p. 23-47). IGI Global. DOI: 10.4018/979-8-3693-3172-9.ch002

Aarabe, M., Khizzou, N. B., Alla, L., & Benjelloun, A. (2024b). Smart Tourism Experience and Responsible Travelers' Behavior : A Systematic Literature Review. In *Promoting Responsible Tourism With Digital Platforms* (p. 128-147). IGI Global. DOI: 10.4018/979-8-3693-3286-3.ch008

Abrokwah-Larbi, K., & Awuku-Larbi, Y. (2023). The impact of artificial intelligence in marketing on the performance of business organizations : Evidence from SMEs in an emerging economy. *Journal of Entrepreneurship in Emerging Economies*. https://www.emerald.com/insight/content/doi/10.1108/JEEE-07-2022-0207/full/html

Agrawal, P., Navgotri, S., & Nagesh, P. (2023). Impact of emerging technologies on digital manufacturing : Insights from literature review. *Materials Today: Proceedings*. Advance online publication. DOI: 10.1016/j.matpr.2023.03.187

Akpan, I. J., Udoh, E. A. P., & Adebisi, B. (2022). Small business awareness and adoption of state-of-the-art technologies in emerging and developing markets, and lessons from the COVID-19 pandemic. *Journal of Small Business and Entrepreneurship*, 34(2), 123–140. DOI: 10.1080/08276331.2020.1820185

Al-Haidari, N. N., Kabanda, S., & Almukhaylid, M. M. (2021). The Challenges Of Implementing Social Media Marketing In The Tourism Industry : A Systematic Review. *Conference: 19th International Conference e-Society 2021*.

Aldebert, B., & Gueguen, G. (2013). TIC et performance : Rôle du dirigeant de PME touristiques. *Revue internationale PME, 26*(3), 213-233.

Ali Qalati, S., Li, W., Ahmed, N., Ali Mirani, M., & Khan, A. (2020). Examining the factors affecting SME performance : The mediating role of social media adoption. *Sustainability (Basel)*, 13(1), 75. DOI: 10.3390/su13010075

Alla, L., Kamal, M., & Bouhtati, N. (2022). Big data et efficacité marketing des entreprises touristiques : Une revue de littérature. *Alternatives Managériales Economiques, 4*(0), Article 0. DOI: 10.48374/IMIST .PRSM/ame-v1i0.36928

Ansari, N., Tyagi, S., Mehrwal, N., Rastogi, N., Chibber, S., Memoria, M., Kumar, R., & Gupta, A. (2022). A critical insight into the impact of technology in transformation of tourist business into smart tourism. *2022 International Conference on Machine Learning, Big Data, Cloud and Parallel Computing (COM-IT-CON), 1*, 832-837. https://ieeexplore.ieee.org/abstract/document/9850779/

Arce, C. G. M., Valderrama, D. A. C., Barragán, G. A. V., & Santillán, J. K. A. (2024). Optimizing business performance : Marketing strategies for small and medium businesses using artificial intelligence tools. *Migration Letters : An International Journal of Migration Studies*, 21(S1), 193–201. DOI: 10.59670/ml.v21iS1.6008

Ashari, H. A., Heidari, M., & Parvaresh, S. (2014). Improving SMTEs' business performance through strategic use of information communication technology : ICT and tourism challenges and opportunities. *International Journal of Academic Research in Accounting. Finance and Management Sciences*, 4(3), 1–20.

Aziz, S., & RAHOUA, F. (2020). L'orientation parties prenantes et performance organisationnelle, cas des structures d'hébergement touristique en milieu rural. *Revue Internationale des Sciences de Gestion*, 3(1). https://revue-isg.com/index.php/home/article/download/188/170

Bag, S., Gupta, S., Kumar, A., & Sivarajah, U. (2021). An integrated artificial intelligence framework for knowledge creation and B2B marketing rational decision making for improving firm performance. *Industrial Marketing Management*, 92, 178–189. DOI: 10.1016/j.indmarman.2020.12.001

Bentalha, B., Hmioui, A., & Alla, L. (2020). La performance des entreprises de services : Un cadrage théorique d'un concept évolutif. *Alternatives Managériales Economiques*, 2(1), Article 1. DOI: 10.48374/IMIST.PRSM/ame-v2i1.19435

Bobillier Chaumon, M.-É. (2021). Technologies émergentes et transformations digitales de l'activité : Enjeux pour l'activité et la santé au travail. *Psychologie du Travail et des Organisations*, 27(1), 17–32. DOI: 10.1016/j.pto.2021.01.002

Bocconcelli, R., Cioppi, M., Fortezza, F., Francioni, B., Pagano, A., Savelli, E., & Splendiani, S. (2018). SMEs and Marketing : A Systematic Literature Review. *International Journal of Management Reviews*, 20(2), 227–254. DOI: 10.1111/ijmr.12128

Boukis, A. (2019). Exploring the implications of blockchain technology for brand-consumer relationships : A future research agenda. *Journal of Product and Brand Management*, 29(3), 307–320. Advance online publication. DOI: 10.1108/JPBM-03-2018-1780

Buhalis, D. (2019). Technology in tourism-from information communication technologies to eTourism and smart tourism towards ambient intelligence tourism : A perspective article. *Tourism Review*, 75(1), 267–272. DOI: 10.1108/TR-06-2019-0258

Camilleri, M. A. (2019). The use of data-driven technologies in tourism marketing. In *Entrepreneurship, Innovation and Inequality* (p. 182-194). Routledge. https://www.taylorfrancis.com/chapters/edit/10.4324/9780429292583-11/use-data-driven-technologies-tourism-marketing-mark-anthony-camilleri

Chintalapati, S., & Pandey, S. K. (2022). Artificial intelligence in marketing : A systematic literature review. *International Journal of Market Research*, 64(1), 38–68. DOI: 10.1177/14707853211018428

Coltey, E., Alonso, D., Vassigh, S., & Chen, S.-C. (2022). Towards an AI-Driven Marketplace for Small Businesses During COVID-19. *SN Computer Science*, 3(6), 441. DOI: 10.1007/s42979-022-01349-w PMID: 35975091

Cranmer, E., & Jung, T. (2017). The value of augmented reality from a business model perspective. *e-Review of Tourism Research*, 8. https://e-space.mmu.ac.uk/617802/

Cranmer, E., Urquhart, C., Claudia tom Dieck, M., & Jung, T. (2021). Developing augmented reality business models for SMEs in tourism. *Information & Management*, 58(8), 103551. DOI: 10.1016/j.im.2021.103551

Cranmer, E. E., Tom Dieck, M. C., & Jung, T. (2018). How can Tourist Attractions Profit from Augmented Reality? In Jung, T., & Tom Dieck, M. C. (Eds.), *Augmented Reality and Virtual Reality* (pp. 21–32). Springer International Publishing., DOI: 10.1007/978-3-319-64027-3_2

Cuevas Vargas, H., Fernández Escobedo, R., Cortés Palacios, H. A., & Ramírez Lemus, L. (2021). *The relation between adoption of information and communication technologies and marketing innovation as a key strategy to improve business performance.* https://addi.ehu.es/handle/10810/52894

Davenport, T., Guha, A., Grewal, D., & Bressgott, T. (2019). How artificial intelligence will change the future of marketing. *Journal of the Academy of Marketing Science*, 48(1), 1–19. DOI: 10.1007/s11747-019-00696-0

Davenport, T., Guha, A., Grewal, D., & Bressgott, T. (2020). How artificial intelligence will change the future of marketing. *Journal of the Academy of Marketing Science*, 48(1), 24–42. DOI: 10.1007/s11747-019-00696-0

Deltour, F., & Lethiais, V. (2014). L'innovation en PME et son accompagnement par les TIC : Quels effets sur la performance? *Systèmes d'information et management, 19*(2), 45-73.

Ertemel, A. V. (2019). *Implications of Blockchain Technology on Marketing* (SSRN Scholarly Paper 3351196). https://papers.ssrn.com/abstract=3351196

Favre-Bonté, V., & Tran, S. (2013). L'apport d'internet aux petites entreprises (PE) touristiques dans la construction de leur positionnement stratégique : Le cas des hébergeurs. *Revue internationale P.M.E (Norwalk, Conn.)*, 26(1), 45–64. DOI: 10.7202/1024270ar

Gafa, Y. (2020). Effet médiateur de l'innovativité dans la relation orientation-marché et performance commerciale des Très Petites Entreprises (TPE) de métiers. *REVUE AFRICAINE DE MANAGEMENT, 3*(5), Article 5. DOI: 10.48424/IMIST.PRSM/ram-v5i3.20156

Gleim, M., & Stevens, J. (2021). Blockchain : A game changer for marketers? *Marketing Letters*, 32(1), 1–6. DOI: 10.1007/s11002-021-09557-9

Godé, C. (2021). Propos introductif : Technologies émergentes et digitalisation des organisations. *Recherche et Cas en Sciences de Gestion*, (22). Advance online publication. DOI: 10.3917/rcsg.022.0007

Grewal, D., Hulland, J., Kopalle, P. K., & Karahanna, E. (2020). The future of technology and marketing : A multidisciplinary perspective. *Journal of the Academy of Marketing Science*, 48(1), 1–8. DOI: 10.1007/s11747-019-00711-4

Haleem, A., Javaid, M., Asim Qadri, M., Pratap Singh, R., & Suman, R. (2022). Artificial intelligence (AI) applications for marketing : A literature-based study. *International Journal of Intelligent Networks*, 3, 119–132. DOI: 10.1016/j.ijin.2022.08.005

Han, R., Lam, H. K. S., Zhan, Y., Wang, Y., Dwivedi, Y. K., & Tan, K. H. (2021). Artificial intelligence in business-to-business marketing : A bibliometric analysis of current research status, development and future directions. *Industrial Management & Data Systems*, 121(12), 2467–2497. DOI: 10.1108/IMDS-05-2021-0300

Hoffman, D. L., & Novak, T. P. (2018). Consumer and Object Experience in the Internet of Things : An Assemblage Theory Approach. *The Journal of Consumer Research*, 44(6), 1178–1204. DOI: 10.1093/jcr/ucx105

Komppula, R., & Reijonen, H. (2006). Performance determinants in small and micro tourism business. *Tourism Review*, 61(4), 13–20. DOI: 10.1108/eb058482

Kotler, P., Kartajaya, H., & Setiawan, I. (2021). *Marketing 5.0 : Technology for Humanity*. John Wiley & Sons.

Kumar, V., Ramachandran, D., & Kumar, B. (2021a). Influence of new-age technologies on marketing : A research agenda. *Journal of Business Research*, 125, 864–877. DOI: 10.1016/j.jbusres.2020.01.007

Kumar, V., Ramachandran, D., & Kumar, B. (2021b). Influence of new-age technologies on marketing : A research agenda. *Journal of Business Research*, 125, 864–877. DOI: 10.1016/j.jbusres.2020.01.007

Lara, J. C. B., García, J. C. P., & Chico, C. O. (2017). Tourism SMEs in a digital environment : Literature review. *European Scientific Journal*, 13(28), 429. DOI: 10.19044/esj.2017.v13n28p429

Loufrani-Fedida, S., & Aldebert, B. (2013). Le management stratégique des compétences dans un processus d'innovation : Le cas d'une TPE touristique. *Revue de Gestion des Ressources Humaines*, 3(89), 56–72. DOI: 10.3917/grhu.089.0056

Lythreatis, S., Singh, S. K., & El-Kassar, A.-N. (2022). The digital divide : A review and future research agenda. *Technological Forecasting and Social Change*, 175, 121359. DOI: 10.1016/j.techfore.2021.121359

Makhloufi, A. (2021). L'entrepreneuriat innovant : Variables stimulant l'innovation dans les PMEs du secteur touristique au Maroc. *Revue Internationale du Chercheur*, 2(3). https://www.revuechercheur.com/index.php/home/article/view/238

Mariani, M., Baggio, R., Fuchs, M., & Höepken, W. (2018). Business intelligence and big data in hospitality and tourism : A systematic literature review. *International Journal of Contemporary Hospitality Management*, 30(12), 3514–3554. DOI: 10.1108/IJCHM-07-2017-0461

Mateo, S. (2020). Procédure pour conduire avec succès une revue de littérature selon la méthode PRISMA. *Kinésithérapie, la Revue*, 20(226), 29–37. DOI: 10.1016/j.kine.2020.05.019

Mikalef, P., & Gupta, M. (2021). Artificial intelligence capability : Conceptualization, measurement calibration, and empirical study on its impact on organizational creativity and firm performance. *Information & Management*, 58(3), 103434. DOI: 10.1016/j.im.2021.103434

Moher, D., Liberati, A., Tetzlaff, J., & Altman, D. G.The PRISMA Group. (2009). Preferred Reporting Items for Systematic Reviews and Meta-Analyses : The PRISMA Statement. *PLoS Medicine*, 6(7), e1000097. DOI: 10.1371/journal.pmed.1000097 PMID: 19621072

Moher, D., Shamseer, L., Clarke, M., Ghersi, D., Liberati, A., Petticrew, M., Shekelle, P., & Stewart, L. A.Prisma-P Group. (2015). Preferred reporting items for systematic review and meta-analysis protocols (PRISMA-P) 2015 statement. *Systematic Reviews*, 4(1), 1. DOI: 10.1186/2046-4053-4-1 PMID: 25554246

Nabaoui, A. (2023). Performance : Concepts, approches et modèles. *Revue Française d'Economie et de Gestion*, 4(11), 11. https://www.revuefreg.fr/index.php/home/article/view/1348

Niang, B. (2024). La participation à la prise de décision et performance organisationnelle dans les PMET au Sénégal. *Revue Internationale des Sciences de Gestion*, 7(1). https://revue-isg.com/index.php/home/article/view/1505

Nizeyimana, J. B., Mukanteri, A., & L'Institut Régional IRIMAG/CFM. (2023). L'impact du marketing numérique sur les Petites et Moyennes Entreprises. *RUFSO Journal of Social Science and Engineering, 35*(03). DOI: 10.55272/rufso.rjsse.35.3.2

Nuryyev, G., Wang, Y.-P., Achyldurdyyeva, J., Jaw, B.-S., Yeh, Y.-S., Lin, H.-T., & Wu, L.-F. (2020). Blockchain technology adoption behavior and sustainability of the business in tourism and hospitality SMEs : An empirical study. *Sustainability (Basel)*, 12(3), 1256. DOI: 10.3390/su12031256

O'Connor, P. (2023). Small-and medium-sized tourism enterprises and smart tourism : Tourism agenda 2030 perspective article. *Tourism Review*, 78(2), 339–343. DOI: 10.1108/TR-09-2022-0431

Panno, A. (2020). Performance measurement and management in small companies of the service sector; evidence from a sample of Italian hotels. *Measuring Business Excellence*, 24(2), 133–160. DOI: 10.1108/MBE-01-2018-0004

Pattinson, C. (2015). Emerging technologies and their environmental impact. *Green Information Technology*, 11-26.

Perera, N. (2021). Impact of digital transformation in measuring business performance of small & medium scale businesses in Sri Lanka. *International Journal of Economics. Business and Management Research*, 5(7), 1–25.

Phillips, P., & Louvieris, P. (2005). Performance Measurement Systems in Tourism, Hospitality, and Leisure Small Medium-Sized Enterprises : A Balanced Scorecard Perspective. *Journal of Travel Research*, 44(2), 201–211. DOI: 10.1177/0047287505278992

Pothineni, S. (2023). The Impact of Data Strategy and Emerging Technologies on Business Performance. [IJBSA]. *International Journal of Business Strategy and Automation*, 4(1), 1–19. DOI: 10.4018/IJB-SA.334022

Rosário, A. T., & Dias, J. C. (2023). How has data-driven marketing evolved : Challenges and opportunities with emerging technologies. *International Journal of Information Management Data Insights*, 3(2), 100203. DOI: 10.1016/j.jjimei.2023.100203

Samara, D., Magnisalis, I., & Peristeras, V. (2020). Artificial intelligence and big data in tourism : A systematic literature review. *Journal of Hospitality and Tourism Technology*, 11(2), 343–367. DOI: 10.1108/JHTT-12-2018-0118

Sánchez-Amboage, E., Crespo-Pereira, V., Membiela-Pollán, M., & Jesús Faustino, J. P. (2024). Tourism marketing in the metaverse : A systematic literature review, building blocks, and future research directions. *PLoS One*, 19(5), e0300599. DOI: 10.1371/journal.pone.0300599 PMID: 38728243

Saoudi, L., Aubry, M., Gomot, T., & Renaud, A. (2023). Transformation digitale et performance des PME : Une analyse bibliométrique pour comprendre et agir. *Revue internationale PME, 36*(2), 13-38.

Seow, A. N., Choong, Y. O., & Ramayah, T. (2021). Small and medium-size enterprises' business performance in tourism industry : The mediating role of innovative practice and moderating role of government support. *Asian Journal of Technology Innovation*, 29(2), 283–303. DOI: 10.1080/19761597.2020.1798796

Setiowati, R., Daryanto, H. K., & Arifin, B. (2015). The effects of ICT adoption on marketing capabilities and business performance of Indonesian SMEs in the fashion industry. *The Journal of Business and Retail Management Research*, 10(1). https://jbrmr.com/cdn/article_file/i-22_c-206.pdf

Shah, S. M. A., El-Gohary, H., & Hussain, J. G. (2015). An Investigation of Market Orientation (MO) and Tourism Small and Medium-Sized Enterprises' (SMEs) Performance in Developing Countries : A Review of the Literature. *Journal of Travel & Tourism Marketing*, 32(8), 990–1022. DOI: 10.1080/10548408.2014.957372

Shaikh, S. (2022). Internet of Things : Designing Digital Eco-Systems for Competitive Tourism Related Micro and Small Enterprises in Pakistan. In Hassan, A. (Ed.), *Technology Application in Tourism in Asia : Innovations, Theories and Practices* (pp. 349–365). Springer Nature., DOI: 10.1007/978-981-16-5461-9_21

Shamseer, L., Moher, D., Clarke, M., Ghersi, D., Liberati, A., Petticrew, M., Shekelle, P., Stewart, L. A., & the PRISMA-P Group. (2015). Preferred reporting items for systematic review and meta-analysis protocols (PRISMA-P) 2015 : Elaboration and explanation. *BMJ, 349*(jan02 1), g7647-g7647. DOI: 10.1136/bmj.g7647

Sharma, A., & Sharma, S. (2024). Adoption of digital marketing in tourism SMEs : A review and research agenda. *Management Research Review*, 47(7), 1077–1095. DOI: 10.1108/MRR-08-2021-0597

Stallone, V., Wetzels, M., & Klaas, M. (2021). Applications of Blockchain Technology in marketing—A systematic review of marketing technology companies. *Blockchain: Research and Applications*, 2(3), 100023. DOI: 10.1016/j.bcra.2021.100023

Stone, M., Aravopoulou, E., Ekinci, Y., Evans, G., Hobbs, M., Labib, A., Laughlin, P., Machtynger, J., & Machtynger, L. (2020). Artificial intelligence (AI) in strategic marketing decision-making : A research agenda. *The Bottom Line (New York, N.Y.)*, 33(2), 183–200. DOI: 10.1108/BL-03-2020-0022

Topsakal, Y., Icoz, O., & Icoz, O. (2022). *Digital Transformation and Tourist Experiences*., DOI: 10.4018/978-1-7998-8528-3.ch002

Verma, S., Sharma, R., Deb, S., & Maitra, D. (2021). Artificial intelligence in marketing : Systematic review and future research direction. *International Journal of Information Management Data Insights*, 1(1), 100002. DOI: 10.1016/j.jjimei.2020.100002

Vlačić, B., Corbo, L., Costa e Silva, S., & Dabić, M. (2021). The evolving role of artificial intelligence in marketing : A review and research agenda. *Journal of Business Research*, 128, 187–203. DOI: 10.1016/j.jbusres.2021.01.055

Wamba-Taguimdje, S.-L., Fosso Wamba, S., Kala Kamdjoug, J. R., & Tchatchouang Wanko, C. E. (2020). Influence of artificial intelligence (AI) on firm performance : The business value of AI-based transformation projects. *Business Process Management Journal*, 26(7), 1893–1924. DOI: 10.1108/BPMJ-10-2019-0411

Zamani, S. Z. (2022). Small and Medium Enterprises (SMEs) facing an evolving technological era : A systematic literature review on the adoption of technologies in SMEs. *European Journal of Innovation Management*, 25(6), 735–757. DOI: 10.1108/EJIM-07-2021-0360

ADDITIONAL READING

Achsa, A., Verawati, D. M., & Novitaningtyas, I. (2023). Implementation of Marketing Strategy Innovation and Business Model Development: Study of SMEs in Tourism Village. *Airlangga Journal of Innovation Management*, 4(2), 172–184. DOI: 10.20473/ajim.v4i2.49859

Asmawati, A., Ahmad, I., Suwarni, E., Alita, D., & Hasrina, C. D. (2024). Online Marketing Readiness of MSMEs in Indonesia: A Perspective of Technology Organizational Environmental Framework. *Journal of Economics, Business, and Accountancy Ventura*, 27(1), 145–155. DOI: 10.14414/jebav.v27i1.3399

Badoc-Gonzales, B. P., Mandigma, M. B. S., & Tan, J. J. (2022). SME resilience as a catalyst for tourism destinations: A literature review. *Journal of Global Entrepreneurship Research*, 12(1), 23–44. DOI: 10.1007/s40497-022-00309-1

Delevska, A., & Osorio, S. C. (2024). Innovation in times of crisis: responses from Australian tourism and hospitality SMEs during Covid-19. In *Handbook of Tourism Entrepreneurship* (pp. 142–158). Edward Elgar Publishing.

Dewhurst, H., Dewhurst, P., & Livesey, R. (2007). Tourism and hospitality SME training needs and provision: A sub-regional analysis. *Tourism and Hospitality Research*, 7(2), 131–143. DOI: 10.1057/palgrave.thr.6050037

Font, X., & Wood, M. E. (2007). *Sustainable tourism certification marketing and its contribution to SME market access.*

Hallak, R., Brown, G., & Lindsay, N. J. (2013). Examining tourism SME owners' place attachment, support for community and business performance: The role of the enlightened self-interest model. *Journal of Sustainable Tourism*, 21(5), 658–678. DOI: 10.1080/09669582.2012.709861

Lee, C., & Hallak, R. (2020). Investigating the effects of offline and online social capital on tourism SME performance: A mixed-methods study of New Zealand entrepreneurs. *Tourism Management*, 80, 104128. DOI: 10.1016/j.tourman.2020.104128

Maduku, D. K. (2021). Antecedents of mobile marketing adoption by SMEs: Does industry variance matter? *Journal of Organizational Computing and Electronic Commerce*, 31(3), 222–249. DOI: 10.1080/10919392.2021.1956847

Manyara, G., & Jones, E. (2005). Policy options for the development of an indigenous tourism SME sector in Kenya. In *Tourism SMEs, service quality and destination competitiveness* (pp. 59–72). CABI Publishing. DOI: 10.1079/9780851990118.0059

Mohamad, N. (2022). Social media and small and medium enterprises in the Malaysian tourism industry. In *Handbook of technology application in tourism in Asia* (pp. 1041–1064). Springer Nature Singapore. DOI: 10.1007/978-981-16-2210-6_47

Pongtanalert, K., & Assarut, N. (2022). Entrepreneur mindset, social capital and adaptive capacity for tourism SME resilience and transformation during the COVID-19 pandemic. *Sustainability (Basel)*, 14(19), 12675. DOI: 10.3390/su141912675

Surya, B., Hernita, H., Salim, A., Suriani, S., Perwira, I., Yulia, Y., Ruslan, M., & Yunus, K. (2022). Travel-business stagnation and SME business turbulence in the tourism sector in the era of the COVID-19 pandemic. *Sustainability (Basel)*, 14(4), 2380. DOI: 10.3390/su14042380

KEY TERMS AND DEFINITIONS

Agility: The capacity of organizations to modify the system in response to changes and movements in the market is a crucial factor in determining their ability to adapt and remain competitive.

Business Model: It is a document that describes the revenue and profit generation plan; it details the value proposition, customer segments, partners, and strategies.

Customer Engagement: A consumer's emotional relationship with a brand developed through positive experiences.

Customer personalization: The practice of aligning products, services, and communications with individual customer preferences is designed to enhance satisfaction and loyalty.

Innovation: is the process of developing an idea and its final output as a product/service.

Return on investment (ROI): A performance measure used to evaluate the efficiency of an investment.

Sustainability: is to drive economies in such a way as to meet the needs of the present without compromising those of future generations based on economic, social, and ecological considerations.

Technology Adoption: The process by which organizations integrate new technologies into their operations to improve their efficiency and competitiveness.

Value proposition: This is the answer to the question of how the product/service solves a problem or provides a specific benefit to the customer.

Chapter 11
Research on the Promotion and Fostering of Entrepreneurship in SMEs:
A Bibliometric Study

Jorge Espinoza-Benavides
https://orcid.org/0000-0002-3459-624X
Universidad Catolica de la Santisima Concepcion, Chile

Nelson Andres Andrade-Valbuena
https://orcid.org/0000-0002-4873-8915
Universidad Catolica de la Santisima Concepcion, Chile

Amanda Arias-Ramírez
Universidad Catolica de la Santisima Concepcion, Chile

Delia Leon-Castro
https://orcid.org/0000-0003-1036-6316
Universidad Catolica de la Santisima Concepcion, Chile

ABSTRACT

The study delves into the realm of Promotion and Fostering of Entrepreneurship (PFE) research, a domain of scholarly interest due to its potential to shape a future where economic growth aligns with societal well-being. This article presents the first-ever bibliometric analysis of academic research dedicated to PFE, spanning from 1956 to 2021. Utilizing bibliometric techniques as performance analysis and graphical mapping, the research examines academic output using the Scopus database, categorizing articles, authors, and institutions. Noteworthy journals like Journal of Business Venturing feature prominently. Crucial articles by authors like Walter, Auer, and Ritter gain attention, while influential institutions like the University of Toronto are emphasized. Graphical mapping of Keywords highlights the growing importance of PFE research, with a notable surge in studies over the last decade. Entrepreneurship ecosystems and the integration of PFE with sustainability and social responsibility issues stand out as new and prominent perspectives.

DOI: 10.4018/979-8-3693-4046-2.ch011

INTRODUCTION

Joseph Schumpeter's contributions to entrepreneurship theory, particularly for small and medium-sized enterprises (SMEs), have long been foundational. His influential works, "The Theory of Economic Development" (1934) and "Capitalism, Socialism, and Democracy" (1942), established a framework for understanding entrepreneurship's role in economic change, highlighting the critical part SMEs play. This understanding has underscored the importance of nurturing entrepreneurship in SMEs as a driver of economic growth and societal well-being (Galindo-Martín et al., 2021). SMEs, as key components of the entrepreneurial ecosystem, face unique opportunities and challenges that require continuous innovation and external support. Technological advancements enable SMEs to optimize operations, reach new markets, and create value. Additionally, engaging in collaborative networks with other firms, academic institutions, or governmental bodies can enhance access to knowledge, capital, and markets. Building organizational resilience is also crucial for SMEs to adapt to market changes and withstand economic fluctuations. These strategies not only help SMEs survive but also thrive, contributing to overall economic growth. Understanding how to encourage entrepreneurship has been strategically crucial for societal advancement over the past sixty years (Urbano, Aparicio & Querol, 2016). This has led to significant academic outputs focused on advancing entrepreneurship theories and methodologies (Bergman & McMullen, 2020). For example, a simple query in the Scopus database for "entrepreneurship" yields over 30,000 scholarly outputs in business and management. This growth justifies the need for a bibliometric analysis of the field's conceptual structure.

Researchers across disciplines have used bibliometric methods to categorize and rank vast academic data, offering insights into diverse subjects (Andrade-Valbuena, Merigó-Lindahl, & Olavarrieta, 2018). These approaches have explored topics like ethical considerations in entrepreneurial decision-making (Vallaster et al., 2019) and corporate entrepreneurship in the public sector (Funko, Vlačić, & Dabić, 2023). However, there has yet to be a comprehensive study on the Promotion and Fostering of Entrepreneurship (PFE), which could significantly advance research in this crucial area. For instance, entrepreneurial orientation has consistently shown positive and significant effects on the economic performance of SMEs. Promoting and fostering entrepreneurship, therefore, enhances SME competitiveness, not only through corporate entrepreneurship but also through the creation of new competitive enterprises, such as science and technology-based ventures (Hornsby et al. 2002; Walter et al. 2006; Keh et al. 2007).

This article aims to provide an extensive overview of nearly seventy years of research on PFE (from 1956 to 2021) using bibliometric methodologies, addressing the following research questions:

1. What are the most visible and prominent research outputs in PFE, particularly in the field of SMEs, from 1956 to 2021?
2. Who are the most relevant authors and institutions in PFE research within the Scopus database?
3. What does the intellectual framework of PFE research look like, based on the most prominent keywords used by authors in the Scopus database?

This evaluation reveals statistical trends within the academic material (Andrade-Valbuena, Valenzuela-Fernández & Merigó, 2022) and applies science mapping, a network analysis using authors' keywords, to explore knowledge dynamics among research topics, providing a holistic view (Andrade-Valbuena, Baier-Fuentes & Gaviria Marin, 2022).

The chapter is structured as follows: Introduction, providing background on PFE; Methodology, describing the perspectives and methods used; Results, presented in sub-themes addressing the research questions, including the identification of the most prominent journals, articles, authors, and institutions, and a performance analysis visualized using VOS viewer software; solutions, future research directions; and conclusions.

BACKGROUND

Promotion and fostering of entrepreneurship

The Promotion and Fostering of Entrepreneurship (PFE) is a multifaceted phenomenon crucial for driving economic development, innovation, and job creation in contemporary societies (Penrose 1959). Emerging from foundational works like Schumpeter's (1934; 1942), PFE has become a significant research focus, deeply rooted in various theories, including Entrepreneurial Ecosystem Theory (Shane & Venkataraman 2000), Organizational and Management Theory (Sandberg 1992; Alvarez & Barney 2004), Sociology (Powell & Baker 2014; Fauchart & Gruber 2011), and Psychology (Baron 1998; Mitchell et al. 2002). This section recognizes the intricate connections among these foundational studies and introduces key theories that explore PFE research, enhancing our understanding of its complexities.

For instance, although there is no universally accepted definition of PFE, by considering some of the most cited articles on the subject, we can propose the following definition: 'PFE refers to all resources and actions available to external and internal agents to strengthen an organization's entrepreneurial orientation, thereby fostering growth in sales, improving profitability, performance, and competitiveness, especially in SMEs' (Hornsby et al. 2002; Siegel et al. 2004; Wennekers et al. 2005; Walter et al. 2006; Keh et al. 2007).

PFE research is grounded in the **Entrepreneurial Ecosystem Theory (EET)** (Spigel 2017; Spigel & Harrison 2018), which examines the dynamic network of factors shaping the entrepreneurial environment (Autio et al. 2018). EET explores how interactions among institutions, policies, culture, education, infrastructure, and financial resources influence entrepreneurship (Roundy & Burke-Smalley 2022). This theory emphasizes a holistic view that considers both tangible and intangible factors in fostering innovation and economic growth (Spigel 2017). Collaboration among stakeholders—entrepreneurs, investors, academia, government, and industry—is crucial for creating a supportive ecosystem (Ratinho et al. 2020).

Within the EET, the **Triple Helix model** highlights the interaction between academia, industry, and government in promoting innovation and entrepreneurship (Etzkowitz & Leydesdorff 2000). It emphasizes collaboration for knowledge transfer, technology commercialization, and new venture creation (Zhou & Etzkowitz 2021). SMEs are often studied from this perspective, with research showing how their failure impacts economic, social, psychological, and physiological aspects (Singh et al. 2007). Organizational and management theory supports SMEs in obtaining and using information for marketing decision-making (Keh et al. 2007).

SMEs, as drivers of innovation and economic dynamism, rely heavily on their ability to navigate the entrepreneurial ecosystem. Government policies, educational institutions, and access to venture capital are critical for reducing operational costs, scaling operations, and enhancing market presence. By leveraging these resources, SMEs can improve their competitive positioning and contribute to the sustainability of the ecosystem.

Organizational and management research, particularly **Institutional Theory**, explains how formal and informal rules shape the resources available to entrepreneurs, influencing their behaviors and outcomes (Bruton et al. 2010). Regulatory frameworks, government policies, and cultural norms significantly impact entrepreneurial activity (Scott 1995). Institutional theory also explores how institutional pressures can lead to isomorphism, helping ventures gain social acceptance or competitive advantage (Nicholls 2010).

The **Resource-Based View (RBV)** theory is central to understanding PFE, emphasizing the importance of resources and capabilities in achieving competitive advantage and superior performance (Barney 1991). RBV highlights the role of human capital, financial capital, social capital, and technological capabilities in entrepreneurial success (Foss et al. 2008).

Social Network Theory (SNT) explores how entrepreneurs and SME owners connect with mentors, peers, investors, and stakeholders, influencing their access to resources, information, and support (Granovetter, 1973). SNT emphasizes the impact of social relationships on resource acquisition, information diffusion, risk mitigation, and market access (Zhang, 2010; Lee & Baek, 2023). SNT is particularly relevant in PFE research for its focus on fostering innovation, collaboration, and knowledge sharing (Huggins & Thompson, 2015).

Cultural and psychological perspectives have also contributed to PFE research by recognizing the influence of mindsets, attitudes, and values on entrepreneurship (Powell & Baker, 2014; Morrison, 2000). **Cultural norms** related to risk-taking, failure tolerance, and success perception impact entrepreneurial activities (Toghraee & Monjezi, 2017; Wennberg et al., 2013). Psychological factors, such as entrepreneurial self-efficacy and opportunity recognition, shape engagement in entrepreneurship and influence marketing decisions for SMEs (McGee et al., 2009; Lumpkin et al., 2004; Keh et al., 2007).

INTEGRATING THEORETICAL PERSPECTIVES TO ENHANCE PFE FOR SMES

Institutional Theory explains how formal institutions, like regulations, and informal institutions, such as cultural norms, shape the entrepreneurial environment. These institutions impact resource availability, market entry, and the overall business climate, either promoting or hindering entrepreneurship. Linking Institutional Theory with PFE shows how effective policies and institutional support foster a conducive environment for entrepreneurship by lowering barriers, providing resources, and encouraging risk-taking.

Entrepreneurial Ecosystem Theory (EET) highlights the interconnected ecosystem components—finance, markets, human capital—that support entrepreneurship. The success of PFE initiatives often depends on the ecosystem's strength. For example, promoting entrepreneurship through training is more effective when the ecosystem offers funding and market access. Integrating EET with PFE shows that fostering entrepreneurship requires addressing various ecosystem facets simultaneously.

The Resource-Based View (RBV) focuses on internal capabilities and resources that firms need for a competitive advantage. RBV, linked with PFE, suggests promoting entrepreneurship requires both external institutional support and internal resource development, such as skills and knowledge. This integration underscores the importance of both external and internal resources in fostering entrepreneurship.

Social Network Theory (SNT) shows how SME Entrepreneurs use networks to access resources, information, and opportunities. SNT, connected with PFE, emphasizes strong social networks' role in providing critical support, especially in resource-limited environments. These networks facilitate knowledge transfer, mentorship, and partnerships, vital for entrepreneurial success.

Cultural and psychological perspectives contribute to PFE by recognizing how mindsets, attitudes, and values influence entrepreneurship. Promoting entrepreneurship involves not just providing resources but also shaping the cultural and psychological environment. By fostering a culture of innovation, risk-taking, and resilience, PFE initiatives create a more favorable environment for entrepreneurship.

This chapter integrates multiple theoretical perspectives to provide a comprehensive understanding of PFE in SMEs. EET offers a macro-level view of interconnected ecosystem components, RBV focuses on the internal resources SMEs need for competitive advantage, and SNT bridges these levels by highlighting networks' role in accessing external resources. Cultural and psychological perspectives further enrich this framework by acknowledging the impact of mindsets and values on entrepreneurial behavior. Together, these approaches present a cohesive framework that captures the complex dynamics of PFE, particularly the challenges and opportunities faced by SMEs.

The entrepreneurial ecosystem framework provides a lens for viewing SME operations' interactions and interdependencies. EET emphasizes the dynamic, interconnected factors influencing entrepreneurship. Our bibliometric analysis supports and expands these insights, showing SMEs as active ecosystem participants, shaping and being shaped by interactions with financial institutions, government bodies, and educational institutions. This bidirectional influence highlights SMEs' importance in the ecosystem's vitality, validating the theoretical models discussed.

MAIN FOCUS OF THE CHAPTER

Methodology

Study Design

This study examines the Promotion and Fostering of Entrepreneurship (PFE) through a bibliometric analysis, providing an overview of scientific production, key articles, authors, journals, and institutions. It also includes graphical visualizations to illustrate trends and relationships within PFE research (Andrade-Valbuena & Merigo, 2018; Llanos-Herrera & Merigo, 2018; Merigó et al., 2015).

Data Source

The primary data source is the Scopus database, chosen for its extensive coverage and high-quality scholarly data (Merigó et al., 2015; Mongeon & Paul-Hus, 2016). Relevant documents from additional sources were referenced to enhance the study's comprehensiveness.

Keyword Selection and Sample Collection

The dataset was generated using the keywords "entrepreneur*" AND "foster*" OR "promotion*" (subject). The search, conducted on October 22, 2022, yielded 5,761 publications spanning from 1956 to 2021, providing a historical overview of PFE research.

Bibliometric Indicators

Bibliometric indicators, such as publication numbers, citation counts, and H-index, were used to assess the impact of PFE research, highlighting the most influential authors, journals, and institutions.

Data Analysis

The dataset was analyzed to identify document types, their totals, and citation counts. Table 1 presents the distribution of document types, with articles comprising 67.70% of documents and 86.68% of citations, followed by reviews, conference papers, and book chapters.

Graphical Visualization

Science mapping techniques, including co-authorship and keyword co-occurrence analysis, were employed to visualize the intellectual structure and collaboration networks within PFE research, revealing relationships between themes and knowledge dynamics.

Table 1 presents the types of PFE documents found and their total accumulated citations. In summary, published papers have accumulated 91,653 citations, with articles contributing 86.68% of the total, followed by reviews at 5.25% and conference papers at 3.04%.

Table 1.Types of documents in PFE in Scopus

Type of document	Number	Total document type	Total citations	% citations
Article	3,900	67.70%	79,443	86.68%
Book	153	2.66%	2,579	2.81%
Book Chapter	620	10.76%	1,574	1.72%
Conference Paper	772	13.40%	2,790	3.04%
Conference Review	27	0.47%	0	0.00%
Editorial	30	0.52%	388	0.42%
Erratum	3	0.05%	0	0.00%
Letter	1	0.02%	2	0.00%
Note	8	0.14%	47	0.05%
Retracted	6	0.10%	0	0.00%
Review	233	4.04%	4,813	5.25%
Short Survey	8	0.14%	17	0.02%
Total	5,761	100%	91,653	100%

Source: Own elaboration based on Scopus 2022.

PERFORMANCE ANALYSIS OF PFE RESEARCH

To analyze journals, articles, authors, and institutions in Promotion and Fostering of Entrepreneurship (PFE), various indicators have been calculated. These include productivity, total citations, and the H-index (Hirsch, 2005). Productivity indicates the number of publications by journals, authors, or institutions, highlighting leaders in the field. The H-index, as described by Blanco-Mesa et al. (2019), relates to the number of citations and published papers, reflecting the importance of journals, institutions, authors, and countries. Total citations represent the number of citations received by publications, providing an indication of their impact. The VOS Viewer software has been used to generate graphical maps and visualize bibliometric information on keywords (Van Eck & Waltman, 2010; Waltman et al., 2010).

Top 30 Journals In PFE

Scientific journals have the function of disseminating contributions and research, speaking specifically in the development of this article with the theme of entrepreneurship and its promotion or encouragement (PFE), hence it is essential to locate the most influential journals in the field. Table 3 contains the list of the Top 30 most productive and prominent journals in PFE. The rankings presented in Table 2, along with Tables 3, 4, and 5, are determined by three primary criteria. The initial criterion is the H-index, which in this study is assessed based on publications concerning PFE. If a tie occurs, the second criterion applied is the total number of papers published in the field of PFE research. Should a tie persist, the final criterion used is the total number of citations each work has received.

The leading journal is Sustainability Switzerland (SS), which has 85 publications on PFE with 885 citations on the topic. In second place is the Journal of Business Venturing (JBV) with 48 published articles, it is the most cited journal with 6945 total citations and has the highest h-index of 35. In addition, this journal has 8 articles ranked among the top 30 most cited articles in PFE (the N30, this list is presented in the next section). In third place is Small Business Economics (SBE), with an output of 47 papers, has 3596 citations, with 3 articles in the N30 in PFE and with an H-index of 28.

The five leading journals identified in our analysis are pivotal in shaping PFE research. Sustainability (Switzerland) focuses on the intersection of sustainability and entrepreneurship, vital as SMEs integrate sustainable practices. Together, these journals disseminate essential research and guide the development of new theories and practices in PFE. The Journal of Business Venturing is foundational in entrepreneurship research, offering key insights into venture creation and innovation, crucial for understanding entrepreneurial ecosystems. Small Business Economics examines economic factors affecting small business performance, emphasizing policy implications for SMEs. The International Journal of Entrepreneurial Behavior and Research enhances understanding of entrepreneurial behavior and socio-psychological aspects, fostering entrepreneurial mindsets. Lastly, the International Entrepreneurship and Management Journal connects entrepreneurship with management practices, offering a global view on challenges and opportunities for SMEs.

Table 2.Top 30 journals in PFE

R	Journal	P-PFE	%PPFE	H-PFE	TC	IF	N50	≥700	≥500	≥250	≥100	≥50	≥25	Q1	Q2	Q3	Q4	Q5
1	Sustainability (Switzerland)	85	1.48%	16	885	5.0	-	-	-	-	-	2	7	85	-	-	-	-
2	Journal of Business Venturing	48	0.83%	35	6945	14.6	8	1	2	4	17	8	6	19	11	13	5	-
3	Small Business Economics	47	0.82%	28	3596	10.7	3	1	-	2	9	5	13	35	5	6	1	-
4	International Journal of Entrepreneurial Behavior and Research	45	0.78%	21	1251	8.0	-	-	-	-	2	3	14	39	6	-	-	-
5	International Entrepreneurship and Management Journal	44	0.76%	22	1171	9.7	-	-	-	-	1	4	15	38	6	-	-	-
6	Journal of Small Business and Enterprise Development	37	0.64%	17	817	5.4	-	-	-	-	-	4	7	20	13	4	-	-
7	International Journal of Entrepreneurship and Small Business	36	0.62%	12	415	1.3	-	-	-	-	-	1	3	26	10	-	-	-
8	Industry and Higher Education	35	0.61%	10	301	2.3	-	-	-	-	-	-	2	17	14	4	-	-
9	Entrepreneurship and Regional Development	32	0.56%	22	2109	8.0	-	-	-	-	8	5	9	16	11	3	2	-
10	Education and Training	29	0.50%	16	715	4.8	-	-	-	-	-	5	5	21	8	-	-	-
11	Management Decision	29	0.50%	16	1119	7.9	1	-	-	1	1	1	11	25	2	2	-	-
12	Journal of Business Research	28	0.49%	18	940	11.2	-	-	-	-	1	6	7	27	1	-	-	-
13	Technological Forecasting and Social Change	27	0.47%	16	684	13.7	-	-	-	-	1	3	6	24	1	1	1	-
14	Contributions to Management Science	23	0.40%	4	58	0.7	-	-	-	-	-	-	-	18	5	-	-	-
15	Journal of Cleaner Production	23	0.40%	14	574	15.8	-	-	-	-	-	4	4	20	3	-	-	-
16	Technovation	21	0.36%	17	949	10.1	-	-	-	-	2	6	6	7	10	2	2	-
17	Academy of Entrepreneurship Journal	20	0.35%	3	31	1.1	-	-	-	-	-	-	-	20	-	-	-	-
18	Emerald Emerging Markets Case Studies	20	0.35%	1	4	0.2	-	-	-	-	-	-	-	17	3	-	-	-
19	Journal of Enterprising Communities	20	0.35%	9	223	3.9	-	-	-	-	-	-	2	19	1	-	-	-
20	Journal of Entrepreneurship Education	20	0.35%	5	154	2.7	-	-	-	-	-	1	1	19	1	-	-	-
21	Journal of Technology Transfer	20	0.35%	17	1068	9.2	-	-	-	-	4	5	5	16	2	2	-	-
22	International Journal of Entrepreneurship and Innovation Management	19	0.33%	8	128	1.1	-	-	-	-	-	-	1	9	9	1	-	-
23	Journal of Developmental Entrepreneurship	19	0.33%	6	106	2.0	-	-	-	-	-	-	-	17	2	-	-	-
24	Research Policy	19	0.33%	14	1740	14.0	2	-	-	2	4	4	2	12	6	-	1	-
25	Advances in Intelligent Systems and Computing	18	0.31%	3	17	0.9	-	-	-	-	-	-	-	18	-	-	-	-
26	Journal of Entrepreneurship in Emerging Economies	18	0.31%	10	308	4.6	-	-	-	-	-	2	1	18	-	-	-	-
27	Journal of Small Business and Entrepreneurship	17	0.30%	8	170	5.0	-	-	-	-	-	-	1	6	11	-	-	-
28	Journal of Entrepreneurship and Public Policy	16	0.28%	6	75	1.7	-	-	-	-	-	-	-	16	-	-	-	-
29	Revista de Economia Publica, Social y Cooperativa	15	0.26%	5	58	2.9	-	-	-	-	-	-	-	15	-	-	-	-
30	Entrepreneurial Business and Economics Review	15	0.26%	6	127	3.7	-	-	-	-	-	-	1	15	-	-	-	-

Source: Own elaboration based on Scopus 2022. R: Ranking; J: Journal; P-EFE: Total number of documents published in PFE; %PPFE: Percentage of documents published in PFE; H-PFE: H-index only with PFE; TC: Total citations; IF: Impact Factor; CP: Citations per document; N50: Number of publications among the 50 most cited articles; ≥700: number of articles with more than 700 citations; ≥500: Number of articles with more than 500 citations; ≥250: number of articles with more than 250 citations; ≥100: number of articles with more than 100 citations; ≥50: number of articles with more than 50 citations; ≥25: number of articles with more than 25 citations; Q1: 2012-2021; Q2: 2002-2011; Q3: 1992-2001; Q4: 1982-1991; Q5: 1956-1981.

The 30 most significant articles in PFE

There are some articles that stand out notably for their large number of citations; their influence has a significant impact on the topic. Table 3 shows the Top 30 most cited and therefore fundamental articles on the topic of entrepreneurship and its promotion or fostering (PFE). The same criteria of Table 2 are followed. Overall, within the Entrepreneurial Ecosystem Theory (EET), the top 10 most cited papers shed light on various aspects of the external environment, particularly relevant for small and medium-sized enterprises (SMEs).

Walter et al., (2006) delve into the relationships and interactions between university spin-offs and their external environment, emphasizing the role of networks and relationships in shaping spin-off performance, which is crucial for SMEs seeking to establish themselves in competitive markets. Similarly, Siegel et al., (2004) explore the emergence of technology transfer offices (TTOs) in research universities, analyzing their role in university/industry technology transfer (UITT) and underscoring the significance of organizational and managerial practices in optimizing knowledge transfer, which can be valuable for SMEs seeking to innovate and grow.

Focusing on societal, cultural, and psychological aspects influencing women entrepreneurs, Brush et al. (2009) highlights the impact of institutionalized social structures (markets, money, management, motherhood, and meso/macro environment) in fostering female entrepreneurship, a segment often represented by SMEs. Wennekers et al. (2005) underscore the influence of cultural and institutional factors in developed countries compared to underdeveloped ones, acknowledging the importance of incentive structures, exploitation of scientific findings, and management education in shaping entrepreneurial dynamics, including those of SMEs. Notably, they found evidence of a U-shaped correlation between nascent entrepreneurship and both per capita income and economic development, which can have implications for SME growth strategies.

Most of the top 10 most cited papers focus on the organizational and management framework, offering valuable insights for SMEs. Stopford & Baden-Fuller (1994) examine corporate entrepreneurship, linking organizational change and performance, which can guide SMEs in innovation and expansion. Keh et al. (2007) emphasize the importance of SMEs' proactive engagement in the entrepreneurial ecosystem, highlighting the need for thorough information acquisition for effective marketing strategies, crucial for SMEs in dynamic markets.

Henri (2006) discusses the role of organizational culture in fostering entrepreneurial activities, offering insights for SMEs to cultivate a culture that supports innovation and growth. Hornsby et al. (2002) explore factors influencing corporate entrepreneurship, providing a scale to evaluate a firm's internal entrepreneurial environment, useful for SMEs encouraging entrepreneurial behavior. Abrahamson and Fairchild (1999) study the evolution of management practices from an institutional perspective, offering insights for SMEs adapting to business trends.

Finally, Cope (2011) addresses venture failure during economic downturns, exploring entrepreneurs' experiences and the importance of relational recovery, providing SMEs with insights on resilience and learning from setbacks to continue their entrepreneurial journey.

Table 3:Top 30 articles in PFE

R	Article	Author	TC	PY
1	The impact of network capabilities and entrepreneurial orientation on university spin-off performance	Walter A.; Auer M.; Ritter T.	735	2006
2	Nascent entrepreneurship and the level of economic development	Wennekers S.; Van Wennekers A.; Thurik R.; Reynolds P.	730	2005
3	Management fashion: Lifecycles, triggers, and collective learning processes	Abrahamson E.; Fairchild G.	672	1999

continued on following page

Table 3:Top 30 articles in PFE Continued

R	Article	Author	TC	PY
4	Middle managers' perception of the internal environment for corporate entrepreneurship: Assessing a measurement scale.	Hornsby J.S.; Kuratko D.F.; Zahra S.A.	587	2002
5	Management control systems and strategy: A resource-based perspective	Henri J.-F.	574	2006
6	Toward a model of the effective transfer of scientific knowledge from academicians to practitioners: Qualitative evidence from the commercialization of university technologies.	Siegel D.S.; Waldman D.A.; Atwater L.E.; Link A.N.	535	2004
7	Entrepreneurial learning from failure: An interpretative phenomenological analysis.	Cope J.	503	2011
8	A gender-aware framework for women's entrepreneurship	Brush C.G.; de Bruin A.; Welter F.	486	2009
9	The effects of entrepreneurial orientation and marketing information on the performance of SMEs	Keh H.T.; Nguyen T.T.M.; Ng H.P.	475	2007
10	Creating corporate entrepreneurship	Stopford J.M.; Baden-Fuller C.W.F.	444	1994
11	The gender of social capital	Burt R.S.	440	1998
12	Entrepreneurship and bank credit availability	Black S.E.; Strahan P.E.	429	2002
13	How effective are technology incubators? Evidence from Italy	Colombo M.G.; Delmastro M.	416	2002
14	Which factors affect entrepreneurial intention of university students?	Turker D.; Selcuk S.S.	398	2009
15	Social capital, knowledge, and the international growth of technology-based new firms	Yli-Renko H.; Autio E.; Tontti V.	395	2002
16	The evolution of the entrepreneurial university	Etzkowitz H.	394	2004
17	Social entrepreneurship - a new look at the people and the potential	Thompson J.; Alvy G.; Lees A.	393	2000
18	Institutional environments for entrepreneurship: Evidence from emerging economies in Eastern Europe	Manolova T.S.; Eunni R.V.; Gyoshev B.S.	366	2008
19	City Marketing, Image Reconstruction and Urban Regeneration	Paddison R.	365	1993
20	Gambling and the health of the public: adopting a public health perspective.	Korn D.A.	347	1999
21	Entrepreneurial legacy: Toward a theory of how some family firms nurture transgenerational entrepreneurship.	Jaskiewicz P.; Combs J.G.; Rau S.B.	337	2015
22	Toward a process theory of entrepreneurial ecosystems	Spigel B.; Harrison R.	333	2018
23	Burst Bubbles or Build Steam? Entrepreneurship Education, Entrepreneurial Self-Efficacy, and Entrepreneurial Intentions.	Piperopoulos P.; Dimov D.	330	2015
24	Growth regimes over time and space	Audretsch D.B.; Fritsch M.	321	2002
25	The effects of industry growth and strategic breadth on new venture performance and strategy content	McDougall P.P.; Covin J.G.; Robinson R.B.; Jr.; Herron L.	319	1994
26	Building an innovation hub: A case study of the transformation of university roles in regional technological and economic development.	Youtie J.; Shapira P.	313	2008
27	Technology Transfer and Universities' Spin-Out Strategies	Lockett A.; Wright M.; Franklin S.	310	2003
28	Regulatory focus theory and the entrepreneurial process	Brockner J.; Higgins E.T.; Low M.B.	305	2004
29	Underpricing and entrepreneurial wealth losses in IPOs: Theory and evidence.	Habib M.A.; Ljungqvist A.P.	304	2001
30	Looking inside the spiky bits: a critical review and conceptualisation of entrepreneurial ecosystems	Brown R.; Mason C.	302	2017

Source: Own elaboration based on Scopus 2022. R: Ranking; J: Journal; TC: Total citations; PY: Year of publication.

To complement, on the Scopus database on the subject of PFE, some articles and reviews stand out with more than 400 citations each, so they could be considered among the most influential documents: "The cognitive perspective: a valuable tool for answering entrepreneurship's basic why questions" by Baron, (2004), "Legitimacy as a social process" by Johnson, Dowd and Ridgeway, (2006), and "The effects of the interactive use of management control systems on product innovation" by Bisbe and Otley, (2004).

The 30 most influential authors in PFE

In the field of PFE, several major authors have significantly contributed to the development of theories and knowledge. Table 4 presents the 30 most influential researchers in this field. The same criteria of Table 2 are used. Urbano holds the top position, having the most publications in PFE with a total of 24 articles. He has an H-index of 13 and a total of 841 citations, making him the second most cited author. Most of Urbano's publications are within the Q1 period (2012-2021). Following closely is Audretsch, with 14 articles and 1267 citations, making him the most cited author in PFE. One of Audretsch's articles is among the N30 most cited articles in the field.

Among the notable authors is Link, who, despite having only 6 publications, has accumulated 723 citations, making him the fourth most cited author. Link's articles have the highest average number of citations at 120.5, and most of his work is published in the Q1 period. This indicates the high impact and recognition of his contributions to PFE research.

The five leading authors in our analysis have significantly contributed to Promotion and Fostering of Entrepreneurship (PFE). Collectively, these authors have shaped the theoretical foundations of PFE and provided practical insights guiding global policy and entrepreneurial practices. David Urbano is known for his work on how institutional environments influence entrepreneurial activities, particularly in SMEs. David Audretsch has advanced understanding of the relationship between entrepreneurship, innovation, and economic growth, with a focus on SMEs' role in regional and national development. Vanessa Ratten has explored sport entrepreneurship and innovation, showing how entrepreneurial practices can be nurtured in various contexts, including SMEs. Peter A. Singer's work, while broader, has impacted the understanding of ethical and social dimensions in entrepreneurship, crucial for sustainable business practices. João J.M. Ferreira is recognized for his research on strategic management and entrepreneurship, emphasizing how SMEs can leverage strategic resources for competitive advantage.

Table 4.Top 30 authors in PFE

R	Authors	Country	P-PFE	%PEFE	H-PFE	TC	CP	N50	Q1	Q2	Q3	Q4	Q5
1	Urbano, D.	ESP	24	37.79%	13	841	35.04	-	23	1	-	-	-
2	Audretsch, D.	USA	14	22.04%	9	1267	90.50	1	6	6	2	-	-
3	Ratten, V.	AUS	14	22.04%	10	383	27.36	-	13	1	-	-	-
4	Singer P.A.	CAN	14	22.04%	9	333	23.79	-	1	13	-	-	-
5	Ferreira, J.J.M.	PRT	14	22.04%	10	291	20.79	-	14	-	-	-	-
6	Guerrero, M.	CHL	11	17.32%	8	338	30.73	-	10	1	-	-	-
7	Daar A.S.	UGA	11	17.32%	9	323	29.36	-	-	11	-	-	-

continued on following page

Table 4. Continued

R	Authors	Country	P-PFE	%PEFE	H-PFE	TC	CP	N50	Q1	Q2	Q3	Q4	Q5
8	Marques, C.S.	PRT	10	15.75%	6	141	14.10	-	10	-	-	-	-
9	Quach, U.	CAN	9	14.17%	9	315	35.00	-	-	9	-	-	-
10	Thorsteinsdóttir, H.	CAN	9	14.17%	9	315	35.00	-	-	9	-	-	-
11	Urban, B.	ZAF	9	14.17%	6	103	11.44	-	9	-	-	-	-
12	Alvarez, C.	COL	8	12.60%	6	362	45.25	-	7	1	-	-	-
13	Kraus, S.	ITA	8	12.60%	6	254	31.75	-	8	-	-	-	-
14	Meoli, M.	ITA	8	12.60%	8	187	23.38	-	8	-	-	-	-
15	Santos, S.	USA	8	12.60%	4	104	13.00	-	8	-	-	-	-
16	Cumming D.	ITA	7	11.02%	6	591	84.43	-	4	3	-	-	-
17	García-Morales, V.	ESP	7	11.02%	7	423	60.43	-	6	1	-	-	-
18	Brettel, M.	DEU	7	11.02%	6	280	40.00	-	7	-	-	-	-
19	Mok K.H.	HKG	7	11.02%	6	206	29.43	-	6	1	-	-	-
20	Peris-Ortiz, M	ESP	7	11.02%	4	144	20.57	-	6	1	-	-	-
21	Welter, F	DEU	7	11.02%	5	743	106.14	1	2	5	-	-	-
22	Fernandes, C.	PRT	7	11.02%	5	141	20.14	-	7	-	-	-	-
23	Williams, N.	GBR	7	11.02%	5	96	13.71	-	7	-	-	-	-
24	Link, A.N.	USA	6	9.45%	4	723	120.50	-	5	1	-	-	-
25	Westhead, P.	GBR	6	9.45%	5	413	68.83	1	3	2	1	-	-
26	Lehmann, E.E.	DEU	6	9.45%	5	280	46.67	-	5	1	-	-	-
27	Carayannis, E	USA	6	9.45%	6	219	36.50	-	3	2	1	-	-
28	Lans, T.	NLD	6	9.45%	5	208	34.67	-	5	1	-	-	-
29	Secundo, G.	ITA	6	9.45%	5	132	22.00	-	6	-	-	-	-
30	Zabala-Iturriagagoitia, J.M.	ESP	6	9.45%	4	111	18.50	-	5	1	-	-	-

Source: Own elaboration based on Scopus 2022; R: Ranking; P-PFE: total documents published in PFE; %PFE: Percentage of documents published in PFE: HPFE: H-index only with PFE; TC: Total Citations; CP: Citations per document; N50: Number of publications among the 50 most cited articles; Q1: 2012-2021; Q2: 2002-2011; Q3: 1992-2001; Q4: 1982-1991; Q5: 1956-1981.

The 30 most influential institutions in PFE

Institutions such as universities support and enable academic research in certain areas and the promotion of entrepreneurship is one of them. Table 5 shows the top 30 universities that have promoted the development of PFE. The same criteria of previous Tables are respected. The University of Toronto leads this ranking with 49 publications, has 1451 total citations and most of its papers are from the Q2 AND Q1 period. The Universitat de València has 37 publications, 475 total citations, most of its publications are Q1. It is followed by the Universitat Autònoma de Barcelona, with a total of 36 publications, has

1301 citations, most of its papers are Q1 and the University of Indiana Bloomington with 32 publications, 322 citations, most of its papers are Q1.

Another interesting indicator is the total cited (TC), in this criterion Erasmus Universiteit Rotterdam is the most outstanding institution due to the work of this university with most of its TC in 1997, Jönköping International Business School also stands out with 1018 TC and the University of Nottingham with 950 TC. The universities with papers within the N50 of most cited articles are the University of Toronto, University of Indiana Bloomington, Erasmus Universiteit Rotterdam and Jönköping International Business School all with a total of 2 publications within this top.

The five leading institutions in our analysis are pivotal in advancing research on Promotion and Fostering of Entrepreneurship (PFE). Together, these institutions have shaped the global PFE research landscape, providing insights that influence policy and practice worldwide. The University of Toronto excels in exploring ethical, social, and innovative aspects of entrepreneurship, key for sustainable SME practices. The University of Valencia has contributed significantly to understanding how institutional environments shape entrepreneurial activities, particularly in Europe. The Autonomous University of Barcelona is known for its interdisciplinary approach, integrating economic, social, and technological perspectives in PFE. Indiana University Bloomington has been influential in studying the economic impacts of entrepreneurship, especially SMEs' role in regional and national development. The University of Sevilla is recognized for its research on cultural and institutional factors influencing entrepreneurship, offering insights on how SMEs can thrive in complex environments.

Table 5.Top 30 institutions in PFE

R	INSTITUTIONS	C	PPFE	%PPFE	HPFE	TC	CP	T50	Q1	Q2	Q3	Q4	Q5
1	University of Toronto	CAN	49	0.85%	19	1451	29.6	2	19	24	4	2	-
2	University of Valencia	ESP	37	0.64%	12	475	12.8	0	32	4	1	-	-
3	Autonomous University of Barcelona	ESP	36	0.62%	18	1301	36.1	0	32	4	-	-	-
4	University of Indiana Bloomington	USA	32	0.55%	16	322	10.1	2	23	6	2	1	-
5	University of Sevilla	ESP	27	0.47%	11	343	12.7	0	22	5	-	-	-
6	University of Beira Interior	PRT	26	0.45%	13	558	21.5	0	23	3	-	-	-
7	George Washington University	USA	24	0.42%	12	476	19.8	0	15	6	1	2	-
8	Polytechnic University of Valencia	ESP	24	0.42%	10	424	17.7	0	22	2	-	-	-
9	University of California, Berkeley	USA	23	0.40%	11	502	21.8	1	15	6	2	-	-
10	Stanford University	USA	22	0.38%	10	432	19.6	0	18	4	-	-	-
11	University of the Witwatersrand, Johannesburg	ZAF	22	0.38%	9	265	12.0	0	19	1	2	-	-
12	Politecnico di Milano	ITA	22	0.38%	11	855	38.9	1	18	4	-	-	-
13	Iscte - University Institute of Lisbon	PRT	21	0.36%	9	297	14.1	0	20	1	-	-	-
14	HSE University	RUS	20	0.35%	9	250	12.5	0	19	1	-	-	-
15	Lunds Universitet	SWE	20	0.35%	8	366	18.3	0	16	3	1	-	-
16	Pennsylvania State University	USA	19	0.33%	9	231	12.2	0	12	5	-	2	-
17	Wageningen University & Research	NLD	19	0.33%	10	375	19.7	0	16	3	-	-	-
18	Tecnologico of Monterrey	MEX	19	0.33%	6	99	5.2	0	17	2	-	-	-

continued on following page

Table 5. Continued

R	INSTITUTIONS	C	PPFE	%PPFE	HPFE	TC	CP	T50	Q1	Q2	Q3	Q4	Q5
19	University of Extremadura	ESP	19	0.33%	6	154	8.1	0	18	1	-	-	-
20	University of Michigan, Ann Arbor	USA	19	0.33%	9	362	19.1	0	8	10	-	1	-
21	University of Granada	ESP	19	0.33%	12	651	34.3	0	16	3	-	-	-
22	Alma Mater Studiorum Università di Bologna	ITA	19	0.33%	11	856	45.1	0	12	6	-	1	-
23	Universiti Kebangsaan Malaysia	MYS	18	0.31%	5	91	5.1	0	14	4	-	-	-
24	KU Leuven	BEL	18	0.31%	7	282	15.7	0	11	7	-	-	-
25	University of Oxford	GBR	18	0.31%	11	478	26.6	0	14	4	-	-	-
26	Newcastle Business School	GBR	18	0.31%	9	263	14.6	0	18	-	-	-	-
27	Massachusetts Institute of Technology	USA	17	0.29%	8	577	33.9	1	8	8	-	-	1
28	HEC Montreal	CAN	16	0.28%	6	244	15.3	0	13	1	2	-	-
29	University for development	CHL	16	0.28%	11	338	21.1	0	16	-	-	-	-
30	University of Porto	PRT	16	0.28%	5	74	4.6	0	15	1	-	-	-

Source: Own elaboration based on Scopus 2022; R: Ranking; P-PFE: total documents published in PFE; %PFE: Percentage of documents published in PFE; HPFE: H-index only with PFE; TC: Total Citations; CP: Citations per document; N50: Number of publications among the 50 most cited articles; Q1: 2012-2021; Q2: 2002-2011; Q3: 1992-2001; Q4: 1982-1991; Q5: 1956-1981.

SCIENCE MAPPING OF PFE RESEARCH

Co-occurrence of Keywords in PFE

In this section, the analysis of bibliographic information using the VOS viewer software revealed several key insights, particularly in relation to small and medium-sized enterprises (SMEs).

Firstly, the co-occurrence of authors' keywords in Promotion and Fostering of Entrepreneurship (PFE) documents highlights the most common and frequent keywords found in the same papers. Among these keywords, "entrepreneurship," "innovation," "entrepreneurship education," "social entrepreneurship," and "sustainability" emerge as the most prevalent, indicating a strong focus on these areas within the context of SMEs.

Additionally, the clustering of terms into distinct areas provides further insight into potential research orientations. For example, the yellow cluster, centered around the keyword "entrepreneurship," includes terms like economic and regional development, venture capital, and policies. These terms suggest a research focus on the economic and policy implications of entrepreneurship, particularly in the context of SMEs.

The green cluster, which is strongly related to PFE, includes terms such as innovation, sustainability, social entrepreneurship, corporate social responsibility, and creativity. This cluster highlights the importance of sustainable and socially responsible practices in entrepreneurship, particularly relevant for SMEs looking to differentiate themselves in competitive markets.

The blue cluster, encompassing terms like leadership, culture, employment, social media, start-ups, and SMEs, indicates a focus on the organizational and cultural aspects of entrepreneurship, with a specific emphasis on the challenges and opportunities faced by SMEs in these areas.

Overall, the analysis underscores the diverse and multidimensional nature of research on PFE, particularly in relation to SMEs, and highlights key areas of focus for future research in this field.

Figure 1. Co-occurrence of keywords in PFE. Source: Own elaboration based on VOS Viewer (Van Eck & Waltman, 2010b).

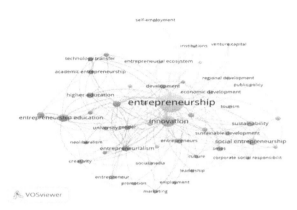

DISCUSSION

This study offers detailed insights into research on the Promotion and Fostering of Entrepreneurship (PFE), with a focus on small and medium-sized enterprises (SMEs). The discussion synthesizes the analysis, integrating theoretical foundations with empirical data to provide a comprehensive view of the current and future directions of PFE research.

1. Research Question 1: Visibility and Prominence of Research Outputs in PFE: The bibliometric analysis shows a significant increase in PFE research output, particularly in the last decade. This surge reflects growing interest in entrepreneurship related to SMEs. Journals like "Journal of Business Venturing" and "Sustainability Switzerland" have become key platforms, emphasizing sustainability and innovation. The prominence of these journals signals a shift towards understanding how sustainable practices and innovation strategies enhance SMEs' resilience and competitiveness in a global market.

2. Research Question 2: Key Contributors to PFE Research: Leading authors, universities, and countries highlight the collaborative nature of PFE research. Scholars such as Urbano and Audretsch have shaped the field by developing frameworks for entrepreneurial practice and policy. The University of Toronto, as a key institution, has advanced PFE research, especially on innovation ecosystems and their impact on SMEs. The concentration of research in countries like the USA and the UK indicates a need for more geographically diverse studies to address the unique challenges SMEs face in different contexts.

3. Research Question 3: Intellectual Framework and Keyword Analysis: The keyword co-occurrence analysis identifies dominant themes in PFE research, such as "entrepreneurship," "innovation," and "sustainability." These interconnected themes reflect the complex nature of entrepreneurship. The rise of "entrepreneurship ecosystems" as a central concept underscores the importance of systemic factors in entrepreneurial success, particularly for SMEs. This concept highlights the need for sup-

portive environments that provide capital access, favorable regulations, and strong collaborative networks. The analysis suggests future research may increasingly explore the intersections between these themes, focusing on how innovation and sustainability can drive SME growth within entrepreneurship ecosystems.

Integration of Theoretical Models with Empirical Findings

The discussion of these research questions is further enriched by integrating the theoretical models explored earlier in the chapter. By connecting these theoretical insights with the empirical data, this study offers a nuanced understanding of how SMEs can navigate and thrive within entrepreneurial ecosystems. The Entrepreneurial Ecosystem Theory (EET), for instance, provides a useful framework for understanding the interactions between different ecosystem components and their impact on SMEs. The empirical findings from the bibliometric analysis support the EET model by highlighting the importance of networks, institutions, and policies in shaping the entrepreneurial landscape. The data also aligns with the Resource-Based View (RBV) theory, which emphasizes the role of unique resources and capabilities in driving SME success.

SOLUTIONS AND RECOMMENDATIONS

This study represents the first exploration of Promotion and Fostering of Entrepreneurship (PFE) research using bibliometric techniques. Through performance analytics, it examines the scientific impact and citations of various agents in PFE research. By applying science mapping, the study visualizes the structure of scientific inquiry and collaboration in the intellectual and relational aspects of PFE. Specifically, it analyzes intellectual production from 1956 to 2021 in the Scopus database, aiming to:

1. Identify the most significant research contributions in PFE, including prominent journals and articles.
2. Recognize key authors and universities contributing to PFE research.
3. Investigate the intellectual structure of PFE research by analyzing key keywords through science mapping.

The analysis of PFE research from 1956 to 2021 in the Scopus database reveals key findings. Articles are the predominant output, with 5,761 publications and 91,653 citations. The top three journals by the number of articles are "Sustainability" (SS), the "Journal of Business Venturing" (JBV), and the "Small Business Economics" (SBE). The most cited article discusses the impact of network capabilities and entrepreneurial orientation on university spin-off performance. The University of Toronto is the leading institution, with 49 publications and 1,451 citations. Keyword analysis highlights themes such as entrepreneurship, innovation, education, social entrepreneurship, and sustainability.

Implications for Policy and Practice

The findings have significant implications for policymakers, practitioners, and researchers. For policymakers, the focus on sustainability and innovation suggests the need for policies that support SMEs in adopting these practices, such as incentives for sustainable practices, access to innovation hubs, and supportive regulatory frameworks. For practitioners, particularly SME owners and managers, the study emphasizes the importance of engaging with the entrepreneurial ecosystem, leveraging networks and resources to enhance competitiveness. For researchers, the study highlights the value of bibliometric methods in mapping the intellectual landscape of entrepreneurship research, identifying gaps, and opportunities for future studies.

FUTURE RESEARCH DIRECTIONS

The authors believe this article will be valuable to researchers, as it identifies research trends and patterns across diverse levels of analysis, including the macro-environment. While the primary goal is to provide a comprehensive overview of the most prolific and influential PFE research, some limitations arise from the methodology used. For example, H-index calculations were based on full authorship for each paper, but this limitation was mitigated by using science mapping techniques like co-authorship counting. Another limitation is the exclusion of factors that could lead to different results, such as alternative metrics or data from other scholarly sources like specialized associations or conferences. However, efforts were made to include additional relevant sources not covered by Scopus, including books and select journals from professional associations related to PFE, as well as conference papers.

While this study offers a comprehensive overview of PFE research, further investigation is needed in several areas. First, there is a need for more geographically diverse studies that explore the unique challenges SMEs face in different regions. Second, future research should examine the role of digital transformation in shaping entrepreneurial ecosystems, especially after the COVID-19 pandemic. Finally, more interdisciplinary research is needed to connect entrepreneurship with fields like environmental science, public health, and social innovation, exploring how these intersections can contribute to more resilient and sustainable SMEs.

CONCLUSION

In conclusion, this study underscores the vital role of SMEs within the broader framework of Promotion and Fostering of Entrepreneurship (PFE). The bibliometric analysis not only maps existing research but also highlights the growing importance of themes like innovation, sustainability, and entrepreneurial ecosystems. These themes are crucial for SMEs, which, despite limited resources, have the potential to drive significant economic growth and innovation. By leveraging components of the entrepreneurial ecosystem, such as government support, educational partnerships, and access to capital, SMEs can overcome challenges and achieve sustained success. The findings enhance our understanding of SMEs' strategic importance in the entrepreneurial ecosystem and offer practical insights for policymakers, researchers, and entrepreneurs aiming to foster a more inclusive and dynamic environment.

A key conclusion of this study comes from comparing the five clusters in Figure 1 with the content analysis of the 10 most cited articles (section 1.2). Four of these clusters align with the main themes of these articles. For instance, the yellow and red clusters emphasize the importance of the external environment on entrepreneurship: the yellow cluster focuses on institutional and public policy perspectives, while the red cluster highlights the role of higher education institutions in promoting entrepreneurship through education and technology transfer, particularly beneficial for SMEs.

The blue cluster relates to organizational aspects of entrepreneurship, such as leadership, culture, and the role of SMEs, emphasizing their crucial role in the entrepreneurial ecosystem.

Although we did not conduct a time evolution analysis of PFE-related keywords, a review of recent articles among the 30 most cited suggests that the green cluster encompasses current relevant topics, such as sustainability, corporate social responsibility, and social entrepreneurship—areas where SMEs can significantly impact. Moreover, we confirmed that the most prominent current topic in PFE is the entrepreneurial ecosystem perspective, leading to the following key proposition: "PFE has evolved over the last decades, with the entrepreneurial ecosystem (EE) framework becoming its main conceptual framework."

The body of knowledge on PFE has consistently shown a structured focus on the role of the external environment and organizational levels, with less emphasis on the individual level. Entrepreneurship ecosystems and the integration of PFE with sustainability and social responsibility are emerging as significant perspectives, particularly relevant for SMEs.

REFERENCES

Abrahamson, E., & Fairchild, G. (1999). Management fashion: Lifecycles, triggers, and collective learning processes. *Administrative Science Quarterly*, 44(4), 708–740. DOI: 10.2307/2667053

Alvarez, S. A., & Barney, J. B. (2004). Organizing rent generation and appropriation: Toward an entrepreneurial theory of the firm. *Journal of Business Venturing*, 19(5), 621–635. DOI: 10.1016/j.jbusvent.2003.09.002

Alvarez, S. A., Ireland, R. D., & Reuer, J. J. (2006). Entrepreneurship and strategic alliances. *Journal of Business Venturing*, 21(4), 401–404. DOI: 10.1016/j.jbusvent.2005.03.001

Ameh, A. A., & Udu, A. A. (2016). Social networks and entrepreneurship orientation among students in nigerian universities: A study of social network size and risk disposition. *Business and Management Research*, 5(2), 1–11. DOI: 10.5430/bmr.v5n2p1

Andrade-Valbuena, N., Baier-Fuentes, H., & Gaviria-Marin, M. (2022). An Overview of Sustainable Entrepreneurship in Tourism, Destination, and Hospitality Research Based on the Web of Science. *Sustainability (Basel)*, 14(22), 14944. DOI: 10.3390/su142214944

Andrade-Valbuena, N. A., & Merigo, J. M. (2018). Outlining new product development research through bibliometrics: Analyzing journals, articles and researchers. *Journal of Strategy and Management*, 11(3), 328–350. DOI: 10.1108/JSMA-08-2017-0061

Andrade-Valbuena, N. A., Merigo-Lindahl, J. M., & Olavarrieta, S. (2018). Bibliometric analysis of entrepreneurial orienta-tion. *World Journal of Entrepreneurship, Management and Sustainable Development*, 15(1), 45–69. DOI: 10.1108/WJEMSD-08-2017-0048

Andrade-Valbuena, N. A., Valenzuela Fernández, L., & Merigó, J. M. (2022). Thirty-five years of strategic management research. A country analysis using bibliometric techniques for the 1987-2021 period. *Cuadernos de Gestión*, 22(2), 7–22. DOI: 10.5295/cdg.211441na

Audretsch, D. B., & Fritsch, M. (2002). Growth regimes over time and space. *Regional Studies*, 36(2), 113–124. DOI: 10.1080/00343400220121909

Audretsch, D. B., & Thurik, A. R. (2000). Capitalism and democracy in the 21st century: From the managed to the entrepreneurial economy. *Journal of Evolutionary Economics*, 10(1-2), 17–34. DOI: 10.1007/s001910050003

Autio, E., Nambisan, S., Thomas, L. D., & Wright, M. (2018). Digital affordances, spatial affordances, and the genesis of entrepreneurial ecosystems. *Strategic Entrepreneurship Journal*, 12(1), 72–95. DOI: 10.1002/sej.1266

Baron, R. A. (1998). Cognitive mechanisms in entrepreneurship: Why and when entrepreneurs think differently than other peo-ple. *Journal of Business Venturing*, 13(4), 275–294. DOI: 10.1016/S0883-9026(97)00031-1

Baron, R. A. (2004, August). Opportunity recognition: a cognitive perspective. in *Academy of management proceedings* briarcliff manor, ny 10510: Academy of management (vol. 2004, no. 1, pp. a1-a6). DOI: 10.5465/ambpp.2004.13862818

Bergman, B. J.Jr, & McMullen, J. S. (2020). Entrepreneurs in the making: Six decisions for fostering entrepreneurship through maker spaces. *Business Horizons*, 63(6), 811–824. DOI: 10.1016/j.bushor.2020.07.004

Bisbe, J., & Otley, D. (2004). The effects of the interactive use of management control systems on product innova-tion. *Accounting, Organizations and Society*, 29(8), 709–737. DOI: 10.1016/j.aos.2003.10.010

Blanco-Mesa, F., León-Castro, E., & Merigó, J. M. (2019). A bibliometric analysis of aggregation operators. *Applied Soft Computing*, 81, 105488. DOI: 10.1016/j.asoc.2019.105488

Brush, C. G., De Bruin, A., & Welter, F. (2009). A gender-aware framework for women's entrepreneurship. *International Journal of Gender and Entrepreneurship*, 1(1), 8–24. DOI: 10.1108/17566260910942318

Bruton, G. D., Ahlstrom, D., & Li, H. L. (2010). Institutional theory and entrepreneurship: Where are we now and where do we need to move in the future? *Entrepreneurship Theory and Practice*, 34(3), 421–440. DOI: 10.1111/j.1540-6520.2010.00390.x

Cope, J. (2011). Entrepreneurial learning from failure: An interpretative phenomenological analysis. *Journal of Business Venturing*, 26(6), 604–623. DOI: 10.1016/j.jbusvent.2010.06.002

Eijdenberg, E. L., Thompson, N. A., Verduijn, K., & Essers, C. (2019). Entrepreneurial activities in a developing country: An institutional theory perspective. *International Journal of Entrepreneurial Behaviour & Research*, 25(3), 414–432. DOI: 10.1108/IJEBR-12-2016-0418

Etzkowitz, H., & Leydesdorff, L. (2000). The dynamics of innovation: From National Systems and "Mode 2" to a Triple Helix of university–industry–government relations. *Research Policy*, 29(2), 109–123. DOI: 10.1016/S0048-7333(99)00055-4

Fauchart, E., & Gruber, M. (2011). Darwinians, communitarians, and missionaries: The role of founder identity in entrepre-neurship. *Academy of Management Journal*, 54(5), 935–957. DOI: 10.5465/amj.2009.0211

Foss, N. J., Klein, P. G., Kor, Y. Y., & Mahoney, J. T. (2008). Entrepreneurship, subjectivism, and the resource-based view: To-ward a new synthesis. *Strategic Entrepreneurship Journal*, 2(1), 73–94. DOI: 10.1002/sej.41

Funko, I. S., Vlačić, B., & Dabić, M. (2023). Corporate entrepreneurship in public sector: A systematic literature review and research agenda. *Journal of Innovation & Knowledge*, 8(2), 100343. DOI: 10.1016/j.jik.2023.100343

Galindo-Martín, M. Á., Castaño-Martínez, M. S., & Méndez-Picazo, M. T. (2021). The role of entrepreneurship in different economic phases. *Journal of Business Research*, 122, 171–179. DOI: 10.1016/j.jbusres.2020.08.050

Granovetter, M. S. (1973). The strength of weak ties. *American Journal of Sociology*, 78(6), 1360–1380. DOI: 10.1086/225469

Habib, M. A., & Ljungqvist, A. P. (2001). Underpricing and entrepreneurial wealth losses in IPOs: Theory and evidence. *Review of Financial Studies*, 14(2), 433–458. DOI: 10.1093/rfs/14.2.433

Henri, J. F. (2006). Management control systems and strategy: A resource-based perspective. *Accounting, Organizations and Society*, 31(6), 529–558. DOI: 10.1016/j.aos.2005.07.001

Hirsch, J. E. (2005). An index to quantify an individual's scientific research output. *Proceedings of the National Academy of Sciences of the United States of America*, 102(46), 16569–16572. DOI: 10.1073/pnas.0507655102 PMID: 16275915

Hopp, C., & Stephan, U. (2012). The influence of socio-cultural environments on the performance of nascent entrepreneurs: Community culture, motivation, self-efficacy and start-up success. *Entrepreneurship and Regional Development*, 24(9-10), 917–945. DOI: 10.1080/08985626.2012.742326

Hornsby, J. S., Kuratko, D. F., & Zahra, S. A. (2002). Middle managers' perception of the internal environment for corporate entrepreneurship: Assessing a measurement scale. *Journal of Business Venturing*, 17(3), 253–273. DOI: 10.1016/S0883-9026(00)00059-8

Huggins, R., & Thompson, P. (2015). Entrepreneurship, innovation and regional growth: A network theory. *Small Business Economics*, 45(1), 103–128. DOI: 10.1007/s11187-015-9643-3

Johnson, C., Dowd, T. J., & Ridgeway, C. L. (2006). Legitimacy as a social process. *Annual Review of Sociology*, 32(1), 53–78. DOI: 10.1146/annurev.soc.32.061604.123101

Keh, H. T., Nguyen, T. T. M., & Ng, H. P. (2007). The effects of entrepreneurial orientation and marketing information on the performance of SMEs. *Journal of Business Venturing*, 22(4), 592–611. DOI: 10.1016/j.jbusvent.2006.05.003

Krueger, N. F.Jr, Reilly, M. D., & Carsrud, A. L. (2000). Competing models of entrepreneurial intentions. *Journal of Business Venturing*, 15(5-6), 411–432. DOI: 10.1016/S0883-9026(98)00033-0

Lee, E. B., & Baek, H. (2023). Prediction of Information Diffusion of New Products: Based on Product Launch and Media Difference. *Journal of the Knowledge Economy*, 15(2), 1–30. DOI: 10.1007/s13132-023-01385-8

Llanos-Herrera, G. R., & Merigo, J. M. (2018). Overview of brand personality research with bibliometric indicators. *Kybernetes*, 48(3), 546–569. DOI: 10.1108/K-02-2018-0051

Lumpkin, G. T., Hills, G. E., & Shrader, R. C. (2004). Opportunity recognition. Entrepreneurship: The way ahead, 73-90.

Mahoney, J. T. (2001). A resource-based theory of sustainable rents. *Journal of Management*, 27(6), 651–660. DOI: 10.1177/014920630102700603

McGee, J. E., Peterson, M., Mueller, S. L., & Sequeira, J. M. (2009). Entrepreneurial self efficacy: Refining the measure. *Entrepreneurship Theory and Practice*, 33(4), 965–988. DOI: 10.1111/j.1540-6520.2009.00304.x

Merigó, J. M., Mas-Tur, A., Roig-Tierno, N., & Ribeiro-Soriano, D. (2015). A bibliometric overview of the Journal of Business Research between 1973 and 2014. *Journal of Business Research*, 68(12), 2645–2653. DOI: 10.1016/j.jbusres.2015.04.006

Mitchell, R. K., Busenitz, L., Lant, T., McDougall, P. P., Morse, E. A., & Smith, J. B. (2002). Toward a theory of entrepreneurial cognition: Rethinking the people side of entrepreneurship research. *Entrepreneurship Theory and Practice*, 27(2), 93–105. DOI: 10.1111/1540-8520.00001

Mongeon, P., & Paul-Hus, A. (2016). The journal coverage of Web of Science and Scopus: A comparative analysis. *Scientometrics*, 106(1), 213–228. DOI: 10.1007/s11192-015-1765-5

Morrison, A. (2000). Entrepreneurship: What triggers it? *International Journal of Entrepreneurial Behaviour & Research*, 6(2), 59–71. DOI: 10.1108/13552550010335976

Nicholls, A. (2010). The legitimacy of social entrepreneurship: Reflexive isomorphism in a pre–paradigmatic field. *Entrepreneurship Theory and Practice*, 34(4), 611–633. DOI: 10.1111/j.1540-6520.2010.00397.x

Østergaard, A., & Marinova, S. T. (2018). Human capital in the entrepreneurship ecosystem. *International Journal of Entrepreneurship and Small Business*, 35(3), 371–390. DOI: 10.1504/IJESB.2018.095907

Penrose, E. (1959). The productive opportunity of the firm and the entrepreneur. In *The Theory of the Growth of the Firm* (pp. 31–42). Oxford University Press.

Powell, E. E., & Baker, T. (2014). It's what you make of it: Founder identity and enacting strategic responses to adversity. *Academy of Management Journal*, 57(5), 1406–1433. DOI: 10.5465/amj.2012.0454

Ratinho, T., Amezcua, A., Honig, B., & Zeng, Z. (2020). Supporting entrepreneurs: A systematic review of literature and an agenda for research. *Technological Forecasting and Social Change*, 154, 119956. DOI: 10.1016/j.techfore.2020.119956

Roundy, P. T., & Burke-Smalley, L. (2022). Leveraging entrepreneurial ecosystems as human resource systems: A theory of meta-organizational human resource management. *Human Resource Management Review*, 32(4), 100863. DOI: 10.1016/j.hrmr.2021.100863

Sandberg, W. R. (1992). Strategic management's potential contributions to a theory of entrepreneurship. *Entrepreneurship Theory and Practice*, 16(3), 73–90. DOI: 10.1177/104225879201600305

Schumpeter, J. (1934). *The theory of economic development*. Harvard University Press.

Schumpeter, J. (1942). *Capitalism, socialism and democracy*. George Allen and Unwin.

Scott, W. R. (1995). *Institutions and Organizations. Thousands Oaks*. Sage Publications.

Shane, S., & Venkataraman, S. (2000). The promise of entrepreneurship as a field of research. *Academy of Management Review*, 25(1), 217–226. DOI: 10.5465/amr.2000.2791611

Siegel, D. S., Waldman, D. A., Atwater, L. E., & Link, A. N. (2004). Toward a model of the effective transfer of scientific knowledge from academicians to practitioners: Qualitative evidence from the commercialization of university technolo-gies. *Journal of Engineering and Technology Management*, 21(1-2), 115–142. DOI: 10.1016/j.jengtecman.2003.12.006

Singh, S., Corner, P., & Pavlovich, K. (2007). Coping with entrepreneurial failure. *Journal of Management & Organization*, 13(4), 331–344. DOI: 10.5172/jmo.2007.13.4.331

Spigel, B. (2017). The relational organization of entrepreneurial ecosystems. *Entrepreneurship Theory and Practice*, 41(1), 49–72. DOI: 10.1111/etap.12167

Spigel, B., & Harrison, R. (2018). Toward a process theory of entrepreneurial ecosystems. *Strategic Entrepreneurship Journal*, 12(1), 151–168. DOI: 10.1002/sej.1268

Stopford, J. M., & Baden-Fuller, C. W. (1994). Creating corporate entrepreneurship. *Strategic Management Journal*, 15(7), 521–536. DOI: 10.1002/smj.4250150703

Tan, J., Shao, Y., & Li, W. (2013). To be different, or to be the same? An exploratory study of isomorphism in the cluster. *Journal of Business Venturing*, 28(1), 83–97. DOI: 10.1016/j.jbusvent.2012.02.003

Toghraee, M. T., & Monjezi, M. (2017). Introduction to cultural entrepreneurship: Cultural entrepreneurship in developing countries. *International Review of Management and Marketing*, 7(4), 67–73.

Urbano, D., Aparicio, S., & Querol, V. (2016). Social progress orientation and innovative entrepreneurship: An international analysis. *Journal of Evolutionary Economics*, 26(5), 1033–1066. DOI: 10.1007/s00191-016-0485-1

Vallaster, C., Kraus, S., Lindahl, J., & Nielsen, A. (2019). Ethics and entrepreneurship: A bibliometric study and literature review. *Journal of Business Research*, 99, 226–237. DOI: 10.1016/j.jbusres.2019.02.050

Van Eck, N., & Waltman, L. (2010a). Software survey: VOSviewer, a computer program for bibliometric mapping. *Scientometrics*, 84(2), 523–538. DOI: 10.1007/s11192-009-0146-3 PMID: 20585380

Van Eck, N., & Waltman, L. (2010b). VOSviewer (version 1.6.20). [Software]. https://www.vosviewer.com/

Walter, A., Auer, M., & Ritter, T. (2006). The impact of network capabilities and entrepreneurial orientation on university spin-off performance. *Journal of Business Venturing*, 21(4), 541–567. DOI: 10.1016/j.jbusvent.2005.02.005

Waltman, L., Van Eck, N. J., & Noyons, E. C. (2010). A unified approach to mapping and clustering of bibliometric networks. *Journal of Informetrics*, 4(4), 629–635. DOI: 10.1016/j.joi.2010.07.002

Wennberg, K., Pathak, S., & Autio, E. (2013). How culture moulds the effects of self-efficacy and fear of failure on entrepre-neurship. *Entrepreneurship and Regional Development*, 25(9-10), 756–780. DOI: 10.1080/08985626.2013.862975

Wennekers, S., Van Wennekers, A., Thurik, R., & Reynolds, P. (2005). Nascent entrepreneurship and the level of economic development. *Small Business Economics*, 24(3), 293–309. DOI: 10.1007/s11187-005-1994-8

Zhang, J. (2010). The problems of using social networks in entrepreneurial resource acquisition. *International Small Business Journal*, 28(4), 338–361. DOI: 10.1177/0266242610363524

Zhou, C., & Etzkowitz, H. (2021). Triple helix twins: A framework for achieving innovation and UN sustainable development goals. *Sustainability (Basel)*, 13(12), 6535. DOI: 10.3390/su13126535

KEY TERMS AND DEFINITIONS

Bibliometrics: A research field using quantitative analysis to study publication patterns, citations, and bibliographic data. It analyzes written documents like academic articles and patents to understand authorship, publication trends, citation patterns, and the impact on the scholarly community.

Entrepreneurial Ecosystem Theory (EET): A framework viewing entrepreneurship as a system influenced by environmental factors. Success depends not only on individual traits but also on the ecosystem, including government policies, cultural norms, access to capital, and infrastructure.

H-index: A metric combining publication quantity and citation impact to measure a researcher's productivity and influence.

Keyword Co-occurrence Analysis: Identifying frequently paired keywords in documents to reveal main themes or topics in a field.

Promotion and Fostering of Entrepreneurship (PFE): Activities aimed at encouraging entrepreneurship in a region or group, including resources, education, mentorship, networking, and financial support.

Resource-Based View (RBV): A theory in strategic management suggesting that a firm's competitive advantage is primarily based on its resources and capabilities rather than external factors.

Science Mapping: Also known as bibliometric mapping, it visually represents the structure and dynamics of scientific knowledge within a field, identifying patterns and relationships between research areas, topics, or authors.

Social Network Theory (SNT): A perspective examining how social structures influence behavior and interactions within a network, focusing on the relationships and connection patterns between actors.

Chapter 12
SMEs in VUCA and Populist Environments:
The Need for Media Education and Information Literacy

Jaime Andrés Wilches Tinjacá
Institución Universitaria Politécnico Grancolombiano, Colombia

María Camila Cuello Saumeth
https://orcid.org/0000-0003-0236-9146
Fundación Universitaria del Área Andina, Colombia

Herman Eduardo Dávila Aguja
Institución Universitaria Politécnico Grancolombiano, Colombia

ABSTRACT

The chapter aims to substantiate the significance of cultivating media education and information literacy, which empower civil society sectors to confront the VUCA environment and cater to their interests and needs. As a result, they fuel the economy and enable the establishment of small and large businesses. With the recognition that populism has an impact on the bonds of trust within civil society that are needed for creating sustainable, supportive, and cooperative economies, as well as production levels that strive for equity and creativity, the prolongation of a scenario marked by volatility, uncertainty, complexity and ambiguity becomes possible.

INTRODUCTION

There is growing concern regarding the ability of populism to exploit socio-economic VUCA environments to reinforce its authority and advance its goals. On the one hand, in times of volatility and turmoil, populist leaders frequently attempt to single out groups or entities that can be blamed for the issues and difficulties confronting society. These alleged "scapegoats" may include immigrants, ethnic or religious minorities, economic or political elites, or even international organizations. By attributing

DOI: 10.4018/979-8-3693-4046-2.ch012

responsibility to these groups, populist leaders redirect the population's discontent and anxiety towards them, thereby strengthening their support.

In VUCA environments with elevated uncertainty and anxiety, populists offer promises of swift and radical changes to tackle social issues. However, these individuals often lack explicit plans for implementation despite proposing economic, political or social reforms as immediate solutions.

In addition to this, a VUCA environment represents a significant challenge for small and medium-sized enterprises (SMEs), as they operate in an increasingly dynamic and changing business context. Volatility and uncertainty can make strategic decisions difficult, while complexity and ambiguity can hinder rapid adaptation to new market conditions. In this sense, SMEs need strong media education and information literacy to successfully navigate VUCA environments.

This implies the ability to understand and effectively use digital tools and available information sources, as well as to discern between relevant and superfluous information. In this way, SMEs can improve their ability to anticipate and respond to market changes, adopt innovative strategies, and stay competitive in an increasingly challenging business environment.

Populism may emerge and thrive in environments defined by Volatility, Uncertainty, Complexity, and Ambiguity (VUCA). During periods of economic crisis, demographic changes, accelerated technological transformations, or social tensions, individuals tend to seek straightforward and expedited solutions to the obstacles they confront. Therefore, populist leaders may appeal to those who feel disoriented or disaffected in a VUCA environment by providing solutions that appear direct and easy to comprehend.

However, there is a possibility that certain economic actors employ populism to advance their interests or create uncertainty in society. This may happen, for instance, through the manipulation of information, whereby data is presented in a biased way to foster insecurity and panic among the population. Alternatively, it could transpire through the use of populist rhetoric to divert attention from structural economic challenges or inequalities that these actors may have had a hand in creating. Finally, this may also occur through the backing of populist leaders who can influence the development of economic policies that benefit their interests.

In accordance with the above, it is understood that the VUCA environment refers not only to the market's volatility, uncertainty, complexity and ambiguity understood in purely economic terms but also to how volatile, uncertain, complex and ambiguous the socioeconomic environment can be given certain economic and social changes such as financial crises, demographic changes, labor trends, inequality, and the consequences of populist measures or speeches.

The chapter aims to substantiate the significance of cultivating media education and information literacy, which empower civil society sectors to confront the VUCA environment and cater to their interests and needs. As a result, they fuel the economy and enable the establishment of small and large businesses. With the recognition that populism has an impact on the bonds of trust within civil society that are needed for creating sustainable, supportive, and cooperative economies, as well as production levels that strive for equity and creativity, the prolongation of a scenario marked by volatility, uncertainty, complexity and ambiguity becomes possible.

The chapter aims to substantiate the significance of cultivating media education and information literacy, which empower civil society sectors to confront the VUCA environment and cater to their interests and needs. As a result, they fuel the economy and enable the establishment of small and large businesses. With the recognition that populism has an impact on the bonds of trust within civil society that are needed for creating sustainable, supportive, and cooperative economies, as well as production levels that strive for equity and creativity, the prolongation of a scenario marked by volatility, uncertainty, complexity and ambiguity becomes possible.

The chapter aims to substantiate the significance of cultivating media education and information literacy, which empower civil society sectors to confront the VUCA environment and cater to their interests and needs. As a result, they fuel the economy and enable the establishment of small and large businesses. With the recognition that populism has an impact on the bonds of trust within civil society that are needed for creating sustainable, supportive, and cooperative economies, as well as production levels that strive for equity and creativity, the prolongation of a scenario marked by volatility, uncertainty, complexity and ambiguity becomes possible.

The chapter aims to substantiate the significance of cultivating media education and information literacy, which empower civil society sectors to confront the VUCA environment and cater to their interests and needs. As a result, they fuel the economy and enable the establishment of small and large businesses. With the recognition that populism has an impact on the bonds of trust within civil society that are needed for creating sustainable, supportive, and cooperative economies, as well as production levels that strive for equity and creativity, the prolongation of a scenario marked by volatility, uncertainty, complexity and ambiguity becomes possible.

The chapter aims to substantiate the significance of cultivating media education and information literacy, which empower civil society sectors to confront the VUCA environment and cater to their interests and needs. As a result, they fuel the economy and enable the establishment of small and large businesses. With the recognition that populism has an impact on the bonds of trust within civil society that are needed for creating sustainable, supportive, and cooperative economies, as well as production levels that strive for equity and creativity, the prolongation of a scenario marked by volatility, uncertainty, complexity and ambiguity becomes possible.

Contextualization and Definition of the VUCA Environment

In essence, it is necessary to grasp the definition of the VUCA environment (Volatility, Uncertainty, Complexity and Ambiguity). In today's business landscape, VUCA has become a fundamental perspective for comprehending the hardships organizations encounter in a constantly evolving and turbulent world. Fuentealba et al. (2023) note that the concept of VUCA, which stands for volatility, uncertainty, complexity, and ambiguity, first emerged in 2008 and saw a significant rise in scientific publications in 2020. This increase is attributed to global instability and the COVID-19 pandemic. It is worth mentioning that no institution has emerged as a significant or moderate producer of publications related to VUCA.

The VUCA environment encompasses the current context in which organizations operate, characterized by volatility, uncertainty, complexity, and ambiguity. Its origins lie in the 1990s, when American soldiers first coined the acronym composed of the terms Volatility (V), Uncertainty (U), Complexity (C), and Ambiguity (A) which became prominent in the English language (Quiroga Gil, 2021).

Therefore, the VUCA acronym can be perceived as follows:

Volatility refers to turbulence or the unexpected increased by dynamics of change; Uncertainty refers to the lack of predictability of issues and events; Complexity refers to the confounding of issues and surrounding factors; and Ambiguity to the haziness of reality and the mixed meaning of conditions. (Sarid & Levanon, 2023, p.1376)

In this context, volatility describes the rate and extent of changes in an environment. Within a volatile world, conditions can drastically transform within short periods. Numerous factors -including swift technological advancements, sudden political changes and unforeseen global events- contribute to volatility, resulting in a business landscape that requires constant adaptability. Therefore, the "V" in the acronym VUCA connotes volatility, indicating that challenges are unpredictable. The nature, velocity, volume, and scale of change do not conform to a predictable pattern (Hwa Ang, 2018).

Uncertainty pertains to the absence of predictability and the impossibility of wholly anticipating forthcoming events. In circumstances of uncertainty, organizations encounter obstacles when devising long-term strategic plans. Capricious economic, geopolitical, and societal factors intensify uncertainty, resulting in a more complicated exercise of decision-making. The terms "U" and "C" denote uncertainty and complexity, respectively, in relation to issues and events whose predictability is hindered by a lack of information or the presence of interconnected variables (Hwa Ang, 2018).

Complexity describes the difficulty in fully comprehending the environment due to the interconnection of contributing factors. Technical terminology will be explained upon first use. In a complex environment, various factors interact simultaneously, giving rise to a complex web of relationships that can be challenging to grasp. These factors include globalization, interdependence of markets, and cultural diversity.

Lastly, VUCA's "A" represents ambiguity, which indicates a lack of clarity about an event's meaning owing to an uncertain causal connection (Hwa Ang, 2018). Ambiguity refers to contradictory information that can obstruct accurate interpretation. Companies operating in ambiguous environments may face difficulties in analyzing market signals or interpreting changes in consumer preferences. Digital transformation and an abundance of data contribute to a state of ambiguity.

As such, the VUCA environment can present a range of challenges for companies, institutions, and individuals in multiple dimensions.

These include not only global health challenges like COVID-19 but also many other challenges: ecological (e.g. climate change, biodiversity loss, extreme weather), social (e.g. involuntary migration, food and water scarcity), political (e.g. interstate conflict, crises of state authority/legitimacy, hypernationalism), and economic (e.g. under-/un-employment, sprawling debt, affordability crises, austerity). (Stein, 2021, p.482)

In light of the aforementioned considerations, comprehension and recognition of the VUCA environment are crucial for the development of successful business strategies. According to Stein, "Developing critical literacy, including around the socio-historical patterns and conditions that led us to our current VUCA context, is a crucial dimension of any reimagined GCE (global citizenship education)" (2021, p.489). Institutions that embrace agile and proactive strategies for managing volatility, uncertainty, complexity, and ambiguity are better positioned to navigate this dynamic environment successfully. Rather than regarding VUCA as an insurmountable challenge, it should be utilized as an opportunity to promote critical literacy, innovation, and resilience in a constantly changing world.

1. THE ROLE OF CIVIL SOCIETY AND ECONOMIC DEVELOPMENT IN A VUCA ENVIRONMENT

In the current context, the VUCA (Volatility, Uncertainty, Complexity, and Ambiguity) environment plays a significant role in shaping global reality. This environment, which comprises unpredictable and swift changes, contributes to a great extent towards the general public's lack of trust in established institutions. The high levels of volatility and uncertainty, driven by unforeseen events and a lack of clarity about the future, lead to immense confusion in society.

The challenges that public managers face, reflecting upon a world characterized by volatility, uncertainty, complexity, and ambiguity (VUCA). Government organizations and officials are increasingly met with distrust and cynicism from their constituents, while the demand for more resilient, effective, and accountable public action continues to rise. (Park, 2018, p.299)

This atmosphere of mistrust and confusion creates fertile ground for the rise of populist movements. These movements often capitalize on widespread uncertainty and discontent, offering simplistic solutions and appealing to emotions rather than effectively addressing the complex challenges facing society. These simplistic solutions are welcome because:

The ugly truth of the VUCA world is that clarity gets rewarded, even if it's wrong, because there is such a need to cut through the confusion. A lot of people can't live with the current level of confusion, so they find simplistic solutions attractive. And of course that can be very dangerous. What you need is to be clear and simple without being simplistic. And then finally, ambiguity yields to agility. In the VUCA world, you have to be an athlete to thrive. I think things like physical fitness and mental fitness and nutrition and healthy lifestyles have always been important, but for leaders in today's world, they are not optional. (Johansen & Euchner, 2013, p.10)

Similarly, in a world that is becoming increasingly globalized and technologically advanced, the inadequacy of media education exacerbates this predicament. Civil society, which plays an essential role in determining a country's direction, is frequently ill-prepared to comprehend and analyze information disseminated via various channels. The lack of comprehensive media education places the population in a vulnerable position, susceptible to information manipulation and lacking discernment within a VUCA environment.

VUCA seems to accurately describe the Fourth Industrial Revolution in which machine intelligence and, more broadly, technology, are transforming almost every field of human endeavor—all against a backdrop of climate change, societal and political turmoil, and enormous and growing wealth inequity. Such a world requires agility and the kind of organizational shape shifting that can quickly respond to opportunities and threats. Rigid and siloed organizations will be increasingly brittle in a VUCA world. (LeBlanc, 2018, p.23)

For these reasons, it is crucial to acknowledge the necessity of enhancing media education and information literacy as integral parts of civil society's formation. A population that is well-informed and critically aware is essential to counteract the negative impacts of the VUCA environment and its exploitation by populist actors, thereby creating a more durable society capable of confronting current challenges.

1.1. Trust in Colombian Institutions Over the Past Five Years

Colombia is a country with numerous public institutions serving society; however, media surveys reveal societal grievances, concerns, and a high level of distrust. One such institution is the National Police, which has faced complaints about its handling of the ongoing national strike and has received its lowest ratings in the 9-year history of the survey. With 64% disapproval and only 31% approval, this institution is among those most impacted by the lack of trust it generates (Infobae, 2021).

Figure 1.Trust in the National Police

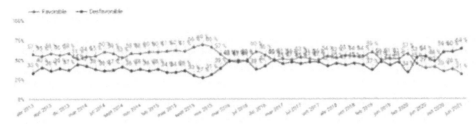

Note. Taken from Infobae (2021).

The Attorney General's Office is the second public institution under scrutiny. Carlos Camargo, in particular, has been deemed controversial for his management during the national strike. In a recent poll, 53% of respondents expressed disapproval, marking the first time such a figure has surpassed approval ratings in the pollster's history (Infobae, 2021).

Figure 2.Trust in the Attorney General's Office

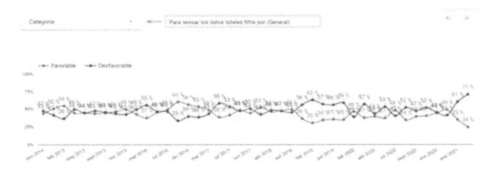

Note. Taken from Infobae (2021).

In third place is the Supreme Court of Justice, which had already reported higher rejection numbers, above 68%. In front of a 19% approval.

Figure 3.Trust in the Supreme Court of Justice

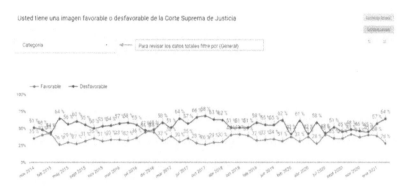

Note. Taken from Infobae (2021).

"The Constitutional Court received disapproval from a maximum of 61% with only 30% showing support. Similarly, the Council of State experienced its highest level of unpopularity with 67%" (Infobae, 2021). Furthermore, the citizens' assessment of Congress of the Republic resulted in an historic high of 86% of disapproval and only 10% approval. The political parties fared no better, with 84% of disapproval.

Figure 4.Trust in the Congress of the Republic

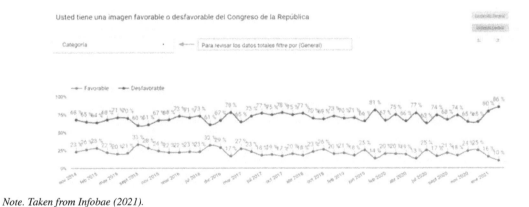

Note. Taken from Infobae (2021).

Seeing the low level of approval that Colombian society has in these institutions, the question arises: do Colombians trust any power entity? The answer is yes, and it is demonstrated in the survey carried out by Invamer "Edelman Trust Barometer" (Galvis, 2023).

Figure 5.Trust in other institutions

Note. Taken from Galvis (2023).

According to the survey, 58% of respondents viewed the country's businessmen positively, while only 36% lacked confidence in the business sector. As for the media, 53% of respondents found them unreliable, while 43% held a favorable opinion of them.

Figure 6.X-ray of trust in Colombia

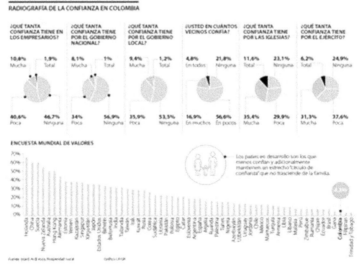

Note. Taken from INCP (2020).

Researchers from the Alliances for Reconciliation program of the United States Agency (USAID) and Acdi-Voca have concluded that Colombia ranks among emerging countries where the population holds greater reservations about companies' operations, as reflected by a general average rating of 4.13% when compared to other nations. Additionally, the lack of trust among Colombians is pervasive and affects both institutional and everyday contexts. Research shows that only 4.8% of those surveyed trust their neighbors, 16.9% trust the majority, 56.6% trust few, and 21.8% trust none (INCP, 2020).

1.2. Civil society sectors: Key actors driving the economy

Civil society sectors play a critical role in driving the economy, serving as the primary actors that generate dynamism, innovation, and sustainability. These sectors encompass a diverse range of entities, including individuals, small businesses, cooperatives, nonprofits, and social enterprises.

The concept of social capital is a recent development in the social sciences that describes the presence of trust, social relationships, and associations between individuals, groups, communities, and organizations. Free association is not only a human right but also a factor that promotes economic and institutional development (Salas Rodas, 2014). The power of social capital is exemplified in the United Kingdom.

Achieving every national goal the UK has - from economic growth, to health and wellbeing, to the green transition – relies on the contribution of a thriving civil society. Social sector organisations are leading creators of social capital, which is an essential component of both economic growth and social cohesion. (Law Family Commission on Civil Society, 2023, p.17)

On the other hand, micro, small, and medium-sized businesses (MSMEs) are a significant driving force in the economy. They represent an essential part of the business landscape and contribute greatly to employment. MSMEs demonstrate agility, flexibility, and innovation, which enable them to adapt efficiently to changing market conditions.

Small and medium-sized enterprises (MSMEs) differ from large corporations and economic empires in that the latter focus solely on generating profits for their shareholders, disregarding their obligation to social responsibility. This leads to a decline in recognition, productivity, and competitiveness. As a result, they cease to contribute to social capital by failing to participate in building social networks and fostering trust (Salas Rodas, 2014).

In the same way, other civil society organizations play an indispensable role in economic development through the influence they exert on political institutions:

Civil society organisations play an invaluable part in helping councils to address the challenges they face, working as partners to help overcome the barriers to engagement experienced by particular groups. This allows government to speak with those audiences through trusted local messengers, and enable everyone to have their say in our democratic processes. Participatory democracy methods, such as Citizens' Juries, can make a profound difference to people's lives: evidence shows that enabling people to participate in the decisions that affect them improves people's confidence in dealing with local issues, builds bridges between citizens and the government, fosters more engagement, and increases social capital. It also increases people's understanding of how decisions are taken, and leads to authorities making better decisions and developing more effective solutions to issues as a broader range of expertise can be tapped into to solve public issues. (HM Government, 2018, p.53)

Nonprofit organizations and social enterprises are essential components of civil society and play a vital role in promoting social and environmental well-being. These entities concentrate on addressing specific problems and generating positive impacts in the community, contributing to the construction of a more equitable and sustainable society through their initiatives.

Those civil society actors working positively to reduce societal harms and increase societal benefits. They aim to improve social cohesion; increase levels of economic and social development; reduce the burdens of poverty, ill-health and inequality; promote the interests of marginalized groups; extend the protection of social, civil and political rights; protect the environment; and provide services such as health, education and other forms of community development. (World Economic Forum, 2013, p.8)

Effective solutions to economic and social challenges require cooperation and collaboration between civil society actors. Partnerships among businesses, non-profit organizations, and government entities can produce comprehensive results.

Civil society contributes to any number of national goals and priorities. From economic growth to health and wellbeing, social sector organisations provide insight, services and the underlying social capital without which progress is impossible. The public recognise the variety of roles played by the social sector, and value its contributions both to service provision and social change. (Law Family Commission on Civil Society, 2023, pp.17-18)

Consequently, civil society sectors play a critical role in both the social fabric and the economy. Their capacity to create jobs, foster innovation, and tackle social and environmental issues contributes substantially to sustainable economic growth. Therefore, civil society organizations have identified opportunities to participate in the 2030 Agenda for Sustainable Development and the Sustainable Development Goals (SDGs) through alliances, platforms, and transnational networks. By utilizing these mechanisms, they can exert influence on decision-making and play a crucial role in accomplishing sustainable development objectives (Guerra Rondón & Bosch, 2023).

1.3. Trust and economic development: A directly proportional relationship

The connection between trust and economic development is fundamental, although intricate. Trust, defined as the reliance in the integrity, honesty, and abilities of others, as well as the dependability of institutions and systems, significantly impacts economic activity and societal advancement. For instance, Liendo (2011) cites Lipset's argument that countries generally evolve towards democracy as their economic development advances. This approach has been supported by recent literature on presidential breakdowns, confirming a direct link between economic development and a president's likelihood of remaining in office. In other words, in economically prosperous nations, the risk of presidential removal is reduced (Liendo, 2011).

In the case of Latin America, citizens' trust in their institutions is affected by various factors. These factors that contribute to trusting institutions include the perception of fair elections, equality under the law, the belief that voting has a tangible influence (in generating mandates), and the absence of corrupt or self-serving behavior by officials. Additionally, trust is closely connected to the perception of competent economic management (Del Tronco, 2013).

Accordingly, citizens generally exhibit greater trust in their institutions, particularly political entities, when they witness a positive economic outlook. As a result, trust levels tend to be lower in complicated economic situations:

One possible explanation of the decline in trust in government that occurred in some countries is that this is a result of the 2008 financial crisis and the ensuing recession. Economic insecurity due to globalisation and technological progress, in combination with the sharp increase in unemployment in Europe after the crisis, may also be partly responsible for such decline. Indeed, unemployment and trust in government are negatively associated. At the same time, governments were often blamed for allowing income inequality to worsen both before and in the aftermath of the crisis, as the rich got richer while the middle class and poorer households experienced slow growth (if not a decline) in their living standards. (Murtini et al., 2018, p.29)

Improved Version: Greater trust is essential for economic development due to various factors such as facilitating cooperation among individuals and companies, enabling entrepreneurs and civil society to access financial resources, stimulating innovation, or attracting foreign investment. Multiple studies have indicated that trust, in both institutions and individuals, is fundamental for social and economic advancement. This factor has been linked to per capita income, economic growth, health, related behaviors, crime rates, and subjective well-being (Murtini et al., 2018).

However, proper media education and information literacy are necessary for trust to exist. Cognitive skills developed through education contribute to a stronger understanding of government functions, resulting in greater trust in public institutions (Murtini et al., 2018). "However, trust is strongly related to variables of economic development that promote growth but also affect trust, which gives rise to a reverse effect from growth to trust, especially in the long run" (Zakharov et al., 2020, p.313).

Trust serves as a crucial component in economic interactions by fostering growth, investment, innovation, cooperation, and sustainable economic development. Conversely, a dearth of trust could impede economic progress by breeding uncertainty, thwarting investment, and leading to ineffective collaboration:

An extensive body of literature shows that trust in public institutions is a necessary condition for the processes of investment, innovation, and trade that drive economic growth. But trust in public institutions is needed not only in the economic sphere. It is also inextricably linked to state legitimacy and is indispensable to the functioning of several governance processes. (Sapienza, 2021, p.1)

Likewise, trust plays a pivotal role in creating a positive business environment. Business entities flourish in settings with political stability, effective law enforcement, and secure property rights. Therefore, the smooth functioning of government and social institutions necessitates trust. Trust empowers individuals to engage in democratic processes and supports law enforcement when institutions operate in a clear and equitable way. As Perry (2021) argues, trust is essential for any thriving society:

Trust is integral to the functioning of any society. Trust in each other, in our public institutions and in our leaders are all essential ingredients for social and economic progress, allowing people to cooperate with and express solidarity for one another. It allows public bodies to plan and execute policies and deliver services. Greater public trust has been found to improve compliance in regulations and tax collections, even respect for property rights. It also gives confidence to consumers and investors, crucial to creating jobs and the functioning of economies more broadly. (p.1)

In a VUCA environment, trust in institutions acts as a stabilizer in situations of uncertainty. The fact that people trust their leaders and the stability of the environment will make them more willing to take risks and plan for the long term.

Arrow (1972) attributed the backwardness of an economy with a low level of trust, or none at all since any economic transaction has a trust factor. Thus, he argued that a significant number of developing countries could not accelerate economic development due to a lack of mutual trust. (Zakharov et al., 2020, p.303)

In conclusion, prior research on social capital suggests that trust plays a crucial role in promoting economic growth, impacting both macro and microlevels of the economy (Zakharov et al., 2020). The strong relationship between trust and economic development, particularly in a VUCA environment, highlights the need to cultivate trust in institutional and interpersonal relationships to foster an environment conducive to economic progress at various levels. Understanding this link is essential to designing strategies that strengthen trust and, therefore, drive sustainable economic development.

1.4. Macroeconomic variables, VUCA environments and SMEs confidence

VUCA environments are also generators of macroeconomic variables that affect the confidence of small and medium-sized entrepreneurs: for example, the size of firms is inversely proportional to their probability of mortality, as long as the right strategies are not used. In the case of Peru, as a Latin American context, "the concept of business mortality includes bankruptcy, voluntary liquidation and merger" (León Mendoza, 2021 p.405). Thus, some of the macroeconomic variables that may have a causal relationship with this mortality are: The level of growth of the Gross Domestic Product (GDP), the inflation rate, unemployment, interest rates, "the degree of openness of the economy to foreign trade and the exchange rate" (León Mendoza, 2021, p.406).

However, the macroeconomic variables that have a statistically significant influence on business mortality are "the GDP growth rate, inflation, the degree of openness to foreign trade, the tax burden, and the credit of the financial system. The level of GDP per capita and the unemployment rate are not statistically significant" (León Mendoza, 2021, p.418); although the growth rate of GDP per capita can have an inverse influence on business mortality.

Consequently, the places with the highest inflation rates will surely have a higher business mortality, and those with a higher degree of openness to foreign trade also allow "the mortality of companies to increase, so that the departments that allocate a greater proportion of their GDP to international exports show a greater number of closures" (León Mendoza, 2021, p.421).

In this vein, macroeconomic variables such as GDP growth, unemployment rate, inflation and fiscal policy can influence the financial and operational health of SMEs. In VUCA environments, where volatility and uncertainty are the norm, SMEs are especially vulnerable to changes in these macroeconomic variables, as they can affect their access to financing, market demand, production costs, and profitability.

2. THE IMPACT OF POPULISM ON CIVIL SOCIETY: EFFECTS OF POPULISM ON BONDS OF TRUST

2.1. The ability of populism to erode trust in civil society.

Populism has a unique capacity to erode trust in civil society due to its simplistic and often polarizing approach. Populist movements strive to establish charismatic leaders and adopt discourses that resonate with popular emotions but can undermine trust in existing institutions. Such erosion results in a widespread distrust of the established political, economic, and social systems.

2.2. Researchers have focused on the many reasons behind populism, including cultural backlash, economic uncertainty, and lack of trust. But no previous study has focused on the role of civil society. Civil society has long been recognized as a key defence of liberal democracy. [...] Thus, one can find arguments for civil society being a protective shield against populism or a vehicle of the populist ideology and the role of civil society in the rise of populism is an empirical matter. (Boeri et al., 2018, p.21)

Until the early 21st century, Western societies may have experienced overconfidence, according to Ponce Alberca. However, after the fall of the Berlin Wall, a new perspective emerged, reinforcing the belief that democracy is the sole political system and the market economy is an inevitable economic system (Alberca, 2022). Against this backdrop, populist rhetoric emerges, creating a climate of mistrust and antagonism between different sectors of civil society by dividing them into simple categories of "us" against "them" or "the good" against "the bad". Simplifying complex issues and attributing blame to particular groups can generate hostility and undermine trust in diversity and cooperation.

According to Laclau, the notion that the State serves as the possible and necessary epicenter for transforming social relations is a recurring feature in Latin American populisms. This belief has far-reaching consequences beyond the realm of populist politics, including the idea that a country's economic rejuvenation hinges on the State's implementation of extraordinary measures. However, populism as a political form has declined due to the erosion of trust in supposed miraculous solutions in recent decades (Laclau, 1987).

According to Hardy (2019), trust has been deteriorating across all areas, with the underlying feeling of insecurity leading to fear. This fear has provided fertile ground for the emergence of not only political populist solutions but also authoritarian approaches. The erosion of trust is worsened by the unpredictability of populism. Populist leaders, concentrating on a charismatic personality instead of sound structural policies, can instill uncertainty and distrust in institutions and their capacity to effectively address challenges.

Thus, the erosion of confidence in civil society caused by populism may have long-term repercussions. Maintaining trust is crucial to the proper operation of civil society, and populism, by subverting these foundations, can harm social harmony and society's capacity to collectively deal with intricate issues.

Figure 7. Populism index of political discourse

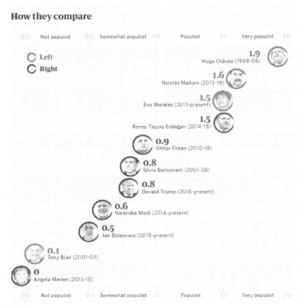

How they compare

0.0 Not populist	0.5 Somewhat populist	1.0 Populist	1.5 Very populist	2.0

○ Left
○ Right

1.9
Hugo Chávez (1999-06)

1.6
Nicolás Maduro (2013-18)

1.5
Evo Morales (2015-present)

1.5
Recep Tayyip Erdoğan (2014-18)

0.9
Viktor Orbán (2010-18)

0.8
Silvio Berlusconi (2001-06)

0.8
Donald Trump (2016-present)

0.6
Narendra Modi (2014-present)

0.5
Jair Bolsonaro (2019-present)

0.1
Tony Blair (2001-05)

0
Angela Merkel (2013-18)

0.0 Not populist	0.5 Somewhat populist	1.0 Populist	1.5 Very populist	2.0

Note. Taken from Lewis et al. (2019).

This perception exists that government decisions prioritize partisan interests over the welfare of the general public, eroding the fundamental basis of a society in which institutions aim to work for the collective benefit. This can lead to long-term consequences on stability and social cohesion. However, as political analyst Sandra Borda has pointed out: "Not in vain did Trump emerge, as that is where leaders go to communicate their shared sentiments and pledge satisfaction of their constituents' needs. A direct relationship is cultivated with the people, while representative institutions take a secondary role" (Canal Capital, 2021).

In Colombia, Kurt Weyland has stated that Álvaro Uribe attempted to consolidate power through the use of the Plebiscite in 2003 and reelection in 2010. However, the institutions played an essential role in preventing this as the Constitutional Court did not permit it. Populist leaders tend to undermine institutions, aspiring to hegemony, which is a significant risk for liberal democracy that is founded on the separation of powers (Canal Capital, 2021).

Thus, it is imperative to consider issues related to trust, such as the complete loss of trust by voters towards different types of elites, including political, traditional, business, union, or religious. Once trust is lost, populations are prone to seek a messianic leader, and populist politicians offer the promise of solving all problems. However, in actuality, they fail to fulfill such expectations (Inter-American Development Bank, 2019).

2.3. Consequences of populism for the development of sustainable and cooperative economies

Populism, as a political phenomenon, has significant consequences for the development of sustainable and cooperative economies. Additionally, it can lead to a lack of accountability, transparency, and inclusivity in decision-making processes, which are essential for sustainable and cooperative economic development. Populist leaders often adopt economic policies that prioritize short-term goals and rhetoric over long-term stability and sound economic planning. Such an approach can result in decisions driven by popularity rather than long-term viability, negatively affecting economic sustainability. Furthermore, "all these types of leftist populist forces are inclined to favor significant state intervention in the economy and are at odds with many elements of economic globalization, in particular with a deregulated financial sector that operates at the global level" (Rovira Kaltwasser, 2019, p.6).

In cooperative economies, populism can sometimes create distrust in institutions and cooperation across different societal sectors. Polarizing rhetoric and confrontational decisions can impede the necessary collaboration for successful cooperative businesses, which rely on the trust and active involvement of their members. This confrontation can lead to detrimental consequences, as noted by Rovira Kaltwasser:

Conceived as a set of ideas that pits "the pure people" against "the corrupt elites," populism can have both positive and negative effects on the economy. [...] negative effects refer to a worsening of the economic situation that can lead to severe crises and deterioration in quality of life for large swathes of the population. [...] Populism can generate high economic uncertainty by making the politics of coalition formation more difficult and unstable. Populism can foster the legitimization of corrupt practices and clientelistic exchanges with the aim of supporting "the pure people" (2019, p.7)

Furthermore, populist economic policies may generate market uncertainty, which can discourage long-term investments and commitments. A lack of stability can impede sustainable economic growth and the ability of cooperatives to plan and expand effectively. This is particularly relevant in the context of left-wing populism, which is prevalent in Latin America:

Inclusionary populism is particularly at odds with the business community and their political allies, since they allegedly control political power to construct a development model that generates poverty. It is not a coincidence that this type of populist discourse usually comes together with the defense of policies that seek growing economic regulation, increasing (capital) taxation and more socioeconomic redistribution. (Rovira Kaltwasser, 2018, p.206)

Similarly, in Latin American nations, populist economic policies often aim for comprehensive economic restructuring to align with their preferences. Referring to Boumans' (2017) work, "in Latin America respondents indicated a decline in populism; which nevertheless continues to taint economic policymaking. [...] In Asia the populist agenda seems to favour tax cuts, while in developing countries economic restructuring seems the preferred policy option" (p.43).

Populism can significantly impact the development of sustainable and cooperative economies by prioritizing short-term popularity over long-term stability and cooperation. This can lead to significant, long-lasting repercussions. For instance, while a temporary increase in fiscal and monetary measures often leads to short-term economic growth, this initial boost ultimately results in a long-term slowdown. This is because of the forthcoming limitations in the fiscal sphere, coupled with the added burden of debt and the rise in inflation (Benczes & Szabó, 2023). Hence, it is imperative to comprehend these effects to endorse policies promoting equal and sustainable economic growth.

3. MEDIA EDUCATION AND INFORMATION LITERACY

3.1. Definition and fundamentals.

The concept of media education differs in its interpretation across regions. For instance, in Canada, the process of acquiring media literacy is conceptualized as obtaining the ability to critically comprehend the nature, techniques, and impacts of media messages and productions. Conversely, in the United Kingdom, Ofcom defines it as the capacity to access, understand, and generate communication within diverse contexts (Lee & So, 2014).

In this context, Lee and So's (2014) definition of media literacy refers to a range of communication skills that involve accessing, analyzing, evaluating, and transmitting information in various ways. This definition is considered a subset of information literacy. Additionally, the concept of Media Information Literacy (MIL), as defined by Corona-Rodríguez, primarily pertains to a specific set of skills relating to interpreting, managing, and handling socio-digital content and information in the media. Its aim is to cultivate the abilities and expertise that can revolutionize how individuals engage with media and information in their surroundings (2021).

In the 21st century, Media and Information Literacy (MIL) is widely regarded as a notion that is openly expressed, acknowledging the universal necessity of socio-cultural diversity (Santos Martínez, 2014). On the other hand, information literacy refers to the competency of accessing, evaluating, and utilizing data efficiently. This includes skills related to information searches, source quality evaluations, copyright comprehension, and ethical information usage.

Information literacy is more related to information storage, processing, and use, while media literacy is concerned more with media content, media industry, and social effects. Despite their differences, however, they have a number of common concerns. Information literacy and media literacy share common goals and future directions. They overlap in the core skills they aim to develop. They both aim at cultivating literate individuals who can make informed judgments regarding the use of information in the digital age (Lee & So, 2014, p.144)

Media education and information literacy are concepts that focus on the skills needed to comprehend, evaluate, and effectively use digital information. In 2008, UNESCO aimed to unify this field by adopting the term media and information literacy, which encompasses interdependent and convergent competencies for interacting with communications and content through a variety of institutions, including libraries, media, and companies (Azoulay, 2019). It is crucial to maintain cohesion between these concepts, because "although media literacy and information literacy look like two separate fields, both concepts share the common goal of cultivating people's ability to access, understand, use, and create media messages or information" (Lee & So, 2014, p.138).

3.2. Relevance of media Education and Information Literacy in the VUCA context.

In a rapidly evolving environment, media education and information literacy serve as crucial resources for comprehending and navigating available information. Yet, the surge of digital technologies and the increasing significance of new media in the daily lives of many have resulted in considerable social and cultural transformations that present significant educational challenges (Valdivia-Barrios et al., 2018).

While John Dewey saw education as the sole avenue to democracy, media education today enables new forms of democratic participation. Media and Information Literacy (MIL) presents a vital educational challenge and is recognized as an inclusive human right (Velez, 2017).

In today's society, technology and media hold significant importance in daily life. As a result, having information literacy skills is critical as it allows individuals to assess information critically, differentiate between dependable and undependable sources, and comprehend how media impacts the generation of knowledge. Additionally, media education enables individuals to dissect and comprehend media messages, identify biases, interpret intentions, and participate actively and thoughtfully in media culture.

Therefore, education bears the responsibility of equipping prospective citizens with the capacity to comprehend and interpret the intricacies of political, economic, and cultural domains. This is vital for effective functioning within a society characterized by ambiguity, adaptation to novel professions, and involvement in group endeavors in an era marked by "glocalization," where changes are incessant and swift (Monreal Guerrero et al., 2017).

Additionally, in a current climate where trust in institutions is eroded due to the impact of populism, the promotion of media education and information literacy helps to enhance bonds of trust in civil society. These efforts enable individuals to become informed and engaged citizens, a vital step towards promoting economic development.

3.3. Media Education: Empowering civil society and strengthening citizen participation.

As mentioned earlier, media education equips individuals with the necessary tools and skills to understand, analyze, and critically engage with media content and public discourse. Over the years, studies in the field of educommunication have shifted towards a more humanistic approach that emphasizes social impact. Recent research focuses on the various ways in which media literacy, when properly directed, can drive social change (Gil & Marzal-Felici, 2023).

Neglecting media education may widen digital disparities, reinforce social injustice, and perpetuate the division between digitally literate and illiterate communities. The use and comprehension of technology are not only influenced by individual autonomy, but also cultural and social factors. Thus, media literacy should not be viewed as a solely self-contained and personal pursuit, but rather as a catalyst for motivating young individuals to actively engage in their communities (Dias-Fonseca & Potter, 2016). In other terms:

To be a citizen today is to be a media citizen, and that means cultivating and acquiring an education in those competences necessary in order to use the media and communicative technologies in their broadest and most integral sense. For example in law and politics, the Internet is being configured as a platform that enables direct citizen participation in various areas of public interest on a national and international level. (Gozálvez-Pérez & Contreras-Pulido, 2014, pp. 130-131)

The digital revolution necessitates a type of literacy that surpasses mere functionality and concentrates on constructing digital citizenship. This form of media literacy could promote critical-reflexive awareness to tackle the inequalities created in the digital society regarding gender, social exclusion, diversity, and poverty (Monreal Guerrero et al., 2017). "A reflection on the civic use of the media and communicative technologies points to a new form of citizenship: media citizenship, which is citizenship in and by the grace of the media, be they traditional or interactive" (Gozálvez-Pérez & Contreras-Pulido, 2014, p.131).

Digital education or literacy necessitates the cultivation of critical and ethical principles, encompassing the ethical utilization of media, information, and technology, along with democratic participation and intercultural discourse. In summary, according to Monreal Guerrero et al. (2017), it is crucial to promote critical participation amongst prosumers as it defines our existence.

3.4. Relationship between Information Literacy and informed decision making.

Different information literacy programs nowadays take an action-oriented approach that supports real-life problem-solving and decision-making. In an age where data and news overwhelm us, the ability to distinguish factual information from misinformation is essential. Research has shown that information literacy equips individuals with the necessary tools to analyze sources, verify facts, and understand the context in which information is presented.

However, media education and information literacy training have not been strong points in Colombian society. Especially, in the educational field, for (Sideri et al., 2017):

Education aims principally at active citizenship configuration promoting open dialogue, participation and cooperation. So it is controversial and rather surprising that even though Education promotes cooperation for co-joint decisions, that even though social media are utilized in a number of activities in educational settings and are used for the purpose of citizens' engagement in public participatory processes, literature hasn't recorded social media usage for participatory processes that lead to decision making in educational settings. (p.2876)

The prevalence of unfiltered information, with questionable authenticity and reliability, is particularly discouraging. This underscores the need to cultivate information literacy skills, which entail the ability to make decisions, troubleshoot, and conduct autonomous investigations. Information literacy is a vital skill that enables individuals to take charge of their personal growth and be ready for continuous learning (González Flores, 2012).

Moreover, information literacy fosters autonomy and informed decision-making. When people possess the abilities to analyze information critically and access various sources, they become better prepared to make informed decisions instead of relying solely on biased narratives or perspectives. Information literacy is a vital factor in enabling individuals to make well-informed decisions within today's information network.

CONCLUSION

An attempt has been made to illustrate how VUCA environments (Volatility, Uncertainty, Complexity, Ambiguity) create an ideal scenario for populism to flourish in the form of a political figure offering solutions to issues of trust at the foundation of societies. This results in decision-making motivated by partisan interests that neglects the general well-being and values short-term gains. Similarly, the creation of a polarized environment necessitates mutual trust among different sectors of society, which weakens economic sustainability and exacerbates the sense of dissatisfaction among civil organizations. Given the inadequacy of information management and lack of media skills, social networks have become a breeding ground for populist discourses that demonize and reinforce dichotomous ideas. Given the inadequacy of information management and lack of media skills, social networks have become a breeding ground for populist discourses that demonize and reinforce dichotomous ideas. These discourses easily penetrate the information membrane of citizens, generating biased opinions and societal fragmentation.

Given the inadequacy of information management and lack of media skills, social networks have become a breeding ground for populist discourses that demonize and reinforce dichotomous ideas. This text highlights the issues of content oversaturation, mediamorphosis, and pseudo-content due to misinformation. Aguaded and Romero-Rodríguez (2015) examined these phenomena. The response to these challenges has led to varying info-diet options and the use of artificial intelligence to detect false content (Flores Vivar, 2019). However, it is acknowledged that while information must first pass through human filters, other mechanisms can be employed to balance the populism debate in a VUCA environment.

This is where media education and information literacy are vital in counteracting the vast amount of information encountered on a daily basis. Rather than attempting to stop it altogether, it is necessary to learn how to live with it. In a VUCA world, the public is the primary filter for populist discourses as they are ultimately the ones who reproduce them. Media literacy can play a critical role in developing individuals who are capable of consuming information in a vigilant manner, identifying the portrayal of political actors in media, comprehending the underlying motives, and recognizing emotions portrayed in positive yet superficial discourses (Romero-Rodríguez et al., 2018).

One noteworthy proposal amidst calls to action by academic and social groups is to establish interdisciplinary teams that implement a communication strategy and maintain an active presence on social media. The aim is to promote the availability and dissemination of accurate information, countering the proliferation of false content propagated by pseudoscientific and populist movements (López-Borrull and Ollé, 2019). In addition to the aforementioned content curation, the proposal for media education revolves around implementing it in secondary school curricula with the school leading the training processes.

It is imperative to reassess the approach to the term "media" when proposing implementation of education in media and information literacy. This is necessary in order to acknowledge that social networks and digital platforms are already being used for informative communication purposes (Aguilar, 2019). Comprehensive training plans in ICT and different narratives must be approached from various perspectives, recognizing the unique storytelling methods and distinct uses of each medium. Ultimately, analyzing the communicative spectrum from a transmedia perspective is crucial (Scolari, 2009).

Accessing the media or the Internet alone and having the ability to publish or use available tools is inadequate for attaining literacy; an all-encompassing and guided process is necessary in citizen education (Lotero-Echeveri, 2014). Acknowledging this responsibility necessitates collective effort that considers the diverse social structures and challenges in the political culture of Colombia, particularly given the lack of trust in its primary organizations. The challenge is to build an informed, critical, participatory and above all cooperative society, which has social capital aimed at generating cohesion, promoting the constitution of civil actors and healthy societies and learning communities, capable of producing: Innovation, change and cultural transformation.

An attempt has been made to visualize how VUCA environments (Volatility, Uncertainty, Complexity, Ambiguity) are the ideal scenario for populism, represented in a political figure, to emerge as a solution to problems of trust at the base of societies. The above leads to decision-making driven by partisan interests, which does not aim for the general well-being and seeks a short-term path. Likewise, a polarized environment is generated that requires mutual trust between sectors of society to work together, weakening economic sustainability and intensifying the feeling of discontent among civil organizations. And it is there, where, given the inadequate management of information and lack of skills in the media scenario, it becomes a favorable space for the exponential replication of populist discourses, which reinforce the dichotomous idea and demonization of the enemy, which can easily cross the information membrane of citizens.

They have found a "sounding board" on social networks, causing opinions to be biased and fragmentation to be generated in society. This, plus the existing misinformation that produces content oversaturation, mediamorphosis (change of media within the ecosystem to adapt to new digital contexts) and pseudo-content (Aguaded and Romero-Rodríguez, 2015). The response to the previous triad has varied in terms of info-diet options or even the capture of false content through artificial intelligence (Flores Vivar, 2019). However, it is recognized that by first passing the information through a human filter, other mechanisms may be the ones that balance the debate between populism and the VUCA environment.

This is where media education and information literacy come to play an important role in counteracting the sea of information to which one is exposed on a daily basis, understanding that rather than stopping it, one must learn to live with it. This is why, in a VUCA world, the first filter for populist discourses must be the people, since in the end, they are the ones who end up reproducing the discourses. And there, media literacy can be the key to creating individuals who are critical of information consumption, capable of discovering the representation of political actors in the media, reading the underlying interests and discerning their emotions in the face of euphoric but empty discourses (Romero-Rodríguez et al., 2018).

One of the proposals that stands out compared to the call for action by various academic and social groups is the formation of interdisciplinary work teams that contain a communication plan and presence in social media, in order to increase the presence and prescription of revised contents, where the provision of false content reigns and is used by pseudosciences and populist movements (López-Borrull and Ollé, 2019). In addition to the content curation proposed above, the proposal that it leads regarding media education is about its implementation in secondary school curricula, and that it is the school that leads the training processes.

It is relevant to highlight that when talking about implementing proposals regarding media education and information literacy, the approach to the term "media" must be reevaluated to ensure that it is understood that social networks and digital platforms are already used as means of communication. informative nature (Aguilar, 2019). Consequently, comprehensive training plans in ICT, and the different narratives, must be dimensioned from all angles, understanding that each medium has its different way of telling stories, but also its uses are different. In conclusion, it is to visualize the communicative spectrum from a transmedia perspective (Scolari, 2009).

Accessing the Internet or the media in general, being able to publish or having the tools available, is not a sufficient process for literacy; a more guided and transversal process must be carried out in citizen education (Lotero-Echeveri, 2014). Assuming this responsibility requires collective work that recognizes the different social structures and challenges in Colombian political culture, given the distrust in its main organizations. The challenge is to build an informed, critical, participatory and above all cooperative society, which has social capital aimed at generating cohesion, promoting the constitution of civil actors and healthy societies and learning communities, capable of producing: Innovation, change and cultural transformation.

Finally, the importance of understanding the relationship between these macroeconomic variables that generate, to a large extent, the mortality of SMEs in VUCA environments is highlighted, as this is crucial to develop effective risk mitigation strategies and to promote business resilience in a dynamic and changing economic context, which is dominated by vulnerability, uncertainty, complexity and ambiguity.

REFERENCES

Aguaded, J., & Romero-Rodríguez, L. M. (2015). Mediamorfosis y desinformación en la infoesfera: Alfabetización mediática, digital e informacional ante los cambios de hábitos de consumo informativo. *Education in the knowledge society: EKS*. DOI: 10.14201/eks20151614457

Aguilar, I. (2019). *La Alfabetización Mediática e Informacional como conocimiento transversal en la Educación Secundaria Obligatoria* [Tesis de maestría]. Universidad Autónoma de Barcelona.

Azoulay, A. (2019). *Global Standards for Media and Information Literacy Curricula Development Guidelines*. United Nations Educational, Scientific and Cultural Organization UNESCO. https://www .unesco.org/sites/default/files/medias/files/2022/02/Global%20Standards%20for%20Media%20and%20 Information%20Literacy%20Curricula%20Development%20Guidelines_EN.pdf

Banco Interamericano de Desarrollo, B. I. D. (2019). *El colapso de la confianza y el auge del populismo*. https://www.iadb.org/es/historia/el-colapso-de-la-confianza-y-el-auge-del-populismo

Benczes, I., & Szabó, K. (2023). An Economic Understanding of Populism: A Conceptual Framework of the Demand and the Supply Side of Populism. *Political Studies Review*, 21(4), 680–696. DOI: 10.1177/14789299221109449

Boeri, T., Mishra, P., Papageorgiou, C., & Spilimbergo, A. (2018). Populism and Civil Society. Populism and Civil Society. International Monetary Fund WP/18/24. https://www.imf.org/en/Publications/WP/ Issues/2018/11/17/Populism-and-Civil-Society-46324

Boumans, D. (2017). *Does Populism Influence Economic Policy Making? Insights from Economic Experts Around the World*. CES ifo DICE Report. https://www.cesifo.org/DocDL/dice-report-2017-4 -boumans-december.pdf

Canal Capital. (2021). *El populismo en Colombia y en América Latina | A las Palabras.*https://www .canalcapital.gov.co/noticias-capital-migracion/el-populismo-colombia-y-america-latina-las-palabras

Corona-Rodríguez, J. (2021). La importancia de la Alfabetización Mediática Informacional en el contexto pandémico: propuesta de actualización y nuevas preguntas. *Diálogos sobre educación. Temas actuales en investigación educativa, 12*(22). https://doi.org/DOI: 10.32870/dse.v0i22.979

Del Tronco, J. (2013). Desconfianza y "Accountability" ¿las causas del Populismo en América Latina? *Latin American Research Review*, 48(2), 55–78. https://www.jstor.org/stable/43670076. DOI: 10.1353/ lar.2013.0026

Dias-Fonseca, D., & Potter, J. (2016). La educación mediática como estrategia de participación cívica on-line en las escuelas portuguesas. *Comunicar, 24*(49), 9-18. https://www.revistacomunicar.com/verpdf .php?numero=49&articulo=49-2016-01

Flores Vivar, J. M. (2019). Inteligencia artificial y periodismo: Diluyendo el impacto de la desinformación y las noticias falsas a través de los bots. *Doxa Comunicación*, 29, 197–212. DOI: 10.31921/ doxacom.n29a10

Fuentealba, D., Flores-Fernández, C., & Carrasco, R. (2023). Análisis bibliométrico y de contenido sobre VUCA. *Revista Española de Documentación Científica*, 46(2), e354. Advance online publication. DOI: 10.3989/redc.2023.2.1968

Galvis, A. (2023). Colombianos tienen mayor confianza en el sector empresarial que en el Gobierno. *Asuntos Legales*.https://www.asuntoslegales.com.co/actualidad/en-colombia-se-tiene-mas-confianza-en -el-sector-empresarial-que-en-gobierno-y-medios-3605773

Gil, I., & Marzal-Felici, J. (2023). ¿Cómo impulsar la educomunicación y la alfabetización mediática desde el sistema educativo en España? Diagnóstico, problemática y propuestas por los expertos. *Revista Mediterránea de Comunicación/Mediterranean. Journal of Communication*, 14(2), 207–226. https:// www.doi.org/10.14198/MEDCOM.24011

González Flores, I. (2012). Necesidad de la alfabetización informacional en la Educación Superior. Vivat Academia, (121),65-76. https://www.redalyc.org/articulo.oa?id=525752951006

Government, H. M. (2018). *Civil Society Strategy: building a future that works for everyone*. Policy paper. https://assets.publishing.service.gov.uk/media/5b6b282440f0b62ec1fa611d/Civil_Society_Strategy _-_building_a_future_that_works_for_everyone.pdf

Gozálvez-Pérez, V., & Contreras-Pulido, P. (2014). Empowering media citizenship through educommunication. *Comunicar*, 42(42), 129–136. DOI: 10.3916/C42-2014-12

Guerra Rondón, L., & Bosch, F. (2023). *Participación de la sociedad civil: conceptos y prácticas en el contexto de los órganos subsidiarios y las reuniones intergubernamentales de la Comisión Económica para América Latina y el Caribe (CEPAL)*. Santiago, Comisión Económica para América Latina. el Caribe (CEPAL). https://repositorio.cepal.org/server/api/core/bitstreams/c902b3c5-d4ab-4e73-96d1 -5b9b03f9b1b0/content

Hardy, C. (2019). Desconfianza y desigualdades: amenazas para la democracia. *En Tejiendo confianza para la cohesión social: una mirada a la confianza en América Latina*, (pp.31-40). https://eurosocial .eu/wp-content/uploads/2019/07/07_tejiendo-confianza.pdf

Hwa Ang, P. (2018). Communicating with Power in a Volatile, Uncertain, Complex, and Ambiguous World. *Journal of Communication*, 68(1), 1–5. DOI: 10.1093/joc/jqx010

Infobae. (2021). *Desconfianza institucional en Colombia: ciudadanos "rajan" a las principales entidades públicas*.https://www.infobae.com/america/colombia/2021/06/22/desconfianza-institucional-en -colombia-ciudadanos-rajan-a-las-principales-entidades-publicas/

Instituto Nacional de Contadores Públicos (INCP). (2020). *Precaria confianza de los colombianos en instituciones del país*.https://incp.org.co/precaria-confianza-los-colombianos-instituciones-del-pais/

Johansen, B., & Euchner, J. (2013). Navigating the VUCA World: An Interview with Bob Johansen. *Research Technology Management*, 56(1), 10–15. DOI: 10.5437/08956308X5601003

Laclau, E. (1987). Populismo y transformación del imaginario político en América Latina. *Boletín de Estudios Latinoamericanos y del Caribe*, 42, 25–38. https://www.jstor.org/stable/25675327

Law Family Commission on Civil Society. (2023). *Unleashing the power of civil society*.https://ci vilsocietycommission.org/wp-content/uploads/2023/01/FINAL-Unleashing-the-power-of-civil-society ---for-upload.pdf

LeBlanc, P. (2018). Higher Education in a VUCA World. *Change*, 50(3-4), 23–26. DOI: 10.1080/00091383.2018.1507370

Lee, A., & So, C. (2014). Media literacy and information literacy: Similarities and differences. *Comunicar*, 42(42), 137–146. DOI: 10.3916/C42-2014-13

León Mendoza, J. (2021). Influencia del contexto macroeconómico en la mortalidad de empresas en Perú. *Cuadernos de Economía (Santiago, Chile)*, 40(83), 403–430. DOI: 10.15446/cuad.econ.v40n83.81957

Lewis, P., Barr, C., Clarke, S., Voce, A., Levett, C., & Gutiérrez, P. (2019). Revealed: the rise and rise of populist rhetoric. *The Guardian*.https://www.theguardian.com/world/ng-interactive/2019/mar/06/ revealed-the-rise-and-rise-of-populist-rhetoric

Liendo, N. (2011). El crecimiento económico y la confianza en las instituciones de gobierno: Un análisis comparado de la evolución en las percepciones de las élites y los ciudadanos de América Latina. *Boletín PNUD Instituto de Iberoamérica*.http://hdl.handle.net/10366/108650

López-Borrull, A., & Ollé, C. (2019). La curación de contenidos como respuesta a las noticias ya la ciencia falsas. *Anuario ThinkEPI*, 13. Advance online publication. DOI: 10.3145/thinkepi.2019.e13e07

Lotero-Echeverri, G. J. (2014). Educación para la ciudadanía en la era de las wikis. *Poliantea*, 10(19), 199–212. DOI: 10.15765/plnt.v10i19.579

Monreal Guerrero, I. M., Parejo Llanos, J. L., & Cortón de las Heras, M. de la O. (2017). Alfabetización mediática y cultura de la participación: retos de la ciudadanía digital en la Sociedad de la Información. *EDMETIC, 6*(2), 148–167. https://doi.org/DOI: 10.21071/edmetic.v6i2.6943

Murtini, F., Fleischeri, L., Siegerinki, V., Aassveii, A., Alganiii, Y., Boarinii, R., Gonzálezi, S., Lontii, Z., Grimaldaiv, G., Hortala Vallvev, R., Kimvi, S., Leevi, D., Puttermanvii, L., & Smithi, C. (2018). Trust and its determinants: Evidence from the Trustlab experiment. *Working Paper No. 89. Organisation for Economic Co-operation and Development*.https://one.oecd.org/document/SDD/DOC(2018)2/En/pdf

Park, S. (2018). Challenges and Opportunities: The 21st Century Public Manager in a VUCA World. *Journal of Public Administration: Research and Theory*, 28(2), 299–301. DOI: 10.1093/jopart/mux042

Perry, J. (2021). *Trust in public institutions: Trends and implications for economic security*. United Nations Department of Economic and Social Affairs., DOI: 10.18356/df7eed76-en

Ponce Alberca, J. (2022). Presentación. El populismo como problema histórico: Algunas reflexiones. *El Futuro Del Pasado*, 13, 17–34. DOI: 10.14201/fdp.27438

Quiroga Gil, M. (2021). Los entornos digitales y el mundo VUCA. In Quiroga, M., Martin, M., & Baldivieso, S. (Eds.), *Entornos Digitales y Mundo Vuca. Libro de Resúmenes y Presentaciones de la 1° Jornada Entornos Digitales y Mundo VUCA* (pp. 8–15). Nueva Editorial Universitaria - UNSL., http:// www.neu.unsl.edu.ar/wp-content/uploads/2021/09/Entornos-digitales-y-mundo-VUCA.pdf

Romero-Rodríguez, L. M., Chaves-Montero, A., & Torres-Toukoumidis, Á. (2018). Neopopulismo, poder y control social: las competencias mediáticas en ideología y valores como defensa de la ciudadanía. *Lumina, 12*(1), 40-54. https://n2t.net/ark:/13683/pHPH/MRs

Rovira Kaltwasser, C. (2018). Studying the (Economic) Consequences of Populism. *AEA Papers and Proceedings. American Economic Association*, 108, 204–207. https://www.jstor.org/stable/26452733. DOI: 10.1257/pandp.20181125

Rovira Kaltwasser, C. (2019). Populism and the Economy: An Ambivalent Relationship. Friedrich Ebert Stiftung. https://library.fes.de/pdf-files/iez/15244.pdf

Salas Rodas, L. (2014). Estado, empresa privada y sector social: Una relación entre sectores que fortalece a la sociedad civil. *Revista de Trabajo Social*, (5), 107–129. https://revistas.udea.edu.co/index.php/revistraso/article/view/20440

Santos Martínez, C. J. (2014). Educación Mediática e Informacional en el contexto de la actual Sociedad del Conocimiento. *Historia y Comunicación Social*, 18(0), 781–794. DOI: 10.5209/rev_HICS.2013.v18.44365

Sapienza, E. (2021). *Policy Brief: Trust in Public Institutions. A conceptual framework and insights for improved governance programming.* United Nations Development Programme UNDP. https://www.undp.org/sites/g/files/zskgke326/files/migration/oslo_governance_centre/Trust-in-Public-Institutions-Policy-Brief_FINAL.pdf

Sarid, A., & Levanon, M. (2023). Embracing dualities: Principles of education for a VUCA world. *Educational Philosophy and Theory*, 55(12), 1375–1386. DOI: 10.1080/00131857.2022.2162384

Scolari, C. A. (2009). Transmedia Storytelling: Implicit Consumers, Narrative Worlds, and Branding in Contemporary Media Production. *International Journal of Communication, 3*(2013), 586-606. https://ijoc.org/index.php/ijoc/article/view/477

Sideri, M., Filippopoulou, A., Rouvalis, G., Kalloniatis, C., & Gritzalis, S. (2017). Social media use for decision making process in educational settings: The Greek case for Leadership's views and attitude in Secondary and Tertiary Education. *HICCS*. https://core.ac.uk/download/pdf/77239811.pdf

Stein, S. (2021). Reimagining global citizenship education for a volatile, uncertain, complex, and ambiguous (VUCA) world. *Globalisation, Societies and Education*, 19(4), 482–495. DOI: 10.1080/14767724.2021.1904212

Valdivia-Barrios, A., Pinto-Torres, D., & Herrera-Barraza, M. (2018). Media Literacy and Learning. Conceptual Contribution in the Field of Media Education. *Revista Electrónica Educare*, 22(2), 1–16. DOI: 10.15359/ree.22-2.8

Velez, I. (2017). Políticas públicas en alfabetización mediática e informacional: el legado de John Dewey. *Revista Fuentes, 19*(2), 39-57. https://revistascientificas.us.es/index.php/fuentes/article/download/4237/3989/13728

World Economic Forum. (2013). *The Future Role of Civil Society.* https://www3.weforum.org/docs/WEF_FutureRoleCivilSociety_Report_2013.pdf

Zakharov, D., Bezruchuk, S., Poplavska, V., Laichuk, S., & Khomenko, H. (2020). The ability of trust to influence GDP per capita. *Problems and Perspectives in Management*, 18(1), 302–314. DOI: 10.21511/ppm.18(1).2020.26

Chapter 13
Sustainability and Strategic Organizational Management of SMEs in Bogota in Uncertain Environments

María Teresa Ramírez Garzón
Universidad de La Salle, Colombia

Carlos Mario Muñoz-Maya
https://orcid.org/0000-0003-1451-1648
Universidad de La Salle, Colombia

Olga Lucia Diaz-Villamizar
https://orcid.org/0000-0003-1451-1648
Universidad Militar Nueva Granada, Colombia

ABSTRACT

The objective of this research is to identify whether there is an association between sustainability and organizational management strategies in uncertain environments in micro and small enterprises. For this purpose, a survey was applied to 377 directors of MSEs in Bogota. To carry out the correlation, two dependent variables were considered: 1) sustainability and 2) organizational strategic management. Uncertainty was considered as an independent variable. Each of these variables was compared to different components. Empirical evidence of the relationship between uncertainty and organizational management and sustainability is shown, no correlation is found between the uncertainty variable and the main strategy variable of the company or between the main strategy of the company and the main problem of the company. There is a slight negative correlation between the uncertainty variable and the main problem variable of the company. Finally, a moderate positive correlation is found between the uncertainty variable and the sustainability and organizational management variable.

DOI: 10.4018/979-8-3693-4046-2.ch013

INTRODUCTION

Companies must increasingly operate in uncertain business or organizational environments due to external or internal factors derived from the country's economic situation, insecurity and violence, new trends in consumption, political instability and increased concern for sales, affecting decision-making and strategic management.

Strategic planning becomes a crucial element for the success of any organization (Gonzalez Hernandez, et al., 2023), this being understood as a process that involves establishing the results that are intended to be achieved, which means determining the future conditions and the elements that are required to effectively achieve these results. Given the above, planning involves making appropriate decisions about what will be done in the future, thus minimizing the risk of what may happen in the organization (Garcia Guiliany et al., 2023, quoting Sarmenteros and Mora and Riapira et al.). Therefore, strategic planning becomes a cornerstone for the implementation of any project within the organization, thus achieving the proposed objectives and goals in the short, medium and long term (Garcia Guiliany et al., 2023, quoting Salazar and Romero and Leyva, Cavazos and Espejel).

Today's organizations are permanently interacting with a highly changing environment (Shamira, 2023), which is characterized by the speed at which technology advances and its impact on the environment, so much so that if they do not keep up to date they may disappear, decrease market share or lose competitiveness (Martinez, et al., 2017). Uncertainty management is closely linked to business management in general. Companies that succeed in integrating uncertainty management practices into their culture and operations tend to be more innovative and are better prepared to face the challenges of the future.

The key is to understand the nature of uncertainty, adopt resilient leadership, communicate effectively, and foster a culture that embraces change (Sanchez Rodriguez, et al., 2024). By doing so, leaders and managers can not only guide their organizations through difficult times but also emerge stronger and more prepared for the future (Eude, 2024).

This study contributes to the existing body of knowledge by exploring the relationship between uncertainty and organizational management and sustainability in MSEs. Uncertainty management is a vital area of research that requires continuous attention. This work adds to the academic dialogue, providing a fresh perspective on how companies can strengthen their capacity to manage uncertainty in a rapidly changing business world.

For the development of this research, a descriptive analysis was carried out on how the independent latent variable of uncertainty affects the dependent latent variable of sustainability and organizational strategic management. It is mainly concluded that this study contributes to the literature related to the management of organizations and sustainability, since it empirically shows the relationship between uncertainty and organizational management and sustainability in the MSEs in the sample.

This chapter delves into issues related to the strategic management of organizations, sustainability and uncertainty. The methodology used for the development of the research is explained, the results obtained are shown and discussed. Finally, the conclusions reached in this study are explained.

BACKGROUND

Organizational Strategic Management

Strategic planning is considered as a systemic process that allows organizations to develop and implement plans with the purpose of achieving the proposed objectives. It becomes a primary tool for decision-making in terms of how to act and the path they should follow to achieve the proposed objectives (Garcia Guiliany, 2023, quoting Muñiz-Jaime et al., and Delgado, Bravo and Pinzon).

Organizations over time have faced different situations in complex and uncertain environments and many times due to the lack of good organizational strategic management, they have been forced to close their businesses. For example, by 1929 at the time of the American "Great Depression," many organizations failed and went bankrupt. To reverse this situation, different proposals were developed that helped companies move forward. For this reason, in 1954, Peter Drucker proposed the Management by Objective (MBO) process, which consists of:

measuring work (performance-results) against predefined objectives... It is a process in which the senior manager and the subordinate of an organization come together to identify the specific objectives defined in each major area of individual responsibility, in terms of expected results of the subordinate, and use this measurement as a guide to the operation of the unit, evaluating the contribution of each of its members (Martinez et al., 2022, p. 97).

The evolution of administrative practices and theories can be observed in administration with MBO, this being part of the postulates of the neoclassical theory of management. In this way, in order to structure and apply MBO, Drucker questions himself by saying, "What is our business or what should it be?" Based on this questioning, Kaplan and Norton reformulate it in order to structure the strategy and ask themselves: what business do we participate in and why? (Martinez et al., 2022).

Some studies have shown the importance and impact that organizational strategic management based on the achievement of objectives can have. This is the case of the study carried out by Salamanca et al. (2014), who state that organizational strategic management based on the achievement of objectives is influenced by the interaction between the development of people, working conditions and productivity. Organizations are information, communication and decision-making systems, and their success or failure depends on the participation that their collaborators can have in them. This means that a successful organization is defined by the relationships between its members, since people are the ones who carry out the different processes immersed in a context of effective communication, adequate information management and proper decision-making, which leads to the achievement of the proposed objectives.

Bejarano-Auqui (2024), carried out research, the objective of which was to design a business management model based on the theory of managerial thinking and the premise of the study was that business management is a characteristic feature of entrepreneurs. Through surveys to 101 entrepreneurs from MSEs in the Eastern Cone of Lima-Peru and literature research on topics related to business management models, the following was concluded: Knowledge and innovation management (KMI) is fundamental for the economic performance of micro and small enterprises since its management under good leadership allows solving productivity problems and facing the threats of globalization; therefore, the KMI must become a primary source of intangible capital to drive innovation and growth in the operations of organizations. Administration and leadership of results-oriented economy management (EM) have a direct and positive influence over control management, directly affecting long-term relationships with different internal and external stakeholders, which translates into added value for the company.

In the dynamics of strategic management, it translates into an integrated tool that provides solutions to activities related to change and innovation in management, production and sales in a sustainable way. EM is also conclusive for MSEs since the measurement of the achievement of the financial objectives proposed in the strategic planning of the organization and its result determine not only profitability but also financial solvency or insolvency. Finally, Bejarano-Auqui (2024) concludes that for MSEs in the Eastern Cone of Lima and worldwide to be competitive and profitable, it is important that managers implement transformational business management and leadership that helps them improve the quality of administrative, productive, and service levels.

Mora Riapira et al. (2015), conducted a study the objective of which was to analyze the relationship between the strategic planning dimension and competitiveness in commercial MSMEs located in Bogota, Colombia. The methodology used was to carry out a contextualization of the sector and an assessment of competitiveness by applying the Competitiveness Map of the Inter-American Development Bank (IDB) as a tool. Through direct and partial correlation tests using SPSS software, they found that strategic planning has a significant impact on the performance of other dimensions related to organizational management and on the competitiveness of the MSMEs analyzed.

Among the results found by Mora Riapira et al. (2015), the following are highlighted: "there is a direct and significant relationship between strategic planning and the competitiveness dimension of MSMEs in the trade sector in Bogota." (p. 86). However, in the specific case of micro-enterprises, a low performance in the different dimensions is observed, affecting in a global way the competitiveness of the commerce sector. As for small companies, a better performance is observed, especially in those that have exported. Improving management processes is a condition for achieving competitiveness in international business.

Finally, Mora Riapira et al. (2015) conclude that there is a correlation between the strategic planning dimension and the procurement and marketing dimensions. In addition, they infer that strategic planning and management control tools contribute to the improvement of the performance of organizations and have an impact on the consolidation and growth of businesses, thus achieving greater competitiveness that allows them to face the risks of the entry of foreign companies and allows them to project the offering of their products or services at the international level.

Strategic management has consolidated over time (arguably since the 1960's), as an intervention model that allows organizations to increase their profitability and productivity which makes them more competitive in uncertain environments (Niebles-Nuñez et al., 2022; Perez-Uribe, 2018).

According to David (2017), for organizations to achieve success, strategic management should focus on integrating the management of different areas of the organization such as finance and accounting, marketing, production and operations, research, development and innovation (R+D+I), as well as information.

A good organizational strategic management requires managers with visible leadership from the top management in two ways "from top to bottom and vice versa", thus achieving the commitment of all members of the organization and a continuous harmony between the different levels and areas of the company, also including the different stakeholders such as "suppliers, customers, community, government, contractors, shareholders, among others". (Perez-Uribe, 2016, p. 5).

According to Perez-Uribe (2016), talking about the strategic aspect requires internal analyses of the organization and how it relates to its environment in the present, also taking into account a vision of its future. Organizations must be managed with a holistic sense and within the concept of organizational synergy.

Strategically managing an organization requires highly qualified managers and strategists capable of meeting the objectives set in the organization, which implies correctly managing the company's resources. Top management must make decisions related to the formulation of assertive strategies, which aim to achieve the goals and objectives proposed. The follow-up of the activities to be carried out should allow them to obtain timely information to improve the processes implemented (Luciano Alipio et al., 2023).

The function of strategic planning is to guide companies to know the economic opportunities that are attractive to their market, which means that they must adapt their resources and capabilities in such a way as to allow them to establish competitive strategies, define short, medium and long-term objectives, specify their mission as a company and determine a long-term vision that will help them to maintain themselves over time and face the threats of the environment that surrounds them (Garcia Guiliany, 2023, quoting Gonzalez et al., and Peralta et al.).

Given the above, strategic management implies having a planning process of what is intended to be done, organizing the necessary resources to carry out what is planned, directing the actions that will be carried out by those involved in the process and controlling the activities and the fulfillment of the achievement of the objectives in order to propose improvement actions when necessary (Luciano Alipio et al., 2023).

Sustainability

Understanding corporate sustainability means conceiving it as an ethical action that is carried out in a planned, organized, directed and controlled manner, which allows the organization to become aware of social and environmental problems, thus giving it the opportunity to reduce the possible negative impacts that the organization may generate in its immediate environment, and benefiting at the same time in the increase of its profitability in the long term (Ortiz et al., 2021).

In the same sense, for Miranda Pegueros et al. (2022), sustainability in organizations should not only be limited to satisfying their stakeholders but should go beyond that; the company should be characterized by being a renewing entity of society that provides both an economic income and a benefit to society. Savitz and Weber (quoted by Miranda Pegueros et al., 2022), propose that there should be an exchange of benefits between stakeholders and the company; therefore, there must be a breakeven point in which both parties are satisfied and this is called "The Sustainability Sweet Spot"; at this point, the company's profits and the common good converge, thus forging opportunities to generate new jobs, products, processes, markets, businesses and management methods.

Sustainability is a commitment of every organization and therefore MSEs cannot be oblivious to this ethical action. According to Velasquez Chacon (2022), micro and small enterprises must integrate sustainability into their strategic management, taking into account the economic and environmental impact that their production process or the provision of a service can generate, in addition to the social impact it can have on the community and the different stakeholders. In the same vein, Gambaro and Garcia (2021) and Merino-Martin & Pastorino (2013) state that companies should not only be concerned with achieving profitability-related objectives to maximize shareholder wealth but should also take into account environmental and social objectives, thus demonstrating concern for the environment and the community.

Sustainability implies existing over time, therefore, in order for MSEs to last, it is necessary for them to perceive sustainable management as "a strategic factor that involves the entire value chain" (p. 4). Achieving this will help them to be more competitive since implementing sustainability as a strategy, will allow to reduce operating costs in the internal processes and generate a profit margin that will be reflected in the profitability of the organization. Velasquez Chacon (2022) proposes different actions so that MSEs can put sustainability management into practice. Among others, it is worth mentioning:

…changing lighting installations to more efficient ones, complying with occupational health and safety laws, and striving to close gaps in wages, and even to demand and support strategic partners to do the same. They may also involve other changes such as starting to measure the carbon or water footprint, measuring the waste generated when producing or implementing an occupational health and safety management system and promoting participation programs with the surrounding community. (p.4)

The foregoing shows that MSEs only need interest to involve sustainability in their strategic plan as a commitment that will impact not only their internal management but also their different stakeholders.

Uncertainty

When there are a series of threats to the fulfillment of organizational objectives, an environment of uncertainty is generated, putting the profitability, liquidity, and market share of the organization at risk. This uncertainty also affects the decision-making process, making planning within the organization difficult (Khandwalla, quoted by Galicia-Gopar et al., 2020).

Cameron, Kim and Whetten, Tushman and Anderson, Li and Atuahene-Gima, Lin and Germain and Power and Reid (quoted by Galicia-Gopar et al., 2020), state that uncertainty has a negative effect on organizations resulting in a price war in the market, imitation of products and services and solutions that are implemented in the short term.

Another of the negative effects of uncertainty is the deficiency in the organization's performance. Managers do not have enough information to respond assertively to the different situations they have to face, which generates feelings of crisis, anxiety, and stress. In environments of uncertainty, the organization avoids planning for the long term, does not invest in innovation, increases staff retirement, which in turn generates feelings of guilt, demotivation, internal conflicts, and loss of credibility (Rivera, Ramirez-Gaston, quoted by Galicia-Gopar et al., 2020).

Muñoz-Maya et al. (2021), found a study by Suarez & Zambrano (20215) in which they state that the leaders of MSEs are characterized by defining short-term objectives that are not part of a previously structured strategic plan. This means that when they are faced with moments of uncertainty, they react by avoiding the risk situation they are facing. In situations of uncertainty, Vizuete Muñoz (2021) state that it is necessary to "break the classic paradigms of administration" (p. 27); on the contrary, it is necessary to propose radical changes when managing this situation. In their study, they propose cognitive flexibility because managing flexibility in organizations is not difficult and, on the contrary, it becomes a great option for immediate solutions to be achieved in situations of uncertain environments. For Vizuete Muñoz (2021), "flexible management is an alternative to lift or keep organizations in force in difficult environments and times of crisis. (p. 27).

For Vizuete Muñoz (2021), the strategic level of the organization is responsible for managing moments of uncertainty, which is why spaces must be generated that allow collaborative work through group and participatory interaction in which the situation is discussed in a mature and effective way, to propose strategies that help them overcome this moment and thus achieve the proposed objectives.

In their management, companies are faced with external factors, among which it is worth mentioning those derived from the political environment or the economic instability of a country or region, which have not been contemplated in their planning, and on many occasions become uncontrollable. In addition to these factors, the managers of organizations are faced with problems that threaten the life cycle of their business and, if they do not adopt forceful strategies, they could disappear from the market. These aspects generate uncertainty for organizations and, therefore, assertive decisions must be made to enable them to remain in the market (Vizuete Muñoz, 2021; Orozco Gutierrez & Henao Vasquez, 2023).

Mses

Aguilar Rascon (2023) states that globally, MSEs account for more than 90% of the business sector and generate more than 33% of the gross domestic product, as they employ more than 45% of the economically active population. Hence the importance of providing studies that allow to know more about their business reality.

It is generally said that MSEs have economic deficiencies; however, it is important to know that there are new financing methods through public and private programs that can help them stay in the market. For this reason, Muñoz Bonilla, & Soriano Flores (2023) consider that the cause of their low survival is not only due to financial aspects, but also to the lack of a practical management model. MSEs require strategic administrative management that allows them to optimize the scarcity of resources. Having a well-structured improvement plan is critical to the survival of these organizations.

As MSEs are the engine of the local economy worldwide, it is crucial that they achieve business sustainability, which is why strategic management is essential for micro and small enterprises to achieve the required development that helps them generate new jobs, improve the quality of life of their employees, to provide benefits to the community and be a good choice for consumers of their products or services (Luciano Alipio, et al., 2023).

Although the economic contribution of MSEs is relevant, in many cases the conditions of the environment reduce their competitiveness and their possibility of being the engine of the economy of the country to which they belong, especially in situations of uncertainty (Muñoz-Maya et al., 2021, quoting Revista Semana).

Internal and external factors affect the production capacity of MSEs. Muñoz-Maya et al. (2021), mention that studies by the National Association of Financial Institutions (Association that leads the defense of Colombian private economy) show that MSEs have shortcomings in their organizational strategic management because of their short-term planning (maximum 1 year), and because their priority is to attend to the day to day issues and do not give importance to the aspects that help them generate added value to make them more competitive. Their difficulty in accessing the financial system does not allow them to invest in innovation projects that can help them grow and enter new markets.

Ayula et al. (2023), conducted a study that aimed to assess "the contribution of micro and small enterprises to the sustainable livelihoods of the Emba Alaje community, Wereda, Ethiopia" (p. 7561). They found that micro and small businesses are more influential than other sectors because they generate income and employment opportunities. It is important for micro enterprises to be well managed and to establish appropriate intervention approaches to increase employment opportunities and contribute to alleviating poverty in nations. Their results showed that micro and small enterprises contribute to economic growth and therefore to the creation of new jobs, thus generating income for the local population. In situations such as low per capita income, poverty and unemployment, MSEs create an entrepreneurial culture and a safe economy in rural regions.

Ayula et al. (2023) also found that micro and small enterprises in both developed and developing economies become a fundamental tool to address economic and social problems and to achieve the sustainable development goals.

MAIN FOCUS OF THE CHAPTER

Methodology

Type of research

This research is descriptive because it analyzes how a phenomenon, and its components are and how they manifest themselves. In this case, it analyzes how the independent variable of uncertainty affects the dependent variable of sustainability and that of organizational strategic management.

The study considers 2 dependent variables:

1. Sustainability which is measured from the social, economic, and environmental components.
2. Organizational strategic management based on the components of leadership, management by objectives, competitive strategy, and performance.

The independent variable is uncertainty and is measured on the basis of new trends, loyalty actions, the country's economic situation, insecurity and violence, concern about sales and political instability.

In addition, it is correlational, because the purpose of this type of study is "to know the relationship or degree of association that exists between two or more concepts, categories or variables in a particular sample or context (Hernandez Sampieri, et al., 2014, p. 93). The research evaluates the degree of association between the dependent variables of sustainability and organizational strategic management and the independent variable of uncertainty.

Hypothesis

According to Hernndez et al., (2014), hypotheses tentatively explain a phenomenon under study and given that the scope of the research is correlational, the following hypotheses are proposed:

H_1. There is a relationship between the uncertainty variable and the company's main strategy variable in the MSEs studied.

H_2. There is a relationship between the uncertainty variable and the company's main problem variable in the MSEs studied.

H_3. There is a relationship between the company's main strategy variable and the company's main problem variable in the MSEs studied.

H_4. There is a relaationship between the uncertainty variable and the sustainability variable in the MSEs studied.

H_5. There is a relationship between the uncertainty variable and the organizational management variable in the MSEs studied.

Sample

For purposes of this research, 377 managers of micro and small enterprises participated in the application of the questionnaire. Students collaborated in the collection of the information.

Data collection instrument

An instrument validated by the Red de Estudios Latinoamericanos en Administración y Negocios (Relayn) was used, and 3 questions related to the description of the companies investigated and 3 questions for the description of the respondents were selected, as presented in Table 1.

Table 1. Questions related to the description of the sample companies and respondents.

Category	Question	Scale
Description of the companies in the sample	Year of start of operations	Numeric
	Type of company	5 response options
	Number of employees	Numeric
Description of respondents	Age	Numeric
	Sex	Male Female
	Level of education	List of options

Note. Own elaboration.

The dependent and independent variables and their components selected from the questionnaire are presented in Table 2.

Table 2. Dependent and independent variables of the structural equation model.

Type of Variable	Variable	Component
Dependent	Sustainability	Social (8 questions)
		Economic (6 questions)
		Environmental (3 questions)
	Organizational strategic management	Direction
		Management by objective
		Competitive strategy
		Performance
Independent	Uncertainty	New trends
		Customer loyalty actions
		Economic situation of the country
		Concern about insecurity and violence
		Concern about sales
		Political instability

Note. Own elaboration.

Data analysis

For the data analysis, the SPSS statistical package was used, since it is a tool that allows to carry out, among other analyses, the multivariate and regression analysis of the different variables under study.

FINDINGS AND DISCUSSION

Instrument Reliability

Cronbach's alpha of 0.788 indicates that the internal consistency of the measuring instrument is good and that the questions of the test are measuring what they are expected to measure, as presented in Table 3.

Table 3. Reliability Statistics

Cronbach's Alpha	N of elements
.788	17

Note. Own elaboration.

Description of the companies in the sample

The sample consisted of 379 micro enterprises, where 67.8% of the organizations started operations before 2015, 21.9% between 2015 and 2019, and 9.5% between 2020 and 2022. The type of company that predominates is the organization incorporated as a company with 45.4%, followed by the company without registration in the Chamber of Commerce or the DIAN with 28.2% and in third place the natural person with business activity with 24.8%. On average, MSEs have 7.38 workers.

With respect to the people surveyed, 64.1% are men and 35.9% are women, where 46.1% have a basic primary and secondary education level, 43.8% are technicians, technologists and mainly professionals and 10.1% have mainly specialization, some have a master's degree or doctorate. The average age is 46.35 years, with a minimum of 17 years and a maximum of 76 years.

Relationship Between the Uncertainty Variable and the Company's Main Strategy Variable

The result of Pearson's correlation coefficient of 0.012 with a significance level of 0.814 indicates that there is no relationship between the two variables of uncertainty and the company's main strategy. Since the value is close to zero, there is no significant relationship between these two variables. In other words, there is no strong linear association between uncertainty and business strategy, as presented in Table 4.

Table 4. Pearson's correlation between the uncertainty variable and the company's main strategy variable

		Consolidated Uncertainty
Main strategy	Pearson's correlation	.012
	Sig. (bilateral)	.814

Note. Own elaboration.

The results indicate that uncertainty does not necessarily predict how business strategy will develop and would imply that these types of companies must be flexible and adaptive in their strategic approach. They cannot rely exclusively on a rigid strategy, as changing conditions require constant adjustments. Also, that in an uncertain environment, companies may consider diversifying their strategies. This involves exploring different approaches and not betting everything on a single strategy.

Moreover, this can be interpreted to mean that uncertainty is a variable present in the MSEs in the sample, since they face a challenging environment at all times, but managers are forced to make decisions on multiple fronts such as getting enough customers to consolidate the company, fine-tuning products/services to make them attractive to customers, achieving the personal financial balance between income and expenses to survive, getting the business to work without requiring so much time from the owner, investing the profits well to grow the company and consolidating the growth of the company. According to Ortiz et al. (2021), the lack of correlation between the uncertainty variable and the main strategy adopted by the company is a wake-up call to organizations to think about organizational management in a planned, organized, directed, and controlled manner, and that uncertainty requires continuous monitoring of the external and internal factors that affect the company. Strategies must be adjusted according to circumstances.

Relationship between the uncertainty variable and the company's main problem variable

The result of Pearson's correlation coefficient of -0.178 with a significance level of 0.001 indicates that there is a slight negative correlation between the two variables of uncertainty and the main problem of the company. This suggests that as uncertainty related to external factors such as the economic situation, insecurity, and political instability increases, there is a slight tendency for the company's core concerns, such as time management, hiring talented staff, financial organization, and customer management, to decline. In other words, when faced with an uncertain environment, priority may be given to adapt to external conditions over optimizing the company's internal situation. However, it is worth mentioning that the degree of this correlation is low, which implies that other factors not considered in this analysis could be influencing the company's main problems, as presented in Table 5.

Table 5. Pearson's correlation between the uncertainty variable and the company's main problem variable

		Company's main problems
Consolidated uncertainty	Pearson's correlation	-.178**
	Sig. (bilateral)	.001

Note. Own elaboration.

Although the correlation is weak, as suggested by Rivera and Ramirez-Gaston, quoted by Galicia-Gopar et al. (2020), that despite the fact that in environments of uncertainty, the organization avoids long-term planning, the strategies of MSEs could benefit from a more balanced approach that addresses both external influences and the internal needs of the company. The results also imply that companies must be flexible and adaptive to address uncertainty, and that there is the need to assess and mitigate uncertainty risks effectively, hence, business strategy must consider uncertainty as a key factor.

Relationship between the company's main strategy variable and the company's main problem variable

The result of Pearson's correlation coefficient of 0.038 with a significance level of 0.463 indicates that there is no correlation between the two variables of main strategy and uncertainty. In other words, there is no strong linear association between the main strategy and the main problem of the company, as shown in Table 6.

Table 6. Pearson's correlation between the main problem variable and the company's main strategy

		Company's main strategy
Company's main problems	Pearson's correlation	.038
	Sig. (bilateral)	.463

Note. Own elaboration.

Given the low correlation value, companies should consider addressing the main issue in a specific way. They cannot rely solely on a general strategy; they must adapt to the specific circumstances and, therefore, identifying the specific problems that affect the company is crucial. This involves a thorough analysis of the relevant areas to address the obstacles, suggesting that strategic decisions should be based on data and evidence.

The practical interpretation of these results could be that the company's day-to-day concerns, such as time management, customer management, and talent organization, are not directly related to the company's main strategy of consolidation and growth as indicated by Khandwalla, quoted by Galicia-Gopar et al (2020) in the sense that this uncertainty also affects the decision-making process, making planning difficult within the organization. This may be because long-term strategies, such as customer consolidation and profit investing, operate at a different level and may not be affected by day-to-day operational issues. In other words, MSEs may be managing their day-to-day challenges effectively without this having a direct and significant impact on their long-term strategies.

Relationship Between Uncertainty and Sustainability Variables

The results of Pearson's correlation coefficient indicate that there is a moderately positive correlation between the uncertainty variable and social, economic and environmental sustainability. This means that in general, as uncertainty increases, so does the sustainability of the company and implies that sustainability requires the ability to adjust to unexpected changes and maintain a long-term focus. Additionally, that companies must assess and manage risks effectively to maintain their commitment to sustainability and that they can seek creative solutions to address challenges and maintain their commitment to sustainability.

This suggests that as uncertainty related to factors such as new trends, customer loyalty, the economic situation, security, sales, and political stability increases, there is a corresponding increase in the social, economic, and environmental sustainability of the company. In other words, companies that are more exposed to uncertainty or that manage uncertainty better tend to have better sustainability practices, as presented in Table 7.

Table 7. Pearson's correlation between uncertainty and social, economic and environmental sustainability

		Social Sustainability	Economic sustainability	Environmental Sustainability	Consolidated sustainability
Consolidated uncertainty	Pearson's correlation	.358**	.354**	.432**	.485**
	Sig. (bilateral)	.000	.000	.000	.000

Note. Own elaboration.

The positive correlation could be interpreted as a sign that companies facing an uncertain environment may be more motivated to implement sustainability strategies as a way to mitigate risks and ensure their long-term viability. For example, a company that cares about insecurity and violence could invest more in responsible social practices, while concern about the country's economic situation could lead a company to adopt sustainable economic measures to ensure its survival and continued growth, in line with Velasquez Chacon (2022), who mentions the need to integrate sustainability into strategic management taking into account the economic and environmental impact that its production process or the provision of a service can generate, in addition to the social impact it can have on the community and the different stakeholders.

Relationship Between the Uncertainty Variable and the Organizational Management Variable

The results of Pearson's correlation coefficient indicate that there is a moderately positive correlation between the uncertainty variable and the organizational management variable. Given the positive correlation coefficient, it can be inferred that as uncertainty increases, so does the need for more effective organizational management. In other words, when conditions are uncertain, the company must adapt and take strategic steps to meet the challenges.

This suggests that as uncertainty factors such as new trends, customer loyalty, the economic situation, insecurity, sales, and political instability increase, organizational management also improves in terms of direction, management by objectives, competitive strategy, and performance, as presented in Table 8.

Table 8. Pearson's correlation between the uncertainty variable and organizational management

		Organizational Management				
		Direction	Management by Objectives	Competitive Strategy	Performance	Consolidated Organizational Management
Consolidated Uncertainty Variable	Pearson's correlation	.176**	.299**	.136**	.361**	.328**
	Sig. (bilateral)	.001	.000	.008	.000	.000

Note. Own elaboration.

Organizational management is made up of several key aspects, such as direction, management by objectives, competitive strategy, and performance. Let's see how they relate to uncertainty:

- Direction: In uncertain situations, direction becomes crucial. Companies must establish a clear vision and strategic objectives to guide their actions and decisions.
- Management by Objectives: Uncertainty requires careful planning. Management by objectives helps define specific goals, allocate resources, and evaluate progress.
- Competitive Strategy: Uncertainty affects market dynamics. Companies must adapt their competitive strategy to stay relevant and face changes.

In other words, positive correlation can be interpreted to mean that organizations that are more exposed to uncertainty or that are able to adapt to it, tend to develop a more effective management. It is possible for these organizations to take a proactive approach to dealing with uncertainty, thereby improving their ability to steer, setting clear goals, defining competitive strategies, and ultimately achieving superior performance. The statistical significance of 0.00 reinforces the reliability of these results, indicating that it is highly unlikely that the observed correlation is the product of chance.

CONCLUSION

This research contributes to the literature on organizational management and sustainability, as it shows empirical evidence of the relationship between uncertainty and organizational management and sustainability in the MSEs of the sample.

Although there is no strong correlation between the uncertainty variable and the company's main strategy variable, uncertainty plays a crucial role in business decision-making. Uncertainty does not predict how business strategy will play out, but it does demand an open-mindedness to explore different approaches. In addition, it suggests that directors should make multifaceted decisions and consider several fronts. Following the recommendations of Ortiz et al. (2021), uncertainty requires continuous monitoring of the internal and external factors that affect the company. Constant adaptation is essential for maintaining sustainability and success.

There is also no strong relationship between the company's main strategy and the company's main problem, which suggests that the day-to-day concerns in the company's operation would not be directly related to strategies for consolidation and permanence of the company over time.

In relation to the uncertainty variable and the Company's main problem variable, the correlation is negative and slight, which suggests that this type of organization gives priority to day-to-day work and adaptation to external conditions over internal optimization, which requires more of a long-term planning. In other words, according to Rivera and Ramirez-Gaston (quoted by Galicia-Gopar et al., 2020), although MSEs' strategies usually avoid long-term planning in uncertain environments, they could benefit from a more balanced approach.

A moderate positive correlation is found between the uncertainty variable and the sustainability and organizational management variable, which suggests with respect to the former that, according to Velasquez-Chacon (2022), sustainability must be integrated to the company's strategic management. The foregoing involves considering the economic, environmental and social impact of business decisions and generating sustainability strategies to mitigate risks and seek durability over time, and this generates a proactive approach to face uncertainty, positively impacting the organizational management variable. With respect to organizational management, strategic direction, management by objectives, competitive strategy and performance are intrinsically related to the company's ability to face uncertainty and achieve exceptional performance. Those companies that take a proactive approach to dealing with uncertainty can achieve a clear direction, set strategic objectives, and define competitive strategies that ensure their long-term feasibility.

Uncertainty is not an obstacle, but an engine of adaptation. MSEs that embrace flexibility and strategic diversification will be better prepared to meet the changing challenges of the business environment. This wake-up call urges us to rethink organizational management and to recognize that uncertainty is an opportunity to grow and prosper.

In general, the results indicate the need for MSEs to guide organizational management and sustainability with a long-term approach that addresses external influences as well as internal requirements.

For this reason, from a strategic orientation, the company should seek to differentiate its work by incorporating into its management the process of formulating objectives, implementation and evaluation of functional strategies in uncertain environments.

RECOMMENDATIONS

To ensure long-term sustainability and success, MSEs must adopt a flexible and complex approach to their strategic management, given that uncertainty is a constant in the business environment. In the first place, this implies that the managers of these companies have an open and proactive mentality and are willing to explore and adapt strategies in a timely and effective manner to changing market conditions.

Second, MSEs must operate in an environment of balance between daily operational management and long-term planning that allows them to meet day-to-day needs while building a solid foundation for the future. The lack of a strong association between short-term and long-term strategies suggests a tendency to focus on immediate problem solving rather than long-term strategic consolidation.

Third, sustainability should be a central component in the strategic management of MSEs, based on strategies that not only mitigate risks or provide solutions to day-to-day operating problems, but also promote sustainability over time by considering the economic, environmental and social impact of decisions. The implementation of sustainable practices in this type of organizations strengthens resilience and competitiveness and contributes to social and environmental responsibility.

Finally, a clear direction based on strategic objectives increases a MSEs ability to deal with uncertainty. Uncertainty should be seen as an opportunity for adaptation and growth and not as an obstacle to meeting the company's goal. A long-term strategic framework will allow MSEs not only to survive in a volatile environment, but also to thrive and grow.

NEW RESEARCH

New research can continue to be carried out on the relationship between uncertainty and organizational management and the sustainability of organizations, insofar as it is a phenomenon that affects all types of companies at both the national and international level. Also, research that seeks to identify successful companies in the management of uncertainty that have positively impacted their organizational management and sustainability.

REFERENCES

Aguilar Rascon, O. C. (2023). El impacto de la dirección en el desempeño en las micro y pequeñas empresas: Un análisis sistémico. *Contaduría y Administración*, 68(3), 46–78. DOI: 10.22201/fca.24488410e.2023.3295

Ayula, G., Abbay, A. G., & Azadi, H. (2023). The role of micro- and small-scale enterprises in enhancing sustainable community livelihood: Tigray, Ethiopia. *Environment, Development and Sustainability*, 25(8), 7561–7584. DOI: 10.1007/s10668-022-02359-7

Bejarano-Auqui, J. F. (2024). Model of Business Management Based on the Theories of Management Thinking of the Mypes. (2024). *Academic Journal of Interdisciplinary Studies*, 13(1), 98. DOI: 10.36941/ajis-2024-0008

David, F. D., & David, F. R. (2017). *Strategic management. A competitive advantage approach, concepts and cases.* (6a edit.). Pearson.

Eude (2024). *Gestión del Cambio en Tiempos de Incertidumbre: Consejos y estrategias para líderes y gerentes.* (15) Gestión del Cambio en Tiempos de Incertidumbre: Consejos y estrategias para líderes y gerentes | LinkedIn

Galicia-Gopar, M. A., Mendoza-Ramirez, L., & Espinosa-Trujillo, M. A. (2020). Estrategias de supervivencia y desempeño de mipymes en un ambiente de incertidumbre. *Ciencias Administrativas. Teoría y Praxis*, 16(2), 31–47.

Gambaro, E., & García, L. N. (2021). Empresas B: Una gestión estratégica apoyada en el conocimiento. *Actualidad Contable Faces*, 24(42), 125–149. DOI: 10.53766/ACCON/2021.42.05

Garcia Guiliany, J., Pizarro de la Hoz, A., Barragán Morales, C., & Villarreal, F. (2023). Planeación estratégica para la competitividad de pequeñas y medianas empresas del sector construcción e inmobiliario. *Revista de Ciencias Sociales*, 29(2), 315–326. DOI: 10.31876/rcs.v29i2.39978

Gonzalez Hernandez, M. E., Portillo Lovo, J. L., Benítez Ramírez, D., & Moran De Villalta, D. (2023). *Planificación estratégica para el centro escolar juan manuel rodríguez.* [Doctoral dissertation, Universidad de El Salvador]. https://oldri.ues.edu.sv/id/eprint/33553/

Hernandez, R., Fernandez, C., & Baptista, P. (2014). *Metodología de la investigación (6a* (McGraw, H. I., Ed.).

Luciano Alipio, R. A., Sotomayor Chahuaylla, J. A., Garcia Juarez, H. D., & Pelaez Camacho, H. Y. (2023). Gestión empresarial en el desarrollo de las MYPES en zonas mineras del Perú. *Revista Venezolana de Gerencia*, 28(103), 1174–1189. DOI: 10.52080/rvgluz.28.103.16

Martinez, L. E., Farfan, E. A., Osto, R. N. Un acercamiento epistémico a la administración por objetivos. *Actualidad Contable FACES,* (45), 93-104.

Martinez, M., Gomez, H., and Martinez, J, (2017). *La gestión de la incertidumbre: Empresas inteligentes con trabajadores del conocimiento.* Vista de La gestión de la incertidumbre: empresas inteligentes con trabajadores del conocimiento (redipe.org)

Merino-Martin, N. H., & Pastorino, A. H. (2013). Perception about sustainable development of sme in Peru. *Revista de Administración de Empresas, 53*(3), 290-302. Doi DOI: 10.1590/S0034-75902013000300006

Miranda Pegueros, M., Lopez Castro, E. M., & Vega Zarate, C. (2022). Hacia una perspectiva integral de gestión en sostenibilidad empresarial. *Trascender, contabilidad y gestión, 7*(19), 150-164.

Mora Riapira, E. H., Vera Colina, M. A., & Melgarejo Molina, Z. A. (2015). Planificación estratégica y niveles de competitividad de las Mipymes del sector comercio en Bogotá. *Estudios Gerenciales*, 31(134), 79–87. DOI: 10.1016/j.estger.2014.08.001

Muñoz Bonilla, H. A., & Soriano Flores, E. (2023). Formulación de proyectos en Mypes: Evidencia empírica de la ausencia de un modelo práctico. *Project. Design and Management*, 5(1), 27–43. DOI: 10.35992/pdm.5vi1.1152

Muñoz-Maya, C. M., Ramirez-Garzón, M. T., & Velazquez, R. P. (2021). Management Practices in Chaotic Environments of SMEs in Bogota. In R. Perez-Uribe, D. Ocampo-Guzman, N. Moreno-Monsalve, & W. Fajardo-Moreno (Eds.), *Handbook of Research on Management Techniques and Sustainability Strategies for Handling Disruptive Situations in Corporate Settings* (pp. 70-88). IGI Global. https://doi .org/DOI: 10.4018/978-1-7998-8185-8.ch004

Niebles-Nuñez, W., Rojas-Martinez, C., Pacheco-Ruiz, C., & Hernandez-Palma, H. G. (2022). Desarrollo de estrategias de direccionamiento estratégico para la gestión de calidad en empresas del sector industrial. *Información Tecnológica*, 33(6), 145–156. DOI: 10.4067/S0718-07642022000600145

Orozco Gutiérrez, T., & Henao Vásquez, G. A. (2023). La toma de decisiones al interior de las organizaciones en momentos de incertidumbre. *Universidad Libre*. chrome-extension://efaidnbmnnnibpcajp-cglclefindmkaj/https://repository.unilibre.edu.co/bitstream/handle/10901/24463/Orozco%20Guti%C3 %A9rrez%20-%20Henao%20V%C3%A1squez.pdf?sequence=1

Ortiz, L. E. M., Mero, M. J. V., Castro, L. M. U., & Sanchez, L. M. C. (2021). Proceso administrativo y sostenibilidad empresarial del sector hotelero de la parroquia Crucita, Manabí-Ecuador. *Revista de Ciencias Sociales*, 27(2), 367–385.

Perez-Uribe, R. I. (2018). *Gerencia estratégica corporativa*. ECOE Ediciones.

Salamanca, Y. T., Cortina, A. D., & Garcia Rios, D. (2014). Modelo de gestión organizacional basado en el logro de objetivos. *Suma de Negocios*, 5(11), 70–77. DOI: 10.1016/S2215-910X(14)70021-7

Sanchez Rodriguez, L. Z., Cejas Martinez, M. F., & Tovar Velasquez, S. J. (2024). *Las competencias del gerente financiero*. CIDE, editorial. chrome-extension://efaidnbmnnnibpcajpcglclefindmkaj/https:// repositorio.cidecuador.org/bitstream/123456789/2944/3/No%2039%20Libro%20Las%20Competencias %203-1-2024.pdf

Shamira, A., Rosas, S. C. Z., & Tusa, F. (2023). Competencias organizacionales del Comunicador Social del ECU 911 ante situaciones de crisis. #. *PerDebate*, 7(1), 106–139. DOI: 10.18272/pd.v7i1.3107

Velasquez Chacon, E. (2022). MSEs and sustainability in times of pandemic in Arequipa, Peru: A structural equation model. *VISUAL REVIEW. International Visual Culture Review Revista Internacional de cultura visual, 10*(4), 1–11. https://doi.org/DOI: 10.37467/revvisual.v9.3624

Vizuete Muñoz, J. M. (2021). La gestión flexible en las organizaciones, en entornos de incertidumbre. *Revista Gestión y Desarrollo Libre, 6*(11), (22-46). https://revistas.unilibre.edu.co/index.php/gestion_libre/article/view/8077/9551

KEY TERMS AND DEFINITIONS

Strategic organizational management: Strategic management comprises all future-oriented decisions made by the management of a company, with a long-term impact. Its main objective is to set the direction and ensure the growth and feasibility of the organization. This management coordinates employee activities around common goals, involving actions such as planning, organization, talent recruitment and retention strategy, as well as the implementation and supervision of the strategic plan.

MSEs: Micro and small enterprises which, under decree 657 of 2019, are classified according to the economic sector they belong to (manufacturing, service and commercial) and their size is determined based on the income from annual ordinary activities represented in Tax Value Units (TVU).

Strategies: Strategy is a process for making decisions in specific situations and it is designed to achieve one or more previously established objectives. In short, it consists of the plan or route to follow to achieve certain objectives.

Sustainability: Sustainability is about meeting the needs of current generations without compromising the needs of future generations, while ensuring a balance between economic growth, respect for the environment and social well-being.

Uncertainty: Organizational uncertainty refers to the lack of clarity or predictability about events, conditions, or situations that affect an organization. This can include changes in the market, technology, competition, government regulations, among other external and internal factors. Uncertainty can make decision-making and strategic planning difficult, as organizations may struggle to anticipate and respond appropriately to changes in their environment. Effective uncertainty management involves adopting flexible strategies, gathering and analyzing relevant information, and the ability to adapt quickly to changing circumstances.

Strategic planning: Strategic planning is a process by which an organization defines its long-term objectives and the actions necessary to achieve them. It involves identifying goals and formulating detailed plans to achieve those goals, taking into account both the organization's internal resources and external factors of the environment in which it operates, such as competition, market opportunities, and changes in the industry or the political and economic context.

Chapter 14
Supply Chain Risk Management in the Business Sector:
The Modern Perspective

Froilan Delute Mobo
https://orcid.org/0000-0002-4531-8106
Philippine Merchant Marine Academy, Philippines

Mohammad Shahparan
https://orcid.org/0009-0007-2850-6598
Silk Road International University of Tourism and Cultural Heritage, Uzbekistan

Abigail Gomez
https://orcid.org/0000-0001-5614-2778
Cavite State University, Philippines

Michael Bongalonta
https://orcid.org/0009-0001-9989-626X
Sorsogon State University, Philippines

ABSTRACT

ABSTRACT The paper indicates to the study of supply chain sustainability strategies, when the risks faced by all business farm in supply chains are so complex, diverse and sudden that it becomes more difficult than ever to predict and determine the probability of their materialization. It substantiates the relevance of supply chain management (Supply Chain Management SCM). It has been determined that in order to competitive advantages in the market sector, business sector need to improve supply chain management properly, which will reduce the cost of production to delivery, optimize times, as well as customer satisfaction. It is proposed to consider the risk management mechanism in business sector as a set of mutually agreed methods, procedures, management tools, taking into account the role of each subject of the supply chain. It is concluded that the correct risk assessment mechanism in the supply chain for business sector should constitute an appropriate tool for assessing the effectiveness of risk management from the point of view of all business sector in the supply chain.

DOI: 10.4018/979-8-3693-4046-2.ch014

INTRODUCTION

The study of aspects of strategic management is of particular interest. This is because for strategic management, now it is possible to analyze and develop a behavioral model for the effective development of the business sector. It is on strategic management that the competitive advantage The concept of supply chain management (SCM) has been a cornerstone of business operations, particularly in industrialized nations, since the 1990s. However, despite its widespread application, there remains a lack of consensus among logistics professionals regarding its precise definition. Some experts view SCM through the lens of logistics integration, emphasizing the coordination of various logistics functions to optimize efficiency. Others perceive SCM as primarily focused on managing distribution logistics, where the movement and storage of goods from point of origin to point of consumption are key. A third perspective, which has gained prominence in recent years, conceptualizes SCM as the implementation of advanced information platforms and management techniques that position the supply chain as a focal point of business strategy.

The onset of the COVID-19 pandemic in 2019 brought unprecedented challenges to global supply chains, exposing vulnerabilities that had previously gone unnoticed. Lockdowns, travel restrictions, and other containment measures severely disrupted supply chain operations across the globe, leading to delays, shortages, and increased costs. This period underscored the fragility of global supply chains and the urgent need for businesses to reassess and fortify their SCM strategies to withstand future disruptions.

In addition to the pandemic, other factors such as natural disasters, geopolitical tensions, and cyber-attacks have further complicated supply chain management. These challenges have increased operational costs and forced businesses to operate in a state of heightened risk awareness. The period of 2021-2022 marked a significant shift in the business sector, with many organizations recognizing that the absence of a stable operating environment had become the new "normal." For supply chain managers, this new reality necessitated a continuous readiness to manage and mitigate risks as they arise.

In the modern business environment, SCM has become more critical than ever. The increasing complexity and interconnectedness of global supply chains have made risk management a central focus for businesses seeking to ensure continuity and resilience. To address these challenges, it is imperative to develop robust supply chain risk management (SCRM) strategies that align with the overarching goals and objectives of the business.

This chapter delves into the dual nature of supply chain risks—both internal and external—that businesses must contend with in today's volatile environment. Internal risks might include operational inefficiencies, supplier failures, or disruptions within the company's own logistics network. External risks, on the other hand, encompass a broader range of threats such as natural disasters, geopolitical instability, and cybercrime. Both types of risks are analyzed in detail, with an emphasis on understanding their sources and implementing effective management strategies.

The growing importance of SCRM in the business sector can be attributed to the increasing frequency and severity of disruptions, driven by factors such as geopolitical conflicts, environmental changes, and the ongoing digital transformation. As businesses strive to enhance their resilience, there is a greater emphasis on developing collaborative capabilities within the supply chain. Effective collaboration not only mitigates risks but also fosters innovation and adaptability, enabling businesses to thrive in an increasingly complex and uncertain world.

The findings of this study suggest that the development of new strategies and organizational measures for assessing and managing supply chain risks is crucial for maintaining stability and profitability in the modern business landscape. The chapter will explore the various dimensions of SCRM, including the critical role of sustainable practices in enhancing supply chain performance. By adopting a holistic approach to risk management, businesses can not only protect their supply chains from potential disruptions but also create a competitive advantage in the marketplace.

age of the company in the market for the sale of goods and the provision of services, as well as the duration of maintaining competitiveness, depends. It is the study and analysis of the behavior of competitors, and the use of modern methods and forms in the competitive struggle that will affect the ability of long-term leadership in a particular product segment.

In the business sector strategic supply chain management is a complex, comprehensive, and integrated type of planning applied to gain increased chain competitiveness. As a rule, it is achieved by increasing the added value or improving the quality of service, which is responsible for the satisfaction of the buyer, and also guessing his needs in the future.

The implementation of strategies depends entirely on the company, its vision of the situation, anticipation of all possible risks, opportunities, and human resources because the success of operations to improve the supply chain lies entirely on the skillful management and organization of resources, competent setting of tasks and planning, a real vision of the opportunities and needs of the company.

The concept of supply chain risk management in the business sector is very broad: from the point of view of the dictionary approach, the term is interpreted as a possible danger or an action at random in the hope of a happy outcome. As an economic unit, the risk is damage, the probabilistic occurrence of which can occur when certain decisions are made; from the point of view of statistical evaluation, supply chain management risk in the business sector is the mathematical expectation of the loss function as a result of the chosen solution. Risk does not consider only damage or negative results in the business process activity; it also leads the positive effects.

In the supply chain management system, the risk is an unfavorable outcome, which consists of the deviation of the actual parameters of supply chain management flows from those planned in the process of implementing supply chain activities.

Supply chain management risks are diverse and to adopt effective management methods, they should be divided into categories depending on the classification feature. There are so many kinds of risks such as external and internal, permanent and temporary, insured and non-insurable risks, and systematic and specific risks. These can be risks of a single link in the supply chain management system (planning risks, transportation risks, storage risks, risks of interaction with suppliers) and risks of the supply chain management system as a whole. According to the degree of influence, the scale of supply chain management risks starts from zero, minimal, and acceptable and ends with critical and catastrophic. According to the results of the logistics activities of the system, commercial, technical, environmental risks, risks of loss of property, and others are distinguished.

Supply chain management risk profiles help to continue to change as business operating models become more standard, modern, and transport networks. It also helps more diverse and interdependent. In the 21st century, most businesses depend on dependent suppliers and partners in many countries. They generate such kind of risk and they are exposed to risks at various steps from the search for raw materials to the assignment of products and services. These risks are not always within the control of the company.

The major disruptions of the latter, including the pandemic, terrorist threats, floods, and the earthquake in Turkey, have intensified public discussion of risk-awareness in supply chains and transport networks.

The modern business sector needs to be more flexible and easier to develop performance in risky and negative environmental effects. On the other hand, the business sector also needs proper decision supply tools to handle various categories of supply chain risks. The modern business sector should be proposing a new framework for assessing the impact of risks of supply change performance. In the last two decades supply chain management increased randomly but business companies face increasing uncertainties that require better supply chain risk management. To improve the supply chain risk management there is a need to consider more real conditions and factors such as demand and time, managing the entire supply chain. It helps not only focus on mitigation strategies but also reduce the dependence on significant suppliers and find out the risk.

Supply chain risk management is getting more attention in almost every business sector. Collaboration and positive approaches can improve the supply chain resilience and robust business side. The global supply chain provides the food, medicine, and products that support our way of life. The ever-growing supply chains have created new challenges that traditional risk management must be equipped to handle. Supply chain risk management is the more popular day by day. Supply chain risk management is an integral function of the supply network. Supply chain risk management is a common issue for the modern business sector who face unpredictable challenges due to the globalization and economic policies of countries. Discuss about supply chain risk management can promote the competitiveness in business sector. One important thing is that risk mitigation strategies can reduce the impact of natural and human-made disasters on supply chains.

SOLUTION AND DISCUSSION

Recent research by Allianz Insurance Company identifies the most pressing risks facing businesses worldwide. At the forefront of these concerns are cyber incidents, which include cybercrime, IT failures, and data breaches, accounting for 44% of the total risk landscape. These incidents have escalated in frequency and sophistication, posing a severe threat to the integrity of supply chains. The growing reliance on digital platforms and interconnected systems has made supply chains particularly vulnerable to cyberattacks, where a single breach can disrupt operations, compromise sensitive information, and erode customer trust.

1. Cyber Incidents and Their Impact on Supply Chains

The digital transformation of supply chains, while enhancing efficiency and transparency, has also introduced new vulnerabilities. Cyber incidents such as ransomware attacks, phishing scams, and hacking attempts can cripple a supply chain by halting operations, corrupting data, or leading to the theft of proprietary information. The interconnectedness of global supply chains means that a cyber incident at one node can quickly ripple through the entire network, causing widespread disruption.

To address these challenges, businesses must prioritize cybersecurity as a core component of their supply chain risk management (SCRM) strategies. This involves implementing robust cybersecurity protocols, conducting regular risk assessments, and fostering a culture of cybersecurity awareness among employees and partners. Additionally, businesses should invest in advanced technologies such as blockchain and AI-driven security solutions that can detect and mitigate threats in real time, ensuring that supply chains remain resilient against cyber incidents.

2. Business Interruption and Supply Chain Disruption

The second most significant risk, with 42% of the global risk share, is business interruption, which includes disruptions to the supply chain. Business interruptions can arise from a variety of sources, including natural disasters, geopolitical conflicts, pandemics, and supplier insolvency. The COVID-19 pandemic is a stark reminder of how quickly and profoundly supply chains can be disrupted, leading to shortages, delays, and increased costs.

To mitigate the risk of business interruptions, businesses must adopt a proactive approach to supply chain management. This includes diversifying their supplier base, developing contingency plans, and investing in supply chain visibility tools that provide real-time insights into potential disruptions. By building a more agile and flexible supply chain, businesses can quickly adapt to changing conditions and minimize the impact of disruptions.

Furthermore, businesses should consider adopting Just-in-Case (JIC) inventory strategies, where critical components or products are stockpiled to buffer against potential supply chain disruptions. While this approach may increase inventory costs, it can also provide a crucial safety net in times of crisis, ensuring that operations can continue without significant delays.

3. The Role of Technological Advancements

Technological advancements play a crucial role in mitigating supply chain risks. For example, predictive analytics can help businesses anticipate potential disruptions by analyzing historical data and identifying patterns that may indicate future risks. Similarly, IoT (Internet of Things) devices can provide real-time monitoring of supply chain activities, allowing businesses to respond quickly to emerging issues.

Blockchain technology, with its decentralized and immutable ledger system, offers significant potential for enhancing supply chain security and transparency. By providing a tamper-proof record of all transactions within the supply chain, blockchain can reduce the risk of fraud, ensure product authenticity, and streamline compliance with regulatory requirements.

4. Collaboration and Resilience Building

Collaboration is another key factor in enhancing supply chain resilience. Businesses must work closely with suppliers, customers, and other stakeholders to develop a shared understanding of risks and coordinate responses to potential disruptions. This collaborative approach can help to build stronger, more resilient supply chains that are better equipped to withstand shocks and recover quickly from disruptions.

Developing strong partnerships with suppliers and investing in long-term relationships can also contribute to supply chain resilience. By fostering trust and transparency, businesses can work more effectively with their suppliers to identify and mitigate risks, ensuring that the supply chain remains robust and responsive to changing conditions.

5. Sustainability as a Risk Mitigation Strategy

Sustainability is increasingly recognized as a key component of supply chain risk management. By adopting sustainable practices, businesses can reduce their exposure to risks such as resource scarcity, regulatory changes, and reputational damage. For example, sourcing materials from environmentally responsible suppliers can help to ensure the long-term availability of critical resources, while reducing the risk of regulatory non-compliance.

Moreover, sustainable supply chains are often more resilient to disruptions. For instance, businesses that prioritize energy efficiency and renewable energy sources may be less vulnerable to fluctuations in energy prices or disruptions to the energy supply. Similarly, companies that invest in sustainable packaging and transportation methods may be better positioned to adapt to changing environmental regulations and consumer preferences.

The functioning of the supply chain management is also affected by sanctions pressure in the world. Now there are restrictions on the capacity of transport capacities, rising fuel prices, an imbalance in supply and demand, a gap in business processes, macroeconomic instability, currency risks, etc. Restoring the work of all logistics links in the chain will require a lot of time and financial resources.

It should be noted that logistical risks have a mostly negative outcome, which has a strong impact on the stability and efficiency of the economic system, which emphasizes the importance of system management tools as a whole.

Discussion

Explanatory Dictionary of the Russian Language, authored by S.I. Ozhegov, the term risk is interpreted as "possible danger, action at random in the hope of a happy outcome." Considered an economic unit, the risk is the damage that is likely to occur when certain decisions are made; from the point of view of statistical evaluation, the risk is the mathematical expectation of the loss function as a result of the chosen solution. (Anikin B.A. Logistics and supply chain management. Theory and practice. Supply chain management: textbook / edited by B.A. Anikin and T.A. Rodkina. - M: Prospekt,2015 - 2016)

During the course work, I was guided by a wide search for publications and articles on the topic of risks in supply chain management, related to risk management by group, focusing on risk management infiltrating production and chain of choice management. There are several reasons not including papers published before 2000. First, traditionally risk and uncertainty have always been an important issue associated with supply chain management. The term "supply chain risk" is relatively new to the literature. Secondly, the problem of supply chain risk management has gained much attention after a series of events, with a serious impact on the supply chain, including floods, earthquakes, and other external as well as internal problems of the region and the country as a whole, resulting in a large supply chain.

According to Malhotra and Grover (1998), the various methodologies used by different researchers fall into five categories, which include conceptual, descriptive, empirical, exploratory cross-sectional, and exploratory longitudinal. Most of it was based on a descriptive approach in methodology. Thus, descriptive and empirical studies occupy about 70-80% of all studies.

The concept is intended to present a research methodology that describes the fundamental concepts of supply chain risk management. In this classification, most papers propose a conceptual methodology for supply chain risk management. For example, Cucchiella and Gastaldi (2006) developed a framework for managing supply chain uncertainty to minimize firm risk. To increase firm flexibility, the authors used risk as a means of dealing with uncertainty in the supply chain. Some of the papers in this category also clarify some of the issues related to supply chain and supply chain risk management, including their definition. Peck (2006) explored the term "supply chain", "supply chain management", and then the combination of supply chain management with risk. The author then argued that supply chain risk should not be considered solely in terms of functional SCM but requires cross-functional considerations.

Descriptive is a methodology that describes, formulates, and develops a supply chain risk management model. For example, there are models developed as the basis for supply chain management that include the identification, analysis, and prioritization of mitigation actions.

The main methods of risk management in the supply chain system include:

1. Checking business partners and proper transactions is most important. This is one kind of method of avoiding the risk.
2. The method of localization (labor-intensive method) – the allocation of the most dangerous link from the logistics system to implement point control to minimize (avoid) the risk.
3. Distribution of funds in different areas. It can be helpful if any side loses automatically other side will cover up for successes.
4. The distribution of common risk by combining with other participants associated with the process of managing supply chain flows.
5. Limiting method - development and installation of appropriate limit constraints (upper / lower thresholds), for example, limiting the share of logistics costs for a particular category.

The transfer of risk for a certain fee is called insurance. To determine the effectiveness of supply chain risk management methods, quantitative and qualitative assessments are used. A qualitative approach to the assessment gives an understanding of the sources, factors, and type of risk, a quantitative assessment:

- Measures the magnitude of the risk of the supply chain management system or part of it. The main quantification methods include:
- Statistical methods (calculation of variance, mathematical expectation, coefficient of variation, regression, multifactorial models);
- Expert method (risk assessment by auditors, experts). The disadvantage is the subjective opinion of a specialist.
- Calculation of the break-even point;
- analogy method (comparison with already known analogous process);
- "Decision tree" (graphic construction of various situations/options);

FUTURE RESEARCH DIRECTIONS

Supply Chain Risk Management (SCRM) has become increasingly significant in today's globalized and interconnected world, where modern supply chains face a plethora of risks ranging from natural disasters and geopolitical tensions to cyber threats and pandemics. The need for robust SCRM strategies has never been more critical. This chapter explores future research directions in SCRM, emphasizing areas such as digital transformation, sustainability, globalization, and cybersecurity.

One promising avenue for future research is the exploration of blockchain technology's potential to enhance transparency, traceability, and security within supply chains. Kshetri (2018) suggests that blockchain could be instrumental in verifying product authenticity and streamlining supply chain processes. Future research should delve into how blockchain can be effectively implemented in various supply chain contexts to mitigate risks associated with fraud and inefficiencies.

Artificial Intelligence (AI) and Machine Learning (ML) also offer substantial opportunities for enhancing SCRM. As Dubey et al. (2020) highlight, AI and ML can significantly improve predictive analytics, risk assessment, and decision-making in supply chains. Investigating AI-driven models to predict disruptions, optimize inventory management, and enhance overall supply chain resilience could prove invaluable. Moreover, research could examine the ethical implications of AI in SCRM, particularly concerning data privacy and algorithmic bias.

The Internet of Things (IoT) presents another critical area for future research, particularly in its capacity to enable real-time monitoring and management of supply chain activities. Ben-Daya et al. (2019) emphasize the importance of integrating IoT devices into existing supply chain frameworks to provide real-time data and enhance risk management. Further research could explore the challenges and benefits of scaling IoT solutions across global supply chains, especially concerning data security and system interoperability.

Sustainability is increasingly becoming a vital component of SCRM, especially with the rising emphasis on Environmental, Social, and Governance (ESG) criteria. Hofmann et al. (2014) argue that integrating sustainability into SCRM is crucial for reducing environmental impact while maintaining supply chain efficiency. Future studies could investigate sustainable practices that not only minimize environmental footprints but also contribute to the long-term resilience of supply chains.

Building resilient supply chains that can withstand various disruptions is another essential focus area. Ivanov and Dolgui (2020) suggest that developing frameworks and strategies to enhance supply chain resilience, particularly in risk identification, mitigation, and recovery, is vital. Research could explore the use of digital twins, scenario planning, and other advanced tools to simulate potential disruptions and assess the effectiveness of resilience strategies.

Geopolitical risks continue to pose significant challenges to global supply chains. He et al. (2013) highlight the impact of geopolitical changes on supply chain dynamics, emphasizing the need for strategies that mitigate risks arising from geopolitical instability. Future research should investigate approaches such as supplier diversification, reshoring of critical production, and the balancing act between globalization and regionalization in supply chain strategies.

Changes in global trade policies and regulations are another area of concern for SCRM. Hilmola et al. (2015) note that shifts in trade policies can have profound effects on supply chains, necessitating adaptive strategies. Future research could explore how businesses can navigate these changes, with a focus on maintaining compliance while optimizing supply chain performance.

Cybersecurity is an increasingly critical issue in supply chain management, particularly as digitalization expands. Kshetri (2014) underscores the growing threat of cyber-attacks on supply chains, advocating for research focused on identifying vulnerabilities and developing robust cybersecurity measures. Further studies could investigate the integration of cybersecurity protocols within supply chain management systems and the role of collaboration among supply chain partners in enhancing cybersecurity.

Data privacy is closely related to cybersecurity, particularly in the context of compliance with regulations such as the General Data Protection Regulation (GDPR). Kshetri (2013) suggests that future research should explore strategies for balancing data privacy with operational efficiency. This could include investigating the impact of emerging data privacy laws on global supply chain operations and the development of privacy-preserving technologies.

Advanced risk assessment models that incorporate modern risk factors are necessary for effective SCRM. Ho et al. (2015) propose that future research should focus on developing sophisticated models to predict and manage supply chain risks more effectively. This could involve the integration of AI and ML in risk modeling, as well as the use of real-time data and analytics to enhance decision-making processes.

Collaborative risk management among supply chain partners can significantly enhance overall resilience. Simangunsong et al. (2012) argue that future research should investigate the benefits and challenges of collaborative approaches in SCRM, including the development of shared risk assessment tools and joint contingency planning. Additionally, studies could explore the role of trust and communication in fostering effective collaboration.

Effective crisis management strategies are essential for maintaining supply chain resilience. Ivanov (2020) suggests that research should explore agile response strategies, the role of digital tools in crisis management, and the integration of crisis management plans into broader SCRM frameworks. Evaluating the long-term impacts of crises, such as pandemics and natural disasters, on supply chains can provide valuable insights for future preparedness (Chopra & Sodhi, 2014).

Leadership plays a crucial role in effective SCRM. Jüttner et al. (2003) propose that research should explore the impact of different leadership styles and strategies on supply chain risk management outcomes. This could include investigating how leadership influences decision-making, risk tolerance, and the development of a risk-aware culture within organizations.

Training programs to enhance risk awareness and preparedness among employees are vital for effective SCRM. Rao and Goldsby (2009) suggest that future research should examine the effectiveness of various training methods, including simulations, workshops, and e-learning, in improving risk management skills. Moreover, studies could explore the role of continuous learning and professional development in maintaining a high level of risk awareness.

Innovation in SCRM practices can significantly enhance risk management capabilities. Pettit et al. (2013) argue that future research should explore new technologies and methods that can be adopted to mitigate supply chain risks, such as AI-driven risk assessment tools, blockchain-based transparency solutions, and IoT-enabled monitoring systems. Further studies could investigate the barriers to innovation in SCRM and strategies for overcoming them.

Startups and SMEs face unique challenges in managing supply chain risks due to limited resources and expertise. Mandal (2013) suggests that future research should investigate specific strategies and tools that can help these businesses manage risks effectively. This could include exploring the role of technology, collaboration, and government support in enhancing SCRM capabilities for smaller enterprises.

Financial aspects of supply chain risk, including currency fluctuations, credit risks, and cash flow management, are crucial for maintaining supply chain stability. Tang (2006) proposes that future research should focus on strategies to manage these financial risks and their impact on supply chain operations. Additionally, studies could explore the role of financial instruments, such as hedging and insurance, in mitigating financial risks.

Economic downturns and uncertainty can significantly impact supply chains, leading to reduced demand, supply disruptions, and financial constraints. Wagner and Bode (2006) suggest that future research should explore strategies to manage supply chain risks in uncertain economic environments, including the development of flexible supply chain models, cost reduction strategies, and diversification of revenue streams.

Finally, combining insights from fields such as engineering, economics, sociology, and environmental science can lead to the development of holistic SCRM strategies. Olson and Wu (2010) argue that interdisciplinary research is essential for addressing complex supply chain risks, particularly those that span multiple domains. Future studies could encourage such interdisciplinary approaches to develop more comprehensive and innovative solutions for managing supply chain risks.

CONCLUSION

In conclusion, supply chain risk management (SCRM) in the business sector encompasses a wide range of risks that may manifest at various points within the supply chain, each with its characteristics and complexities. The sustainability and efficiency of a supply chain are largely determined by the effectiveness of the risk management tools employed and the accuracy with which risks are assessed. The successful application of a comprehensive risk assessment mechanism can lead to the development of a resilient delivery system, characterized by efficient control over goods transportation and the seamless integration of various supply chain components into a unified information network, all tailored to the needs and priorities of consumers.

However, it is important to recognize that uncertainty in the supply chain poses significant challenges, making it difficult to guarantee the complete fulfillment of customer obligations. A key insight from this analysis is that addressing global risks in supply chains requires collective action and collaboration among all stakeholders. As such, the implementation of a universal risk assessment mechanism should result in the creation of more robust tools to counter contemporary threats, ensuring that supply chains can adapt to and mitigate risks effectively.

In today's highly competitive international environment, the necessity of applying realistic and context-specific risk assessment methods cannot be overstated. These methods must align with actual business processes and provide actionable insights. When appropriately selected, a supply chain risk assessment tool can serve as a vital instrument for evaluating the effectiveness of SCRM strategies, offering valuable perspectives to all participants involved in the supply chain. Ultimately, the strategic application of these tools and methodologies will enhance the resilience, sustainability, and overall performance of supply chains in the modern business landscape.

REFERENCES

Ben-Daya, M., Hassini, E., & Bahroun, Z. (2019). Internet of things and supply chain management: A literature review. *International Journal of Production Research*, 57(15-16), 4719–4742. DOI: 10.1080/00207543.2017.1402140

Chopra, S., & Sodhi, M. S. (2014). Reducing the risk of supply chain disruptions. *MIT Sloan Management Review*, 55(3), 73–80.

Christopher, M., & Peck, H. (2004). Building the resilient supply chain. *International Journal of Logistics Management*, 15(2), 1–14. DOI: 10.1108/09574090410700275

Cucchiella, F., & Gastaldi, M. (2006). Risk management in supply chain: A real option approach. *Journal of Manufacturing Technology Management*, 17(6), 700–720. DOI: 10.1108/17410380610678756

Dubey, R., Gunasekaran, A., Childe, S. J., Blome, C., Papadopoulos, T., & Singh, T. (2020). Big data and predictive analytics and manufacturing performance: Integrating institutional theory, resource-based view and big data culture. *British Journal of Management*, 31(2), 341–361. DOI: 10.1111/1467-8551.12355

He, Y., Keung Lai, K., Sun, H., & Chen, Y. (2013). The impact of supplier integration on customer integration and new product performance: The mediating role of manufacturing flexibility under trust theory. *Industrial Management & Data Systems*, 113(3), 367–388. DOI: 10.1108/02635571311312640

Hilmola, O. P., Hilletofth, P., & Kovács, G. (2015). Supply chain management and enterprise resource planning systems: A Finnish perspective. *Journal of Manufacturing Technology Management*, 26(5), 728–755. DOI: 10.1108/JMTM-11-2013-0143

Ho, W., Zheng, T., Yildiz, H., & Talluri, S. (2015). Supply chain risk management: A literature review. *International Journal of Production Research*, 53(16), 5031–5069. DOI: 10.1080/00207543.2015.1030467

Hofmann, H., Busse, C., Bode, C., & Henke, M. (2014).

Kshetri, N. (2013). *Cybercrime and cybersecurity in the global south*. Springer. DOI: 10.1057/9781137021946

Kshetri, N. (2014). The impacts of cloud computing and big data applications on developing world-based smallholder farmers.

Kshetri, N. (2018). 1 Blockchain's roles in meeting key supply chain management objectives. *International Journal of Information Management*, 39, 80–89. DOI: 10.1016/j.ijinfomgt.2017.12.005

Malhotra, M. K., & Grover, V. (1998). An assessment of survey research in POM: From constructs to theory. *Journal of Operations Management*, 16(4), 407–425. DOI: 10.1016/S0272-6963(98)00021-7

Mandal, S., Sarathy, R., Korasiga, V. R., Bhattacharya, S., & Dastidar, S. G. (2016). Achieving supply chain resilience: The contribution of logistics and supply chain capabilities. *International Journal of Disaster Resilience in the Built Environment*, 7(5), 544–562. DOI: 10.1108/IJDRBE-04-2016-0010

Olson, D. L., & Wu, D. D. (2010). A review of enterprise risk management in supply chain. *Kybernetes*, 39(5), 694–706. DOI: 10.1108/03684921011043198

Pettit, T. J., Croxton, K. L., & Fiksel, J. (2013). Ensuring supply chain resilience: Development and implementation of an assessment tool. *Journal of Business Logistics*, 34(1), 46–76. DOI: 10.1111/jbl.12009

Rao, S., & Goldsby, T. J. (2009). Supply chain risks: A review and typology. *International Journal of Logistics Management*, 20(1), 97–123. DOI: 10.1108/09574090910954864

Tang, C. S. (2006). Perspectives in supply chain risk management. *International Journal of Production Economics*, 103(2), 451–488. DOI: 10.1016/j.ijpe.2005.12.006

Wagner, S. M., & Bode, C. (2006). An empirical investigation into supply chain vulnerability. *Journal of Purchasing and Supply Management*, 12(6), 301–312. DOI: 10.1016/j.pursup.2007.01.004

Chapter 15
The Impact of FinTech on Entrepreneurial Intentions Among Young Indian Entrepreneurs Using Crowdfunding, Blockchain, and Mobile Payments

Mushtaq Ahmad Shah
https://orcid.org/0000-0002-3177-9622
Lovely Professional University, India

ABSTRACT

This study examines the influence of FinTech technologies like crowdfunding, blockchain, and mobile payments on the entrepreneurial intentions of young Indian entrepreneurs. A quantitative research design was used to collect data from 150 respondents using a structured questionnaire. The study used exploratory factor analysis (EFA) and reliability tests to validate the components and analyze the links between these technologies and entrepreneurial inclinations. The findings show that crowdfunding lowers financial obstacles and raises entrepreneurial confidence, blockchain improves transparency and operational efficiency, and mobile payments increase transaction convenience and consumer reach. These findings demonstrate FinTech's major role in promoting entrepreneurship among young Indians.

INTRODUCTION

The Indian government has acknowledged the crucial role of technology entrepreneurs in driving India's sustained growth in the digital age, leading to the launch of various initiatives since 2016. These initiatives include programs like Startup India, aimed at fostering entrepreneurship and innovation Verma (2022), as well as the Technology Entrepreneurship (TE) ecosystem to support the evolution of techno-entrepreneurial firms in India (Sharma & Ritu, 2023). The emphasis is on three major areas:

DOI: 10.4018/979-8-3693-4046-2.ch015

liberating entrepreneurship from bureaucratic barriers, providing institutional frameworks for innovation, and assisting young innovators and businesses. Progress is already being made, with around 10 million young entrepreneurs benefiting from the Skill India programme each year, receiving specialised training in new technological areas such as artificial intelligence, IoT, robotics, and big data analytics, all of which will be required for tomorrow's corporations. Enabled by these emerging technologies, FinTech has significantly transformed the global financial services industry, offering numerous benefits to entrepreneurs (Taherdoost, 2023).

India is leading the FinTech adoption race with an adoption rate of 87%, substantially higher than the world average of 64% (Das & Pachoni 2022). The promising Indian FinTech market is expected to reach $1 trillion in AUM and $200 billion in revenue by 2030. Over the past decade, financial technology (fintech) has significantly transformed the global economic landscape, with a notable impact on emerging markets like India. Fintech innovations, including mobile payments, online banking, blockchain technology, and artificial intelligence in financial services, have played a crucial role in enhancing financial inclusion and empowering young Indian entrepreneurs to overcome historical financial barriers and compete globally. Research highlights the synergy between online payment development, P2P lending, artificial intelligence, and blockchain, emphasizing their potential to revolutionize the financial industry. (Zhao, 2023). The evolution of fintech reflects a broader trend of technological disruption in the financial sector, offering new opportunities for innovation and growth among young entrepreneurs (Rîmniceanu, 2023). This transformation is particularly evident in emerging markets like India, where a burgeoning population of young entrepreneurs is leveraging fintech innovations to overcome historical financial barriers. Fintech encompasses a wide range of applications, from mobile payments and online banking to blockchain technology and artificial intelligence in financial services. These advancements have not only facilitated greater financial inclusion but have also empowered a new generation of Indian entrepreneurs to innovate and compete on a global scale.

The current landscape of fintech in India is characterized by rapid growth and diversification. Key technologies driving this evolution include mobile payment platforms like Paytm and Google Pay, peer-to-peer lending, crowdfunding, digital wallets, and blockchain-based solutions. Mobile payments, in particular, have seen widespread adoption, with the Unified Payments Interface (UPI) becoming a cornerstone of India's digital payment infrastructure. Furthermore, advancements in artificial intelligence and machine learning are enhancing risk assessment, fraud detection, and personalized financial services, making them more accessible and efficient (Han et al., 2023). The integration of these technologies is transforming how young entrepreneurs manage their finances, access capital, and engage with customers, fostering an environment ripe for innovation and economic growth.

Despite the significant progress, several theoretical gaps remain in understanding the impact of fintech on young Indian entrepreneurs. There is a need for a comprehensive framework that captures the relationship between different fintech innovations and entrepreneurial activities. There is limited research on the differential impact of fintech across various demographic and socioeconomic groups among young entrepreneurs. This chapter aims to address these gaps by providing a nuanced analysis of the fintech landscape as it pertains to young Indian entrepreneurs. This book chapter explores the changing environment of fintech ecosystems, with a focus on how advances in cutting-edge technology like as crowdfunding, Blockchain and Mobile Payment influence entrepreneurial intention. By achieving these objectives, the research seeks to offer a holistic understanding of how cutting-edge technologies are shaping the entrepreneurial ecosystem in India. This chapter not only aims to fill the existing knowledge gaps but also aspires to contribute to the broader discourse on fintech and entrepreneurship in emerging markets. By focusing on the unique context of young Indian entrepreneurs, it highlights the transformative potential of fintech while providing actionable insights for policymakers, practitioners, and researchers interested in the intersection of technology, finance, and entrepreneurship.

Background of the study

Entrepreneurship, particularly in the digital businesses, has seen significant technological growth since the 1980s. Internet, social media, mobile communications, big data, cloud computing, blockchain, AI, IoT, etc. have created a favourable technological ecology for entrepreneurship (Satjaharuthai & Lakkhongkha, 2023). As a result, digital businesses have turned to business analytics, data homogeneity, re-programmability, and other self-referential results to foster entrepreneurship creativity. Many current digital innovations have been aided by entrepreneurship-facilitated technological resources. A typical business model on a digital platform offers new opportunities for value creation and entrepreneurship. Digital businesses have successfully bridged the physical divide and motivated entrepreneurs through hybrid work environments including work from home. Innovative business platforms that financial companies use to develop new products, services, processes, and models through incremental and disruptive innovations form the core concepts of the fintech environment (Puschmann, 2017). For example, the application of emerging technologies such as decentralized distributed ledgers (blockchains) and peer-to-peer (P2P) systems is transforming the financial sector by leveraging new capabilities (Gozman, Liebenau & Mangan, 2018). Leong and Sung (2018) broadly define fintech as an innovative ecosystem that enhances financial services by integrating technology into business scenarios, adopting disruptive concepts and models that revolutionize the entire industry. Fintech provides all the services traditionally offered by banks, but with significantly reduced margins. Focusing on fintech as a component of the entrepreneurial ecosystem, Santoso, & Oetomo (2016) pointed out the use of information technology significantly influences entrepreneurial intentions. Their research indicated that Indonesian students with a solid understanding and usage of information technology exhibit higher entrepreneurial intentions compared to those without such knowledge. Additionally, having financial capital and a strong entrepreneurial intention further boosts these intentions. Conversely, a lack of capital is one of the primary barriers preventing students from pursuing entrepreneurial ventures

Crowdfunding and Entrepreneurial Intention

Crowdfunding for business involves raising small amounts of money from a large number of individuals through online platforms, such as Kickstarter or GoFundMe, to support new business endeavours (Dubey et al., 2023). This method broadens the pool of potential investors beyond traditional sources like venture capitalists, allowing entrepreneurs to access necessary financing for their ventures. Crowdfunding plays a significant role in shaping entrepreneurial intention by influencing various factors. Studies have shown that factors like the need for achievement and the desire for financial power positively impact entrepreneurs' intention to adopt crowdfunding (Ndumbaro, Mofulu, & Ndaki 2023). Additionally, backer engagement and value creation are crucial aspects that influence backer funding intention in reward-based crowdfunding, highlighting the importance of project novelty and platform interactivity (Wu et al., 2023). Moreover, the perceived benefits of crowdfunding, including economic benefits, convenience, and social support, significantly influence an entrepreneur's intention to use crowdfunding platforms, with gender moderation showing an insignificant relationship in this context (Jamil et al., 2023). Furthermore, the value co-creation through knowledge sharing and interaction between backers and campaign actors is essential for backers' participation in crowdfunding initiatives, emphasizing the experiential benefits for campaign success (Gangi et al., 2023). These findings underscore the relationship between crowdfunding and entrepreneurial intention, showcasing the multifaceted impact of crowdfunding on entrepreneurial endeavours (Polas et al., 2022).

Crowdfunding has emerged as a pivotal tool for fostering entrepreneurial intention, particularly among young and aspiring entrepreneurs. By leveraging online platforms to pool small amounts of capital from a large number of individuals, crowdfunding democratizes the fundraising process, making it accessible to entrepreneurs who might otherwise struggle to secure traditional funding. This approach not only provides the necessary financial resources but also validates the market demand for the proposed products or services. Studies have shown that crowdfunding can significantly enhance entrepreneurial intention by reducing the barriers to entry and providing a proof-of-concept. For instance, the ability to attract backers and raise funds through platforms like Kickstarter or Indiegogo offers entrepreneurs early-stage validation and market feedback, which are critical for refining their business ideas. Furthermore, the social aspect of crowdfunding, where entrepreneurs can directly engage with potential customers and supporters, fosters a sense of community and belonging, which can be highly motivating for entrepreneurs. Moreover, the transparency and accountability inherent in crowdfunding campaigns compel entrepreneurs to meticulously plan and present their business ideas, thereby enhancing their business acumen and strategic thinking. This process not only builds their confidence but also prepares them for future interactions with investors and stakeholders. Moreover, the success of a crowdfunding campaign can serve as a powerful signal to other investors and financial institutions, potentially opening doors to additional funding opportunities.

Mobile Payments and Entrepreneurial Intention

Mobile payments, as a key component of financial technology (FinTech), play a significant role in influencing entrepreneurial intention. Research indicates that mobile money (MoMo) positively impacts women's entrepreneurial intention by serving as a proxy for FinTech adoption, while also fostering financial inclusion (Haq & Dawood 2023). Factors such as crowdfunding, blockchain, and knowledge about FinTech contribute positively to entrepreneurial intention in emerging economies like Tunisia, showcasing the potential of FinTech ecosystems to influence decision-making processes (Festa et al., 2022). Additionally, factors like service quality, perceived ease of use, security, and trust influence consumers' continuance intention to use mobile payments, emphasizing the importance of these aspects in driving adoption and usage of mobile payment services (Fadhil & Subriadi, 2023)

The advent and proliferation of mobile payments have profoundly reshaped the financial landscape, particularly influencing entrepreneurial activities. With the increasing accessibility of the Internet through smartphones, the digital economy has experienced significant transformations, and mobile payments stand out as a critical component of this shift. Telecom operators, financial institutions, and merchants have rapidly advanced in promoting mobile services, leveraging the ubiquitous presence of mobile phones to enhance the adoption and utilization of these services (Mishra, Walsh & Srivastava (2022). The integration of mobile payments into daily transactions has simplified financial processes for entrepreneurs, allowing them to conduct business more efficiently and reach a broader customer base. This technology enables instant, secure transactions, reducing the dependency on cash and traditional banking systems, which can be particularly beneficial in regions with limited banking infrastructure.

As a result, mobile payments can lower entry barriers for new businesses, facilitating entrepreneurial ventures by providing a seamless and accessible financial ecosystem (Braido Klein & Papaleo 2021).

Despite the potential risks associated with mobile payments, including security breaches and fraud, their overall impact on entrepreneurial intention is largely positive. Mobile payments provide entrepreneurs with a robust tool for financial management and customer engagement, fostering innovation and business growth. The ability to quickly and efficiently process transactions enhances operational efficiency and customer satisfaction, crucial elements for entrepreneurial success.

Blockchain and Entrepreneurial Intention

Blockchain technology plays a significant role in influencing entrepreneurial intention by fostering innovation and sustainability. Studies have shown that blockchain technology positively impacts entrepreneurial ecosystems by enhancing green innovation practices, leading to a sustainable green economy (Festa et al., 2022). Additionally, the intention to use blockchain technology mediates the relationship between sustainability orientation and the adoption of green innovation, further promoting green economic sustainability (Polas et al., 2022). Furthermore, blockchain's influence extends to retail supply chains, where it enhances transparency, authenticity, and trust, ultimately affecting employees' behavioral intention to adopt blockchain technology in the retail sector (Ruangkanjanase et al., 2023). Blockchain technology has the potential to positively influence entrepreneurial intention by improving trust, security, and relationship quality, thereby encouraging its adoption in various sectors and entrepreneurial endeavours (Mukherjee et al., 2023). Blockchain technology has emerged as a transformative force within the entrepreneurial ecosystem, significantly influencing entrepreneurial intention and the broader landscape of business innovation. At its core, blockchain is a decentralized digital ledger that ensures the integrity and transparency of transactions through a network of distributed nodes. This technology facilitates the tokenization of assets, allowing them to be represented digitally and traded securely and transparently. The implications of blockchain extend far beyond simple financial transactions, impacting various facets of entrepreneurship, from fundraising to operational efficiency.

Blockchain technology plays a crucial role in shaping entrepreneurial structures and fostering new business models, particularly through the emergence of decentralized autonomous organizations (Zheng, Huang & Xu 2023). By leveraging blockchain, entrepreneurs can decentralize ownership structures, enhance value propositions through nonfungible tokens (NFTs), and implement smart contract-enabled consensus mechanisms, thereby promoting innovation and competition in the market (Lee & Kim, 2023). These dApps can disrupt traditional business models by providing more equitable and efficient alternatives, thus driving entrepreneurial activity and growth. Moreover, blockchain's ability to streamline supply chain management and ensure the provenance of goods can significantly enhance operational efficiency for entrepreneurs. By providing an immutable record of transactions, blockchain enables better tracking of products and materials, reducing fraud, and improving traceability. This capability is particularly valuable in industries such as agriculture, pharmaceuticals, and luxury goods, where authenticity and origin are critical. However, the widespread adoption of blockchain is not without challenges. Issues such as scalability, regulatory uncertainty, and the technical complexity of blockchain systems can pose significant hurdles. Entrepreneurs must navigate these challenges to fully harness the potential of blockchain technology.

Data analysis and discussion

To understand the impact of Fintech and Cutting-Edge Technology's Impact on Young Indian Entrepreneurs. This study adopts a quantitative research design to investigate the impact of crowdfunding, blockchain, and mobile payments on the entrepreneurial intentions of young Indian entrepreneurs. The study employed a purposive sampling technique to select 150 young entrepreneurs from various regions in India. The participants were chosen based on their engagement with FinTech technologies and their entrepreneurial activities. The sample comprised individuals aged between 18 and 35 years, ensuring a focus on young entrepreneurs. The demographic details of the respondents were collected, including gender, age, education level, and experience in leading entrepreneurial projects.

Data Collection: Data was collected using a structured questionnaire designed to measure the impact of crowdfunding, blockchain, and mobile payments on entrepreneurial intention. The questionnaire consisted of three sections, each addressing one of the three FinTech technologies. Each section included multiple items measured on a five-point Likert scale, ranging from 1 (strongly disagree) to 5 (strongly agree). The questionnaire items were developed based on a comprehensive review of existing literature and refined through a pilot test with a small group of respondents to ensure clarity and relevance. The final questionnaire included 16 items after dropping less relevant items based on initial factor analysis. The items focused on various aspects such as ease of securing funding, market validation, transparency, security, and operational efficiency.

Validity and Reliability: To ensure the validity and reliability of the questionnaire, several steps were taken. Content validity was established through expert review and pilot testing. Construct validity was assessed using factor analysis, and internal consistency was measured using Cronbach's Alpha. The Kaiser-Meyer-Olkin (KMO) measure and Bartlett's Test of Sphericity were conducted to confirm the suitability of the data for factor analysis. The KMO value was 0.888, indicating strong sampling adequacy, and Bartlett's Test was significant ($p < 0.000$), confirming the data's suitability.

Factor Analysis

Exploratory factor analysis (EFA) was performed using Principal Component Analysis (PCA) with Varimax rotation to identify the underlying factors influencing entrepreneurial intentions. The analysis aimed to reduce the data into meaningful factors and to validate the constructs measured by the questionnaire. Items with low factor loadings or cross-loadings were removed to ensure clear factor structure. The final factor analysis resulted in three distinct components: Crowdfunding, Blockchain, and Mobile Payments. Descriptive statistics were used to summarize the demographic characteristics of the respondents. Inferential statistics, including factor analysis and reliability analysis, were employed to test the hypotheses and validate the constructs. The reliability of the constructs was assessed using Cronbach's Alpha, with values exceeding 0.85 for all factors, indicating high internal consistency.

Demographic Profile of the respondent

This questionnaire was administered to 150 respondents to collect data on the impact of crowdfunding, blockchain, and mobile payments on young entrepreneurial intention. The table 1 given presents the demographic details of respondents in three key aspects: gender, age, and education.

Table 1. Demographic Details

Gender of Respondents		
Gender	**Frequency**	**Percentage**
Male	118	78.50%
Female	32	21.50%
Total	150	100%
Age of Respondents		
Age Group	Frequency	Percentage
18-24 years	24	16.00%
25-29 years	87	58.10%
30-34 years	27	18.00%
35+ years	12	8.00%
Total	150	100%
Education of Respondents		
Education Level	Frequency	Percentage
Secondary School	24	15.75%
High School	23	15.37%
Diploma/Bachelor's	90	59.96%
Postgraduate	13	8.92%
Total	150	100%

As evident from the above table out of the total 150 respondents, 118 (78.50%) identified as male, while 32 (21.50%) identified as female. The majority of respondents, 87 (58.10%), fell within the age group of 25-29 years, followed by 27 (18.00%) in the 30-34 years age bracket. A smaller proportion of respondents were distributed across the age groups of 18-24 years (24 respondents, 16.00%) and 35+ years (12, 8.00%). Among the 150 respondents, the highest proportion, 90 (59.96%), held a Diploma or Bachelor's degree. This was followed by 24 (15.75%) respondents with education up to Secondary School level and 23 (15.37%) with education up to High School level. A smaller portion of respondents, 13 (8.92%), were classified as Postgraduates. The above tables provide a comprehensive snapshot of the demographic composition of the respondent population, offering insights into their gender distribution, age distribution, and educational backgrounds

Latent construct and associated items

A literature review was used to identify the items for crowdfunding, blockchain, and mobile payments. The latent constructions and items are labelled in table 2. The questionnaire on five-point Likert scale was used to assess the impact of crowdfunding, blockchain, and mobile payments on young entrepreneurial intention. Respondents were requested to indicate their level of agreement with each statement, where 1 = Strongly Disagree, 2 = Disagree, 3 = Neutral, 4 = Agree, and 5 = Strongly Agree.

Table 2. Latent construct and associated items

Item	Statement	
Crowdfunding		
CF1	Crowdfunding has made it easier for me to secure initial funding for my business idea.	
CF2	The success of my crowdfunding campaign has increased my confidence in pursuing entrepreneurship.	
CF3	Crowdfunding platforms provide valuable market validation for my business concepts.	
CF4	The ability to reach a broad audience through crowdfunding motivates me to innovate.	
CF5	The feedback from backers on crowdfunding platforms helps improve my business idea.	
CF6	Crowdfunding reduces the financial barriers to starting a new business.	
Blockchain		
BC1	Blockchain technology enhances the transparency of business transactions, increasing my trust in the process.	
BC2	The use of blockchain simplifies the process of raising capital for my startup.	
BC3	Blockchain provides a secure way to manage and verify business records.	
BC4	The decentralized nature of blockchain reduces my reliance on traditional financial institutions.	
BC5	Blockchain technology opens new business model opportunities that I am eager to explore.	
BC6	The implementation of smart contracts through blockchain makes business operations more efficient.	
Mobile Payments		
MP1	Mobile payments have made financial transactions more convenient for my business.	
MP2	The ease of using mobile payments increases my willingness to engage in entrepreneurial activities.	
MP3	Mobile payment systems enhance customer satisfaction by providing flexible payment options.	
MP4	The security features of mobile payments increase my confidence in handling business finances.	
MP5	Mobile payments reduce the costs associated with traditional banking.	
MP6	The widespread adoption of mobile payments makes it easier to reach a larger customer base.	

Factor Analysis

Factor analysis is a statistical method used to identify underlying relationships between measured variables. It aims to reduce data dimensionality by grouping correlated variables into factors. This helps in understanding the structure of the data and identifying key constructs. Before proceeding to factor analysis, KMO and Bartlett's Test was conducted to understand weather the dataset is suitable for factor analysis.

Table 3. KMO and Bartlett's Test

Kaiser-Meyer-Olkin Measure of Sampling Adequacy.		.888
Bartlett's Test of Sphericity	Approx. Chi-Square	5186.047
	Df	105
	Sig.	.000

The KMO value is 0.888, which falls into the range of "admirable" according to Kaiser (1974). Values between 0.8 and 0.9 indicate that the sample is very adequate for factor analysis. The Bartlett's Test of Sphericity shows a high chi-square value of 5186.047 with 105 degrees of freedom and a significance level of 0.000. This test is significant ($p < 0.05$), indicating that the variables are sufficiently correlated for factor analysis.

The results of the KMO and Bartlett's Test indicate (table 3) that the dataset is highly suitable for factor analysis. The KMO value of 0.888 signifies strong sampling adequacy, suggesting that there is a significant amount of shared variance among the items. The significant Bartlett's Test of Sphericity confirms that the correlations among variables are appropriate for conducting a factor analysis table 4, validating the adequacy of the dataset for extracting meaningful factors.

Table 4. Rotated Component Matrix

	Component		
	1	2	3
CF1			.860
CF2			.781
CF4			.844
CF6			.761
BC1		.783	
BC2		.870	
BC3		.885	
BC4		.882	
BC6		.831	
MP1	.857		
MP2	.847		
MP3	.867		
MP4	.880		
MP5	.870		
MP6	.828		

Extraction Method: Principal Component Analysis.
Rotation Method: Varimax with Kaiser Normalization.
a. Rotation converged in 4 iterations.

Discussion on extracted components

Component 1: Mobile Payments

This component reflects the impact of mobile payments on entrepreneurial activities, emphasizing convenience, security, cost reduction, and customer satisfaction. Mobile payments have made financial transactions more convenient for businesses (0.857). The ease of using mobile payments increases willingness to engage in entrepreneurial activities (0.847). Additionally, mobile payment systems enhance customer satisfaction by providing flexible payment options (0.867). The security features of mobile payments increase confidence in handling business finances (0.880). Moreover, mobile payments reduce the costs associated with traditional banking (0.870). Finally, the widespread adoption of mobile payments makes it easier to reach a larger customer base (Loading: 0.828) This component captures the impact of mobile payments on entrepreneurial activities, highlighting convenience, security, cost reduction, and customer satisfaction as key factors. These aspects are critical for entrepreneurs as they navigate financial transactions, manage business finances securely, reduce operational costs, and expand their market reach, all of which are facilitated by mobile payment solutions. The high factor loadings suggest that these variables are strong indicators of the positive influence of mobile payments on entrepreneurial activities.

Component 2: Blockchain

This component emphasizes the role of blockchain technology in enhancing transparency, security, and efficiency in business operations, as well as reducing reliance on traditional financial institutions. Blockchain technology increases trust in business transactions through enhanced transparency (0.783). It simplifies the process of raising capital for startups (0.870) and provides a secure method for managing and verifying business records (0.885). The decentralized nature of blockchain reduces reliance on traditional financial institutions (0.882), and the implementation of smart contracts improves the efficiency of business operations (0.831). This component emphasizes the role of blockchain technology in enhancing transparency, security, and efficiency in business operations, as well as reducing reliance on traditional financial institutions.

Component 3: Crowdfunding

This component highlights the role of crowdfunding in facilitating entrepreneurial activities by making it easier to secure initial funding, boosting confidence, and reducing financial barriers. Crowdfunding simplifies securing initial funding for business ideas (0.860). The success of crowdfunding campaigns increases confidence in pursuing entrepreneurship (0.781) and motivates innovation by enabling access to a broad audience (0.844). Additionally, crowdfunding reduces financial barriers to starting a new business (0.761). This component reflects the impact of crowdfunding on securing initial funding, boosting entrepreneurial confidence, fostering innovation, and reducing financial barriers for new ventures

The factor analysis results, after reducing the items, reveal three distinct components that are well-defined and significant. The mobile payments component highlights the practical benefits of mobile payment systems, the blockchain component underscores the advantages of blockchain technology in enhancing business operations, and the crowdfunding component demonstrates the positive effects of crowdfunding on entrepreneurial activities. Each component is supported by high loadings, indicating that the items within each factor are highly correlated and represent their respective constructs effectively.

Reliability

The Cronbach's Alpha values for all three latent variables (Crowdfunding, Blockchain, and Mobile Payments) was calculated to check internal consistency and reliability of the respective items.

Table 5. Cronbach's Alpha

Latent Variable	Extracted Items	Cronbach's Alpha
Crowdfunding (CF)	4	0.859
Blockchain (BC)	5	0.92
Mobile Payments (MP)	6	0.928

The Cronbach's Alpha values for all three latent variables (Crowdfunding, Blockchain, and Mobile Payments) indicate strong internal consistency and reliability of the respective items table 5. This ensures that the items within each factor are consistently measuring the intended constructs, making the results of the factor analysis robust and dependable.

CONCLUSION OF THE STUDY

This study provides an in-depth investigation of how FinTech innovations such as mobile payments, blockchain, and crowdfunding affect young Indian entrepreneurs' intentions to start their own businesses. The findings demonstrate how these technologies have the capacity to transform the entrepreneurial environment by making it more accessible, effective, and creative. These innovative tools allow young entrepreneurs to get past traditional obstacles including lack of trust, operational inefficiencies, and cash availability. The demographic analysis indicated a well-educated sample, predominantly male and aged between 25 and 29, leading projects primarily in India. The high KMO value (0.888) and significant Bartlett's Test of Sphericity ($p < 0.000$) confirmed the suitability of the data for factor analysis, ensuring the robustness of the findings.

The factor analysis revealed three distinct components that influence entrepreneurial intentions: the convenience and security of mobile payments, the transparency and efficiency of blockchain technology, and the financial accessibility provided by crowdfunding. The reliability of these constructs was validated with Cronbach's Alpha values exceeding 0.85 for all factors, indicating strong internal consistency and reliability of the measurement items. The study highlights the critical role of mobile payments in making financial transactions more convenient and secure, thus reducing operational costs and expanding customer reach. Blockchain technology emerged as a key factor in enhancing trust through transparent and secure transactions, simplifying capital raising processes, and enabling innovative business models. Crowdfunding was identified as a significant enabler of entrepreneurial activities by reducing financial barriers and providing market validation and feedback, thereby boosting entrepreneurial confidence and motivation.

Future Scope and Recommendations

The study's conclusions provide various directions for further investigation. First of all, making the sample larger and include a more varied population might improve the results' generalizability. A more thorough knowledge of the influence of FinTech technology on entrepreneurial ambitions may be obtained by including entrepreneurs from different industries, geographical areas, and educational backgrounds. These kinds of research might monitor the development of company owners over time and offer insights into the ways that consistent usage of mobile payments, blockchain, and crowdfunding affects the expansion, scalability, and sustainability of businesses. Additionally, examining the relationship between these technologies and other factors such as regulatory environments, market conditions, and cultural influences can offer a more nuanced understanding of their impact. There is also a need for more in-depth qualitative research to explore the experiences and perspectives of young entrepreneurs using these technologies.

Policymakers and educators can play critical roles in creating an entrepreneurial ecosystem that maximises the benefits of FinTech. Policies that promote the development and use of these technologies, such as advantageous regulatory frameworks, innovation incentives, and investments in digital infrastructure, are critical. Educational institutions should include FinTech literacy into their curricula, providing future entrepreneurs with the information and skills needed to properly employ these technologies. This study reveals the strong favourable influence of crowdsourcing, blockchain, and mobile payments on youthful entrepreneurial intents in India. It establishes a solid platform for future research, policy development, and educational programmes targeted at supporting a thriving and inclusive entrepreneurial environment by giving practical insights and compelling empirical data. The continuous research and development of FinTech technologies will be critical in realising the full potential of young entrepreneurs, generating economic growth, and fostering innovation.

REFERENCES

Alshebami, A. S. (2022). Crowdfunding platforms as a substitute financing source for young Saudi entrepreneurs: Empirical evidence. *SAGE Open*, 12(3), 21582440221126511. DOI: 10.1177/21582440221126511

Braido, G., Klein, A., & Papaleo, G. (2021). Facilitators and barriers faced by mobile payment fintechs in the Brazilian context. *BBR.Brazilian Business Review*, 18(1), 22–44. DOI: 10.15728/bbr.2021.18.1.2

Das, G., & Pachoni, P. (2022). Pduamt. *Business Review*.

Dubey, A. K., Shingte, S. C., Siddiqui, M. S., & Patil, S. (2023, May). Crowdfunding using Blockchain for Startups and Investors. In *2023 7th International Conference on Intelligent Computing and Control Systems (ICICCS)* (pp. 1400-1405). IEEE. DOI: 10.1109/ICICCS56967.2023.10142310

Fadhil, M. K., & Subriadi, A. P. (2023, February). Factor Affecting Behavior Intention To Use Mobile Payment Adoption: An Analysis Of Literature Review. In *2023 International Conference on Computer Science, Information Technology and Engineering (ICCoSITE)* (pp. 847-852). IEEE. DOI: 10.1109/ICCoSITE57641.2023.10127839

Festa, G., Elbahri, S., Cuomo, M. T., Ossorio, M., & Rossi, M. (2022). FinTech ecosystem as influencer of young entrepreneurial intentions: Empirical findings from Tunisia. *Journal of Intellectual Capital*, 24(1), 205–226. DOI: 10.1108/JIC-08-2021-0220

Gangi, F., Daniele, L. M., Scuotto, V., & Tani, M. (2023). Uncovering Backers' Intention to Participate in Reward-Based Crowdfunding: The Role of Value Cocreation. *IEEE Transactions on Engineering Management*.

Gozman, D., Liebenau, J., & Mangan, J. (2018). The innovation mechanisms of fintech start-ups: Insights from SWIFT's innotribe competition. *Journal of Management Information Systems*, 35(1), 145–179. DOI: 10.1080/07421222.2018.1440768

Han, Y., Chen, J., Dou, M., Wang, J., & Feng, K. (2023). The Impact of Artificial Intelligence on the Financial Services Industry. *Academic Journal of Management and Social Sciences*, 2(3), 83–85. DOI: 10.54097/ajmss.v2i3.8741

HAQ, Z., & Dawood, M. (2023). Does FinTech promote entrepreneurial intention among women? Studying the mediating role of financial inclusion

Jamil, S., Shah, F., Khan, S., & Imran, I. (2023). The The influence of potential outcome on entrepreneurs' decisions to participate in Crowdfunding in Pakistan (Karachi). *International journal of social science & entrepreneurship, 3*(1), 1-24.

Lee, G., & Kim, T. (2023). An Economic Appraisal of Blockchain's Impact on Finance and Market Competition. *Journal of Student Research*, 12(2). Advance online publication. DOI: 10.47611/jsrhs.v12i2.4407

Leong, K., & Sung, A. (2018). FinTech (Financial Technology): What is it and how to use technologies to create business value in fintech way? *International Journal of Innovation, Management and Technology*, 9(2), 74–78. DOI: 10.18178/ijimt.2018.9.2.791

Mishra, V., Walsh, I., & Srivastava, A. (2022). Merchants' adoption of mobile payment in emerging economies: The case of unorganised retailers in India. *European Journal of Information Systems*, 31(1), 74–90. DOI: 10.1080/0960085X.2021.1978338

Mukherjee, S., Baral, M. M., Lavanya, B. L., Nagariya, R., Singh Patel, B., & Chittipaka, V. (2023). Intentions to adopt the blockchain: Investigation of the retail supply chain. *Management Decision*, 61(5), 1320–1351. DOI: 10.1108/MD-03-2022-0369

Ndumbaro, F., Mofulu, G., & Ndaki, D. P. (2023). Extrinsic Motivation toward Entrepreneurs' Intention to Adopt Crowdfunding: The Case of Kiva Lending Crowdfunding. *African Journal of Innovation and Entrepreneurship*, 2(1), 103–128. DOI: 10.31920/2753-314X/2023/v2n1a5

Polas, M. R. H., Kabir, A. I., Sohel-Uz-Zaman, A. S. M., Karim, R., & Tabash, M. I. (2022). Blockchain technology as a game changer for green innovation: Green entrepreneurship as a roadmap to green economic sustainability in Peru. *Journal of Open Innovation*, 8(2), 62. DOI: 10.3390/joitmc8020062

Puschmann, T. (2017). Fintech. *Business & Information Systems Engineering*, 59(1), 69–76. DOI: 10.1007/s12599-017-0464-6

Rîmniceanu, R. (2023, May). Innovation in the Financial Sector (FinTech): Paradigms, Causes, Effects and Perspectives. In *Proceedings of the International Conference on Cybersecurity and Cybercrime-2023* (pp. 21-33). Asociatia Romana pentru Asigurarea Securitatii Informatiei. DOI: 10.19107/CYBERCON.2023.03

Ruangkanjanases, A., Qhal, E. M. A., Alfawaz, K. M., & Hariguna, T. (2023). Examining the antecedents of blockchain usage intention: An integrated research framework. *Sustainability (Basel)*, 15(4), 3500. DOI: 10.3390/su15043500

Santoso, D. S., & Oetomo, B. (2016). Relationship between entrepreneurial skills, entrepreneurial orientation, and information technology to entrepreneurship intention: Cases in Indonesia. *International Journal of Management Sciences and Business Research*, 5(4).

Satjaharuthai, K., & Lakkhongkha, K. (2023). The Role of Entrepreneurs in Driving the Success of their Businesses in the Digital Era. *International Journal of Professional Business Review: Int.J. Prof. Bus. Rev.*, 8(7), 109.

Sharma, A., & Ritu, N. R. (2023). Role of Government Schemes in Supporting Startups in India: A Quantitative Investigation. [EEL]. *European Economic Letters*, 13(1), 276–280.

Srivastava, S. C., & Shainesh, G. (2015). Bridging the service divide through digitally enabled service innovations. *Management Information Systems Quarterly*, 39(1), 245–268. DOI: 10.25300/MISQ/2015/39.1.11

Taherdoost, H. (2023). Fintech: Emerging trends and the future of finance. *Financial Technologies and DeFi: A Revisit to the Digital Finance Revolution*, 29-39.

Verma, J. (2022). Assessing Government Initiatives Towards the Development of Entrepreneurship in India. In *Institutions, Resilience, and Dynamic Capabilities of Entrepreneurial Ecosystems in Emerging Economies* (pp. 44-53). IGI Global. DOI: 10.4018/978-1-6684-4745-1.ch004

Wu, C. H. J., Atmaja, F. T., Ko, Y. C., & Guttena, R. K. (2023). Backer funding intention in reward-based crowdfunding: Service-dominant logic and stimulus-organism-response perspectives. *International Journal of Bank Marketing*, 41(2), 289–311. DOI: 10.1108/IJBM-03-2022-0127

Yifan, Z. (2023). The Fintech Revolution: Innovations Reshaping the Financial Industry. DOI: 10.54097/hbem.v15i.9327

Zhao, Y. (2023). The Fintech Revolution: Innovations Reshaping the Financial Industry. *Highlights in Business. Economics and Management*, 15, 123–128.

Zheng, C., Huang, X., & Xu, Y. (2023). The Impact of Blockchain on Enterprises Sharing Real Data Based on Dynamic Evolutionary Game Analysis. *Sustainability (Basel)*, 15(12), 9439. DOI: 10.3390/su15129439

Chapter 16
Case Imark Group S.A.S. (IGS)

Rafael Ignacio Pérez-Uribe
https://orcid.org/0000-0001-9924-6657
Universidad de La Salle, Colombia

Catalina Gomez-Hurtado
https://orcid.org/0000-0002-9540-4467
Imark S.A.S., Colombia

Nelson Andres Andrade-Valbuena
https://orcid.org/0000-0002-4873-8915
Universidad Catolica de la Santisima Concepcion, Chile

María Teresa Ramírez-Garzón
Universidad de La Salle, Colombia

ABSTRACT

Imark group S.A.S is a micro-company dedicated for 13 years to advising multiple Colombian companies in advertising communication, organizational communication, as well as in providing digital and lithographic printing solutions and sale of promotional material. The company has also provided advice on research of markets and design of digital marketing campaigns.The objective of this work is to show how, from a consultancy to a Colombian microenterprise, a strategic direction is formulated and how to relate it to business results in terms of better competitiveness, in this case of the company IMARK SAS. This work was carried out with the support of the owner of the company, the participation of the General Management and the accounting and financial support staff.The activities that were carried out through the application of the corporate strategic management (CSM) model which allowed the companies to structure their medium-term strategic direction and short-term action plan.

DOI: 10.4018/979-8-3693-4046-2.ch016

INTRODUCTION

To talk about strategic management, it is important to understand well what its evolution over time has been, beginning in the mid-50s of the 20th century, which is the decade of the formal birth of companies producing export goods and the beginning of colonization of multinationals in the global arena (Căpu neanu et al., 2021).

"There were few companies in the world that had the luxury of mass production and that could place their products in markets that required them. Companies where it was relatively easy to project sales and production to five and up to ten years (long term) and prepare budgets organized by fixed items that served as guides for decision making (...), and on an operational scale, detailed plans were used by work areas" (Perez-Uribe, 2018, p. 11).

Since the end of the 1960s and the beginning of the 1970s, the proliferation of companies began to be evident in the environment, which gave customers more options to satisfy their needs and expectations with a greater diversity of goods and services. The environment became highly competitive, and companies began to introduce the concept of strategy within their organizations. Experts on the subject were hired and specialized teams were created to technically design strategic planning in companies (both single-product and diversified multinationals, and conglomerates). The strategy was explicit, designed by planning experts, which had an impact on the organizational structure of the companies and made them create strategic entrepreneurial units or more commonly known as strategic business units (Kurt, 2022).

At the end of the seventies and the beginning of the eighties of the 20th century, a positive action in the ways of doing business, supported by the evolution in technology, mainly in the field of information systems, began to change economic trends. In the United States, Western Europe, and Japan, governments emerged with a clear vision of the future and immediately began supporting business, negotiating with unions, cutting levels of government bureaucracy, and bringing a new marketing system to the public sector (Taylor and Harrison, 1991, pp. xiii-xvi).

The speed and level at which changes occurred at the end of the 20th century and in the first two decades of the 21st century, required organizations to be much more adaptable to the environment. Some of the pressures for production, management and adaptation to change at the local and global level were the consequence of factors such as: The introduction of new technologies (automation, internet, smartphones); widespread deregulation and privatization; the development of world markets and direct investment by multifocal and transnational companies; the contraction and restructuring of the retail and wholesale markets; the decline of the manufacturing sector and heavy industry and a shift towards high value-added product and service industries; the rise of corporate invaders, ready to seize those companies about to be liquidated for their deficient financial resources, to take advantage of their assets, as well as those with high potential; and shortages of key skills despite continued high unemployment in areas such as electronics, computer and system design, marketing, and finance (Barbosa et al., 2019; Ghemawat, 2000).

The objective of this chapter is to present step by step the methodology, based on a model called Corporate Strategic Management (Perez-Uribe, 2018), which was used by the IMARK GROUP company, to formulate the strategic direction that makes it easier to achieve its business objectives. This objective arises from the problem presented in the last year of opening new markets with new projects. One of the limitations of this chapter is that although the competitive analysis was carried out in the sector in which IMARK operates based on the key success factors in the sector, this study is not shown in the case due to having confidential data.

IMARK Group S.A.S is a micro-enterprise that began to operate on March 5th., 2013 and develops the main activity of providing advertising services nationwide with headquarters in Bogota, Colombia, with the following lines of work: Advertising design, graphic production, Digital Marketing, Web Design and promotional items. To date, it has four permanent employees and works by project, in such a way that the required people are hired for each one.

BACKGROUND

Business Results

It is said in all management literature that organizations should be guided by a series of corporate objectives generally directed towards a series of expected results such as: efficiency and productivity; business sustainability that includes social responsibility in terms of comprehensive quality in the administration of human beings and environmental management; effectiveness and profitability (Aghina, et al., 2020):

Efficiency or Productivity

Refers to the ability to generate products (goods and/or services) considering the way the various inputs were used in a production process (Shah et al., 2022). In this sense, it is understandable, only because of managerial action, in which the capacity of the worker up to the business management are involved, going through the technique and technology incorporated in the production process. It encapsulates the central subject of administration "to make a better and greater use of the available resources" considering that the advances in productivity allow a more effective and efficient use of the available means of production, obtaining the greatest possible quantity of goods. and services at a lower cost (Coccia, 2009).

In this field, productivity and efficiency are synonymous and must be understood as the result of a process that includes education, organizational culture management, human resources management, adaptation of technology (soft and hard) to changes of the environment, research and development, and strategic management of companies (Nakamura et al., 2018).

Business sustainability that includes social responsibility, quality in the administration of the human being and environmental management

At this point, there is no intention to delve into the complex world of business sustainability, but rather leave some basic ideas about this subject and give it the importance it deserves as a concept, considering the relevance it has as an organizational result alongside effectiveness, efficiency and profitability. Garzon & Ibarra (2014) assure that: "Sustainability and, consequently, the green economy depends essentially on the use or consumption that is made of resources, as well as on the capacity of the environment to absorb the waste that we generate" (pp. 54-55).

"Sustainable development implies the use and consumption of resources, considering that the consumption of the resource does not exceed its regeneration capacity. This should be the concern of company managers, while continuing to exploit basic resources, to allow their recovery, as it occurs in agriculture or fishing" (Perez-Uribe and Ramirez Salazar, 2023, p. 6).

According to Cardenas & Rios (2016)

Social responsibility is the capacity to respond that a company or an entity has, in the face of the effects and implications of its actions on the different groups with which it is related (stakeholders or groups of interest). In this way, companies are socially responsible when the activities they carry out are oriented towards satisfying the needs and expectations of their members, the society and those who benefit from their commercial activity, as well as caring for and preserving the environment (p.6).

From this definition, the following factors involved in the managerial decision to work with a philosophy of social responsibility linked to organizational sustainability are extracted (table 1):

Table 1. Factors involved in corporate responsibility.

FACTOR	WHAT IT ENTAILS
Values and principles	Defining them, deploying them, and leading them permanently in front of the stakeholders
Harmony work environment	Construction and maintenance of a harmonious work environment among all stakeholders
Sustainable development	Generation by the senior management of the organizations of the necessary conditions to work the processes that allow sustainable development. To be addicted to sustainable development.
Dynamic balance	Work for the dynamic balance in the management of available resources and generated because of the production process.
Great Place to Work	In relation to the human being, work as much as possible along the lines of the Great Place to Work approach.
Environmental management	Work with the concept of environmental management, understood as a process that is aimed at resolving, mitigating and/or preventing environmental problems, with the purpose of achieving sustainable development, understood as one that allows man to develop its potential and its biophysical and cultural heritage, guaranteeing its permanence in time and space.

Source. Own elaboration

Effectiveness

"From the Latin verb "*efficere*": to execute, carry out, effect, produce, obtain as a result. Relationship between the results, planned and unforeseen, and the objectives" (Rojas, et al., 2017).

Talking about effectiveness is talking about generating a true and direct impact on improving life and satisfying the needs of a niche market by delivering products (goods and services) that add value and exceed customer expectations. The effectiveness is the quantification of the fulfillment of the goal and the real results delivered to any stakeholder (Camue et al., 2017).

Effectiveness is the ability to achieve the desired or expected effect. Efficacy is understood as the process of reaching or exceeding the objectives or expected results and is preferably applied to things, but it can also be applied to people in the sense of competent (Akporiaye, 2023).

Profitability

According to Barauskaite & Streimikiene (2021) profitability is the ability to produce benefits or income. Relationship between the amount of a certain investment and the profits obtained after deducting commissions and taxes. Profitability, unlike magnitudes such as income or profit, is always expressed in relative terms.

There are different ways to measure profitability, but it is usually done through indicators that are the result of comparing one account with another (Hristov & Chirico, 2019). "Mathematically speaking, it is the quotient between two figures that show the balances of the accounts that you want to analyze with each other (...) which can be the Balance, the Results or both" (Arias, 2014, p. 46).

In addition to those described above and to complement the concepts of profitability, the following table is presented, which explains some notions on this subject (table 2).

Table 2. Fundamentals of profitability

Types of profitability	Measurement and Calculation
Over sales	It is measured by the margin on sales, that is, by the relationship between profits and net sales.
Economic	It is calculated by the rate of return of the asset, that is, by the relationship between net profit and total assets (liabilities plus equity).
Financial	It is equal to the product of its economic profitability by its financial leverage.
Of a project or product	It is measured by the relationship between the forecasted or real profit and the investment necessary to carry out the project in order to market the product.
Financial performance	**Liquidity:** • **Working capital**: a company that has adequate working capital is able to pay its commitments when due and, at the same time, satisfy contingencies and uncertainties. Insufficient working capital is the main cause of late payments and serious financial difficulties (current assets – current liabilities). • **Current ratio**: indicates the company's ability to meet its short-term obligations (current assets / current liabilities). • **Acid test**: measures more severely the degree of liquidity of companies since, in some circumstances, inventories and other short-term assets can be difficult to liquidate ((Available + temporary investments + debtors) / current liabilities). • **Current liabilities / inventories:** in percentage terms, it shows how much the settlement of current liabilities depends on the sale of inventories (Current liabilities / inventories). **Indebtedness:** for indebtedness indicators, the upper quartile typifies a situation of high indebtedness while the lower one typifies a low level of indebtedness. This means that, contrary to what was found in other groups of indicators, the companies with the highest risk are typified by the upper quartile. • **Net worth:** It is a more conservative measure of Liquid Equity since it may be the case that it has been amplified by valuations without real support (Liquid Equity - valuations). • **Level of indebtedness** corresponds to the degree of leverage used and indicates the participation of creditors over the assets of the company (Total liabilities / total assets) **Of activity:** • **Net equity turnover** shows the volume of sales generated by the investment made by the shareholders (Net sales / net equity). • **Turnover of total assets** corresponds to the volume of sales generated by total assets (Net sales / total assets).

Source. Own elaboration from Sari et al., (2023), Husain & Sunardi (2020) and Brealey and Myers quoted by Arias (2014).

Competitiveness

Organization with better effectiveness, efficiency, profitability, and business sustainability will be the most competitive in the same economic sector or comparatively with different companies and from other economic sectors (Perez-Uribe, 2018, p. 10). Francis (2023) defines competitiveness as the ability to reach a greater number of customers in products with similar characteristics for the same market, through lower prices, higher quality, image, etc. Some of the characteristics of a more competitive organization are (table 3).

Table 3. Characteristics of a competitive organization

CHARACTERISTICS	DESCRIPTION
Greater market share	Having a greater market share, which means having the highest sales or operating income compared to the competition.
Firm positioning	Increase the positioning of the firm in a specific sector.
Better business results	Possess the best effectiveness, efficiency, profitability, and sustainability in the economic sector in which the organization operates.
Supplier	To be the supplier of choice for the customer.
Products	To achieve high competitiveness, innovative, improved and quality products (goods and services) are required.
Comparative advantages	It means to achieve, sustain, and improve a certain better position in the social and economic environment. The comparative advantage of a company would be in its ability, resources, knowledge, and attributes available to it, the same ones that its competitors lack or that they have to a lesser extent, which make it possible to obtain higher returns than those of the others.

Source. Own elaboration

Corporate Strategic Management (CSM). The model

Three fundamental concepts make up this model:

Management

This CSM model should only be brought to the reality of each organization with the leadership of the management, from the top to the lowest levels and from these to senior management. Here the fundamental task of the management of each entity is to achieve the passion of all workers with their work in a sustainable manner, including all stakeholders in favor of the expected results of each organization (suppliers, customers, community, government, contractors, workers, shareholders, and families of workers, among others) (Prasad, 2020).

Strategic

The strategic makes the company energize from the internal to its environment and vice versa, both in the present and towards its future (Perez-Uribe et al., 2016), because this concept "leads to carry out a rational analysis of the opportunities offered by the environment, of the strengths and weaknesses of the form and the selection of a strategic commitment", to achieve the objectives (Ansoff et al., 1983, p. 9; Capusneanu et al., 2021).

Corporate

Because many of the components that are part of the CSM model emphasize that the company must be managed as a unit with a "holistic" sense, understood as the concept enunciated by Weaver and quoted by Luengo (2018), of the confrontation that organizations have to "the many problems of disorganized complexity in which there is a very high or even infinite number of variables or elements" (p.2), within the concept of organizational synergy "understood as the coordinated collaborative action of various entities to carry out a function" (Polo Sanchez, 2017, p. 2).

Corporate Strategic Management (CSM): The benefits

The concept of Corporate Strategic Management (CSM) arises by uniting the three previous constructs; it is much more than a simple forecasting process, since it requires establishing clear objectives and strategies to develop them during specific periods, to achieve and build the planned future situation. This action results in a visible strategic direction, materialized in a document that serves as a logbook for the operation of an organization. This process may remain static over time unless it becomes a fundamental tool for managerial decision-making with regard to the stakeholders of the institution.

Some of the benefits shown by the organizations in which this CSM model has been implemented are the following (Perez-Uribe, 2018, pp. 80-81):

Table 4. CSM model implementation benefits

BENEFITS	DESCRIPTION
Theoretical framework for action	It provides the theoretical framework for action found in the mindset of the organization and its employees, enabling managers and others in the company to similarly assess strategic situations, analyze alternatives in a common language, and decide on the actions (based on a set of shared opinions and values) that should be undertaken within a reasonable period of time.
Release organizational energy	It allows company leaders to unleash the energy of the organization behind a shared vision and believe that it is possible to carry it out.
Improve organizational capacity	Increases the organization's capacity to implement the strategic plan reflected in its direction in a complete and timely manner.
Develop, organize and use tools	It helps the organization develop, organize, and use tools for a better understanding and management of the environment, industry or field in which it operates, as well as its clients (current and potential) and its own capabilities and limitations.
Provide a periodic basis in time to adjust	It provides a periodic basis in time, to constantly adjust to the current events and actions of competitors.
Anticipate the opponent's moves	This concept is analogous to the way world-class chess players think. Not only do they have to decide their immediate moves, but they have to watch the opponent's moves, consider their possible responses, and plan various moves in advance. The same is true with strategic planning: the planning team must anticipate the opponent's moves, consider requirements of their plans, and then base additional plans on those requirements.
Maintain a solid management approach	It is a solid approach that facilitates the achievement of business results (effectiveness, efficiency, profitability, and social responsibility). The understanding of the strategies of the competitors is improved and a better positioning of the image in the sector is achieved.

continued on following page

Table 4. Continued

BENEFITS	DESCRIPTION
Organizations and proactive people	The CSM makes organizations and the people that integrate them proactive (they build the sector where they move and prepare or could quickly adapt to unforeseen changes). Having clarity where to go, improvement of the commitment of all personnel and synergy and better collaboration between processes and work areas are generated.
Awareness of reality	Greater awareness of environmental opportunities and threats and greater clarity of the weaknesses and strengths of each process or work area is acquired, which favors a company's capabilities in terms of problem prevention.
Better business results	It allows to develop more clarity regarding the allocation of resources, significantly improve revenue, profitability and productivity and avoid decreases in revenue and profits.

Source. Own elaboration

CSM Definition

Perez-Uribe (2018) assures that CSM is the "Process of formulating, implementing, evaluating and providing feedback on inter-functional and cross decisions that allow the organization to facilitate the achievement of its business or organizational results" (p.81). This definition implies that strategic management integrates mission, as well as support and strategic processes (administration, marketing, finance, information technology, production, logistics, operation, and human resources, among others) to achieve the success of the organization. In other words, those who make decisions in an organization obtain, process, and analyze internal and external information to assess the present situation and the level of competitiveness of a company with the purpose of anticipating and deciding on the strategic direction (figure 1).

Figure 1. Corporate Strategic Management Definition

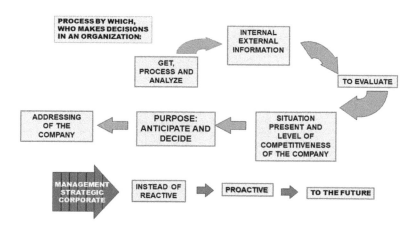

Source. Authors

348

General steps of a CSM process

The model is applied in three large steps, which will be explained more clearly with the development of the case in the methodology part of this chapter (Kabeyi, 2019):

1) The Formulation of strategies, which in turn has the following items: a) The current strategic identification of the company, which is made up of a brief history of the organization, its corporate purpose, the description of its products, vision, mission, principles, policies, values, objectives, strategies and organization chart, b) The strategic diagnosis: internal, external and competitiveness, c) The strategic conclusions that gather the results of the two previous points, and d) The approach of a strategic direction to the future, which integrates the vision (long term), mission (short and medium term), principles (long term), policies (short term), values (long term), objectives and strategies in the medium term (figure 2).

Figure 2. Step One: Strategy Formulation

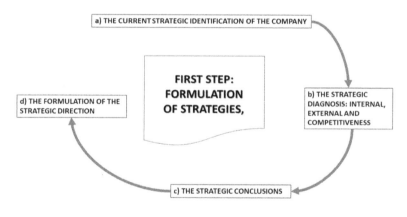

2) The execution of strategies: This is the second big step in this model. It is developed through the structuring of an action plan, tactical or operational, in the short term (less than a year), with which each of the strategies proposed in the medium term are specified and disaggregated. Each action plan contains goals or expected results, management indicators, activities, responsible parties, start and end dates, and resources required for its development. The implementation or execution of strategies involves developing a culture of commitment, an effective organizational structure, modifying marketing activities, preparing budgets, developing, and using information systems, as well as linking employee compensation to company results. It is the active stage of the strategic direction, which means making workers and managers bring the formulated strategies to reality. This stage is often considered the most difficult in strategic management and requires discipline, dedication, and personal sacrifice (Fuertes et al., 2020).

The success of the implementation of the strategies lies in the ability of managers to create the right conditions to motivate employees, which is more of an art than a science. There is no point in formulating strategies if there is no intention to implement them and to bring them to reality, the ability to relate to others is extremely important. The implementation challenge is to stimulate managers and workers throughout the organization to work with pride and enthusiasm to achieve the objectives set (Ahmad, I., & Ahmad, S., 2021).

Figure 3. Step Two: Strategy Implementation

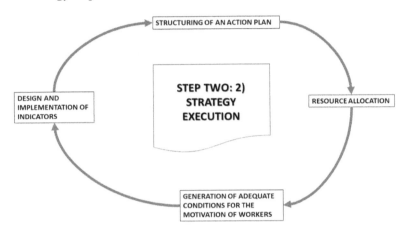

Note. Authors

3) Monitoring and evaluation of strategies: This third step is carried out most of the time when the action plan is being developed. It is verification that what was planned is being executed and the observance that the expected results really occurred and can be carried out in the execution of the strategies or once some of its activities are carried out in accordance with the defined action plan (Garcia et al., 2017). Managers must know when certain strategies are not working well; this stage is the fundamental means to obtain this information (Peñafiel et al., 2020). Many of the strategies must be adjusted along the way, because internal and external factors change permanently and it is necessary to assess them because today's success does not guarantee tomorrow's triumph (Ore et al., 2020).

The three fundamental activities to evaluate the strategies are (Naidoo, 2019): a) periodic review of the activities that were defined in the action plan b) performance measurement through management indicators and c) application of corrective actions (figure 4).

Figure 4. Step Three: Strategy Monitoring and Evaluation

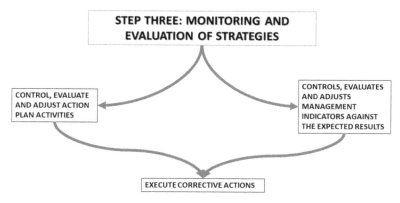

STEP THREE: MONITORING AND EVALUATION OF STRATEGIES

CONTROL, EVALUATE AND ADJUST ACTION PLAN ACTIVITIES

CONTROLS, EVALUATES AND ADJUSTS MANAGEMENT INDICATORS AGAINST THE EXPECTED RESULTS

EXECUTE CORRECTIVE ACTIONS

Note. Own elaboration

MAIN FOCUS OF THE CHAPTER

At this point, the Issues, Controversies and Problems are presented considering the explanation of the methodology used to formulate the strategic direction of the company and the application of the first two steps of the corporate strategic management model that, with the tools used, allow them to be presented in a clear manner.

Methodology

As mentioned in the summary of this chapter, the development of the CSM model in the IMARK company was carried out by applying the five steps explained in the theoretical framework of this chapter (figure 5): 1) Current strategic identification, 2) Strategic diagnosis: internal - WEST - identification of weaknesses and strengths; external -OPT- identification of opportunities and threats, 3) With the above information, strategic conclusions were drawn using cross-analysis matrices to formulate strategic options to mitigate weaknesses, take advantage of opportunities and countering threats. Of these strategic options, the most important were selected considering the BST (Behavioral Science Technology) matrix (Perez-Uribe, 2018, p.197), which allows them to be prioritized against the feasibility of implementing them from the point of cost to do so and the power that each one has to achieve objectives and develop the company mission.

Figure 5. Five steps for the implementation of the CSM model in IMARK

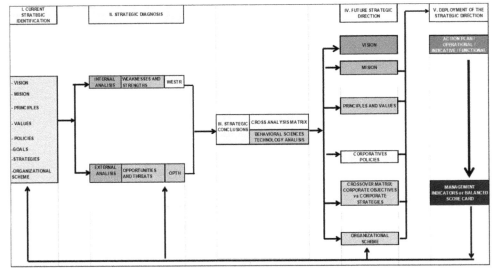

Source. *Pérez-Uribe (2018, p.97)*

Strategic identification of the Company (Gomez, 2023).

Vision. The company does not currently have a vision.

Mission. "We are an advertising and organizational communication agency, founded more than 13 years ago in Bogota, Colombia. Our purpose is to provide a high-quality service through the implementation of digital technology and analytical tools that help not only improve the scope of communications but also allow our clients to make efficient decisions".

Principles

Love for our work: we do our work with passion and the desire for everything to turn out very well.

Attention to the needs of our clients: we pay special attention to the needs of our clients; they are the center of our work.

Jobs well done from the beginning: we take care of every detail to avoid rework in the projects.

We speed up time to meet objectives: we know that time is very important to our clients, which is why we seek it to be our main ally, monitoring it in each process.

We serve our clients with joy: because we know that good service is synonymous with satisfaction.

Values.

Passion, customer service, responsibility, compliance, and kindness

Objectives.

Does not have clearly defined objectives.

Strategies.

The main strategy is based on compliance in the delivery time of the works and in their quality.

Quality policy.

Quality is the consequence of a belief that values customer satisfaction and the positive results of the company.

Encourage participation and teamwork for correct decision-making.

Provide human, technical and financial resources to achieve permanent improvement and respect for the environment.

Raise awareness among employees in order to focus on the most profitable areas of the activity and thus achieve the best business results.

Organization chart.

The company currently has the General Management and four Directorates: Finance, marketing, design, and digital marketing.

Strategic Diagnosis of the Company

Internal Analysis

Weaknesses Analysis.

The list of weaknesses drawn up by management and some selected workers is the result of a meeting in which, in addition to agreeing on the aspects in which the company could improve, the group qualifies them according to the criteria defined by the CSM model (table 5).

Table 5. Criteria for qualifying weaknesses

CRITERIA	LEVEL	QUALIFICATION RANGE	LEVEL DESCRIPTION
Magnitude: Relative weight of the existence of the weakness is to give a rating on a scale from 1 to 10 according to the following parameters	Very high	(10-8)	Its permanent. It is a weakness with which the company lives on a day-to-day basis at work.
	High	(7.9-6)	It is repeated frequently. It depends on the type of organization; this level could be weekly or monthly
	Medium	(5.9-3)	It shows up sometimes. If the previous high level is weekly, this average level will be monthly. If the high level is monthly, this level will be semi-annual.
	Low	(2.9-1)	It occurs rarely. Depending on previous levels, it could be every year.

continued on following page

Table 5. Continued

CRITERIA	LEVEL	QUALIFICATION RANGE	LEVEL DESCRIPTION
Business importance: The importance expresses that each of the listed weaknesses negatively affects the fulfillment of the company's mission, taking into account the following criteria:	Very high	(10-8)	It negatively and directly affects in an extreme way the fulfillment of the mission of the organization
	High	(7.9-6)	It affects considerably and negatively the fulfillment of the mission
	Medium	(5.9-3)	It affects somewhat negatively the fulfillment of the mission
	Low	(2.9-1)	It affects very little in a negative way the fulfillment of the mission

Source. Authors from Perez-Uribe (2018, pps.149-150)

The analysis of weaknesses based on table 5, in IMARK turned out like this (table 6):

Table 6. Matrix Description of Weaknesses

No.	WEAKNESSES DEFINITION	MAG.	BI
1.	Disorder in financial management	10	10
2	There is no separation of assets between owner and company	7.9	7
3	Lack of budget planning	10	5.9
4	Personnel assessment system is not adequate	8	6
5	Lack of human management policies	7	7.9
6	No document for contractor management	10	5.9
7	Lack of staff wellness programs	10	2.9
AVERAGE		**8.99**	**6.51**

Note. Own elaboration.

The information from table 6 is taken to the weakness dispersion matrix (figure 6), resulting in the following priority analysis: In quadrant I, the following weaknesses were of high priority: No.1; Disorder in financial management and in quadrant II of prevention, No.3 Lack of budget planning and No. 5 there are no human management policies.

Figure 6. Weakness Dispersion Matrix

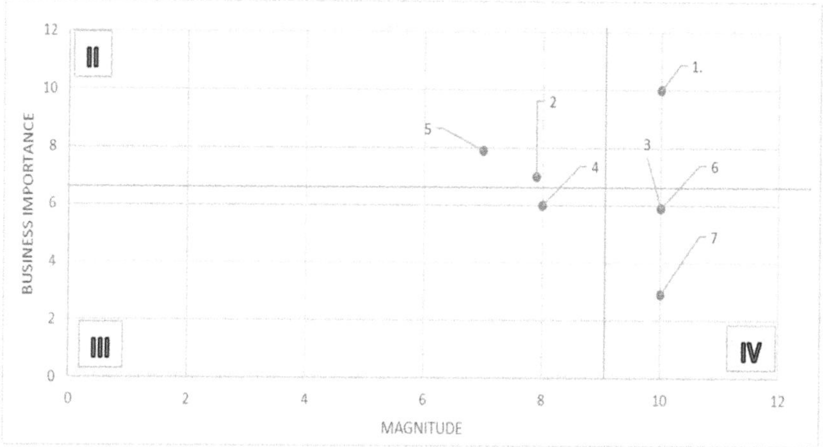

Strengths Analysis.

This analysis was carried out with the management and some selected workers using the Nominal Group Technique (NGT) and they were qualified to observe the importance of each one to develop the mission of the company. For this exercise, the nominal group technique can be observed in Table 7. The following strengths (with a value above the median) are the ones that impact with the greatest weight for the fulfillment of the mission: No.2, Positioning in the market; No.3, state-of-the-art equipment; No.5, exclusivity in customer service and No.4, Innovation in design technology.

Table 7. Strengths NGT Matrix

NOMINAL GROUP TECHNIQUE (NGT)					
ITEM	STRENGTHS	EVALUATORS			RESULTS
		CATALINA	FELIPE	ANA	
1	Experience in the sector	3	2	4	9
2	Market positioning	7	5	6	18
3	Latest technology equipment	5	6	7	18
4	Innovation in design technology	2	7	3	12
5	Exclusivity in customer service	6	4	5	15
6	Innovation of introduction of new products	1	3	2	6
7	Program innovation for supplier management	4	1	1	6
MEDIAN					12.00

Source. Own elaboration from Pérez-Uribe (2018, pps. 155-156)

External Analysis

Basically, at this point, from the analysis of external variables: political, economic, social, technological, environmental, legal and competitive (PESTELC) (Çitilci & Akbalık, 2020), those that directly affect the competitive position of the company are listed, in such a way that they can become opportunities and threats that are or would be affecting it in the short term and are classified according to the criteria explained in tables 8, 9 and 10.

Table 8. Criteria for analyzing and prioritizing the probability of occurrence for opportunities and threats.

CRITERIA	LEVEL	QUALIFICATION RANGE	LEVEL DESCRIPTION
Probability of occurrence: How likely it is that it will occur or that there is an opportunity, or the threat analyzed. The existence of the factors analyzed is rated from 1 to 10.	Very high	(10-8)	Currently exists
	High	(7.9-6)	It could occur in the immediate future (from a week to a month). This period will depend on each economic sector in which each company is located.
	Medium	(5.9-3)	It could happen soon (one month to six months). This period will depend on the criteria defined above.
	Low	(2.9-1)	It is remote that it happens. It could be presented from six months onwards (this period will depend on what is defined in the previous criteria)

Source. Perez-Uribe (2018, pp. 129-130)

Table 9. Criteria for analyzing and prioritizing the potential effect on the business of opportunities and threats

CRITERIA	LEVEL	QUALIFICATION RANGE	LEVEL DESCRIPTION
Potential effect on the business of opportunities: ¿How much does the analyzed opportunity affect the fulfillment of the company's mission? How much they affect opportunities is scored from 1 to 10 according to the following criteria:	Excellent	(10-8)	It strongly and positively affects the fulfillment of the company's mission.
	Positive	(7.9-6)	It affects considerably the fulfillment of the mission of the company
	Moderate	(5.9-3)	Affects somewhat positively the fulfillment of the company's mission
	Light	(2.9-1)	It affects very little the fulfillment of the mission of the company

continued on following page

Table 9. Continued

CRITERIA	LEVEL	QUALIFICATION RANGE	LEVEL DESCRIPTION
Potential effect on the business of opportunities: ¿How much does the analyzed threats affect the fulfillment of the company's mission? How much they affect threats is scored from 1 to 10 according to the following criteria:	Catastrophic	(10-8)	Critically negatively affects the fulfillment of the company's mission
	Severe	(7.9-6)	Significantly negatively affects mission accomplishment
	Moderate	(5.9-3)	It affects somewhat negatively the fulfillment of the mission
	Light	(2.9-1)	It affects very little the fulfillment of the mission of the company

Source. Perez-Uribe (2018, p. 130)

Opportunities Analysis

The result of the application of the previous criteria in IMARK was the following in terms of opportunities (table 10):

Table 10. List of Opportunities

No.	OPPORTUNITIES DEFINITION	PO	POWER EFFECT ON THE BUSINESS
1.	Sector competitiveness allows raising the quality of service by positioning the best companies	8	7.9
2.	Economies of scale allow competition when price is relevant to customers	8	10
3.	Customer needs in terms of time and resources	10	7.9
4.	Market segments that have not been covered	7.9	10
5.	Availability of suppliers to manufacture new products according to needs.	7	5.9
6.	Customers with post-sale support needs	8	6
7	Orientation of the Sector towards the satisfaction of the client's needs.	8.5	9
AVERAGE		8.20	8.10

Source. Own elaboration

The data is taken to the opportunity dispersion matrix to select the most important ones from the upper right (I) and left (II) quadrants. In the upper right quadrant are the opportunities: No.7, Orientation of the sector towards the needs of the client. In the left contingency quadrant: No. 2, Economies of scale allow competition when price is relevant to customers and No. 4, Market segments that have not been covered (Figure 7).

Figure 7. Opportunity Dispersion Matrix

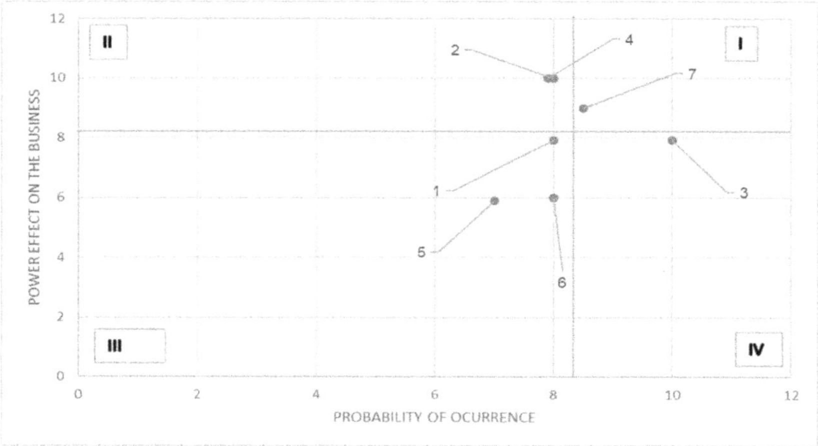

Threats Analysis

The result of the application of the previous criteria in IMARK was the following in terms of threats (table 11):

Table 11. List of Threats

No.	THREATS DEFINITION	PO	POWER EFFECT ON THE BUSINESS
1	Creation of new taxes by the government	5.9	10.0
2	Economic opening allows the entry of products that would increase the supply in the market by reducing prices.	4	7.9
3	International impositions that oblige the State to take tariff and fiscal measures on companies	3	4
4	The competition has management of media, promotion, advertising and dynamic web page that facilitate the management of information with the client.	10	5.9
5	Selection of products by price (Less technical specification) and not by Quality by the end customer.	8	9
6	High power of associativity of the suppliers in front of the final customer of the company, represented in the demand to execute contracts with suppliers in the area.	8	10
AVERAGE		6.5	7.8

Source. Own elaboration

The data is taken to the threat dispersion matrix to select the most important ones from the upper right (I) and left (II) quadrants. In the upper right quadrant are the opportunities: No.6, High power of associativity of the suppliers in front of the final customer of the company, represented in the demand to carry out contracts with suppliers in the area and No. 5, Selection of products by price (Less technical specification) and not by Quality by the end customer. In the left quadrant of contingency No. 1, Creation of new taxes by the government and No. 2, Economic opening allows the entry of products that would increase the supply in the market by reducing prices (figure 8).

Figure 8. Threats Dispersion Matrix

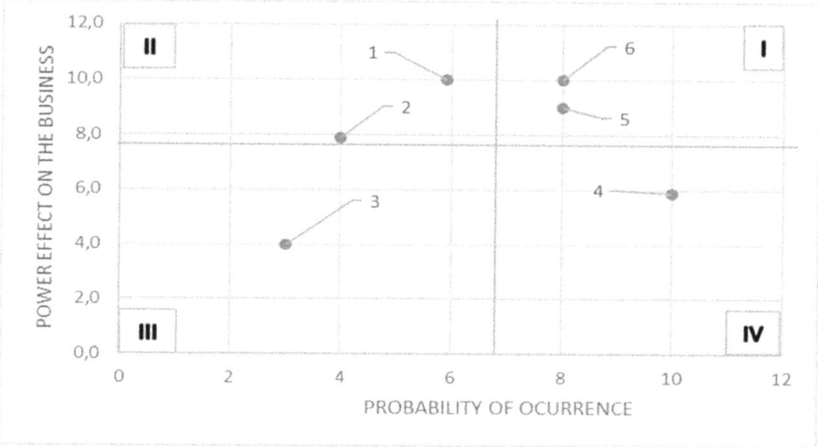

SOLUTIONS AND RECOMMENDATIONS

The solutions and recommendations for this company begin from the development of the strategic conclusions (third step of the CSM model) reached by the IMARK analysis group, using the tools of the SCM model for this purpose (Perez-Uribe, 2018), which consisted of organizing the information from the previous points in a priority manner that allowed management to focus on the most important items of all the information analyzed, both in the current strategic identification and in the internal and external diagnosis. Cross-analysis matrices were mainly used, which facilitated the formulation of strategic options to mitigate weaknesses, countering threats and take advantage of opportunities, selecting those strengths that were selected to put them into practice. The following matrices were worked on matrix of weaknesses strategic activities (strategic options) (WSAS) with their respective strengths; Matrix of opportunities for which exploitation strategies (strategic options) (OUSS) were formulated with their respective strengths; and matrix with strategies to counter threats with their respective strengths (TCSS). The Behavioral Science technology (BST) matrix was also used to prioritize the strategic options in terms of the feasibility of carrying them out and how powerful they were for the fulfillment of the mission, as shown below.

WSAS Matrix

Those weaknesses of the internal strategic diagnosis, which were found to be priorities in quadrants 1 and 2 of the matrix analysis in the internal analysis, are selected and taken to the first column (table 12). Those activities or strategic options that would allow them to be mitigated (second column) (Table 12) were formulated from different sources, and the existing strengths (from the internal strengths analysis) that will allow the implementation of said options or strategic activities (third column) were selected) (table 12).

Table 12. WSAS Matrix

WSAS		
WEAKNESSES	**STRATEGIC ACTIVITIES**	**STRENGTHS**
Disorder in financial management	Development of a reinvestment plan and cash flow.	Innovation of inventory control programs
	Development of management indicators that allow the priorities to be identified at each stage of a project, in compliance with the proposed goals	Experience in the sector
Lack of budget planning	Generation of work fronts that allow the fulfillment of the proposed goals.	Innovation of supplier control programs
Lack of documentation of knowledge	Implementation of a management system to document the processes	Innovation in the development of measurement equipment
Lack of human management policies	Implementation of human management program	Experience in the sector

Source. Own elaboration

OUSS Matrix

Those opportunities from the external strategic diagnosis, which were found to be priorities in quadrants 1 and 2 of the matrix analysis in the external analysis, were selected and moved to the first column (Table 13). Those strategies or strategic options that would make it possible to take advantage of them (second column) (table 13) were formulated from different sources, and the existing strengths (from the internal strengths analysis) that will allow the implementation of said options or strategies of use were selected (third column) (table 13).

Table 13. OUSS Matrix

OUSS		
OPPORTUNITIES	**USE STRATEGIES**	**STRENGTHS**
Economies of scale allow competition when price is relevant to customers	Development of volume discount strategies and early payment so that customers perceive the price benefit	Market Positioning
Market segments that have not been covered	Development of search strategies and selection of unexplored market niches to publicize the company	
Orientation of the Sector towards the satisfaction of the client's needs.	Development of exclusivity strategies for clients of different categories with minimum contracts for 1 year	Exclusivity in customer service

Source. Own elaboration

TCSS Matrix

Those threats from the external strategic diagnosis, which were found to be priorities in quadrants 1 and 2 of the matrix analysis in the external analysis, were selected and moved to the first column (table 14). The strategies or strategic options that would make it possible to counteract them (second column) (table 14) were formulated from different sources, and the existing strengths (from the internal strengths analysis) that will allow the implementation of said options or counter strategies (third column) were selected. (table 14).

Table 14. TCSS Matrix

TCSS		
THREATS	**COUNTER STRATEGIES**	**STRENGTHS**
Creation of new taxes by the government	Launch of new services based on digital service solutions can be created that may be exempt from TAXES	New product introduction innovation
Economic opening allows the entry of products that would increase the supply in the market by reducing prices.	Development of positioning strategies through social networks to achieve greater reach and permanent communication that allows competition for quality rather than price	Market positioning
Selection of products by price (Less technical specification) and not by Quality by the end customer.	Design of new alternatives based on the price-quality relationship to avoid competing for price in the market	Innovation in design technology

Source. Own elaboration

BST Matrix

Once the strategic options have been defined, they are prioritized according to the following criteria of Behavioral Science Technology (BST) (table 15):

Table 15. BST Matrix

VARIABLES	GRADES	DESCRIPTION
FEASIBILITY	1	Difficult to achieve. Requires a lot of money
	2	It is moderately feasible to perform. The resources can be obtained to implement the strategic option
	3	It is easy to develop with the resources available in the short and medium term.
POWER	1	Slightly powerful
	2	Medium powerful
	3	Very powerful

Source. Perez-Uribe (2018, pp. 197-198)

With the previous analysis criteria (table 15), the following table was structured for IMARK:

Table 16. BST Matrix applied in IMARK.

BST			
STRATEGIC OPTIONS	**FEASIBILITY**	**POWER**	**TOTAL = (FEAS. * POWER)**
STRATEGIC ACTIVITIES			
Development of a reinvestment plan and cash flow.	3	3	9
Generation of work fronts that allow the fulfillment of the proposed goals.	3	2	6
Implementation of a management system to document the processes	2	2	4
Implementation of human management program	3	3	9
Development of management indicators that allow the priorities to be identified at each stage of a project, in compliance with the proposed goals	3	3	9
COUNTER STRATEGIES			
Launch of new services based on digital service solutions can be created that may be exempt from TAXES	2	3	6
Development of positioning strategies through social networks to achieve greater reach and permanent communication that allows competition for quality rather than price	3	2	6
Design of new alternatives based on the price-quality relationship to avoid competing for price in the market	2	3	6
USE STRATEGIES			
Development of volume discount strategies and early payment so that customers perceive the price benefit	2	3	6
Development of search strategies and selection of unexplored market niches to publicize the company	3	3	9

Note. Own elaboration

Strategic Direction

The recommendations that are delivered to the management of IMARK, are related to the implementation of the strategic direction (It becomes the company's road map) integrated by the following directional parameters: vision 2030, mission, principles, values, policies, crossing matrix, organizational structure and the action plan:

Vision (2030)

The IMARK GROUP S.A.S publicity agency wishes to position itself in the market as a leading company in the development of creative and environmentally sustainable innovation processes, leading a continuous improvement strategy and applying new technologies for the efficient communication of our clients.

Mission

We are a publicity and organizational communication agency that provides a high-quality service through the implementation of digital technology and analytical tools that help not only to improve the reach of communications but also allow our clients to make efficient decisions. Our strategic allies have extensive experience in the sector and have permanent support and advanced organizational development to closely support our clients.

Principles and values

Love for our work: we do our work with passion and the desire for everything to turn out very well.

Attention to the needs of our clients: we pay special attention to the needs of our clients; they are the center of our work.

Jobs well done from the beginning: we take care of every detail to avoid rework in the projects.

We speed up time to meet objectives: we know that time is very important to our clients, which is why we seek it to be our main ally, supporting them in each process.

We serve our clients with joy: because we know that good service is synonymous with satisfaction.

Policies

- Develop business campaigns to promote their activities and services on the website and social networks.
- Take advantage of the quality of products, to expand the customer database.
- Continue with the corporate purpose of the company, with caution, in the management of clients, suppliers and investments while the reforms to be developed by the government in office are known.

Organization Chart

Figure 9. Organization chart

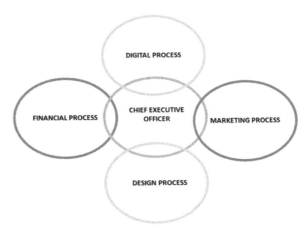

Note. Own elaboration

Crossover Matrix

This matrix (table 17) is the summary of the previous steps developed in the IMARK company, and is made up of the final and selected strategies of the BST and linked to each corporate objective that the company must achieve (table 17):

Table 17. IMARK Crossover Matrix

CORPORATE STRATEGIES (2023-2025)	GOALS	EXPECTED RESULTS
1. Development of a reinvestment plan and cash flow.	Maintain the ROA percentage between current 13.11% and 14.11% by 2024	PROFITABILITY
2. Creation and release new services based on digital service solutions (can be created that may be exempt from TAXES)		
3. Development of positioning strategies through social networks to achieve greater reach and permanent communication that allows competition for quality rather than price	Develop five new projects by 2025	EFFECTIVENESS
4. Design of new alternatives based on the price-quality relationship to avoid competing for price in the market		
5. Generation of work fronts that allow the fulfillment of the proposed goals.		

continued on following page

Table 17. Continued

CORPORATE STRATEGIES (2023-2025)	GOALS	EXPECTED RESULTS
6. Implementation of a management system to document the processes	Optimize production processes to reduce costs and response times by 20%	EFFICIENCY
7. Development of management indicators that allow the priorities to be identified at each stage of a project, in compliance with the proposed goals	100% measure the development of the activities of each area of the company by documenting each process to optimize them and generate continuous improvement	
8. Creation and Implementation of human management program	Create two alliances with educational institutions to achieve the training and updating of 100% of the workers	SUSTAINIBILITY

Note. Own elaboration

Action Plan (short term - less than a year-)

In addition, it is recommended that the company's management implement the action plan with its respective schedule between 2023 and 2024, which will allow it to carry out each proposed strategy and therefore achieve the expected objectives. The Format for the implementation of the action plan in less than one year contains the following sections: the title of each definitive strategy; For each strategy, the pertinent activities must be defined to bring it to reality; each activity must be assigned the corresponding responsible person; the start and end date of each activity must be specified; If an additional budget is required to develop each activity; define the evaluation dates of the development of each activity and in the last column the observations on the implementation of each activity are to be recorded (table 18 and figure 10).

Table 18. IMARK action plan

1. Development of a reinvestment plan and cash flow.						
Activities	Responsible	Date		Aditional Budget (US $)	Evaluation Date	Evaluation Observations
		Start	Ends			
1. Creation and implementation of the financial committee. Define functions of the Committee	Committee (CEO and financial advisor)	1/09/2023	30/09/2023			
2. Review Financial Statements focused on financial and accounting indicators such as: ROE, ROA, Indebtedness, Leverage, Operating Cash Flow, EBITDA, Inventory Turnover and Operating Margins.		Dates established by the Committee				
3. Bimonthly evaluation meetings						
TOTAL ANNUAL				3.600.oo		

2. Creation of new services based on digital service solutions (be exempt from TAXES)						
Activities	Responsible	Date		Aditional Budget (US $)	Evaluation Date	Evaluation Observations
		Start	Ends			
1. Carrying out a study on tax-exempt products	CEO and Consultant in design of publicity products	1/09/2023	1/12/2023			
2. Creation and release of 4 new products		1/1/2024	31/10/2024			
3. Bimonthly evaluation meetings from the year 2024		30/1/2024	31/10/2024			
TOTAL ANNUAL				1.000.oo		

3. Development of positioning strategies through social networks to achieve greater reach and permanent communication that allows competition for quality rather than Price						
Activities	Responsible	Date		Aditional Budget (US $)	Evaluation Date	Evaluation Observations
		Start	Ends			
1. Analysis of the social networks that have the best impact for advertising issues	CEO and Consultant in marketing and social networks	1/09/2023	31/10/2023			
2. Creation, release and evaluation of 4 positioning messages		1/11/2023	31/11/2024			
3. Bimonthly evaluation meetings		1/11/2023	31/11/2024			
TOTAL ANNUAL				1.000.oo		

4. Design of new alternatives based on the price-quality relationship to avoid competing for price in the market						
Activities	Responsible	Date		Aditional Budget (US $)	Evaluation Date	Evaluation Observations
		Start	Ends			
1. Analysis of the competitors similar to IMARK	CEO and Consultant in marketing and social networks	1/09/2023	31/10/2023			
2. Creation, release and evaluation of 4 new alternatives		1/11/2023	31/11/2024			
3. Bimonthly evaluation meetings		1/11/2023	31/11/2024			
TOTAL ANNUAL				1.000.oo		

5. Generation of work fronts that allow the fulfillment of the proposed goals.						
Activities	Responsible	Date		Aditional Budget (US $)	Evaluation Date	Evaluation Observations
		Start	Ends			
1. Analysis of new market niches	CEO and Consultant in marketing and social networks	1/09/2023	31/10/2023			
2. Combination of strategies 2 to 4 to enter the new markets defined in activity 1.		1/11/2023	31/11/2024			
3. Bimonthly evaluation meetings		1/11/2023	31/11/2024			
TOTAL ANNUAL				1.000.oo		

6. Implementation of a management system to document the processes						
Activities	Responsible	Date		Aditional Budget (US $)	Evaluation Date	Evaluation Observations
		Start	Ends			
1. Analysis, improvement and documentation of financial processes	CEO and Consultant in processes	1/10/2023	31/10/2023			
2. Analysis, improvement and documentation of marketing processes		1/11/2023	31/11/2023			
3. Analysis, improvement and documentation of digital processes		1/12/2023	31/1/2024			
4. Analysis, improvement and documentation of design processes		1/2/2024	28/2/2024			
5. Implementation and evaluation processes		31/11/2023	31/11/2024			
6. Bimonthly evaluation meetings		31/11/2023	31/11/2024			

continued on following page

Table 18. Continued

TOTAL ANNUAL				1.000.oo		

7. Development of management indicators that allow the priorities to be identified at each stage of a project, in compliance with the proposed goals

Activities	Responsible	Date		Aditional Budget (US $)	Evaluation Date	Evaluation Observations
		Start	Ends			
1. Analysis and definition of indicators	CEO and Consultant in indicators	1/09/2023	31/10/2023			
2. Starting up the indicator battery		1/11/2023	31/11/2024			
3. Bimonthly evaluation meetings		1/11/2023	31/11/2024			
TOTAL ANNUAL				1.000.oo		

8. Creation and Implementation of human management program

Activities	Responsible	Date		Aditional Budget (US $)	Evaluation Date	Evaluation Observations
		Start	Ends			
1. Design and implementation of training plan	CEO and Consultant in Human Resources	1/09/2023	31/10/2023			
2. Review and update of corporate policies and competencies of strategic allies		1/11/2023	31/11/2023			
3. Review the organizational and specific competencies of the company by process.		1/12/2023	31/1/2024			
4. Review the company benefits plan.		1/09/2023	31/1/2024			
5. Creation of a more participatory organizational culture in which all stakeholders are aware of what is being done at IMARK		1/09/2023	31/10/2024			
3. Bimonthly evaluation meetings		1/11/2023	31/10/2024			
TOTAL ANNUAL				1.000.oo		

Note. Own elaboration

Figure 10. Action plan Schedule (I) IMARK

Note. Own elaboration

Figure 11. Action plan Schedule (II) IMARK

IMARK ACTION PLAN SCHEDULE (II)														
STRATEGIES ACTIVITIES	DURATION IN MONTHS	1	2	3	4	5	6	7	8	9	10	11	12	
5. Generation of work fronts that allow the fulfillment of the proposed goals.														
1. Analysis of new market niches	1													
2. Combination of strategies 2 to 4 to enter the new markets defined in activity 1.	11													
6. Implementation of a management system to document the processes														
1. Analysis, improvement and documentation of financial processes	1													
2. Analysis, improvement and documentation of marketing processes	1													
3. Analysis, improvement and documentation of digital processes	1													
4. Analysis, improvement and documentation of design processes	1													
5. Implementation and evaluation processes	11													
7. Development of management indicators that allow the priorities to be identif														
1. Analysis and definition of indicators	1													
2. Starting up the indicator battery	11													
8. Creation and Implementation of human management program														
1. Design and implementation of training plan	1													
2. Review and update of corporate policies and competencies of strategic allies	1													
3. Review the organizational and specific competencies of the company by process.	1													
4. Review the company benefits plan.	5													
5. Creation of a more participatory organizational culture in which all stakeholders are aware of what is being done at IMARK	12													
Bimonthly evaluation meetings for the 8 strategies and activities	12													

Note. Own elaboration

FUTURE RESEARCH DIRECTIONS

This case is a clear example to structure a strategic direction step by step with its corresponding action plan, in such a way that it can serve as a guide for other micro-enterprises to carry out theirs. In addition, several similar cases that have applied this CSM model could be collected, to write down the common strengths, weaknesses, opportunities and threats between those applications and thus facilitate new strategy formulation exercises. Likewise, show the strategies and common objectives to have them as a reference for new applications.

CONCLUSION

In the case explained in detail in this chapter, several fundamental aspects are observed that make the formulation, implementation and evaluation of a strategic direction successful. The first aspect is the commitment and acceptance of management to get involved in the process (Mahmood, 20121). The second, is to be guided by a strategic management model that allows the participants who are involved in this strategic process of the company to preserve a logical order for the strategic approach (Amalia & Mohammad, 2023). The third aspect is the commitment to the execution and evaluation of the plan (Kabeyi, 2019) and the fourth aspect, is the development of the adjustments that must be made in the strategies and their activities, in such a way that allows the company to adapt to the events that arise and affect both positively and negatively its competitive position (Wiltsey et al., 2019).

REFERENCES

Aghina, W., Handscomb, C., Ludolph, J., Rona, D., & West, D. (2020). *Enterprise agility: Buzz or business impact?*https://www.mckinsey.com/~/media/McKinsey/Business%20Functions/Organization/Our%20Insights/Enterprise%20agility%20Buzz%20or%20business%20impact/Enterprise-agility-Buzz-or-business-impact-vF.pdf

Ahmad, I., & Ahmad, S. B. (2021). Effect of managerial skills on the performance of small-and medium-sized enterprises: A case study in Pakistan. *The Journal of Asian Finance. Economics and Business*, 8(4), 161–170.

Akporiaye, A. (2023). Evaluating the effectiveness of oil companies' corporate social responsibility (CSR). *The Extractive Industries and Society*, 13, 101221. DOI: 10.1016/j.exis.2023.101221

Amalia, S. I., & Mohammad, W. (2023). Mintzberg's 5Ps Strategic Management Model at Yuda Curtain Shop. *Himeka: Journal of Interdisciplinary Social Sciences*, 1(1), 83–89.

Ansoff, I., Declerck, R. P., & Hayes, R. L. (1983). *El planteamiento estratégico*. Editorial Trillas.

Arias Gamboa, M.A. (2014). *La gestión administrativa y su impacto en la rentabilidad financiera de la empresa SEISMICCORP SERVICE S.A.* Facultad de contabilidad y auditoría. Dirección de posgrado maestría en administración financiera y comercio internacional. Trabajo de Titulación Previo a la obtención del Grado Académico de Magister en Administración Financiera y Comercio Internacional. Ambato – Ecuador. Universidad Técnica de Ambato.

Barauskaite, G., & Streimikiene, D. (2021). Corporate social responsibility and financial performance of companies: The puzzle of concepts, definitions and assessment methods. *Corporate Social Responsibility and Environmental Management*, 28(1), 278–287. DOI: 10.1002/csr.2048

Barbosa, F., Romero, F. C., & Cunha, J. (2019). Innovation, Sustainability, and Organizational Change in a Social Portuguese Organization: A Strategic Management Perspective. In I. Management Association (Ed.), *Social Entrepreneurship: Concepts, Methodologies, Tools, and Applications* (pp. 304-327). IGI Global. DOI: 10.4018/978-1-5225-8182-6.ch016

Camue Álvarez, A., Carballal del Río, E., & Toscano Ruiz, D. F. (2017). Concepciones teóricas sobre la efectividad organizacional y su evaluación en las universidades. *Cofin Habana, 11*(2), 136-152. http://scielo.sld.cu/scielo.php?script=sci_arttext&pid=S2073-60612017000200010&lng=es&tlng=es

Căpu neanu, S., Topor, D. I., Constantin, D. M., Barbu, C. M., & Hint, M. S. (2021). Strategic Management Accounting: Dimensions and Strategic Tools. In Oncioiu, I., Căpu neanu, S., Topor, D., & Constantin, D. (Eds.), *Sustainability Reporting, Ethics, and Strategic Management Strategies for Modern Organizations* (pp. 1–29). IGI Global., DOI: 10.4018/978-1-7998-4637-6.ch001

Cárdenas Flórez, D., & Ríos Zuluaga, M. (2016*). Diagnóstico de la responsabilidad social empresarial con enfoque en discapacitados físicamente, entre las pymes y en algunos talleres de confecciones de la ciudad de Pereira y Dosquebradas; con una propuesta de fortalecimiento de responsabilidad social empresarial.* Universidad Tecnológica de Pereira. Facultad de Tecnología Industrial Pereira. https://repositorio.utp.edu.co/server/api/core/bitstreams/7792aea2-1ca1-4b26-bd4d-a2325539c4c3/content

Çitilci, T., & Akbalık, M. (2020). The importance of PESTEL analysis for environmental scanning process. In *Handbook of Research on Decision-Making Techniques in Financial Marketing* (pp. 336–357). IGI Global. DOI: 10.4018/978-1-7998-2559-3.ch016

Coccia, M. (2009, March). What is the optimal rate of R&D investment to maximize productivity growth? *Technological Forecasting and Social Change*, 76(3), 433–446. DOI: 10.1016/j.techfore.2008.02.008

Francis, A. (2023). The concept of competitiveness. In *The competitiveness of european industry* (pp. 5-20). Routledge. Francis, A. (2023). The concept of competitiveness. In *The competitiveness of european industry* (pp. 5-20). Routledge. DOI: 10.4324/9781003369820-2

Fuertes, G., Alfaro, M., Vargas, M., Gutiérrez, S., Ternero, R., & Sabattin, J. (2020). Conceptual framework for the strategic management: A literature review descriptive. *Journal of Engineering*, 2020, 1–21. DOI: 10.1155/2020/6253013

Garcia Guiliany, J., Duran, S., Cardeño Pórtela, E., Prieto Pulido, R., Garcia Cali, E. & Paz Marcano, A. (2017). Proceso de planificación estratégica: Etapas ejecutadas en pequeñas y medianas empresas para optimizar la competitividad. *Revista Espacio*. Vol. 38 (N.º 52) Año 2017. Pág. 16.

Garzón, M. A., & Ibarra, A. (2014). Revisión Sobre la Sostenibilidad Empresarial. *Revista de Estudios Avanzados de Liderazgo*, 2014, Volumen 1, Número 3. https://www.regent.edu/acad/global/publications/real/vol1no3/4-castrillon.pdf

Ghemawat, P. (2000). *La estrategia en el panorama del negocio*. Prentice Hall.

Gómez-Hurtado, C. (2023). Current strategic identification of IMARK. Interview by Rafael Perez in june 2023. Bogotá-Colombia.

Hristov, I., & Chirico, A. (2019). The role of sustainability key performance indicators (KPIs) in implementing sustainable strategies. *Sustainability (Basel)*, 11(20), 5742. DOI: 10.3390/su11205742

Husain, T., & Sunardi, N. (2020). Firm's Value Prediction Based on Profitability Ratios and Dividend Policy. *Finance & Economics Review*, 2(2), 13–26. DOI: 10.38157/finance-economics-review.v2i2.102

Kabeyi, M. (2019). Organizational strategic planning, implementation and evaluation with analysis of challenges and benefits. *International Journal of Applied Research*, 5(6), 27–32. DOI: 10.22271/allresearch.2019.v5.i6a.5870

Kurt, Y. (2022). Improving Society as a Business Strategy: A Review From a Strategic Management Perspective. In Goi, C. (Ed.), *Innovative Economic, Social, and Environmental Practices for Progressing Future Sustainability* (pp. 121–135). IGI Global., DOI: 10.4018/978-1-7998-9590-9.ch007

Luengo González, E. (2018). *Las vertientes de la complejidad: pensamiento sistémico, ciencias de la complejidad, pensamiento complejo, paradigma ecológico y enfoques holistas*. ITESO., https://rei.iteso.mx/bitstream/handle/11117/5686/Las%20Vertientes%20de%20la%20complejidad%20REI.pdf?sequence=4&isAllowed=y

Mahmood Aziz, H., Jabbar Othman, B., Gardi, B., Ali Ahmed, S., Sabir, B. Y., Burhan Ismael, N., & Anwar, G. (2021). Employee commitment: The relationship between employee commitment and job satisfaction. *Aziz, HM, Othman, BJ, Gardi, B., Ahmed, SA, Sabir, BY, Ismael, NB, Hamza, PA, Sorguli, S., Ali, BJ, Anwar, G.(2021). Employee Commitment: The Relationship between Employee Commitment And Job Satisfaction.The Journal of Humanistic Education and Development*, 3(3), 54–66.

Naidoo, P. (2019). *Monitoring and evaluating the effectiveness of business operational strategies that enhance competitive advantage for facility management companies: a case study of ten (10) facility management companies in Gauteng, South Africa* (Doctoral dissertation).

Nakamura, k., Kaihatsu, S. & Yagi, T. (2018) Productivity Improvement and Economic Growth. Bank of Japan. *Working Paper Series.* No.18-E-10 May 2018.

Ore, H., Olortegui, E., & Ponce, D. (2020). Planeamiento estratégico como instrumento de gestión en las empresas: Revisión Bibliográfica. *Revista Pakamuros,* Volumen 8, Número 4, Octubre –Diciembre, 2020, páginas 31-44. http://190.119.95.85/index.php/pakamuros/article/view/147/127

Peñafiel Nivela, G. A., Acurio Armas, J. A., Manosalvas Gómez, L. R., & Burbano Castro, B. E. (2020). Formulación de estrategias para el desarrollo empresarial de la constructora Emanuel en el cantón La Maná. *Revista Universidad y Sociedad*, 12(4), 45–55.

Pérez–Uribe, R. (2018). *Gerencia estratégica Corporativa.* Ediciones Ecoe Ltda. Primera Edición. ISBN: 978-958-771-630-6. eISBN: 978-958-771-631-3. 259 p. abril.

Pérez-Uribe, R., & Ocampo Guzmán, D. Ospina&Bermeo, J., Cifuentes Valenzuela, J., & Cubillos Leal, C.A. (2016). *MIIGO - Modelo de Intervención e Innovación para el direccionamiento estratégico.* Ediciones EAN. ISBN: 978-958-756-414-3. 98 p.

Pérez-Uribe, R., Ocampo-Guzmán, D., Salcedo-Pérez, C., Piñeiro-Cortes, L., and Ramírez-Salazar, MDP. (2020). *Increasing the Competitiveness of SMEs.* January 20. Pages: 550. DOI: .DOI: 10.4018/978-1-5225-9425-3

Polo Sánchez, A. C. (2017). *Estrategia administrativa de Claro: resiliencia o sinergia organizacionales.* https://ciencia.lasalle.edu.co/administracion_de_empresas/1465

Prasad, L. M. (2020). *Principles and practice of management.* Sultan Chand & Sons.

Rojas, M., Jaimes, L. & Valencia, (2017). Efectividad, eficacia y eficiencia en equipos de trabajo. *Revista espacios.* Vol. 39 (N.° 06) Año 2018. Pág. 11. 23/10/2017. https://www.revistaespacios.com/a18v39n06/a18v39n06p11.pdf

Sari, D. P., Nabella, S. D., & Fadlilah, A. H. (2022). The Effect of Profitability, Liquidity, Leverage, and Activity Ratios on Dividend Policy in Manufacturing Companies in the Food and Beverage Industry Sector Listed on the Indonesia Stock Exchange in the 2016-2020 Period. *Jurnal Mantik*, 6(2), 1365–1375.

Shah, W. U. H., Hao, G., Zhu, N., Yasmeen, R., Padda, I. U. H., & Abdul Kamal, M. (2022). A cross-country efficiency and productivity evaluation of commercial banks in South Asia: A meta-frontier and Malmquist productivity index approach. *PLoS One*, 17(4), e0265349. DOI: 10.1371/journal.pone.0265349 PMID: 35385496

Taylor, B., & Harrison, J. (1991). Planeación estratégica exitosa. Legis editores SA. Colombia

Wiltsey Stirman, S., Baumann, A. A., & Miller, C. J. (2019). The FRAME: An expanded framework for reporting adaptations and modifications to evidence-based interventions. *Implementation Science : IS*, 14(1), 1–10. DOI: 10.1186/s13012-019-0898-y PMID: 31171014

KEY TERMS AND DEFINITIONS

BST Matrix: Methodology that serves to prioritize the strategic options in terms of the feasibility in money and how powerful they are to develop the mission of the company.

Crossover Matrix: Methodology that serves to show the link that must exist between the definitive strategies and the objectives that must be achieved in the medium term.

CSM.: Corporate Strategic Management is a model that serves to formulate a strategic direction. This model has five steps for its development.

Opportunities: Environmental variables that positively affect the competitive position of the company in some way.

OUSS Matrix: Methodology that serves to cross information in terms of opportunities, the strategies that are used to take advantage of them and the strengths that are required to implement said strategies.

PESTELC: Analysis of political, economic, technological, environmental, legal and competitive variables, on which the opportunities and threats that affect a company are listed.

Strengths: Capacities and resources that have been managed well and have aspects that have allowed to fulfill the mission of the company.

Threats: Environmental variables that negatively affect the competitive position of the company in some way.

TCSS Matrix: Methodology that serves to cross information in terms of threats, the strategies that serve to counteract them and the strengths that are required to implement these strategies.

Weaknesses: Aspects that can be improved. These may be problems that make it impossible to fulfill the mission of the Company.

WSAS Matrix: Methodology that serves to cross information in terms of weaknesses, the strategic activities that serve to mitigate them and the strengths that are required to implement said activities.

Compilation of References

Aarabe, M., Khizzou, N. B., Alla, L., & Benjelloun, A. (2024a). Marketing Applications of Emerging Technologies : A Systematic Literature Review. In *AI and Data Engineering Solutions for Effective Marketing* (p. 23-47). IGI Global. DOI: 10.4018/979-8-3693-3172-9.ch002

Aarabe, M., Khizzou, N. B., Alla, L., & Benjelloun, A. (2024b). Smart Tourism Experience and Responsible Travelers' Behavior : A Systematic Literature Review. In *Promoting Responsible Tourism With Digital Platforms* (p. 128-147). IGI Global. DOI: 10.4018/979-8-3693-3286-3.ch008

Abada, T., Hou, F., & Lu, Y. (2014). Choice or necessity: Do immigrants and their children choose self-employment for the same reasons? *Work, Employment and Society*, 28(1), 78–94. DOI: 10.1177/0950017013511870

Abbasian, S., & Yazdanfar, D. (2013). Exploring the financing gap between native born women- and immigrant women-owned firms at the start-up stage. *International Journal of Gender and Entrepreneurship*, 5(2), 157–173. DOI: 10.1108/17566261311328837

Abrahamson, E., & Fairchild, G. (1999). Management fashion: Lifecycles, triggers, and collective learning processes. *Administrative Science Quarterly*, 44(4), 708–740. DOI: 10.2307/2667053

Abrokwah-Larbi, K., & Awuku-Larbi, Y. (2023). The impact of artificial intelligence in marketing on the performance of business organizations : Evidence from SMEs in an emerging economy. *Journal of Entrepreneurship in Emerging Economies*. https://www.emerald.com/insight/content/doi/10.1108/JEEE-07-2022-0207/full/html

Acquaah, M. (2011). Business strategy and competitive advantage in family businesses in Ghana: The role of social networking relationships. *Journal of Developmental Entrepreneurship*, 16(01), 103–126. DOI: 10.1142/S1084946711001744

Addo, P. A. (2017). "Is It Entrepreneurship, or Is It Survival?': Gender, Community, and Innovation in Boston's Black Immigrant Micro-Enterprise Spaces [Article]. *Societies, 7*(3), 19, Article 20. https://doi.org/DOI: 10.3390/soc7030020

Aghina, W., Handscomb, C., Ludolph, J., Rona, D., & West, D. (2020). *Enterprise agility: Buzz or business impact?*https://www.mckinsey.com/~/media/McKinsey/Business%20Functions/Organization/Our%20Insights/Enterprise%20agility%20Buzz%20or%20business%20impact/Enterprise-agility-Buzz-or-business-impact-vF.pdf

Agrawal, P., Navgotri, S., & Nagesh, P. (2023). Impact of emerging technologies on digital manufacturing : Insights from literature review. *Materials Today: Proceedings*. Advance online publication. DOI: 10.1016/j.matpr.2023.03.187

Aguaded, J., & Romero-Rodríguez, L. M. (2015). Mediamorfosis y desinformación en la infoesfera: Alfabetización mediática, digital e informacional ante los cambios de hábitos de consumo informativo. *Education in the knowledge society: EKS*. DOI: 10.14201/eks20151614457

Aguilar Rascon, O. C. (2023). El impacto de la dirección en el desempeño en las micro y pequeñas empresas: Un análisis sistémico. *Contaduría y Administración*, 68(3), 46–78. DOI: 10.22201/fca.24488410e.2023.3295

Aguilar, I. (2019). *La Alfabetización Mediática e Informacional como conocimiento transversal en la Educación Secundaria Obligatoria* [Tesis de maestría]. Universidad Autónoma de Barcelona.

Aguinis, H., & Gottfredson, R. K. (2010). Best-practice recommendations for estimating interaction effects using moderated multiple regression Estimating Interaction Effects Using Multiple Regression. *Journal of Organizational Behavior*, 31(6), 776–786. DOI: 10.1002/job.686

Agustina, Y., & Nurulistanti, L. (2022). How money circulates in indonesian smes: An analysis of financial literacy, business performance, financial management behavior, and financial attitude. Educational Administration: *Theory and Practice,* 28(2), 122-132. *Scopus.* Advance online publication. DOI: 10.17762/kuey.v28i02.425

Ahmad, I., & Ahmad, S. B. (2021). Effect of managerial skills on the performance of small-and medium-sized enterprises: A case study in Pakistan. *The Journal of Asian Finance. Economics and Business*, 8(4), 161–170.

Akomea, S. Y., Agyapong, A., Ampah, G., & Osei, H. V. (2023). Entrepreneurial orientation, sustainability practices and performance of small and medium enterprises: Evidence from an emerging economy. *International Journal of Productivity and Performance Management*, 72(9), 2629–2653. DOI: 10.1108/IJPPM-06-2021-0325

Akpan, I. J., Udoh, E. A. P., & Adebisi, B. (2022). Small business awareness and adoption of state-of-the-art technologies in emerging and developing markets, and lessons from the COVID-19 pandemic. *Journal of Small Business and Entrepreneurship*, 34(2), 123–140. DOI: 10.1080/08276331.2020.1820185

Akporiaye, A. (2023). Evaluating the effectiveness of oil companies' corporate social responsibility (CSR). *The Extractive Industries and Society*, 13, 101221. DOI: 10.1016/j.exis.2023.101221

Albats, E., et al. (2020). Networks for Innovation: Accelerating Innovation through Networked Relationships.

Aldebert, B., & Gueguen, G. (2013). TIC et performance : Rôle du dirigeant de PME touristiques. *Revue internationale PME, 26*(3), 213-233.

Aldén, L., & Hammarstedt, M. (2016). Discrimination in the Credit Market? Access to Financial Capital among Self-employed Immigrants. *Kyklos*, 69(1), 3–31. https://doi.org/https://doi.org/10.1111/kykl.12101. DOI: 10.1111/kykl.12101

Al-Haidari, N. N., Kabanda, S., & Almukhaylid, M. M. (2021). The Challenges Of Implementing Social Media Marketing In The Tourism Industry : A Systematic Review. *Conference: 19th International Conference e-Society 2021.*

Ali Qalati, S., Li, W., Ahmed, N., Ali Mirani, M., & Khan, A. (2020). Examining the factors affecting SME performance : The mediating role of social media adoption. *Sustainability (Basel)*, 13(1), 75. DOI: 10.3390/su13010075

Aliaga-Isla, R., & Rialp, A. (2013). Systematic review of immigrant entrepreneurship literature: Previous findings and ways forward. *Entrepreneurship and Regional Development*, 25(9-10), 819–844. DOI: 10.1080/08985626.2013.845694

Ali, B. J., & Anwar, G. (2021). Business strategy: The influence of Strategic Competitiveness on competitive advantage. International Journal of Electrical. *Electronics and Computers*, 6(2), 1–9.

Alkahtani, A., Nordin, N., & Khan, R. U. (2020). Does government support enhance the relation between networking structure and sustainable competitive performance among SMEs? *Journal of Innovation and Entrepreneurship*, 9(1), 1–16. DOI: 10.1186/s13731-020-00127-3

Alla, L., Kamal, M., & Bouhtati, N. (2022). Big data et efficacité marketing des entreprises touristiques : Une revue de littérature. *Alternatives Managériales Economiques, 4*(0), Article 0. DOI: 10.48374/IMIST .PRSM/ame-v1i0.36928

Almeida, F. (2024). Causes of Failure of Open Innovation Practices in Small- and Medium-Sized Enterprises. *Administrative Sciences*, 14(3), 50. https://www.mdpi.com/2076-3387/14/3/50. DOI: 10.3390/ admsci14030050

Alrubaiee, L., Alzubi, H. M., Hanandeh, R. E., & Al Ali, R. (2015). Investigating the relationship between knowledge management processes and organizational performance the mediating effect of organizational innovation. *International Review of Management and business research, 4*(4 Part 1), 989.

Alshammari, M. (2020). The impact of training on Employee performance: A study of the banking sector in Saudi Arabia. *International Journal of Business and Management*, 15(3), 1–12. DOI: 10.5539/ijbm. v15n3p1

Alshebami, A. S. (2022). Crowdfunding platforms as a substitute financing source for young Saudi entrepreneurs: Empirical evidence. *SAGE Open*, 12(3), 21582440221126511. DOI: 10.1177/21582440221126511

Alvarez, S. A., & Barney, J. B. (2004). Organizing rent generation and appropriation: Toward an entrepreneurial theory of the firm. *Journal of Business Venturing*, 19(5), 621–635. DOI: 10.1016/j. jbusvent.2003.09.002

Alvarez, S. A., Ireland, R. D., & Reuer, J. J. (2006). Entrepreneurship and strategic alliances. *Journal of Business Venturing*, 21(4), 401–404. DOI: 10.1016/j.jbusvent.2005.03.001

Alzate, BA, Giraldo, LT, & Barbosa, AF (2012). *Technological surveillance: methodologies and applications* . Electronic Journal of People Management and Technology, 5(13).

Amagir, A., van den Brink, H. M., Groot, W., & Wilschut, A. (2022). SaveWise: The impact of a real-life financial education program for ninth grade students in the Netherlands. *Journal of Behavioral and Experimental Finance, 33.Journal of Behavioral and Experimental Finance*, 33, 100605. Advance online publication. DOI: 10.1016/j.jbef.2021.100605

Amalia, S. I., & Mohammad, W. (2023). Mintzberg's 5Ps Strategic Management Model at Yuda Curtain Shop. *Himeka: Journal of Interdisciplinary Social Sciences*, 1(1), 83–89.

Amal, M., Awuah, G. B., Raboch, H., & Anderson, S. (2013). Differences and similarities of the internationalization processes of multinational companies from developed and emerging countries. *European Business Review*, 25(5), 411–428. DOI: 10.1108/EBR-08-2012-0048

Ameh, A. A., & Udu, A. A. (2016). Social networks and entrepreneurship orientation among students in nigerian universities: A study of social network size and risk disposition. *Business and Management Research*, 5(2), 1–11. DOI: 10.5430/bmr.v5n2p1

Anand, J., McDermott, G., Mudambi, R., & Narula, R. (2021). Innovation in and from emerging economies: New insights and lessons for international business research. *Journal of International Business Studies*, 52(4), 545–559. DOI: 10.1057/s41267-021-00426-1

Andrade-Valbuena, N. A., & Merigo, J. M. (2018). Outlining new product development research through bibliometrics: Analyzing journals, articles and researchers. *Journal of Strategy and Management*, 11(3), 328–350. DOI: 10.1108/JSMA-08-2017-0061

Andrade-Valbuena, N. A., Merigo-Lindahl, J. M., & Olavarrieta, S. (2018). Bibliometric analysis of entrepreneurial orienta-tion. *World Journal of Entrepreneurship, Management and Sustainable Development*, 15(1), 45–69. DOI: 10.1108/WJEMSD-08-2017-0048

Andrade-Valbuena, N. A., Valenzuela Fernández, L., & Merigó, J. M. (2022). Thirty-five years of strategic management research. A country analysis using bibliometric techniques for the 1987-2021 period. *Cuadernos de Gestión*, 22(2), 7–22. DOI: 10.5295/cdg.211441na

Andrade-Valbuena, N., Baier-Fuentes, H., & Gaviria-Marin, M. (2022). An Overview of Sustainable Entrepreneurship in Tourism, Destination, and Hospitality Research Based on the Web of Science. *Sustainability (Basel)*, 14(22), 14944. DOI: 10.3390/su142214944

Andreeva, T., & Kianto, A. (2012). Does knowledge management really matter? Linking knowledge management practices, competitiveness and economic performance. *Journal of Knowledge Management*, 16(4), 617–636. DOI: 10.1108/13673271211246185

Ansari, N., Tyagi, S., Mehrwal, N., Rastogi, N., Chibber, S., Memoria, M., Kumar, R., & Gupta, A. (2022). A critical insight into the impact of technology in transformation of tourist business into smart tourism. *2022 International Conference on Machine Learning, Big Data, Cloud and Parallel Computing (COM-IT-CON), 1*, 832-837. https://ieeexplore.ieee.org/abstract/document/9850779/

Ansoff, I., Declerck, R. P., & Hayes, R. L. (1983). *El planteamiento estratégico*. Editorial Trillas.

Antonak, R. F., & Livneh, H. (1988). *The measurement of attitudes toward people with disabilities: Methods, psychometrics and scales*. Charles C Thomas, Publisher.

Anwar, M., & Shah, S. Z. (2021). Entrepreneurial orientation and generic competitive strategies for emerging SMEs: Financial and nonfinancial performance perspective. *Journal of Public Affairs*, 21(1), e2125. DOI: 10.1002/pa.2125

Appiah, T., & Agblewornu, V. V. (2024). Financial Literacy, Financial Access, and Small Business Performance in Secondi-Takoradi Metropolis of Ghana: The Mediating Effect of Financial Capability. *African Journal of Business & Economic Research*, 19(2), 299–321. DOI: 10.31920/1750-4562/2024/v19n2a13

Arce, C. G. M., Valderrama, D. A. C., Barragán, G. A. V., & Santillán, J. K. A. (2024). Optimizing business performance : Marketing strategies for small and medium businesses using artificial intelligence tools. *Migration Letters : An International Journal of Migration Studies*, 21(S1), 193–201. DOI: 10.59670/ml.v21iS1.6008

Archuleta, K. L., Dale, A., & Spann, S. M. (2013). College students and financial distress: Exploring debt, financial satisfaction, and financial anxiety. *Financial Counseling and Planning*, 24(2), 50–62.

Arias Gamboa, M.A. (2014). *La gestión administrativa y su impacto en la rentabilidad financiera de la empresa SEISMICCORP SERVICE S.A.* Facultad de contabilidad y auditoría. Dirección de posgrado maestría en administración financiera y comercio internacional. Trabajo de Titulación Previo a la obtención del Grado Académico de Magister en Administración Financiera y Comercio Internacional. Ambato – Ecuador. Universidad Técnica de Ambato.

Arnold, H. J. (1982). Moderator variables: A clarification of conceptual, analytic, and psychometric issues. *Organizational Behavior and Human Performance*, 29(2), 143–174. DOI: 10.1016/0030-5073(82)90254-9

Arslan, A., Kamara, S., Zahoor, N., Rani, P., & Khan, Z. (2022). Survival strategies adopted by microbusinesses during COVID-19: an exploration of ethnic minority restaurants in northern Finland. *International Journal of Entrepreneurial Behavior & Research*. https://doi.org/https://doi-org.ezproxy.inn.no/10.1108/IJEBR-05-2021-0396

Arun, K., & Yildirim Ozmutlu, S. (2024). The effect of environmental competitiveness, customer and competitor orientation on export performance. *Journal of Business and Industrial Marketing*, 39(2), 142–160. DOI: 10.1108/JBIM-01-2022-0019

Ashari, H. A., Heidari, M., & Parvaresh, S. (2014). Improving SMTEs' business performance through strategic use of information communication technology : ICT and tourism challenges and opportunities. *International Journal of Academic Research in Accounting. Finance and Management Sciences*, 4(3), 1–20.

Atarama, T., & Vega, D. (2020). *Comunicación corporativa y branded content en Facebook: un estudio de las cuentas oficiales de las universidades peruanas*. Revista de Comunicación.

Atkinson, A., & Messy, F. A. (2012). Measuring financial literacy: Results of the OECD/International Network on Financial Education (INFE) pilot study. OECD Working Papers on Finance, Insurance and Private Pensions, No. 15. *OECD Publishing*.

Audretsch, D. B., & Fritsch, M. (2002). Growth regimes over time and space. *Regional Studies*, 36(2), 113–124. DOI: 10.1080/00343400220121909

Audretsch, D. B., & Keilbach, M. (2004). Entrepreneurship and Regional Growth: An Evolutionary Interpretation. *Journal of Evolutionary Economics*, 14(5), 605–616. DOI: 10.1007/s00191-004-0228-6

Audretsch, D. B., & Thurik, A. R. (2000). Capitalism and democracy in the 21st century: From the managed to the entrepreneurial economy. *Journal of Evolutionary Economics*, 10(1-2), 17–34. DOI: 10.1007/s001910050003

Augier, M., & Teece, D. J. (2009). Dynamic capabilities and the role of managers in business strategy and economic performance. *Organization Science*, 20(2), 410–421. DOI: 10.1287/orsc.1090.0424

Auh, S., & Menguc, B. (2005). Balancing exploration and exploitation: The moderating role of competitive intensity. *Journal of Business Research*, 58(12), 1652–1661. DOI: 10.1016/j.jbusres.2004.11.007

Aulakh, P. S., Kotabe, M., & Teegen, H. (2000). Export strategies and performance of firms from emerging economies: Evidence from Brazil, Chile, and Mexico. *Academy of Management Journal*, 43(3), 342–361. DOI: 10.2307/1556399

Autio, E., Kenney, M., Mustar, P., Siegel, D., & Wright, M. (2014). Entrepreneurial innovation: The importance of context. *Research Policy*, 43(7), 1097–1108. https://doi.org/https://doi.org/10.1016/j.respol.2014.01.015. DOI: 10.1016/j.respol.2014.01.015

Autio, E., Nambisan, S., Thomas, L. D., & Wright, M. (2018). Digital affordances, spatial affordances, and the genesis of entrepreneurial ecosystems. *Strategic Entrepreneurship Journal*, 12(1), 72–95. DOI: 10.1002/sej.1266

Aydin, A. E., & Akben Selcuk, E. (2019). An investigation of financial literacy, money ethics and time preferences among college students: A structural equation model. *International Journal of Bank Marketing, 37*(3), 880-900. *Scopus*. Advance online publication. DOI: 10.1108/IJBM-05-2018-0120

Ayula, G., Abbay, A. G., & Azadi, H. (2023). The role of micro- and small-scale enterprises in enhancing sustainable community livelihood: Tigray, Ethiopia. *Environment, Development and Sustainability*, 25(8), 7561–7584. DOI: 10.1007/s10668-022-02359-7

Ayyagari, M., Demirguc-Kunt, A., & Maksimovic, V. (2021). "Small vs. Young Firms across the World: Contribution to Employment, Job Creation, and Growth." Policy Research Working Paper, World Bank.

Aziz, S., & RAHOUA, F. (2020). L'orientation parties prenantes et performance organisationnelle, cas des structures d'hébergement touristique en milieu rural. *Revue Internationale des Sciences de Gestion, 3*(1). https://revue-isg.com/index.php/home/article/download/188/170

Azoulay, A. (2019). *Global Standards for Media and Information Literacy Curricula Development Guidelines*. United Nations Educational, Scientific and Cultural Organization UNESCO. https://www.unesco.org/sites/default/files/medias/files/2022/02/Global%20Standards%20for%20Media%20and%20Information%20Literacy%20Curricula%20Development%20Guidelines_EN.pdf

Bag, S., Gupta, S., Kumar, A., & Sivarajah, U. (2021). An integrated artificial intelligence framework for knowledge creation and B2B marketing rational decision making for improving firm performance. *Industrial Marketing Management*, 92, 178–189. DOI: 10.1016/j.indmarman.2020.12.001

Bagwell, S. (2018). From mixed embeddedness to transnational mixed embeddedness. *International Journal of Entrepreneurial Behaviour & Research*, 24(1), 104–120. DOI: 10.1108/IJEBR-01-2017-0035

Bailey, S. (2014). *Academic writing: A handbook for international students*. Routledge. DOI: 10.4324/9781315768960

Bajo, O. (1991). *Theories of international trade*. Antoni Bosh.

Baláž, V. (2004). Knowledge-intensive business services in transition economies. *Service Industries Journal*, 24(4), 83–100. DOI: 10.1080/0264206042000275208

Banco Interamericano de Desarrollo, B. I. D. (2019). *El colapso de la confianza y el auge del populismo*. https://www.iadb.org/es/historia/el-colapso-de-la-confianza-y-el-auge-del-populismo

Baporikar, N. (2015a). *5. Innovation Knowledge Management Nexus. Innovation Management*. GRUYTER.

Baporikar, N. (2015b). Drivers of Innovation. In Ordoñez de Pablos, P., Turró, L., Tennyson, R., & Zhao, J. (Eds.), *Knowledge Management for Competitive Advantage During Economic Crisis* (pp. 250–270). Business Science Reference. DOI: 10.4018/978-1-4666-6457-9.ch014

Baporikar, N. (2016a). Organizational Barriers and Facilitators in Embedding Knowledge Strategy. In *Business Intelligence: Concepts, Methodologies, Tools, and Applications* (pp. 1585–1610). Business Science Reference. DOI: 10.4018/978-1-4666-9562-7.ch079

Baporikar, N. (2016b). Understanding Knowledge Management Spectrum for SMEs in Global Scenario. [IJSODIT]. *International Journal of Social and Organizational Dynamics in IT*, 5(1), 1–15. DOI: 10.4018/IJSODIT.2016010101

Baporikar, N. (2017a). Knowledge Management for Excellence in Indian Public Sector. [IJSESD]. *International Journal of Social Ecology and Sustainable Development*, 8(1), 49–65. DOI: 10.4018/IJSESD.2017010104

Baporikar, N. (2017b). Knowledge Transfer Issues in Teaching: Learning Management. In Baporikar, N. (Ed.), *Innovation and Shifting Perspectives in Management Education* (pp. 58–78). Business Science Reference. DOI: 10.4018/978-1-5225-1019-2.ch003

Baporikar, N. (2018). *Global Practices in Knowledge Management for Societal and Organizational Development*. IGI Global. DOI: 10.4018/978-1-5225-3009-1

Baporikar, N. (2019). Knowledge Management Dynamics and Public Sector Organization Development. In Albastaki, Y., Al-Alawi, A., & Abdulrahman Al-Bassam, S. (Eds.), *Handbook of Research on Implementing Knowledge Management Strategy in the Public Sector* (pp. 55–71). IGI Global. DOI: 10.4018/978-1-5225-9639-4.ch003

Baporikar, N. (2020). Role and Room for Knowledge Management in Small and Medium Enterprises. In Idemudia, E. (Ed.), *Handbook of Research on Social and Organizational Dynamics in the Digital Era* (pp. 115–134). IGI Global. DOI: 10.4018/978-1-5225-8933-4.ch006

Baporikar, N. (2021). Knowledge Management for Business Sustainability. In Geada, N., & Anunciação, P. (Eds.), *Reviving Businesses With New Organizational Change Management Strategies* (pp. 30–44). IGI Global. DOI: 10.4018/978-1-7998-7452-2.ch002

Baporikar, N. (2022). Strategies to Manage and Preserve Indigenous Knowledge. In Tshifhumulo, R., & Makhanikhe, T. (Eds.), *Handbook of Research on Protecting and Managing Global Indigenous Knowledge Systems* (pp. 207–222). IGI Global. DOI: 10.4018/978-1-7998-7492-8.ch012

Baporikar, N. (2023). Intergenerational Leadership for Improved Knowledge Transfer. In Polat, S., & Çelik, Ç. (Eds.), *Perspectives on Empowering Intergenerational Relations in Educational Organizations* (pp. 114–139). IGI Global. DOI: 10.4018/978-1-6684-8888-1.ch005

Barauskaite, G., & Streimikiene, D. (2021). Corporate social responsibility and financial performance of companies: The puzzle of concepts, definitions and assessment methods. *Corporate Social Responsibility and Environmental Management*, 28(1), 278–287. DOI: 10.1002/csr.2048

Barbosa, F., Romero, F. C., & Cunha, J. (2019). Innovation, Sustainability, and Organizational Change in a Social Portuguese Organization: A Strategic Management Perspective. In I. Management Association (Ed.), *Social Entrepreneurship: Concepts, Methodologies, Tools, and Applications* (pp. 304-327). IGI Global. DOI: 10.4018/978-1-5225-8182-6.ch016

Barnett, W. P. (1997). The dynamics of competitive intensity. *Administrative Science Quarterly*, 42(1), 128–160. DOI: 10.2307/2393811

Barney, J. (1991). Firm resources and sustained competitive advantage. *Journal of Management*, 17(1), 99–120. DOI: 10.1177/014920639101700108

Baron, R. A. (2004, August). Opportunity recognition: a cognitive perspective. in *Academy of management proceedings* briarcliff manor, ny 10510: Academy of management (vol. 2004, no. 1, pp. a1-a6). DOI: 10.5465/ambpp.2004.13862818

Baron, R. A. (1998). Cognitive mechanisms in entrepreneurship: Why and when entrepreneurs think differently than other peo-ple. *Journal of Business Venturing*, 13(4), 275–294. DOI: 10.1016/S0883-9026(97)00031-1

Barrafrem, K., Västfjäll, D., & Tinghög, G. (2024). Financial Homo Ignorans: Development and validation of a scale to measure individual differences in financial information ignorance. *Journal of Behavioral and Experimental Finance*, 42, 100936. DOI: 10.1016/j.jbef.2024.100936

Barrera-Ortegon, A., Medina-Ricaurte, G. F., & Jimenez-Hernandez, P. R. (2024). Organizational Elements to Confront Turbulent and Fragile VUCA to BANI Scenarios. In *Organizational Management Sustainability in VUCA Contexts* (pp. 20–43). IGI Global. DOI: 10.4018/979-8-3693-0720-5.ch002

Barsky, R. B., Juster, F. T., Kimball, M. S., & Shapiro, M. D. (1997). Preference Parameters and Behavioral Heterogeneity: An Experimental Approach in the Health and Retirement Study*. *The Quarterly Journal of Economics*, 112(2), 537–579. DOI: 10.1162/003355397555280

Beattie, M. (2020). 'Like an American but without a gun'?": Canadian national identity and the Kids in the Hall. *Participations*, 17(2). https://www.participations.org/Volume%2017/Issue%202/2.pdf

Beck, T., Demirguc-Kunt, A., & Levine, R. (2005). SMEs, Growth, and Poverty: Cross-Country Evidence. *Journal of Economic Growth*, 10(3), 199–229. DOI: 10.1007/s10887-005-3533-5

Bejarano-Auqui, J. F. (2024). Model of Business Management Based on the Theories of Management Thinking of the Mypes. (2024). *Academic Journal of Interdisciplinary Studies*, 13(1), 98. DOI: 10.36941/ajis-2024-0008

Beleska-Spasova, E., Glaister, K. W., & Stride, C. (2012). Resource determinants of strategy and performance: The case of British exporters. *Journal of World Business*, 47(4), 635–647. DOI: 10.1016/j.jwb.2011.09.001

Belue, R., Tayllor, K., Anakwe, A., Bradford, N., Coleman, A., & Ahmed, M., & D, A. (2024). Poner la Cultura en primer lugar en la planificación estratégica organizativa de la Comunidad. *Organization Development Journal*, ●●●, 80–90.

Benczes, I., & Szabó, K. (2023). An Economic Understanding of Populism: A Conceptual Framework of the Demand and the Supply Side of Populism. *Political Studies Review*, 21(4), 680–696. DOI: 10.1177/14789299221109449

Ben-Daya, M., Hassini, E., & Bahroun, Z. (2019). Internet of things and supply chain management: A literature review. *International Journal of Production Research*, 57(15-16), 4719–4742. DOI: 10.1080/00207543.2017.1402140

Bentalha, B., Hmioui, A., & Alla, L. (2020). La performance des entreprises de services : Un cadrage théorique d'un concept évolutif. *Alternatives Managériales Economiques, 2*(1), Article 1. DOI: 10.48374/IMIST.PRSM/ame-v2i1.19435

Bergman, B. J.Jr, & McMullen, J. S. (2020). Entrepreneurs in the making: Six decisions for fostering entrepreneurship through maker spaces. *Business Horizons*, 63(6), 811–824. DOI: 10.1016/j.bushor.2020.07.004

Berrone, P., Cruz, C., & Gomez-Mejia, L. R. (2012). Socioemotional Wealth in Family Firms: Theoretical Dimensions, Assessment Approaches, and Agenda for Future Research. *Family Business Review*, 25(3), 258–279. DOI: 10.1177/0894486511435355

Bhatti, Y., & Ventresca, M. (2013). How Can 'Frugal Innovation' Be Conceptualized? SSRN Electronic Journal.

Billiones, R. (2019). Thriving (and not just surviving) in a VUCA healthcare industry. *Medical Writing*, 28(1), 67–69.

Bisbe, J., & Otley, D. (2004). The effects of the interactive use of management control systems on product innova-tion. *Accounting, Organizations and Society*, 29(8), 709–737. DOI: 10.1016/j.aos.2003.10.010

Blanchet, N. (2021). *Immigrant-led SME exporters in Canada*. /https://www.international.gc.ca/trade-commerce/assets/pdfs/inclusive_trade-commerce_inclusif/Immigrant-led-SME-Exporters-canada-en.pdf

Blanco-Mesa, F., León-Castro, E., & Merigó, J. M. (2019). A bibliometric analysis of aggregation operators. *Applied Soft Computing*, 81, 105488. DOI: 10.1016/j.asoc.2019.105488

Bobillier Chaumon, M.-É. (2021). Technologies émergentes et transformations digitales de l'activité : Enjeux pour l'activité et la santé au travail. *Psychologie du Travail et des Organisations*, 27(1), 17–32. DOI: 10.1016/j.pto.2021.01.002

Bocconcelli, R., Cioppi, M., Fortezza, F., Francioni, B., Pagano, A., Savelli, E., & Splendiani, S. (2018). SMEs and Marketing : A Systematic Literature Review. *International Journal of Management Reviews*, 20(2), 227–254. DOI: 10.1111/ijmr.12128

Bocken, N. M. P., Short, S. W., Rana, P., & Evans, S. (2014). A literature and practice review to develop sustainable business model archetypes. *Journal of Cleaner Production*, 65, 42–56. DOI: 10.1016/j.jclepro.2013.11.039

Boehe, D. M., & Cruz, L. B. (2010). Corporate social responsibility, product differentiation strategy and export performance. *Journal of Business Ethics*, 91(2), 325–346. DOI: 10.1007/s10551-010-0613-z

Boeri, T., Mishra, P., Papageorgiou, C., & Spilimbergo, A. (2018). Populism and Civil Society. Populism and Civil Society. International Monetary Fund WP/18/24. https://www.imf.org/en/Publications/WP/Issues/2018/11/17/Populism-and-Civil-Society-46324

Bollen, K. A., & Stine, R. (2014). Direct and indirect effetcs: Classical and bootstrap estimates of variability. *Sociological Methodology*, 20, 115–140. DOI: 10.2307/271084

Bonaccorsi, A. (1992). On the relationship between firm size and export intensity. *Journal of International Business Studies*, 23(3), 605–635. DOI: 10.1057/palgrave.jibs.8490280

Bonilla, M., & Martínez, M. (2009). *Analysis of the methodology for evaluating competitiveness: the case of the World Economic Forum and the Colombian business reality*. Bogotá, Colombia: Universidad del Rosario.

Bonin, H., Constant, A., Tatsiramos, K., & Zimmermann, K. F. (2009). Native-migrant differences in risk attitudes. *Applied Economics Letters*, 16(15), 1581–1586. DOI: 10.1080/13504850701578926

Boons, F., & Lüdeke-Freund, F. (2013). Business models for sustainable innovation: State-of-the-art and steps towards a research agenda. *Journal of Cleaner Production*, 45, 9–19. DOI: 10.1016/j.jclepro.2012.07.007

Boso, N., Story, V. M., Cadogan, J. W., Micevski, M., Kadic-Maglajlic, S., & Kadić-Maglajlić, S. (2013). Firm innovativeness and export performance: Environmental, networking, and structural contingencies. *Journal of International Marketing*, 21(4), 62–87. DOI: 10.1509/jim.13.0052

Boukis, A. (2019). Exploring the implications of blockchain technology for brand-consumer relationships : A future research agenda. *Journal of Product and Brand Management*, 29(3), 307–320. Advance online publication. DOI: 10.1108/JPBM-03-2018-1780

Boumans, D. (2017). *Does Populism Influence Economic Policy Making? Insights from Economic Experts Around the World*. CES ifo DICE Report. https://www.cesifo.org/DocDL/dice-report-2017-4-boumans-december.pdf

Braido, G., Klein, A., & Papaleo, G. (2021). Facilitators and barriers faced by mobile payment fintechs in the Brazilian context. *BBR.Brazilian Business Review*, 18(1), 22–44. DOI: 10.15728/bbr.2021.18.1.2

Brinckmann, J., Grichnik, D., & Kapsa, D. (2010). Should entrepreneurs plan or just storm the castle? A meta-analysis on contextual factors impacting the business planning–performance relationship in small firms. *Journal of Business Venturing*, 25(1), 24–40. https://doi.org/https://doi.org/10.1016/j.jbusvent.2008.10.007. DOI: 10.1016/j.jbusvent.2008.10.007

Briones, G. (1981). *Methods and Techniques of Research for the Social Sciences. The Formulation of Social Research Problems*. Uniandes.

Brush, C. G., De Bruin, A., & Welter, F. (2009). A gender-aware framework for women's entrepreneurship. *International Journal of Gender and Entrepreneurship*, 1(1), 8–24. DOI: 10.1108/17566260910942318

Bruton, G. D., Ahlstrom, D., & Li, H. L. (2010). Institutional theory and entrepreneurship: Where are we now and where do we need to move in the future? *Entrepreneurship Theory and Practice*, 34(3), 421–440. DOI: 10.1111/j.1540-6520.2010.00390.x

Buckley, P. J., Pass, C. L., & Prescott, K. (1991). Measures of International Competitiveness: A Critical Survey. *Journal of Marketing Management*, 4(2), 175–200. DOI: 10.1080/0267257X.1988.9964068

Buhalis, D. (2019). Technology in tourism-from information communication technologies to eTourism and smart tourism towards ambient intelligence tourism : A perspective article. *Tourism Review*, 75(1), 267–272. DOI: 10.1108/TR-06-2019-0258

Burinskienė, A., & Daškevič, D. (2023). CONTEMPORARY CONCEPT OF BUSINESS COMPETI-TIVENESS. *Management/Vadyba (16487974), 39* (1).

ca/guides/spotlight-pleins_feux/intercultural-business-interculturelle-des-affaires.aspx?lang=eng

Caballero-Morales, S. O. (2021). Innovation as recovery strategy for SMEs in emerging economies during the COVID-19 pandemic. *Research in International Business and Finance*, 57, 101396. DOI: 10.1016/j.ribaf.2021.101396 PMID: 33558782

Cadrazco-Parra, W., Zapata-Domínguez, Á., & Lombana-Coy, J. (2021). Capacidades dinámicas: Aportes y tendencias. *Revista Lasallista de Investigacion*.

Camilleri, M. A. (2019). The use of data-driven technologies in tourism marketing. In *Entrepreneurship, Innovation and Inequality* (p. 182-194). Routledge. https://www.taylorfrancis.com/chapters/edit/10.4324/9780429292583-11/use-data-driven-technologies-tourism-marketing-mark-anthony-camilleri

Camilleri, M. A., & Valeri, M. (2021). Thriving family businesses in tourism and hospitality: A systematic review and a synthesis of the relevant literature. *Journal of Family Business Management, ahead-of-print*(ahead-of-print). https://doi.org/DOI: 10.1108/JFBM-10-2021-0133

Camisón, C., & Villar-López, A. (2010). Effect of SMEs' international experience on foreign intensity and economic performance: The mediating role of internationally exploitable assets and competitive strategy. *Journal of Small Business Management*, 48(2), 116–151. DOI: 10.1111/j.1540-627X.2010.00289.x

Camue Álvarez, A., Carballal del Río, E., & Toscano Ruiz, D. F. (2017). Concepciones teóricas sobre la efectividad organizacional y su evaluación en las universidades. *Cofin Habana, 11*(2), 136-152. http://scielo.sld.cu/scielo.php?script=sci_arttext&pid=S2073-60612017000200010&lng=es&tlng=es

Canada.ca. (n.d). The Honourable Rechie Valdez. https://www.pm.gc.ca/en/cabinet/honourable-rechie
-valdez

Canadian Women's Foundation and Platform. (2021). *Resetting normal: Gender, intersectionality and leadership.*https://fw3s926r0g42i6kes3bxg4i1-wpengine.netdna-ssl.com/wp-content/uploads/2021/04/
Resetting-Normal-Gender-Intersectionality-and-Leadership-Report-Final-EN.pdf

Canal Capital. (2021). *El populismo en Colombia y en América Latina | A las Palabras.*https://www
.canalcapital.gov.co/noticias-capital-migracion/el-populismo-colombia-y-america-latina-las-palabras

Căpu neanu, S., Topor, D. I., Constantin, D. M., Barbu, C. M., & Hint, M. S. (2021). Strategic Management Accounting: Dimensions and Strategic Tools. In Oncioiu, I., Căpu neanu, S., Topor, D., & Constantin, D. (Eds.), *Sustainability Reporting, Ethics, and Strategic Management Strategies for Modern Organizations* (pp. 1–29). IGI Global., DOI: 10.4018/978-1-7998-4637-6.ch001

Cárdenas Flórez, D., & Ríos Zuluaga, M. (2016*). Diagnóstico de la responsabilidad social empresarial con enfoque en discapacitados físicamente, entre las pymes y en algunos talleres de confecciones de la ciudad de Pereira y Dosquebradas; con una propuesta de fortalecimiento de responsabilidad social empresarial.* Universidad Tecnológica de Pereira. Facultad de Tecnología Industrial Pereira. https://
repositorio.utp.edu.co/server/api/core/bitstreams/7792aea2-1ca1-4b26-bd4d-a2325539c4c3/content

Carlson, M. B., Nelson, J. S., & Skimmyhorn, W. L. (2016). Military personal finance research. *Handbook of consumer finance research*, 251-264.

Carlson, N. A. (2023). Differentiation in microenterprises. *Strategic Management Journal*, 44(5), 1141–1167. DOI: 10.1002/smj.3463

Cascio, 2020 Facing the Age of Chaos https://medium.com/@cascio/facing-the-age-of-chaos-
b00687b1f51d

Catacataca, P. D. (n.d). *The use of Filipino in official transactions, communication, and correspondence.*https://ncca.gov.ph/about-ncca-3/subcommissions/subcommission-on-cultural-disseminationscd/
language-and-translation/the-use-of-filipino-in-official-transactions-communication-and-
correspondence/

Cavusgil, S. T., & Zou, S. (1994). Marketing strategy-performance relationship: An investigation of the empirical link in export market ventures. *Journal of Marketing*, 58(1), 1–21. DOI: 10.1177/002224299405800101

Cazau, P. (2006). Introducción a la investigación en ciencias sociales.

Cerda Hugo. (2002). The Elements of Research. Editorial el Buho Ltda. Bogotá. 3rd reprint.

Chambi, P. (2023). *Segmentación de mercado: Machine Learning en marketing en contextos de covid-19*. Industrial Data.

Charbonneau, J. (2017). *To win at trade with ASEAN, Canada must also focus on security and Culture.* https://www.asiapacific.ca/blog/win-trade-asean-canada-must-also-focus-security-and-culture

Chesbrough, H. W. (2003). *Open Innovation: The new imperative for creating and profiting from technology*. Harvard Business School Press.

Chikwendu, J. E., & Mutambara, E. (2020). Sociological factors influencing the success of African immigrant-owned micro businesses in South Africa. *Entrepreneurship and Sustainability Issues, 8*(1), 972-982. https://doi.org/https://doi.org/10.9770/jesi.2020.8.1(65)

Chintalapati, S., & Pandey, S. K. (2022). Artificial intelligence in marketing : A systematic literature review. *International Journal of Market Research*, 64(1), 38–68. DOI: 10.1177/14707853211018428

Chopra, S., & Sodhi, M. S. (2014). Reducing the risk of supply chain disruptions. *MIT Sloan Management Review*, 55(3), 73–80.

Christensen, C. M. (1997). *The Innovator's Dilemma: When New Technologies Cause Great Firms to Fail*. Harvard Business Review Press.

Christensen, C. M., Raynor, M. E., & McDonald, R. (2015). What is disruptive innovation? *Harvard Business Review*, 93(12), 44–53. PMID: 17183796

Christopher, M., & Peck, H. (2004). Building the resilient supply chain. *International Journal of Logistics Management*, 15(2), 1–14. DOI: 10.1108/09574090410700275

Chumarina, G. & Abulkhanova, G. (2021). Corporate Social Responsibility Management. *International Journal of Financial Research.* Vol 12 No. 1.

Chung, H. F. L., & Ho, M. H.-W. (2021). International competitive strategies, organizational learning and export performance: A match and mis-match conceptualization strategies. *European Journal of Marketing*, 55(10), 2794–2822. DOI: 10.1108/EJM-04-2019-0309

CIMA, R. (2018). Identify and understand clients' money scripts: A framework for using the KMSI-R. *Journal of Financial Planning*, 31(3), 46–55.

Çitilci, T., & Akbalık, M. (2020). The importance of PESTEL analysis for environmental scanning process. In *Handbook of Research on Decision-Making Techniques in Financial Marketing* (pp. 336–357). IGI Global. DOI: 10.4018/978-1-7998-2559-3.ch016

City of Toronto. (n.d.). *Strong economy.*https://www.toronto.ca/business-economy/invest-in-toronto/strong-economy/

Clark, R., Lusardi, A., & Mitchell, O. S. (2020). Financial fragility during the COVID-19 pandemic. *NBER Working Paper No. 28207.* National Bureau of Economic Research.

Coccia, M. (2009, March). What is the optimal rate of R&D investment to maximize productivity growth? *Technological Forecasting and Social Change*, 76(3), 433–446. DOI: 10.1016/j.techfore.2008.02.008

Cohen, W. M., & Levinthal, D. A. (1990). Absorptive capacity: A new perspective on learning and innovation. *Administrative Science Quarterly*, 35(1), 128–152. DOI: 10.2307/2393553

Collins, J. (2003). Cultural diversity and entrepreneurship: Policy responses to immigrant entrepreneurs in Australia. *Entrepreneurship and Regional Development*, 15(2), 137–149. DOI: 10.1080/0898562032000075168

Colombian Political Constitution. 1991, Congress of the Republic, Law 27 of 1992.

Coltey, E., Alonso, D., Vassigh, S., & Chen, S.-C. (2022). Towards an AI-Driven Marketplace for Small Businesses During COVID-19. *SN Computer Science*, 3(6), 441. DOI: 10.1007/s42979-022-01349-w PMID: 35975091

Congress of the Republic, Law 87 of 1993. file:///C:/Users/User/Downloads/Dialnet-FormacionDel-TalentoHumano-2934638.pdf file:///C:/Users/User/Downloads/KarlPolany_Economy-as-an-institutionalized-activity%20(1).pdf

Constant, A., & Zimmermann, K. F. (2006). The Making of Entrepreneurs in Germany: Are Native Men and Immigrants Alike? *Small Business Economics*, 26(3), 279–300. DOI: 10.1007/s11187-005-3004-6

Cope, J. (2011). Entrepreneurial learning from failure: An interpretative phenomenological analysis. *Journal of Business Venturing*, 26(6), 604–623. DOI: 10.1016/j.jbusvent.2010.06.002

Corona-Rodríguez, J. (2021). La importancia de la Alfabetización Mediática Informacional en el contexto pandémico: propuesta de actualización y nuevas preguntas. *Diálogos sobre educación. Temas actuales en investigación educativa, 12*(22). https://doi.org/DOI: 10.32870/dse.v0i22.979

Cranmer, E., & Jung, T. (2017). The value of augmented reality from a business model perspective. *e-Review of Tourism Research, 8*. https://e-space.mmu.ac.uk/617802/

Cranmer, E. E., Tom Dieck, M. C., & Jung, T. (2018). How can Tourist Attractions Profit from Augmented Reality? In Jung, T., & Tom Dieck, M. C. (Eds.), *Augmented Reality and Virtual Reality* (pp. 21–32). Springer International Publishing., DOI: 10.1007/978-3-319-64027-3_2

Cranmer, E., Urquhart, C., Claudia tom Dieck, M., & Jung, T. (2021). Developing augmented reality business models for SMEs in tourism. *Information & Management*, 58(8), 103551. DOI: 10.1016/j.im.2021.103551

Cucchiella, F., & Gastaldi, M. (2006). Risk management in supply chain: A real option approach. *Journal of Manufacturing Technology Management*, 17(6), 700–720. DOI: 10.1108/17410380610678756

Cuevas Vargas, H., Fernández Escobedo, R., Cortés Palacios, H. A., & Ramírez Lemus, L. (2021). *The relation between adoption of information and communication technologies and marketing innovation as a key strategy to improve business performance.* https://addi.ehu.es/handle/10810/52894

Dabab, M., & Weber, C. (2018). Business Intelligence and Data Analytics as a Driver of Dynamic Capability Strategic Approach. *Portland International Conference on Management of Engineering and Technology (PICMET)*, 1-9. DOI: 10.23919/PICMET.2018.8481750

Dabić, M., Maley, J., Dana, L. P., Novak, I., Pellegrini, M. M., & Caputo, A. (2020). Pathways of SME internationalization: A bibliometric and systematic review. *Small Business Economics*, 55(3), 705–725. DOI: 10.1007/s11187-019-00181-6

Dabić, M., Vlačić, B., Paul, J., Dana, L.-P., Sahasranamam, S., & Glinka, B. (2020). Immigrant entrepreneurship: A review and research agenda. *Journal of Business Research*, 113, 25–38. https://doi.org/ https://doi.org/10.1016/j.jbusres.2020.03.013. DOI: 10.1016/j.jbusres.2020.03.013

Dalkey, N., & Helmer, O. (1962). An Experimental Application of the Dephi Metod to the Use of Experts. *Rand Co*, 27. https://www.rand.org/content/dam/rand/pubs/research_memoranda/2009/RM727.1.pdf

Damayanti, R., Al-Shami, S. S. A., Bin Rahim, A. B. R., & Marwati, F. S. (2018). Factors that influence financial literacy on small medium enterprises: A literature review. [Scopus.]. *Opción*, 34(86), 1540–1557.

Darvin, R. (2016). Mediating identities: Language, media, and Filipinos in Canada. https://dx.doi.org/ DOI: 10.14288/1.0347617

Das, G., & Pachoni, P. (2022). Pduamt. *Business Review.*

Davenport, T. H., & Prusak, L. (2005). What do we talk about when we talk about knowledge? *I. NONAKA, Hg. Knowledge management. Critical perspectives on business and management. London: Routledge*, 301-321.

Davenport, T. H., & Prusak, L. (1998). *Working knowledge: How organizations manage what they know.* Harvard Business Press.

Davenport, T., Guha, A., Grewal, D., & Bressgott, T. (2019). How artificial intelligence will change the future of marketing. *Journal of the Academy of Marketing Science*, 48(1), 1–19. DOI: 10.1007/s11747-019-00696-0

David, F. R. (2003). Conceptos de Administración Estratégica. Naucalpan de Juárez: Pearson Education.

David, F. D., & David, F. R. (2017). *Strategic management. A competitive advantage approach, concepts and cases.* (6a edit.). Pearson.

Davies, A. (2019). Carrying out systematic literature reviews: An introduction. *British Journal of Nursing (Mark Allen Publishing)*, 28(15), 1008–1014. DOI: 10.12968/bjon.2019.28.15.1008 PMID: 31393770

de Leon, F. M., Jr. (n.d.). *Understanding the Filipino* [PowerPoint Slides]. SlidePlayer. https://slideplayer.com/slide/4211242/

De Vita, L., Mari, M., & Poggesi, S. (2014). Women entrepreneurs in and from developing countries: Evidences from the literature. *European Management Journal*, 32(3), 451–460. DOI: 10.1016/j.emj.2013.07.009

Del Tronco, J. (2013). Desconfianza y "Accountability" ¿las causas del Populismo en América Latina? *Latin American Research Review*, 48(2), 55–78. https://www.jstor.org/stable/43670076. DOI: 10.1353/lar.2013.0026

Deltour, F., & Lethiais, V. (2014). L'innovation en PME et son accompagnement par les TIC : Quels effets sur la performance? *Systèmes d'information et management, 19*(2), 45-73.

Departamento Nacional de Planeación [DNP]. (2020). Política nacional de inclusión y educación económica y financiera. *Documento CONPES 4005, 1*, 94.

Department of Foreign Affairs. (n.d.). *Mission, vision, and core values.* https://dfa.gov.ph/about/mission-vision-core-values

Department of Tourism. (n.d.). *National tourism development plan.* http://www.tourism.gov.ph/NTDP.aspx

Department of Trade and Industry. (n.d). *ASEAN 50: 50th year of being one ASEAN.* Association of Southeast Asian Nations. https://www.dti.gov.ph/asean/

Dervitsiotis, K. N. (2010). Developing full-spectrum innovation capability for survival and success in the global economy. *Total Quality Management & Business Excellence*, 21(2), 159–170. DOI: 10.1080/14783360903549865

Dias-Fonseca, D., & Potter, J. (2016). La educación mediática como estrategia de participación cívica on-line en las escuelas portuguesas. *Comunicar, 24*(49), 9-18. https://www.revistacomunicar.com/verpdf.php?numero=49&articulo=49-2016-01

Dosi, G. (1982). Technological paradigms and technological trajectories: A suggested interpretation of the determinants and directions of technical change. *Research Policy*, 11(3), 147–162. DOI: 10.1016/0048-7333(82)90016-6

Drucker, P. F. (1954). The Practice of Management: A Study of the Most Important Function in America Society. *Harper & Brothers.*

Drucker, P. F. (2020). *The essential drucker.* Routledge. DOI: 10.4324/9780429347979

Duan, C., & Sandhu, K. (2022). Immigrant entrepreneurship motivation – scientific production, field development, thematic antecedents, measurement elements and research agenda. *Journal of Enterprising Communities: People and Places in the Global Economy*, 16(5), 722–755. DOI: 10.1108/JEC-11-2020-0191

Dubey, A. K., Shingte, S. C., Siddiqui, M. S., & Patil, S. (2023, May). Crowdfunding using Blockchain for Startups and Investors. In *2023 7th International Conference on Intelligent Computing and Control Systems (ICICCS)* (pp. 1400-1405). IEEE. DOI: 10.1109/ICICCS56967.2023.10142310

Dubey, R., Gunasekaran, A., Childe, S. J., Blome, C., Papadopoulos, T., & Singh, T. (2020). Big data and predictive analytics and manufacturing performance: Integrating institutional theory, resource-based view and big data culture. *British Journal of Management*, 31(2), 341–361. DOI: 10.1111/1467-8551.12355

Durant, A., & Shepherd, I. (2009). 'Culture' and 'communication' in intercultural communication. *European journal of English studies*, 13(2), 147-162. Page 4

Duranton, G., & Puga, D. (2004). Micro-Foundations of Urban Agglomeration Economies. In Henderson, J. V., & Thisse, J.-F. (Eds.), *Handbook of Regional and Urban Economics* (Vol. 4, pp. 2063–2117). Elsevier., https://doi.org/https://doi.org/10.1016/S1574-0080(04)80005-1

Edeh, J. N., Obodoechi, D. N., & Ramos-Hidalgo, E. (2020). Effects of innovation strategies on export performance: New empirical evidence from developing market firms. *Technological Forecasting and Social Change*, 158, 120167. DOI: 10.1016/j.techfore.2020.120167

Efron, B. (1988). Bootstrap Confidence Intervals: Good or bad? *Psychological Bulletin*, 104(2), 293–296. DOI: 10.1037/0033-2909.104.2.293

Eggers, F. (2020). Masters of Disasters? Challenges and Opportunities for SMEs in Times of Crisis. *Journal of Business Research*, 116, 199–208. DOI: 10.1016/j.jbusres.2020.05.025 PMID: 32501306

Eijdenberg, E. L., Thompson, N. A., Verduijn, K., & Essers, C. (2019). Entrepreneurial activities in a developing country: An institutional theory perspective. *International Journal of Entrepreneurial Behaviour & Research*, 25(3), 414–432. DOI: 10.1108/IJEBR-12-2016-0418

Eisenhardt, K. M., & Martin, J. A. (2000). Dynamic capabilities: What are they? *Strategic Management Journal*, 21(10-11), 1105–1121. DOI: 10.1002/1097-0266(200010/11)21:10/11<1105::AID-SMJ133>3.0.CO;2-E

Embassy of the Philippines in Hague. (n.d.). *General information*. https://thehaguepe.dfa.gov.ph/79-about-us/98-general-information#:~:text=Two%20official%20languages%20%E2%80%94%20Filipino%20and,of%20instruction%20in%20higher%20education

Embassy of the Philippines in Ottawa. (n.d.). *Filipinos in Canada: The Filipino diaspora in Canada*. https://ottawape.dfa.gov.ph/index.php/2016-04-12-08-34-55/filipino-diaspora

Ertemel, A. V. (2019). *Implications of Blockchain Technology on Marketing* (SSRN Scholarly Paper 3351196). https://papers.ssrn.com/abstract=3351196

Ertorer, S. E., Long, J., Fellin, M., & Esses, V. M. (2020). Immigrant perceptions of integration in the Canadian workplace. *Equality, Diversity and Inclusion*, Vol. ahead-of-print No. ahead-of-print. https://doi.org/DOI: 10.1108/EDI-02-2019-0086

Etzkowitz, H., & Leydesdorff, L. (2000). The dynamics of innovation: From National Systems and "Mode 2" to a Triple Helix of university–industry–government relations. *Research Policy*, 29(2), 109–123. DOI: 10.1016/S0048-7333(99)00055-4

Eude (2024). *Gestión del Cambio en Tiempos de Incertidumbre: Consejos y estrategias para líderes y gerentes*. (15) Gestión del Cambio en Tiempos de Incertidumbre: Consejos y estrategias para líderes y gerentes | LinkedIn

Eulerich, M., Eulerich, A., & Fligge, B. (2023). Analyzing the strategy–performance relationship in Germany – can we still use the common strategic frameworks? *Journal of Strategy and Management*, 16(3), 516–532. DOI: 10.1108/JSMA-09-2022-0157

European Commission. (2021). *Annual Report on European SMEs*

Evason, N. (2016a). *Canadian Culture: Business Culture*. https://culturalatlas.sbs.com.au/canadian-culture/canadian-culture-business-culture

Evason, N. (2016b). *Canadian Culture: Dates of Significance*. https://culturalatlas.sbs.com.au/canadian-culture/canadian-culture-dates-of-significance

Evason, N. (2016c). *Canadian Culture: Religion*. https://culturalatlas.sbs.com.au/canadian-culture/canadian-culture-religion

Fadhil, M. K., & Subriadi, A. P. (2023, February). Factor Affecting Behavior Intention To Use Mobile Payment Adoption: An Analysis Of Literature Review. In *2023 International Conference on Computer Science, Information Technology and Engineering (ICCoSITE)* (pp. 847-852). IEEE. DOI: 10.1109/ICCoSITE57641.2023.10127839

Fagerberg, J. (1996). Technology and Competitiveness. *Oxford Review of Economic Policy*, 12(3), 39–51. DOI: 10.1093/oxrep/12.3.39

Fagerberg, J., Mowery, D. C., & Nelson, R. R. (2013). *The Oxford Handbook of Innovation*. Oxford University Press.

Faherty, U., & Stephens, S. (2016). Innovation in micro enterprises: Reality or fiction? *Journal of Small Business and Enterprise Development*, 23(2), 349–362. DOI: 10.1108/JSBED-11-2013-0176

Fahey, L., & Narayanan, V. K. (1986). *Macroenviromental Analysis for Strategic Management*. West Publishing Company.

Fairlie, R. W., & Fossen, F. M. (2020). Defining Opportunity versus Necessity Entrepreneurship: Two Components of Business Creation. In Polachek, S. W., & Tatsiramos, K. (Eds.), *Change at Home, in the Labor Market, and On the Job* (Vol. 48, pp. 253–289). Emerald Publishing Limited., DOI: 10.1108/ S0147-912120200000048008

Fairlie, R. W., & Lofstrom, M. (2015). Immigration and entrepreneurship. In *Handbook of the economics of international migration* (Vol. 1, pp. 877–911). Elsevier.

Falahati, L., & Paim, L. H. (2011). Gender differences in financial well-being among college students. *Australian Journal of Basic and Applied Sciences*, 5(9), 1765–1776.

Falahat, M., & Migin, M. W. (2017). Export performance of international new ventures in emerging market. *International Journal of Business and Globalisation*, 19(1), 111–125. DOI: 10.1504/IJBG.2017.085119

Falavigna, G., Ippoliti, R., & Manello, A. (2019). Judicial Efficiency and Immigrant Entrepreneurs. *Journal of Small Business Management*, 57(2), 421–449. DOI: 10.1111/jsbm.12376

Farida, I., & Setiawan, D. (2022). Business strategies and competitive advantage: The role of performance and innovation. *Journal of Open Innovation*, 8(3), 163. DOI: 10.3390/joitmc8030163

Fauchart, E., & Gruber, M. (2011). Darwinians, communitarians, and missionaries: The role of founder identity in entrepre-neurship. *Academy of Management Journal*, 54(5), 935–957. DOI: 10.5465/ amj.2009.0211

Favre-Bonté, V., & Tran, S. (2013). L'apport d'internet aux petites entreprises (PE) touristiques dans la construction de leur positionnement stratégique : Le cas des hébergeurs. *Revue internationale P.M.E (Norwalk, Conn.)*, 26(1), 45–64. DOI: 10.7202/1024270ar

Fernandes, D., Lynch, J. G.Jr, & Netemeyer, R. G. (2014). Financial Literacy, Financial Education, and Downstream Financial Behaviors. *Management Science*, 60(8), 1861–1883. https://www.jstor.org/stable/ 42919641. DOI: 10.1287/mnsc.2013.1849

Ferraz, J. C., Kupfer, D., & Iootty, M. (2004). Industrial competitiveness in Brazil. 10 years after liberalization. *CEPAL Review*, 82(82), 91–119. DOI: 10.18356/a99f5747-en

Festa, G., Elbahri, S., Cuomo, M. T., Ossorio, M., & Rossi, M. (2022). FinTech ecosystem as influencer of young entrepreneurial intentions: Empirical findings from Tunisia. *Journal of Intellectual Capital*, 24(1), 205–226. DOI: 10.1108/JIC-08-2021-0220

Flores Vivar, J. M. (2019). Inteligencia artificial y periodismo: Diluyendo el impacto de la desinformación y las noticias falsas a través de los bots. *Doxa Comunicación*, 29, 197–212. DOI: 10.31921/doxacom.n29a10

Flores, J., Pincay, D., & Vargas, P. (2018). Esquema de alineamiento estratégico: Una perspectiva teórica desde la consultoría empresarial y la gerencia aplicada. *CIENCIA UNEMI*, 41-56.

Forcadell, F. (2004). *Business growth from a resource-based approach. Towards an integrative model.* Rey Juan Carlos University.

Foss, N. J., Klein, P. G., Kor, Y. Y., & Mahoney, J. T. (2008). Entrepreneurship, subjectivism, and the resource-based view: To-ward a new synthesis. *Strategic Entrepreneurship Journal*, 2(1), 73–94. DOI: 10.1002/sej.41

Francis, A. (2023). The concept of competitiveness. In *The competitiveness of european industry* (pp. 5-20). Routledge. Francis, A. (2023). The concept of competitiveness. In *The competitiveness of european industry* (pp. 5-20). Routledge. DOI: 10.4324/9781003369820-2

Fred, R. (2008). *Strategic Management Concepts* (11th ed.). Pearson education.

Friberg, J. H., & Midtbøen, A. H. (2018). Ethnicity as skill: Immigrant employment hierarchies in Norwegian low-wage labour markets. *Journal of Ethnic and Migration Studies*, 44(9), 1463–1478. DOI: 10.1080/1369183X.2017.1388160

Fuchs, M., & Kostner, M. (2016). Antecedents and consequences of firm' s export marketing strategy. An empirical study of Austrian SMEs (a contingency perspective). *Management Research Review*, 39(3), 329–355. DOI: 10.1108/MRR-07-2014-0158

Fuentealba, D., Flores-Fernández, C., & Carrasco, R. (2023). Análisis bibliométrico y de contenido sobre VUCA. *Revista Española de Documentación Científica*, 46(2), e354. Advance online publication. DOI: 10.3989/redc.2023.2.1968

Fuertes, G., Alfaro, M., Vargas, M., Gutiérrez, S., Ternero, R., & Sabattin, J. (2020). Conceptual framework for the strategic management: A literature review descriptive. *Journal of Engineering*, 2020, 1–21. DOI: 10.1155/2020/6253013

Funko, I. S., Vlačić, B., & Dabić, M. (2023). Corporate entrepreneurship in public sector: A systematic literature review and research agenda. *Journal of Innovation & Knowledge*, 8(2), 100343. DOI: 10.1016/j.jik.2023.100343

Gafa, Y. (2020). Effet médiateur de l'innovativité dans la relation orientation-marché et performance commerciale des Très Petites Entreprises (TPE) de métiers. *REVUE AFRICAINE DE MANAGEMENT*, 3(5), Article 5. DOI: 10.48424/IMIST.PRSM/ram-v5i3.20156

Galicia-Gopar, M. A., Mendoza-Ramirez, L., & Espinosa-Trujillo, M. A. (2020). Estrategias de supervivencia y desempeño de mipymes en un ambiente de incertidumbre. *Ciencias Administrativas. Teoría y Praxis*, 16(2), 31–47.

Galindo-Martín, M. Á., Castaño-Martínez, M. S., & Méndez-Picazo, M. T. (2021). The role of entrepreneurship in different economic phases. *Journal of Business Research*, 122, 171–179. DOI: 10.1016/j.jbusres.2020.08.050

Galvis, A. (2023). Colombianos tienen mayor confianza en el sector empresarial que en el Gobierno. *Asuntos Legales*.https://www.asuntoslegales.com.co/actualidad/en-colombia-se-tiene-mas-confianza-en-el-sector-empresarial-que-en-gobierno-y-medios-3605773

Gambaro, E., & García, L. N. (2021). Empresas B: Una gestión estratégica apoyada en el conocimiento. *Actualidad Contable Faces*, 24(42), 125–149. DOI: 10.53766/ACCON/2021.42.05

Gangi, F., Daniele, L. M., Scuotto, V., & Tani, M. (2023). Uncovering Backers' Intention to Participate in Reward-Based Crowdfunding: The Role of Value Cocreation. *IEEE Transactions on Engineering Management*.

Gans, J. (2016). *The Disruption Dilemma*. MIT Press. DOI: 10.7551/mitpress/9780262034487.001.0001

Garcia Guiliany, J., Duran, S., Cardeño Pórtela, E., Prieto Pulido, R., Garcia Cali, E. & Paz Marcano, A. (2017). Proceso de planificación estratégica: Etapas ejecutadas en pequeñas y medianas empresas para optimizar la competitividad. *Revista Espacio*. Vol. 38 (N.º 52) Año 2017. Pág. 16.

Garcia Guiliany, J., Pizarro de la Hoz, A., Barragán Morales, C., & Villarreal, F. (2023). Planeación estratégica para la competitividad de pequeñas y medianas empresas del sector construcción e inmobiliario. *Revista de Ciencias Sociales*, 29(2), 315–326. DOI: 10.31876/rcs.v29i2.39978

Garrido, S. (2003). *Direccion estrategica*. Mc Graw Hill.

Garzón, M. A., & Ibarra, A. (2014). Revisión Sobre la Sostenibilidad Empresarial. *Revista de Estudios Avanzados de Liderazgo*, 2014, Volumen 1, Número 3. https://www.regent.edu/acad/global/publications/real/vol1no3/4-castrillon.pdf

Gazette, O. (n.d.). *Philippine Government*. https://www.officialgazette.gov.ph/about/gov/

Gazette, O. (n.d.). *The Philippines*. https://www.officialgazette.gov.ph/about/philippines /

Geissdoerfer, M., Savaget, P., & Evans, S. (2017). The Cambridge business model innovation process. *Journal of Cleaner Production*, 142, 1550–1567.

Gemünden, H. G. (1991). Success factors of export marketing: A meta-analytic critique of the empirical studies. In Paliwoda, S. (Ed.), *Perspectives on International Marketing - Re-Issued* (pp. 222–246). Routeldge Library Edition International Business., DOI: 10.4324/9780203076613-8

Ghemawat, P. (2000). *La estrategia en el panorama del negocio*. Prentice Hall.

Gil, I., & Marzal-Felici, J. (2023). ¿Cómo impulsar la educomunicación y la alfabetización mediática desde el sistema educativo en España? Diagnóstico, problemática y propuestas por los expertos. *Revista Mediterránea de Comunicación/Mediterranean. Journal of Communication*, 14(2), 207–226. https://www.doi.org/10.14198/MEDCOM.24011

Giraldo, A. M., Arango, M. J., & Castillo, M. B. (2006). *Training of human talent: a strategic factor for the development of sustainable productivity and competitiveness in organizations. Guillermo de Ockham: Scientific Journal, 4* (1), 43-81._https://www.redalyc.org/articulo.oa?id=477847114019 https://www .researchgate.net/profile/Marco-Vivarelli/publication/228001376_Impacto_social_de_la_globalizacion _en_los_paises_en_desarrollo/links/5a02fb77a6fdcc6b7c9a4f94/Impacto-social-de-la-globalizacion -en-los-paises-en-desarrollo.pdf https://www.scielo.sa.cr/scielo.php?script=sci_arttext&pid=S1659 -49322020000200006

Gleim, M., & Stevens, J. (2021). Blockchain : A game changer for marketers? *Marketing Letters*, 32(1), 1–6. DOI: 10.1007/s11002-021-09557-9

Global Affairs Canada. (2022). *Minister Ng establishes the Canada-Philippines joint economic commission.*https://www.canada.ca/en/global-affairs/news/2022/05/minister-ng-establishes-the-canada -philippines-joint-economic-commission.html

Godé, C. (2021). Propos introductif : Technologies émergentes et digitalisation des organisations. *Recherche et Cas en Sciences de Gestion*, (22). Advance online publication. DOI: 10.3917/rcsg.022.0007

Godet, M., Monti, R., Meunier, F., & Roubelat, F. (2000). *La caja de herramientas de la Prospectiva.* Librairie des Arts et Métiers.

Gomber, P., Koch, J.-A., & Siering, M. (2017). Digital Finance and FinTech: Current research and future research directions. *Journal of Business Economics*, 87(5), 537–580. DOI: 10.1007/s11573-017-0852-x

Gómez, G. (2021). Los cibergéneros especializados: Análisis sobre la modalidad de gestión de contenidos en weblogs independientes de moda. *Cuadernos del Centro de Estudios en Diseño y Comunicación. Ensayos.*

Gómez-Hurtado, C. (2023). Current strategic identification of IMARK. Interview by Rafael Perez in june 2023. Bogotá-Colombia.

Gonzales, L. (2017). Gestión estratégica de la Comunidad Colombiana de Cómputo Avanzado 3CoA® mediante análisis DOFA y cocreación. *Ingeniare. Revista Chilena de Ingeniería*, 25(3), 464–476. DOI: 10.4067/S0718-33052017000300464

González Flores, I. (2012). Necesidad de la alfabetización informacional en la Educación Superior. Vivat Academia, (121),65-76. https://www.redalyc.org/articulo.oa?id=525752951006

Gonzalez Hernandez, M. E., Portillo Lovo, J. L., Benítez Ramírez, D., & Moran De Villalta, D. (2023). *Planificación estratégica para el centro escolar juan manuel rodríguez.* [Doctoral dissertation, Universidad de El Salvador]. https://oldri.ues.edu.sv/id/eprint/33553/

Götz, O., Kerstin, L.-G., & Krafft, M. (2010). Evaluation of Structural Equation Models Using Partial Least Square (PLS) Approach. In Esposito Vinzi, V., Chin, W., Henseler, J., & Wang, H. (Eds.) *Handbook of Partial Least Squares*. Springer Handbooks of Computational Statistics (pp. 691–711). Springer, Berlin, Heidelberg. DOI: 10.1007/978-3-540-32827-8_30

Gouvernement du Québec. (2022). *Importance of French in Quebec.*https://www.quebec.ca/en/ immigration/french-in-quebec#:~:text=According%20to%20the%20Charter%20of,work

Government of Canada. (2012). *Discover Canada – Canada's economy.*https://www.canada.ca/en/immigration-refugees-citizenship/corporate/publications-manuals/discover-canada/read-online/canadas-economy.html

Government of Canada. (2016a). *Effective interactive communication.*https://www.canada.ca/en/revenue-agency/corporate/careers-cra/information-moved/cra-competencies-standardized-assessment-tools/canada-revenue-agency-competencies-april-2016/effective-interactive-communication.html

Government of Canada. (2016b). *Key leadership competency profile and examples of effective and ineffective behaviors.*https://www.canada.ca/en/treasury-board-secretariat/services/professional-development/key-leadership-competency-profile/examples-effective-ineffective-behaviours.html

Government of Canada. (2017). *About official languages and bilingualism.*https://www.canada.ca/en/canadian-heritage/services/official-languages-bilingualism/about.html

Government of Canada. (2018a). *About the Crown.*https://www.canada.ca/en/canadian-heritage/services/crown-canada/about.html

Government of Canada. (2018b). *Mandate - Immigration, Refugees, Citizenship Canada.*https://www.canada.ca/en/immigration-refugees-citizenship/corporate/mandate.html

Government of Canada. (2020a). *Community support, multiculturalism, and anti-racism initiatives program.*https://www.canada.ca/en/canadian-heritage/services/funding/community-multiculturalism-anti-racism.html

Government of Canada. (2020b). *The creation of Canada.*https://www.canada.ca/en/canadian-heritage/services/origin-name-canada.html

Government of Canada. (2021a). *Aging and chronic diseases: A profile of Canadian seniors.*https://www.canada.ca/en/public-health/services/publications/diseases-conditions/aging-chronic-diseases-profile-canadian-seniors-report.html

Government of Canada. (2021b). *Canada welcomes the most immigrants in a single year in its history.* https://www.canada.ca/en/immigration-refugees-citizenship/news/2021/12/canada-welcomes-the-most-immigrants-in-a-single-year-in-its-history.html

Government of Canada. (2021c). *Responsible business conduct abroad: Canada's strategy for the future.* https://www.international.gc.ca/trade-commerce/rbc-cre/strategy-2022-strategie.aspx?lang=eng

Government of Canada. (2021d). *The constitutional distribution of legislative powers.*https://www.canada.ca/en/intergovernmental-affairs/services/federation/distribution-legislative-powers.html

Government of Canada. (2021e). *Spotlight on intercultural business.*https://www.tradecommissioner.gc

Government of Canada. (2022a). *Job enhancement and essential skills.*

Government of Canada. (2022b). *What is gender-based analysis plus.* https://women-gender-equality.canada.ca/en/gender-based-analysis-plus/what-gender-based-analysis-plus.html

Government of Canada. (2023). *Canada opens operations centre in the Philippines to boost global immigration processing capacity.*https://www.canada.ca/en/immigration-refugees-citizenship/news/2023/03/canada-opens-operations-centre-in-the-philippines-to-boost-global-immigration-processing-capacity.html

Government of Canada. (2023). *Notice – Supplementary information for the 2024-2026 immigration level plans.*https://www.canada.ca/en/immigration-refugees-citizenship/news/notices/supplementary-immigration-levels-2024-2026.html

Government of Canada. (2024a). *Canada-Philippines relations.*https://www.international.gc.ca/country-pays/philippines/relations.aspx?lang=eng

Government of Canada. (2024b). *Canada's chairing of the CPTPP Commission in 2024.*https://www.international.gc.ca/trade-commerce/trade-agreements-accords-commerciaux/agr-acc/cptpp-ptpgp/commission-2024.aspx?lang=eng

Government of Canada. (2024c). *State of trade 2023: Inclusive trade.*https://www.international.gc.ca/transparency-transparence/state-trade-commerce-international/2023.aspx?lang=eng. ISSN 2562-8321

Government of Prince Edward Island. (n.d.). *Canadian citizenship.*http://www.gov.pe.ca/photos/original/WI_KCanadianCit.pdf

Government, H. M. (2018). *Civil Society Strategy: building a future that works for everyone.* Policy paper. https://assets.publishing.service.gov.uk/media/5b6b282440f0b62ec1fa611d/Civil_Society_Strategy_-_building_a_future_that_works_for_everyone.pdf

Gozálvez-Pérez, V., & Contreras-Pulido, P. (2014). Empowering media citizenship through educommunication. *Comunicar*, 42(42), 129–136. DOI: 10.3916/C42-2014-12

Gozman, D., Liebenau, J., & Mangan, J. (2018). The innovation mechanisms of fintech start-ups: Insights from SWIFT's innotribe competition. *Journal of Management Information Systems*, 35(1), 145–179. DOI: 10.1080/07421222.2018.1440768

Graham, J. (2010, April). The influence of national culture on SME management practices. In *Proceedings of the Management Challenges in the 21st Century Conference*, Bratislava, Slovakia (pp. 91-99).

Granovetter, M. S. (1973). The strength of weak ties. *American Journal of Sociology*, 78(6), 1360–1380. DOI: 10.1086/225469

Grant, M. J., & Booth, A. (2009). A typology of reviews: An analysis of 14 review types and associated methodologies. *Health Information and Libraries Journal*, 26(2), 91–108. DOI: 10.1111/j.1471-1842.2009.00848.x PMID: 19490148

Green, B. N., Johnson, C. D., & Adams, A. (2006). Writing narrative literature reviews for peer-reviewed journals: Secrets of the trade. *Journal of Chiropractic Medicine*, 5(3), 101–117. https://doi.org/doi. DOI: 10.1016/S0899-3467(07)60142-6 PMID: 19674681

Grewal, D., Hulland, J., Kopalle, P. K., & Karahanna, E. (2020). The future of technology and marketing : A multidisciplinary perspective. *Journal of the Academy of Marketing Science*, 48(1), 1–8. DOI: 10.1007/s11747-019-00711-4

Guan, J., & Ma, N. (2003). Innovative capability and export performance of Chinese firms. *Technovation*, 23(9), 737–747. DOI: 10.1016/S0166-4972(02)00013-5

Guerra Rondón, L., & Bosch, F. (2023). *Participación de la sociedad civil: conceptos y prácticas en el contexto de los órganos subsidiarios y las reuniones intergubernamentales de la Comisión Económica para América Latina y el Caribe (CEPAL).* Santiago, Comisión Económica para América Latina. el Caribe (CEPAL). https://repositorio.cepal.org/server/api/core/bitstreams/c902b3c5-d4ab-4e73-96d1-5b9b03f9b1b0/content

Gupta, R. (2024). Exploring the impact of socio-cultural factors on entrepreneurship development in emerging markets. DOI: 10.21203/rs.3.rs-3938479/v1

Gutiérrez, R., Martínez, C., Sfeir-Younis, A., Fairbanks, M., Lindsay, S., Holden, P., & Brugger, E. (1998). Challenges for the new millennium in Latin America. Sustainable development, competitiveness and second-generation reforms. Bogotá, Colombia.

Gutter, M. S., Copur, Z., & Garrison, S. (2010). Which students are more likely to experience financial socialization opportunities? Exploring the relationship between financial behaviors and financial well-being of college students. *Journal of Family and Economic Issues*, 31(3), 387–397. PMID: 20835377

Habib, M. A., & Ljungqvist, A. P. (2001). Underpricing and entrepreneurial wealth losses in IPOs: Theory and evidence. *Review of Financial Studies*, 14(2), 433–458. DOI: 10.1093/rfs/14.2.433

Hack-Polay, D., Tenna Ogbaburu, J., Rahman, M., & Mahmoud, A. B. (2020). Immigrant entrepreneurs in rural England – An examination of the socio- cultural barriers facing migrant small businesses in Lincolnshire [Article]. *Local Economy*, 35(7), 676–694. DOI: 10.1177/0269094220988852

Haddad, M. I., Williams, I. A., Hammoud, M. S., & Dwyer, R. J. (2020). Strategies for implementing innovation in small and medium-sized enterprises. *World Journal of Entrepreneurship, Management and Sustainable Development*, 16(1), 12–29. DOI: 10.1108/WJEMSD-05-2019-0032

Hair, J. F., Hult, G. T., Ringle, C. M., & Sarstedt, M. (2014). A Primer on Partial Least Squares Structural Equation Modeling (PLS-SEM). *Sage (Atlanta, Ga.)*.

Hair, J. F., Ringle, C. M., & Sarstedt, M. (2011). PLS-SEM: Indeed a silver bullet. *Journal of Marketing Theory and Practice*, 19(2), 139–152. DOI: 10.2753/MTP1069-6679190202

Haleem, A., Javaid, M., Asim Qadri, M., Pratap Singh, R., & Suman, R. (2022). Artificial intelligence (AI) applications for marketing : A literature-based study. *International Journal of Intelligent Networks*, 3, 119–132. DOI: 10.1016/j.ijin.2022.08.005

Halikias, J., & Salavou, H. E. (2014). Generic business strategies of Greek exporting firms. *European Journal of International Management*, 8(2), 127–140. DOI: 10.1504/EJIM.2014.059579

Hall, J. K., & Vredenburg, H. (2012). The challenge of innovating for sustainable development. *MIT Sloan Management Review*, 45(1), 61–68.

Hanel, P. H. P., Maio, G. R., Soares, A. K. S., Vione, K. C., de Holanda Coelho, G. L., Gouveia, V. V., Patil, A. C., Kamble, S. V., & Manstead, A. S. R. (2018). Cross-cultural differences and similarities in human value instantiation. *Frontiers in Psychology*, 9(849), 849. Advance online publication. DOI: 10.3389/fpsyg.2018.00849 PMID: 29896151

Han, R., Lam, H. K. S., Zhan, Y., Wang, Y., Dwivedi, Y. K., & Tan, K. H. (2021). Artificial intelligence in business-to-business marketing : A bibliometric analysis of current research status, development and future directions. *Industrial Management & Data Systems*, 121(12), 2467–2497. DOI: 10.1108/IMDS-05-2021-0300

Han, Y., Chen, J., Dou, M., Wang, J., & Feng, K. (2023). The Impact of Artificial Intelligence on the Financial Services Industry. *Academic Journal of Management and Social Sciences*, 2(3), 83–85. DOI: 10.54097/ajmss.v2i3.8741

HAQ, Z., & Dawood, M. (2023). Does FinTech promote entrepreneurial intention among women? Studying the mediating role of financial inclusion

Haq, M., Johanson, M., Davies, J., Dana, L.-P., & Budhathoki, T. (2021). Compassionate customer service in ethnic minority microbusinesses. *Journal of Business Research*, 126, 279–290. https://doi.org/ https://doi.org/10.1016/j.jbusres.2020.12.054. DOI: 10.1016/j.jbusres.2020.12.054

Hardy, C. (2019). Desconfianza y desigualdades: amenazas para la democracia. *En Tejiendo confianza para la cohesión social: una mirada a la confianza en América Latina*, (pp.31-40). https://eurosocial .eu/wp-content/uploads/2019/07/07_tejiendo-confianza.pdf

Hasler, A., Lusardi, A., & Oggero, N. (2020). Financial fragility in the US: Evidence and implications. *NBER Working Paper No. 26383*. National Bureau of Economic Research.

Hays, J. (2015). *Filipino character and personality: Hiya, amor propio, emotions and the influences of Catholicism, Asia and Spain. Facts and Details.*https://factsanddetails.com/southeast-asia/Philippines/ sub5_6c/entry-3867.html

Healthcare of Ontario Pension Plan. (2022). *2022 Canadian retirement survey.*

Heenkenda, H. M. J. C. B., Xu, F., Kulathunga, K. M. M. C. B., & Senevirathne, W. A. R. (2022). The role of innovation capability in enhancing sustainability in SMEs: An emerging economy perspective. *Sustainability (Basel)*, 14(17), 10832. DOI: 10.3390/su141710832

Helfat, C. E., Finkelstein, S., Mitchell, W., Peteraf, M. A., Singh, H., Teece, D. J., & Winter, S. G. (2007). *Dynamic Capabilities: Understanding Strategic Change in Organizations*. Blackwell Publishing.

Henager, R. (2017). Financial Behaviors of Military Households: The Role of Financial Literacy and Financial Education. *Consumer Interests Annual, 63.*

Henchoz, C., Coste, T., & Wernli, B. (2019). Culture, money attitudes and economic outcomes. *Swiss Journal of Economics and Statistics, 155*(1). *Swiss Journal of Economics and Statistics*, 155(1), 2. Advance online publication. DOI: 10.1186/s41937-019-0028-4

Henderson, R. M., & Clark, K. B. (1990). Architectural innovation: The reconfiguration of existing product technologies and the failure of established firms. *Administrative Science Quarterly*, 35(1), 9–30. DOI: 10.2307/2393549

Henri, J. F. (2006). Management control systems and strategy: A resource-based perspective. *Accounting, Organizations and Society*, 31(6), 529–558. DOI: 10.1016/j.aos.2005.07.001

Henseler, J., & Chin, W. W. (2010). A comparison of approaches for the analysis of interaction effects between latent variables using partial least squares path modeling. *Structural Equation Modeling*, 17(1), 82–109. DOI: 10.1080/10705510903439003

Hernandez, J., Chumaceiro, C., & Atencio, E. (2009). Quality of Service and Human Resources: Case study of a department store. *Revista Venezolana de Gerencia*.

Hernandez, R., Fernandez, C., & Baptista, P. (2014). *Metodología de la investigación (6a* (McGraw, H. I., Ed.).

Herzallah, A. M., Gutiérrez-gutiérrez, L., & Munoz, J. F. (2014). Total quality management & business excellence total quality management practices, competitive strategies and financial performance: The case of the Palestinian industrial SMEs. *Total Quality Management & Business Excellence*, 25(6), 635–649. DOI: 10.1080/14783363.2013.824714

He, Y., Keung Lai, K., Sun, H., & Chen, Y. (2013). The impact of supplier integration on customer integration and new product performance: The mediating role of manufacturing flexibility under trust theory. *Industrial Management & Data Systems*, 113(3), 367–388. DOI: 10.1108/02635571311312640

Hill, M., Ireland, R., & Hoskisson, R. (2004). *Global Economy. Strategic Management, Competitiveness and Concepts of Globalization*. Thomson.

Hilmola, O. P., Hilletofth, P., & Kovács, G. (2015). Supply chain management and enterprise resource planning systems: A Finnish perspective. *Journal of Manufacturing Technology Management*, 26(5), 728–755. DOI: 10.1108/JMTM-11-2013-0143

Hirsch, J. E. (2005). An index to quantify an individual's scientific research output. *Proceedings of the National Academy of Sciences of the United States of America*, 102(46), 16569–16572. DOI: 10.1073/pnas.0507655102 PMID: 16275915

Hoffman, D. L., & Novak, T. P. (2018). Consumer and Object Experience in the Internet of Things : An Assemblage Theory Approach. *The Journal of Consumer Research*, 44(6), 1178–1204. DOI: 10.1093/jcr/ucx105

Hofmann, H., Busse, C., Bode, C., & Henke, M. (2014).

Hofstede, G. (2011). Dimensionalizing Cultures: The Hofstede Model in Context. *Online Readings in Psychology and Culture*, 2(1). Advance online publication. DOI: 10.9707/2307-0919.1014

Hofstede, G. J., Jonker, C. M., & Verwaart, T. (2009). Modeling power distance in trade. In David, N., & Sichman, J. S. (Eds.), Lecture Notes in Computer Science: Vol. 5269. *Multi-agent-based simulations IX. MABS 2008*. Springer., DOI: 10.1007/978-3-642-01991-3_1

Hopp, C., & Stephan, U. (2012). The influence of socio-cultural environments on the performance of nascent entrepreneurs: Community culture, motivation, self-efficacy and start-up success. *Entrepreneurship and Regional Development*, 24(9-10), 917–945. DOI: 10.1080/08985626.2012.742326

Hornsby, J. S., Kuratko, D. F., & Zahra, S. A. (2002). Middle managers' perception of the internal environment for corporate entrepreneurship: Assessing a measurement scale. *Journal of Business Venturing*, 17(3), 253–273. DOI: 10.1016/S0883-9026(00)00059-8

Ho, W., Zheng, T., Yildiz, H., & Talluri, S. (2015). Supply chain risk management: A literature review. *International Journal of Production Research*, 53(16), 5031–5069. DOI: 10.1080/00207543.2015.1030467

Hristov, I., & Chirico, A. (2019). The role of sustainability key performance indicators (KPIs) in implementing sustainable strategies. *Sustainability (Basel)*, 11(20), 5742. DOI: 10.3390/su11205742

https://hoopp.com/docs/default-source/default-document-library/abacusresearch2022_execsummary.pdf

https://www.canada.ca/en/services/jobs/training/initiatives/skills-success/tools/job-enhancement.htm l

Huggins, R., & Thompson, P. (2015). Entrepreneurship, innovation and regional growth: A network theory. *Small Business Economics*, 45(1), 103–128. DOI: 10.1007/s11187-015-9643-3

Husain, T., & Sunardi, N. (2020). Firm's Value Prediction Based on Profitability Ratios and Dividend Policy. *Finance & Economics Review*, 2(2), 13–26. DOI: 10.38157/finance-economics-review.v2i2.102

Hwa Ang, P. (2018). Communicating with Power in a Volatile, Uncertain, Complex, and Ambiguous World. *Journal of Communication*, 68(1), 1–5. DOI: 10.1093/joc/jqx010

Ibeh, K. I., & Wheeler, C. N. (2005). A resource-centred interpretation of export performance. *The International Entrepreneurship and Management Journal*, 1(4), 539–556. DOI: 10.1007/s11365-005-4777-4

IFAC (2020). The Foundation for Economies Worldwide Is Small Business. IFAC Report.

INE. (2017). *Censo Geral da População de Moçambique*. Instituto Nacional de Estatística.

Infobae. (2021). *Desconfianza institucional en Colombia: ciudadanos "rajan" a las principales entidades públicas.*https://www.infobae.com/america/colombia/2021/06/22/desconfianza-institucional-en -colombia-ciudadanos-rajan-a-las-principales-entidades-publicas/

Instituto Nacional de Contadores Públicos (INCP). (2020). *Precaria confianza de los colombianos en instituciones del país.*https://incp.org.co/precaria-confianza-los-colombianos-instituciones-del-pais/

International Labour Organization. (n.d.). *Labour migration in the Philippines.*https://www.ilo.org/manila/areasofwork/labour-migration/lang--en/index.htm

International Monetary Fund. (2022). *Philippines: Datasets.*https://www.imf.org/external/datamapper/profile/PHL

International Trade Centre. (2020). *Promoting SME competitiveness in the Philippines: Compete, connect, and change to build resilience to crises.* ITC.

Investing in Women. (2017). *Filipino women in leadership: Government and industry.*https://investinginwomen.asia/knowledge/filipino-women-leadership-government-industry/

Ishikawa, K. (1995). *The Essence of Quality Control.* Available in https://jrvargas.files.wordpress.com/2011/02/que_es_el_control_total_de_la_ calidad_- _ -**kauro_ishikawa.pdf**.

Islami, X., & Topuzovska Latkovikj, M. (2022). There is time to be integrated: The relationship between SCM practices and organizational performance - The moderated role of competitive strategy. *Cogent Business and Management*, 9(1), 1–26. DOI: 10.1080/23311975.2021.2010305

Istipliler, B., Bort, S., & Woywode, M. (2023). Flowers of adversity: Institutional constraints and innovative SMEs in transition economies. *Journal of Business Research*, 154, 113306. https://doi.org/https://doi.org/10.1016/j.jbusres.2022.113306. DOI: 10.1016/j.jbusres.2022.113306

Jamil, S., Shah, F., Khan, S., & Imran, I. (2023). The The influence of potential outcome on entrepreneurs' decisions to participate in Crowdfunding in Pakistan (Karachi). *International journal of social science & entrepreneurship, 3*(1), 1-24.

Jantunen, A., Puumalainen, K., Saarenketo, S., & Kylaheiko, K. (2005). Entrepreneurial orientation, dynamic capabilities and export performance. *Journal of International Entrepreneurship*, 3(3), 223–243. DOI: 10.1007/s10843-005-1133-2

Jaworski, B. J., & Kohli, A. K. (1993). Market orientation: Antrcendent and consequences. *Journal of Marketing*, 57(1), 53–70. DOI: 10.1177/002224299305700304

Jimenez-Ramírez, M. H. (2006). Modelo de competitividad empresarial. *Umbral científico*, (9), 115-125.

Johansen, B., & Euchner, J. (2013). Navigating the VUCA World: An Interview with Bob Johansen. *Research Technology Management*, 56(1), 10–15. DOI: 10.5437/08956308X5601003

Johanson, J., & Vahlne, J. E. (1977). The internationalization process of a firm - A model of knowledge foreign and increasing market commitments. *Journal of International Business Studies*, 8, 23–32. DOI: 10.1057/palgrave.jibs.8490676

Johnson, C., Dowd, T. J., & Ridgeway, C. L. (2006). Legitimacy as a social process. *Annual Review of Sociology*, 32(1), 53–78. DOI: 10.1146/annurev.soc.32.061604.123101

Jones, K., Ksaifi, L., & Clark, C. (2023). 'The biggest problem we are facing is the running away problem': Recruitment and the paradox of facilitating the mobility of immobile workers. *Work, Employment and Society*, 37(4), 841–857. DOI: 10.1177/09500170221094764

Jones, T., Ram, M., Edwards, P., Kiselinchev, A., & Muchenje, L. (2014). Mixed embeddedness and new migrant enterprise in the UK. *Entrepreneurship and Regional Development*, 26(5-6), 500–520. DOI: 10.1080/08985626.2014.950697

Jones, T., Ram, M., & Villares-Varela, M. (2019). Diversity, economic development and new migrant entrepreneurs. *Urban Studies (Edinburgh, Scotland)*, 56(5), 960–976. DOI: 10.1177/0042098018765382

Kabeyi, M. (2019). Organizational strategic planning, implementation and evaluation with analysis of challenges and benefits. *International Journal of Applied Research*, 5(6), 27–32. DOI: 10.22271/allresearch.2019.v5.i6a.5870

Kaivo-oja, JRL and Lauraeus, IT (2018), " *The VUCA approach as a solution concept to corporate foresight challenges and global technological disruption* ", foresight, Vol. 20 No. 1, pp. 27 - 49 .

Kang, J. W., & Latoja, M. C. (2022). COVID-19 and overseas Filipino workers: Return migration and reintegration into the home country – the Philippine case. *ADB Southeast Asia Working Paper Series*, 21. https://dx.doi.org/DOI: 10.22617/WPS220002-2

Kauffeld, S., & Lehmann- Willenbrock, N. (. (2019). The role of training in improving organizational competitiveness: A systematic review. *Journal of Business Research*, 101, 1–12. DOI: 10.1016/j.jbusres.2019.01.011

Kaufmann, F. (2020). *PME. Pequenas e Médias Empresas em Moçambique—Situação e Desafios.* ExperTS GIZ.

Keh, H. T., Nguyen, T. T. M., & Ng, H. P. (2007). The effects of entrepreneurial orientation and marketing information on the performance of SMEs. *Journal of Business Venturing*, 22(4), 592–611. DOI: 10.1016/j.jbusvent.2006.05.003

Kerr, S. K., & Kerr, W. (2020). Immigrant entrepreneurship in America: Evidence from the survey of business owners 2007 & 2012. *Research Policy*, 49(3), 103918. https://doi.org/https://doi.org/10.1016/j.respol.2019.103918. DOI: 10.1016/j.respol.2019.103918

Keskin, H., Ayar Şentürk, H., Tatoglu, E., Gölgeci, I., Kalaycioglu, O., & Etlioglu, H. T. (2021). The simultaneous effect of firm capabilities and competitive strategies on export performance: The role of competitive advantages and competitive intensity. *International Marketing Review*, 38(6), 1242–1266. DOI: 10.1108/IMR-09-2019-0227

Khan, H., & Khan, Z. (2021). The efficacy of marketing skills and market responsiveness in marketing performance of emerging market exporting firms in advanced markets : The moderating role of competitive intensity. *International Business Review*, 30(6), 101860. DOI: 10.1016/j.ibusrev.2021.101860

Khan, K. S., Kunz, R., Kleijnen, J., & Antes, G. (2003). Five steps to conducting a systematic review. *Journal of the Royal Society of Medicine*, 96(3), 118–121. DOI: 10.1177/014107680309600304 PMID: 12612111

Khin, S., & Ho, T. C. (2019). Digital technology, digital capability and organizational performance: A mediating role of digital innovation. *International Journal of Innovation Science*, 11(2), 177–195. DOI: 10.1108/IJIS-08-2018-0083

Kipping, M., & Clark, T. (2012). *The Oxford Handbook of Management Consulting.* Oxford University Press.

Klontz, B. T., & Britt, S. L. (2012). How clients' money scripts predict their financial behaviors. *Journal of Financial Planning*, 25(11), 33–43.

Klontz, B., Britt, S. L., Mentzer, J., & Klontz, T. (2011). Money beliefs and financial behaviors: Development of the Klontz Money Script Inventory. *Journal of Financial Therapy*, 2(1), 1–22. DOI: 10.4148/jft.v2i1.451

Klontz, B., & Klontz, T. (2009). *Mind over money: Overcoming the money disorders that threaten our financial health*. Crown Currency.

Kloosterman, R. C. (2003). Creating opportunities. Policies aimed at increasing openings for immigrant entrepreneurs in the Netherlands. *Entrepreneurship and Regional Development*, 15(2), 167–181. DOI: 10.1080/0898562032000075159

Koe, J. H. N., & Yeoh, K. K. (2021). Factors influencing financial planning for marriage amongst young malaysian couples. *International Journal of Business and Society, 22*(1), 33-54. *Scopus*. Advance online publication. DOI: 10.33736/ijbs.3161.2021

Komppula, R., & Reijonen, H. (2006). Performance determinants in small and micro tourism business. *Tourism Review*, 61(4), 13–20. DOI: 10.1108/eb058482

Koontz, H. (1998). *Management: A Global Perspective*. McGraw- Hill.

Kor, Y. Y., Mahoney, J. T., Siemsen, E., & Tan, D. (2016). Penrose's The Theory of the Growth of the Firm. *Production and Operations Management Society*, 1727-1744.

Kotler, P., Kartajaya, H., & Setiawan, I. (2021). *Marketing 5.0 : Technology for Humanity*. John Wiley & Sons.

Kotler, P., & Keller, K. (2012). *Marketing Management*. Addison-Wesley.

Krippendorff, K. (1990). *Content analysis methodology: theory and practice*. Editorial Paidos.

Krueger, N. F.Jr, Reilly, M. D., & Carsrud, A. L. (2000). Competing models of entrepreneurial intentions. *Journal of Business Venturing*, 15(5-6), 411–432. DOI: 10.1016/S0883-9026(98)00033-0

Krugman, P., & Obstfeld, M. (2000). *International Economics: Theory and Policy*. Addison-Wesley.

Kshetri, N. (2014). The impacts of cloud computing and big data applications on developing world-based smallholder farmers.

Kshetri, N. (2013). *Cybercrime and cybersecurity in the global south*. Springer. DOI: 10.1057/9781137021946

Kshetri, N. (2018). 1 Blockchain's roles in meeting key supply chain management objectives. *International Journal of Information Management*, 39, 80–89. DOI: 10.1016/j.ijinfomgt.2017.12.005

Kubr, M. (1997). La consultoría de empresas: Guía para la profesión. Geneva.

Kuivalainen, O., Sundqvist, S., & Servais, P. (2007). Firms' degree of born-globalness, international entrepreneurial orientation and export performance. *Journal of World Business*, 42(3), 253–267. DOI: 10.1016/j.jwb.2007.04.010

Kumar, V., Ramachandran, D., & Kumar, B. (2021a). Influence of new-age technologies on marketing : A research agenda. *Journal of Business Research*, 125, 864–877. DOI: 10.1016/j.jbusres.2020.01.007

Kump, B., Engelmann, A., Kessler, A., & Schweiger, C. (2019). Toward a dynamic capabilities scale: Organizational measuring sensing, seizing, and transforming capacities. *Industrial and Corporate Change*, 28(5), 1149–1172.

Kurt, Y. (2022). Improving Society as a Business Strategy: A Review From a Strategic Management Perspective. In Goi, C. (Ed.), *Innovative Economic, Social, and Environmental Practices for Progressing Future Sustainability* (pp. 121–135). IGI Global., DOI: 10.4018/978-1-7998-9590-9.ch007

Kushnirovich, N., Heilbrunn, S., & Davidovich, L. (2018). Diversity of Entrepreneurial Perceptions: Immigrants vs. Native Population. *European Management Review*, 15(3), 341–355. https://doi.org/https://doi.org/10.1111/emre.12105. DOI: 10.1111/emre.12105

Labarca, N. (2007). *Consideraciones Teóricas de la Competitividad Empresarial*. Zulia: OMNIA 13.

Labarca, N. (2008). Evolución del pensamiento estratégico en la formación de la estrategia empresarial. *Publicaciones científicas Universidad de Zulia*.

Laclau, E. (1987). Populismo y transformación del imaginario político en América Latina. *Boletin de Estudios Latinoamericanos y del Caribe*, 42, 25–38. https://www.jstor.org/stable/25675327

Lara, J. C. B., García, J. C. P., & Chico, C. O. (2017). Tourism SMEs in a digital environment : Literature review. *European Scientific Journal*, 13(28), 429. DOI: 10.19044/esj.2017.v13n28p429

Law 1499 of 2017.

Law Family Commission on Civil Society. (2023). *Unleashing the power of civil society.*https://civilsocietycommission.org/wp-content/uploads/2023/01/FINAL-Unleashing-the-power-of-civil-society---for-upload.pdf

Lawrence, K. (2013). *Developing leaders in a VUCA environment*. UNC Executive Development.

Le Thanh, T., Huan, N. Q., & Hong, T. T. T. (2021). Determinants for competitiveness in the context of international integration pressure: Case of small and medium enterprises in emerging economy–Vietnam. *Cogent Business & Management*, 8(1), 1893246. DOI: 10.1080/23311975.2021.1893246

Leal Rodríguez, A. L., Leal Millán, A., Roldán Salgueiro, J. L., & Ortega Gutiérrez, J. (2013). Knowledge management and the effectiveness of innovation outcomes: The role of cultural barriers. *Electronic Journal of Knowledge Management*, 11(1), 62–71.

LeBlanc, P. (2018). Higher Education in a VUCA World. *Change*, 50(3-4), 23–26. DOI: 10.1080/00091383.2018.1507370

Lechner, C., & Gudmundsson, S. V. (2014). Entrepreneurial orientation, firm strategy and small firm performance. *International Small Business Journal*, 32(1), 36–60. DOI: 10.1177/0266242612455034

Lee, A., & So, C. (2014). Media literacy and information literacy: Similarities and differences. *Comunicar*, 42(42), 137–146. DOI: 10.3916/C42-2014-13

Lee, E. B., & Baek, H. (2023). Prediction of Information Diffusion of New Products: Based on Product Launch and Media Difference. *Journal of the Knowledge Economy*, 15(2), 1–30. DOI: 10.1007/s13132-023-01385-8

Lee, G., & Kim, T. (2023). An Economic Appraisal of Blockchain's Impact on Finance and Market Competition. *Journal of Student Research*, 12(2). Advance online publication. DOI: 10.47611/jsrhs.v12i2.4407

Lee, N. (2015). Migrant and ethnic diversity, cities and innovation: Firm effects or city effects? [Article]. *Journal of Economic Geography*, 15(4), 769–796. DOI: 10.1093/jeg/lbu032

Lee, N., Sameen, H., & Cowling, M. (2020). Access to Finance for Innovative SMEs since the Financial Crisis. *Research Policy*, 49(2), 103900.

Leguizamon, M. (2020). Análisis de ataques informáticos mediante Honeypots en la Universidad Distrital Francisco José de Caldas. *Ingeniería y competitividad*.

Leifer, R., McDermott, C. M., O'Connor, G. C., Peters, L. S., Rice, M., & Veryzer, R. W. (2000). *Radical Innovation: How Mature Companies Can Outsmart Upstarts*. Harvard Business Review Press.

Leitner, K., & Guldenberg, S. (2010). Generic strategies and firm performance in SMEs : A longitudinal study of Austrian SMEs. *Small Business Economics*, 35(2), 169–189. DOI: 10.1007/s11187-009-9239-x

Lengler, J. F., Sousa, C. M., & Marques, C. (2014). Examining the relationship between market orientation and export performance: The moderating role of competitive intensity. In *Advances in International Marketing* (Vol. 24, pp. 75–102). Emerald Group Publishing Limited., DOI: 10.1108/S1474-7979(2013)0000024008

Lengler, J. F., Sousa, C. M., Perin, M. G., Sampaio, C. H., & Martínez-López, F. J. (2016). The antecedents of export performance of Brazilian small and medium-sized enterprises (SMEs): The non-linear effects of customer orientation. *International Small Business Journal*, 34(5), 701–727. DOI: 10.1177/0266242615588837

León Mendoza, J. (2021). Influencia del contexto macroeconómico en la mortalidad de empresas en Perú. *Cuadernos de Economía (Santiago, Chile)*, 40(83), 403–430. DOI: 10.15446/cuad.econ.v40n83.81957

Leong, K., & Sung, A. (2018). FinTech (Financial Technology): What is it and how to use technologies to create business value in fintech way? *International Journal of Innovation, Management and Technology*, 9(2), 74–78. DOI: 10.18178/ijimt.2018.9.2.791

Leonidou, L. C., Fotiadis, T. A., Christodoulides, P., Spyropoulou, S., & Katsikeas, C. S. (2015). Environmentally friendly export business strategy: Its determinants and effects on competitive advantage and performance. *International Business Review*, 24(5), 798–811. DOI: 10.1016/j.ibusrev.2015.02.001

Le, T. T., & Ikram, M. (2022). Do sustainability innovation and firm competitiveness help improve firm performance? Evidence from the SME sector in Vietnam. *Sustainable Production and Consumption*, 29, 588–599. DOI: 10.1016/j.spc.2021.11.008

Lewis, P., Barr, C., Clarke, S., Voce, A., Levett, C., & Gutiérrez, P. (2019). Revealed: the rise and rise of populist rhetoric. *The Guardian*.https://www.theguardian.com/world/ng-interactive/2019/mar/06/revealed-the-rise-and-rise-of-populist-rhetoric

Liendo, N. (2011). El crecimiento económico y la confianza en las instituciones de gobierno: Un análisis comparado de la evolución en las percepciones de las élites y los ciudadanos de América Latina. *Boletín PNUD Instituto de Iberoamérica*.http://hdl.handle.net/10366/108650

Lin, H. F., & Lee, G. G. (2005). Impact of organizational learning and knowledge management factors on e-business adoption. *Management Decision*, 43(2), 171–188. DOI: 10.1108/00251740510581902

Liu, C.-W., & Cheng, J.-S. (2018). Exploring Driving Forces of Innovation in the MSEs: The Case of the Sustainable B&B Tourism Industry. *Sustainability (Basel)*, 10(11), 3983. https://www.mdpi.com/2071-1050/10/11/3983. DOI: 10.3390/su10113983

Llanos-Herrera, G. R., & Merigo, J. M. (2018). Overview of brand personality research with bibliometric indicators. *Kybernetes*, 48(3), 546–569. DOI: 10.1108/K-02-2018-0051

Lombana, J., & Rozas Gutiérrez, S. (2009). *Analytical framework of competitiveness: Foundations for the study of regional competitiveness. Thought & management, (26), 1-38.* Porter.

Lopez, E., Sepulveda, C., & Arenas, A. (2010). La consultoría de Gestión Humana en empresas medianas. *Estudios Gerenciales*, 146-168.

López-Borrull, A., & Ollé, C. (2019). La curación de contenidos como respuesta a las noticias ya la ciencia falsas. *Anuario ThinkEPI*, 13. Advance online publication. DOI: 10.3145/thinkepi.2019.e13e07

Lopez-Torres, G. C. (2023). The impact of smes' sustainability on competitiveness. *Measuring Business Excellence*, 27(1), 107–120. DOI: 10.1108/MBE-12-2021-0144

Lotero-Echeverri, G. J. (2014). Educación para la ciudadanía en la era de las wikis. *Poliantea*, 10(19), 199–212. DOI: 10.15765/plnt.v10i19.579

Loufrani-Fedida, S., & Aldebert, B. (2013). Le management stratégique des compétences dans un processus d'innovation : Le cas d'une TPE touristique. *Revue de Gestion des Ressources Humaines*, 3(89), 56–72. DOI: 10.3917/grhu.089.0056

Loux, M. D. (2021). *Strategies to Provide Financial Literacy to Military Students.* Colorado Technical University.

Luciano Alipio, R. A., Sotomayor Chahuaylla, J. A., Garcia Juarez, H. D., & Pelaez Camacho, H. Y. (2023). Gestión empresarial en el desarrollo de las MYPES en zonas mineras del Perú. *Revista Venezolana de Gerencia*, 28(103), 1174–1189. DOI: 10.52080/rvgluz.28.103.16

Luengo González, E. (2018). *Las vertientes de la complejidad: pensamiento sistémico, ciencias de la complejidad, pensamiento complejo, paradigma ecológico y enfoques holistas.* ITESO., https://rei.iteso.mx/bitstream/handle/11117/5686/Las%20Vertientes%20de%20la%20complejidad%20REI.pdf?sequence=4&isAllowed=y

Lumpkin, G. T., Hills, G. E., & Shrader, R. C. (2004). Opportunity recognition. Entrepreneurship: The way ahead, 73-90.

Lundmark, L., Ednarsson, M., & Karlsson, S. (2014). International Migration, Self-employment and Restructuring through Tourism in Sparsely Populated Areas. *Scandinavian Journal of Hospitality and Tourism*, 14(4), 422–440. DOI: 10.1080/15022250.2014.967995

Lusardi, A., & Mitchell, O. S. (2017). How ordinary consumers make complex economic decisions: Financial literacy and retirement readiness. *The Quarterly Journal of Economics*, 122(1), 207–252.

Luther, R. K., Leech, I. E., & Garman, E. T. (1998). The employer's cost for the personal financial management difficulties of workers: Evidence from the US Navy. *Personal Finances and Worker Productivity, 2*(1).

Luu, T. D. (2023). Fostering strategic entrepreneurship of smes: The role of organisational change forces. *Management Decision*, 61(3), 695–719. DOI: 10.1108/MD-08-2021-1024

Lythreatis, S., Singh, S. K., & El-Kassar, A.-N. (2022). The digital divide : A review and future research agenda. *Technological Forecasting and Social Change*, 175, 121359. DOI: 10.1016/j.techfore.2021.121359

Mahamadou, Z. (2021). Internationalization processes for sub-Saharan Africa' s small and medium-sized enterprises: The case of Ivory Coast. *Thunderbird International Business Review*, 63(4), 437–449. DOI: 10.1002/tie.22190

Mahmood Aziz, H., Jabbar Othman, B., Gardi, B., Ali Ahmed, S., Sabir, B. Y., Burhan Ismael, N., & Anwar, G. (2021). Employee commitment: The relationship between employee commitment and job satisfaction. *Aziz, HM, Othman, BJ, Gardi, B., Ahmed, SA, Sabir, BY, Ismael, NB, Hamza, PA, Sorguli, S., Ali, BJ, Anwar, G.(2021). Employee Commitment: The Relationship between Employee Commitment And Job Satisfaction.The Journal of Humanistic Education and Development*, 3(3), 54–66.

Mahmood, A., & Ezeala-Harrison, F. (2000). *Comparative versus competitive advantage, and competitiveness in developing countries. Socioeconomic Development in the 21st Century*. International Institute for Development Studies.

Mahoney, J. T. (2001). A resource-based theory of sustainable rents. *Journal of Management*, 27(6), 651–660. DOI: 10.1177/014920630102700603

Mahr, D., Lievens, A., & Blazevic, V. (2014). The value of customer cocreated knowledge during the innovation process. *Journal of Product Innovation Management*, 31(3), 599–615. DOI: 10.1111/jpim.12116

Makhloufi, A. (2021). L'entrepreneuriat innovant : Variables stimulant l'innovation dans les PMEs du secteur touristique au Maroc. *Revue Internationale du Chercheur*, 2(3). https://www.revuechercheur.com/index.php/home/article/view/238

Malavé, J. (1996). Competitiveness: Current state of the debate. *IBM Debates*, 3, 38.

Malerba, R. C., & Ferreira, J. J. (2021). Immigrant entrepreneurship and strategy: A systematic literature review. *Journal of Small Business and Entrepreneurship*, 33(2), 183–217. DOI: 10.1080/08276331.2020.1804714

Malhotra, M. K., & Grover, V. (1998). An assessment of survey research in POM: From constructs to theory. *Journal of Operations Management*, 16(4), 407–425. DOI: 10.1016/S0272-6963(98)00021-7

Malki, B., Uman, T., & Pittino, D. (2022). The entrepreneurial financing of the immigrant entrepreneurs: A literature review. *Small Business Economics*, 58(3), 1337–1365. DOI: 10.1007/s11187-020-00444-7

Mandal, S., Sarathy, R., Korasiga, V. R., Bhattacharya, S., & Dastidar, S. G. (2016). Achieving supply chain resilience: The contribution of logistics and supply chain capabilities. *International Journal of Disaster Resilience in the Built Environment*, 7(5), 544–562. DOI: 10.1108/IJDRBE-04-2016-0010

Mankiw, N. G. (1998). *Principles of Macroeconomics*. Mc Graw-Hill.

Manotas, E. C., & Gonzalez-Perez, M. A. (2020). Internationalization and performance of small and medium-sized enterprises from emerging economies: Using hazards methodology for competitiveness study. *Competitiveness Review*, 30(5), 635–663. DOI: 10.1108/CR-03-2019-0028

Maqsoom, A., Arif, I., Shafi, K., Umer, M., Nazir, T., & Nawab, S. (2021). Motives and competitive assets for internationalization: A comparison between emerging and developed economy international construction contracting firms. *Applied Economics*, 53(22), 2539–2553. DOI: 10.1080/00036846.2020.1863321

Mariani, M., Baggio, R., Fuchs, M., & Höepken, W. (2018). Business intelligence and big data in hospitality and tourism : A systematic literature review. *International Journal of Contemporary Hospitality Management*, 30(12), 3514–3554. DOI: 10.1108/IJCHM-07-2017-0461

Mariño, A., Cortez, F., & Luis, G. (2008). Herramienta de software para la enseñanza y entrenamiento en la construcción de la matriz DOFA. *Ing. Investig.*

Markovic, S., Koporcic, N., Arslanagic-Kalajdzic, M., Kadic-Maglajlic, S., Bagherzadeh, M., & Islam, N. (2021). Business-to-business open innovation: COVID-19 lessons for small and medium-sized enterprises from emerging markets. *Technological Forecasting and Social Change*, 170, 120883. DOI: 10.1016/j.techfore.2021.120883

Martinez, L. E., Farfan, E. A., Osto, R. N. Un acercamiento epistémico a la administración por objetivos. *Actualidad Contable FACES*, (45), 93-104.

Martinez, M., Gomez, H., and Martinez, J, (2017). *La gestión de la incertidumbre: Empresas inteligentes con trabajadores del conocimiento*. Vista de La gestión de la incertidumbre: empresas inteligentes con trabajadores del conocimiento (redipe.org)

Martinez, A. (2023). A paper about the influence of Philippines' unique social culture in business. *ASEAN Journal of CI-EL and Applied Philosophy*, 1(1). Advance online publication. DOI: 10.22146/arcelap.v1i1.9732

Martin-Montaner, J., Serrano-Domingo, G., & Requena-Silvente, F. (2018). Networks and self-employed migrants. *Small Business Economics*, 51(3), 735–755. DOI: 10.1007/s11187-017-9962-7

Matenge, T. (2011). Small firm internationalization – A developing country perspective. *International Journal of Business Administration*, 2(4), 103–111. DOI: 10.5430/ijba.v2n4p103

Mateo, S. (2020). Procédure pour conduire avec succès une revue de littérature selon la méthode PRISMA. *Kinésithérapie, la Revue*, 20(226), 29–37. DOI: 10.1016/j.kine.2020.05.019

Mateus and Brasset (2002). Globalization: its effects and benefits. *Economy and Development, 1* (1).

McGee, J. E., Peterson, M., Mueller, S. L., & Sequeira, J. M. (2009). Entrepreneurial self efficacy: Refining the measure. *Entrepreneurship Theory and Practice*, 33(4), 965–988. DOI: 10.1111/j.1540-6520.2009.00304.x

McGuinness, N. W., & Little, B. (1981). The influence of product characteristics on the export performance of new industrial products. *Journal of Marketing*, 45(2), 110–122. DOI: 10.1177/002224298104500211

Mehjabeen, M., & Khan, S. N. (2024). Motivating factors affecting formalization of small informal enterprises: Evidence from an emerging economy. *Business Strategy & Development*, 7(3), e426. DOI: 10.1002/bsd2.426

Mendoza, C., Morén-Alegret, R., & McAreavey, R. (2020). (Lifestyle) immigrant entrepreneurs in Spanish small villages: Rethinking international immigration in rural Alt Empordà, Catalonia. *Belgeo. Revue belge de géographie*(1). https://doi.org/https://doi.org/10.4000/belgeo.44107

Merigó, J. M., Mas-Tur, A., Roig-Tierno, N., & Ribeiro-Soriano, D. (2015). A bibliometric overview of the Journal of Business Research between 1973 and 2014. *Journal of Business Research*, 68(12), 2645–2653. DOI: 10.1016/j.jbusres.2015.04.006

Merino-Martin, N. H., & Pastorino, A. H. (2013). Perception about sustainable development of sme in Peru. *Revista de Administración de Empresas*, 53(3), 290-302. Doi DOI: 10.1590/S0034-75902013000300006

Mikalef, P., & Gupta, M. (2021). Artificial intelligence capability : Conceptualization, measurement calibration, and empirical study on its impact on organizational creativity and firm performance. *Information & Management*, 58(3), 103434. DOI: 10.1016/j.im.2021.103434

Minority Rights Group International. (n.d.). *Philippines: Indigenous peoples.*https://minorityrights.org/minorities/indigenous-peoples-6/#:~:text=The%20other%20concentration%20of%20indigenous,Talandig%2C%20and%20Tiruray%20or%20Teduray

Mintzberg, H., & Quinn, B. (1993). *El proceso estratégico: Conceptos, Contextos y casos*. Prentice Hall.

Miranda Pegueros, M., Lopez Castro, E. M., & Vega Zarate, C. (2022). Hacia una perspectiva integral de gestión en sostenibilidad empresarial. *Trascender, contabilidad y gestión*, 7(19), 150-164.

Mishra, M., Chaubey, A., Khatwani, R., & Nair, K. (2023). Overcoming barriers in automotive smes to attain international competitiveness: An ism approach modelling. *Journal of Business and Industrial Marketing*, 38(12), 2713–2730. DOI: 10.1108/JBIM-12-2022-0546

Mishra, V., Walsh, I., & Srivastava, A. (2022). Merchants' adoption of mobile payment in emerging economies: The case of unorganised retailers in India. *European Journal of Information Systems*, 31(1), 74–90. DOI: 10.1080/0960085X.2021.1978338

Mitchell, R. K., Busenitz, L., Lant, T., McDougall, P. P., Morse, E. A., & Smith, J. B. (2002). Toward a theory of entrepreneurial cognition: Rethinking the people side of entrepreneurship research. *Entrepreneurship Theory and Practice*, 27(2), 93–105. DOI: 10.1111/1540-8520.00001

Moher, D., Liberati, A., Tetzlaff, J., & Altman, D. G. (2009). Preferred reporting items for systematic reviews and meta-analyses: The PRISMA statement. *PLoS Medicine*, 6(7), e1000097. DOI: 10.1371/journal.pmed.1000097 PMID: 19621072

Moher, D., Shamseer, L., Clarke, M., Ghersi, D., Liberati, A., Petticrew, M., Shekelle, P., & Stewart, L. A.Prisma-P Group. (2015). Preferred reporting items for systematic review and meta-analysis protocols (PRISMA-P) 2015 statement. *Systematic Reviews*, 4(1), 1. DOI: 10.1186/2046-4053-4-1 PMID: 25554246

Mojica, F. J. (2006). Concepto y aplicación de la prospectiva estratégica. *Revista Med Volumen 14.*, 122-131. https://www.redalyc.org/pdf/910/91014117.pdf

Molina, I. (1998). *Fundamental Concepts of Political Science*. Alianza Editorial.

Moncada, L., Zambrano, L., Falcones, J., & Angulo, R. (2022). Company "Corp. Naula S.A.S" and the Importance of an Audit of the Human Talent Department. *Universidad y Sociedad*.

Moncayo, J, E. (2003). *New Theories and Approaches*

Mongeon, P., & Paul-Hus, A. (2016). The journal coverage of Web of Science and Scopus: A comparative analysis. *Scientometrics*, 106(1), 213–228. DOI: 10.1007/s11192-015-1765-5

Monreal Guerrero, I. M., Parejo Llanos, J. L., & Cortón de las Heras, M. de la O. (2017). Alfabetización mediática y cultura de la participación: retos de la ciudadanía digital en la Sociedad de la Información. *EDMETIC*, 6(2), 148–167. https://doi.org/DOI: 10.21071/edmetic.v6i2.6943

Montenegro-Velandia and Alvarez-Rodriguez. (2011). Approach to the concept of organizational competitiveness. *National Research Journal, 9* (16).

Mora Riapira, E. H., Vera Colina, M. A., & Melgarejo Molina, Z. A. (2015). Planificación estratégica y niveles de competitividad de las Mipymes del sector comercio en Bogotá. *Estudios Gerenciales*, 31(134), 79–87. DOI: 10.1016/j.estger.2014.08.001

Moreira, A. C., Ribau, C. P., & Borges, M. I. (2024). Internationalisation of SMEs: A comparative perspective between Africa and Latin America. *International Journal of Entrepreneurship and Small Business*, 51(4), 513–541. DOI: 10.1504/IJESB.2024.136944

Morgan, N. A., Kaleka, A., & Katsikeas, C. S. (2004). Antecedents of export venture performance: A theoretical model and empirical assessment. *Journal of Marketing*, 68(1), 90–108. DOI: 10.1509/jmkg.68.1.90.24028

Morrison, A. (2000). Entrepreneurship: What triggers it? *International Journal of Entrepreneurial Behaviour & Research*, 6(2), 59–71. DOI: 10.1108/13552550010335976

Moshtari, M., & Safarpour, A. (2023). Challenges and strategies for the internationalization of higher education in low-income East African countries. *Higher Education*, ●●●, 1–21. PMID: 36713135

Mosquera, S., & Jardim da Palma, P. (Eds.). (2020). *Multidisciplinary Approach to Entrepreneurship Education for Migrants*. IGI Global. DOI: 10.4018/978-1-7998-2925-6

Mueller, E. (2014). Entrepreneurs from low-skilled immigrant groups in knowledge-intensive industries: Company characteristics, survival and innovative performance. *Small Business Economics*, 42(4), 871–889. DOI: 10.1007/s11187-013-9498-4

Mukherjee, S., Baral, M. M., Lavanya, B. L., Nagariya, R., Singh Patel, B., & Chittipaka, V. (2023). Intentions to adopt the blockchain: Investigation of the retail supply chain. *Management Decision*, 61(5), 1320–1351. DOI: 10.1108/MD-03-2022-0369

Mukhopadhyay, S. (n.d.). *International Projects* [PowerPoint Slides]. SlidePlayer., https://slideplayer.com/slide/13936018/

Munkejord, M. C. (2017). His or her work–life balance? Experiences of self-employed immigrant parents. *Work, Employment and Society*, 31(4), 624–639. DOI: 10.1177/0950017016667041

Muñoz Bonilla, H. A., & Soriano Flores, E. (2023). Formulación de proyectos en Mypes: Evidencia empírica de la ausencia de un modelo práctico. *Project. Design and Management*, 5(1), 27–43. DOI: 10.35992/pdm.5vi1.1152

Muñoz-Maya, C. M., Ramirez-Garzón, M. T., & Velazquez, R. P. (2021). Management Practices in Chaotic Environments of SMEs in Bogota. In R. Perez-Uribe, D. Ocampo-Guzman, N. Moreno-Monsalve, & W. Fajardo-Moreno (Eds.), *Handbook of Research on Management Techniques and Sustainability Strategies for Handling Disruptive Situations in Corporate Settings* (pp. 70-88). IGI Global. https://doi .org/DOI: 10.4018/978-1-7998-8185-8.ch004

Murnieks, C. Y., Klotz, A. C., & Shepherd, D. A. (2020). Entrepreneurial motivation: A review of the literature and an agenda for future research. *Journal of Organizational Behavior*, 41(2), 115–143. https:// doi.org/https://doi.org/10.1002/job.2374. DOI: 10.1002/job.2374

Murtini, F., Fleischeri, L., Siegerinki, V., Aassveii, A., Alganiii, Y., Boarinii, R., Gonzálezi, S., Lontii, Z., Grimaldaiv, G., Hortala Vallvev, R., Kimvi, S., Leevi, D., Puttermanvii, L., & Smithi, C. (2018). Trust and its determinants: Evidence from the Trustlab experiment. *Working Paper No. 89. Organisation for Economic Co-operation and Development.* https://one.oecd.org/document/SDD/DOC(2018)2/En/pdf

Musik and Romo. (2005). On the concept of competitiveness. *Foreign Trade, 55* (3).

Musso, F., & Francioni, B. (2014). International strategy for SMEs: Criteria for foreign markets and entry modes selection. *Journal of Small Business and Enterprise Development*, 21(2), 301–312. DOI: 10.1108/JSBED-10-2013-0149

Nabaoui, A. (2023). Performance : Concepts, approches et modèles. *Revue Française d'Economie et de Gestion*, 4(11), 11. https://www.revuefreg.fr/index.php/home/article/view/1348

Naidoo, P. (2019). *Monitoring and evaluating the effectiveness of business operational strategies that enhance competitive advantage for facility management companies: a case study of ten (10) facility management companies in Gauteng, South Africa* (Doctoral dissertation).

Najmaei, A. (2011). Dynamic Business Model Innovation: An Analytical Archetype. *3rd International Conference on Information and Financial Engineering*, 12, 165-171. IACSIT Press, Singapore.

Nakamura, k., Kaihatsu, S. & Yagi, T. (2018) Productivity Improvement and Economic Growth. Bank of Japan. *Working Paper Series*. No.18-E-10 May 2018.

Naradda Gamage, S. K., Ekanayake, E. M. S., Abeyrathne, G. A. K. N. J., Prasanna, R. P. I. R., Jayasundara, J. M. S. B., & Rajapakshe, P. S. K. (2020). A review of global challenges and survival strategies of small and medium enterprises (SMEs). *Economies*, 8(4), 79. DOI: 10.3390/economies8040079

Naudé, W., Siegel, M., & Marchand, K. (2017). Migration, entrepreneurship and development: Critical questions. *IZA Journal of Migration*, 6(1), 5. DOI: 10.1186/s40176-016-0077-8

Navarro-García, A., Arenas-Gaitán, J., Rondán-Cataluña, F. J., & Rey-Moreno, M. (2016). Global model of export performance: Moderator role of export department. *Journal of Business Research*, 69(5), 1880–1886. DOI: 10.1016/j.jbusres.2015.10.073

Ndalira, D. W., Ngugi, J. K., & Chepkulei, B. (2013). Effect of the type of innovation on the growth of small and medium enterprises in Kenya: A case of garment enterprises in Jericho, Nairobi. *European Journal of Management Sciences and Economics*, 1(2).

Ndesaulwa, A. P., & Kikula, J. (2016). The impact of innovation on performance of small and medium enterprises (SMEs) in Tanzania: A review of empirical evidence. *Journal of Business and Management Sciences*, 4(1), 1–6.

Ndumbaro, F., Mofulu, G., & Ndaki, D. P. (2023). Extrinsic Motivation toward Entrepreneurs' Intention to Adopt Crowdfunding: The Case of Kiva Lending Crowdfunding. *African Journal of Innovation and Entrepreneurship*, 2(1), 103–128. DOI: 10.31920/2753-314X/2023/v2n1a5

Nelson, R. (1992). Recent Writings on Competitiveness: Boxing the Compass. *California Management Review*, 34(2), 127–137. DOI: 10.2307/41166697

Neville, F., Orser, B., Riding, A., & Jung, O. (2014). Do young firms owned by recent immigrants out-perform other young firms? *Journal of Business Venturing*, 29(1), 55–71. https://doi.org/https://doi.org/10.1016/j.jbusvent.2012.10.005. DOI: 10.1016/j.jbusvent.2012.10.005

Newland, K., & Tanaka, H. (2010). *Mobilizing diaspora entrepreneurship for development*. Migration Policy Institute Washington.

NHO. (2022). *Fakta om små og mellomstore bedrifter (SMB) [Facts about small and medium sized enterprises]* Norwegian Confederation of Businss. Retrieved 12 December from https://www.nho.no/tema/sma-og-mellomstore-bedrifter/artikler/sma-og-mellomstore-bedrifter-smb/

Niang, B. (2024). La participation à la prise de décision et performance organisationnelle dans les PMET au Sénégal. *Revue Internationale des Sciences de Gestion*, 7(1). https://revue-isg.com/index.php/home/article/view/1505

Nicholls, A. (2010). The legitimacy of social entrepreneurship: Reflexive isomorphism in a pre–paradigmatic field. *Entrepreneurship Theory and Practice*, 34(4), 611–633. DOI: 10.1111/j.1540-6520.2010.00397.x

Niebles-Nuñez, W., Rojas-Martinez, C., Pacheco-Ruiz, C., & Hernandez-Palma, H. G. (2022). Desarrollo de estrategias de direccionamiento estratégico para la gestión de calidad en empresas del sector industrial. *Información Tecnológica*, 33(6), 145–156. DOI: 10.4067/S0718-07642022000600145

Nizeyimana, J. B., Mukanteri, A., & L'Institut Régional IRIMAG/CFM. (2023). L'impact du marketing numérique sur les Petites et Moyennes Entreprises. *RUFSO Journal of Social Science and Engineering*, 35(03). DOI: 10.55272/rufso.rjsse.35.3.2

Norwegian Government Security and Service Organisation. (2002). *Prosjekt – DIFFERENSIERT regelverk for mikrobedrifter og nyetablert [Project - DIFFERENTIATED regulations for micro-enterprises and newly established]*.

Nuryyev, G., Wang, Y.-P., Achyldurdyyeva, J., Jaw, B.-S., Yeh, Y.-S., Lin, H.-T., & Wu, L.-F. (2020). Blockchain technology adoption behavior and sustainability of the business in tourism and hospitality SMEs : An empirical study. *Sustainability (Basel)*, 12(3), 1256. DOI: 10.3390/su12031256

O'Connor, P. (2023). Small-and medium-sized tourism enterprises and smart tourism : Tourism agenda 2030 perspective article. *Tourism Review*, 78(2), 339–343. DOI: 10.1108/TR-09-2022-0431

O'Reilly, C. A., & Tushman, M. L. (2020). *Lead and Disrupt: How to Solve the Innovator's Dilemma.* Stanford University Press.

OECD (2021). SME and Entrepreneurship Outlook 2021. OECD Report.

OECD, & Scalabrini Migration Center. (2017). *Interrelations between public policies, migration and development in the Philippines. OECD Development Pathways.* https://doi.org/DOI: 10.1787/9789264272286-en

OECD. (2017). SME and entrepreneurship policy in Canada. OECD Studies on SMEs and Entrepreneurship. *OECD Publishing, Paris.* https://doi-org.lib-ezproxy.concordia.ca/10.1787/9789264273467-en

OECD. K. (2018). *OECD science, technology and innovation outlook 2018.* Paris: OECD publishing.

Olson, D. L., & Wu, D. D. (2010). A review of enterprise risk management in supply chain. *Kybernetes*, 39(5), 694–706. DOI: 10.1108/03684921011043198

Ordoñez de Pablos, P. (Ed.). (2014). *Knowledge management for competitive advantage during economic crisis.* IGI Global.

Ore, H., Olortegui, E., & Ponce, D. (2020). Planeamiento estratégico como instrumento de gestión en las empresas: Revisión Bibliográfica. *Revista Pakamuros,* Volumen 8, Número 4, Octubre –Diciembre, 2020, páginas 31-44. http://190.119.95.85/index.php/pakamuros/article/view/147/127

Orozco Gutiérrez, T., & Henao Vásquez, G. A. (2023). La toma de decisiones al interior de las organizaciones en momentos de incertidumbre. *Universidad Libre.* chrome-extension://efaidnbmnnnibpcajp-cglclefindmkaj/https://repository.unilibre.edu.co/bitstream/handle/10901/24463/Orozco%20Guti%C3%A9rrez%20-%20Henao%20V%C3%A1squez.pdf?sequence=1

Ortiz, L. E. M., Mero, M. J. V., Castro, L. M. U., & Sanchez, L. M. C. (2021). Proceso administrativo y sostenibilidad empresarial del sector hotelero de la parroquia Crucita, Manabí-Ecuador. *Revista de Ciencias Sociales*, 27(2), 367–385.

Østergaard, A., & Marinova, S. T. (2018). Human capital in the entrepreneurship ecosystem. *International Journal of Entrepreneurship and Small Business*, 35(3), 371–390. DOI: 10.1504/IJESB.2018.095907

Ostrovsky, Y., & Picot, G. (2021). Innovation in immigrant-owned firms [Article]. *Small Business Economics*, 57(4), 1857–1874. DOI: 10.1007/s11187-020-00376-2

Ozili, P. K. (2018). Impact of digital finance on financial inclusion and stability. *Borsa Istanbul Review*, 18(4), 329–340. DOI: 10.1016/j.bir.2017.12.003

Page, M. J., McKenzie, J. E., Bossuyt, P. M., Boutron, I., Hoffmann, T. C., Mulrow, C. D., Shamseer, L., Tetzlaff, J. M., Akl, E. A., Brennan, S. E., Chou, R., Glanville, J., Grimshaw, J. M., Hróbjartsson, A., Lalu, M. M., Li, T., Loder, E. W., Mayo-Wilson, E., McDonald, S., & Moher, D. (2021). The PRISMA 2020 statement: An updated guideline for reporting systematic reviews. *BMJ (Clinical Research Ed.)*, 372(71), n71. Advance online publication. DOI: 10.1136/bmj.n71 PMID: 33782057

Palacios Rodríguez, M. Á. (2020). Strategic Planning, a functional instrument within organizations. *National Journal of Administration*, 11(2).

Pandey, A., Ashta, A., Spiegelman, E., & Sutan, A. (2020). Catch them young: Impact of financial socialization, financial literacy and attitude towards money on financial well-being of young adults. *International Journal of Consumer Studies, 44*(6), 531-541. *Scopus.* Advance online publication. DOI: 10.1111/ijcs.12583

Panno, A. (2020). Performance measurement and management in small companies of the service sector; evidence from a sample of Italian hotels. *Measuring Business Excellence*, 24(2), 133–160. DOI: 10.1108/MBE-01-2018-0004

Paola, A., & Sánchez, F. C. (2015). *Análisis del Proceso Productivo de una Empresa de Confecciones: Modelación y Simulación.* Ciencia e Ingeniería Neogranadina.

Pappas, N., Caputo, A., Pellegrini, M. M., Marzi, G., & Michopoulou, E. (2021). The complexity of decision-making processes and IoT adoption in accommodation SMEs. *Journal of Business Research*, 131, 573–583. DOI: 10.1016/j.jbusres.2021.01.010

Park, S. (2018). Challenges and Opportunities: The 21st Century Public Manager in a VUCA World. *Journal of Public Administration: Research and Theory*, 28(2), 299–301. DOI: 10.1093/jopart/mux042

Parnell, J. A. (2006). Generic strategies after two decades: A reconceptualization of competitive strategy. *Management Decision*, 44(8), 1139–1154. DOI: 10.1108/00251740610690667

Pattinson, C. (2015). Emerging technologies and their environmental impact. *Green Information Technology*, 11-26.

Pavlou, P. A., & El Sawy, O. A. (2011). Understanding the Black Box of Dynamic Capabilities: A Dynamic Process Model of Sensing, Seizing, and Transforming. *Academy of Management Review*, 35(1), 60–79.

Peñafiel Nivela, G. A., Acurio Armas, J. A., Manosalvas Gómez, L. R., & Burbano Castro, B. E. (2020). Formulación de estrategias para el desarrollo empresarial de la constructora Emanuel en el cantón La Maná. *Revista Universidad y Sociedad*, 12(4), 45–55.

Penrose, E. (1959). The productive opportunity of the firm and the entrepreneur. In *The Theory of the Growth of the Firm* (pp. 31–42). Oxford University Press.

Perera, N. (2021). Impact of digital transformation in measuring business performance of small & medium scale businesses in Sri Lanka. *International Journal of Economics. Business and Management Research*, 5(7), 1–25.

Peres, J. A. H., Geldes, C., Kunc, M. H., & Flores, A. (2023). The effect of local institutions on the competitive strategies of exporters. The case of emerging economies in Latin America. *Journal of Business Research*, 169, 114256. https://doi.org/https://doi.org/10.1016/j.jbusres.2023.114256. DOI: 10.1016/j.jbusres.2023.114256

Perez, L., Vasquez, C., & Luna, M., & J, P. (2011). Indicadores estratégicos para incrementar la efectividad de las inspecciones para las operadoras del servicio eléctrico Venezolano. *Universidad, Ciencia y Tecnología.*

Pérez–Uribe, R. (2018). *Gerencia estratégica Corporativa*. Ediciones Ecoe Ltda. Primera Edición. ISBN: 978-958-771-630-6. eISBN: 978-958-771-631-3. 259 p. abril.

Pérez-Uribe, R., & Ocampo Guzmán, D. Ospina&Bermeo, J., Cifuentes Valenzuela, J., & Cubillos Leal, C.A. (2016). *MIIGO - Modelo de Intervención e Innovación para el direccionamiento estratégico*. Ediciones EAN. ISBN: 978-958-756-414-3. 98 p.

Pérez-Uribe, R., Ocampo-Guzmán, D., Salcedo-Pérez, C., Piñeiro-Cortes, L., and Ramírez-Salazar, MDP. (2020). *Increasing the Competitiveness of SMEs*. January 20. Pages: 550. DOI: .DOI: 10.4018/978-1-5225-9425-3

Perez-Uribe, R. I. (2018). *Gerencia estratégica corporativa*. ECOE Ediciones.

Perry, J. (2021). *Trust in public institutions: Trends and implications for economic security*. United Nations Department of Economic and Social Affairs., DOI: 10.18356/df7eed76-en

Pettit, T. J., Croxton, K. L., & Fiksel, J. (2013). Ensuring supply chain resilience: Development and implementation of an assessment tool. *Journal of Business Logistics*, 34(1), 46–76. DOI: 10.1111/jbl.12009

Pett, T., & Wolff, J. (2017). Exploring competitive strategies: The role of managerial perceptions and motivations on internationalisation of SMEs. *International Journal of Entrepreneurial Venturing*, 9(2), 181–202. DOI: 10.1504/IJEV.2017.086484

Philippine Statistics Authority. (2022). *2020 overseas Filipino workers (final results)*. https://psa.gov.ph/content/2020-overseas-filipino-workers-final-results

Phillips, P., & Louvieris, P. (2005). Performance Measurement Systems in Tourism, Hospitality, and Leisure Small Medium-Sized Enterprises : A Balanced Scorecard Perspective. *Journal of Travel Research*, 44(2), 201–211. DOI: 10.1177/0047287505278992

Pikkemaat, B., Peters, M., & Bichler, B. F. (2019). Innovation research in tourism: Research streams and actions for the future. *Journal of Hospitality and Tourism Management*, 41, 184–196. https://doi.org/https://doi.org/10.1016/j.jhtm.2019.10.007. DOI: 10.1016/j.jhtm.2019.10.007

Pinzon, M. J. L. (2021). *Defamiliarized family: The "Anak ng OFWs" emergent narratives on mediated communication and parent-child relationships*. https://scholar.archive.org/work/fm6e4hv6nzgvtctoivd3uujohu/access/wayback/http://www.plarideljournal.org/download/6098/

Pitre, R., Builes, S., & Hernández, H. (2021). *Impacto del marketing digital a las empresas colombianas emergentes*. Revista Universidad y Empresa.

Polanyi, K. (2015). The economy as an institutionalized activity. Journal of critical economics, (20), 192-207.

Polas, M. R. H., Kabir, A. I., Sohel-Uz-Zaman, A. S. M., Karim, R., & Tabash, M. I. (2022). Blockchain technology as a game changer for green innovation: Green entrepreneurship as a roadmap to green economic sustainability in Peru. *Journal of Open Innovation*, 8(2), 62. DOI: 10.3390/joitmc8020062

Polisetty, A., Lalitha, N., & Singu, H. B. (2021). Factors affecting financial literacy among budding entrepreneurs. *Universal Journal of Accounting and Finance, 9*(5), 1085-1092. *Scopus.* Advance online publication. DOI: 10.13189/ujaf.2021.090518

Polo Sánchez, A. C. (2017). *Estrategia administrativa de Claro: resiliencia o sinergia organizacionales.* https://ciencia.lasalle.edu.co/administracion_de_empresas/1465

Ponce Alberca, J. (2022). Presentación. El populismo como problema histórico: Algunas reflexiones. *El Futuro Del Pasado*, 13, 17–34. DOI: 10.14201/fdp.27438

Popper, R. (2008). How are foresight methods selected? *foresight, 10*(6), 62-89.

Porter, M. (1980). *Las 5 fuerzas de Porter.* Harvard Business School.

Porter, M. (1991). *The competitive advantage of nations.* Ed. Vergara.

Porter, M. (2000). *Being competitive. New contributions and conclusions.* CECSA.

Porter, M. E. (1980). *Competitive Advantage.* The Free Press.

Pothineni, S. (2023). The Impact of Data Strategy and Emerging Technologies on Business Performance. [IJBSA]. *International Journal of Business Strategy and Automation*, 4(1), 1–19. DOI: 10.4018/IJB-SA.334022

Powell, E. E., & Baker, T. (2014). It's what you make of it: Founder identity and enacting strategic responses to adversity. *Academy of Management Journal*, 57(5), 1406–1433. DOI: 10.5465/amj.2012.0454

Prasad, L. M. (2020). *Principles and practice of management.* Sultan Chand & Sons.

Prusak, R. (2019). Analysis of selected elements of knowledge management in the context of the size of the enterprise and the specifics of its activity. *Management*, 23(1), 90–104. DOI: 10.2478/manment-2019-0006

Puschmann, T. (2017). Fintech. *Business & Information Systems Engineering*, 59(1), 69–76. DOI: 10.1007/s12599-017-0464-6

Quigley, B. Z., & Rustagi, N. K. (2018). Level of Education and Family Dynamics among Immigrant and Nonimmigrant Business Owners in the Case of Arlington County, VA. *Competition Forum, 16*(2), 90-95. https://login.ezproxy.inn.no/login?url=https://search.ebscohost.com/login.aspx?direct=true&db=s3h&AN=132606003&site=ehost-live&scope=site

Quiroga Gil, M. (2021). Los entornos digitales y el mundo VUCA. In Quiroga, M., Martin, M., & Baldivieso, S. (Eds.), *Entornos Digitales y Mundo Vuca. Libro de Resúmenes y Presentaciones de la 1° Jornada Entornos Digitales y Mundo VUCA* (pp. 8–15). Nueva Editorial Universitaria - UNSL., http://www.neu.unsl.edu.ar/wp-content/uploads/2021/09/Entornos-digitales-y-mundo-VUCA.pdf

Radicic, D., & Petković, S. (2023). Impact of digitalization on technological innovations in small and medium-sized enterprises (SMEs). *Technological Forecasting and Social Change*, 191, 122474. DOI: 10.1016/j.techfore.2023.122474

Radjou, N., Prabhu, J., & Ahuja, S. (2012). *Jugaad Innovation: Think Frugal, Be Flexible, Generate Breakthrough Growth*. Jossey-Bass.

Ramirez, C., & Ramirez, M. (2016). *Fundamentos de Administración*. Ediciones ECOE.

Ramonet, I. (2001). *Impact of globalization on developing countries. Memoria magazine, 143* .

Rao, S., & Goldsby, T. J. (2009). Supply chain risks: A review and typology. *International Journal of Logistics Management*, 20(1), 97–123. DOI: 10.1108/09574090910954864

Rasheed, B., & Ahmad, M. (2022). Competitive intensity: Bridging the gap between corporate social responsibility and competitive advantage. *Journal of Strategy and Management*, 15(4), 745–765. DOI: 10.1108/JSMA-08-2021-0177

Rath, J., & Swagerman, A. (2016). Promoting Ethnic Entrepreneurship in European Cities: Sometimes Ambitious, Mostly Absent, Rarely Addressing Structural Features. *International Migration (Geneva, Switzerland)*, 54(1), 152–166. https://doi.org/https://doi.org/10.1111/imig.12215. DOI: 10.1111/imig.12215

Ratinho, T., Amezcua, A., Honig, B., & Zeng, Z. (2020). Supporting entrepreneurs: A systematic review of literature and an agenda for research. *Technological Forecasting and Social Change*, 154, 119956. DOI: 10.1016/j.techfore.2020.119956

Reimann, C. K., Carvalho, F. M., & Duarte, M. P. (2022). Adaptive marketing capabilities, market orientation, and international performance: The moderation effect of competitive intensity. *Journal of Business and Industrial Marketing*, 37(12), 2533–2543. DOI: 10.1108/JBIM-08-2021-0391

Restrepo Restrepo, A. M., & Montoya Restrepo Restrepo, I. A. (2003). Organizations and methods of understanding them. *Innovar (Universidad Nacional de Colombia)*, 13(22), 63–72.

Reyes, J. A. L. (2015). Environmental attitudes and behaviors in the Philippines. *Journal of Educational and Social Research*, 4(6), 87–102. DOI: 10.5901/jesr.2014.v4n6p87

Riaz, S., Khan, H. H., Sarwar, B., Ahmed, W., Muhammad, N., Reza, S., & Ul Haq, S. M. N. (2022). Influence of Financial Social Agents and Attitude Toward Money on Financial Literacy: The Mediating Role of Financial Self-Efficacy and Moderating Role of Mindfulness. *SAGE Open, 12*(3). *SAGE Open*, 12(3). Advance online publication. DOI: 10.1177/21582440221117140

Ribau, C. P., Moreira, A. C., & Raposo, M. (2017). Export performance and the internationalisation of SMEs. *International Journal of Entrepreneurship and Small Business*, 30(2), 214–240. DOI: 10.1504/IJESB.2017.081438

Ribau, C. P., Moreira, A. C., & Raposo, M. (2018). SME internationalization research: Mapping the state of the art. *Canadian Journal of Administrative Sciences*, 35(2), 280–303. https://onlinelibrary.wiley.com/doi/pdf/10.1002/cjas.1419. DOI: 10.1002/cjas.1419

Ricardo, D., & Reeder, J. (1817). *Principles of Political Economy and Taxation*. Pyramid Editions.

Rîmniceanu, R. (2023, May). Innovation in the Financial Sector (FinTech): Paradigms, Causes, Effects and Perspectives. In *Proceedings of the International Conference on Cybersecurity and Cybercrime-2023* (pp. 21-33). Asociatia Romana pentru Asigurarea Securitatii Informatiei. DOI: 10.19107/CY-BERCON.2023.03

Rivera, J. P. R., & Tullao, T. S. Jr. (2020). Investigating the link between remittances and inflation: Evidence from the Philippines. *South East Asia Research*, 28(3), 301–326. DOI: 10.1080/0967828X.2020.1793685

Rodriguez, A. and Rodriguez, Y. (2015), " *Metaphors for today's leadership: VUCA world, millennial, and cloud leaders* ", Journal of Management Development, Vol. 34 No. 7, pp . 854 - 866.

Rojas, M., Jaimes, L. & Valencia, (2017). Efectividad, eficacia y eficiencia en equipos de trabajo. *Revista espacios*. Vol. 39 (N.º 06) Año 2018. Pág. 11. 23/10/2017. https://www.revistaespacios.com/a18v39n06/a18v39n06p11.pdf

Romero-Rodríguez, L. M., Chaves-Montero, A., & Torres-Toukoumidis, Á. (2018). Neopopulismo, poder y control social: las competencias mediáticas en ideología y valores como defensa de la ciudadanía. *Lumina, 12*(1), 40-54. https://n2t.net/ark:/13683/pHPH/MRs

Rosário, A. T., & Dias, J. C. (2023). How has data-driven marketing evolved : Challenges and opportunities with emerging technologies. *International Journal of Information Management Data Insights*, 3(2), 100203. DOI: 10.1016/j.jjimei.2023.100203

Rosli, M. M., & Sidek, S. (2013). The Impact of innovation on the performance of small and medium manufacturing enterprises: Evidence from Malaysia. *Journal of Innovation Management in Small & Medium Enterprises*, 2013, 1–16. DOI: 10.5171/2013.885666

Roundy, P. T., & Burke-Smalley, L. (2022). Leveraging entrepreneurial ecosystems as human resource systems: A theory of meta-organizational human resource management. *Human Resource Management Review*, 32(4), 100863. DOI: 10.1016/j.hrmr.2021.100863

Rousseau, D. M., Manning, J., & Denyer, D. (2008). 11 Evidence in management and organizational science: Assembling the field's full weight of scientific knowledge through syntheses. *The Academy of Management Annals*, 2(1), 475–515. DOI: 10.5465/19416520802211651

Rovira Kaltwasser, C. (2019). Populism and the Economy: An Ambivalent Relationship. Friedrich Ebert Stiftung. https://library.fes.de/pdf-files/iez/15244.pdf

Rovira Kaltwasser, C. (2018). Studying the (Economic) Consequences of Populism. *AEA Papers and Proceedings. American Economic Association*, 108, 204–207. https://www.jstor.org/stable/26452733. DOI: 10.1257/pandp.20181125

Rowe, A., & Mason, K. D. (1982). *Strategic Management and Business Policy: A Methodological Approach*. Addison-Wesley.

Ruangkanjanases, A., Qhal, E. M. A., Alfawaz, K. M., & Hariguna, T. (2023). Examining the antecedents of blockchain usage intention: An integrated research framework. *Sustainability (Basel)*, 15(4), 3500. DOI: 10.3390/su15043500

Ruan, M. D., Baskaran, A., & Zhou, S. S. (2022). Mainland Chinese Immigrant-owned SMEs in Malaysia: Case Studies [Article]. *Millennial Asia, 13*(1), 5-34. *Article*, 0976399620977026. Advance online publication. DOI: 10.1177/0976399620977026

Rua, O., França, A., & Fernández Ortiz, R. (2018). Key drivers of SMEs export performance: The mediating effect of competitive advantage. *Journal of Knowledge Management*, 22(2), 257–279. DOI: 10.1108/JKM-07-2017-0267

Safari, A., Saleh, A. S., & Balicevac Al Ismail, V. (2022). Enhancing the export activities of small and medium-sized enterprises in emerging markets. *Journal of Business and Industrial Marketing*, 37(5), 1150–1166. DOI: 10.1108/JBIM-08-2020-0388

Sahoo, S. (2022). Lean practices and operational performance: The role of organizational culture. *International Journal of Quality & Reliability Management*, 39(2), 428–467. DOI: 10.1108/IJQRM-03-2020-0067

Salamanca, Y. T., Cortina, A. D., & Garcia Rios, D. (2014). Modelo de gestión organizacional basado en el logro de objetivos. *Suma de Negocios*, 5(11), 70–77. DOI: 10.1016/S2215-910X(14)70021-7

Salas Rodas, L. (2014). Estado, empresa privada y sector social: Una relación entre sectores que fortalece a la sociedad civil. *Revista de Trabajo Social*, (5), 107–129. https://revistas.udea.edu.co/index.php/revistraso/article/view/20440

Salas, E., Tannenbaum, S. I., Kraiger, K., & Smith-Jentsch, K. A. (2012). The science of training and development in organizations: What matters in practice. *Psychological Science in the Public Interest*, 13(2), 74–101. DOI: 10.1177/1529100612436661 PMID: 26173283

Salim, I. M., & Sulaiman, M. (2011). Organizational learning, innovation and performance: A study of Malaysian small and medium sized enterprises. *International Journal of Business and Management*, 6(12), 118. DOI: 10.5539/ijbm.v6n12p118

Salvatore Dominick. (1996) *Microeconomics*. Mc Graw Hill, Third Edition. Mexico.

Samara, D., Magnisalis, I., & Peristeras, V. (2020). Artificial intelligence and big data in tourism : A systematic literature review. *Journal of Hospitality and Tourism Technology*, 11(2), 343–367. DOI: 10.1108/JHTT-12-2018-0118

Sam, P. A., Frimpong, S., & Kendie, S. (2022). Personal finance behaviour: A reasoned action approach. *International Journal of Social Economics*, 49(8), 1119–1131. DOI: 10.1108/IJSE-02-2021-0097

Sanchez Rodriguez, L. Z., Cejas Martinez, M. F., & Tovar Velasquez, S. J. (2024). *Las competencias del gerente financiero*. CIDE, editorial. chrome-extension://efaidnbmnnnibpcajpcglclefindmkaj/https://repositorio.cidecuador.org/bitstream/123456789/2944/3/No%2039%20Libro%20Las%20Competencias%203-1-2024.pdf

Sánchez-Amboage, E., Crespo-Pereira, V., Membiela-Pollán, M., & Jesús Faustino, J. P. (2024). Tourism marketing in the metaverse : A systematic literature review, building blocks, and future research directions. *PLoS One*, 19(5), e0300599. DOI: 10.1371/journal.pone.0300599 PMID: 38728243

Sanchez, P. A. (2002). Soil fertility and hunger in Africa. *Science*, 295(5562), 2019–2020. DOI: 10.1126/science.1065256 PMID: 11896257

Sandberg, W. R. (1992). Strategic management's potential contributions to a theory of entrepreneurship. *Entrepreneurship Theory and Practice*, 16(3), 73–90. DOI: 10.1177/104225879201600305

Sanford, L. & Moskowitz. (2015). The Small and Medium-Sized Enterprise (SME). DOI: 10.1016/B978-0-12-800353-4.00004-X

Santos Martínez, C. J. (2014). Educación Mediática e Informacional en el contexto de la actual Sociedad del Conocimiento. *Historia y Comunicación Social*, 18(0), 781–794. DOI: 10.5209/rev_HICS.2013.v18.44365

Santoso, D. S., & Oetomo, B. (2016). Relationship between entrepreneurial skills, entrepreneurial orientation, and information technology to entrepreneurship intention: Cases in Indonesia. *International Journal of Management Sciences and Business Research*, 5(4).

Saoudi, L., Aubry, M., Gomot, T., & Renaud, A. (2023). Transformation digitale et performance des PME : Une analyse bibliométrique pour comprendre et agir. *Revue internationale PME, 36*(2), 13-38.

Sapienza, E. (2021). *Policy Brief: Trust in Public Institutions. A conceptual framework and insights for improved governance programming*. United Nations Development Programme UNDP. https://www.undp.org/sites/g/files/zskgke326/files/migration/oslo_governance_centre/Trust-in-Public-Institutions-Policy-Brief_FINAL.pdf

Sari, D. E., Narimo, S., & Saputra, R. C. (2020). The effect of financial literacy and pocket money on consumer behavior of universitas muhammadiyah surakarta (Ums) students. [Scopus.]. *International Journal of Scientific and Technology Research*, 9(2), 4235–4237.

Sari, D. P., Nabella, S. D., & Fadlilah, A. H. (2022). The Effect of Profitability, Liquidity, Leverage, and Activity Ratios on Dividend Policy in Manufacturing Companies in the Food and Beverage Industry Sector Listed on the Indonesia Stock Exchange in the 2016-2020 Period. *Jurnal Mantik*, 6(2), 1365–1375.

Sarid, A., & Levanon, M. (2023). Embracing dualities: Principles of education for a VUCA world. *Educational Philosophy and Theory*, 55(12), 1375–1386. DOI: 10.1080/00131857.2022.2162384

Sarwar, H., Aftab, J., Ishaq, M. I., & Atif, M. (2023). Achieving business competitiveness through corporate social responsibility and dynamic capabilities: An empirical evidence from emerging economy. *Journal of Cleaner Production*, 386, 135820. DOI: 10.1016/j.jclepro.2022.135820

Saskatchewan. (n.d.). *Key economic sectors.*https://www.saskatchewan.ca/business/investment-and-economic-development/key-economic-sectors

Satjaharuthai, K., & Lakkhongkha, K. (2023). The Role of Entrepreneurs in Driving the Success of their Businesses in the Digital Era. *International Journal of Professional Business Review: Int.J. Prof. Bus. Rev.*, 8(7), 109.

Schilke, O. (2014). On the contingent value of dynamic capabilities for competitive advantage: The non-linear moderating effect of environmental dynamism. *Strategic Management Journal*, 35(2), 179–203. DOI: 10.1002/smj.2099

Schiuma, G. (2012). Managing knowledge for business performance improvement. *Journal of Knowledge Management*, 16(4), 515–522. DOI: 10.1108/13673271211246103

Schumpeter, J. (1934). *The theory of economic development*. Harvard University Press.

Schumpeter, J. (1942). *Capitalism, socialism and democracy*. George Allen and Unwin.

Schumpeter, J. A. (1934). *The theory of economic development: An inquiry into profits, capital, credit, interest, and the business cycle*. Harvard University Press.

Schwab, K. (2018). The Global Competitiveness Report 2018. World Economic Forum.

Scolari, C. A. (2009). Transmedia Storytelling: Implicit Consumers, Narrative Worlds, and Branding in Contemporary Media Production. *International Journal of Communication, 3*(2013), 586-606. https://ijoc.org/index.php/ijoc/article/view/477

Scott, B. R., & Lodge, G. C. (1985). US Competitiveness in the World Economy. *Harvard Business Review*.

Scott, W. R. (1995). *Institutions and Organizations. Thousands Oaks*. Sage Publications.

Scroope, C. (2017a). *Filipino culture: Business culture*.https://culturalatlas.sbs.com.au/filipino-culture/filipino-culture-business-culture

Scroope, C. (2017b). *Filipino culture: Religion*.https://culturalatlas.sbs.com.au/filipino-culture/filipino-culture-religion

Seba, I., & Rowley, J. (2010). Knowledge management in UK police forces. *Journal of Knowledge Management*, 14(4), 611–626. DOI: 10.1108/13673271011059554

Sedziniauskiene, R., Sekliuckiene, J., & Zucchella, A. (2019). Networks' Impact on the Entrepreneurial Internationalization: A Literature Review and Research Agenda. *MIR. Management International Review*, 59(5), 779–823. DOI: 10.1007/s11575-019-00395-6

Selvarajah, C., Le, T. D., & Sukunesan, S. (2019). The Vietnam project: Developing conceptual knowledge on cross-cultural skills for training in SME internationalization. *Asia Pacific Business Review*, 25(3), 338–366. DOI: 10.1080/13602381.2019.1598076

Semrau, T., Ambos, T., & Kraus, S. (2016). Entrepreneurial orientation and SME performance across societal cultures: An international study. *Journal of Business Research*, 69(5), 1928–1932. DOI: 10.1016/j.jbusres.2015.10.082

Seow, A. N., Choong, Y. O., & Ramayah, T. (2021). Small and medium-size enterprises' business performance in tourism industry : The mediating role of innovative practice and moderating role of government support. *Asian Journal of Technology Innovation*, 29(2), 283–303. DOI: 10.1080/19761597.2020.1798796

Servantie, V., & Rispal, M. H. (2020). Bricolage, effectuation, and causation shifts over time in the context of social entrepreneurship. In *Social Entrepreneurship and Bricolage* (pp. 49–74). Routledge. DOI: 10.4324/9780429263767-3

Setiowati, R., Daryanto, H. K., & Arifin, B. (2015). The effects of ICT adoption on marketing capabilities and business performance of Indonesian SMEs in the fashion industry. *The Journal of Business and Retail Management Research*, 10(1). https://jbrmr.com/cdn/article_file/i-22_c-206.pdf

Shah, S. H., Angeles, L. C., & Harris, L. M. (2017). Worlding the intangibility of resilience: The case of rice farmers and water-related risk in the Philippines. *World Development*, 98, 400–412. DOI: 10.1016/j.worlddev.2017.05.004

Shah, S. M. A., El-Gohary, H., & Hussain, J. G. (2015). An Investigation of Market Orientation (MO) and Tourism Small and Medium-Sized Enterprises' (SMEs) Performance in Developing Countries : A Review of the Literature. *Journal of Travel & Tourism Marketing*, 32(8), 990–1022. DOI: 10.1080/10548408.2014.957372

Shah, W. U. H., Hao, G., Zhu, N., Yasmeen, R., Padda, I. U. H., & Abdul Kamal, M. (2022). A cross-country efficiency and productivity evaluation of commercial banks in South Asia: A meta-frontier and Malmquist productivity index approach. *PLoS One*, 17(4), e0265349. DOI: 10.1371/journal.pone.0265349 PMID: 35385496

Shaikh, S. (2022). Internet of Things : Designing Digital Eco-Systems for Competitive Tourism Related Micro and Small Enterprises in Pakistan. In Hassan, A. (Ed.), *Technology Application in Tourism in Asia : Innovations, Theories and Practices* (pp. 349–365). Springer Nature., DOI: 10.1007/978-981-16-5461-9_21

Shamira, A., Rosas, S. C. Z., & Tusa, F. (2023). Competencias organizacionales del Comunicador Social del ECU 911 ante situaciones de crisis. #. *PerDebate*, 7(1), 106–139. DOI: 10.18272/pd.v7i1.3107

Shamseer, L., Moher, D., Clarke, M., Ghersi, D., Liberati, A., Petticrew, M., Shekelle, P., Stewart, L. A., & the PRISMA-P Group. (2015). Preferred reporting items for systematic review and meta-analysis protocols (PRISMA-P) 2015 : Elaboration and explanation. *BMJ, 349*(jan02 1), g7647-g7647. DOI: 10.1136/bmj.g7647

Shane, S., & Venkataraman, S. (2000). The promise of entrepreneurship as a field of research. *Academy of Management Review*, 25(1), 217–226. DOI: 10.5465/amr.2000.2791611

Sharma, A., & Ritu, N. R. (2023). Role of Government Schemes in Supporting Startups in India: A Quantitative Investigation. [EEL]. *European Economic Letters*, 13(1), 276–280.

Sharma, A., & Sharma, S. (2024). Adoption of digital marketing in tourism SMEs : A review and research agenda. *Management Research Review*, 47(7), 1077–1095. DOI: 10.1108/MRR-08-2021-0597

Sharma, B., & Fisher, T.Sharma and Fisher. (1997). Functional strategies and competitiveness: An empirical analysis using data from Australian manufacturing. *Benchmarking for Quality Management & Technology*, 4(4), 286–294. DOI: 10.1108/14635779710195122

Sharma, S., Durand, R. M., & Gur-arie, O. (1981). Identification and analysis of moderator variables. *JMR, Journal of Marketing Research*, 18(3), 291–300. DOI: 10.1177/002224378101800303

Sharma, S., & Sharma, S. K. (2020). Probing the links between team resilience, competitive advantage, and organizational effectiveness: Evidence from information technology industry. *Business Perspectives and Research*, 8(2), 289–307. DOI: 10.1177/2278533719887458

Shim, S., Barber, B. L., Card, N. A., Xiao, J. J., & Serido, J. (2010). Financial socialization of first-year college students: The roles of parents, work, and education. *Journal of Youth and Adolescence*, 39(12), 1457–1470. DOI: 10.1007/s10964-009-9432-x PMID: 20938727

Sideri, M., Filippopoulou, A., Rouvalis, G., Kalloniatis, C., & Gritzalis, S. (2017). Social media use for decision making process in educational settings: The Greek case for Leadership's views and attitude in Secondary and Tertiary Education. *HICCS*. https://core.ac.uk/download/pdf/77239811.pdf

Siegel, D. S., Waldman, D. A., Atwater, L. E., & Link, A. N. (2004). Toward a model of the effective transfer of scientific knowledge from academicians to practitioners: Qualitative evidence from the commercialization of university technolo-gies. *Journal of Engineering and Technology Management*, 21(1-2), 115–142. DOI: 10.1016/j.jengtecman.2003.12.006

Singh, S., Corner, P., & Pavlovich, K. (2007). Coping with entrepreneurial failure. *Journal of Management & Organization*, 13(4), 331–344. DOI: 10.5172/jmo.2007.13.4.331

Smaliukiene, R., & Bekesiene, S. (2020). Towards sustainable human resources: How generational differences impact subjective wellbeing in the military? *Sustainability (Basel)*, 12(23), 10016. DOI: 10.3390/su122310016

Smith, A. (1776). *The Wealth of Nations: Books I-II-III and selection of Books IV and V.* Alianza editorial.

Smith, S. (1995). Elaborate World Class Competitiveness. *Managing Service Quality*, 5(5), 36–42. DOI: 10.1108/09604529510100387

Solano, V., Chalco, F., & Luis, N. (2023). Estrategias de gestión de talentos humanos en pequeñas y medianas empresas peruanas. *Revista Venezolana de Gerencia*.

Soloviov, V. (2022). Re-examining the links between cultural values and innovation. *Economics & Sociology (Ternopil)*, 15(2), 41–59. DOI: 10.14254/2071-789X.2022/15-2/3

Sousa, C. M. P. (2004). Export performance measurement: An evaluation of the empirical research in the literature. *Academy of Marketing Science Review*, 9, 1–23.

Sousa, C. M. P., Martínez-López, F. J., & Coelho, F. (2008). The determinants of export performance: A review of the research in the literature between 1998 and 2005. *International Journal of Management Reviews*, 10(4), 343–374. DOI: 10.1111/j.1468-2370.2008.00232.x

Spigel, B. (2017). The relational organization of entrepreneurial ecosystems. *Entrepreneurship Theory and Practice*, 41(1), 49–72. DOI: 10.1111/etap.12167

Spigel, B., & Harrison, R. (2018). Toward a process theory of entrepreneurial ecosystems. *Strategic Entrepreneurship Journal*, 12(1), 151–168. DOI: 10.1002/sej.1268

Srivastava, S. C., & Shainesh, G. (2015). Bridging the service divide through digitally enabled service innovations. *Management Information Systems Quarterly*, 39(1), 245–268. DOI: 10.25300/MISQ/2015/39.1.11

Stallone, V., Wetzels, M., & Klaas, M. (2021). Applications of Blockchain Technology in marketing—A systematic review of marketing technology companies. *Blockchain: Research and Applications*, 2(3), 100023. DOI: 10.1016/j.bcra.2021.100023

Statistics Canada. (2021). *Table 10-10-0137-01 Representation of women and men elected to national Parliament and of ministers appointed to federal Cabinet.* https://doi.org/DOI: 10.25318/1010013701-eng

Stein, S. (2021). Reimagining global citizenship education for a volatile, uncertain, complex, and ambiguous (VUCA) world. *Globalisation, Societies and Education*, 19(4), 482–495. DOI: 10.1080/14767724.2021.1904212

Stone, M., Aravopoulou, E., Ekinci, Y., Evans, G., Hobbs, M., Labib, A., Laughlin, P., Machtynger, J., & Machtynger, L. (2020). Artificial intelligence (AI) in strategic marketing decision-making : A research agenda. *The Bottom Line (New York, N.Y.)*, 33(2), 183–200. DOI: 10.1108/BL-03-2020-0022

Stopford, J. M., & Baden-Fuller, C. W. (1994). Creating corporate entrepreneurship. *Strategic Management Journal*, 15(7), 521–536. DOI: 10.1002/smj.4250150703

Storti, L. (2014). Being an entrepreneur: Emergence and structuring of two immigrant entrepreneur groups. *Entrepreneurship and Regional Development*, 26(7-8), 521–545. DOI: 10.1080/08985626.2014.959067

Storz, C., Ten Brink, T., & Zou, N. (2022). Innovation in emerging economies: How do university-industry linkages and public procurement matter for small businesses? *Asia Pacific Journal of Management*, 39(4), 1439–1480. DOI: 10.1007/s10490-021-09763-z

Strömbäck, C., Lind, T., Skagerlund, K., Västfjäll, D., & Tinghög, G. (2017). Does self-control predict financial behavior and financial well-being? *Journal of Behavioral and Experimental Finance*, 14, 30–38. DOI: 10.1016/j.jbef.2017.04.002

Sulistyo, H., & Ayuni, S. (2020). Competitive advantages of SMEs: The roles of innovation capability, entrepreneurial orientation, and social capital. *Contaduría y Administración*, 65(1), 156. DOI: 10.22201/fca.24488410e.2020.1983

Surya, B., Menne, F., Sabhan, H., Suriani, S., Abubakar, H., & Idris, M. (2021). Economic growth, increasing productivity of SMEs, and open innovation. *Journal of Open Innovation*, 7(1), 20. DOI: 10.3390/joitmc7010020

Susilowati, N., & Latifah, L. (2017). College student financial behavior: An empirical study on the mediating effect of attitude toward money. *Advanced Science Letters, 23*(8), 7468-7472. *Scopus.* Advance online publication. DOI: 10.1166/asl.2017.9500

Swank, G. (2019). *The importance of building lasting relationships for your organization.* https://www.inc.com/young-entrepreneur-council/the-importance-of-building-lasting-relationships-for-your -organization.html

Syrek, C. J., Weigelt, O., Kühnel, J., & de Bloom, J. (2018). All I want for Christmas is recovery–changes in employee affective well-being before and after vacation. *Work and Stress*, 32(4), 313–333. DOI: 10.1080/02678373.2018.1427816

Szeiner, Z., Ladislav, M., Horbulak, Z., & Póor, J. (2020). *Management Consulting Trends in Slovakia In the Light of Global and Regional tendencies.* IEECA. DOI: 10.15549/jeecar.v7i2.390

Szkudlarek, B., & Wu, S. X. (2018). The culturally contingent meaning of entrepreneurship: Mixed embeddedness and co-ethnic ties. *Entrepreneurship and Regional Development*, 30(5-6), 585–611. DOI: 10.1080/08985626.2018.1432701

Taherdoost, H. (2023). Fintech: Emerging trends and the future of finance. *Financial Technologies and DeFi: A Revisit to the Digital Finance Revolution*, 29-39.

Takeuchi, H., & Nonaka, I. (2000). Classic work: Theory of organizational knowledge creation.

Tang, C. S. (2006). Perspectives in supply chain risk management. *International Journal of Production Economics*, 103(2), 451–488. DOI: 10.1016/j.ijpe.2005.12.006

Tan, J., Shao, Y., & Li, W. (2013). To be different, or to be the same? An exploratory study of isomorphism in the cluster. *Journal of Business Venturing*, 28(1), 83–97. DOI: 10.1016/j.jbusvent.2012.02.003

Tanyushcheva, N. Y., & Kunitsyna, N. N. (2021). Assessment of public opinion on compliance with anti-cleaning legislation. *Monitoring Obshchestvennogo Mneniya: Ekonomicheskie i Sotsial'nye Per*emeny, 2, 213-233. *Scopus*. Advance online publication. DOI: 10.14515/monitoring.2021.2.1730

Tariq, M. U. (2024). Multidisciplinary service learning in higher education: Concepts, implementation, and impact. In S. Watson (Ed.), *Applications of service learning in higher education* (pp. 1-19). IGI Global. https://doi.org/DOI: 10.4018/979-8-3693-2133-1.ch001

Tariq, M. U. (2024). Emotional intelligence in understanding and influencing consumer behavior. In Musiolik, T., Rodriguez, R., & Kannan, H. (Eds.), *AI impacts in digital consumer behavior* (pp. 56–81). IGI Global., DOI: 10.4018/979-8-3693-1918-5.ch003

Tariq, M. U. (2024). Enhancing cybersecurity protocols in modern healthcare systems: Strategies and best practices. In Garcia, M., & de Almeida, R. (Eds.), *Transformative approaches to patient literacy and healthcare innovation* (pp. 223–241). IGI Global., DOI: 10.4018/979-8-3693-3661-8.ch011

Tariq, M. U. (2024). Fintech startups and cryptocurrency in business: Revolutionizing entrepreneurship. In Kankaew, K., Nakpathom, P., Chnitphattana, A., Pitchayadejanant, K., & Kunnapapdeelert, S. (Eds.), *Applying business intelligence and innovation to entrepreneurship* (pp. 106–124). IGI Global., DOI: 10.4018/979-8-3693-1846-1.ch006

Tariq, M. U. (2024). Leveraging artificial intelligence for a sustainable and climate-neutral economy in Asia. In Ordóñez de Pablos, P., Almunawar, M., & Anshari, M. (Eds.), *Strengthening sustainable digitalization of Asian economy and society* (pp. 1–21). IGI Global., DOI: 10.4018/979-8-3693-1942-0.ch001

Tariq, M. U. (2024). Metaverse in business and commerce. In Kumar, J., Arora, M., & Erkol Bayram, G. (Eds.), *Exploring the use of metaverse in business and education* (pp. 47–72). IGI Global., DOI: 10.4018/979-8-3693-5868-9.ch004

Tata, J., & Prasad, S. (2015). Immigrant family businesses: Social capital, network benefits and business performance [Article]. *International Journal of Entrepreneurial Behaviour & Research*, 21(6), 842–866. DOI: 10.1108/IJEBR-06-2014-0111

Taylor, B., & Harrison, J. (1991). Planeación estratégica exitosa. Legis editores SA. Colombia

Teece, DJ (2019). A capability theory of the firm: an economics and (strategic)

Teece, D. J. (2018). Business models and dynamic capabilities. *Long Range Planning*, 51(1), 40–49. DOI: 10.1016/j.lrp.2017.06.007

Teece, D. J., Pisano, G., & Shuen, A. (1998). Dynamic Capabilities and Strategic Management. *Strategic Management Journal*.

Teece, D., Peteraf, M., & Leih, S. (2016). Dynamic capabilities and organizational agility: Risk, uncertainty, and strategy in the innovation economy. *California Management Review*, 58(4), 13–35. DOI: 10.1525/cmr.2016.58.4.13

Thaler, R. H. (2016). Behavioral economics: Past, present, and future. *The American Economic Review*, 106(7), 1577–1600. DOI: 10.1257/aer.106.7.1577

Thaler, R. H., & Sunstein, C. R. (2008). *Nudge: Improving decisions about health, wealth, and happiness*. Yale University Press.

The Culture Factor club (n.d). *Country Comparison tool Hofstede Insigths.*https://www.hofstede-insights.com/country-comparison-tool?countries=canada https://www.hofstede-insights.com/country-comparison-tool?countries=philippinies

The Philippine Atmospheric Geophysical and Astronomical Services Administration. (2022). *Flood information.*https://www.pagasa.dost.gov.ph/flood#flood-information

The Philippine Atmospheric Geophysical and Astronomical Services Administration. (n.d.). *Climate of the Philippines.*https://www.pagasa.dost.gov.ph/information/climate-philippines#:~:text=Using%20temperature%20and%20rainfall%20as,season%2C%20from%20December%20to%20May

The World Bank. (2021). *GDP (current US$).*https://data.worldbank.org/indicator/NY.GDP.MKTP.CD

Tidd, J., & Bessant, J. (2018). *Managing Innovation: Integrating Technological, Market and Organizational Change*. Wiley.

Tileva, A. (2022). Anything but micro-no small change: Informality practices at a nonprofit microlender in Washington, DC. *Economic Anthropology*, 9(1), 72–83. DOI: 10.1002/sea2.12193

TodayTranslations. (n.d.). Doing business in Canada. https://www.todaytranslations.com/consultancy-services/business-culture-and-etiquette/doing-business-in-canada/

Toghraee, M. T., & Monjezi, M. (2017). Introduction to cultural entrepreneurship: Cultural entrepreneurship in developing countries. *International Review of Management and Marketing*, 7(4), 67–73.

Tomos, F. A., Thurairaj, S., Balan, O., & Hy.ams-Ssekasi, D. (2020). Effects of Culture on Women Entrepreneurs' Success: A Cross-Country Study. *Gender Studies, Entrepreneurship and Human Capital.*, 269-295. .DOI: 10.1007/978-3-030-46874-3_15

Topsakal, Y., Icoz, O., & Icoz, O. (2022). *Digital Transformation and Tourist Experiences.*, DOI: 10.4018/978-1-7998-8528-3.ch002

Trade, S. (2022). *Canada: Business practices.* https://santandertrade.com/en/portal/establish-overseas/canada/business-practices

Truong, L. (2019). *Corporate Social Responsibility and Job Pursuit Intention: A Study of Moderating Role of Personal Values.* RCISS's Working Papers.

Ujar, A. C., Ramos, C. D., Hernandez, H. E., & Lopez, J. (2013). *Organizational Culture: evolution in measurement. Management Studies. vol.29 no.128 Cali.* http://www.scielo.org.co/scielo.php?pid=S0123-59232013000300010&script=sci_arttext

United Nations Office for Disaster Risk Reduction. (2019). *Disaster risk reduction in the Philippines: Status report 2019.* https://www.unisdr.org/files/68265_682308philippinesdrmstatusreport.pdf

United Nations. (2022). *Severe downturns in labour-intensive sectors spell trouble for global inequality.* United Nations. Retrieved January 15 from https://www.un.org/tr/desa/severe-downturns-labour-intensive-sectors-spell-trouble-global-inequality

Urbano, D., Aparicio, S., & Querol, V. (2016). Social progress orientation and innovative entrepreneurship: An international analysis. *Journal of Evolutionary Economics*, 26(5), 1033–1066. DOI: 10.1007/s00191-016-0485-1

Valdivia-Barrios, A., Pinto-Torres, D., & Herrera-Barraza, M. (2018). Media Literacy and Learning. Conceptual Contribution in the Field of Media Education. *Revista Electrónica Educare*, 22(2), 1–16. DOI: 10.15359/ree.22-2.8

Vallaster, C., Kraus, S., Lindahl, J., & Nielsen, A. (2019). Ethics and entrepreneurship: A bibliometric study and literature review. *Journal of Business Research*, 99, 226–237. DOI: 10.1016/j.jbusres.2019.02.050

Van Eck, N., & Waltman, L. (2010b). VOS viewer (version 1.6.20). [Software]. https://www.vosviewer.com/

Van Eck, N., & Waltman, L. (2010a). Software survey: VOS viewer, a computer program for bibliometric mapping. *Scientometrics*, 84(2), 523–538. DOI: 10.1007/s11192-009-0146-3 PMID: 20585380

Van Hulten, A., & Ahmed, A. D. (2013). Migrant entrepreneurs' access to business finance in Australia. *Journal of Developmental Entrepreneurship*, 18(01), 1350003. DOI: 10.1142/S1084946713500039

Vandor, P. (2021). Are voluntary international migrants self-selected for entrepreneurship? An analysis of entrepreneurial personality traits. *Journal of World Business*, 56(2), 101142. https://doi.org/https://doi.org/10.1016/j.jwb.2020.101142. DOI: 10.1016/j.jwb.2020.101142

Varcoe, K. P., Emper, N., & Lees, N. (2002). Working with military audiences to improve financial well-being. *Journal of Family and Consumer Sciences*, 94(1), 33.

Vătămănescu, E. M., Cegarra-Navarro, J. G., Andrei, A. G., Dincă, V. M., & Alexandru, V. A. (2020). SMEs Strategic Networks and Innovative Performance: A Relational Design and Methodology for Knowledge Sharing. *Journal of Knowledge Management*, 24(6), 1291–1316. DOI: 10.1108/JKM-01-2020-0010

Velasquez Chacon, E. (2022). MSEs and sustainability in times of pandemic in Arequipa, Peru: A structural equation model. *VISUAL REVIEW. International Visual Culture Review Revista Internacional de cultura visual, 10*(4), 1–11. https://doi.org/DOI: 10.37467/revvisual.v9.3624

Velez, I. (2017). Políticas públicas en alfabetización mediática e informacional: el legado de John Dewey. *Revista Fuentes, 19*(2), 39-57. https://revistascientificas.us.es/index.php/fuentes/article/download/4237/3989/13728

Verma, J. (2022). Assessing Government Initiatives Towards the Development of Entrepreneurship in India. In *Institutions, Resilience, and Dynamic Capabilities of Entrepreneurial Ecosystems in Emerging Economies* (pp. 44-53). IGI Global. DOI: 10.4018/978-1-6684-4745-1.ch004

Verma, S., Sharma, R., Deb, S., & Maitra, D. (2021). Artificial intelligence in marketing : Systematic review and future research direction. *International Journal of Information Management Data Insights*, 1(1), 100002. DOI: 10.1016/j.jjimei.2020.100002

Vermeir, I., & Verbeke, W. (2016). Sustainable food consumption among young adults in Belgium: Theory of planned behaviour and the role of confidence and values. *Ecological Economics*, 64(3), 542–553. DOI: 10.1016/j.ecolecon.2007.03.007

Vijaykumar, J. H. (2022). The Association of Financial Socialization with Financial Self-Efficacy and Autonomy: A Study of Young Students in India. *Journal of Family and Economic Issues, 43*(2), 397-414. *Scopus.* Advance online publication. DOI: 10.1007/s10834-021-09797-x

Villarino, R. T. H., Villarino, M. L. F., Temblor, M. C. L., Bernard, P., & Plaisent, M. (2022). Developing a health and well-being program for college students: An online intervention. *World Journal on Educational Technology.*, 14(1), 65–78. DOI: 10.18844/wjet.v14i1.6638

Vizuete Muñoz, J. M. (2021). La gestión flexible en las organizaciones, en entornos de incertidumbre. *Revista Gestión y Desarrollo Libre, 6*(11), (22-46). https://revistas.unilibre.edu.co/index.php/gestion_libre/article/view/8077/9551

Vlačić, B., Corbo, L., Costa e Silva, S., & Dabić, M. (2021). The evolving role of artificial intelligence in marketing : A review and research agenda. *Journal of Business Research*, 128, 187–203. DOI: 10.1016/j.jbusres.2021.01.055

Wagner, S. M., & Bode, C. (2006). An empirical investigation into supply chain vulnerability. *Journal of Purchasing and Supply Management*, 12(6), 301–312. DOI: 10.1016/j.pursup.2007.01.004

Walter, A., Auer, M., & Ritter, T. (2006). The impact of network capabilities and entrepreneurial orientation on university spin-off performance. *Journal of Business Venturing*, 21(4), 541–567. DOI: 10.1016/j.jbusvent.2005.02.005

Waltman, L., Van Eck, N. J., & Noyons, E. C. (2010). A unified approach to mapping and clustering of bibliometric networks. *Journal of Informetrics*, 4(4), 629–635. DOI: 10.1016/j.joi.2010.07.002

Wamba-Taguimdje, S.-L., Fosso Wamba, S., Kala Kamdjoug, J. R., & Tchatchouang Wanko, C. E. (2020). Influence of artificial intelligence (AI) on firm performance : The business value of AI-based transformation projects. *Business Process Management Journal*, 26(7), 1893–1924. DOI: 10.1108/BPMJ-10-2019-0411

Wang, Q. (2012). Ethnic Entrepreneurship Studies in Geography: A Review1. *Geography Compass*, 6(4), 227–240. https://doi.org/https://doi.org/10.1111/j.1749-8198.2012.00482.x. DOI: 10.1111/j.1749-8198.2012.00482.x

Wang, X., Han, R., & Zheng, M. (2024). Competitive strategy and stock market liquidity: A natural language processing approach. *Information Technology and Management*, 25(1), 99–112. DOI: 10.1007/s10799-023-00401-2

Wasserman, T., & Wasserman, L. (2020). Motivation: State, Trait, or Both. In Wasserman, T., & Wasserman, L. (Eds.), *Motivation, Effort, and the Neural Network Model* (pp. 93–101). Springer International Publishing., DOI: 10.1007/978-3-030-58724-6_8

Wennberg, K., Pathak, S., & Autio, E. (2013). How culture moulds the effects of self-efficacy and fear of failure on entrepre-neurship. *Entrepreneurship and Regional Development*, 25(9-10), 756–780. DOI: 10.1080/08985626.2013.862975

Wennekers, S., Van Wennekers, A., Thurik, R., & Reynolds, P. (2005). Nascent entrepreneurship and the level of economic development. *Small Business Economics*, 24(3), 293–309. DOI: 10.1007/s11187-005-1994-8

Wernerfelt, B. (1984). A Resource-Based View of the Firm. *Strategic Management Journal*, 5(2), 171–180. DOI: 10.1002/smj.4250050207

Westhead, P., Ucbasaran, D., & Binks, M. (2004). Internationalization strategies selected by established rural and urban SMEs. *Journal of Small Business and Enterprise Development*, 11(1), 8–22. DOI: 10.1108/14626000410519065

West, J., & Bogers, M. (2014). Leveraging external sources of innovation: A review of research on open innovation. *Journal of Product Innovation Management*, 31(4), 814–831. DOI: 10.1111/jpim.12125

Weston, J., & Copeland, T. (1992). *Finanzas en administración* (9th ed., Vol. I). McGraw Hill.

Wiltsey Stirman, S., Baumann, A. A., & Miller, C. J. (2019). The FRAME: An expanded framework for reporting adaptations and modifications to evidence-based interventions. *Implementation Science : IS*, 14(1), 1–10. DOI: 10.1186/s13012-019-0898-y PMID: 31171014

World Bank (2020). Micro, Small and Medium Enterprises Economic Indicators. World Bank Report.

World Economic Forum. (2013). *The Future Role of Civil Society.*https://www3.weforum.org/docs/WEF_FutureRoleCivilSociety_Report_2013.pdf

Wu, C. H. J., Atmaja, F. T., Ko, Y. C., & Guttena, R. K. (2023). Backer funding intention in reward-based crowdfunding: Service-dominant logic and stimulus-organism-response perspectives. *International Journal of Bank Marketing*, 41(2), 289–311. DOI: 10.1108/IJBM-03-2022-0127

Wu, Y.-L. (2022). Entrepreneurship Experiences among Vietnamese Marriage Immigrant Women in Taiwan. *Sustainability (Basel)*, 14(3), 1489. https://www.mdpi.com/2071-1050/14/3/1489. DOI: 10.3390/su14031489

Xiao, Y., & Watson, M. (2019). Guidance on Conducting a Systematic Literature Review. *Journal of Planning Education and Research*, 39(1), 93–112. DOI: 10.1177/0739456X17723971

Yachin, J. M. (2019). The entrepreneur–opportunity nexus: Discovering the forces that promote product innovations in rural micro-tourism firms. *Scandinavian Journal of Hospitality and Tourism*, 19(1), 47–65. DOI: 10.1080/15022250.2017.1383936

Yazdanfar, D., Abbasian, S., & Brouder, P. (2015). Business advice strategies of immigrant entrepreneurs in Sweden. *Baltic Journal of Management*, 10(1), 98–118. DOI: 10.1108/BJM-01-2014-0018

Yeasmin, N., & Koivurova, T. (2019). A factual analysis of sustainable opportunity recognition of immigrant entrepreneurship in Finnish Lapland: Theories and practice. *Journal of Entrepreneurship, Management and Innovation*, 15(2), 57-84. https://doi.org/https://doi.org/10.7341/20191523

Yifan, Z. (2023). The Fintech Revolution: Innovations Reshaping the Financial Industry. DOI: 10.54097/hbem.v15i.9327

Yi, J., Wang, C., & Kafouros, M. (2013). The effects of innovative capabilities on exporting: Do institutional forces matter? *International Business Review*, 22(2), 392–406. DOI: 10.1016/j.ibusrev.2012.05.006

Young, S., Hamill, J., Wheeler, C., & Davies, J. R. (1989). *International Market Entry and Development*. Harvester Wheatsheaf.

Yudistira, Y., Arkeman, Y., Andati, T., & Jahroh, S. (2022). A bibliometric review on dynamic capability. *Indonesian Journal of Business and Entrepreneurship*, 8(1), 158–167. DOI: 10.17358/ijbe.8.1.158

Zaied, R. M. B., Louati, H., & Affes, H. (2015). The relationship between organizational innovations, internal sources of knowledge and organizational performance. *International Journal of Managing Value and Supply Chains*, 6(1), 53–67. DOI: 10.5121/ijmvsc.2015.6105

Zakharov, D., Bezruchuk, S., Poplavska, V., Laichuk, S., & Khomenko, H. (2020). The ability of trust to influence GDP per capita. *Problems and Perspectives in Management*, 18(1), 302–314. DOI: 10.21511/ppm.18(1).2020.26

Zamani, S. Z. (2022). Small and Medium Enterprises (SMEs) facing an evolving technological era : A systematic literature review on the adoption of technologies in SMEs. *European Journal of Innovation Management*, 25(6), 735–757. DOI: 10.1108/EJIM-07-2021-0360

Zastempowski, M. (2022). What Shapes Innovation Capability in Micro-Enterprises? New-to-the-Market Product and Process Perspective. *Journal of Open Innovation*, 8(1), 59. https://doi.org/https://doi.org/10.3390/joitmc8010059. DOI: 10.3390/joitmc8010059

Zeschky, M., Widenmayer, B., & Gassmann, O. (2014). Frugal innovation in emerging markets. *Research Technology Management*, 57(4), 38–45. DOI: 10.5437/08956308X5404007

Zhang, J. (2010). The problems of using social networks in entrepreneurial resource acquisition. *International Small Business Journal*, 28(4), 338–361. DOI: 10.1177/0266242610363524

Zhao, Y. (2023). The Fintech Revolution: Innovations Reshaping the Financial Industry. *Highlights in Business. Economics and Management*, 15, 123–128.

Zheng, C., Huang, X., & Xu, Y. (2023). The Impact of Blockchain on Enterprises Sharing Real Data Based on Dynamic Evolutionary Game Analysis. *Sustainability (Basel)*, 15(12), 9439. DOI: 10.3390/su15129439

Zhou, C., & Etzkowitz, H. (2021). Triple helix twins: A framework for achieving innovation and UN sustainable development goals. *Sustainability (Basel)*, 13(12), 6535. DOI: 10.3390/su13126535

Zou, S., & Stan, S. (1998). The determinants of export performance: A review of the empirical literature between 1987 and 1997. *International Marketing Review*, 15(5), 333–356. DOI: 10.1108/02651339810236290

About the Contributors

Rafael Perez-Uribe Doctor of Business Sciences, U. Nebrija. Diploma of Advanced Studies in applied economics, U. Nebrija. Master's Degree in Organizational Management, EAN University. Maître es Sciences, University of Quebec to Chicoutimi. Specialist in Evaluation and Construction of Management Indicators for Higher Education, School of Business Administration. Postgraduate Studies as Kenkyusei (Associate Researcher) in Total Quality Control and Quality Circles, Fukushima University, Japan. Business Administrator, Universidad Jorge Tadeo Lozano. Former director of the research group on the management of large, small and medium-sized enterprises (G3pymes) and Professor attached to the Management of Research of EAN University. Currently professor and Researcher at La Salle University in Bogotá-Colombia.

David Ocampo Guzmán Master in Science, Universiteé Du Quebec a Chicoutimi. Máster in Organizational, Management, Universidad EAN. Business Administrator Universidad EAN. Expert in defining, aligning and addressing strategic planning and directing for companies and organizations, especially Small and Medium sized firms. (SMEs). Very competent in attending organizational restructuring requirements for both private companies as well as public entities, leading assessment and evaluation processes procuring a profound and thorough organizational diagnosis, allowing the implementation of new management models and/or the upgrade of current ones, which include designing and applying Key Performance Indicators (KPIs).

Luz Janeth Lozano-Correa Doctor in Administration, Master in Organizational Management, Specialist in Human Resources Management and Psychologist. Certified Master Coach. Experience as a consultant in national and multinational companies related to corporate human talent management processes oriented towards humanistic and organizational training.; planning, design, development and monitoring of alternative processes of excellence to the organizational value chain, coaching and feedback, Train the trainer, development of management skills, effective management skills, Change Management and strategies, Strengthening of Teamwork and Internalization of Corporate Values and Competencies, experiential education, commercial growth workshops, diagnosis, evaluation and intervention of organizational climate, management and business improvement. University teacher-researcher in undergraduate and postgraduate courses in management areas related to human development and organizational management. National and international speaker on issues of management and strategic processes in organizations and on the development of skills, human talent, coaching-mentoring, emotional intelligence, quality of work life, occupational health, customer service, leadership, development of "human talents". " through entrepreneurship, change management, development of high-performance teams, among others. Speaker at different events on topics related to Human Talent, Coaching and Social Responsibility.

***

Mourad Aarabe PhD student at the National School of Business and Management of Fez, Sidi Mohamed de Ben Abdellah University. His research focuses on tourism, marketing, digital marketing, and management

Lhoussaine ALLA, professor in management sciences at the National School of Applied Sciences, researcher at the LAREMEF laboratory, Sidi Mohamed Ben Abdellah University, Fez, Morocco. He is a permanent professor of various marketing management modules at Sidi Mohamed Ben Abdellah University in Fez (Morocco) and in several public and private business graduate schools. He is an accredited professional expert in the fields of Training Engineering, Professional Coaching and Mentoring young entrepreneurs. After a PhD thesis on creating value for the customer and its impact on the overall performance of companies, Prof. Lhoussaine ALLA invested more in scientific research in marketing, through various scientific contributions in the form of participation in international conferences and symposia and scientific publications, in various themes inherent to Marketing (customer value creation, customer behaviour, e-marketing, customer experience, sales performance, Marketing Data Analytics, territorial marketing, territorial attractiveness, territorial economic intelligence, ...), finance (stock market performance, financial analysts, financing package,...), entrepreneurship (entreprene

Maria Lavina Alonzo is a graduate of Master of Management Major in Public Management from the University of the Philippines. She gained international experience by working at the Canadian Embassy in Manila (Philippines). After a research scholarship from the Canada-ASEAN program, she pursued advanced studies at Concordia University. Her research interests revolve around women empowerment, intercultural communication, and management theories. She currently works as a Manager of Administration and Development at a nonprofit organization in Quebec, Canada.

Nelson A. Andrade-Valbuena is an Associate Professor at the Faculty of Economics and Business Administration, Universidad Católica de la Santísima Concepción. Dr. Andrade holds a PhD in Management from the University of Chile (Chile), a Master and Business Administration (MBA) from Universita Degli Studi Guglielmo Marconi (Italy), and a bachelor degree in Business Administration from EAN University (Colombia). He is Assistant Editor at Revista Estudios de Administración. He has several publications in journals, books and conference proceedings. His research has been published in Technological Forecasting and Social Change journal, World Journal of Entrepreneurship, Management and Sustainable Development, Journal of Strategy and Management, among others. He is currently interested on innovation, entrepreneurship, and strategic management.

Albert Dario Arias Ardila Business Administrator, Specialist in Finance at University of Rosario, and master's in business management from the University of Université du Québec à Chicoutimi (Canada). Professional experience of more than 20 years in the areas of finance, grants and funds, personal finance, and financial risk management. He has experience of more than 13 years in higher education as a professor, researcher and consultant on issues related to finance, finance behavior and strategic management and entrepreneurship. Expertise in different fields such as financial sector, education sector in public and private organizations.

Amanda A. Arias-Ramírez is a PhD student in Management at the Faculty of Economics and Business Administration, Universidad Católica de la Santísima Concepción (UCSC), and holds a Bachelor's degree in Business Administration from UCSC, Chile. She serves as an assistant investigator in the Administration Department at the Faculty of Economics and Business Administration, UCSC. She played an essential role as a research assistant in a Regional Project FIC on sectoral indices in Chile. Distinguished at the university for her academic performance, she served as an assistant professor during her bachelor's degree at UCSC. She is currently interested in Entrepreneurship, Marketing, and Organizational Behavior.

Neeta Baporikar is currently Professor/Director(Business Management) at Harold Pupkewitz Graduate School of Business, Namibia University of Science and Technology, Namibia. Prior to this, she was Head-Scientific Research, with the Ministry of Higher Education CAS-Salalah, Sultanate of Oman, Professor (Strategy and Entrepreneurship) at IIIT Pune and BITS India. With a decade-plus of experience in the industry, consultancy, and training, she made a lateral switch to research and academics in 2000. Prof Baporikar holds D.Sc. (Management Studies) USA, Ph.D. (Management), SP Pune University, INDIA with MBA (Distinction) and Law (Hons.) degrees. Apart from this, she is an external reviewer, Oman Academic Accreditation Authority, an Accredited Management Teacher, a Qualified Trainer, an FDP from EDII, a Doctoral Guide, and Board Member of Academic Advisory Committee in accredited B-Schools. She has to her credit many conferred doctorates, 350+ scientific publications and authored 30+ books in the area of Strategy, Entrepreneurship, Management and Higher Education. She is also a member of the international and editorial advisory board, reviewer for Emerald, IGI, Inderscience, Wiley, etc.

Andrea Barrera Associate Professor of UNAD. Business Administrator from the National University of Colombia, Doctorate Student in Administration from the University of Celaya, Master in Administration from the Technological Institute of Monterrey, Specialist in Process Engineering and Quality Management from the EAN University, Member of the Research Group PHOENIX, Principal investigator of the project Management tools to face BANI scenarios. Co-investigator of the project The political stability of nation-states is a determining factor for the growth of the economy. Academic Peer of the Ministry of National Education, Experience in University Academic Management, Course Director of the Master's Degree in Administration of Organizations of the National Open and Distance University-UNAD-. andrea.barrera@unad.edu.co

Nouhaila Ben Khizzou is a PhD student at the National School of Business and Management of Fez, Sidi Mohamed de Ben Abdellah University. His research focuses on tourism, marketing, digital marketing, and management

Ahmed Benjelloun, Teacher-researcher at the National School of Business and Management of Fez, Sidi Mohamed de Ben Abdellah University

Prosper Bernard is a professor of management at the University of Quebec in Montréal where he was previously vice-rector and member of the BOARD of TRUSTEES of the university. He is also Chairman of the Board of the University Consortium of the Americas in Florida. He holds several degrees including a PhD from City University of New York. He has served successively as Director of the PHD program in management, and managed a PHD consortium including McGill university,Director of the department of management and technology, Director of the MBA program locally and abroad, namely in China, the only one Executive MBA officially recognized by the Chinese government. Lately, China's Jiangsu Province presented him with the prestigious Friendship Medal and the Labor Prize for his contribution to university education. He has published numerous books and articles in academic conferences and scopus, IEEE and other prestigious journals.

Camila Cuello Professional in Business and International Relations. Master's in Interdisciplinary Social Research. Professor. Experience as a research professional, manager of inter-institutional agreements for the formulation of international cooperation projects and participation in the organization of national and international events. Researcher in topics related to the area of business and social sciences.

Olga Diaz Villamizar, Phd in management with extensive research experience.

Jorge Espinoza Benavides is a researcher in entrepreneurship, with emphasis on business failure, re-entrepreneurship, management in adverse contexts and innovation management in small businesses. He has published his research papers in mainstream journals related to entrepreneurship, such as: SBEJ, IEMJ, IJEBR, among others. He is also currently the director of innovation at his university (Universidad Católica de la Santísima Concepción, Chile).

Abigail C. Gomez is an Assistant Professor IV from Cavite State University Imus Campus. She graduated with the degrees Bachelor of Arts in Communication from De La Salle University Dasmariñas and Master of Arts in Educational Management major in Educational Supervision from Philippine Christian University. Currently, she is part of the faculty roster of the Department of Languages and Mass Communication and as a beginner faculty researcher, has published various researches indexed in Google Scholar with 19 citations.

Catalina Gomez PhD Candidate in Business Administration - DBA at the Universidad de la Salle (Colombia). Master in Marketing Management from the Viña del Mar University (Chile). Specialist in Organizational Communication from the Pontificia Universidad Javeriana (Colombia). Professional in Publicity from the Catholic University of Manizales (Colombia). Professor at University Institutions in Bogotá. General Director and Founder of the Publicity agency Imark Group S.A.S. Adviser and consultant in multiple national and international companies in the field of publicity communication. National and international speaker.

Irma Gutierrez Almendarez Project finance manager and process leader who can handle complex and challenging tasks in budgeting, cash flow analysis, and financial statement analysis. She developed strong skills in HR recruitment, negotiation, procurement, and corporate legal matters, with over 20 years of experience enabling her to effectively manage diverse teams and stakeholders. As an educator, she is passionate about sharing her knowledge and experience with the next generation of leaders and innovators.

Atle Hauge is a social geographer and professor of service innovation at the Inland Norway University of Applied Sciences. His primary research interests are innovation and regional development. He has also conducted extensive research on cultural and creative industries and led the Knowledge Centre (Kunnskaptverket) – National Centre for Cultural Industries.

Adolfo Hernández Hernández Business Administrator, Specialist in Logistics Management and master's in supply chain and Logistics Management from the University of Warwick (United Kingdom). Professional experience of more than 18 years in the areas of demand planning, production management, transportation management, purchasing and strategic sourcing. Experience of more than 11 years in higher education as a professor, researcher, and consultant on Operations Management, Logistics and Supply Chain issues. Great trajectory in the design and development of logistics solutions supported by technological products of Industry 4.0.

Nydia Hernandez Mora I am a Business Administrator, with a Master's Degree in Finance and more than 20 years of experience in the financial, business and academic sector. I have an important career in the administration of academic programs

Pedro Jimenez_Hernandez, Business Administrator from the National University of Colombia, MBA emphasis in Finance from the European Postgraduate Institute, Specialist in Financial Administration from the EAN University, Project Accountant Worley-Jacobs, Professor at the Nueva Granada Military University

Terry Lantai graduated with a Bachelor of Tourism at Central Queensland University (CQU) in 2004. He pursued a Master of Science in Hotel and Hospitality Management at University of Stavanger (UIS), which was completed in 2016. Besides having worked many years in the industry in sales and marketing, he is currently a PhD fellow at Inland Norway University of Applied Sciences. His research interests include consumer behaviour, entrepreneurship, innovation and diversity management.

Delia Angélica León Castro is a PhD student in Management at the Universidad Católica de la Santísima Concepción (Chile). She holds a Master's degree in Management focused on Finance from the Universidad Autónoma de Sinaloa (Mexico), a Bachelor's degree in Accounting from the Universidad Autónoma de Occidente (Mexico), and a Bachelor's degree in Law from the Universidad Autónoma de Sinaloa (Mexico). Her research interests focus on corporate finance and governance, sustainability, and management.

Ronald Martinez Contreras I am a Business Administrator, with a Master's Degree in Finance and more than 20 years of experience in the financial, business and academic sector. I have an important career in the administration of academic programs

German Medina Economist, Master in Organization Administration, Specialist in Public Management, Specialist in Pedagogy for the development of Autonomous Learning, Associate Professor at the National Open and Distance University UNAD, member of the Fénix research group. Principal researcher The political stability of nation states is a determining factor for the growth of the economy. Co-investigator in the project Consumer Behavior and its decision-making process in relation to the use of neuromarketing (neuroscience) in mass consumption products. german.medina@unad.edu.co

Xiang Ying Mei is an associate professor in marketing at Inland Norway University of Applied Sciences. She holds a Ph.D. in tourism management from the University of Queensland, Australia. In addition to years of practical experiences in the service industries, her research interests range from government policies, innovation, regional development, tourism management and development, experience economy, consumer behavior and marketing, to digital learning tools and student engagement in higher education. Mei has previously published in journals such as Journal of Applied Research in Higher Education, Library and Information Science Research, International Review of Retail Distribution & Consumer Research, Tourism Management Perspective, Current Issues in Tourism, Anatolia, Tourism Analysis, European Journal of Tourism Research, Scandinavian Journal of Hospitality and Tourism Research and Tourism and Hospitality Research.

Froilan Mobo He is a Doctor of Public Administration graduate from the Urdaneta City University Class of 2016 and a graduate of the 2nd Doctorate Degree (Ph.D.) in Development Education program at the Central Luzon State University, Nueva Ecija, Philippines, Class of 2022. On March 11, 2024, Dr. Mobo was accredited and reclassified by the Commission on Higher Education (CHED) to the position of Professor II in the Philippine Merchant Marine Academy (PMMA), and this allowed him to work with different international research institutions, such as the Director and Research Consultant of the IKSAD Research Institute, Turkey. At present, he is in the process of finishing his 3rd master's degree, leading to social studies education at Bicol University. Recently, Dr. Mobo passed Batch 3—Certified Research Professional—and ranked in the top 5 in the National Examination.

António C. Moreira obtained a Bachelor's degree in Electrical Engineering and a Master's degree in Management, both from the University of Porto, Portugal. He received his Ph.D. in Management from the University of Manchester, England. He has a solid international background in industry leveraged working for a multinational company in Germany as well as in Portugal. He has also been involved in consultancy projects and research activities. He is an Associate Professor at the Department of Economics, Management, Industrial Engineering, and Tourism, University of Aveiro, Portugal. He is a member of the GOVCOPP research unit.

Carlos Muñoz-Maya, Phd in management with extensive research experience. Associate Professor at La Salle University.

Eurico C. Navaia obtained a Bachelor's degree in Economics and Management, a Master's degree in Business Administration from the Catholic University of Mozambique, and a doctorate in Marketing and Strategy from Aveiro University, Portugal. He has a solid background in research and consultancy activities in innovation and performance of SMEs. He is an assistant at the Faculty of Social Sciences and Humanities at Zambeze University, Mozambique.

Michel Plaisent is a full professor in the University of Québec in Montréal (Canada). After a bachelor in Information technology, a M.Sc. in project management and a Ph.D. in Information Technology Management, he joined the Business school in 1980 where he held different position while developing his research career, namely IT program director for 6 years. His doctoral research was pioneer as he studied the use of computer mediated communication systems by CEO. Since then, Dr. Plaisent's researches continue to focus human factors of IT, namely cognitive ergonomics, learning problems and personal productivity tools for managers. Among his new researches namely: Education 4.0 concepts and tools, and more broadly the impact of internet on life and society. He has published more than 25 books and more than one hundred of articles in international conferences and academic indexed journals. He is engaged in China EMBA program and he manages for UQAM research collaboration protocols with three South-Asia universities.

Maria Ramìrez PhD in Administration from the University of Celaya (Mexico), master's in teaching from the University of La Salle, specialist in Human Resources Management and Business Administration from the EAN University, with extensive experience in teaching at a national and international level. Experience as a researcher and co-investigator in topics such as organization management, competitiveness, sustainable management and corruption in micro, small and medium-sized companies and as an advisor and consultant on issues related to organization management in both private and public companies. Ability to lead groups and work as a team in the development of research projects in which articles, book chapters and books have been published. Ability to make decisions in a professional manner and to assess projects and products resulting from research as a Peer Evaluator.

Claudia Pires Ribau holds a Ph.D. in Marketing and Strategy from the University of Aveiro; she is a Marketing Specialist; she has a postgraduate degree in Marketing and a bachelor's degree in Business Communication. She has been teaching in higher education since 2004 in the areas of marketing, international marketing, relational marketing, digital marketing and communication, communication, integrated marketing communication, communication and advertising, international business, consumer behavior, human resources management, and organizational management. She was the pedagogical coordinator of the Department of Communication and Marketing (DETCOM), a member of the Pedagogical Council, and a member of the Permanent Commission of the Technical-Scientific Council, at a Polytechnic Institute. As a coordinator, she led new pedagogical projects and was responsible for the development of new courses (at both undergraduate and graduate levels), pedagogical coordination, and coordination of the teaching staff. She participates as a jury member in several academic examinations. In her technical-scientific production, she focuses her research in the area of international marketing, particularly in SMEs. She is currently involved in a post-doctoral program. In addition to her technical-scientific performance (in research) and pedagogical ability, she also has over 25 years of professional experience in the industry in the areas of marketing, communication, and human resources management. Since 2002-2024, she has been the marketing manager in a B2B context-industrial SME, having previously held functional responsibilities in the areas of communication, strategic human resources management, and integrated human resources management. She is involved in several projects, not only in the specifically marketing field (especially industrial), but also in strategic management, being a member of the board of directors.

Carlos Salcedo-Pérez, Phd In Business. M.S. in Economic Development. B.S. in Business Administration. University profesor and researcher.

Mushtaq Ahmad Shah is a finance expert with a PhD in Infrastructure Finance. He teaches banking, finance and economics at Lovely Professional University in India. Dr. Shah has over 8 years of experience teaching and researching at various institutions. He's written articles in academic journals and presented his work at conferences on banking, partnerships between public and private sectors, and behavioral finance.

Mohammad Shahparan has a Master's degree in Logistics(By Tourism Direction) from "Silk Road"International University of Tourism and Cultural Heritage, Samarkand, Uzbekistan. He is now working as a full-time lecturer at the Department of Tourism at the same university. The authors research is focused on Tourism logistics, Transport logistics and Transport Economics. In these fields, he has published several articles in prestigious journal related to tourism and transport.

Muhammad Usman Tariq has more than 16+ year's experience in industry and academia. He has authored more than 200+ research articles, 100+ case studies, 95+ book chapters and several books other than 4 patents. He is founder and CEO of The Case HQ, a unique repository for courses, narrative and video case studies. He has been working as a consultant and trainer for industries representing six sigma, quality, health and safety, environmental systems, project management, and information security standards. His work has encompassed sectors in aviation, manufacturing, food, hospitality, education, finance, research, software and transportation. He has diverse and significant experience working with accreditation agencies of ABET, ACBSP, AACSB, WASC, CAA, EFQM and NCEAC. Additionally, Dr. Tariq has operational experience in incubators, research labs, government research projects, private sector startups, program creation and management at various industrial and academic levels. He is Certified Higher Education Teacher from Harvard University, USA, Certified Online Educator from HMBSU, Certified Six Sigma Master Black Belt, Lead Auditor ISO 9001 Certified, ISO 14001, IOSH MS, OSHA 30,

Resti Tito Villarino is a registered nurse and a licensed professional teacher in the Philippines. He is a Canada ASEAN – SEED (Scholarships and Educational Exchanges for Development) research scholar at the Université du Québec à Montréal, Montreal, Quebec, Canada. Moreover, he is a Sigma Theta Tau International Honor Society of Nursing (Psi Beta Chapter) member, an AACCUP (Accrediting Agency of Chartered Colleges and Universities in the Philippines, Inc.) accreditor, and an associate member of the National Research Council of the Philippines-Medical Sciences Division. He is a peer-reviewer for Scopus and Web of Science-indexed journals. He has published and presented research articles globally with international collaborations, including Canada, France, England, Lebanon, Vietnam, China, and South Africa. His educational qualifications include a Doctorate in Development Education, a Master of Arts in Education, and units in Psychiatric Nursing. His research interests include Science, Health, Education, Climate Change, and Translational Research

Index

A

action plan 191, 341, 349, 350, 363, 365, 368
Administrative Modernization 57, 58
Agility 53, 97, 102, 115, 154, 155, 157, 158, 168, 233, 242, 271, 275, 369
AI 49, 154, 155, 160, 167, 171, 220, 222, 223, 228, 229, 230, 233, 235, 236, 237, 240, 241, 316, 320, 321, 327
Artificial Intelligence 49, 65, 108, 109, 154, 155, 166, 168, 172, 218, 219, 222, 223, 227, 228, 229, 230, 231, 233, 234, 235, 236, 237, 238, 239, 240, 241, 285, 286, 320, 326, 338
Augmented Reality 65, 223, 229, 232, 233, 236, 237

B

Bibliometrics 261, 266
Blockchain 167, 168, 218, 219, 220, 222, 227, 228, 229, 230, 231, 236, 237, 239, 240, 316, 317, 319, 321, 323, 325, 326, 327, 328, 329, 330, 331, 332, 335, 336, 337, 338, 339, 340
Budget 206, 354, 360, 365, 366, 367
Business Constraints 2, 8, 9, 10, 15, 24
business results 341, 343, 346, 347, 348, 353

C

Canada 8, 10, 69, 70, 71, 73, 74, 75, 76, 77, 78, 79, 80, 81, 82, 83, 84, 85, 87, 88, 89, 90, 91, 92, 282
Chain Value 198
Competitive Advantage 23, 25, 26, 30, 40, 43, 44, 45, 98, 99, 100, 101, 102, 103, 105, 107, 111, 114, 115, 156, 157, 158, 159, 161, 169, 170, 173, 179, 181, 182, 194, 196, 198, 199, 200, 201, 202, 203, 204, 205, 206, 208, 209, 213, 214, 215, 246, 247, 253, 266, 309, 314, 315, 371
competitive intensity 25, 26, 27, 31, 32, 33, 34, 35, 36, 38, 39, 40, 42, 43, 44, 45
Competitiveness 39, 40, 47, 48, 49, 50, 51, 52, 53, 55, 56, 59, 61, 63, 64, 65, 66, 67, 70, 71, 90, 91, 95, 96, 97, 98, 99, 100, 101, 102, 105, 106, 107, 108, 109, 110, 111, 112, 113, 114, 115, 116, 151, 153, 154, 155, 159, 161, 163, 165, 168, 169, 170, 171, 195, 199, 200, 201, 204, 206, 208, 209, 211, 212, 213, 220, 221, 222, 224, 227, 230, 231, 232, 233, 234, 242, 244, 245, 257, 259, 275, 294, 296, 299, 307, 315, 316, 341, 346, 348, 349, 357, 370, 371
Competitive strategy 25, 26, 28, 32, 33, 35, 36, 42, 43, 44, 100, 214, 300, 301, 305, 306, 307
Corporate Training 48, 65
Crowdfunding 162, 325, 326, 327, 328, 330, 331, 332, 335, 336, 337, 338, 339, 340
cultural transformation 285, 286

D

Digital Transformation 152, 153, 154, 155, 166, 168, 172, 217, 218, 222, 239, 240, 259, 270, 314, 316, 319

E

economic policies 268, 281, 316
Economies 3, 7, 8, 16, 17, 18, 19, 25, 26, 27, 29, 31, 37, 38, 40, 44, 63, 64, 70, 96, 97, 102, 113, 151, 153, 161, 162, 166, 168, 170, 171, 172, 204, 205, 226, 235, 242, 250, 252, 267, 268, 269, 277, 281, 300, 328, 339, 357, 361
Emerging technologies 65, 108, 109, 167, 217, 218, 219, 222, 223, 224, 225, 227, 228, 229, 230, 231, 232, 233, 234, 235, 239, 326, 327
Entrepreneurial Intention 252, 326, 327, 328, 329, 330, 331, 338
Entrepreneurship 2, 3, 4, 6, 7, 8, 9, 10, 11, 12, 17, 18, 19, 20, 21, 22, 23, 30, 40, 42, 43, 44, 72, 89, 90, 91, 92, 111, 114, 115, 152, 154, 164, 166, 170, 171, 226, 227, 235, 236, 241, 243, 244, 245, 246, 247, 249, 250, 251, 252, 253, 254, 255, 256, 257, 258, 259, 260, 261, 262, 263, 264, 265, 266, 325, 326, 327, 329, 332, 335, 338, 339, 369
environment 11, 12, 23, 26, 30, 31, 32, 49, 50, 54, 55, 57, 59, 61, 62, 64, 65, 70, 72, 78, 83, 95, 96, 98, 99, 100, 102, 103, 105, 106, 107, 108, 109, 110, 113, 116, 118, 151, 152, 154, 157, 158, 159, 160, 161, 162, 163, 164, 166, 167, 168, 169, 173, 175, 178, 179, 180, 182, 195, 198, 199, 201, 202, 205, 209, 210, 222, 234, 238, 245, 246, 247, 251, 252, 259, 260, 263, 267, 268, 269, 270, 271, 276, 277, 278, 283, 285, 286, 294, 296, 297, 298, 299, 303, 305, 307, 308, 309, 311, 314, 322, 323, 326, 327, 336, 337, 342, 343, 344, 346, 347, 353
export performance 25, 26, 27, 28, 29, 30, 31, 32, 33, 34, 35, 36, 37, 38, 39, 40, 41, 42, 43, 44, 45, 170

302, 303, 304, 306, 307, 308, 310, 311

Milton Keynes UK
Ingram Content Group UK Ltd.
UKHW031840301024
450366UK00010B/100

9 798369 351